GW00418080

# PSYCHOLOGY OF INFANCY

SAGE LIBRARY IN DEVELOPMENTAL PSYCHOLOGY

# PSYCHOLOGY OF INFANCY

## VOLUME III
*Motor Development, Spatial Awareness and Multisensory Perception*

Edited by

## J. Gavin Bremner and Alan M. Slater

Los Angeles | London | New Delhi
Singapore | Washington DC

Los Angeles | London | New Delhi
Singapore | Washington DC

SAGE Publications Ltd
1 Oliver's Yard
55 City Road
London EC1Y 1SP

SAGE Publications Inc.
2455 Teller Road
Thousand Oaks, California 91320

SAGE Publications India Pvt Ltd
B 1/I 1 Mohan Cooperative Industrial Area
Mathura Road
New Delhi 110 044

SAGE Publications Asia-Pacific Pte Ltd
3 Church Street
#10-04 Samsung Hub
Singapore 049483

© Introduction and editorial arrangement by
J. Gavin Bremner and Alan M. Slater, 2014

First published 2014

Typeset by R.S. Prints, New Delhi

Printed on paper from sustainable resources

**Library of Congress Control Number: 2013947741**

**British Library Cataloguing in Publication Data**

A catalogue record for this book is available from the
British Library

MIX
Paper from
responsible sources
FSC
www.fsc.org    FSC® C013604

Printed in Great Britain by
CPI Group (UK) Ltd, Croydon, CR0 4YY

ISBN: 978-1-4462-6717-2 (set of six volumes)

# Contents

## Volume III: Motor Development, Spatial Awareness and Multisensory Perception

Introduction: Motor Development, Spatial Awareness and
Multisensory Perception   *J. Gavin Bremner and Alan M. Slater*        vii

### 8. Motor Development and Relations between Perception and Action

35. Newborn Stepping: An Explanation for a "Disappearing" Reflex        3
    *Esther Thelen and Donna M. Fisher*
36. Development of Reaching in Infancy        25
    *Neil E. Berthier and Rachel Keen*
37. A Pick-Me-Up for Infants' Exploratory Skills: Early Simulated
    Experiences Reaching for Objects Using 'Sticky Mittens' Enhances
    Young Infants' Object Exploration Skills        47
    *Amy Needham, Tracy Barrett and Karen Peterman*
38. How Do You Learn to Walk? Thousands of Steps and Dozens of
    Falls Per Day        67
    *Karen E. Adolph, Whitney G. Cole, Meghana Komati,*
    *Jessie S. Garciaguirre, Daryaneh Badaly, Jesse M. Lingeman,*
    *Gladys L.Y. Chan and Rachel B. Sotsky*
39. Specificity of Learning: Why Infants Fall over a Veritable Cliff        83
    *Karen E. Adolph*

### 9. Spatial Orientation

40. Egocentric versus Allocentric Spatial Coding in Nine-Month-Old
    Infants: Factors Influencing the Choice of Code        99
    *J. Gavin Bremner*
41. The Role of Self-Produced Movement and Visual Tracking in Infant
    Spatial Orientation        115
    *Linda P. Acredolo, Anne Adams and Susan W. Goodwyn*
42. The Development of Relational Landmark Use in Six- to
    Twelve-Month-Old Infants in a Spatial Orientation Task        131
    *Adina R. Lew, J. Gavin Bremner and Leonard P. Lefkovitch*
43. Spatial Updating and Training Effects in the First Year of
    Human Infancy        151
    *D. Tyler and B.E. McKenzie*

44. The Contribution of Visual and Vestibular Information to Spatial
    Orientation by 6- to 14-Month-Old Infants and Adults          167
    *J. Gavin Bremner, Fran Hatton, Kirsty A. Foster and Uschi Mason*
45. Effect of Self-Produced Locomotion on Infant Postural Compensation
    to Optic Flow                                                 191
    *Carol I. Higgins, Joseph J. Campos and Rosanne Kermoian*
46. Travel Broadens the Mind                                      205
    *Joseph J. Campos, David I. Anderson, Marianne A. Barbu-Roth,
    Edward M. Hubbard, Matthew J. Hertenstein and David Witherington*

## 10. Multisensory Perception

47. The Development of Intersensory Temporal Perception: An Epigenetic
    Systems/Limitations View                                      279
    *David J. Lewkowicz*
48. Intersensory Redundancy Guides the Development of Selective
    Attention, Perception, and Cognition in Infancy               341
    *Lorraine E. Bahrick, Robert Lickliter and Ross Flom*
49. The Effects of Auditory Information on 4-Month-Old Infants'
    Perception of Trajectory Continuity                           349
    *J. Gavin Bremner, Alan M. Slater, Scott P. Johnson, Uschi C. Mason
    and Jo Spring*
50. Crossmodal Learning in Newborn Infants: Inferences about
    Properties of Auditory-Visual Events                          367
    *Barbara A. Morrongiello, Kimberley D. Fenwick and Graham Chance*
51. Intermodal Perception at Birth: Intersensory Redundancy Guides
    Newborn Infants' Learning of Arbitrary Auditory–Visual Pairings  381
    *Alan Slater, Paul C. Quinn, Elizabeth Brown and Rachel Hayes*
52. Preverbal Infants' Sensitivity to Synaesthetic Cross-Modality
    Correspondences                                               391
    *Peter Walker, J. Gavin Bremner, Uschi Mason, Jo Spring, Karen Mattock,
    Alan Slater and Scott P. Johnson*
53. Sound Symbolism in Infancy: Evidence for Sound–Shape
    Cross-Modal Correspondences in 4-Month-Olds                   399
    *Ozge Ozturk, Madelaine Krehm and Athena Vouloumanos*

# Introduction: Motor Development, Spatial Awareness and Multisensory Perception

*J. Gavin Bremner and Alan M. Slater*

## Motor Development and Relations between Perception and Action

Infants are born with a set of action capabilities. These have traditionally been identified as reflexes stimulated by specific stimuli, and many appear to die out before being supplanted by emerging action. These include primitive grasp reflex, startle reflex, Moro reflex and such like, and tend to be identified as vestiges of our evolutionary past. One of the more complex behaviours is the walking reflex, an elaborate left-right sequence of leg movements elicited when the infant is held upright. This, like other reflexes disappears following birth, leading to speculation that the behaviour was really an adaptation to the uterine environment, accomplishing reorientation. However, Thelen and Fisher (1982) [35] claim that stepping dies out due to increases in leg mass, which are not compensated by increases in muscle strength. This leaves open the likelihood that newborn stepping is a precursor of later walking, though the link may be due to the fact that left-right movements naturally emerge from the biodynamics of the legs.

Another focus of research on motor development concerns the development of reaching and grasping. A common assumption was that reaching would become more rapid with age. However, the development of sophisticated motion analysis systems has provided better evidence, and on the basis of longitudinal data from reach onset through to 20 months of age, Berthier and Keen (2006) [36] detected a sequence in which reaching actually slowed initially. Elbow flexion increased during development and smoothness of reaching increased rather than reaching speed. The ability to grasp objects also develops considerably during infancy. This ability is important in terms of achieving goals, but also leads to tactile exploration to supplement visual exploration. Needham et al. (2003) [37] demonstrate a means of enriching young infants' tactile experience by providing sticky mittens that support grasping. After play sessions using the mittens, infants scored higher on measures of object engagement than infants without this experience.

Locomotion is another key motor skill that infants acquire. Typically they crawl before they walk, and one question is why, if crawling works, infants progress to the apparently more hazardous skill of walking. Adolph et al. (2012) [38] gathered detailed data on crawlers and walkers in naturalistic settings, which demonstrated that on transition to walking infants did not fall more than they had while crawling, and basically acquired the benefits of upright posture without an increase in hazard. Despite the transition from crawling to walking, through accumulated experience infants progressively move further and more safely. In interesting contrast, the information that infants gain regarding hazards tends to be specific to the action domain. For instance, infants who are competent at sitting show avoidance of a hazardous gap while sitting but not when in a crawling posture (Adolph, 2000) [39].

## Spatial Orientation

Locomotor ability brings benefits for mobility but also provides new problems for infants as they attempt to find their way around the environment. An early question was whether infants were capable of taking account of bodily reorientation. One approach to this is to hide an object in one of two locations, with the infant watching, but to move the infant to a new location before allowing search. This method indicated that 9-month-olds only took account of their movement in relocating the object if there were strong spatial landmarks to indicate the object's position (Bremner, 1978) [40]. Although this finding might suggest that infants define the object's location relative to external landmarks, Acredolo et al. (1984) [41] demonstrated that the more successful infants tracked the location of the target more during their movement, and when tracking was prevented, 12-month-olds' performance declined markedly. In contrast, 18-month-olds track less and perform accurately even when tracking is prevented.

Earlier work indicated a reliance on direct landmarks by infants around 9 months of age. However, more recent work indicated that infants of this age were capable of using landmarks indirectly, anticipating an event at a location between two distinct markers (Lew et al., 2000) [42]. In addition, other workers demonstrated that under some circumstances young infants could reorient after rotation without the aid of landmarks (Tyler & McKenzie, 1990) [43]. These investigators suggested that this indicated that infants were relying on vestibular information to reorient. However, visual flow information was also present, and Bremner et al. (2011) [44] demonstrated that infants tended to rely more on visual flow information for reorientation, except at 9 months when vestibular information predominated.

It is around 8 or 9 months that infants begin to crawl. Higgins et al. (1996) [45] demonstrated that infants with locomotor experience responded more to peripheral optic flow than pre-locomotor infants. Why then the finding that at around that age infants rely more on vestibular information? This is possibly because in the process of active locomotion they calibrate information from the vestibular system relative to visual flow information, and so vestibular information becomes temporarily more salient as part of that process. But there certainly seems to be no simple relationship between locomotion onset and spatial orientation. As Campos et al. (2000) [46] point out, many factors ranging from perceptual calibration to how parents react to hazards are liable to be altered as a result of the infant becoming mobile, and these changes are likely to alter infants' spatial awareness as a result.

## Multisensory Perception

Although most work on infant perception concerns ability within a single modality, usually vision, there is a considerable literature on intersensory perception, particularly auditory-visual perception. One commonly investigated intersensory event concerns temporal coincidence between sight and sound, for instance in a case in which an object hits a surface. Thus one focus of intersensory research concerns the temporal domain. Reviewing the evidence, Lewkowicz (2000) [47] argues that intersensory temporal perception develops in an orderly fashion, with detection of synchrony, duration, temporal rate and rhythm developing in sequence. Lewkowicz argues that this sequence reflects a complexity hierarchy, and proposes an epigenetic model in which development occurs through lower-level abilities supporting the emergence of higher-level abilities.

Rather than seeing intersensory perception as developing following perceptual development in single modalities, it is argued that the congruence that frequently occurs in intersensory events has a vital function in development, recruiting infants' attention and enhancing perceptual development (Bahrick et al., 2004) [48]. This opens up the possibility that infant abilities have been underestimated by the predominant focus on single modalities. Looking back to the work on perception of trajectory continuity (Volume II), there is evidence that adding auditory information for movement supports 4-month-olds' perception of trajectory continuity in an event in which an object passes behind an occluder (Bremner et al., 2012) [49].

As in any area of infancy research, one can ask when intersensory perception can first be detected. There is now good evidence that even newborns are capable of intersensory perception, associating sights and sounds through their common location in space (Morrongiello et al., 1998) [50] and learning arbitrary correspondences between sounds and shapes (Slater et al., 1999) [51].

A new and controversial branch of infant intersensory research concerns some associations that are rather unexpected, at least in the infancy literature. As adults, we unconsciously form associations, such as between pitch of sound and height in the visual field or sharpness of an object, that do not have obvious bases in the everyday world. One popular view is that these associations have a linguistic basis (e.g. *high* refers both to pitch and spatial height). However, there is now evidence that these associations are spontaneously detected by prelinguistic infant. Four-month-olds detect an association between high-pitched sound and the sharpness of an object and its height in the visual field (Walker et al., 2010) [52], and the pitch-sharpness association is also detected when speech sounds are used (Ozturk et al. 2013) [53]. Thus, instead of having a basis in language, these associations appear to be innate and may explain the linguistic associations that formerly were seen as their source.

# 8. Motor Development and Relations between Perception and Action

# Newborn Stepping: An Explanation for a "Disappearing" Reflex

*Esther Thelen and Donna M. Fisher*

When newborn infants are held under their arms in an upright position, tilted slightly forward, with the soles of their feet touching a surface, they will often perform coordinated movements that look remarkably like mature, erect locomotion. This stepping reflex becomes increasingly difficult to elicit after the first few weeks and usually disappears entirely by about 2 months of age.[1] Infants do not show such erect "walking" movements again until the last months of the first year.

Why should a comparatively complex and well-executed movement be lost at the same time that the infant is becoming motorically more competent? Why should the same movement reappear many months later? The most widely accepted explanation is that maturing cortical centers inhibit a primitive stepping reflex, just as the other neonatal reflexes such as the Moro, tonic neck, palmar grasp, and plantar grasp are suppressed as the motor tracts develop (Andre-Thomas & Autgaerden, 1966; Peiper, 1963; Touwen, 1976). Although the overt behavior of stepping disappears, it is unlikely that the neural mechanism responsible for the stepping movements dissolves completely only to reappear at a later age. Rather, the early stepping coordinations may be dominated by other movement patterns (Touwen, 1976) or suppressed by "higher centers" (Menkes, 1980). The patterns later reappear and are incorporated into erect walking (McGraw, 1932). The idea that the developing cortex inhibits early reflexes is further supported by the observation of certain fetal and neonatal reflexes in adult humans and other animals with

**Source:** *Developmental Psychology*, 18(5) (1982): 760–775.

neurological lesions or senile degeneration (Paulson & Gottlieb, 1968; Peiper, 1963; Teitelbaum, Wolgin, De Ryck & Marin, 1976).

A complementary hypothesis to the notion of cortical inhibition is that neonatal reflexes may be phylogenetically programmed to disappear because they are no longer functional. For example, Oppenheim (1981) has recently argued that infant reflexes may not be necessarily either vestigal behaviors or primitive antecedents of later movements but transient movements themselves with genuine adaptive functions. For example, the Moro and grasp reflexes may aid clinging (Peiper, 1963). Similarly, stepping movements may indeed function to position the fetus in the normal vertex position for birth (Oppenheim, 1981).

The nature of the disappearing infant reflexes is a highly controversial issue. Those who believe these reflexes are isomorphic with later behavior, or at least essential components of that behavior, advocate intervention in the exercise of the early reflexes (Bower, 1976; Konner, 1973; Zelazo, 1976). Those who see infant reflexes as lower level organizations competing with the development of voluntary control (e.g., DiLeo, 1967; Molnar, 1978) claim that active efforts to retain these reflexes may, in fact, retard normal development (Pontius, 1973) or may even cause neuromuscular abnormalities (Gotts, 1972; Simpkiss & Raikes, 1972).

In this article we seek to resolve the controversy over the stepping reflex by proposing a new explanation. When infants are supported upright, the homology between their stepping movements and mature walking is striking. Although leg movements are common when infants are lying down, at first glance this kicking bears little resemblence to erect locomotion. Consequently, kicking has been ignored or discounted as a locomotor precursor (Peiper, 1963). However, using kinematic techniques, we recently showed a dramatic similarity between spontaneous kicking in 1-month old infants in the supine position and the topographical and temporal patternings of the mature step cycle (Thelen, Bradshaw, & Ward, 1981). We suggested that early kicking was a manifestation of a muscle synergism later used for locomotion and was expressed before the infants' legs could support their weight in upright locomotion and before voluntary control of the legs had matured. In other words, this spontaneous behavior may be a component of later walking.

This discovery raised the possibility that newborn stepping and spontaneous kicking were not different movements but reflections of the same muscle synergisms seen when infants are held upright or placed lying down. Kicking differs from stepping in an essential dimension, however. Unlike erect stepping, supine kicking does not disappear. Kicking remains in the infant's repertoire in similar form and indeed increases both in frequency and in ease of elicitation throughout the first 6 or 7 months (Thelen, 1979, 1981a). If kicking and stepping are indeed the same movement, the clue to the disappearance of stepping and the increase of kicking might appear to be in the consequences of the infant's posture rather than in some yet unknown central neural processes.

The purposes of this article are first to demonstrate the identity between neonatal stepping and kicking. To do this, we compare topographical, temporal, electromyographic, and motivational characteristics of stepping and kicking in the same newborns. We argue that these data support a view of kicking and stepping as the same underlying movement – probably isomorphic with later locomotion – but differentially influenced by the biomechanical demands of the supine versus upright posture. A second purpose is to show, from this and additional kinesiological reasoning, that straightforward biomechanical demands can, in a simple manner, account for the disappearance of the stepping reflex, the increase of spontaneous kicking, and the retention of stepping through practice.

## Method

### Subjects

Subjects were eight normal infants recruited by telephone from published birth announcements and by word of mouth. Four of the infants were boys. Two of the girls were normal, full-term monozygotic twins delivered by Caesarian section (zygosity determined by a common placenta). Seven of the infants were exactly 2 weeks old when observed; Male 1 was 5 days old. Birth weights averaged 3,333 g (range, 2,835 g to 3,855 g). Five additional infants were observed, but their data were not used because stepping could not be elicited in three infants, neither kicking nor stepping was seen in the fourth infant, and the fifth infant fell asleep. This percentage of infants failing to show the stepping response at any one test session is consistent with studies reported by Beintema(1968).

### Procedure

The design of these observations was a combination of frame-by-frame movement microanalysis, using videotape recordings and concurrent electromyography (EMG) of four major muscle groups of the legs. This "neuroethological" technique has the advantage of providing both detailed kinematic data and a behavioral framework for understanding the muscle activations. Behaviorally, identical movements may result from dissimilar patterns of muscle contractions; at the same time EMG recordings are nearly impossible to interpret without corresponding movement analysis, especially in infants who cannot voluntarily contract muscles on command (Bekoff, 1978).

Because both kicking (Thelen, 1981a; Thelen et al., 1981) and stepping (Beintema, 1968; Peiper, 1963) are most easily elicited in infants who are awake and moving, fussing, or crying, we asked parents to bring infants to the laboratory about an hour before an anticipated feeding. If the infants were asleep, the handling required to attach the electrodes usually woke them up. Infants were prepared for recording by wiping the electrode sites with Omni Prep (D. O. Weaver Co.) and attaching Beckman miniature bipotential surface electrodes. Electrodes were attached to the bellies of the following muscles on the right leg: tibialis anterior, medial gastrocnemius, rectus femoris, and medial hamstring. Each recording electrode was referred to a second electrode placed about 1 cm away on the same muscle group. To further secure the electrodes and minimize movement artifact, stretch nylon infant tights and socks, cut off at the knee and ankle, were placed on the infant. These procedures resulted in consistently low skin resistance readings, which were monitored at each application; no movement artifact; and a minimum of electrical spread between muscles despite their small distances apart (O'Connell & Gardner, 1963). Finally, the joints were marked with 3 mm white tape squares affixed to small strips of black tape. Muscle activity was amplified on a Grass Model 7D polygraph with 7DA driver amplifiers and 7P3 AC preamplifiers.

Behavioral recording used two cameras and two Sony VO 2800 video recorders. One camera recorded a lateral view of the right leg. The second camera, positioned directly over the supine infant, recorded movements of both legs in the frontal plane. Two TEL VC-405 frame markers simultaneously labeled video fields on both the lateral and frontal tapes and provided a signal on a special polygraph channel (60 frames/sec). Thus movement in both the sagittal and frontal planes could be correlated precisely to the polygraph records. The stepping reflex was produced by standing the infant on a pressure-sensitive mat, which was also amplified and recorded on the polygraph.

After the infants were prepared, the recording session began with 5 minutes of spontaneous kicking in the supine position. No specific stimuli were presented to the infants. Immediately after the kicking, the observer lifted the infant under the arms and placed the soles of the feet gently on the surface of the pressure mat. Testing sessions for stepping ranged from .5 to 1.9 in ($M = 1.3$ min) and were terminated if the infant became unduly distressed.

During the recording session, an observer recorded the infant's state every $16^{2}/_{3}$ sec (1,000 frames) by using instantaneous sampling. Infants were scored on an arousal scale as follows: 1 = asleep; 2 = drowsy; 3 = awake, quiet, no or few gross movements; 4 = awake, moving; 5 = fussy; 6 = crying. Interobserver reliabilities were determined for half the observations, and these, as percentage of agreement, were 77%. To obtain rate, alternation, and laterality data, observers scored right and left leg kicks from the frontal view videotapes using an event recorder activated by two finger keys. Interobserver reliabilities in eight pilot and three subject tapes were .98 for the rate, .95 for alternation, and .94 for laterality.

Kinematic data were obtained by scanning the videotapes frame by frame, using procedures described previously (Thelen et al., 1981). Half the videotapes were scored twice; reliabilities, as determined by previous methods, were 78%. Over 180,000 frames were scanned in this study.

In brief, kicks and steps were characterized by four phases. During the flexion phase, ankle, knee, and hip were flexed, and the leg was brought toward the torso. The intramovement-pause phase was the time between the end of the movement of the flexion and the initiation of motion. In the third, or extension, phase, there was an increase in joint angles and movement away from the torso. The intermovement interval was the duration between the termination of movement in the extension phase and the start of the next flexion. For temporal data, observers noted the frame numbers of the start and termination of the flexion and extension phases, according to predetermined criteria (see Thelen et al., 1981). In addition, the position of the marked knee joint at each of the four movement change points was also recorded by using a transparent 5 mm grid placed over the video screen. This resulted in measurements of displacement of the knee in the $x$ and $y$ planes during the movement phases – a reflection of the amplitude of the movement. Electromyographic descriptions were obtained by finding the movement change points by frame number on the polygraph chart and qualitatively relating the videotaped movements and the preceding and succeeding events to their EMG counterparts.

## Results

### Motivation and Elicitation of Kicking and Stepping

Of the 13 newborn infants originally brought to the laboratory, eight showed both kicking and stepping movements in the single continuous recording session; these data are reported here. Table 1 shows the individual rates of kicks and steps in these infants. (The data from the twins, Females 3 and 4, proved no more alike than unrelated subjects in all respects, and they are therefore treated as individual subjects.) There is no overall difference in the rates of kicking and stepping, nor is there a correlation between kicking and stepping rates in individual infants (Spearman's $r = .639$, ns). Some infants kicked more than they stepped; for some the reverse was true; but in most the rate stayed about the same.

The upright posture, therefore, was no more effective in eliciting locomotorlike movements in newborns than was the supine posture. Likewise, the tactile stimuli from the soles of the feet as they are placed on the surface do not uniquely release these movements. Infants just as readily perform leg movements when the soles of their feet do not contact a surface or bear weight.

Previous research has shown that spontaneous kicking and other stereotyped movements are more likely to be seen when infants are fussy or excited than when they are alert and quiet (Thelen, 1981a; Thelen

**Table 1:** Rate, alternations, and laterality in newborn kicking and stepping

| | Rate | | Alternations % of total movements | | Laterality % right-leg movements | | Laterality Side of first step |
|---|---|---|---|---|---|---|---|
| Subject | Kicks/min. | Steps/min. | Kicks | Steps | Kicks | Step | |
| Female | | | | | | | |
| 1 | 42.7 | 20.8 | 46.8 | 37.5 | 59.4 | 54.3 | L |
| 2 | 20.2 | 10.5 | 45.8 | 75.0 | 31.8 | 50.0 | L |
| 3 | 20.5 | 21.0 | 68.1 | 66.7 | 60.6 | 52.3 | L |
| 4 | 13.6 | 25.0 | 71.6 | 47.8 | 47.7 | 34.8 | R |
| Male | | | | | | | |
| 1 | 15.2 | 26.0 | 92.1 | 100.0 | 50.0 | 59.0 | L |
| 2 | 16.8 | 12.6 | 65.0 | 52.4 | 36.0 | 57.0 | R |
| 3 | 11.3 | 10.0 | 37.3 | 83.3 | 77.1 | 50.0 | L |
| 4 | 11.5 | 10.5 | 70.1 | 73.7 | 55.2 | 42.1 | L |
| M | 19.0 | 17.1 | 62.1 | 67.1 | 52.2 | 48.8 | |

*Note:* L = left. R = right.

et al., 1981). Peiper (1963) and Beintema (1968) also reported more stepping responses when infants were highly aroused. In general, the infants in this study showed moderate to high levels of arousal during the observation. The overall arousal index, a weighted average of time spent in states ranging from 1 (asleep) to 6 (crying), was 4.8. The correlation between individual kicking rates and arousal index did not reach statistical significance (Spearman's $r$ = .642), but there was a tendency for the four fastest kickers to be more aroused than the four slowest kickers (4.72 vs. 4.22). There was also a tendency for infants to be more aroused in the stepping portion of the observation (5.1) than in the kicking portion (4.5), but infants generally became more fussy during the observation, and the stepping test was done at the end of the session. In any case, in this sample, kicking did not require higher degrees of arousal than stepping. Therefore, once infants were aroused enough to show gross motor movements, there apparently was nothing unique about the traditional walking posture for eliciting steplike patterns. Figure 1 illustrates the continuity of kicking and stepping. As the infant is lifted off the table, ongoing kicking movements look like stepping in the air before the feet ever touch the surface.

## Alternation and Laterality of Stepping and Kicking

Descriptions of the newborn stepping reflex emphasize the regular alternation of movements between right and left legs, as in mature locomotion (Andre-Thomas & Autgaerden, 1966; Peiper, 1963; Taft & Cohen, 1967). When the alternations are actually quantified, results show, as in Table 1, that overall, steps with one leg are followed by steps with the contralateral leg about two thirds of the time, although there is individual variability. Kicking also shows

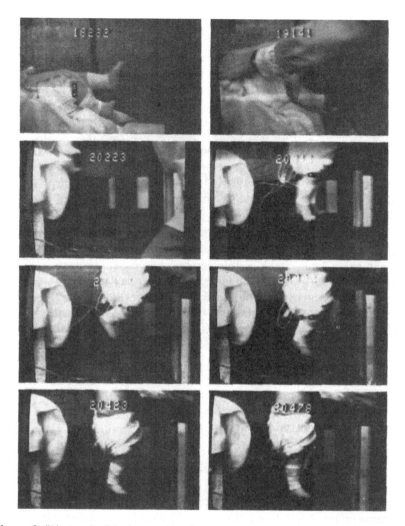

**Figure 1:** "Air-stepping" in the transition from the supine to vertical posture in a 2-week old girl. (Photographed from videomonitor stopped on single frames. Frame numbers have been superimposed on the tape, 60 frames/sec. From the upper left: Frame 18282 [0 sec], supine kicking; Frame 19141 [14.317 sec], observer prepares to lift infant; Frame 20223 [32.350 sec], infant is lifted from cot [note step with right leg]; Frame 20311 [33.817 sec], infant is being lowered to mat, both legs extended; Frame 20353 [34.516 sec], both legs flexed in step; Frame 20392 (35.167 sec) left leg, partially obscured, flexed in step, feet have not yet made contact with substrate; Frame 20423 (35.683 sec), right leg lowered to substrate, right foot still plantar flexed, left leg flexed; Frame 20478 (36.600 sec), right leg fully extended, left leg still flexed in step.).

regular alternation in about the same proportion of movements. Infants who used a single leg more often in kicking tended to do the same in stepping, although the results are not significant in this small sample. Alternation, then, is not confined to movements in the erect posture.

Peters and Petrie (1979) reported that a significant proportion of 24 infants tested commenced stepping with the right leg when their feet were lowered to the surface. As shown in Table 1, these results were not confirmed in our small sample. Infants showed no preference for the right leg to initiate stepping after touching the surface nor was there a consistent, overall laterality preference in either kicking or stepping.

## Kinematic Comparisons between Kicking and Stepping

Figures 2 and 3 show stick diagrams of two typical successive kicks and two typical successive steps in the same infant (Male 4); these diagrams were obtained by plotting the toe, ankle, knee, and hip positions every two frames (33 msec). Qualitative comparisons of the two movements show many similarities in topography. Both movements show rapid and nearly simultaneous flexions in ankle, knee, and hip, followed by an extension characterized by a swing forward of the lower leg and increased plantar flexion of the ankle. (This similarity is best seen by rotating the diagram to the orientation of the other movement posture). There are several differences in the movement patterns as well. Contact with the substrate in stepping prevents the full extent of plantar flexion of the foot. In these examples, the joint angles in knee and hip at the maximally flexed position of kicking are smaller than those at the same joints in stepping, which suggests that the kick flex has a larger amplitude or path than in the step. Extension, however, was often slower and less complete in the kick than in the step. In general, there is a marked congruence in the movement patterns traced by kicking and stepping.

## Electromyography of Kicking and Stepping

Figures 2 and 3 also show the EMG records of the successive kicks and steps in the same infant. A full description of the EMG of leg movements in infancy and their developmental course can be found in Thelen and Fisher (Note 1). In brief, young infants show two main types of stereotyped leg movements in the sagittal plane (*i.e.*, excluding rotations). One type is a slow, ramp-type lift of the leg with knee extended and characterized by moderately high, tonic activation of the rectus femoris (the hip flexor); usually, but not always, there is coactivation of the hamstrings that acts as a stabilizer of the extended knee. Leg lifts may last from a few to many seconds. We have never observed leg lifts while the infant was held in the upright position.

The second type, which is of concern here, is the rapid, steplike kick, illustrated by the diagrams in Figure 2. This kick shows strong, phasic activation in the tibialis anterior, the ankle dorsiflexor, the rectus femoris, (the hip flexor), and usually, but not always, some activity in the hamstrings

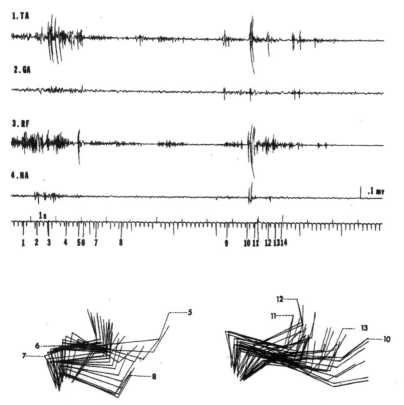

**Figure 2:** Stick-figure diagrams and concurrent electromyographs of kicking movements in a 2-week old boy (Male 4). (Polygraph channels record the following muscles of the right leg: 1. TA = tibialis anterior, ankle dorsiflexor; 2. GA = medial gastrocnemius-plantor flexor of the ankle; it is also a knee stabilizer and has a small role in knee flexion; 3. RF = rectus femoris, hip flexor and knee extensor; 4. HA = medial hamstring, knee flexor, hip extensor, and knee stabilizer. The fifth channel is a timer channel showing seconds [upward] and frames on the videotape; each down stroke marks 10 frames. The numbers added to the fifth channel correspond to movement changes as determined by frame-by-frame scanning of the videotape and also to corresponding points on the stick-figure diagrams: 1. At the beginning of this segment, the leg is lifted and the knee is extended. 2. Onset of the kick from the lifted position; knee and hip are sharply flexed, the ankle is dorsiflexed. 3. Knee is extended, leg is still lifted [hip flexed]. 4. Leg is dropped slightly. 5. Rapid knee and hip flex; leg is dropped slightly during flexion [see diagram]. 6. Rapid flexion movement ends. 7. Leg is slowly flexed further to the maximum flexed position. 8. During extension phase, leg is relaxed and rests on substrate. 9. Leg is slightly lifted with extended knee. 10. At onset of rapid kick, leg is again dropped slightly and then flexed. 11. This is the point of maximum flexion. 12. Extension phase begins. 13. Extension phase ends, knee is extended, hip is still slightly flexed. 14. Leg is lowered to substrate.).

(knee flexors). The flexor burst is almost always about 200 msec in duration. Most significantly, however, the extension phase of the kick, in which the leg is stretched out and away from the body, shows little or no corresponding phasic activation of the extensor muscles. In other words, the extension appears to be simply a relaxation of the leg following the strong activation

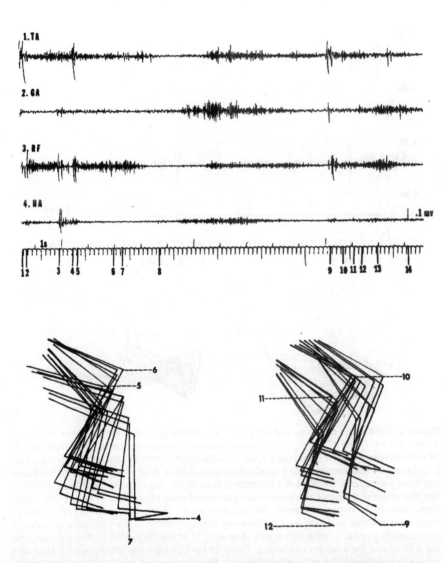

**Figure 3:** Stick figure diagrams and concurrent electromyographs of stepping movements in a 2-week-old boy (Male 4), recorded 4 minutes after the segment shown in Figure 2. (Polygraph channels are labeled similarly to Figure 2. The numbers added to the fifth channel correspond to movement changes as determined by frame-by-frame scanning of the videotape and also to corresponding points on the stick-figure diagrams: 1. Onset of a step. 2. Maximum flexion of step. 3. Leg has been lowered to the surface, and pressure mat indicates weight borne on the leg. 4. Onset of flexion for step [see diagram]. 5. End of flexion movement; leg is held in the flexed position, and there is tonic activation of rectus femoris. 6. Leg begins swing forward and is lowered. 7. Toe touches surface. 8. Foot flat, knee extended, weight borne on leg. 9. Onset of flexion for next step [see diagram]. 10. Maximum flexion. 11. Onset of extension movement; infant has been moved backward slightly by examiner. 12. Toe touches substrate. 13. Plantar flexion of foot [infant "standing on toes"]. 14. Foot is again flat on substrate.).

of the flexion; the momentum of the flexion is sufficient to account for the movement of the leg to the resting position. Occasionally, infants will lie with their legs quite tightly flexed against their bodies; in this case, low levels of tonic co-contraction of the upper leg muscles are observed. Figure 3 shows an EMG record from the same infant during the stepping test, which followed 4 minutes after the kicks shown in Figure 2. During erect posture, EMGs show clear tonic activation of the knee stabilizers, the gastrocnemius, hamstrings, and quadriceps, when the legs are weight bearing. During the step, however, the EMGs are highly similar to those seen in the kick. Note, for example, the impulsive and strong flexor contractions in tibialis and rectus and somewhat weaker response in the hamstrings. (The relatively minor role of the hamstrings in both kick and step flexion may indicate that hip flexion supplies the principal momentum and that the knee flexion is a more passive consequence of strong hip contraction.) When the infant pauses in the flexed position, antigravity tonic activity is seen in the flexors. As in kicks, extensor movement is largely passive. Figure 3 also shows clear gastrocnemius activity during plantar flexion of the ankle. Because strong plantar flexion is much less common in supine kicking than when the foot is weight bearing, the kicking EMG in general shows much less gastrocnemius activity than the stepping EMG. Although there are some understandable differences in the use of stabilizing and weight-bearing muscle combinations, the EMG reveals the step and kick to be identical patterns of muscle contraction.

## Temporal Characteristics of Kicking and Stepping

Frame-by-frame microanalysis was done using the lateral view tapes for the first 30 consecutive right-leg kicks or for the total number of right kicks on the tape if the infant performed less than 30 right-leg kicks. All the right-leg steps in the session were analyzed. The results of this analysis are presented in Table 2. Kicks and steps are very similar in their temporal structure. The mean duration of the flexion phase was just over 300 msec for both kicks and steps, with no significant differences between the phase durations for the sample or for individual infants. Durations of the other movement phase, extension, were slightly longer than flexion; kick extensions averaging 586 msec were significantly longer overall than step extensions averaging 420 msec. Both the intramovement pause and the intermovement interval showed no duration differences between kicking and stepping. The pause, or nonmovement, phases were distinctly more variable than the flexion and extension phases, both in individual infants and for the sample as a whole.

   This asymmetry in the variability of these phases is further illustrated in Figure 4, which shows the frequency histograms of the phase durations pooled for all eight infants. Both flexion and extension phases are tightly clustered around the means. Intramovement pauses also show a large proportion of

**Table 2:** Mean duration of phases of newborn kicking and stepping

| Subject | N | Flexion | Intramove pause | Extension | Intermove interval | Move cycle |
|---|---|---|---|---|---|---|
| | | | *Phase duration (in sec)* | | | |
| | | | **Female** | | | |
| 1 | | | | | | |
| Kicks | 27 | .269 | .363 | .580 | 1.530 | 2.710 |
| Steps | 22 | .374 | .305 | .539 | 2.998 | 4.185 |
| 2 | | | | | | |
| Kicks | 26 | .319 | .171 | .727 | 10.371 | 11.610 |
| Steps | 7 | .395 | .171 | .660 | 12.389 | 13.569 |
| 3 | | | | | | |
| Kicks | 30 | .219 | .491 | .454 | 1.556 | 2.731 |
| Steps | 9 | .183 | .439 | .318 | 5.420 | 6.402 |
| 4 | | | | | | |
| Kicks | 28 | .356 | 1.317[a] | .655 | 5.948 | 8.300 |
| Steps | 11 | .320 | .335 | .435 | 2.317 | 3.440 |
| | | | **Male** | | | |
| 1 | | | | | | |
| Kicks | 30 | .362[b] | .504 | .627[c] | 6.818 | 8.290 |
| Steps | 7 | .243 | .271 | .245 | 2.975 | 3.680 |
| 2 | | | | | | |
| Kicks | 27 | .328 | .458 | .503[d] | 8.810 | 10.115 |
| Steps | 11 | .374 | .822 | .273 | 7.752 | 9.212 |
| 3 | | | | | | |
| Kicks | 30 | .277 | .468 | .476 | 2.277 | 3.513 |
| Steps | 4 | .392 | .417 | .438 | 11.417 | 12.661 |
| 4 | | | | | | |
| Kicks | 30 | .398 | .514 | .689 | 8.630 | 10.207 |
| Steps | 7 | .333 | .638 | .474 | 11.664 | 13.147 |
| Means | | | | | | |
| Kicks | 228 | .315 | .542 | .586[e] | 5.672 | 7.115 |
| SD | | .199 | .734 | .453 | 11.939 | 12.029 |
| Steps | 78 | .324 | .434 | .420 | 5.763 | 6.942 |
| SD | | .243 | .574 | .289 | 7.481 | 7.586 |

Note: [a] Kicks significantly different from steps ($t = 3.80$, $p < .001$). [b] Kicks significantly different from steps ($t = 2.59$, $p < .05$). [c] Kicks significantly different from steps ($t = 2.93$, $p < .01$). [d] Kicks significantly different from steps ($t = 4.33$, $p < .0001$). [e] Kicks significantly different from steps ($t = 3.36$, $p < .001$).

very short intervals, indicating that once the leg is flexed, there is a high probability that the extension will follow within a few hundred milliseconds. The intermovement interval, however, is very variable. Although some kicks and steps will follow almost immediately, often many seconds may elapse between movements. The skewed intervals between movements indicate that kicks and steps are likely to cluster together or occur in bouts.

## Similarities between Stepping, Kicking, and Mature Stepping

Mature locomotion is usually described as having a "swing" phase, in which the foot is off the ground and moving forward, and a "stance" phase, in which the foot is on the ground and the body is moving forward with respect to the weight-bearing leg. In a number of vertebrate and invertebrate species,

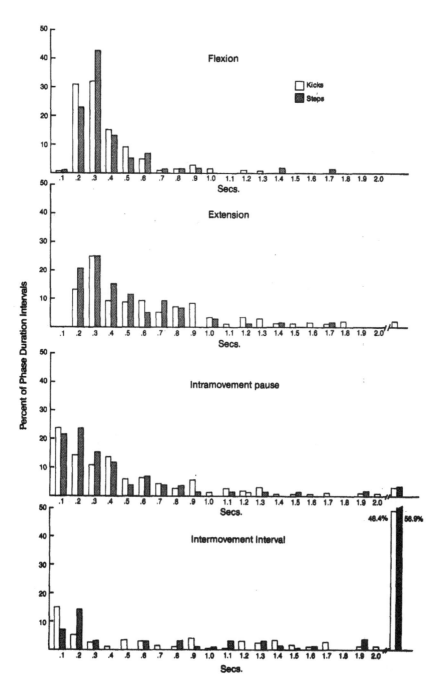

**Figure 4:** Frequency histograms of phase duration intervals of kicking and stepping. (Data are pooled for eight infants. All intervals over 2 sec are summed and included in the final bars.).

including humans, these phases vary differently with the velocity of locomotion. As the speed of walking increases, the stance phase decreases proportionately. In contrast, the swing duration remains relatively constant or decreases only slightly. Thus, increases in speed are accomplished largely by reducing the time the support leg remains on the ground (Pearson, 1976).

An identical phase relationship was found in kicking in 1-month-old infants (Thelen et al., 1981). The sum of the flexion, intrakick pause, and extension phase is analogous to the swing phase, whereas the extended interval between movements is similar to the support, or stance, phase. Regression of kick swing and stance on the cycle time, the reciprocal of the rate, showed that the swing, remained virtually constant in duration. Adjustments in speed were made entirely in the interkick interval, which decreased as the cycle decreased.

This relationship was confirmed for kicking in the younger infants of the present study and extended to stepping as well. In all eight infants, regression $R^2$ for the intermovement interval on the cycle duration ranged from .938 to .999 for kicks and from .962 to .999 for steps, all highly significant at the .0001 level. Regression $R^2$ of swing phase was not significantly related to cycle time for kicks in four infants; it was significantly related in four others, but much less strongly than for the stance phase ($R^2$ ranged from .175 to .405). In only one of the eight infants was step swing related to cycle time ($R^2 = .462$, $p < .03$). When the swing showed a relationship to velocity, the extension phase of the swing accounted for the observed proportional change.

Thus, in newborn stepping and kicking, as in 1-month kicking, adjustments in velocity are made almost entirely by adjusting the time between the movements. In newborn kicking, more rapid kicking is also reflected in slightly faster extension phases. The flexion and intramovement pause durations remain unaffected by the overall rate.

## Amplitude Comparisons between Kicking and Stepping

Amplitude changes during kicking and stepping were quantified by measuring the displacement of the knee during flexion and extension. Any differences in image size from moving the infant from the supine to the erect position were corrected by adjusting the step displacements by a factor that was the ratio of the fixed limb length from knee to ankle in kicking and stepping conditions. The resulting displacements are shown for the individual infants in Figure 5. In order to compare homologous aspects of the movements in each posture, the flexions and extensions are expressed as vectors parallel to the torso ($x$ axis in kicking, $y$ axis in stepping) and a vector perpendicular to the torso ($y$ axis in kicking, $x$ in stepping).

This analysis confirmed our subjective impression that the flexion in kicking was a "bigger" movement than that in stepping, that is, the knee was brought closer to the chest, and the final joint angles were smaller. In five of the eight

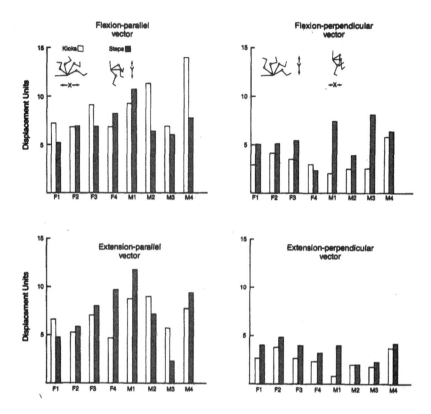

**Figure 5:** Comparisons of kick and step amplitudes during flexion and extension for individual infants. (Amplitudes are expressed as vectors parallel to the torso [x axis in kicks, y axis in steps] and vectors perpendicular to the torso [y axis in kicks, x axis in steps].).

subjects, the parallel vector was greater in kicking than in stepping. Overall, kicks moved 8.3 units compared to 6.9 units in steps. In contrast, steps showed a bigger displacement in the perpendicular flexion vector in seven out of eight infants. Reference to the stick diagrams shows that in supine kicking, the knee is lifted and then lowered toward the chest. This results in a smaller final hip angle and smaller difference between the initiation and final position of the leg than in stepping, where the maximum flex is both lifted and extended from the body. Extension values in the perpendicular vector also reflect the effect of the supine posture on the degree of flexion possible in the hip.

Extension amplitudes in the parallel vector are more variable. Especially interesting are the cases such as Females 3 and 4 and Male 4 in which a large flexion in the kick was followed by comparatively smaller displacement in the extension. The relaxation of the extension, longer in, duration, often resulted in the leg resting on the substrate before the joints were fully extended. In other words, extensions in kicking were sometimes not complete or would consist of an initial relaxation of the leg to a semiflexed position, followed by an extension so gradual that it was undetectable by this analysis (over hundreds of frames). In contrast, extensions in stepping almost always were complete – until the foot touched the surface.

## Discussion

The weight of the evidence presented here suggests that neonatal stepping and supine spontaneous kicking are identical movement patterns ennervated by the same neural pathways. Behaviorally, both movements show identical synergistic flexion at ankle, knee, and hip, followed by a steplike forward extension. There is remarkable correspondence in the temporal organization of kick and step, including the absolute durations of the phase intervals and the variability structure of those intervals. Electromyographically, both step and kick show the same phasic flexor burst, followed by a passive extension phase. It is difficult to imagine that the precise and stereotyped nature of these movements could be controlled by two entirely different neural pattern generators, each for a separate posture.

One of the textbook principles in kinesiology is that muscle function can only be understood in reference to the effects of gravity and body position in terms of support or nonsupport (e.g., Logan & McKinney, 1977, p. 70). Where kicking and stepping do differ, those differences can indeed be readily explained by considering the effects of the upright versus the supine posture and the action of bearing the weight on the legs and the feet. When the soles of the feet contact the surface, the knees straighten and stabilize, and further active plantar flexion is done against the forces of gravity. Plantar flexion in the supine position, in contrast, appears to be a consequence of the passive extensor relaxation and shows little activity in the ankle extensors. Hip flexion in the upright position works entirely against gravity, but that same movement in the supine position is indeed aided by gravity. Thus, the flexion, although of similar duration, travels further in kicking than in stepping. The same muscle impulse, the programmed flexor burst, can exert a greater force when the mass of the leg is working partially with the pull of gravity rather than entirely against it. (Compare, for example, the ease of bringing your knee to your chest while lying down or while standing.)

Extension similarly shows the simple bio-mechanical effects of the infant's posture. In the upright position, suspended by the armpits, the infant's full weight is opposed by the pull of gravity. As the flexor contractions are released, the legs, aided by gravity acting on their mass, are quickly stretched to the full extended position. When the infant is lying down, the weight of the body is supported by the substrate, and the extensor relaxation is neither as short in duration nor as large in amplitude.

Stepping is equally indistinguishable from kicking on motivational or eliciting factors. The traditional literature would lead us to believe, somewhat anthrocentrically, that the upright posture provides some unique stimulus for eliciting steplike movements. This study shows, however, that infants are equally disposed to perform similar leg motions when supine. In either posture, infants should be in a moderate-to-high state of arousal to show these gross motor behaviors. Almost all infants were aroused and somewhat distressed when they were lifted to the stepping-test position. Korner & Grobstein (1966) reported that when crying neonates were picked up to the shoulder they were quieted, but without the soothing shoulder contact, handling and the upright posture increased arousal. It may be that the arousal changes induced by picking up infants and suspending them by the armpits may elicit leg movements, which appear like steps. Although it may seem to the examiner that the adultlike erect position is the stimulus for the reflex, it is likely that generalized tonic arousal, not the posture per se, is the releasing factor (cf. Figure 1 and also Thelen, 1981a, 1981b).

If newborn stepping and kicking are indeed isomorphic, what accounts for the increase in the ease of elicitation and frequency of kicking and the virtual disappearance of stepping? We believe the answer again lies in the all-important differential effects of gravity on muscle function in the two postures. As the infant matures, the mass of the legs increases dramatically, altering the dynamics of the moving limb. It may well be that the strength of the muscle contractions, that is, the rate of the firing of the motor units and/ or the number of motor units recruited may be sufficient to cause frequent and vigorous kicks when the body weight is supported in the supine position and the movement is aided by gravity; however, it may be simply inadequate to lift the legs or support the full weight when the infant is upright. Thus, we are proposing an inequality in the development of the muscle mass and the strength of the muscle contractions, which is noticeable when the muscles must exert work entirely against gravity.

This hypothesis is entirely consistent with Zelazo's (1976) views of the stepping reflex as being a precursor to locomotion, although we do not exclude the possibility of reflexes having ontogenetic, adaptive functions as well as potential ones (see Thelen, 1981b). However, we do offer an alternative explanation for why the reflex normally disappears and why active exercise was effective in prolonging the movement and perhaps accelerating voluntary walking.

We suggest that the experimental infants in the Zelazo, Zelazo, and Kolb (1972) study participated in a program of simple physical training. A textbook principle in physical training is that in order to develop strength, "overload" demands must be made on the muscles; they must work against resistances greater than normally encountered (Logan & McKinney, 1977). Zelazo's passive exercise control infants had their legs moved for them while they were on their backs, whereas those infants in the experimental group were held upright. These authors assumed that the determining variable was that of active versus passive movement (cf. Held & Hein, 1963), but perhaps a more important difference was the posture. The supine position imposes no overload for infants who characteristically assume that posture. In contrast, infants who were encouraged to "walk" were additionally moving against gravity. Similarly, adults impose additional antigravity activity on abdominal and back muscles when they do sit ups. The infants who actively stepped may have, through training, increased their strength to keep up with the increasing mass of their legs.

Was the increase in stepping of the Zelazo et al. (1972) active exercise group a result of instrumental learning as the authors claim? Learning cannot be ruled out as a factor. Work by us (Thelen, 1981a; Thelen & Fisher, in press) and others (reviewed by Rovee-Collier & Gekoski, 1979) shows that supine leg kicking, for example, can be converted from a spontaneous to an instrumental action. However, there are several reasons to argue against learning as the necessary cause for step increasing. First, spontaneous kicking movements in all 20 infants observed naturalistically every 2 weeks increased dramatically from ages 4 weeks to 6 months without any intervention (Thelen, 1979). Infants kicked increasingly more during this period, and they kicked in a wider variety of contexts (Thelen, 1981a). If their physical strength is sufficient, this increase may have also been reflected in "vertical kicking," or stepping. Zelazo et al. (1972) describe one 5-week-old infant who made "vigorous walking motions while the observer suspended him in mid-air over the table" (p. 315). Although these authors interpret this as "little doubt that learning occurred," we show that such "air-stepping" can be seen without any reinforcement or practice, as in Figure 1. Finally, the young infants we have tested in the laboratory looked uncomfortable, not pleasurably reinforced when held under the armpits with legs dangling, although this discomfort may disappear as the infants get older.

The question of why human infants would show this disparity between muscle mass and strength has several possible answers. If functional use of the legs in early infancy has no adaptive significance, there would be no selective pressure for mass and strength development to occur synchronously. It may well be that weight gain and the concomitant benefits of temperature regulation and fat storage are more important adaptive priorities in young infants than motor precocity.

A second and more troubling speculation is that Western infant-care practices do not optimize infant motor strength development. There are many reports of striking motor precocity in infants of peoples of Africa and Central America (e.g., Ainsworth, 1967; Geber & Dean, 1957; Konner, 1976; Leiderman, Babu, Kagia, Kraemer, & Leiderman, 1973; Solomons & Solomons, 1975). Although there is debate over the origins and extent of this precocity (cf. Freedman, 1976; Warren, 1972), there appears to be an association between motor advancement and the practice of continual mother–infant contact, especially in the use of the sling. Konner (1973), for example, noted that in the !Kung hunter–gatherers, parents encouraged a vertical posture in infants in a sling or held them sitting or standing in the mothers' laps. In terms of the physical training hypothesis advanced here, the upright posture may play a very important role in advancing motor control. This position provides the overload training for legs, neck, and trunk that is simply not experienced by a baby who is horizontal for most of the day and night. More work is clearly needed to determine the effect of child-care customs on motor development.

The introduction of this peripheral or bio-mechanical hypothesis is not meant to discount the importance of central mechanisms in motor control or to ignore the possibility of environmentally mediated central changes. For example, recent studies showed that opportunities for physical exercise during development increased specific aspects of cerebellar Purkinje cells in both monkeys (Floeter & Greenough, 1979) and mice (Pysh & Weiss, 1979). It is also premature to assume that mechanisms controlling stepping are identical to those involved in the other so-called primitive reflexes. Nonetheless, the role of the biomechanical properties of muscle and their concomitant developmental changes have been largely ignored in favor of central processes, although recent motor theorists are increasingly focusing on these dynamic aspects of movement control (cf. Kelso, Holt, Rubin, & Kugler, 1981). Since in infants, motor maturity and central nervous system integrity are usually also associated with gains in weight and strength, it is essential to separate these contributing influences on motor development.

## Note

1. There are large discrepancies in the literature over the age of the disappearance of the stepping reflex. For example, in the same volume, Taft and Cohen (1967) place this disappearance at 3–4 months and DiLeo (1967) at 6 weeks.

## Reference Note

1. Thelen, E., & Fisher, D. M. *Kinematic and electromyographic characteristics of spontaneous leg movements in young infants.* Manuscript in preparation, 1982.

## References

Ainsworth, M. D. S. *Infancy in Uganda.* Baltimore, Md.: Johns Hopkins University Press, 1967.

Andre-Thomas, & Autgaerden, S. *Locomotion from pre- to postnatal life.* Lavenham, Suffolk, England: Spastics Society, 1966.

Beintema, D. J. *A neurological study of newborn infants.* Lavenham, Suffolk, England: Spastics Society, 1968.

Bekoff, A. A neuroethological approach to the study of the ontogeny of coordinated behavior. In G. M. Burghardt & M. Bekoff (Eds), *The development of behavior: Comparative and evolutionary aspects.* New York: Garland, 1978.

Bower, T. G. R. Repetitive processes in child development. *Scientific American,* 1976, *235(5),* 38–47.

DiLeo, J. H. Developmental evaluation of very young infants. In J. Hellmuth (Ed.), *Exceptional infant: Vol. 1. The normal infant.* Seattle, Wash.: Special Child Publications, 1967.

Floeter, M. K., & Greenough, W. T., Cerebellar plasticity: Modification of Purkinje cell structure by differential rearing in monkeys. *Science,* 1979, *206,* 227–229.

Freedman, D. B. Comments on "From reflexive to instrumental behavior." In L. P. Lipsitt (Ed.), *Developmental psychobiology: The significance of infancy.* Hillsdale, N.J.: Erlbaum, 1976.

Geber, M., & Dean, R. F. The state of development of newborn African children. *Lancet,* 1957, 1, 1216–1219.

Gotts, E. E. Newborn walking. *Science,* 1972, *177,* 1057–1058.

Held, R., & Hein, A. Movement-produced stimulation in the development of visually guided behavior. *Journal of Comparative and Physiological Psychology,* 1963, *56,* 872–876.

Kelso, J. A. S., Holt, K. G., Rubin, P., & Kugler, P. N. Patterns of human interlimb coordination emerge from the properties of non-linear, limit cycle oscillatory processes: Theory and data. *Journal of Motor Behavior,* 1981, *13,* 226–261.

Konner, M. Newborn walking: Additional data. *Science* 1973, *179,* 397.

Konner, M. Maternal care, infant behavior, and development among the Kalahari Desert San. In R. B. Lee & I. De Vore (Eds.), *Kalahari hunter-gatherers.* Cambridge, Mass.: Harvard University Press, 1976.

Korner, A. F., & Grobstein, R. Visual alertness as related to soothing in neonates: Implications for maternal stimulation and early deprivation. *Child Development,* 1966, *37,* 867–876.

Leiderman, F. H., Babu, B., Kagia, J., Kraemer, H. C., & Leiderman, G. F. African infant precocity and some social influences during the first year. *Nature,* 1973, *242,* 247–249.

Logan, G. A., & McKinney, W. C. *Anatomic kinesiology* (2nd ed.). Dubuque, Iowa: Brown, 1977.

McGraw, M. B. From reflex to muscular control in the assumption of an erect posture and ambulation in the human infant. *Child Development,* 1932, *3,* 291–297.

Menkes, J. H. *Textbook of child neurology.* Philadelphia, Pa.: Lea & Febiger, 1980.

Molnar, G. E. Analysis of motor disorder in retarded infants and young children. *American Journal of Mental Deficiency,* 1978, *83,* 213–222.

O'Connell, A. L., & Gardner, E. B. The use of electromyography in kinesiological research. *Research Quarterly of the American Association of Health and Physical Education,* 1963, *34,* 166–184.

Oppenheim, R. W. Ontogenetic adaptations and retrogressive processes in the development of the nervous system and behaviour: A neuroembryological perspective. In H. F. R. Prechtl & K. Connolly (Eds.), *Maturation and development.* London: Spastics International Medical Publications and William Heinemann Medical Books, 1981.

Paulson, G., & Gottlieb, G. Developmental reflexes: The reappearance of foetal and neonatal reflexes in aged patients. *Brain,* 1968, *91,* 37–52.

Pearson, K. The control of walking. *Scientific American,* 1976, *235(6),* 72–86.

Peiper, A. *Cerebral function in infancy and childhood.* New York: Consultants Bureau, 1963.

Peters, M., & Petrie, B. F. Functional asymmetries in the stepping reflex of human neonates. *Canadian Journal of Psychology,* 1979, *33,* 198–200.

Pontius, A. A. Neuro-ethics of "walking" in the newborn. *Perceptual and Motor Skills,* 1973, *37,* 235–245.

Pysh, J. J., & Weiss, G., M. Exercise during development induces an increase in Purkinje cell dendritic tree size. *Science,* 1979, *206,* 230–231.

Rovee-Collier, C. K., & Gekoski, M. J. The economics of infancy: A review of conjugate reinforcement. *Advances in Child Development and Behavior,* 1979, *13*, 195–255.

Simpkiss, M. J., & Raikes, A. S. Problems resulting from excessive use of baby walkers and baby bouncers. *Lancet,* 1972, *1*, 747.

Solomons, G., & Solomons, H. Motor development in Yucatecan infants. *Developmental Medicine and Child Neurology,* 1975, *17*, 41–46.

Taft, L. T., & Cohen, H. J. Neonatal and infant reflexology. In J. Hellmuth (Ed.), *Exceptional infant: Vol. 1. The normal infant.* Seattle, Wash.: Special Child Publications, 1967.

Teitelbaum, P., Wolgin, D. L., De Ryck, M., & Marin, O. S. M. Bandage-backfall reaction: Occurs in infancy, hypothalamic damage, and catalepsy. *Proceedings of the National Academy of Science,* 1976, 75, 3311–3314.

Thelen, E. Rhythmical stereotypies in normal human infants. *Animal Behaviour,* 1979, *27*, 699–715.

Thelen, E. Kicking, rocking, and waving: Contextual analysis of rhythmical stereotypies in normal human infants. *Animal Behaviour,* 1981, *29*, 3–11. (a)

Thelen, E. Rhythmical behavior in infancy: An ethological perspective. *Developmental Psychology,* 1981, *17*, 237–257. (b)

Thelen, E., Bradshaw, G., & Ward, J. A. Spontaneous kicking in month-old infants. Manifestation of a human locomotor program. *Behavioral and Neural Biology,* 1981, 52, 45–53.

Thelen, E., & Fisher, D. M. From spontaneous to instrumental behavior: Kinematic analysis of movement changes during very early learning. *Child Development,* in press.

Touwen, B. *Neurological development in infancy.* London: Spastics International Medical Publishers, 1976.

Warren, N. African infant precocity. *Psychological Bulletin,* 1972, *78*, 353–367.

Zelazo, P. R. From reflexive to instrumental behavior. In L. P. Lipsitt (Ed.), *Developmental psychobiology: The significance of infancy.* Hillsdale, N.J.: Erlbaum, 1976.

Zelazo, P. R., Zelazo, N., & Kolb, S. "Walking" in the newborn. *Science,* 1972, *176*, 314–315.

# Development of Reaching in Infancy

*Neil E. Berthier and Rachel Keen*

## Introduction

The development of human infant reaching has engendered considerable interest over the last decades. Developmentalists are interested in describing the course of the development of reaching and in using reaching as a model system with which to investigate the processes underlying development. Nondevelopmentalists are interested in understanding the development of reaching as a case of motor learning and in its implications for the understanding of how adults control their reaching movements.

The development of electronic motion-analysis systems in the last decade has led to a burst of reports analyzing the development of reaching. This research provided data that falsified earlier hypotheses about the development of reaching. For example, while it seemed reasonable that infants would reach faster as they become more proficient reachers (Halverson 1933), only Konczak et al. (1995) found an increase in reaching speed with development, and that increase disappeared when reaching speed was normalized by the distance of the reach.

While Konczak et al. (1995, 1997), Konczak and Dichgans (1997), Thelen et al. (1996), and von Hofsten (1991) provide a substantial body of data, the literature on infants reaching for stationary objects is not without controversy. For example, the number of peaks in the hand-speed profile: von Hofsten (1991) observed that the number of peaks decreases with age, but Fetters and Todd (1987) found that the number of peaks is relatively stable with age. This disagreement is important because Berthier (1996), von Hofsten (1979),

**Source:** *Experimental Brain Research*, 169(4) (2006): 507–518.

and von Hofsten (1991) argued that the multiple peaks in infant hand-speed profiles indicated the presence of multiple action or movement units. This suggestion was disputed by Thelen et al. (1993) who contended that the multiplicity of peaks largely reflected the uncontrolled dynamics of the arm. Thelen et al.'s (1993) argument was supported by Berthier et al. (2005) who showed that when two or three actions were applied to a dynamical model of an infant arm, five or six peaks in the speed profile were observed.

Regardless of the controversy concerning what individual kinematic descriptors reflect, the published data conflict. While the discrepancies may reflect differences in experimental procedures (e.g., Fetters and Todd (1987) and von Hofsten (1979) used older video-based methods), they may also be the result of the small number of subjects upon which the reports are based. For example, the three long-term longitudinal studies of infants reaching for stationary objects (Konczak et al. 1997, 1995; Konczak and Dichgans 1997; Thelen et al. 1996; von Hofsten 1991) report data from only a total of 18 infants. Even though these studies provide dense longitudinal data, the fact that they are each based on so few infants, limits their generalizability. For example, Thelen et al. (1993, 1996) intensively studied four infants over the first year and concluded that infants show different developmental trajectories. This leads to the possibility that if Thelen et al. (1993, 1996) had studied a different group of four infants, different developmental patterns would have been observed. Perhaps, a diversity of developmental patterns has led to the discrepancies in the literature. In order to obtain a more complete view of the development of infant reaching, the present paper adds 12 infants' data to the existing corpus of longitudinal data and explicitly examines the kinematics of reaching across studies.

Recent advances in statistics also provide a more powerful and informative way to analyze longitudinal data. Previously, longitudinal data were analyzed using repeated measures analyses of variance, but the development of linear and nonlinear mixed-effects models or hierarchical linear models (Goldstein 2003; Pinheiro and Bates 2000) allows for the linear and nonlinear modeling of longitudinal data without the requirement that the data be balanced. The balanced data requirement of traditional analysis of variance is particularly troubling in long-term longitudinal studies with human infants because missing sessions are common and data loss due to the lack of the infant's compliance is usually substantial. The mixed-effects models also have the important added advantage of being able to estimate the variability of the population from which the sample is drawn. This allows for an estimate of the differences in the patterns of data of different infants, an important theoretical factor that has been emphasized by Thelen et al. (1993, 1996), who concluded that different infants show different patterns of development.

Besides providing a description of the development of the kinematics of infant reaching, we also sought to deepen our understanding of how development occurs. Thelen et al. (1993) argued that the process of development of reaching involves self-organization and discovery of useful patterns, von Hofsten (1993) described development as a search of the task space for actions, while Berthier (1996) and Berthier et al. (2005) have provided models of interactive learning that discover useful patterns of reaching. While reaching in older children and adults involves the use of forward and inverse models (e.g., Jansen-Osmann et al. 2002), it seems unlikely that accurate dynamical models would be employed by 4-month-old infants at the onset of reaching (they are not necessary in simulated reaching, see, Berthier et al. 2005). More likely, action selection involves choosing movements that take the hand to the target rapidly, smoothly, accurately, and with low energetic costs. Thelen et al. (1993) suggested that actions that minimize or counteract the motion-dependent torques that occur during reaching are preferred, a suggestion that was not confirmed by Konczak et al. (1997). Berthier (1996) has suggested that infants attempt to reach targets in minimal time. In considering these various descriptions, Engelbrecht's (2001) discussion of various criteria that could be used to evaluate reaching movements for fitness may be helpful.

Because action selection ultimately operates at the level of limb forces, two groups of investigators have used inverse dynamical models in an attempt to estimate how limb forces change with development (Thelen et al. 1993; Konczak et al. 1997, 1995; Konczak and Dichgans 1997). Those studies show that development leads to both smoother hand paths as well as smoother joint-torque profiles. In the current paper, we not only measured how hand speed and reach straightness change with development, but we also computed the jerk of movements. Jerk is the third derivative of position with respect to time and Flash and Hogan (1995, 1985) have argued that it is optimized to select movements. Jerk is also related to torque change so that computing jerk provides an indirect measure of net joint torque (Uno et al. 1989). We emphasize that we did not attempt to determine which metric is used during development because infants probably do not use a single, quantifiable metric; instead we simply computed descriptive variables that assessed the straightness, smoothness, speed, and jerkiness of reaching, qualities that would all be important to a reacher, determining which movements were good or bad.

But given the dynamical complexity of human limbs, what mechanisms are used by the infants to achieve smooth reach profiles? Bernstein (1967) realized that simple random search would fail because of the large number of possible actions and because of the nonlinear mapping of motor commands to actions. To address this problem, Bernstein (1967) suggested that novices would limit the dynamical complexity of the task by stiffening joints, a simplification that would reduce the nonlinearity of movement as well as reduce the number of possible actions. Joint stiffening in novices has been observed in studies of adults (Vereijken et al. 1992; Newell and van Emmerik 1989) and infants (Berthier et al. 1999; Spencer and Thelen 2000). In infants,

Berthier et al. (1999) showed that during the first week of successful reaching, little change in elbow angle was observed during reaching and Spencer and Thelen (2000) showed that early reaching movements were controlled by the proximal musculature of the shoulder. Halverson (1933) had also previously noted that early reaching is largely accomplished by shoulder movement. Of course, joint stiffening reduces the capabilities of the arm and increases the energetic cost of movement so we can expect to observe joint stiffening only in the initial phases of learning. Our last major goal of the current work is to describe the developmental time course over which infants begin to use the elbow joint in reaching.

## Methods

### Subjects

Twelve infants participated as subjects in the current experiment. All infants were the result of full-term pregnancies and were in good health on the day of testing. Data from some of these infant's first reaching sessions were reported in Berthier et al. (1999). Families received a small gift for each experimental visit (usually a small toy or book). The experimental procedure was reviewed and approved by the institutional human subjects committee. Informed consent was obtained from the infants' parents.

### Equipment and Procedure

Young infants were seated on one of their parent's laps during experimental sessions. The parent was asked to hold their infant firmly around the hips so as to support the infant and allow for free movement of the infant's arms. The parent was further asked to refrain from attempting to influence the infant in any way. Depending on the infant's level of comfort, older infants were seated in an infant booster seat with the seat belt fastened. In both situations, infants reached naturally and because the target object was held within arm's length of the infant, little trunk flexion was observed.

Data was obtained from two longitudinal studies. The first was designed to study reaching for the first several weeks after reach onset and five infants were tested at least once a week in the laboratory from several weeks before to 4 or 5 weeks after reach onset. Typically, infants were tested from 9 to 22 weeks of age in this study. A second study was intended to study the development of reaching from 6 to 20 months of age. Five infants participated in this study and were tested in the laboratory at monthly intervals until a year of age and quarterly intervals thereafter. Lastly, two infants were enrolled in the first study and were also studied until 20 months of age. As with other studies of infants, missing sessions occurred with sickness, vacation, noncompliance of the infants, obstructed motion analysis markers, and fussiness.

Infants younger than 160 days reached exclusively for a colorful plastic toy (Sesame Street's Big Bird, 7 cm length). The toy was attached to a rattle and held by an experimenter who sat facing the infant. Because older infants quickly became uninterested in the single toy, older infants reached for a group of small plastic toys and infants over a year of age were also asked to reach for small oat breakfast cereal (Cheerios). At the beginning of each trial, the presenter attracted the attention of the infant to the toy and slowly brought it forward to a position 15–25 cm away from the infant. To encourage use of the right hand, the toy was presented approximately 30° in the horizontal plane to the infant's right. In all cases, the target object was presented as still as possible when the infant was reaching.

Infants were videotaped throughout the session at 30 frames/s with an infrared camera (Panasonic WV1800) placed to the right of the infant for a side view of the reaches. In addition to the videotape, the reaches were monitored using an Optotrak motion-analysis system. This system consisted of three infrared cameras that generated estimates of a marker's position in three-dimensional coordinates. In the current experiments, four infrared emitting diodes (IREDs) were used as markers. The Optotrak system estimated the positions of these markers at a rate of 100 Hz. Position data were acquired during 10–20 s trials. Two IREDs were taped on the back of the infant's right hand, one just proximal to the joint of the index finger and one on the ulnar surface just proximal to the joint of the little finger. These two IREDs were used on the hand in order to keep at least one in camera view if the infant rotated his or her hand during the reach. Infants tended to ignore the IREDs once they were in place. One IRED was also placed on the apex of the infant's shoulder and one on the lateral edge of infant's elbow. The Optotrak cameras were placed above and to the right of the infants.

The video camera output was fed through a date-timer (For-A) and into a videocassette recorder (Panasonic Model 1950), and a video monitor (Sony Model 1271). The Optotrak system and the date-timer were triggered simultaneously by a second experimenter in order to time-lock the IRED data with the video-recorded behavior for later scoring. The second experimenter was seated out of view, triggered the data collection by the motion analysis system, and observed the infant on the video monitor.

## Kinematic Data Analysis and Computational Methods

Videotapes were first examined for any significant movement of the hand that was made in the presence of the goal object. We defined a reach as a forward movement of the hand toward the goal object that was accompanied by the attention of the infant to the goal object, usually visual attention, and by the viewer's judgment that the infant was in fact attempting to reach for the toy, not simply batting at it or touching it incidentally in a movement toward the mouth, body, or contralateral hand. We also eliminated small arm movements where the infant obtained the goal object through experimenter errors when the presenter presented the object too close to the infant so as to almost place the object in the infants hand without significant movement on the infant's part.

Reach onset was defined as the point in time when the hand started to move forward toward the goal object as judged by frame-by-frame observation of the videotape. Backward, upward, or other preparatory movements before forward movement were not considered part of the reach proper. These preparatory movements were easy to score because they often involved large movements, such as an upward movement from the infant's thigh to their shoulder. The end of the reach was defined by the time of contact with the target object. In practice, segments of the video were scored for when infants made contacts with the target and then the videotape was rewound, frame-by-frame, until the point where the infant's hand first made a discernible forward movement to the target.

The data obtained from the Optotrak system are estimates of the true IRED position at the time of the sample. The dynamic programming method of Busby and Trujillo (1985) was used to estimate the position, velocity, and acceleration of the hand. The algorithm assumes that the marker is a point moving through space and computes a smooth path based on a minimal input control. We used the criteria suggested by Busby and Trujillo for selecting the parameter $B$ and used $B = 1 \times 10^{-11}$ (Berthier 1996; Milner and Ijaz 1990). While exact comparisons are difficult because of the algorithm, the data reported here are similarly smoothed to traditional low-pass filtering with a cutoff frequency of 30–50 Hz.

The data filtering resulted in estimated velocity and acceleration vectors in three-dimensional space for each data sample. The instantaneous jerk (third derivative of position) was estimated by taking the temporal differences of the acceleration vectors. The speed (tangential velocity or resultant speed) was calculated as the magnitude of the velocity vector and the total squared jerk of a movement was estimated by summing the squared instantaneous jerk over the time of the reach.

As we and others have found, young infants reach toward targets using multiple accelerations and decelerations of the hand. We analyzed the amplitude and timing of these individual peaks to determine if there were any dependencies in the peak amplitudes. To determine the time of a speed peak, we smoothed the speed data with a three-point moving average filter. We then defined peaks as times when the two previous samples of the smoothed speed function had positive slopes and the two succeeding samples of the smoothed speed function had negative slopes. Typically, each reach contained a number of distinct speed peaks and the times and amplitudes of these speed peaks were then noted.

Two other variables were calculated from the peaks in the hand-speed profile. First, the largest peak in a reach was identified. One variable was then calculated as the time of that peak in milliseconds from the start of the reach. A second variable, percent peak, was calculated by dividing the time of the largest peak by the movement time of the reach. The value of the latter would be 0.50 if the peak occurred in the middle of the reach and 0.25 if the largest peak occurred one quarter of the way through the reach.

Because our infants made unconstrained reaches in three dimensions, we computed kinematic measures that were relatively reliable, direct, and did not assume any particular kinematic or dynamical model of the arm. For example, instead of attempting to estimate the elbow angle, which would have been difficult with our marker arrangement, we simply used the difference of the hand marker from the shoulder marker. Because the arm is composed of essentially rigid links, the hand–shoulder distance is an increasing monotonic function of the elbow angle.

Previous work showed that the elbow was relatively fixed at the developmental onset of reaching (Berthier et al. 1999; Spencer and Thelen 2000). Because a major goal of the current work was to determine the development of elbow utilization in infants, we computed the change in hand–shoulder distance during a reach as an index of the change in elbow angle during that reach. To this end, we subtracted the shortest hand–shoulder distance during the reach from the largest hand–shoulder distance during that reach. If the elbow was locked during a reach, that difference was zero, if the elbow angle showed a large change during a reach, that difference was large.

The straight-line distance from the position of the hand marker at the start of the reach to the position of the same hand marker at the end of the reach was calculated. The hand-path length was calculated by summing the differences in hand-marker position during the reach. A straightness measure was computed by dividing the path length of the reach by the distance of the reach. Path curvature was not used as a measure of straightness because it is strongly dominated by changes in the direction of the hand and noise of the measurement system at low speeds.

## Results

Infants typically started reaching at about 16 weeks of age. Apart from missed sessions due to illness or vacation, data acquisition with infants over a year of age was especially challenging because some infants would not tolerate the Optotrak markers placed on their hands (this is the reason data collection stopped for infants 1 and 3 and why the session is missing at 16 months for infant 5). When Optotrak data was collected, 35.1% of the reaching trials were

**Table 1:** Description of the sample of usable Optotrak data

| Infant | Age range (days) | Sessions with usable data | Total number of trials with usable data |
|---|---|---|---|
| 1 | 174–394 | 7 | 60 |
| 2 | 114–482 | 13 | 67 |
| 3 | 191–299 | 4 | 46 |
| 4 | 197–381 | 6 | 41 |
| 5 | 168–653 | 7 | 48 |
| 6 | 123–616 | 14 | 94 |
| 7 | 98–651 | 12 | 47 |
| 8 | 95–121 | 5 | 11 |
| 9 | 121–135 | 3 | 10 |
| 10 | 118–146 | 4 | 14 |
| 11 | 126–154 | 4 | 21 |
| 12 | 130–142 | 2 | 3 |

lost because the motion-analysis system lost sight of the markers. Overall, data was obtained from 82 experimental sessions from infants of 95–653 days of age. Table 1 describes the usable data set.

We computed 11 variables that are typically used to assess infant reaching with the purpose of determining whether all of these variables were necessary to provide a full accounting of how infant reaches develop. Was there a smaller set of variables that provides an adequate description of the development of reaching? For example, do average and peak speed furnish us with inde-pendent information and thus both need to be used in our description or do they present highly correlated information that only informs us about a single underlying variable? If variables do not give independent information, how do we determine the key variables that supply critical information? By eliminating redundant information from our computed variables we hope to uncover the underlying processes undergoing developmental change.

Our first step in this analysis was to compute the correlation matrix across the variables for all infant reaches. These calculations did not attempt to remove variance that was due to individual infants or due to age, but simply aggregated all the reaches together in a single data set. If the resulting correlation matrix shows correlations that were small in magnitude, we would conclude that the variables provided independent information and informed us about different aspects of infant reaches. On the other hand, if particular variables showed high correlations, we would suspect that those correlated variables might be informing us about single underlying variables.

Because the distribution of the jerk-dependent variable was strongly skewed to the right, movement jerk was log-transformed for the current analysis. Fig. 1 shows the resulting correlation matrix in graphical form. In the figure, the magnitude of each pair-wise correlation is given by the area of the corresponding disk, with filled disks representing positive correlations and open disks representing negative correlations. For reference, the diagonal of the matrix displays autocorrelations of the variables which are necessarily 1.0. Correlations that were not significant at the 0.05 level are not displayed.

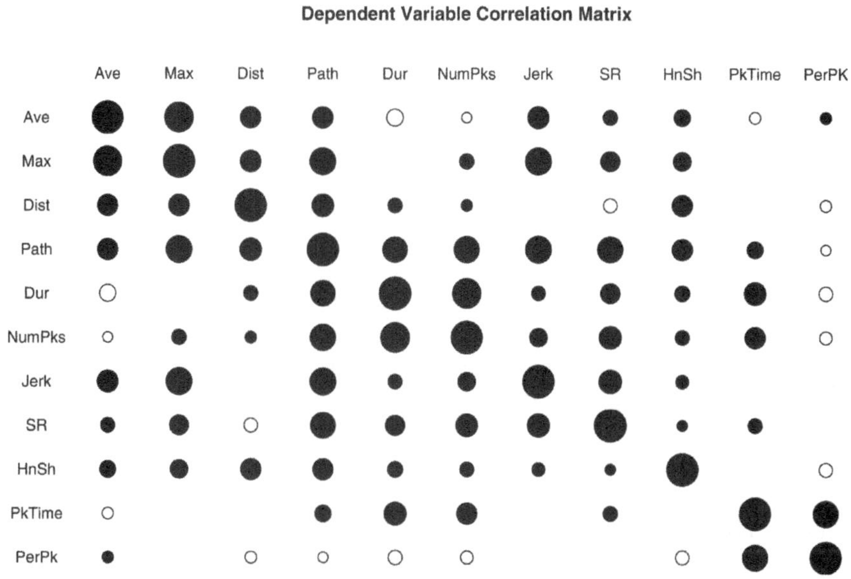

**Dependent Variable Correlation Matrix**

**Figure 1:** Dependent-variable correlation matrix with the magnitude of the correlation represented by the area of each disk, with filled disks being positive correlations and open disks being negative correlations. For scale, the diagonal displays correlations of 1.0. *Ave* average speed, *Max* peak speed, *Dist* straight-line distance of the hand to the target at the start of the reach, *Path* hand path length, *Dur* movement time, *NumPks*, number of speed peaks, *Jerk* total squared jerk, *SR* straightness ratio, *HnSh* hand–shoulder distance change, *Pk Time* time of peak speed in ms, *PerPk* time of peak speed in percent movement time.

Inspection of Fig. 1 indicates that many of the dependent variables were substantially correlated with each other. For example, average speed (Ave) and peak speed (Max) were correlated at the 0.83 level, and the path length (Path), temporal duration (Dur), and number of speed peaks (NumPks) were correlated between 0.60 and 0.68.

The high correlation between the number of speed peaks and the temporal duration and path length suggested that speed peaks were occurring at relatively consistent intervals. Subsequent analysis of peak timing showed that the peaks occurred with a median temporal interval of 190 ms with the central 50% of the inter-peak intervals ranging from 140 to 270 ms.

The large number of nonzero correlations in the matrix indicated significant dependence among our dependent variables and suggested that the observed pattern could be the result of variation in a smaller set of underlying variables. To determine whether a smaller set of underlying variables could be discovered, we performed a maximum-likelihood factor analysis. Factor analysis was chosen over principal component analysis because the aim was more to discover the underlying factors than to generate a compact representation of the data.

We performed our analysis using the factanal procedure in the R statistical package (http://www.cran.r-project.org). The analysis standardized each variable so that scale differences were eliminated. We used a standard varimax rotation and started our analysis with three factors and increased the number of factors until a good model of the data was obtained. The fit of the statistical model to the data was assessed by comparing the model's correlation matrix with the correlation matrix computed from the data. This procedure was used instead of using the overall proportion of variance explained because it assessed the fit of the model at the level of the pair-wise correlations between the variables. A good model of the data would be one that preserves these pair-wise correlations, whereas a model with overall good fit in terms of proportion of variance explained might be deficient in that it distorted the pair-wise relationship between two variables.

With three factors in the model, the largest discrepancy between the two matrices was 0.42, with four factors the largest discrepancy was 0.10 and with five, 0.06. The results of the analysis with five factors are presented in Table 2. The factor analytic model explained 84% of the variance of the data with all the dependent variables being well modeled by the analysis except the variability in hand–shoulder distance which had a high uniqueness (0.74). The first factor heavily loaded on the variables that measure the speed and jerk of the reach; the second, the temporal duration of the reach and the number of speed peaks; the third, the time of peak speed; the fourth, the distance covered by the reach; and the fifth, the straightness of the reach.

In sum, the current 11 dependent variables did not provide independent information and a factor analysis found that infant reaches could be described by a smaller set of five underlying variables. While some of these relationships were expected, others were not. For example, while it is possible that the peak speed of a reach could be independent of the average speed of a reach, a high correlation between the two would be expected. On the other hand, there is no a priori reason to expect that the number of speed peaks in a reach would be highly correlated with the length of the hand path or with the temporal duration of a reach as we observed.

**Table 2:** Results of the factor analysis

| DV | Uniqueness | Factor 1 | Factor 2 | Factor 3 | Factor 4 | Factor 5 |
|---|---|---|---|---|---|---|
| Average speed | 0.13 | 0.80 | −0.32 | | 0.33 | 0.13 |
| Maximum speed | 0.08 | 0.90 | | | 0.30 | 0.14 |
| Distance | 0.16 | 0.22 | | | 0.87 | −0.16 |
| Path length | 0.09 | 0.51 | | | 0.44 | 0.41 |
| Duration | 0.08 | | 0.92 | | 0.21 | 0.15 |
| Number of speed peaks | 0.17 | 0.16 | 0.88 | | | 0.17 |
| Jerk | 0.17 | 0.87 | 0.25 | | | 0.13 |
| Straightness ratio | 0.01 | 0.30 | 0.32 | | −0.16 | 0.88 |
| Hand–shoulder distance | 0.74 | 0.24 | 0.19 | −0.12 | 0.39 | |
| Time of speed peak | 0.18 | | 0.46 | 0.78 | | |
| Percent MT speed peak | 0.005 | 0.10 | −0.21 | 0.96 | −0.14 | |
| Cumulative variance | | 0.25 | 0.47 | 0.61 | 0.74 | 0.84 |

## Changes in Reach Kinematics with Age

Because of the unbalanced nature of our longitudinal data, we used mixed-effects models to analyze the data. Mixed-effects models consider the within- and between-subject variability and produce population and individual regression coefficients that can be tested for significance. We used data from individual reaches in estimating the regression coefficients. In the current work, the nlme package in the R statistical program was used to estimate the regression coefficients.

Mixed-effects modeling allows for both linear and nonlinear regressions. Apart from the hand–shoulder variability measure where we expected an increase and a leveling off with age, we had no strong theoretical reason to assume either a linear or nonlinear model for development. Thus, we explored several types of models in the initial phases of our analysis. We found that nonlinear models did not improve the fit over a standard linear model so linear mixed-effects models were used in the current analyses. The hand–shoulder variability-dependent variable was analyzed separately (see below).

In plotting the prediction residuals of the linear fits, we discovered significant departures from normality. Because normality of the residuals is a requirement of mixed-effects models and because the residuals were positively skewed, we recomputed the linear fits after logarithmic transformation of the data (i.e., $In(y) = b + ax$). This procedure normalized the residuals while at the same time producing approximate homogeneity. Viewed in the untransformed, original coordinates, the logarithmic transformation produces exponential fits of the form: $y = e^b.e^{ax}$, with the $y$-intercept given by the value of $e^b$ and the decay of the exponential function given by $a$. While these exponential fits could in principle show significant curvature in the original coordinate system, the regression curves resulting from the current analysis only slightly departed from straight lines (see Fig. 2). The advantage of this procedure was not that it allowed for curvilinear fits of the data, but that it normalized the regression residuals.

Table 3 shows the results of the linear mixed-effects modeling for our dependent variables. Of primary interest in our investigation was whether the dependent variable varied as a function of age of the infant. A test of this is provided in the test of the $a$ against 0. The $P$-values for these tests are given in the fourth column of the table. Of the ten regressions, four of the decay parameters were significantly different from 0 and all of these were negative in sign indicating a decreasing function of age. Even though these parameters were small in magnitude, because of the nature of the exponential fit the parameters indicate substantial decreases with age. Plots of the overall fits for across infants are given in Fig. 2 and inspection of that figure shows significant downward trend in the prediction with age for some of the dependent variables. Table 3 numerically gives the effect of age in the fifth (intercept) and sixth (2 years) columns which gives the model's predicted value at age

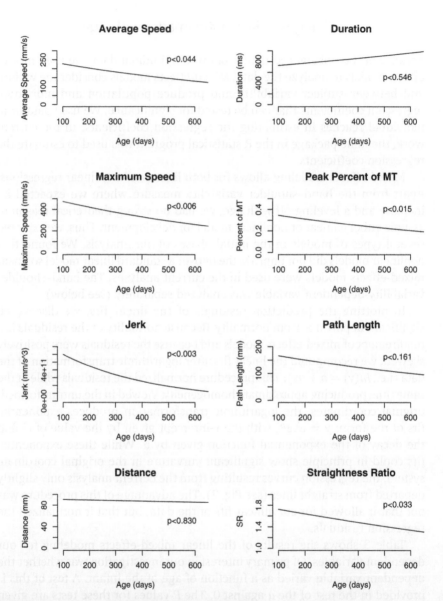

**Figure 2:** Plots of regressions for the dependent variables

0 and at 2 years of age. For example, the predicted peak speeds of the reaches decreases from 535 to 223 mm/s over the first 2 years of life.

Significance test of the decay parameters (fourth column) showed that the average and peak speed and the total jerk of the reach decreased as the infant aged, and that the straightness of the reach increased and that the time of peak speed decreased with age. Fig. 2 shows population plots of the fitted functions for the dependent variables as a function of the infant's age.

**Table 3:** Estimated regression parameters with P-values for tests of the parameters against a null hypothesis that they equal 0

| Dependent variable | a | Between S variability | p | Intercept ($e^b$) | Value at 2 years | Between S variability | p |
|---|---|---|---|---|---|---|---|
| Average speed (mm/s) | -0.0011 | 0.00125 | 0.044 | 254 | 114 | 185–353 | 0.000 |
| Maximum speed (mm/s) | -0.0012 | 0.00088 | 0.006 | 535 | 223 | 410–690 | 0.000 |
| Distance (mm) | -0.0001 | 0.001 | 0.830 | 92 | 86 | 68–120 | 0.000 |
| Path length (mm) | -0.0010 | 0.00125 | 0.161 | 184 | 89 | 116–263 | 0.000 |
| Duration (ms) | 0.0006 | 0.00078 | 0.546 | 689 | 1068 | 436–944 | 0.000 |
| Speed peaks (n) | -0.0002 | 0.00025 | 0.238 | 2.67 | 2.31 | 2.18–3.36 | 0.000 |
| Jerk (mm/s³) | -0.0029 | 0.0024 | 0.003 | $e^{27.5}$ | $e^{25.4}$ | $e^{26.6}$–$e^{28.1}$ | 0.000 |
| Straightness ratio | -0.0005 | 0.00055 | 0.033 | 1.81 | 1.26 | 1.39–2.16 | 0.000 |
| Time of peak Speed (ms) | -0.0004 | 0.00067 | 0.247 | 256 | 191 | 175–375 | 0.000 |
| Time of peak speed (%) | -0.0011 | 0.000938 | 0.015 | .384 | 0.172 | 0.266–0.556 | 0.000 |

The fits were performed on log-transformed data so that the fit equation was $\ln(y) = b + ax$. The column labeled between S variability after the $a$ coefficient is the estimated standard deviation of the $a$ coefficient and that labeled between S variability after the intercept column is the mean plus and minus one standard deviation of the intercept across subjects back-transformed to the original units of the data.

The preceding information describes the development of the average infant, but mixed-effects modeling also provides information about the infant-to-infant variability in development. Fig. 3 shows plots of changes in peak speed, jerk, straightness, and time of the peak speed for the four infants in the study whose data spanned the most time. The plotted lines are the individual regression curves for the four infants and the dots are the means for that dependent variable for that testing session. While the same general trend in the fit can be observed across infants, differences are apparent when different infants are compared. For example, the third infant in each panel showed a dramatic decrease in the speed and jerk of reaching during development, but the other three infants showed more modest decreases in these measures.

Estimates of the infant-to-infant variability are numerically provided in mixed-effects modeling by estimates of the variability of the regression coefficients in the population. This is an estimate of the variability of the data in the population from which the subjects are randomly drawn and should not be confused with confidence limits or error bars around the estimates of the group coefficients. These estimates of variability between subjects in the population are provided in Table 3 in the columns labeled "Between $S$ Variability." The column after the one labeled "$a$" is the estimated standard deviation of the decay parameter across infants, and the one after the column labeled "intercept" is the group average plus and minus one standard deviation of the intercept parameter back-transformed to the original scale of measurement. The latter was done because of the logarithmic transformation of the data.

These estimates of variability between randomly sampled infants are fairly large and confirm that the developmental changes in reach kinematics are quite different from infant to infant. While the variability in the coefficients is considerable, when the individual coefficients were plotted the distribution appeared roughly normal without any grouping or categorical differences between infants. That is, no evidence was found for groups of "slow reachers" and "fast reachers," but rather reaching speeds varied normally across infants.

The dependent variable that measured the use of the elbow degree-of-freedom was analyzed differently. Berthier et al. (1999) had shown that the distance between the hand and shoulder was almost constant when infants began to reach indicating that the elbow was relatively fixed at the onset of reaching. Because the change in the hand–shoulder distance was negligible for most reaches at the onset of reaching, we hypothesized that the change in the hand–shoulder distance would be minimal at the very onset of reaching and increase with increasing age, perhaps leveling off at some point when the elbow was fully employed by infants. Because we expected an increase followed by a leveling off, we used piecewise linear or "broken-stick" regression when modeling the change in hand–shoulder distance with age. Initial regressions indicated a skewed distribution of residuals so the data were again

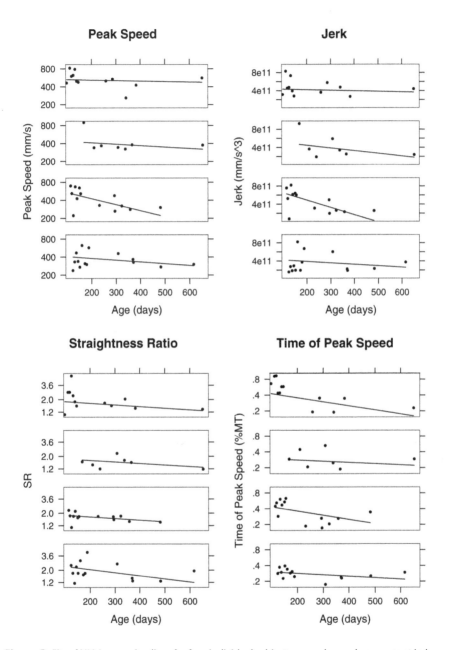

**Figure 3:** Fits of HLM regression lines for four individual subjects on peak speed, movement jerk, straightness ratio, and time of peak speed as a fraction of movement duration. Each panel shows the fit for the four subjects with the broadest range of data. The subjects displayed are numbers 7, 5, 2, and 6, from top to bottom. Because the fits were preformed on log-transformed data, each point in the figure is the geometric mean for that individual's testing session.

log-transformed. Regressions were then performed with two linear segments and the break point between the segments being varied from 150 to 250 days of age in steps of 10 days. We found that the best fit of the data using the AIC criterion was obtained for a break point at 180 days.

The best-fit regression equation with a break at 180 days was

$$y = e^b \, e^{a_1 x}, x \le 180,$$
$$y = e^b \, e^{a_2 x}, x \le 180$$

where $b = 3.530$, $a_1 = 0.013$, and $a_2 = -0.0024$. The P-values for the three coefficients were 0.0001, 0.0043, and 0.179, respectively, indicating a statistically significant increase in hand–shoulder distance variability up to 180 days of age followed by relatively constant hand–shoulder distances over the next year and a half. A plot of the hand–shoulder variability fit as a function of age is shown in Fig. 4.

## Discussion

With the addition of the current data, there are now four studies using modern motion-analysis systems that have longitudinally studied a total of 30 infants in infancy. These studies all agree that successful, goal-directed reaching is observed in infants starting at about 16 weeks of age. A summary of the data sets of these studies and relevant cross-sectional studies is provided in Table 4

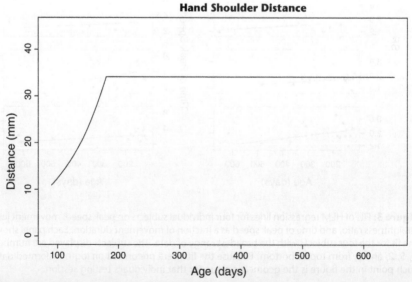

**Figure 4:** Regression of hand–shoulder distance variability on age. The plot is with the right-hand side slope coefficient equal to 0 because the P-value did not indicate a difference of the fit coefficient from 0.

**Table 4:** Results of previously published studies of the development of reaching in human infants

| Paper | Number of subjects | Ages (weeks of age) | Speed (mm/s) | NumPks | MaxSpeed time | Distance | Straightness |
|---|---|---|---|---|---|---|---|
| *Longitudinal* | | | | | | | |
| von Hofsten (1979) (videotape) | 5 | 12–36 | Decreases | 2.7 | | | 4.5–2.0 |
| Fetters and Todd (1987) (film) | 10 | 21–41 | 406–426 (Max; ns) | 4.02–2.44 | | | 2.1 |
| von Hofsten (1991) | 5 | 19–31 | 236–186 (Ave) | 2.38–1.58 | | | 2.19–1.29 |
| Thelen et al. (1993, 1996, 2000) | 4 | 3–52 | 473–348 (Max) | | | | 1.29–1.15 |
| Konczak et al. (1995, 1997) | 9 | 18–156 | 560–1,170 (Max) / 520–760 (Norm; ns) | 5.2–1.5 / 1.2–0.9 (Norm) | 0.50–0.40 | Increases | 3.1–1.3 |
| Current | 12 | 14–93 | 240–140 (Ave) / 490–250 (Max) | 2.5 | 0.35–0.20 | | 1.75–1.38 |
| *Cross-sectional* | | | | | | | |
| Matthew and Cook (1990) (videotape) | 30 | 20, 26, 34 | 102, 131, 173 (Ave) | 5.6–3.1 | | Increases | 2.6–1.6 |
| Berthier and McCarty (1995) | 48 | 22.5, 31.5, 40.5 | 877, 974, 806 (Max) / 389, 338, 378 (Ave) | 3.5–2.4 (Norm) / 1.4, 1.1, 0.8 | | | |
| McCarty and Ashmead (1999) | 48 | 22.5, 31.5, 40.5 | 389, 338, 378 (Ave) | 2.5–2.3 | | | 2.25–1.6 |
| Newman et al. (2001) | 39 | 22.5–75 | 432, 301, 382 (Max) | | 0.40–0.34 | | |

When a hyphenated range is given, the initial number is for the youngest age and the second number is for the oldest age. Berthier and McCarty (1995) and McCarty and Ashmead (1999) are the result of the analysis of the same set of data.

organized by the first five factors in the factor analytic model given in the results section above.

The factor analysis produced several results. First, the analysis showed that the large number of typically computed descriptive variables are highly intercorrelated and that they do not produce independent information about infant reaching. Second, the analysis informed us that infant reaches vary only along about five dimensions: speed/jerk, number of speed peaks/duration, time of peak speed, distance of the reach, and straightness of the reach. The variability along these dimensions is due to both changes with age and differences among infants. To assess how infants differ, we need only to use these five dimensions. Lastly, the analysis provided unexpected information about kinematic differences in that the number of speed peaks was linearly related to the temporal duration of the reach.

Several developmental trends are apparent in the results. First, and not surprisingly, infant reaches are significantly curved at the youngest ages and they become substantially straighter by 2 and 3 years of age. Straightness ratios are generally around two at reach onset and decrease to about 1.3–1.4 by 2 and 3 years of age. The straightness ratio at the end of infancy approaches, but is still substantially different from adult straightness ratios, which are typically close to 1.0 for unobstructed reaching (e.g., Churchill et al. 2000).

The second consistent developmental trend is that the time of maximum hand speed during the reach moves closer to the beginning of the reach with age. The current results together with Konczak et al. (1995, 1997) and Newman et al. (2001) show that the time of the peak hand speed is between 0.35 and 0.50 of the reach at the onset of reaching and that at the oldest ages the time moves to 0.20–0.40 of the reach. Related to this is the finding of von Hofsten (1991) who found that the largest movement unit of a reach moves closer to the beginning of the reach with age. Together, these results are consistent with the development of a transport phase similar to that of adults where the hand moves toward the target and a grasp phase where grasp is accomplished (Jeannerod 1997).

Two other developmental trends are not as consistently observed across studies. While Halverson (1933) concluded that the speed of reaching increases with age in the infant, modern long-term longitudinal studies either find a significant decrease in the average or maximum speed during the reach with age (Fetters and Todd 1987; Thelen et al. 1996), or no change (von Hofsten 1991; Konczak et al. 1995, 1997; Konczak and Dichgans 1997). We note the close agreement of Thelen et al.'s (1996) observed average speed of 186 mm/s and peak speed of 348 mm/s at 1 year of age, with the predicted values of, 170 mm/s for average speed at 1 year and of 345 mm/s for peak speed from the current regressions. This agreement is remarkable in that the infants were supported differently in the two studies, reached for different toys, and likely reached different distances. Comparison of the straightness ratios and numbers of speed peaks between the two studies at 1 year showed less agreement (1.51

vs. 1.15 and 2.48 vs. 1.58, respectively) and indicated that the current infants reached more circuitously than those of Thelen et al. (1996).

Interpretation of differences in reach speed is complicated by that fact that adults show linear increases in reaching speed with increasing distance (e.g., Berthier et al. 1996), and while this relationship was not observed at the very onset of reaching (Berthier et al. 1999), the correlation coefficient between average or maximum speed and distance was 0.42 and 0.43, respectively, in the current data set. Because of this scaling of speed with distance, studies where the distance of the reach increases with age will likely find increases in hand speed with age. For example, Konczak et al. (1995) found that the significant increase in maximum hand speed observed with age become nonsignificant when the speeds were normalized by the distance of the reaches. Thus, the existing data support the conclusion that reaching speed is either stable or decreasing during infancy.

While one might think that a decrease in reaching speed is exactly opposite to what would be expected with an increase in reaching skill, the decrease seems to reflect an increase in the smoothness of reaching. In the current data, average and peak speeds were highly correlated with total jerk of the movement ($r = 0.61$ and 0.76, respectively) and the total jerk decreased more dramatically with age than either average or peak speeds. The observed decrease in reaching speed and jerk is likely the result of increasing ability to modulate net joint torque through anticipation of motion-dependent torques and by more appropriately timing muscle contractions (Konczak et al. 1995, 1997; Konczak and Dichgans 1997).

The overall trend toward a decrease in reaching speed over the first years of life does not discount the possibility that short-term increases and decreases might be observed with development. Indeed, Thelen et al. (1996) concluded that the few weeks around the onset of reaching is a time when reaching speed increases and then decreases, and Berthier and McCarty (1996) and Newman et al. (2001) observed a significant decrease in reaching speed at 7 months followed by a subsequent increase in speed. These results illustrate that development is not a simple monotonic approach to an ideal, but a complex process that depends on the ability, motivation, and goals of the infant.

The current literature also disagrees on how the number of speed peaks or number of movement units change with development. While von Hofsten (1979, 1991), Mathew and Cook (1990), and Konczak et al. (1995) found that the number of movement units and temporal duration of infant reaching decreases dramatically with age; others have found more modest decreases or relatively good stability in the number of speed peaks (Fetters and Todd 1987; Thelen et al. 1996; Berthier and McCarty 1996). Part of the discrepancy is surely due to subtle differences in the filtering of the data and in the definition of a speed peak or movement unit, but even the decreases observed by Mathew and Cook (1990) and Konczak et al. (1995) become minimal when the data are normalized by the increase in reach distance that was observed with age.

The finding of relative stability in the number of speed peaks/movement units combined with the high correlation of number of peaks and duration of the reach ($r = 0.77$) is consistent with the finding of von Hofsten (1991) who argued that the movement units reflect on-line corrections to the reach, and that the primary or transport- movement unit becomes larger and earlier with development. Von Hofsten (1979) also apparently observed a high correlation between the number of movement units and duration when he observed that both decline over the first 6 months of age. Ample data are available that infants can make on-line corrections and that by and large, the hand changes direction between movement units in a way that corrects the hand's heading (Berthier 1996; von Hofsten 1991). However, the fact that the number of peaks is highly correlated with the temporal duration of the reach and that the number is relatively stable with development suggests that either corrections are applied at regular intervals during reaching or that the timing reflects the natural dynamic frequency of the arm. It is clear that not all of speed peaks/ movement units reflect corrections because a single action applied to the arm can result in multiple movement units (Berthier et al. 1999, 2005).

Previously, we found that infants at the onset of reaching adopt a way of reaching that minimizes elbow-flexion and -extension (Berthier et al. 1999). Because we wanted to minimize the errors associated with estimating elbow-joint angle, we used the variability of hand–shoulder distance to assess the elbow movement. At the onset of reaching, this variability was in the order of 1 or 2 cm for a typical reach. Because infants seem highly unlikely to be able to anticipate motion-dependent torques, we concluded that infants were likely employing co-contraction about the elbow to maintain relative fixation. This locking of the elbow was not obligatory as some arm movements showed significant changes in hand–shoulder distance. Spencer and Thelen (2000) showed that infants learning to reach primarily rely on the shoulder musculature to extend the hand to the target. Others have observed limb stiffening in individuals learning to control movements during acquisition of new motor skills (Vereijken et al. 1992; Spencer and Thelen 2000; Newell and van Emmerik 1989).

A key question for the current work was to determine how rapidly after reaching onset, infants begin to use the elbow in reaching movements. We found that the use of the elbow gradually increased, reaching a plateau at about 6 months of age. This period of increasing use of the elbow coincides with the "rapid phase" of motor learning observed by Konczak et al. (1995) and the "active phase" of learning observed by Thelen et al. (1996). The former was a time where the average kinematics across infants showed rapid change and the latter was a time where the speed of reaching increased and then decreased. Particularly in regard to Thelen et al. (1996), our results suggest that early reaching is a time of high speed, high jerk reaches followed by a slowing of the reach over the period of a few weeks. As the latter slowing occurs, our data shows that the elbow is increasingly employed in executing reaches during this period.

As anticipated by Bernstein (1967), the early fixation followed by later use of the elbow may represent a solution to the degrees-of-freedom problem of motor learning. Thelen et al. (1996) concurred and proposed that the "active phase" of motor learning at 6 months where high reaching speeds were observed represented "an enhanced exploration in the speed-parameter space allowing infants to discover a more globally stable and appropriate speed metric both for reaching movements and for movements prior to reaching." (p. 1072). Our results provide the first direct data that the elbow is initially fixed at the onset of reaching and becomes increasingly used in reaching by 6 months of age.

Lastly, our mixed-effect models provide a broad summary of infant kinematics with development and necessarily smooth out week-to-week deviations in kinematics. One benefit of these mixed-effects models is that they estimate the infant-to-infant variation in the dependent variables. As seen in Table 3, this variability can be substantial. However, the between-infant variability was normally distributed in our data and did not support the hypothesis that infants differ categorically in their developmental patterns.

Overall, infant reaching shows dramatic increases in straightness and smoothness over the first 2 years of life, with concomitant decreases in reaching speed and jerk. Kinematics change rapidly over the first 2 or 3 months of reaching with infants gradually employing the distal joints to move the hand to the target object. Development is protracted with kinematic change slowing over the second year of life. Significantly, our results agree with Konczak and Dichgans (1997) in showing that reaching skill must show substantial improvement in smoothness and straightness after 2 years of age to achieve adult levels of control.

## References

Bernstein N (1967) The co-ordination and regulation of movements. Pergamon Press, Oxford

Berthier NE (1996) Learning to reach: a mathematical model. Dev Psychol 32:811–823

Berthier NE, McCarty M (1996) Speed of infant reaching during the first year: Confirmation of a prediction. Infant Behav Dev 19:531

Berthier NE, Clifton R, Gullipalli V, McCall D, Robin D (1996) Visual information and object size in the control of reaching. J Mot Behav. 28:187–197

Berthier NE, Clifton RK, McCall D, Robin D (1999) Proximodistal structure of early reaching in human infants. Exp Brain Res 127:259–269

Berthier NE, Rosenstein MT, Barto AG (2005) Approximate optimal control as a model for motor learning. Psychol Rev 112:329–346

Busby H, Trujillo D (1985) Numerical experiments with a new differentiation filter. J Biomech Eng 107:293–299

Churchill A, Hopkins B, Ronnqvist L, Vogt S (2000) Vision of the hand and environmental context in human prehension. Exp Brain Res 134:81–89

Engelbrecht S (2001) Minimum principles in motor control. J Math Psychol 45:497–542

Fetters L, Todd J (1987) Quantitative assessment of infant reaching movements. J Mot Behav 19:147–166

Flash T, Hogan N (1985) The coordination of arm movements: an experimentally confirmed mathematical model. J Neurosci 5:1688–1703

Flash T, Hogan N (1995) Optimization principles in motor control. In: Arbib MA (ed) The handbook of brain theory and neural networks. The MIT Press, Cambridge, pp 682–685

Goldstein H (2003) Multilevel statistical models, 3rd edn. Hodder Arnold, London

Halverson H (1933) The acquisition of skill in infancy. J Genet Psychol 43:3–48

von Hofsten C (1979) Development of visually directed reaching: the approach phase. J Hum Mov Stud 5:160–178

von Hofsten C (1991) Structuring of early reaching movements: a longitudinal study. J Mot Behav 23:280–292

von Hofsten C (1993) Prospective control: a basic aspect of action development. Hum Dev 36:1046–1057

Jansen-Osmann P, Richter S, Konczak J, Kalveram K-T (2002) Force adaptation transfers to untrained workspace regions in children. Evidence for developing inverse dynamic models. Exp Brain Res 143:212–220

Jeannerod M (1997) The cognitive neuroscience of action. Black-well, Oxford

Konczak J, Dichgans J (1997) The development toward stereotypic arm kinematics during reaching in the first 3 years of life. Exp Brain Res 117:346–354

Konczak J, Borutta M, Topka H, Dichgans J (1995) The development of goal-directed reaching in infants: hand trajectory formation and joint torque control. Exp Brain Res 106:156–168

Konczak J, Borutta M, Dichgans J (1997) The development of goal-directed reaching in infants. Exp Brain Res 113:465–474

Mathew A, Cook M (1990) The control of reaching movements by young infants. Child Dev 61:1238–1257

Milner T, Ijaz M (1990) The effect of accuracy constraints on three-dimensional movement kinematics. Neuroscience 35:365–374

Newell K, van Emmerik R (1989) The acquisition of coordination: preliminary analysis of learning to write. Hum Mov Sci 8:17–32

Newman C, Atkinson J, Braddick O (2001) The development of reaching and looking preferences in infants to objects of different sizes. Dev Psychol 37:1–12

Pinheiro JC, Bates DM (2000) Mixed-effects models in S and S-Plus. Springer, Berlin Heidelberg New York

Spencer J, Thelen E (2000) Spatially specific changes in infants' muscle coactivity as they learn to reach. Infancy 1:275–302

Thelen E, Corbetta D, Kamm K, Spencer JP, Schneider K, Zernicke R (1993) The transition to reaching: mapping intention to intrinsic dynamics. Child Dev 64:1058–1098

Thelen E, Corbetta D, Spencer JP (1996) Development of reaching during the first year: role of movement speed. J Exp Psychol Hum Percept Perform 22:1059–1076

Uno Y, Kawato M, Suzuki R (1989) Formation and control of optimal trajectory in human multijoint arm movement. Biol Cybern 61:89–101

Vereijken B, van Emmerik R, Whiting H, Newell K (1992) Free(z)ing degrees of freedom in skill acquisition. J Mot Behav 24:133–142

# A Pick-Me-Up for Infants' Exploratory Skills: Early Simulated Experiences Reaching for Objects Using 'Sticky Mittens' Enhances Young Infants' Object Exploration Skills

*Amy Needham, Tracy Barrett and Karen Peterman*

## 1. Introduction

A question as old as the study of development itself is how the developing organism is affected by its environment. Traditionally, critical (or sensitive) periods have been proposed to account for the influence of experience on the developing organism. These periods have typically been conceived of as intervals of time during which the organism is especially sensitive to input from the environment. The influence here is largely unidirectional: as long as it comes at the right time, the environment has its effect on the organism. Other formulations of the effects of experience on development explicitly acknowledge the interdependence between the organism and its environment and the complex ways in which these interactions can influence development (Bertenthal & Campos, 1987; Gottlieb, 1991a, 1991b; Greenough, Black, & Wallace, 1987; Hofer, 1981). In the current research, we explore what effect the enrichment of infants' typical early experience as agents acting on objects would have on their object exploration behavior. Infants were given the opportunity to reach for and

**Source:** *Infant Behavior & Development*, 25(3) (2002): 279–295.

"grasp" objects earlier than they would normally do so. The effects of this experience on infants' object exploration behavior were assessed by comparing the exploratory skills of infants who had this early reaching and grasping experience with those who did not.

How are infants' actions influenced by their prior experiences? This question has been addressed by a number of different researchers (Adolph, 1997, 2000; Bertenthal, Campos, & Barrett, 1984; Bertenthal, Campos, & Kermoian, 1994; Clifton, Rochat, Litovsky, & Perris, 1991; Needham, 1999a; see Campos et al., 2000 for a recent review). In a set of influential studies, Campos, Bertenthal, and their colleagues (Bertenthal et al., 1984, 1994; Campos, Hiatt, Ramsay, Henderson, & Svejda, 1978) explored the relation between infants' self-produced locomotion and their reaction to the deep side of the visual cliff. The results of the studies showed that infants who had experience with self-produced locomotion (either their own naturally-acquired experience or artificially-acquired experience using an infant walker) showed evidence of wariness toward the deep side of the cliff. This wariness was shown by an increase in the infants' heart rate when placed on the deep side of the visual cliff, or simple avoidance of the deep side, as compared to infants who did not have locomotor experience. These findings suggest that infants' wariness of heights may develop at least in part as a result of experience with self-produced locomotion, a relation first suggested by Held and Hein's (1963) classic 'kitten carousel' study.

However, the situation is unlikely to be that simple. Adolph's (1997, 2000) elegant work has shown that infants do not acquire a general fear of heights through their early self-produced locomotor experiences (i.e., while crawling) that generalizes to walking postures. Presumably, if infants developed fear of heights via their crawling experiences (either their own visual or vestibular sensations or observing scary emotional responses from parents who find their infants in dangerous situations), these same fears would constrain their behaviors as they began to walk. But Adolph's results show an amazing specificity to infants' learning in this domain – infants must learn all over again what the consequences of dropoffs and steep slopes are for their walking, even though they have already learned what the consequences are for their crawling.

The studies described above indicate that we know relatively little about how infants' experiences in a domain affect their abilities within or outside that domain. The literature suggests that cross-domain influences do occur, although the changes may be less sweeping or far-reaching than originally thought. Despite the domain- or posture-specificity of some motor accomplishments, researchers have claimed that changes in infants' object exploration skills may be influenced by their early actions on objects. Gibson (1988), in her seminal review paper, proposed that the acquisition of new motor skills makes possible a whole new array of exploratory situations which in turn have important implications for cognitive development (see also Bushnell & Boudreau, 1993). Following up on Gibsons's claims, some experimental work has linked developments in object exploratory skills with other non-motor developments such as (a) noting the correspondence in the visual and auditory components of an event involving objects (Eppler, 1995) and (b) determining a boundary between two adjacent objects (Needham, 2000). The current research investigates Gibson's claim about the potentially far-reaching affects of attaining new motor skills by studying the relation between early reaching experiences and the development of infants' object exploration skills. We now review what is known about the development of object exploration during the first few months of life.

Although infants do not systematically reach for objects until approximately 5 months of age, even newborns will sometimes bring objects placed in their hands up to the mouth for oral contact (Butterworth & Hopkins, 1988; Lew & Butterworth, 1997; Rochat, 1993; Rochat & Senders, 1991). Indeed, hand–mouth behavior broadly construed (e.g., thumb-sucking) has been observed even in fetuses (Nillsson & Hamberger, 1990). In one of the only studies to investigate very young infants' object exploration, Rochat (1989) observed many developmental changes in 2- to 5-month-old infants' oral and visual object exploration. One major change is that object exploration becomes more coordinated over different sensory modalities, so that by 4–5 months of age, visual, oral, and manual exploration often occur in concert. This change results in more effective and efficient collection of information over a given period of time (Gibson, 1988; Gibson & Pick, 2000). Infants also engage in significantly more oral and visual exploration over time, with increasing emphasis on visual exploration. One example of this trend is that although 2- and 3-month-old infants' initial exploration of an object tended to be *oral*, 4- and 5-month-old infants' initial exploration tended to be *visual*. By 5 months of age, the visual modality seems to lead and help coordinate the exploration taking place in other modalities (see also Ruff, Saltarelli, Capozzoli, & Dubiner, 1992, who provide evidence that mouthing immediately followed by looking is a clear indication of infants' gathering information about an object).

What abilities come together to produce this rapid increase in exploratory behavior between 2 and 5 months of age? One very basic notion is that in order for infants to engage in longer bouts of object exploration, their gross motor skills (e.g., arm strength, hand strength) must be sufficiently developed (Halverson, 1931, 1933; Jeannerod, 1981, 1984; von Hofsten, 1979). These gross motor skills would presumably allow infants to maintain a grasp of the object for longer periods of time, an important contributor to longer bouts of object exploration when infants must hold the object they explore (as in Rochat, 1989). Further, developments in infants' fine motor skills must also contribute. For example, the development of fingering behavior Rochat observed beginning around 4 months of age requires a certain amount of fine motor control (Bushnell & Boudreau, 1993; Gibson, 1988; Ruff, 1984).

Another factor related to the increase in object exploration could be improvements in hand–eye and hand–mouth coordination (Bruner, 1969; Gesell, 1934; Lockman & Ashmead, 1983; White, 1969). The coordination of these exploratory systems makes possible the increases in multi-modal exploration noted by Rochat (1989). It also seems likely that infants' motivation to explore objects could increase during the time between 2 and 5 months of age. Researchers have long noticed that infants' interest in objects increases dramatically once they develop the ability to reach for objects (Fogel, Dedo, & McEwen, 1992; Gibson, 1988; Gibson & Pick, 2000; Kaye & Fogel, 1980). In one study investigating connections between postural position, reaching ability and visual gaze during mother–infant interactions, Fogel et al. (1992) found that infants who could reach for objects spent less time gazing at their mothers than infants who could not yet successfully reach for objects.

Like Bertenthal's walker studies that explored the role of self-produced locomotion on the development of infants' wariness of heights, we sought to learn more about the factors underlying the development of infants' object exploration skills by giving infants experiences that would simulate prehension earlier than they would normally engage in this behavior. The participants in this study were 3 months of age at the time of testing (i.e., 0.5–1.5 months prior to spontaneous effective reaching and grasping), and were in the midst of the transitions in object exploration skills discovered by Rochat (1989).

The enrichment experience consisted of 12–14 brief parent-led object play sessions held at the infant's home. During the play sessions, the infant sat on a parent's lap at a table and wore mittens with the soft side of Velcro covering the palms. On the table in front of the infant were small, lightweight objects with edges covered in the corresponding side of the Velcro. With a quick swipe of the hand, the infant could easily "pick up" an object as it stuck to the mitten. Our pilot observations of infants wearing these "sticky mittens" led us to believe that they quickly became visually engaged in the objects on the table, possibly as a result of the realization that they were in control of the objects' movements.

After the enrichment phase for the infants in the experimental condition, these infants as well as the infants in the control condition (who did not receive any prior experience) were brought to the lab for an assessment of their prehensile and object exploration skills. Based on the idea that the onset of self-produced locomotion facilitates changes in the infant's life due to the new experiences that accompany the change, we hypothesized that early production of prehensile actions may bring with it new experiences that would lead to changes in infants' object-directed activity. If this hypothesis is correct, experience interacting with toys while wearing the mittens would facilitate the development of infants' object-directed activity both while the mittens were being worn and after they were taken off.

## 2. Method

### 2.1. Participants

Participants were 32 healthy, full-term infants (15 girls, 17 boys) ranging in age from 3 months to 3 months, 19 days ($M$ = 3 months, 9 days, SD = 5.4 days). Half of the infants were in the experimental condition ($M$ = 3 months, 11 days) and half were in the control condition ($M$ = 3 months, 7 days). Data from seven additional infants were collected and eliminated: three due to fussiness during the trials, two because their at-home experience did not exceed the minimum of 80 min, and one due to drowsiness during the session. Data from one infant were excluded because her scores on all measures exceeded two standard deviations from the average scores of the rest of the infants in that condition.

The infants' names for this experiment were obtained from the Durham County vital records office. Parents were contacted via letter and follow-up phone calls. They were offered reimbursement for their travel expenses but were not compensated for their participation.

### 2.2. Apparatus

#### 2.2.1. Home Session

The enrichment sessions received by the infants in the experimental condition featured three different sets of toys. These toys were purchased at a store and altered in the ways described below for this experiment. Set 1 consisted of wooden blocks of various sizes (2 cm × 6 cm × 2 cm, 2 cm × 8 cm × 2 cm, 4 cm × 2 cm × 4 cm, 3 cm × 3 cm × 3 cm) and brightly colored (red, yellow, blue, or orange). Set 2 was made up of black plastic rings of four different shapes: square, oval, triangle, and diamond. Each measured 6.5 cm at its widest point. Set 3 was comprised of plastic cubes, also known as Duplos® blocks, measuring 4.5 cm on each side and with a 2.5 cm dome on the top. Each infant received a set of four blocks that were either blue, red, or yellow.

Tabs of Velcro (the 'hard' side) were placed on each object. The blocks in Set 1 were covered in an average of 11 pieces, each measuring 3.2 cm². The rings in Set 2 had six 1.3 cm width pieces wrapped around at evenly-spaced locations. The plastic cubes in Set 3 received seven pieces, each measuring 6.5 cm².

The mittens were made of soft fleece. Long strips of the Velcro's soft side were sewn horizontally along the palm of the mitten. The length of the strips varied from 7.5 to 10 cm depending on where on the palm it was found. The mitten was secured at the infants' wrist by an adjustable strap that could expand to as large as 9 cm across.

Parents were given a daily log to track the time spent on the enrichment sessions with their infant. The log was used to both quantify the minutes spent on the enrichment, and as a reminder for the parent to incorporate the toys into their daily play.

## 2.2.2. Laboratory Session

The first two laboratory test trials utilized the same kind of plastic cubes and mittens that the experimental infants played with at home. The infants sat on their mothers' laps to explore the plastic cubes at a wooden table that was 74 cm in height. A pillow was placed under an infant if his or her arms could not rest above the table top. The table top was 81 cm from left to right sides and 64 cm from infant to the experimenter, who sat facing the baby. A half circle (23 cm radius) was cut out of the infant's side of the table, so the infant was surrounded by table. The table was covered in a brightly lined white contact paper.

For the object exploration trials, the infants sat in a semireclined "bouncy seat" to give postural support while they held a series of four novel objects (see Fig. 1). These four objects were designed to be either high or low in

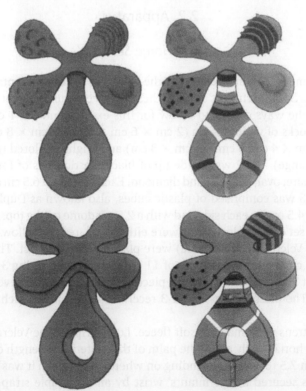

**Figure 1:** Teethers given to the infants in the object exploration portion of the lab visit

visual and oral information. One of the objects (the low-visual/high-oral object) was a commercially available red rubber teether with four mouthable segments that had different orally available textures on them (small bumps, small dimples, one large dimple, and raised straight edges). The high-visual/ high-oral object was an identical teether that was decorated with black, blue, green, and yellow plastic tape. The low-oral objects were smooth wooden replicas of the high-oral objects; they were made to be roughly the same as these objects in size, shape, and weight, and were decorated in the same way as the high-oral objects.

## 2.3. Procedure

### 2.3.1. Home Session

Only the infants in the experimental condition participated in this portion of the study. An experimenter went to the homes of the infants in the experimental condition, bringing with her a set of mittens and toys and a copy of the daily log. The experimenter demonstrated the procedure to the parent and then watched while the parent completed the first 10 min session.

Parents were asked to put the mittens on their baby's hands and play with the toys as instructed, 10 min a day for 2 weeks. This involved setting one of the three sets of toys on a table in front of the infant while the infant was wearing the mittens. Parents were asked to cycle through the three sets of toys in turn, but the timing of presentation of each set was left to the discretion of the parent. The rings and blocks were to be arranged in a pile in front of the infant; whereas, the cubes were arranged in a square. Parents were told that if their infant did not spontaneously swat at the objects, they could tap near the objects and/or place the infant's mittened hand on the objects. If the infant made contact with an object, the parent would then remove the toy(s) from the mitten(s) and place them back in front of the infant to allow them to try again. The parents recorded the time their infant spent engaged with the mittens and toys on the daily log.

### 2.3.2. Laboratory Session

The infants in both the experimental and control conditions participated in this portion of the study. The laboratory session consisted of two kinds of trials: the prehension trials and the object exploration trials. The prehension trials featured objects that had been used in the enrichment sessions. Infants wore the sticky mittens for one of these trials, but not the other. For these trials, we were interested in infants' visual contact with the objects on the table and swiping at these objects. The object exploration trials were designed to assess infants' object exploration skills, and featured novel objects. The infants did not wear the sticky mittens during any of these trials. For these trials, we were interested in infants' visual and oral exploration of the objects. The upright-seated posture and the reclined postures of these two kinds of trials were chosen to facilitate infants' accomplishment of the tasks in each portion of the study. The infants' behaviors in these trials were recorded on videotape and coded using a videocassette recorder and color video monitor.

For the prehension trials, the infant sat on a parent's lap in front of the wooden table. The experimenter sat opposite the infant and introduced objects that had been used in the enrichment sessions. For both trials, the experimenter placed the four plastic cubes of Set 3 together to make a square in front of the infant (these cubes may have been a different color than the infants had experience with in the home enrichment sessions). The infant was allotted approximately 2 min to interact with these objects, and this behavior was recorded. If the infant became inattentive to the objects or experimenter, the experimenter tapped lightly on the table or moved the objects slightly to reorient the infant. The second trial was identical to the first, with one exception: the mittens were placed on the infants' hands prior to the beginning of the trial.

Following the prehension trials, the mittens were removed from the infants' hands in preparation for the object exploration trials. In these trials, the infants sat in a semireclined "bouncy seat" while they held a series of four novel teethers that they could visually, orally, and manually explore. Infants were presented with each red teether (see Fig. 1) in a random order. Each object was brought into the infant's field of view and placed into the infant's hand. The teethers were presented in a vertical orientation, as if they were bouquets of flowers. The length of time the infant held the object was monitored by the experimenter, who used the following decision rules to determine the ends of the trials:

(1) If the infant dropped the object prior to accumulating 30 s of holding, the experimenter put the object back into the infant's hand and continued the trial.
(2) If the infant dropped the object after holding it for 30 s, the experimenter went on to the next trial.
(3) If the infant had held the object for 60 s without dropping it, the object was removed from the infant's hand and the next trial was begun.

Objects were placed alternately in the infants' right and left hands.

Four infants failed to complete the full set of test trials in the lab, due to fussiness: three infants were missing one of the object exploration trials and one infant was missing one of the prehension trials. The remainder of each of these infants' data sets was included in the analyses.

## 2.4. Coding

Duration measures (e.g., Looking time, Holding time, Mouthing time) were determined by trained coders who pressed the trigger of a joystick in a continuous fashion whenever the infant engaged in each behavior. For example, when coding for Looking time, the coder would press the trigger as soon as the infant looked at the object and would keep pressing until the infant looked away. The input from each joystick fed into a program that tabulated duration.

### 2.4.1. Prehension Trials

To determine the effect of the enrichment experience on object exploration, both the amount of time infants spent looking at the plastic cubes and the number of times the infant tried to "pick up" the cubes were measured. Looking time was defined by the amount of time spent looking at the plastic cubes. Looking percentage scores were calculated as Looking time divided by total time of the trial. Total time was the amount of time between the beginning and end of a trial. The beginning of each trial started when the infant was presented with the plastic cubes and the experimenter's hands were taken away. The trial ended when the experimenter retrieved the blocks from the infant. If the mittens fell off or needed to be adjusted, that time was subtracted from the measure of total time.

The number of times an infant tried to "pick up" the cubes was measured by the swats made toward the toy. A swat was defined as a movement of the arm(s) that resulted in manual contact with the blocks. A swat was not counted if the experimenter accidentally pushed the blocks into the infant's hands when presenting them. During the prehension trials, only one swat was counted until the experimenter took the blocks off of the mittens and placed them back in front of the infant.

To assess the intentionality of swatting behavior, swats were further divided into two groups: (1) with visual contact toward the objects immediately prior to the swat or (2) without visual contact toward the objects immediately prior to the swat. We thought that this difference might reflect a difference in the intention behind the action (with prior visual contact suggesting intentional contact with the object and no prior visual contact suggesting unintentional contact). To give an indication of the amount of the infant's general activity with the arm regardless of intention to act upon the objects, both groups of swats were summed to yield the total number of swats for both trials.

### 2.4.2. Object Exploration Trials

Three behaviors (Holding time, Looking time, and Mouthing time) were coded from the videotapes, and additional measures (percentage scores for each of the three main measures, an overall exploration percentage, and a measure of switching between looking and mouthing) were derived from these three main behaviors.

Holding time, Looking time, and Mouthing time were measured in real time as described above. Holding time was the amount of time the infant held each object. Looking time and Mouthing time were coded simultaneously for each baby by two different coders (this was done so switching between looking and mouthing could be determined and so simultaneous looking and mouthing could be measured). Looking time was the amount of time the infant spent visually exploring each teether. Looking percentage scores were determined by finding the proportion of time that the infant looked at each teether over the total time that the infant held it. Mouthing time was the amount of time the infant spent orally exploring each teether (including brushes of the teether against the lips). Mouthing percentage scores were determined by finding the proportion of time that the infant mouthed the teether over the total time that the infant held it.

For each infant and each object, an Exploration percentage was calculated by adding the looking and Mouthing times together and subtracting the time that the infant was engaged in both activities. This score was then divided by the total Holding time to make an Exploration percentage score. This score reflected the percent of the trial time that the infant spent exploring the object (either visually or orally).

To measure the level of coordination between visual and oral exploration, we counted the number of times that each infant switched between exploration in the two modalitites. Switches were determined from the paper printouts of the Looking and Mouthing time coding (which resulted in a continuous record of the infants' looking and mouthing behavior at the tenth-of-second level). A switch was defined as (1) a change from exploration in one modality (looking or mouthing) to exploration in the other modality that took place within 1 s and with less than 1 s of overlap of the two modalities, or (2) the onset and offset of exploration in one modality during a longer bout of exploration in the other modality.

To assess reliability for the Holding time, Looking time, and Mouthing time measures, one-third of all subjects ($N = 10$) was recoded by a trained observer who was aware of the condition of each infant but not aware of the goals or hypotheses of the study. Percent agreement was calculated for each of the following measures: Swatting and Looking time for the prehension trials and Looking time, Mouthing time, and Holding time for the object exploration trials. The range of percent agreement was 87–99% with an average of 93%.

Because the experimenters running the sessions could not be kept unaware of the condition each infant was in (parents who participated in the experimental condition brought the toys and mittens back to the laboratory; parents would also sometimes make comments about the home sessions at various points during the lab visit), we coded a sample of the sessions for the experimenter's and parent's behavior during the test sessions. Although the experimenters tried to keep quiet during the sessions and instructed the parent to do the same, it was not always possible to keep the session perfectly quiet. We were concerned that potential interruptions during the sessions (i.e., the experimenter or parent talking or laughing) could have happened more frequently for either the control or the experimental groups.

To address this possibility, we coded a randomly selected sample of 10 sessions (5 from the experimental condition and 5 from the control condition) for the experimenter's and parent's behavior during the lab session. We counted the number of vocalizations produced by the parent or experimenter during the session, regardless of whether they were directed to the experimenter, parent, or baby. All vocalizations were counted, even if they were so quiet that the infant was unlikely to have heard them. This coding effort determined that the experimental ($M = 22$, SD $= 11$) and control ($M = 18.6$, SD $= 9.3$) groups had approximately equal number of vocalizations, $F(1, 8) = .278, p = .61$. We also counted the number of times that a vocalization during the trial resulted in the baby disengaging in the task (even briefly), and this number was also not different between the experimental ($M = 3$, SD $= 2.6$) and control ($M = 1$, SD $= 1$) groups, $F(1, 8) = 2.67, p = .14$. Thus, any differences in the behaviors of the infants in the experimental and control conditions could not be a result of the experimenters' and parents' behaviors during the sessions.

## 3. Results

### 3.1. Prehension Trials

The results for the prehension trials are shown in Fig. 2. The looking percentage scores and swatting measures were analyzed by means of analysis of variance (ANOVA) to assess differences in looking and swatting between the infants in the experimental and control conditions.

First, a two-factor ANOVA was run to assess differences in infants' visual exploratory behavior depending on whether the infant was in the experimental or control condition (between-subjects factor) and whether they were wearing the mittens or not (within-subjects factor). This analysis revealed that the infants in the experimental condition ($M = 68.3$, SD $= 25.1$) looked at the objects for a greater portion of the trial than infants in the control condition ($M = 33.0$, SD $= 30.4$) whether the infants were wearing the mittens or not, $F(1, 29) = 13.82, p < .001$.

A second ANOVA was conducted on the numbers of swats that the infants produced during the prehension trials, again depending upon whether the infant was in the experimental or control condition (between-subjects factor) and whether they were wearing the mittens or not (within-subjects factor).

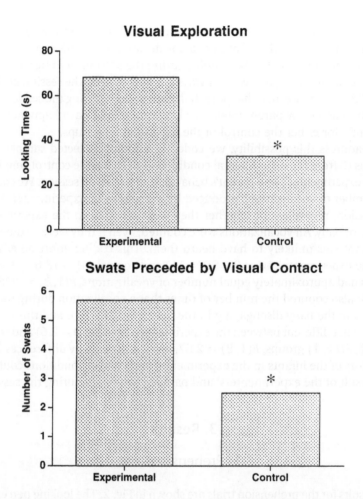

**Figure 2:** Results of the prehension trials portion of the lab visit. The graphs show that the experienced infants looked at the objects more and produced more visually-coordinated swats than the inexperienced infants. An asterisk indicates significance at the $p < .05$ level.

Overall, there was a trend for the infants in the experimental condition ($M = 6.9$, SD $= 4.2$) to exhibit more swatting behavior toward the test objects than the infants in the control condition ($M = 4.8$, SD $= 5.0$), $F(1, 29) = 2.18$, $p = .15$. However, one might reasonably claim that only those swats that were immediately preceded by visual contact with the objects were actually intended to result in contact with the objects. Swats that did not have visual contact leading up to them may actually have been accidental contacts with the objects. When one considers only those swats that were immediately preceded by visual contact, it becomes clear that the infants in the experimental condition ($M = 5.7$, SD $= 4.4$) produced significantly more of these "intentional" swats than the infants in the control condition ($M = 2.5$, SD $= 4.3$), $F(1, 29) = 4.7$, $p < .05$.

### 3.2. Object Exploration Trials

The results for the object exploration trials are shown in Fig. 3. Because the object exploration trials yielded similar values across the four red teethers, each measure was averaged across the teethers for each infant. Simple one-factor ANOVAs were conducted on each measure to determine if the enrichment sessions affected infants' exploration of these novel objects.

These analyses showed that the infants in the experimental condition had higher Exploration percentages than the infants in the control condition, $F(1, 33) = 7.38, p < .05$, indicating that the experimental infants ($M = 47.6$,

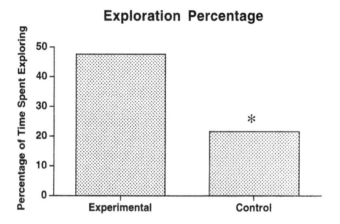

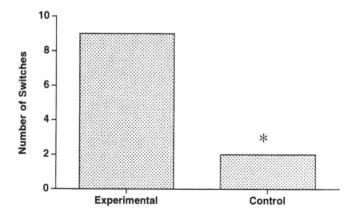

**Figure 3:** Results of the object exploration portion of the lab visit. The graphs show that the experienced infants explored the teethers (both visually and orally) for a greater percentage of time and switched between visual and oral exploration more than the inexperienced infants. An asterisk indicates significance at the $p < .05$ level.

SD = 28) explored the objects orally and visually for a significantly greater portion of the trial than the control infants did ($M$ = 21.6, SD = 21.2). The infants in the experimental condition also had greater Mouthing percentage scores than the infants in the control condition, $F(1, 33)$ = 6.80, $p < .05$, indicating that the infants in the experimental condition ($M$ = 23.2, SD = 19.9) spent a significantly greater portion of the trials engaging in oral exploration of the objects than the infants in the control condition did ($M$ = 8.1, SD = 12.8). Although not quite significant, there was a trend for the infants in the experimental condition to have greater Looking percentage scores ($M$ = 30.0, SD = 25.8) than the infants in the control condition ($M$ = 14.5, SD = 17), $F(1, 33)$ = 2.97, $p$ = .09. Finally, there was significantly more switching between visual and oral exploration of the objects by the infants in the experimental condition ($M$ = 9.0, SD = 11.0) compared to the infants in the control condition ($M$ = 2.0, SD = 3.0), $F(1, 33)$ = 6.75, $p < .05$.

## 4. Discussion

On almost every measure of object exploration and object-directed action obtained, infants who had the 2-week enrichment experience with the sticky mittens significantly outperformed their counterparts who did not have this experience. When seated at the table for the prehension tasks, the experienced infants looked at the objects significantly longer than the control infants both with and without the mittens. The experienced infants also swatted at the objects more during visual contact compared to the control infants whether or not they were wearing the mittens. The fact that this finding held whether or not the infants were wearing the mittens suggests that the experienced infants were not just "trained up" on how to use the mittens to move the objects on the table. Rather, the enrichment experience may have increased their engagement in objects in general, and may have served as a motivator for initiating contact with objects in many situations.

When in the bouncy seat for the object exploration tasks, the experienced infants spent significantly more time exploring (visually and orally) the novel red teether objects than the control infants. The experienced infants spent significantly more time mouthing the objects and their levels of visual exploration during these trials were approaching significance. The experienced infants also switched between visual and oral exploration significantly more than the control infants, indicating that the experienced infants did not just explore more, but were employing exploration strategies that involved more coordination between oral and visual modalities.

Although the results show substantial differences between the infants who received the enrichment experience and those who did not, we do not yet know exactly what about the enrichment experience served to facilitate infants' object exploration skills. One possibility is that noticing the contingency between their own movements and the consequences of those movements for moving and transporting objects was the key reason for the behavior changes we observed. If this is true, then other manipulations that would give infants this same opportunity (e.g., simply connecting the objects to their hands using strings) should produce the same behavior changes. Alternately, the critical component of the experience we created could have been the additional practice bringing objects to the face for visual exploration or to the mouth for oral exploration. If this is true, then experiences in which the parent places objects in the infant's hands for transport to the eyes or mouth should also be effective. The experiences may also have functioned in this way because parents brought infants' attention to the objects in a more systematic fashion than they typically would have. If this is true, then infants tested in the same way as the experimental group in this study, except without the mittens, would show the same effects as we reported here. Finally, it may have been experience with the mittens on their hands that drew infants' attention to their hands and led to the changes in behavior we observed here (see, for example, White, 1971). If this last hypothesis is true, then the stickiness of our mittens was not actually essential, and infants wearing mittens without Velcro should experience the same facilitation as was observed in our current study. Our future research efforts will address these questions and we hope will reveal the exact nature of the effects of these experiences.

These findings lead to a number of conclusions about the development of infants' object exploration skills. First, they suggest that experience acting on objects may be a critical factor in increasing infants' engagement in objects and their object exploration skills. Not only do infants explore objects more after this experience, they employ more sophisticated object exploration strategies that involve more coordination between visual and oral exploration. It seems unlikely that the sticky mittens experience could have had much of a direct effect on infants' fine motor skills, as the mittens themselves would have prevented much fingering activity. It is possible, though, that the mittens experience had an indirect effect on fine motor skills: the mittens experience could have piqued the infants' interest in objects in general and they could have begun more detailed exploration of objects over the 2-week period of the experience sessions that would have facilitated the development of their fine-motor skills.

The fact that there were no significant differences in the infants' actions whether they were wearing the mittens or not suggests that the infants did not just become conditioned to wave their hands around more while wearing the mittens. Rather, the evidence supports the conclusion that the infants generalized what they learned while wearing the mittens to other situations in which they were not wearing the mittens.

One might wonder whether the experienced infants' increase in visual exploration in the prehension trials as compared to the control infants could be a result of those objects being familiar to the experienced infants. However, studies have typically found that increasing an infant's prior experience with an object *decreases* his or her attention to the object at a later time (Cornell, 1979; Fagan, 1970, 1971, 1973, 1974, 1977; Lasky, 1980; Martin, 1975; Rose, 1981; Rose & Slater, 1983). Furthermore, an increase in visual attention to objects for the experienced infants compared to the control infants was also found in the object exploration phase of the study, which involved completely novel objects. Thus, we conclude that the sticky mittens experience led to an increase in infants' engagement in familiar and unfamiliar objects.

One explanation consistent with the current results is that noting the contingency between their own movements and the consequences for object movement facilitate their engagement in objects in a variety of ways. How could this effect be conceptualized? First, one may think of it as a kind of decalage, because infants have already learned how their social actions (facial expressions, gestures, crying) bring about a whole variety of different "observable effects", or responses from the people around them (Adolph, Eppler, & Gibson, 1993; Gibson, 1988; Gibson & Pick, 2000). Of course, the specific ways in which they have an effect in the physical world are so different from the ways in which they have an effect in the social world that they are unlikely to have much 'savings' from one to the other (recall Adolph's (1997, 2000) findings on learning specificity).

Another experimental paradigm that has allowed infants to produce observable actions on objects before they would typically do so on their own is Rovee-Collier's conjugate reinforcement paradigm (see Rovee-Collier & Hayne, 2000). In this paradigm, a ribbon is tied to an infant's ankle and the other end is tied to a mobile stand. What happens in this situation is that infants' rate of leg kicks increases sharply. This is additional evidence that producing actions on objects with observable effects is highly reinforcing for young infants. It remains an open question whether this experience with leg-kicking and mobile-moving would generalize to producing actions with the hands on objects on a table (or objects placed in their hands). If experience moving mobiles did lead infants to become more engaged in objects earlier than they typically would, a strong case could be made for the role of producing actions with observable effects on objects on increases in infants' object attention. It seems possible to us, however, that these two situations would seem so different to these young infants that they would not make the connection between the two.

What are the functions or consequences of infants' increased object exploration? There could be many consequences, of course, but one hypothesis we are investigating is that as infants explore objects more actively, they learn the relation between object features and object boundaries. That is, as they explore objects more actively, they may come to realize that object boundaries exist where there are abrupt changes in an object's shape, color, and pattern. Our lab has already produced evidence that infants who employ more active exploration strategies (exploring more, switching more between oral and visual modalities of exploration) are better able to segregate a visual display into its component parts, as compared to infants who employ less active exploration strategies (Needham, 2000). If it is the case that the active exploration strategies are a key factor in the development of these segregation abilities (presumably as a result of their learning about object properties), then we would predict that infants who have the sticky mittens experience should have advanced exploration skills and, as a result, advanced object segregation skills.

In this framework, we believe that multimodal exploration could serve the special function of amplifying some information, making it easier for infants to attend to it. For example, object shape is available visually, orally, and haptically, whereas color and pattern are only available visually. Because research from our lab has shown that young infants use shape to segregate objects prior to the time that they use color and pattern (Needham, 1999b), our future research will explore the idea that one reason for this difference is that shape is available multimodally whereas color and pattern are not.

These findings give us a glimpse into the processes underlying the development of infants' exploratory skills: specifically, they show that experience acting on objects is an important contributor to the increase in object attention and object exploration that is typically observed by 6 months of age. Although infants typically receive this experience around 4.5–5 months of age, when they do receive it earlier, their object attention and object exploration skills are enhanced. These findings highlight the interrelations between developments in different areas and add to the growing body of research that shows important linkages between infants' perceptual, cognitive, and action-based abilities (e.g., Adolph, 1997, 2000; Gibson & Pick, 2000; McCarty, Clifton, & Collard, 1999, 2001). Future work will provide a better understanding of the complex interdependencies between these abilities as they develop during the first year of life.

## References

Adolph, K. E. (1997). Learning in the development of infant locomotion. *Monographs of the Society for Research in Child Development, 62* (3, Serial No. 251).

Adolph, K. E. (2000). Specificity of learning: Why infants fall over a veritable cliff. *Psychological Science, 11,* 290–295.

Adolph, K. E., Eppler, M. A., & Gibson, E. J. (1993). Development of perception of affordances. In C. Rovee-Collier & L. Lipsitt (Eds.), *Advances in infancy research* (Vol. 8, pp. 51–98), Norwood, NJ: Ablex.

Bertenthal, B. I., & Campos, J. J. (1987). New directions in the study of early experience. *Child Development, 58,* 560–567.

Bertenthal, B. I., Campos, J. J., & Barrett, K. C. (1984). Self-produced locomotion: An organizer of emotional, cognitive, and social development in infancy. In R. Emde & R. Harmon (Eds.), *Continuities and discontinuities in development* (pp. 175–210). New York: Plenum Press.

Bertenthal, B. I., Campos, J. J., & Kermoian, R. (1994). An epigenetic perspective on the development of self-produced locomotion and its consequences. *Current Directions in Psychological Science, 3,* 140–145.

Bruner, J. S. (1969). Eye, hand, and mind. In D. Elkind & J. H. Flavell (Eds.), *Studies in cognitive development, esays in honor of Jean Piaget* (pp. 223–236). New York: Oxford University Press.

Bushnell, E. W., & Boudreau, J. P. (1993). Motor development and the mind: The potential role of motor abilities as a determinant of aspects of perceptual development. *Child Development, 64,* 1005–1021.

Butterworth, G., & Hopkins, B. (1988). Hand–mouth coordination in the new-born baby. *British Journal of Developmental Psychology, 6,* 303–314.

Campos, J. J., Hiatt, S., Ramsay, D., Henderson, C., & Svejda, M. (1978). The emergence of fear on the visual cliff. In M. Lewis & L. Rosenblum (Eds.), *The development of affect* (pp. 149–182). New York: Plenum Press.

Campos, J. J., Anderson, D. I., Barbu-Roth, M. A., Hubbard, E. M., Hertenstein, M. J., & Witherington, D. (2000). Travel broadens the mind. *Infancy, 1,* 149–219.

Clifton, R. K., Rochat, P., Litovsky, R. Y., & Perris, E. E. (1991). Object representation guides infants' reaching in the dark. *Journal of Experimental Psychology: Human Perception and Performance, 17,* 323–329.

Cornell, E. H. (1979). Infants' recognition memory, forgetting, and savings. *Journal of Experimental Child Psychology, 28,* 359–374.

Eppler, M. A. (1995). Development of manipulatory skills and the deployment of attention. *Infant Behavior and Development, 18,* 391–405.

Fagan, J. F. (1970). Memory in the infant. *Journal of Experimental Child Psychology, 9,* 217–226.

Fagan, J. F. (1971). Infants' recognition memory for a series of visual stimuli. *Journal of Experimental Child Psychology, 11,* 244–250.

Fagan, J. F. (1973). Infants' delayed recognition memory and forgetting. *Journal of Experimental Child Psychology, 16,* 424–450.

Fagan, J. F. (1974). Infant recognition memory: The effects of length of familiarization and type of discrimination task. *Child Development, 45,* 351–356.

Fagan, J. F. (1977). Infant recognition memory: Studies in forgetting. *Child Development, 48,* 68–78.

Fogel, A., Dedo, J. Y., & McEwen, I. (1992). Effect of postural position and reaching on gaze during mother–infant face-to-face interaction. *Infant Behavior and Development, 15,* 231–244.

Gesell, A. (1934). *An atlas of infant behavior* (Vol. 1). New Haven, CT: Yale University Press.

Gibson, E. J. (1988). Exploratory behavior in the development of perceiving, acting, and the acquiring of knowledge. *Annual Review of Psychology, 39,* 1–41.

Gibson, E. J., & Pick, A. D. (2000). *An ecological approach to perceptual learning and development.* New York, NY: Oxford University Press.

Gottlieb, G. (1991a). Experiential canalization of behavioral development: Results. *Developmental Psychology, 27,* 35–39.

Gottlieb, G. (1991b). Experiential canalization of behavioral development: Theory. *Developmental Psychology, 27,* 4–13.

Greenough, W. T., Black, J. E., & Wallace, C. S. (1987). Experience and brain development. *Child Development, 58,* 539–559.

Halverson, H. M. (1931). An experimental study of prehension in infants by means of systematic cinema records. *Genetic Psychology Monographs, 10,* 107–283.

Halverson, H. M. (1933). The acquisition of skill in infancy. *Journal of Genetic Psychology, 43*, 3–48.

Held, R., & Hein, A. (1963). Movement-produced stimulation in the development of visually-guided behavior. *Journal of Comparative and Physiological Psychology, 56*, 872–876.

Hofer, M. (1981). *The roots of human behavior*. San Francisco, CA: Freeman.

Jeannerod, M. (1981). Intersegmental coordination during reaching at natural visual objects. In J. Long & A. Baddeley (Eds.), *Attention and performance IX* (pp. 153–168). Hillsdale, NJ: Erlbaum.

Jeannerod, M. (1984). The timing of natural prehension movements. *Journal of Motor Behavior, 16*, 235–254.

Kaye, K., & Fogel, A. (1980). The temporal structure of face-to-face communication between mothers and infants. *Developmental Psychology, 16*, 454–464.

Lasky, R. E. (1980). Length of familiarization and preference for novel and familiar stimuli. *Infant Behavior and Development, 3*, 15–28.

Lew, A. R., & Butterworth, G. (1997). The development of hand–mouth coordination in 2- to 5-month-old infants: Similarities with reaching and grasping. *Infant Behavior and Development, 20*, 59–69.

Lockman, J. J., & Ashmead, D. H. (1983). Asynchronies in the development of manual behavior. In L. P. Lipsitt & C. K. Rovee-Collier (Eds.), *Advances in infancy research* (Vol. 2, pp. 113–136). Norwood, NJ: Ablex.

Martin, R. M. (1975). Effects of familiar and complex stimuli on infant attention. *Developmental Psychology, 11*, 178–185.

Needham, A. (1999a). How infants grasp two adjacent objects: Effects of perceived display composition on infants' actions. *Developmental Science, 2*, 219–233.

Needham, A. (1999b). The role of shape in 4-month-old infants' segregation of adjacent objects. *Infant Behavior and Development, 22*, 161–178.

Needham, A. (2000). Improvements in object exploration skills may facilitate the development of object segregation in early infancy. *Journal of Cognition and Development, 1*, 131–156.

Nillsson, L., & Hamberger, L. (1990). *A child is born*. New York, NY: Delacorte Press.

Rochat, P. (1989). Object manipulation and exploration in 2- to 5-month-old infants. *Developmental Psychology, 25*, 871–884.

Rochat, P. (1993). Hand–mouth coordination in the newborn: Morphology, determinants, and early development of a basic act. In G. J. P. Savelsbergh (Ed.), *The development of coordination in infancy* (pp. 265–288). Amsterdam: North-Holland.

Rochat, P., & Senders, S. J. (1991). Active touch in infancy: Action systems in development. In M. J. S. Weiss & P. R. Zelazo (Eds.), *Newborn attention: Biological constraints and the influence of experience* (pp. 412–442). Norwood, NJ: Ablex.

Rose, S. A. (1981). Developmental changes in infants' retention of visual stimuli. *Child Development, 52*, 227–233.

Rose, D. H., & Slater, A. M. (1983). Infant recognition memory following brief stimulus exposure. *British Journal of Developmental Psychology, 1*, 221–230.

Rovee-Collier, C., & Hayne, H. (2000). Memory in infancy and early childhood. In E. Tulving & F. Craik (Eds), *The Oxford handbook of memory* (pp. 267–282). New York, NY: Oxford University Press.

Ruff, H. A. (1984). Infants' manipulative exploration of objects: Effects of age and object characteristics. *Developmental Psychology, 20*, 9–20.

Ruff, H. A., Saltarelli, L. M., Capozzoli, M., & Dubiner, K. (1992). The differentiation of activity in infants' exploration of objects. *Developmental Psychology, 28*, 851–861.

von Hofsten, C. (1979). Development of visually guided reaching: The approach phase. *Journal of Human Movement Studies, 5*, 160–178.

White, B. L. (1969). The initial coordination of sensorimotor schemas in human infants: Piaget's ideas and the role of experience. In D. Elkind & J. H. Flavell (Eds.), *Studies in cognitive development, essays in honor of Jean Piaget* (pp. 237–256). New York, NY: Oxford University Press.

White, B. L. (1971). *Human infants: Experience and psychological development.* Englewood Cliffs, NJ: Prentice-Hall.

# 38

# How Do You Learn to Walk? Thousands of Steps and Dozens of Falls Per Day

*Karen E. Adolph, Whitney G. Cole, Meghana Komati,*
*Jessie S. Garciaguirre, Daryaneh Badaly, Jesse M. Lingeman,*
*Gladys L.Y. Chan and Rachel B. Sotsky*

How do infants learn to walk? For more than 100 years, researchers have described developmental antecedents of walking, improvements in the kinematics of walking gait, and changes in the neurophysiological correlates of walking (Adolph & Robinson, in press). However, a century of research has proceeded without a natural ecology of infant locomotion. Researchers know nothing about how much infants crawl and walk, how their activity is distributed over time, how far they travel and where they go, how frequently they fall and what motivates them to persevere, and how natural locomotion changes with development. Lack of such descriptive data is a serious omission, unique to motor development. Descriptions of infants' natural activity have been instrumental for constraining theory, guiding clinical interventions, and motivating new research in other areas, such as language acquisition (Hart & Risley, 1995; Hurtado, Marchman, & Fernald, 2008; MacWhinney, 2000), cognitive development (Piaget, 1936/1952), social-emotional development (Barker & Wright, 1951; Messinger, Ruvolo, Ekas, & Fogel, 2010), symbolic play (Tamis-LeMonda & Bornstein, 1996), sleep (Kleitman & Engelmann, 1953), and natural vision (Cicchino, Aslin, & Rakison, 2011; Franchak, Kretch, Soska, & Adolph, 2011; Smith, Yu, & Pereira, 2011). But theories about the development of locomotion and therapies designed to redress atypical locomotor development are not connected to data on infants' real-world experiences with locomotion.

**Source:** *Psychological Science*, 23(11) (2012): 1387–1394.

Why are natural descriptions so conspicuously absent from the literature on infant locomotion? One reason for the absence of data is the traditional emphasis on neuromuscular maturation. The long-held assumption that locomotion develops as a universal series of increasingly erect stages led researchers to focus on the formal structure of prone crawling postures en route to upright walking (Gesell, 1946). Similarly, the search for locomotor "primitives" led to formal comparisons between alternating leg movements in newborn stepping, treadmill-elicited stepping, and independent walking (Dominici et al., 2011; Forssberg, 1985; McGraw, 1945; Thelen, 1986; Zelazo, 1983). But age-related sequences in the topography of locomotion dodge the question of why crawlers ever bother to walk. That is, why would expert crawlers abandon a presumably stable, quadrupedal posture that took months to master in order to move in a precarious, upright posture that involves frequent falling? In fact, the question of why children persist in acquiring new skills that are initially less functional than the skills already in their repertoires is a central but unanswered question in developmental psychology (Miller & Seier, 1994; Siegler, 2000).

A second, related, reason for the lack of data on natural locomotion is that researchers have historically measured aspects of periodic gait – consecutive, regular steps over open ground – rather than natural locomotion in a cluttered environment where deviations from periodic gait can be adaptive and functional. Since the 1930s, researchers have described infants' movements as they take a series of continuous steps over a straight, uniform path (Bril & Breniere, 1993; Dominici et al., 2011; Hallemans, De Clercq, & Aerts, 2006; McGraw, 1945; Shirley, 1931). With the standard paradigm, it is imperative that the infants being assessed walk as quickly and as straight as possible because speed and straightness affect measures such as step length. But the first thing that researchers discover as they try to coax infants along a straight, continuous path is that infants do not readily walk this way. Instead, they stop after a few steps, speed up and slow down, swerve and change direction, and misstep or fall. Typically, such deviations from periodic gait are ignored because they invalidate standard skill measures, and thus trials must be repeated. However, in natural locomotion, modifications in step length, speed, and direction are necessary to cope with variable terrain (Patla, 1997). Without a corpus of natural infant locomotion, researchers cannot know whether standard skill measures such as step length and speed during periodic gait are related to functional skill measures in the everyday environment, such as how much infants crawl or walk, how many steps they take, how far they travel, and how frequently they fall.

A third factor contributing to ignorance about infants' natural experiences with locomotion is that researchers (including the current authors) routinely represent experience as the number of days that have elapsed since an onset date. Researchers report walking experience as the number of days between the first day of walking and the day of testing. However, this definition is misleading: New walkers walk intermittently, vacillating between days when they walk and days when they do not (Adolph, Robinson, Young, & Gill-Alvarez, 2008). More important, this definition is a conceptual misrepresentation of experience. The passage of time is only a proxy for the events that infants actually experience (Adolph & Robinson, in press; Wohlwill, 1970). Although walking experience reliably predicts improvements in standard skill measures such as step length and step width (Adolph, Vereijken, & Shrout, 2003; Bril & Breniere, 1993) and in performance of perceptual-motor tasks such as perceiving affordances of slopes (Adolph, 1997), the number of days since walking onset carries little more meaning than test age (the number of days since birth). Indeed, some researchers refer to the number of days since onset as "walking age" (Clark, Whitall, & Phillips, 1988). Possibly, sheer practice, indexed by accumulated number of steps, facilitates improvements in gait. Alternatively, particular experiences, such as surfaces encountered or falls, may teach infants to walk. Without a natural corpus of infant locomotion, there is no empirical basis for hypothesizing about underlying learning mechanisms.

## The Current Study

The current study provides the first data on natural infant locomotion – time in motion and distribution of activity over time, variety of locomotor paths, and accumulated steps, distance, and falls. We had three aims. First, we compared natural locomotion in experienced crawlers and novice walkers to gain purchase on the question of why crawlers are motivated to walk. Second, we asked whether functional measures of walking skill, such as number of steps and number of falls per hour, improve with test age and walking age, as do standard skill measures like step length and step width. Third, we investigated relations between standard and functional measures of walking skill.

Presumably, most spontaneous walking occurs while infants explore the environment and interact with caregivers. Accordingly, data were collected while infants played freely under caregivers' supervision. We videotaped infants rather than relying on step counters or parent informants – two methods that proved problematic in earlier attempts to quantify infants' natural locomotion (Adolph, 2002). Because video coding was intensely detailed and laborious, we collected representative (15- to 60-min) samples of activity, as is customary in studies of language acquisition (e.g., Hurtado et al., 2008). Most samples were collected in a laboratory playroom to maximize recording quality and to eliminate individual differences in infants' home environments. We also observed infants in their homes to ensure the validity of the laboratory data for estimating natural activity. We focused on 12- to 14-month-old novice walkers, in whom improvements in standard skill measures are most dramatic, but included a sample of older, more experienced 19-month-olds, whose skill measures typically have begun to reach asymptote (Adolph et al., 2003;

Bril & Breniere, 1993; Clark et al., 1988; Hallemans et al., 2006). We also observed a comparison group of 12-month-old expert crawlers.

## Method

### Participants and Procedure

We collected 15 to 60 min of spontaneous activity for 151 infants (72 girls, 79 boys) from the New York City area. Most families were middle-class, and 73% were White. Data from 5 additional infants were excluded because of fussiness or technical problems. We observed 20 crawlers (11.8–12.2 months of age) and 116 walkers (11.8–19.3 months) in a laboratory playroom (8.66 m × 6.10 m) filled with furniture, varied ground surfaces, and toys (Fig. 1a). Infants could move freely throughout the room (Fig. 1b). To ensure that playroom observations were representative of natural locomotion, we also observed fifteen 12.8- to 13.8-month-old walkers in their homes. Caregivers were instructed to interact normally with their infants and to mind their safety. In both settings, an experimenter recorded infants' movements with a handheld camera. In the laboratory, two additional fixed cameras recorded side and overhead views to aid coding.

Crawling and walking age were determined from parental reports of the first day that infants traveled 10 ft across a room without stopping. Walking age was unavailable for 5 infants. Figure 2a shows a frequency distribution of walking age and sex, and whether infants were observed in the lab playroom or in their homes. Figure 2b shows the distribution of crawling and walking ages for the six groups of infants: twenty 12-month-old crawlers (observed in the lab for 20 min), twenty 12-month-old walkers (observed in the lab for 20 min), thirty 13-month-old walkers (observed in the lab for 30 min), thirty-six 14-month-old walkers (observed in the lab for 15 min), thirty 19-month-old walkers (observed in the lab for 30 min), and fifteen 13-month-old walkers (observed at home for 60 min). Notably, in the 12-month-olds, crawling age ($M$ = 97.6 days) was considerably larger than walking age ($M$ = 29.7 days), $t(38)$ = 5.41, $p$ < .01 (see the top two rows of Fig. 2b). Across the entire sample, walking age ranged from 5 to 289 days. Walking age overlapped among the 12- to 14-month-olds, and there was no difference in walking age between 13-month-olds observed at home ($M$ = 47.4 days) and in the lab ($M$ = 45.9 days), $p$ > .10.

At the end of the laboratory sessions, we collected two standard measures of walking skill as infants walked a straight path over a pressure-sensitive mat (3.6 m × 0.89 m; GAITRite System, CIR Systems, www.gaitrite.com; see Fig. 1a): step length (front-to-back distance between consecutive footfalls) and step width (side-to-side distance between feet). We estimated crawlers' average step length (distance between consecutive knee contacts) from the

a

b

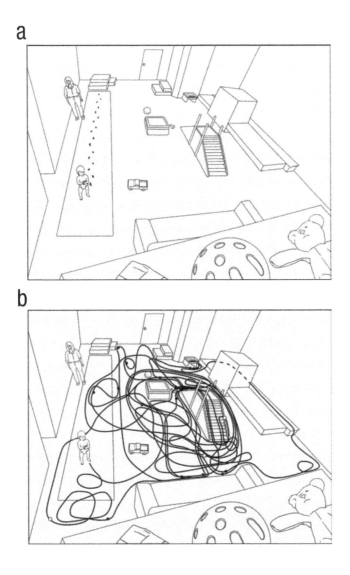

**Figure 1:** Layout of the laboratory playroom (a) and an example of a natural walking path (b). Dimensions are drawn to scale. In (a), the large rectangle on the left shows the location of the gait carpet and a representative walking path over the carpet. The playroom also contained a couch, a padded square pedestal, a slide and small stairs, a narrow catwalk behind a wooden barrier, large steps at the ends of the catwalk, a set of carpeted stairs, a set of wooden stairs, a standing activity table, and a wall lined with shelves of toys. The line superimposed over the diagram in (b) shows the natural walking path of one typical 13-month-old during the first 10 min of spontaneous play. Overlapping lines indicate revisits to the same location. Filled circles represent the location of rest periods longer than 5 s; open circles denote falls.

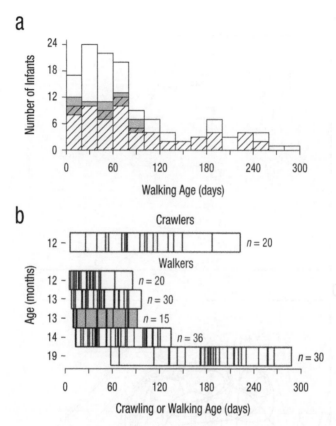

**Figure 2:** Frequency histogram of walking age across the entire sample (a) and distribution of crawling and walking ages for the six groups of infants (b). In (a), striped portions of the bars denote girls, and nonstriped portions denote boys. In both (a) and (b), gray bars denote home observations, and white bars denote lab observations. Each vertical line in (b) represents one infant.

number of steps taken to crawl a 3.6-m path. Three walkers and 1 crawler did not contribute usable data.

## Data Coding

A primary coder scored 100% of the video data for the duration of time crawling or walking, number of crawling or walking steps, and number of falls. *Time crawling or walking* was the duration of a single step or series of steps flanked by rest periods of at least 0.5 s; onsets were scored from the video frame when the walker's foot (or crawler's knee) left the floor, and offsets were scored from the video frame when the foot or knee touched the floor in the last step of the series. Coders did not score time in motion for the home observations because they could not determine bout onsets and offsets reliably. A *step* was considered any up-and-down motion of a leg that changed the infant's location on the floor. *Falls* were scored when infants lost balance while crawling or walking, and their bodies dropped to the floor unsupported. A second coder independently scored 25% of each infant's data. Interrater agreement was high for time crawling or walking, number of steps, and number of falls, $rs > .95$, $ps < .01$.

To characterize the overall amount of natural locomotion, we calculated the accumulated time crawling or walking, number of steps, and number of falls for each infant and then expressed the data as proportions or hourly rates to allow comparisons across groups that were observed for different amounts of time. We estimated the total distance that infants walked, as if stringing their steps together end to end, by multiplying each infant's total step number by his or her average step length on the gait carpet.

## Results

How did functional skill measures compare between 12-month-old crawlers and walkers? As expected, novice walkers fell more times per hour ($M = 31.5$) than expert crawlers did ($M = 17.4$), $t(38) = 2.52$, $p < .02$ (Fig. 3a), although the prevalence of falls in expert crawlers was unexpected. However, walkers walked more than crawlers crawled (Figs. 3b–3d): Walkers spent a larger proportion of time in motion ($M = .33$) than crawlers ($M = .20$), $t(38) = 3.04$, $p < .01$; walkers accumulated more steps per hour ($M = 1,456.1$) than crawlers ($M = 635.9$), $t(38) = 3.78$, $p < .01$; and walkers traveled greater distances per hour ($M = 296.9$ m) than crawlers ($M = 100.4$ m), $t(36) = 4.05$, $p < .01$. When we reconsidered falls taking into account the differences in activity between crawlers and walkers, differences in fall rate disappeared (Figs. 3e–3g): For every fall, walkers accumulated 1.2 min in motion, on average, and crawlers accumulated 1.7 min; walkers accumulated 69.2 steps for each fall, on average, and crawlers accumulated 54.7; walkers traveled 12.5 m for each fall, on average, and crawlers traveled 8.6 m; all $ps > .10$.

Across the entire data set, walking infants averaged 2,367.6 steps per hour, traveled 701.2 m per hour, and fell 17.4 times per hour. However, like periodic gait, natural walking develops (see Fig. S1 in the Supplemental Material available online). As shown in the top two rows of Table 1, test age and walking age were significantly correlated with both standard measures of walking skill (step length, step width) and functional measures of walking skill (proportion of time walking, number of steps per hour, distance traveled per hour, number of falls per hour): Older infants (as identified by both chronological and walking age) took longer, narrower steps during periodic gait over the gait carpet. And during free play, older infants spontaneously spent more time walking, took more steps, traveled farther distances, and fell less frequently, all $ps < .01$. The significant correlations between age and functional skill measures remained even when time in motion was partialed out (Table 2),

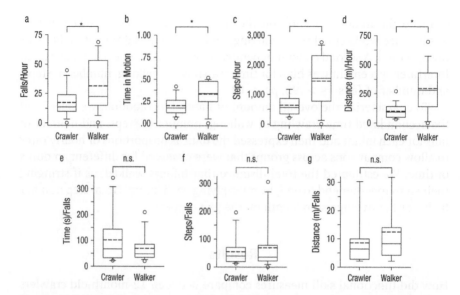

**Figure 3:** Comparisons between 12-month-old expert crawlers and 12-month-old novice walkers: (a) number of falls per hour, (b) proportion of time in motion, (c) number of steps per hour, (d) distance traveled per hour, (e) accumulated time in motion for each fall, (f) accumulated number of steps for each fall, and (g) accumulated distance traveled for each fall. Solid horizontal lines in these box plots denote medians, and dashed horizontal lines denote means; circles denote outliers beyond the 10th and 90th percentiles; boxes include the 25th to 75th percentiles; tails denote the 10th and 90th percentiles. Asterisks indicate significant differences between the two groups, $p < .05$.

all $ps < .01$, which means that functional skill measures reflect more than overall activity level. Also, infants observed in their homes appeared similar to infants observed in the laboratory playroom; $t$ tests comparing home ($n = 15$) and lab ($n = 70$) observations of infants with equivalent walking age showed no differences in number of steps per hour or number of falls per hour, $ps > .10$ (Figs. S1d and S1e).

Infants who were better walkers on the gait carpet were also better walkers during free play: Standard and functional skill measures were significantly correlated (Table 1), and these correlations remained after time in motion was partialed out (Table 2). Time walking, number of steps per hour, and distance traveled per hour were inherently intercorrelated (Table 1) because infants who took more steps had to cover more ground and spend more time in motion. However, number of falls per hour was not correlated with time walking, number of steps per hour, or distance traveled per hour (Table 1) because although infants who walked more had more opportunities to fall, they were also better walkers and thus fell less. When time in motion was partialed out, number of falls per hour was significantly negatively correlated with number of steps per hour and distance traveled per hour (Table 2), and all functional measures were consistent: Better walkers took more steps, traveled farther distances, and fell less frequently.

**Table 1:** Correlations between test age, walking age, and skill measures

| Measure | Walking age | Step length | Step width | Time walking | Steps/hour | Distance/hour | Falls/hour |
|---|---|---|---|---|---|---|---|
| Test age | .86** (124) | .71** (111) | -.60** (111) | .20* (114) | .46** (129) | -.65** (111) | -.35** (129) |
| Walking age | | .74** (106) | -.68** (106) | .28** (109) | .48** (124) | .68** (106) | -.33** (124) |
| Step length | | | -.65** (111) | .28** (111) | .51** (111) | .76** (111) | -.28** (111) |
| Step width | | | | -.24* (111) | -.42** (111) | -.55** (111) | .32** (111) |
| Time walking | | | | | .85** (114) | .72** (111) | .14 (114) |
| Steps/hour | | | | | | .92** (111) | -.09 (129) |
| Distance/hour | | | | | | | -.17 (111) |

*Note:* Degrees of freedom are shown in parentheses.
*p < .05. **p < .01.

**Table 2:** Partial correlations between test age, walking age, and skill measures controlling for time walking

| Measure | Steps/hour | Distance/hour | Falls/hour |
|---|---|---|---|
| Test age | .55** (113) | .75** (110) | −.39** (113) |
| Walking age | .49** (108) | .71** (105) | −.39** (109) |
| Step length | .54** (110) | .84** (110) | −.33** (110) |
| Step width | −.43** (110) | −.57** (110) | .36** (110) |
| Steps/hour | | .84** (110) | −.39** (113) |
| Distance/hour | | | −.40** (110) |

Note: Degrees of freedom are shown in parentheses.
**$p < .01$.

Although standard and functional skill measures were correlated, periodic gait on the gait carpet and natural locomotion during free play looked very different (Figs. 1a and 1b). Our impression from scoring the video files was that infants' natural paths twisted through most of the open space in the room. We confirmed that impression in 7 randomly selected novice walkers (mean walking age = 57.7 days) and 7 experienced walkers (mean walking age = 190.3 days) in the first 10 min of play. We superimposed 105 grid squares over the open areas of the playroom and scored each time the infants entered each square. All infants rambled throughout the room and spontaneously played near the couch and on the slide, pedestal, catwalk, carpeted stairs, and wooden stairs. The number of different grid squares entered was similar between novices ($M = 49$) and experts ($M = 57$), but experts made more return trips to the same squares. Novices entered or reentered 128.3 grid squares, on average, and experts entered or reentered 205.9 grid squares, $t(12) = 2.71, p < .05$.

Although infants accumulated thousands of steps during the observation periods, they spent most of the time stationary. They were under no obligation to move, and one 12-month-old did not take any walking steps. On average, infants walked only 32.3% of the time. Walking was distributed over time in primarily short bursts of activity. The raster plot in Figure S2 in the Supplemental Material shows the even distribution of walking bouts for the 60 infants observed for 30 min, ranked by walking age. Raster plots of the other 56 infants for whom we scored bout duration showed similarly even distributions. On average, 46% of bouts consisted of one to three steps, and 23% consisted of a single step – too short to qualify as periodic gait and too short for calculating standard measures of walking skill. There was no difference in duration, step number, or step rate between walking bouts that ended in falls and those that did not, $ps > .10$.

## Discussion

A remarkable thing about basic skills acquired during infancy is the apparent ease and rapidity of their acquisition. Infants learn to walk, talk, think, play, and perceive objects and events in the course of natural activity. Thus, descriptions of natural activity play a critical role in guiding research, theory, and application. The development of locomotion is a notable exception: Until now, research, theory, and clinical intervention have proceeded without a natural ecology of infant locomotion. By collecting such a corpus, we aimed to address the question of why expert crawlers transition to walking, investigate developmental changes in natural locomotion and whether they relate to improvements on standard measures, and provide an empirical basis for hypothesizing about learning mechanisms.

## Why Walk?

Our inclusion of a comparison group of expert crawlers provided some clues to the long-standing puzzle of why infants who are skilled crawlers abandon crawling for a precarious, new, upright posture. To our surprise, expert crawlers were not more skilled than novice walkers. Functional measures of locomotor skill showed that crawlers crawled less than walkers walked, took fewer steps, and traveled shorter distances. Moreover, falling was common: All but one crawler fell. As expected, falling was far more common in novice walkers: One racked up 69 falls per hour. But when we reconsidered fall rate to take into account the differences in activity between crawlers and walkers, the difference in fall rates disappeared, and walkers were no longer at a disadvantage. In fact, when we reanalyzed standard measures of locomotor skill (measures of crawling or walking over a straight, uniform path) in infants observed longitudinally (originally reported in Adolph, 1997), step length and speed increased steadily from infants' 1st week of crawling to their 19th week of walking, and showed no decrement over the transition from crawling to walking (Adolph, 2008). In other words, assessments of both standard and functional skill measures indicate that new walkers reap all the benefits of an upright posture without incurring additional risk of falling. Thus, part of the answer to "why walk?" is "why not?"

## Development of Natural Locomotion

After 100 years of studying the development of walking by coercing infants to walk at a steady pace along a straight, uniform path, researchers can say with certitude that standard measures of walking skill (e.g., step length and step width) improve with test age and walking age. We replicated that century-old finding. More newsworthy is our finding that natural locomotion also improves: Functional measures of walking skill obtained from spontaneous locomotion during free play (number of steps, distance traveled, and number of falls per hour) improve with test age and walking age. These findings held up after statistically adjusting for time walking, which means that older, more experienced walkers not only walk more, but also walk better. Just as standard skill measures are intercorrelated, functional skill measures were highly consistent. When time walking was partialed out to statistically adjust for activity, analyses showed that infants who took more steps and traveled farther distances fell less frequently.

Moreover, we found that standard and functional skill measures were significantly correlated. Thus, this study provides the first evidence of construct validity for standard skill measures in terms of natural infant walking. This set of findings is remarkable because periodic gait (Fig. 1a) looks notably different from natural locomotion (Fig. 1b).

## Possible Learning Mechanisms

Researchers need to reconsider the long-held tradition of using walking age to represent walking experience. Walking age signifies only the elapsed time since walking onset. Like test age, walking age is a robust predictor of various developmental outcomes, but it is not an explanatory variable. In other areas of developmental research, descriptions of natural activity have informed understanding about learning mechanisms. For example, in language acquisition, the sheer number of utterances and word tokens in mothers' natural talk to infants when they are 18 months old (estimated from 12 min of mother-infant free play in a laboratory playroom) predicts their rate of vocabulary growth and language processing speed at 24 months of age (Hurtado et al., 2008). In contrast, diversity of language (number of word types) is not predictive. In conceptual development, event type rather than sheer quantity of input affects learning about causal agency: A higher proportion of agentive events compared with self-propulsion events (estimated from 1 hr of video collected with a head camera) during natural activity at 3, 8, and 12 months of age influences generalization about causal agency (in habituation tasks) at 10 to 14 months of age (Cicchino et al., 2011). Similarly, a corpus of natural locomotion allows researchers to investigate possible learning mechanisms by analyzing specific measures of locomotor experience. The current study suggests that quantity, distribution, and variety of experiences are viable candidates as factors affecting learning to walk.

Although most people would assume that infants walk and fall a lot, few would guess that the average toddler takes 2,368 steps, travels 701 m – the length of 7.7 American football fields – and falls 17 times per hour. Hourly rates provide only a tantalizing window into the amounts of practice that likely accumulate over a day. For example, a multiplier of 6 hr (approximately half of infants' waking day) would indicate that infants take 14,000 steps daily, travel the length of 46 football fields, and incur 100 falls. Estimates of natural activity are equally enormous for other skills. Middle-class infants hear

2,150 words per hour, more than 30 million words by 3 years (Hart & Risley, 1995). Eleven- to 13-month-olds spend more than 30 min per hour engaged with objects during everyday activity (Karasik, Tamis-LeMonda, & Adolph, 2011). By 2 months of age, infants have executed more than 2.5 million eye movements (Johnson, Amso, & Slemmer, 2003), and by 3.5 months, they have performed 3 to 6 million.

To put these immense numbers into perspective, consider that concert musicians and professional athletes require approximately 4 hr of practice per day to train and fine-tune their perceptual-motor systems (Ericsson, Krampe, & Tesch-Romer, 1993). The consensus in the literature on expertise is that large amounts of regular practice, accumulated over years of training, promote expert performance (Ericsson & Ward, 2007). The same principle could apply to acquiring expertise in walking.

Natural walking was distributed in time and occurred in variable patterns and contexts. Short bursts of walking were separated by longer stationary periods. Walking bouts were frequently too short – one to three steps – to qualify as periodic gait. Moreover, infants started and stopped at will, traveled in winding paths over varying surfaces, took sideways and backward steps, varied their walking speed, switched from upright to other postures, and misstepped and fell. They visited multiple locations and engaged in different activities therein.

Laboratory studies with older children and adults indicate that time-distributed, variable practice is beneficial for motor learning (Gentile, 2000; Schmidt & Lee, 1999). Time-distributed practice is more effective than massed practice because intermittent rest periods allow learning to be consolidated, relieve fatigue, and renew motivation. Variable practice leads to greater flexibility and broader transfer than blocked practice because executing a variety of movements in a variety of contexts helps learners to identify the relevant parameters and their allowable settings. Recent efforts to teach robots to walk provide additional support for the effectiveness of variable practice. The traditional approach is to train robots to walk as fast as possible in a straight line – essentially, to train robots on periodic gait (Kohl & Stone, 2004). But training robots with omnidirectional gait on variable paths – a regimen similar to infants' natural locomotion – led to more adaptive, functional locomotor skill. After 15,000 runs through an obstacle course, robots had fewer falls, took more steps, traveled greater distances, and moved more quickly than they had prior to training. Moreover, in a test not possible with infants, they exhibited elite performance in robot soccer: With a variable training regimen, the UT Austin Villa team won all 24 games in the 2011 RoboCup 3D simulation competition, scoring 136 goals and conceding none (MacAlpine, Barrett, Urieli, Vu, & Stone, 2012; Urieli, MacAlpine, Kalyanakrishnan, Bentor, & Stone, 2011).

# Conclusion

How do infants learn to walk? This corpus of natural locomotion indicates that infants accumulate massive amounts of time-distributed, variable practice. Over days of walking, they take more steps, travel farther distances, and fall less. And they may be motivated to walk in the first place because walking takes them farther faster than crawling without increasing the risk of falling. Traditional studies of infant locomotion during periodic gait could not have revealed these findings.

# References

Adolph, K. E. (1997). Learning in the development of infant locomotion. *Monographs of the Society for Research in Child Development, 62*(3, Serial No. 251).

Adolph, K. E. (2002). Learning to keep balance. In R. Kail (Ed.), *Advances in child development and behavior* (Vol. 30, pp. 1–40). Amsterdam, The Netherlands: Elsevier Science.

Adolph, K. E. (2008). The growing body in action: What infant locomotion tells us about perceptually guided action. In R. L. Klatzky, B. MacWhinney, & M. Behrmann (Eds.), *Embodiment, ego-space, and action* (pp. 275–321). New York, NY: Taylor & Francis Group.

Adolph, K. E., & Robinson, S. R. (in press). The road to walking: What learning to walk tells us about development. In P. Zelazo (Ed.), *Oxford handbook of developmental psychology*. New York, NY: Oxford University Press.

Adolph, K. E., Robinson, S. R., Young, J. W., & Gill-Alvarez, F. (2008). What is the shape of developmental change? *Psychological Review, 115*, 527–543.

Adolph, K. E., Vereijken, B., & Shrout, P. E. (2003). What changes in infant walking and why. *Child Development, 74*, 474–497.

Barker, R. G., & Wright, H. F. (1951). *One boy's day: A specimen record of behavior.* New York, NY: Harper Brothers.

Bril, B., & Breniere, Y. (1993). Posture and independent locomotion in early childhood: Learning to walk or learning dynamic postural control? In G. J. P. Savelsbergh (Ed.), *The development of coordination in infancy* (pp. 337–358). Amsterdam, The Netherlands: Elsevier.

Cicchino, J. B., Aslin, R. N., & Rakison, D. H. (2011). Correspondences between what infants see and know about causal and self-propelled motion. *Cognition, 118*, 171–192.

Clark, J. E., Whitall, J., & Phillips, S. J. (1988). Human interlimb coordination: The first 6 months of independent walking. *Developmental Psychobiology, 21*, 445–456.

Dominici, N., Ivanenko, Y. P., Cappellini, G., D'Avella, A., Mondi, V., Cicchese, M., & . . . Lacquaniti, F. (2011). Locomotor primitives in newborn babies and their development. *Science, 334*, 997–999.

Ericsson, K. A., Krampe, R. T., & Tesch-Romer, C. (1993). The role of deliberate practice in the acquisition of expert performance. *Psychological Review, 100*, 363–406.

Ericsson, K. A., & Ward, P. (2007). Capturing the naturally occurring superior performance of experts in the laboratory: Toward a science of exceptional performance. *Current Directions in Psychological Science, 16*, 346–350.

Forssberg, H. (1985). Ontogeny of human locomotor control I. Infant stepping, supported locomotion, and transition to independent locomotion. *Experimental Brain Research, 57*, 480–493.

Franchak, J. M., Kretch, K. S., Soska, K. C., & Adolph, K. E. (2011). Head-mounted eye tracking: A new method to describe infant looking. *Child Development, 82*, 1738–1750.

Gentile, A. M. (2000). Skill acquisition: Action, movement, and neuromotor processes. In J. Carr & R. Shepard (Eds.), *Movement science: Foundations for physical therapy in rehabilitation* (2nd ed., pp. 111–187). New York, NY: Aspen Press.

Gesell, A. (1946). The ontogenesis of infant behavior. In L. Carmichael (Ed.), *Manual of child psychology* (pp. 295–331). New York, NY: John Wiley.

Hallemans, A., De Clercq, D., & Aerts, P. (2006). Changes in 3D joint dynamics during the first 5 months after the onset of independent walking: A longitudinal follow-up study. *Gait & Posture, 24*, 270–279.

Hart, B., & Risley, T. D. (1995). *Meaningful differences in the everyday experiences of young American children*. Baltimore, MD: Paul H. Brookes.

Hurtado, N., Marchman, V. A., & Fernald, A. (2008). Does input influence uptake? Links between maternal talk, processing speed and vocabulary size in Spanish-learning children. *Developmental Science, 11*, F31–F39.

Johnson, S. P., Amso, D., & Slemmer, J. A. (2003). Development of object concepts in infancy: Evidence for early learning in an eye tracking paradigm. *Proceedings of the National Academy of Sciences, USA, 100*, 10568–10573.

Karasik, L. B., Tamis-LeMonda, C. S., & Adolph, K. E. (2011). The transition from crawling to walking and infants' actions with objects and people. *Child Development, 82*, 1199–1209.

Kleitman, N., & Engelmann, T. G. (1953). Sleep characteristics of infants. *Journal of Applied Physiology, 6*, 269–282.

Kohl, N., & Stone, P. (2004). Policy gradient reinforcement learning for fast quadrupedal locomotion. *Proceedings of the IEEE International Conference on Robotics and Automation, 3*, 2619–2624.

MacAlpine, P., Barrett, S., Urieli, D., Vu, V., & Stone, P. (2012). Design and optimization of an omnidirectional humanoid walk: A winning approach at the RoboCup 2011 3D simulation competition. In *Proceedings of the Twenty-Sixth AAAI Conference on Artificial Intelligence (AAAI-12)* (Vol. 1, pp. 1047–1053). Palo Alto, CA: Association for the Advancement of Artificial Intelligence.

MacWhinney, B. (2000). *The CHILDES project: Tools for analyzing talk*. Mahwah, NJ: Erlbaum.

McGraw, M. B. (1945). *The neuromuscular maturation of the human infant*. New York, NY: Columbia University Press.

Messinger, D., Ruvolo, P., Ekas, N., & Fogel, A. (2010). Applying machine learning to infant interaction: The development is in the details. *Neural Networks, 23*, 1004–1016.

Miller, P. H., & Seier, W. (1994). Strategy utilization deficiencies in children: When, where, and why. In H. Reese (Ed.), *Advances in child development and behavior* (Vol. 25, pp. 107–156). New York, NY: Academic Press.

Patla, A. E. (1997). Understanding the role of vision in the control of human locomotion. *Gait & Posture, 5*, 54–69.

Piaget, J. (1952). *The origins of intelligence in children* (M. Cook, Trans.). New York, NY: International Universities Press. (Original work published 1936)

Schmidt, R. A., & Lee, T. D. (1999). *Motor control and learning: A behavioral emphasis* (3rd ed.). Champaign, IL: Human Kinetics.

Shirley, M. M. (1931). *The first two years: A study of twenty-five babies*. Westport, CT: Greenwood Press.

Siegler, R. S. (2000). The rebirth of children's learning. *Child Development, 71*, 26–35.

Smith, L. B., Yu, C., & Pereira, A. F. (2011). Not your mother's view: The dynamics of toddler visual experience. *Developmental Science, 14*, 9–17.

Tamis-LeMonda, C. S., & Bornstein, M. H. (1996). Variation in children's exploratory, nonsymbolic, and symbolic play: An explanatory multidimensional framework. In C. K. Rovee-Collier & L. R. Lipsitt (Eds.), *Advances in infancy research* (Vol. 10, pp. 37–78). Westport, CT: Ablex.

Thelen, E. (1986). Treadmill-elicited stepping in seven-month-old infants. *Child Development*, *57*, 1498–1506.

Urieli, D., MacAlpine, P., Kalyanakrishnan, S., Bentor, Y. , & Stone, P. (2011). On optimizing interdependent skills: A case study in simulated 3D humanoid robot soccer. In *Proceedings of the 10th International Conference on Autonomous Agents and Multiagent Systems* (Vol. 2, pp. 769–776). Richland, SC: International Foundation for Autonomous Agents and Multiagent Systems.

Wohlwill, J. P. (1970). The age variable in psychological research. *Psychological Review*, *77*, 49–64.

Zelazo, P. R. (1983). The development of walking: New findings on old assumptions. *Journal of Motor Behavior, 2*, 99–137.

# 39

# Specificity of Learning: Why Infants Fall over a Veritable Cliff

*Karen E. Adolph*

Falling over a cliff can have dire consequences for an animal's survival. Since Lashley and Russell's (1934) first demonstrations that dark-reared rats match the force of their jumps to the size of a dropoff, the role of experience in promoting adaptive motor responses to depth information has been of central concern to developmentalists (Walk, Gibson, & Tighe, 1957). Precocial species such as chicks and goats do not require experience to avoid going over the edge of an impossibly large precipice (Gibson & Walk, 1960; Walk, 1966; Walk & Gibson, 1961). In contrast, human infants and other altricial species require a protracted period of locomotor experience (Campos, Bertenthal, & Kermoian, 1992; Held & Hein, 1963; Richards & Rader, 1983). In the classic experimental paradigm, babies are tested on a "visual cliff" to ensure their safety. The apparatus looks like a sheer drop-off because the visible ground surface lies far below a sheet of safety glass. Several studies have shown that the duration of infants' crawling experience predicts avoidance of the visual cliff, independently of the age at which infants begin crawling or their age at testing. For example, at 7.5 to 8.5 months of age, only 35% of inexperienced crawlers (11 days of experience) avoided the visual cliff, but 65% of more experienced crawlers (41 days of experience) steadfastly refused to go across (Bertenthal, Campos, & Barrett, 1984).

Despite strong evidence linking adaptive responses with locomotor experience, the question remains as to what infants may learn via crawling that facilitates the coordination between perception and action. Clearly, avoiding

**Source:** *Psychological Science*, 11(4) (2000): 290–295.

a cliff does not depend solely on depth perception. Months before they begin crawling, infants display sensitivity to depth information (e.g., Campos, Langer, & Krowitz, 1970; Slater & Morison, 1985; Yonas & Hartman, 1993). Several other accounts have been proposed. Most widely cited is Campos and colleagues' (1992) proposal that experience induces fear of heights and fear mediates avoidance responses. Although there is no association between experiences of falling and cliff avoidance (Scarr & Salapatek, 1970), researchers have suggested that wariness may arise from minor scrapes and tumbles and from negative near-falling experiences as infants peer over the edge of sheer drop-offs or vigilant parents grab them at the edge of the bed or changing table (Bertenthal, Campos, & Kermoian, 1994; Thelen & Smith, 1994). According to this account, crawling experience facilitates avoidance responses through repeated associations between depth information and the perceptual consequences of disequilibrium and near-falling. Alternatively, fear of heights may arise from a discrepancy in infants' typical crawling experience on solid ground and the novel perceptual input at the brink of a precipice. Experience locomoting with their faces near the floor may lead infants to expect particular correlations between visual and vestibular input. At the edge of a cliff, visual coding of angular acceleration is quite different because the visible texture elements are farther away from infants' faces. Thus, a discrepancy in expected correlations between visual and vestibular input might promote wariness at the edge of the novel surface (Campos et al., 1992). Finally, other researchers have proposed that experience leads to an appreciation of the properties of the ground surface for supporting the body (e.g., Bertenthal & Campos, 1990; Gibson & Schmuckler, 1989). In particular, experience crawling over solid ground might teach infants that locomotion is impossible without a surface that they can see and feel beneath their bodies.

Recent findings suggest that none of these accounts is sufficient for explaining how experience facilitates adaptive responses to depth information for a drop-off. If infants learn to avoid a discrepancy in depth of the ground surface because they are afraid of heights, associate heights with the perceptual consequences of falling, or know that the body cannot be supported in empty space, then they should show similar avoidance responses regardless of the posture in which they are tested. To the contrary, my colleagues and I found that learning is specific to each postural milestone in development.

## The Sway Model

Typically, motor development in infancy is marked by a series of postural milestones – sitting, crawling, cruising sideways along furniture, and walking. To keep balance in these postures, infants must maintain their bodies within a region of permissible postural sway (Riccio, 1993; Riccio & Stoffregen, 1988). Babies will fall over if their bodies move outside this region because they lack sufficient muscle strength to pull themselves back into position. Variations in surface properties threaten balance control because the region of permissible sway narrows and infants' bodies move more rapidly toward the outer limits. To judge possibilities for action, infants must gauge their available muscle torque for counteracting destabilizing torque relative to surface properties (size of a precipice, degree of slant, etc.).

The sway model proposes that the coordination between perception and action is organized within postural systems, so that experience with an earlier-developing skill does not transfer automatically to a later-developing skill (Adolph & Eppler, 1998, in press). Experience promotes learning about balance control, and infants learn to detect threats to balance and discover compensatory strategies for recovering balance when it is disrupted. Learning may be posture-specific because each postural milestone represents a different perception-action system with different relevant control variables. Sitting, crawling, and walking postures, for example, involve different regions of permissible sway for different key pivots around which the body rotates (e.g., the hips for sitting, the wrists for crawling, and the ankles for walking). In addition, each postural milestone involves different muscle groups for executing movements and for generating compensatory sway; different vantage points for viewing the ground; different patterns of optic flow as the body sways back and forth; different correlations between visual, kinesthetic, and vestibular information; and so on. Thus, extensive experience with each postural milestone in development may be required to define the relevant control variables for the new perception-action system and to facilitate their on-line calibration.

## Specificity of Learning

The disparity in depth at the brink of a steep slope, as on a cliff, presents a challenge for balance control and locomotion. In accordance with the sway model, in a longitudinal study, I found that learning to avoid descent of impossibly steep slopes does not transfer across developmental changes from crawling to walking postures (Adolph, 1997). In their first weeks of crawling, infants observed on an adjustable sloping walkway (0°–36°) plunged headfirst down impossibly steep slopes. Over weeks of crawling, however, the infants' judgments became increasingly accurate. By their last weeks of crawling, they consistently crawled down safe slopes and slid down or avoided risky ones. Surprisingly, in their first weeks of walking, the same babies attempted to walk down the same impossibly risky slopes that they had so recently avoided in the crawling posture. In fact, new walkers showed no transfer from their old, familiar crawling posture to their new, upright walking posture on consecutive trials at the same risky slope. Over weeks of walking experience, errors decreased but learning was no faster the second time around.

The present experiments show that specificity of learning is not limited to locomotion down slopes or to developmental changes from crawling to walking postures. The experiments provided a stronger test of the specificity of learning predicted by the sway model by testing infants in two postures, sitting and crawling, within the same test session. In both postures, babies were perched at the brink of an adjustable gap. They were encouraged to span the gap by leaning forward while extending an arm. At the smallest gap distances, balance was trivial. At intermediate distances, the infants had to gauge the necessary forces required to span the gap. This test is similar to Lashley and Russell's (1934) classic jumping-stand task in which rats launched themselves over an adjustable gap. At the largest distances, gap size exceeded the infants' limit of permissible sway. As on the visual cliff, avoidance was the appropriate response to impossibly large gaps. However, in contrast to the visual cliff, the gap apparatus was a veritable cliff with no protective safety glass. Visual and haptic exploration yielded concordant information for depth. Errors in judgment resulted in falling into the precipice, requiring rescue by the experimenter.

The experimental design capitalized on the fact that most infants display a period of overlap between sitting and crawling milestones. Typically, they have many weeks of experience keeping balance in the sitting posture at the same time that they are novices at maintaining balance in the crawling posture. If experience leads to either fear of heights, negative associations with falling, or knowledge that the body cannot be supported in empty space, infants should respond similarly in these two postural conditions. However, if the coordination between perception and action is organized so that the utilization of depth information is specific to each postural control system, then infants who are experienced at sitting but novices at crawling should show more adaptive responses in their more experienced sitting posture.

## Experiment 1: Sitting and Crawling

### Method

Nineteen 9-month-old infants (11 boys, 8 girls) were tested in an experienced sitting posture ($M = 104$ days of sitting experience) and a less familiar crawling posture ($M = 45$ days of crawling experience). Two additional infants did not complete testing because of fussiness or fatigue. Parents reported infants' prior experiences with sitting, crawling, and falling.

The gaps apparatus was composed of a large, stationary starting platform and a movable landing platform. The landing platform could be moved back and forth to adjust the gap between the platforms (76 cm deep). As shown in Figure 1a, in the sitting condition, infants were encouraged to lean forward and extend their arm out over the gap. Flat toys were attached to the end of a stick to provide infants with an incentive to span the gap. An assistant moved the stick back and forth to create gaps of 0 to 90 cm between the toy and the edge of the starting platform. Gap distance was varied by moving the stick rather than the landing platform to prevent pinching infants' legs in the gap and to keep infants from propping their feet or free hand on the far side of the gap to aid in balance control.

In the crawling condition (see Fig. 1b), infants were encouraged to lean forward and extend their arm toward the landing platform as they crawled over the gap. Toys were placed on the landing platform to provide infants with an incentive to span the gap. An assistant moved the landing platform back and forth to create gaps of 0 to 90 cm between the edges of the two platforms.

In both conditions, parents stood at the far side of the landing platform and coaxed their infants to retrieve the toys. An experimenter (shown in Fig. 1) followed closely alongside infants to ensure their safety but did not provide physical support unless they fell into the gap. Previous research with infants on slopes shows that infants tackle such tasks independently and do not rely on the experimenter to catch them (e.g., Adolph, 1997). Trials lasted 30 s.

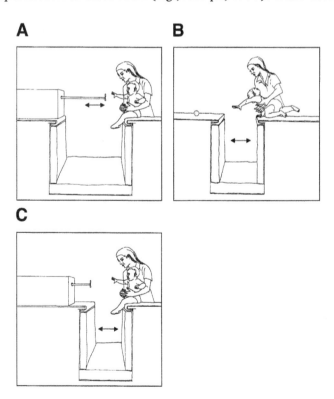

**Figure 1:** The adjustable gap apparatus in various experimental conditions: (a) sitting condition with movable stick (Experiment 1), (b) crawling condition (Experiments 1 and 2), and (c) sitting condition with movable landing platform (Experiment 2).

Because infants of the same age have widely varying body dimensions and motor skill, a psychophysical staircase procedure (Adolph, 1995, 1997) was used to estimate the boundary between gaps that were safe and risky relative to each infant's body size and skill in each condition. The staircase procedure is an on-line method for estimating a threshold using a minimal number of trials. Trials were coded as either successful attempts (contacting the toy safely), failed attempts (falling into the gap), or avoidance (no attempt to span the gap). For the purpose of the staircase procedure, failed attempts and avoidance responses were treated as equivalent, unsuccessful outcomes. After successful trials, the experimenter increased gap size by 6 cm. After unsuccessful trials, the experimenter repeated the same gap size for reliability; then, to maintain infants' motivation, she presented an easy baseline gap (4 cm for crawling and 10 cm for sitting); next, gap size was decreased by 4 cm relative to the last unsuccessful trial. This process of presenting larger and smaller gaps continued until converging on a gap boundary to a 67% criterion (largest gap infant managed successfully on at least 2/3 of trials). The "plus 6 cm, minus 4 cm" rule ensured that gap boundaries were determined in 2-cm increments.

After the gap boundary was identified, additional trials were presented, beginning with safe gaps (6 cm smaller than boundary) and proceeding to increasingly risky gaps (6 cm, 12 cm, and 18 cm larger than boundary), with 2 trials at each gap distance. Infants also received 2 trials at the largest, 90-cm, gap to assess their responses when absolute gap size was the same dimension as the standard visual cliff. In total, infants received 17 to 42 trials in the sitting condition and 21 to 38 trials in the crawling condition. Nine infants were tested first in the sitting condition and then in the crawling condition, and 10 were tested with the conditions in the reverse order.

Data from the staircase trials and the additional trials were re-scored from videotapes in terms of success, failure, and avoidance; interrater reliability showed 97% agreement. In addition, coders noted whether infants tested their region of permissible sway at the edge of gaps by leaning forward while extending an arm without touching the far side of the gap, then leaning backward while retracting the arm; interrater reliability showed 95% agreement.

If infants perceived the depth information accurately in relation to their region of permissible sway, then they would attempt safe gaps, for which the probability of falling was low, and avoid risky gaps, for which the probability of falling was high. Perfect perceptual judgments would be indicated by a match between the probability of avoiding and the probability of falling. Alternatively, if infants did not accurately relate the perceptual information to possibilities for action, then they would fall into impossibly large gaps. If infants learned from falling on one trial, then they would avoid the same gap on the next trial. Most important, if learning about balance control does not transfer across developmental changes in postures, then infants would avoid risky gaps in their more experienced sitting posture, but fall into risky gaps in their less familiar crawling posture.

## Results and Discussion

Gap boundaries were larger for all infants in the sitting condition ($M$ = 26.6 cm) compared with the crawling condition ($M$ = 10.1 cm). However, individual infants differed widely in their gap boundaries (range: 20–32 cm for sitting and 2–18 cm for crawling). Thus, a safe gap for sitting could be risky for crawling, and a safe gap for a more skilled infant could be risky for a less skilled one. The experimental design roughly equated relative amount of risk to allow comparisons between sitting and crawling postures and between infants with different gap boundaries. In the sitting condition, the probability of falling increased from .04 at the gap boundary to .93 at distances 12 cm larger than the boundary. In the crawling condition, the probability of falling increased from .14 at the gap boundary to .94 at gaps 12 cm larger.

The experiment yielded two surprising results that are consistent with the sway model but are not predicted by accounts based on fear of heights, negative associations with falling, or knowledge about ground surfaces. First, avoidance of risky gaps did not generalize across changes in posture. Second, there was no evidence of within-session learning as a result of falling.

With regard to generalization across postures, at every risky gap distance, the rate of adaptive avoidance responses was higher in the experienced sitting posture than in the less familiar crawling posture (see Fig. 2a). All infants closely matched avoidance responses to the probability of falling in the sitting posture, but grossly overestimated their ability to span gaps in the crawling posture. A 2 (postural condition) × 4 (risky gap distance) repeated measures analysis of variance revealed main effects for postural condition, $F(1, 11)$ = 15.76, $p$ < .002, and gap distance, $F(3, 33)$ = 15.51, $p$ < .000. Paired comparisons revealed significant differences between sitting and crawling conditions at each risky gap distance (all $ps$ < .04). In fact, 6 infants showed finely tuned avoidance responses in the sitting posture but no capacity to gauge their ability in the crawling posture. They attempted all gap distances in the crawling posture, including the 90-cm gap, which was tantamount to crawling into thin air. The remaining 13 infants scaled their responses to their gap boundaries in both postures, but much more accurately in the sitting condition. For this group, avoidance responses were significantly higher in the sitting condition than the crawling condition at the boundary and at the +6-cm and +12-cm increments (all $ps$ < .03).

Because the data in Figure 2a are based on relative amount of risk, this analysis raises the possibility that the dissociation between postures was merely a consequence of the fact that infants' gap boundaries for sitting were larger than those for crawling. Hence, if infants simply attempted to

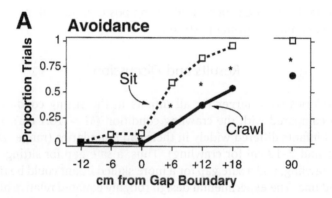

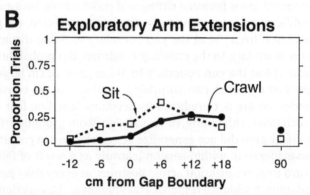

**Figure 2:** Proportion of trials with avoidance responses (a) and exploratory arm extensions (b) in Experiment 1. The data are plotted according to relative degree of risk. The 0 point on the x-axis represents each infant's gap boundary in each condition. Negative numbers on the x-axis denote safe gaps (gaps smaller than the boundary), and positive numbers denote risky gaps (gaps larger than the boundary). Data are also included for the largest, 90-cm, gap. Asterisks denote significant differences between the sitting and crawling conditions.

reach over the same small gaps and avoided the same large gaps in the two postures, this would lead to a spurious dissociation. However, examining the rate of avoidance responses at each absolute gap size shows that this was not the case. Every infant showed different levels of avoidance responses to the same gap size in the sitting and crawling postures. The 6 reckless crawlers obviously showed different responses to the same absolute gap size depending on postural condition because they never avoided the gap while crawling. The remaining 13 infants also showed different levels of avoidance responses to the same gap sizes in sitting and crawling postures. Unlike the reckless crawlers, they were more likely to avoid gaps between 14 cm and 32 cm in the crawling posture than in the sitting posture. But, as Figure 3 shows, this avoidance rate still grossly overestimated their ability to span the gap in the crawling posture; that is, the probability of avoiding was significantly lower than the probability of falling, even when the probability of falling was 1.0.

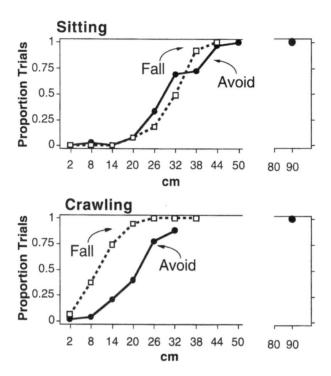

**Figure 3:** Avoidance responses in the 13 infants who showed some sensitivity to gap size in the crawling condition, Experiment 1. The data are plotted according to absolute gap size in both conditions. Solid curves show the probability of avoiding the gap, and dashed curves show the probability of falling.

In contrast, the infants' avoidance rate in the sitting posture closely matched the probability of falling (curves are superimposed).

The second surprising result was that infants showed no evidence of learning from falling. Most infants fussed slightly when they fell, suggesting that falling downward into the gap was aversive. Infants rarely fell in the sitting posture ($M$ = 19% of trials with risky gaps), giving them few opportunities to learn from falling. In the crawling posture, infants fell often ($M$ = 61% of trials with risky gaps), but they showed no evidence of learning from these experiences. Each time that infants fell in their first attempt at a particular gap distance, the same gap size was repeated on the next trial. If the infants had associated depth information with the negative consequences of falling, they would have avoided the gap on the repeated trial. They did not. On 88% of such immediately repeated trials, infants attempted to span the same risky gap distance. Furthermore, there were no effects of condition order to suggest learning from falling on earlier trials. Nor was infants' aversion to falling related to experiencing minor falls at home, and none of the infants had experienced a serious fall incurring injury at home.

In addition, the infants did not simply learn to rely on the experimenter. Because the experimenter provided physical support only after they began to fall, they experienced the perceptual consequences of self-induced disequilibrium in both postures as they swayed to and fro at the brink of the gap. They appeared to test the limits of their region of permissible sway by leaning forward as they extended an arm without contacting the far side of the gap, then leaning backward as they retracted it. Exploratory arm extensions increased on risky gaps, $F(2, 30) = 3.55, p < .04$, and were equally frequent in the two postures (see Fig. 2b). Furthermore, if the infants had merely relied on the experimenter to catch them or considered falling to be a kind of game, then they should have responded indiscriminately to all gap sizes in both postural conditions. However, many infants avoided the largest gaps in the crawling posture (which appeared latest in the test session), there were no effects of condition order, and all children avoided risky gaps in the sitting condition.

## Experiment 2: Replication

A new, mechanized gaps apparatus was constructed to rule out the possibility that the infants in Experiment 1 avoided risky gaps in the sitting posture simply because the landing platform was always 90 cm away. For both postures, gap distance was varied by moving the landing platform along a calibrated track (0–90 cm). In the sitting condition, a toy was presented on the end of a stick, with the toy always perpendicular to the edge of the landing platform (see Fig. 1c). Baseline gap size was increased to 20 cm in the sitting condition to prevent pinching infants' legs inside the apparatus. The experimenter repeated trials on which infants propped their legs or free hand on the far side of the gap to aid in balance control. In the crawling condition, the toy was placed on the landing platform as before. Seventeen infants (6 girls, 11 boys) were tested in an experienced sitting posture ($M$ =104 days) and a less familiar crawling posture ($M$ = 55 days). Four additional babies did not complete testing because of fussiness or fatigue.

    With the new gaps apparatus, Experiment 2 replicated all results from Experiment 1. All infants could safely span larger gaps when sitting ($M$ = 27.29 cm) than when crawling ($M$ = 13.33 cm). Most important, in their experienced sitting posture, all infants closely matched avoidance responses to the probability of falling, but in their less familiar crawling posture, they attempted impossibly risky gaps and fell (see Fig. 4). A 2 (postural condition) × 4 (risky gap distance) repeated measures analysis of variance revealed main effects for postural condition, $F(1, 8) = 7.22, p < .028$, and gap distance, $F(3, 24) = 9.14, p < .000$. Paired comparisons showed significant differences between postures at each risky gap distance (all $ps < .05$). Eight infants fell into the 90-cm gap in the crawling condition but not in the sitting condition, showing striking specificity of knowledge about balance control.

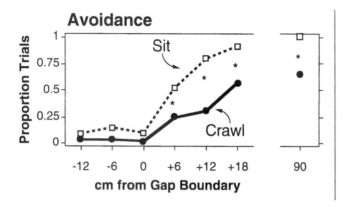

**Figure 4:** Proportion of trials with avoidance responses in Experiment 2. The data are plotted according to relative degree of risk (see Fig. 2). Data are also included for the largest, 90-cm, gap. Asterisks denote significant differences between sitting and crawling conditions.

## General Discussion

The present experiments involving infants reaching over gaps and the earlier longitudinal investigation of infants descending slopes indicate that experience with an earlier-developing skill does not transfer automatically to a later-developing one. Together, these studies point to surprising specificity of learning across three major postural milestones in development – sitting, crawling, and walking. Apparently, the coordination between perception and action that is required to use depth information to plan actions adaptively is specific to the particular postural control system being engaged in the task. This dissociation between postures belies previous accounts suggesting that adaptive responses to disparity in depth of the ground surface depend on a general sort of knowledge such as fear of heights, on associations between depth information and falling, or on knowledge that the body cannot be supported in empty space.

However, a more subtle type of transfer does occur. Apparently, learning transfers from uneventful, everyday experience coping with balance on safe, solid ground to the potentially risky situations in the novel gaps and slopes tasks. In the gaps studies, neither prior experiences of falling or near-falling from heights nor experiences incurred during the test session were related to adaptive avoidance responses to risky gaps. Similarly, in the longitudinal study of infants descending slopes, learning did not depend on experience falling from heights or falling down slopes during testing. Moreover, learning to avoid risky slopes did not depend on experience coping with slopes. Infants in a control group, matched for age and duration of crawling and walking experience, behaved similarly to the babies tested repeatedly on laboratory slopes, and no infants had experience on slopes outside the laboratory.

Within postures, however, infants showed generalization of learning across changes in their own bodies and skills. In the slopes study, it was possible to track changes in infants' body dimensions, locomotor skills, and locomotor experiences on a weekly basis and to relate these factors to changes in the laboratory task. Each week, infants' bodies and skills changed considerably, in ways that affected the biomechanics of keeping balance. Thus, a slope that was risky one week could be safe the next, and a slope that was previously safe could become risky. Despite these changes, within postures, infants' responses continually improved. It was uneventful, everyday experience coping with each posture in development that predicted the adaptiveness of the infants' responses.

Together, the findings from both studies indicate that infants' learning is not confined to acquisition of particular facts about the environment (e.g., a particular gap size is too large or a particular degree of slope is too steep), particular facts about themselves (being a highly skilled sitter or a poorly skilled crawler, having top-heavy body dimensions or more maturely proportioned ones), or any type of fixed association between particular environmental properties and particular motor responses. In fact, such inflexibility in learning would be maladaptive because infants' bodies and skills change from week to week and the everyday terrain is variable. Instead, the results are consistent with the sway model: Infants must learn, posture by posture in the course of development, how to discover on-line their region of permissible sway and to use this information for prospective control of action. According to this account, learning in the course of development may be both far more specific and far more flexible than previously recognized.

## References

Adolph, K.E. (1995). A psychophysical assessment of toddlers' ability to cope with slopes. *Journal of Experimental Psychology: Human Perception and Performance, 21,* 734–750.

Adolph, K.E. (1997). Learning in the development of infant locomotion. *Monographs of the Society for Research in Child Development, 62*(3, Serial No. 251).

Adolph, K.E., & Eppler, M.A. (1998). Development of visually guided locomotion. *Ecological Psychology, 10,* 303–321.

Adolph, K.E., & Eppler, M.A. (in press). Flexibility and specificity in infant motor skill acquisition. In J. Fagan & H. Hayne (Eds.), *Progress in infancy research.* Norwood, NJ: Ablex.

Bertenthal, B.I., & Campos, J.J. (1990). A systems approach to the organizing effects of self-produced locomotion during infancy. In C. Rovee-Collier & L.P. Lipsitt (Eds.), *Advances in infancy research* (Vol. 6, pp. 1–60). Norwood, NJ: Ablex.

Bertenthal, B.I., Campos, J.J., & Barrett, K.C. (1984). Self-produced locomotion: An organizer of emotional, cognitive, and social development in infancy. In R.N. Emde & R.J. Harmon (Eds.), *Continuities and discontinuities in development* (pp. 175–210). New York: Plenum Press.

Bertenthal, B.I., Campos, J.J., & Kermoian, R. (1994). An epigenetic perspective on the development of self-produced locomotion and its consequences. *Current Directions in Psychological Science, 3*, 140–145.

Campos, J.J., Bertenthal, B.I., & Kermoian, R. (1992). Early experience and emotional development: The emergence of wariness of heights. *Psychological Science, 3*, 61–64.

Campos, J.J., Langer, A., & Krowitz, A. (1970). Cardiac responses on the visual cliff. *Science, 170*, 196–197.

Gibson, E.J., & Schmuckler, M.A. (1989). Going somewhere: An ecological and experimental approach to development of mobility. *Ecological Psychology, 1*, 3–25.

Gibson, E.J., & Walk, R.D. (1960). The "visual cliff." *Scientific American, 202*, 64–71.

Held, R., & Hein, A. (1963). Movement-produced stimulation in the development of visually guided behavior. *Journal of Comparative and Physiological Psychology, 56*, 872–876.

Lashley, K.S., & Russell, J.T. (1934). The mechanism of vision: XI. A preliminary test of innate organization. *Journal of Genetic Psychology, 45*, 136–144.

Riccio, G.E. (1993). Information in movement variability about the qualitative dynamics of posture and orientation. In K.M. Newell & D.M. Corcos (Eds.), *Variability and motor control* (pp. 317–357). Champaign, IL: Human Kinetics Publishers.

Riccio, G.E., & Stoffregen, T.A. (1988). Affordances as constraints on the control of stance. *Human Movement Science, 7*, 265–300.

Richards, J.E., & Rader, N. (1983). Affective, behavioral, and avoidance responses on the visual cliff: Effects of crawling onset age, crawling experience, and testing age. *Psychophysiology, 20*, 633–642.

Scarr, S., & Salapatek, P. (1970). Patterns of fear development during infancy. *Merrill-Palmer Quarterly, 16*, 53–90.

Slater, A., & Morison, V. (1985). Shape constancy and slant perception at birth. *Perception, 14*, 337–344.

Thelen, E., & Smith, L.B. (1994). *A dynamic systems approach to the development of cognition and action*. Cambridge, MA: MIT Press.

Walk, R.D. (1966). The development of depth perception in animals and human infants. *Monographs of the Society for Research in Child Development, 31*(5, Serial No. 107), 82–108.

Walk, R.D., & Gibson, E.J. (1961). A comparative and analytical study of visual depth perception. *Psychological Monographs, 75*(15, Whole No. 519).

Walk, R.D., Gibson, E.J., & Tighe, T.J. (1957). Behavior of light- and dark-reared rats on a visual cliff. *Science, 126*, 80–81.

Yonas, A., & Hartman, B. (1993). Perceiving the affordance of contact in four- and five-month-old infants. *Child Development, 64*, 298–308.

# 9. Spatial Orientation

# Egocentric versus Allocentric Spatial Coding in Nine-Month-Old Infants: Factors Influencing the Choice of Code

*J. Gavin Bremner*

A t around the age of 9 months (corresponding to Piaget's sensorimotor Stage 4) infants make important progress in their dealings with the world. For the first time they engage in a form of manual action which has generally been interpreted as search for the hidden object. Piaget (1954) claims that this new behavior marks the beginning of a crucial stage in the development of the infant's concept of objects, interpreting such search as indication that the infant for the first time conceives of an object as something that continues to exist substantially, even when it is out of sight.

This search behavior is quite limited how ever, for although the infant experiences little difficulty in finding an object hidden repeatedly in one place (A), when he sees the object hidden in a new place (B), he continues to search for it back at the old place (A). This phenomenon, which has become known as the Stage 4, or AB̄ (A not B) error, has been replicated in a number of recent studies (Appel, 1971; Bower & Paterson, 1972; Evans & Gratch, 1972; Gratch, Appel, Evans, LeCompte, & Wright, 1974; Gratch & Landers, 1971; Harris, 1973) and is thus a reliable finding.

Piaget believes that the Stage 4 error indicates the limited nature of the infant's object conception. Although the Stage 4 infant has made the important step of engaging in manual search for a hidden object, the object is not yet located in a coherent objective spatial framework, and to this extent remains

**Source:** *Developmental Psychology*, 14(4) (1978): 346–355.

"at disposal in the place where the action has made use of it" (Piaget, 1954, p. 50). He suggests that the infant very rapidly associates the object with a particular place, a place that is specified by the actions made when he originally retrieved the object. Thus, Piaget argues that the infant's object concept is still partially egocentric because the object still remains linked, albeit indirectly, to the infant's action. Similarly, he views the infant's concept of space as egocentric, because it is the object's position that is partially defined by the infant's action.

The validity of Piaget's hypothesis remains to be assessed, because there still seems to be no evidence that gives a convincing answer to the question of why the infant makes the Stage 4 error. However, no matter what may be the reason for this error, it constitutes a fairly consistent phenomenon which may be interpreted as an error to a place. The manner in which the infant defines the place to which he errs is open to investigation, and thus the question of egocentrism can be posed in the spatial context. In this case, definition of position relative to the self may be considered egocentric coding of position. However, definition of position in this way does not necessarily involve the belief that the object is in any way dependent on the self. In this sense, the hypothesis of spatial egocentrism does not make such strong assumptions about the infant's egocentrism as Piaget's hypothesis does. As an alternative to defining positions egocentrically, the infant may define positions relative to some external framework. For the purposes of the present article, any such "nonegocentric" method of coding position will be termed *allocentric.*

The question of how the infant defines the position at which he consistently searches in the Stage 4 task may be tackled by the use of a simple technique. The infant is allowed to find an object several times in one (A) of two places arranged symmetrically to left and right of his midline, and is then moved to the opposite side of the display before the object is again hidden in the same place. If he defines position egocentrically, he should now search at the other position (B) because as a result of his movement, this position now bears the same relation to the infant as Position A did before he was moved. On the other hand, if he specifies position allocentrically, he should not err.

Using this method, Bremner and Bryant (1977) produced evidence strongly supporting the presence of egocentric coding in the 9-month-old infant's spatial judgments. The infant's tendency to use this method was evident despite the fact that the two hiding positions were clearly differentiated to adult eyes, the display being painted so that one position lay on a black background and the other lay on a white background. Infants in the new position responded in a manner consistent with the use of an egocentric code, although this involved making responses to a position that was both visually and spatially distinct from the original.

It is interesting to note that Bremner and Bryant's result was the opposite of that obtained by Tolman, Ritchie, and Kalish (1946) in an experiment with the same basic design, intended to solve a similar problem in animal learning. Tolman et al. showed that rats were considerably better at place learning than at response learning (for instance, always turning left no matter what the starting point). It seems likely that this result arose because rats were able to use salient cues to allocentric location, such as distinctive lighting or olfactory cues (Hilgard & Bower, 1948). This poses the question of whether the provision of more salient spatial cues would allow the 9-month-old infant to employ an allocentric strategy. A recent experiment (Bremner, 1978) has provided evidence suggesting that this is the case. This experiment took the form of a replication of several conditions of Bremner and Bryant's study, with one simple alteration. Instead of using a black and white table with two grey covers, two covers, one black and the other white, were used on a grey table. It was assumed that differentiation of the covers in this manner would provide the infant with a more salient spatial cue than differentiation of the table sides. This proved to be the case, since under these conditions few infants made errors in search from the new side of the table when the object was hidden in the same place (on the table) as they had found it originally, the reverse of Bremner and Bryant's result for this condition. Thus, it may be concluded that the 9-month-old infant is capable of defining positions allocentrically, but that this ability is limited to cases in which allocentric cues are particularly salient.

The second interesting result that arose from this study (Bremner, 1978) was the fact that the use of cover differentiation as a spatial cue only produced a clear change in performance in the condition just described. If, as an alternative, the infant remained in the same place and the covers were exchanged halfway through the session, nearly half of the infants made errors if the object was hidden under the same cover at the new side. From this result, it seems that either the movement of the infant or the stability of the position is important in determining whether or not the infant uses an allocentric code.

One of the problems inherent in the use of a modified Stage 4 task to investigate the infant's spatial abilities is that the infant may not be sufficiently encouraged to take note of the spatial transformation taking place between Stages 1 and 2. This is so because the rotation is made between trials when the infant has found the object that he was seeking and thus has no reason to attend to what is happening. Thus, it is possible that a task of this sort does not constitute a fair test of the infant's spatial understanding.

It may be possible to avoid this problem by the use of a revised technique. Although the infant is not likely to be particularly attentive to changes taking place once he has found the object and before it is hidden again, he is noticeably attentive during the period after the object is hidden and before he has found it. Thus, if the task was modified so that the infant (or the table) is moved after the object is hidden but before he is allowed to search, there is a higher likelihood that he would maintain his attention on the table while he or it was being moved.

The present article sets out to investigate the 9-month-old infant's ability under such conditions. In particular, it investigates the nature of the factors that may contribute to definition of an allocentric position which the infant is capable of holding constant during a movement of himself or of the position.

## Experiment 1

One factor that may be of importance in determining the way in which the infant defines a position is the amount of experience he has had of reaching at that place. The role of action in defining a position is not clear. Although Piaget (1954) assigns a central role to it in his explanation of the Stage 4 error, it has been shown that this error occurs even when the infant has previously only seen the object hidden and revealed at the first place and has not been allowed to search there (Butterworth, 1974; Evans, Note 1). Thus, it seems that overt manual action cannot be the infant's only means of specifying Position A as the place of search.

No matter what its relevance is to the Stage 4 error, the role of action in defining an object's location that changes relative to the subject while the object is hidden remains to be established. There are two possible hypotheses:

1. Action at one position helps to define it as a particular allocentric position to which attention will be directed during movement of the subject or the object.
2. Action at one position promotes response perseveration or leads the infant to use an egocentric or subject-referent definition of position.

Hypothesis 1 predicts that previous action at one place would lead to allocentric responding after the spatial transformation, whereas Hypothesis 2 predicts that such experience would lead to egocentric responding. Although, if anything, evidence from infants' performance in the Stage 4 task lends more support to Hypothesis 2 than to Hypothesis 1, we cannot assume that the same would be the case in the modified task under discussion.

Before any other factors relevant to the infant's spatial abilities can be investigated, it is important to establish which of these hypotheses holds true. Experiment 1 performs this function by comparing performance on rotation trials between two groups: one that was given previous experience of finding the object at Position A and another that was not given such experience.

# Method

## Subjects

Thirty-two healthy babies (mean age: 9 months, 8 days; range: 28 days) completed the experiment. A further 15 babies (mean age: 9 months, 7 days) were seen but were not considered, either because they became upset or because they showed no interest. The 32 babies were divided into two groups of 16, each with 8 boys and 8 girls.

## Apparatus

The baby was seated in a baby chair facing a table with dimensions 30 x 60 cm. Two 8 × 8 cm wells, 3 cm deep and with 1.5 cm rims, were located with their centers 28 cm apart in the long-axis midline of the table. The table was oriented so that its long axis was perpendicular to the direction of the infant's "straight ahead". Two 16 × 16 cm dishcloths were used as covers for the wells. In order to make discrimination between the wells more straightforward, the table was painted so that one well lay on a black background and the other lay on a white background. In all respects mentioned so far, the apparatus was identical to that used by Bremner and Bryant (1977). The baby chair was mounted on a turntable that allowed its rotation around the center point of the table. Additionally, the chair was mounted on wheels that allowed it to be moved toward and away from the table. It was possible to rotate the table about its midpoint.

## Design

The design is summarized in Table 1. All infants underwent a brief familiarization period. For Group A, following familiarization, the experiment consisted of two stages, each consisting of five hiding trials. In Stage 1, the object was hidden each time in the same well, and the infant was allowed to search for it. In Stage 2, which followed immediately, the object was hidden as usual, but the infant was moved to the opposite side of the table before being allowed to search. Group B did not receive Stage 1 trials, proceeding directly from the familiarization period to Stage 2. For both groups, total reliance on an

**Table 1:** Design and results of Experiment 1

| Group | Mean age | Previous experience trials (Stage 1) | Rotation trials (Stage 2) | No. incorrect[a] (Trial 1, Stage 2) | Mean error over five trials (Stage 2) |
|-------|----------|--------------------------------------|---------------------------|-------------------------------------|---------------------------------------|
| A | 277.9 | 5 | 5 | 14 | 3.81 |
| B | 284.5 | 0 | 5 | 6 | 1.81 |

[a] Out of 16.

egocentric definition of position precludes successful performance on Stage 2 trials, since the hiding position (A) ceases to be the one specified by this system after the infant is rotated. If the prior search experience given to Group A in Stage 1 has an effect on these infants' search behavior on rotation trials, this should manifest itself as a difference in Stage 2 performance between the groups.

## Procedure

Infants were tested in their own homes because it was felt that they were less likely to become distracted or upset in this situation than if they were tested in a strange environment. Every effort was made to place the apparatus so that the environment was as near to being symmetrical about the infant's midline as possible. Thus, all infants were tested in a familiar, differentiated environment which provided a stable background relative to the table. The probability that infants would perform better in their home environment was felt to outweigh any disadvantages that might arise from not using the same environment for each infant.

**Familiarization period.** Infants were placed in the chair and allowed to familiarize themselves with the experimenter and with novel objects such as the chair, table, and covers. It was judged important that the infant should become habituated to the covers to ensure that lifting them in the experiment proper was not a result of interest in the covers per se, a possibility suggested by Bower and Wishart (1972). When the infant seemed happy in the situation, a novel toy was introduced (e.g., a padlock and chain, a toy ladybird, etc; the one that interested the infant most was found by trial and error).

Once the infant's attention was captured by the toy, four "warm-up" trials were given. These took the form of partial hiding trials and were given because it has been shown that such experience increases the likelihood that the infant will search for a hidden object on later trials (Miller, Cohen, & Hill, 1970). The object was lowered onto the table and then raised again. The lowering sequence was repeated three times, and the third time the object was left on the table. One cover was then drawn over the object until it was roughly three-quarters covered. During this time, the infant was out of reach of the table. After a 5 sec delay, he was moved forward to the table and allowed to search for the toy. He was allowed to play with it for about 10 sec when he retrieved it. In order to avoid biasing the infant's responses to either side, these trials took place at the midpoint of the table.

During the warm-up trials, the only difference in treatment between the two groups was during the delay period between partial hiding and search. After the object was partially hidden, infants in Group B were rotated through an arc of 90° to a point halfway around the table and then back again to their original position. This was thought to be a necessary precaution against surprise in these infants when they were presented with rotation trials immediately afterwards. The direction of this rotation was always the same as the full rotation on later trials. This procedure was delayed until Stage 1 for infants in Group A.

**Stage 1, preliminary search trials.** Only Group A received these trials. The first trial followed immediately upon completion of the familiarization period. The same lowering sequence was followed in these as in the warm-up trials. However, this took place at one of the wells, and instead of the object being partially hidden, it was completely hidden, both covers being drawn forward simultaneously until they covered both wells completely. The toy was hidden with the infant looking on and always in the same well. Again, 5 sec was allowed to elapse between hiding and search. During this time, the infant was rotated through an arc of 90° to a point halfway around the table, and then back again to his original position. The direction of rotation was always the same as the full rotation during Stage 2, and was to the side at which the object was hidden. (It is possible that this, and the corresponding procedure during the warm-up trials for Group B, could have helped infants to identify the correct position, but since the intention was to produce a task that was not too difficult, this procedure was not avoided). The reason for this 90° degree rotation was again to accustom the infant to movement before the rotation trials took place. The infant was allowed to correct mistakes and to play with the toy for about 10 sec when he retrieved it. The location of the correct side and its color were fully counterbalanced within each group.

**Stage 2, rotation trials.** Both groups received these trials. The trial administration procedure was identical to that of Stage 1, except in the following two aspects: (a) In the interval between the object being hidden and the infant being allowed to search, he was rotated through 180° around the table so that he ended up at its opposite side and had to search from there. In order to encourage the infant to keep track of the object's location, this movement was always past the side of the table at which the object was hidden, (b) The infant was drawn back from the table immediately on making an error, and so was prevented from correcting mistakes. After the infant had searched, he was returned to his original position. This procedure was repeated five times, the object always being hidden in the same well, and with the infant starting at the same side each time. For infants in Group A, the same well was used as in Stage 1.

During the whole test session, the experimenter sat opposite the infant, facing him across the table. When the infant was rotated, the experimenter also moved round and so remained opposite him. The infant's mother normally remained in the room during the test session. She stood behind the experimenter in his position before rotation, and to avoid undue distraction during rotation she remained in that position during the whole session. This was found to be a better arrangement than placing her behind the infant, since in this case he was liable to catch sight of her suddenly during the crucial rotation trials.

During the warm-up trials and Stages 1 and 2, and including the transition interval between stages, the intertrial interval was held as near 15 sec as possible.

## Results

### Stage 1

The scores in Stage 1 show that on the whole, infants in Group A were perfectly well able to search for the object correctly from their initial location. On the first trial of this stage, only 3 of the 16 infants made an error (binomial $p = .011$, one tail), and on average for the five trials only 2 of the 16 infants made errors on any trial. Over the five trials, seven infants made no errors, eight made one error, and one made two errors.

### Stage 2

The crucial trial of this stage is the first one, since the infant's performance on subsequent trials may be affected by his previous Stage 2 experience, as well as by any experience he may have had before this stage. The scores for the first trial are presented in Table 1. In Group A, a larger number of infants made an error than would be expected by chance (binomial $p = .004$, two tail); whereas in Group B the number of infants making an error did not depart significantly from that expected by chance, (binomial $p = .45$, two tail). Furthermore, a significantly larger number of infants erred in Group A compared with Group B, $\chi^2(1) = 6.53, p < .02$, two tail.

There are two possible interpretations of the first trial data for Group B. Either these infants employed no consistent strategy and responded at random, or some of them used a strategy that led them to err while others used a strategy that led to correct performance. Unfortunately, the present data do not allow a choice between these alternatives. An analysis of consistency of response over the five trials would be inconclusive, since on later trials infants might consistently repeat a response that they had initially made at random, especially if this response was successful.

The only support for the second interpretation comes from observing where infants looked while they were being rotated. Because the experimenter was engaged in moving himself and the infant during rotation, he was unable to make detailed observations of the infant's fixations. Two things were noted, however. First, infants almost always fixated the correct location until they were halfway round the table. Second, infants fell into two roughly equal groups with respect to their fixations after the halfway point in the rotation. One group continued to fixate the correct position and usually searched there after the rotation, while the other group began to alternate fixation between the two positions after the halfway point and usually ended up searching in the wrong place. Unfortunately, these observations were not considered sufficiently accurate to merit their report in anything other than anecdotal form. However, they do suggest that at least the first group of infants were not responding randomly.

Finally, the mean error over five trials is shown in Table 1. The mean error for Group A was significantly larger than it was for Group B, $t(30) = 3.9$, $p < .01$, two-tailed.

## Discussion

The results of this experiment provide fairly strong support for the second hypothesis stated in the introduction. That is, that action on one position promotes response perseveration or leads the infant to use an egocentric definition of position. Infants who were given previous search experience (Group A) showed a much stronger tendency to reach in the same direction relative to themselves during the subsequent rotation trials than those who were not given this experience (Group B). It is not clear to what extent the perseverative errors made by Group A were simply the result of a manual response habit acquired during initial trials, or, at a higher level, to an egocentric definition of position. However, the fact that infants still make the Stage 4 error after simply observing the object hidden and revealed at Position A (Butterworth, 1974; Evans, Note 1) provides support for the latter interpretation.

While it is clear that a significant majority of infants in Group A defined the position of search relative to themselves, the results for Group B are not so easily interpreted. As was pointed out, it is not clear whether these infants simply responded randomly or whether some adopted an egocentric strategy while others adopted an allocentric strategy. The observations of the infants' fixations provide very tentative support for the second interpretation, but they do not constitute sufficiently strong evidence to rule out the first interpretation. However, these observations are useful in pointing to a potentially important area for future research.

The results for Group A provide no evidence that the present task is a more sensitive way of measuring the infant's spatial ability than the Stage-4-type task used in previous studies (Bremner & Bryant, 1977; Bremner, 1978). Performance in Group A did not differ significantly from performance in the corresponding condition in Bremner and Bryant's study, where 12 infants out of 16 made an error. However, as the results for Group B show, elimination of previous search experience led to a significant reduction in egocentric responding. It seems likely that if infants have any ability to code position allocentrically in this type of task, they are more likely to do so when the egocentric tendency is reduced. Consequently, it seems important to eliminate previous search experience in further investigation of the factors influencing the infant's spatial coding.

It might be argued that the warm-up trials provided such experience for Group B; however, there was no evidence of infants searching at the central position in the later stages of the experiment, when it was devoid of object and cover. Accordingly, the general procedure used with Group B was adopted in Experiment 2, in the hope that this would provide favorable conditions for the detection of allocentric spatial coding by the 9-month-old infant.

# Experiment 2

This experiment was designed as a test of two hypotheses suggested by previous results (Bremner, 1978). These are (a) that the 9-minth-old infant is more successful in search for a hidden object when the object's position relative to the infant has changed due to the movement of the infant than he is when this relationship has changed due to movement of the object, and (b) that the 9-month-old infant is more successful in search for a hidden object at a position that changes relative to himself, if the position of that object is cued by the color of the cover under which it is hidden rather than by the color of the side of the table at which it is hidden.

## Method

### Subjects

Forty-eight healthy babies (mean age: 9 months, 4 days; range: 33 days) completed the experiment. A further 17 babies (mean age: 9 months, 3 days) were seen but were not considered, either because they became upset or because they showed no interest in the task. The 48 babies were divided into three groups of 16, each with 8 boys and 8 girls.

### Apparatus

The apparatus was identical to that used in Experiment 1, but for the fact that for Groups C and D, a grey table was used instead of a black and white one, and a black and a white cover were used instead of two identical grey covers.

## Design

This experiment sets out to investigate the effects of different cuing conditions and different movement conditions by making systematic changes in the presentation conditions for Group B of Experiment 1. The data for the latter group are included in the analysis, since the design is incomplete without this group. The presentation conditions for the three groups in this experiment are best described in terms of how they differ from those for Group B of Experiment 1. In order to avoid confusion with the groups of the previous experiment, the present groups are labeled C, D, and E.

For Group C, the rotation condition differed from that for Group B of Experiment 1. The object was hidden each time in the same well, but instead of the infant being moved around to the opposite side of the table before being allowed to search, the table was rotated through 180°. For Group D, the cuing condition was different. The same procedure was adopted with this group as with Group B of Experiment 1, but position was cued by a black and a white cover instead of a table with one side black and the other side white. For Group E, both conditions were different. The table was rotated instead of the infant, and cover cues were used instead of table cues. The design is summarized in Table 2.

## Procedure

**Familiarization period.** The procedure during this period was identical to that followed in Experiment 1, apart from slight differences in the administration of the warm-up trials, between the three groups. As in the case of Group B of Experiment 1, Group D infants were moved through an arc of 90° and back between partial hiding and search on each trial, in order to accustom them to movement before rotation trials commenced. The side to which they were moved was always the side past which they were moved on rotation trials. This procedure was not necessary for Groups C and E, since these infants remained at the same side of the table throughout the session. However, in order to accustom these infants to movement of the table before rotation trials commenced, the table was rotated through 90° and back between partial hiding and search. This movement was always made so that the side of

**Table 2:** Design and results of Experiment 2 (including Group B, Experiment 1 for comparison)

| Experiment/Group | Mean age | Rotation trials | Rotation condition | Cuing condition | No. incorrect[a] (Trial 1) | Mean error over five trials |
|---|---|---|---|---|---|---|
| 1  B | 284.5 | 5 | Infant | Table | 6 | 1.81 |
| 2  C | 280.2 | 5 | Table | Table | 12 | 3.00 |
| D | 277.2 | 5 | Infant | Cover | 3 | 1.31 |
| E | 275.1 | 5 | Table | Cover | 6 | 2.50 |

[a]Out of 16.

the table that rotated toward the infant was the same side that passed close to them on the rotation trials.

Finally, the fact that the two covers were distinct in the task presented to Groups D and E, required the precaution of alternating the cover used on warm-up trials in order to reduce the possibility of these infants establishing a response directed to a particular cover during this stage.

**Rotation trials.** The five rotation trials followed immediately. For Group D, the procedure was identical to that used in Experiment 1. For Groups C and E, the only difference was that instead of the infant being rotated through 180° around the midpoint of the table while the object was out of sight, the table was rotated through 180°. Thus, if the object had been hidden on the infant's left, the rotation moved it to the infant's right. The rotation always took place so that the side of the table that passed close to the infant was the one at which the object was hidden. After each trial the table was moved back, so that on the next trial, hiding would take place in the same place relative to the infant and in the same well as before.

## Results

Table 2 shows the results of the experiment both in terms of the number of infants in each group making an error on the first trial and in terms of the mean error over five trials for each group. Again, the crucial rotation trial was the first one, since the infant's performance on subsequent trials may have been affected by experience from previous trials. Two main results stand out. In Group C, more infants than expected by chance made an error on the first trial by responding to the egocentric position that the object had occupied before the table was moved (binomial $p = .038$, one tail), while in Group D fewer infants made an error than expected by chance (binomial $p = .01$, one tail). These results, along with the fact that in Group E, the same number of infants made an error as in Group B of Experiment 1, suggest that the two factors manipulated in the experiment had opposite effects on the infants' performance. Using the cover differentiation cue led to an improvement in performance, with the majority of infants responding allocentrically, while moving the table instead of the infant led to poorer performance, with the majority of infants responding egocentrically.

Pairwise chi-square analyses showed that in Group C, significantly more infants made an error than in all other groups: Groups C versus D, $\chi^2(1) = 8.03$, $p < .005$, one tail; Group C versus Group B and Group E, $\chi^2(1) = 3.17$, $p < .05$, one tail. There were no other significant differences between groups. The first trial data are more easily interpreted in the light of the following two comparisons. First, the number of infants making an error in the infant-movement groups (B and D) is significantly smaller than the corresponding number in the object-movement groups (C and E), $n = 9$ and 18, respectively,

$\chi^2(1) = 4.1$, $p < .025$, one tail. Second, the number of infants making an error in the cover-cue groups (D and E) is significantly smaller than the corresponding number in the table-side-cue groups (B and C), $n = 9$ and 18, respectively, $\chi^2(1) = 4.1$, $p < .025$, one tail. Thus, we can conclude that both a change in the movement condition and a change in the cuing condition produced a significant change in performance.

While the results for Groups C and D are fairly clear, the chance level performance of Group E presents the same problem in interpretation as the data for Group B did in Experiment 1. However, in the light of the results for Groups C and D, it seems likely that Groups B and E were faced with a task that did not let them make a clear choice between egocentric and allocentric responding. Probably as a consequence of this, they either responded randomly, or else some chose to respond allocentrically while others chose to respond egocentrically.

In order to render the error scores over five trials more suitable for parametric analysis, these were transformed according to the formula $X' = (X + .5)^{\frac{1}{2}}$ (Winer, 1962). A two-way analysis of variance (Movement Condition × Cuing Condition) performed on the transformed scores revealed a significant movement condition effect, the mean error for the object movement groups being significantly higher than that for the infant-movement groups, $F(1, 60) = 10.27$, $p < .01$. However, this analysis did not reveal a significant difference between means for the table-side-cue and cover-cue groups, $F(1, 60) = 1.7$, $p > .05$, although this difference was in the same direction as it was in the first trial data. The interaction between these factors was not significant.

## Discussion

The pattern of these results is quite similar to that obtained in previous work (Bremner & Bryant, 1977; Bremner, 1978). Thus, it seems fair to make the following conclusions:

1. The 9-month-old infant's definition of the position of a hidden object need not involve himself as referent.
2. Infants are more likely to use an allocentric definition if position is cued by cover differentiation rather than by table-side differentiation.
3. Infants are more likely to use an allocentric code in searching for a hidden object whose spatial relationship to them has changed, if this change results from movement of the infant rather than of the object.

There are two possible interpretations of the third finding: (a) The infant's movement alerts him to the fact that a change is taking place in the spatial relationship between himself and the object, and as a consequence, he performs better, (b) The infant has the ability to code the position of an object allocentrically, but only if that position remains stable relative to the cover cues *and* relative to an external spatial framework based on other stable cues (in this case, unknown cues within the room). Thus, the suggestion here is that the infant is successful only when he can use two allocentric codes in conjunction, one based on the cover cues and the other based on stable cues in the room.

Unfortunately, a choice between these explanations is not yet possible. However, it may be that both of these factors contributed to the superior performance in the infant-movement conditions. This possibility gains credibility when viewed in the light of a previous hypothesis (Bremner, 1978). According to this hypothesis, two things happen when the infant begins to crawl, an ability that he gains, on the average, between 8 and 9 months of age.

First, as a result of his frequent displacements, more and more situations crop up in which the egocentric code fails to specify the same position over time. Thus, in situations in which he has moved, the infant comes to rely more on other definitions of position. This suggests that the first interpretation of the superior performance of infant-movement groups may be valid.

Second, by observing the results of his active displacements in space, the infant gains information that allows him to define stable positions allocentrically. Clearly, the infant has ample opportunity to observe objects being displaced by adults and to observe the changes that take place when adults move him from place to place. However, in such cases the infant's role is that of observer. Since the present hypothesis is an active hypothesis, much in the spirit of theories of reafference, it predicts progress in spatial organization only when the infant's role in the displacement is that of agent, and when he has direct feedback from the displacement in the form of a change in perspective. Hence, the prediction that the infant will gain the ability to relate his own movements to a stable space before gaining this ability with the displacements of objects.

The fact that in Experiment 1 infants who were given experience of finding an object several times in the same place were strongly disposed toward egocentric response in their search for the object after its position relative to them had changed may have considerable importance for our understanding of the reasons for the Stage 4 error. Piaget stresses the importance of successful action in determining the position of search at this stage. Although it has been shown that infants who simply observe the object hidden and revealed at Position A nevertheless search for it there after they see it hidden at Position B (Butterworth, 1974; Evans, Note 1), such evidence does not rule out the possibility that action defines the position of search. Although manual action on A trials is prevented in this task, there remains the possibility that its position defining role is taken over by the repeated perceptual actions involved in watching the object being repeatedly hidden and revealed at A.

The contribution of the present study to this problem is the suggestion that although previous repeated action may be a particularly potent factor in determining the location of future search, it is not an essential factor. The results of the experiments reported here suggest that the infant has alternative means of definition at his disposal, but that when the task is structured so that the object can initially be found by repetition of a previous action, definition of position in terms of action is chosen in preference to these other, possibly more appropriate means.

Although this study and a previous one (Bremner, 1978) have shown fairly conclusively that conditions exist in which the 9-month-old infant can code position allocentrically, and have pointed out some of the factors important in determining whether or not the infant will use this ability, this is clearly only the starting point. The details of how the infant goes about defining position, both allocentrically and egocentrically, still remain to be established, and in this respect this study poses more questions than it attempts to answer.

## Reference Note

1. Evans, W. F. *The Stage IV error in Piaget's theory of object concept development: An investigation of the role of activity.* Unpublished dissertation proposal, University of Houston, 1973.

## References

Appel, K. J. *Three studies in object conceptualisation: Piaget's sensori-motor stages four and five.* Unpublished doctoral dissertation, University of Houston, 1971.

Bower, T. G. R., & Paterson, J. G. Stages in the development of the object concept. *Cognition,* 1972, *1,* 47–55.

Bower, T. G. R., & Wishart, J. G. The effects of motor skill on object permanence. *Cognition,* 1972, *1,* 165–172.

Bremner, J. G. Spatial errors made by infants: Inadequate Spatial cues or evidence of egocentrism? *British Journal of Psychology,* 1978, *69,* 77–84.

Bremner, J. G., & Bryant, P. E. Place versus response as the basis of spatial errors made by young infants. *Journal of Experimental Child Psychology,* 1977, *23,* 162–177.

Butterworth, G. *The development of the object concept in human infants.* Unpublished Doctor of Philosophy thesis, University of Oxford, 1974.

Evans, W. F., & Gratch, G. The stage IV error in Piaget's theory of object concept development: Difficulties in object conceptualisation or spatial location? *Child Development,* 1972, *43,* 682–688.

Gratch, G., Appel, K. J., Evans, W. F., LeCompte, G. K., & Wright, N. A. Piaget' s stage IV object concept error: Evidence of forgetting or object conception? *Child Development,* 1974, *45,* 71–77.

Gratch, G., & Landers, W. F. Stage IV of Piaget's theory of infants' object concepts: a longitudinal study. *Child Development,* 1911, *42,* 359–372.

Harris, P. L. Perseverative errors in search by young infants. *Child Development,* 1973, *44,* 28–33.

Hilgard, E. R., & Bower, G. H. *Theories of learning.* New York: Appleton-Century-Crofts, 1948.

Miller, D., Cohen, L., & Hill, K. A methodological investigation of Piaget's theory of object concept development in the sensory-motor period. *Journal of Experimental Child Psychology,* 1970, *9,* 59–85.

Piaget, J. [*The construction of reality in the child.*] (Margaret Cook, trans.). New York: Basic Books, 1954. (Originally published 1936.)

Tolman, E. C., Ritchie, B. F., & Kalish, D. Studies in spatial learning IV. Place learning versus response learning. *Journal of Experimental Psychology,* 1946, *36,* 221–229.

Winer, B. J. *Statistical principles in experimental design.* New York: McGraw-Hill, 1962.

# 41

# The Role of Self-Produced Movement and Visual Tracking in Infant Spatial Orientation

*Linda P. Acredolo, Anne Adams and Susan W. Goodwyn*

To date an impressive body of research has accumulated indicating that the younger the infant the more likely he or she is to give priority to egocentric over objective spatial information when trying to remember locations in large-scale spatial environments. In four separate studies, Acredolo (1978), Acredolo and Evans (1980), Cornell and Heth (1979), and Rieser (1979) each noted strong tendencies by infants 6 months or younger to look, in anticipation of an event, in the same direction as had been appropriate before the infant had been moved to a different spot in the environment. Acredolo (1978) and Cornell and Heth (1979) also included older age groups and, consequently, were able to demonstrate that this tendency declines as age increases.

Although the exact nature of this "egocentric" behavior has been debated, that is, whether it reflects dependence on a body-centered organization of space or simply a motor habit (see Acredolo, in press, for a review), the fact remains that infants are increasingly willing or able as they grow older to forego reliance on such information in favor of reliance on landmarks and/or truly coordinated perspectives of the spaces around them. One obvious question that remains is "Why?" What is it that enables or motivates the older infant but not the younger to look beyond the relation of objects and events to his or her own body? It is our belief that a parallel between development

**Source:** *Journal of Experimental Child Psychology*, 38(2) (1984): 312–327.

in this domain and the development of locomotor skills may provide some clues to this developmental mystery.

Recognition of parallel development in these two domains is not new. As early as 1977 Bremner and Bryant pointed out that the rise in objective responding in spatial tasks of this sort cooccurs with changes from sitting to crawling to walking – an observation echoed by Acredolo in 1978. Speculation about a causal relation between the two is tantalizingly plausible, but without some direct evidence of a link between self-produced movement and objective responding, must remain just that – speculation. It was the purpose of the present experiment to provide such evidence, and to do so through the use of a longitudinal design which would allow comparison of early and late locomotor periods.

Our faith in the idea of a link between locomotor development and objective responding is strengthened by existing research with infants showing relationships between self-produced movement and other spatial phenomena. For example, Campos, Svejda, Bertenthal, Benson, and Schmid (1981) have demonstrated that at least some experience with self-produced movement, either in the form of crawling or experience in a "walker" (i.e., an apparatus on wheels which allows even a noncrawling infant to move through space) is necessary for development of the degree of depth perception exhibited by infants who avoid the deep side of a visual cliff. Apparently, moving themselves through space accomplishes for this aspect of spatial knowledge something that passive movement (being carried from place to place) does not. Exactly what that contribution is, is not yet totally clear, although an increase in visual attention to the environment is hypothesized by Campos et al. (1981) to be an important factor.

If visual attention is indeed an important product of self-produced movement, the question remains: Attention to what? At least a partial answer may be attention to the different visual perspectives that result from movement. This suggestion is supported by another study by Campos (Campos, Bertenthal, & Benson, 1980) in which crawling and noncrawling 7½-month-old infants were compared on their ability to extract a constant form from a fluctuating display. Using a habituation paradigm similar to one used by Ruff (1978), Campos et al. (1980) demonstrated that the infants with crawling experience were more likely than noncrawling infants to recognize a form as familiar even though it had been presented from a variety of different viewpoints. If Campos et al. (1980) are indeed correct in interpreting this pattern as indicative of a link between self-produced movement and a tendency to coordinate perspectives, then it seems reasonable to expect self-produced movement to have an equally facilitative effect on the type of spatial orientation task at issue here. After all, an objective response in studies like those of Acredolo (1978) is really a recognition by the infant of "place constancy," analogous to the "shape constancy" studied by Campos et al. (1980).

One final study suggesting we are correct in hypothesizing a connection between self-produced movement and spatial orientation in infants is a brief report of a creative study by Benson and Uzgiris (1981). Eleven-month-old infants were taught to find an object in one of two hiding places in a large, three-sided Plexiglas box. During the training trials the permanently open side was the side farthest from the infants and the wall closest to the infants was removed to allow access to the two covered wells. During the test trials which followed training, the object was once again hidden in the same well, the wall closest to the infants was replaced, and the infants were either carried or allowed to move on their own to the opposite, permanently open side of the box in order to retrieve the object. Just as we would predict, the results indicated significantly fewer egocentric choices on the test trials after "active" movement.

Several factors, however, make us cautious about accepting these results as definitive. It appears that the active and passive conditions differed in several important respects in addition to the type of movement, differences which may have favored the active condition. Specifically, in the active condition infants remained at ground level and could reach for the object as soon as the far corner of the box was rounded. Thus, visual tracking of the correct site was fairly easy to maintain, and the infants were never again confronted with the confusing "one-on-the-right, one-on-the-left" configuration that they would have seen had they been required to reach the middle of the open side before searching. In contrast, in the passive condition, infants were apparently lifted off the ground and set down in the middle of the open side. Consequently, their view of the apparatus was disrupted and their next ground level view was in an important way a replication of their original view: one hiding spot to their right, one to their left. It is conceivable that such a combination could have increased the likelihood of dependence on egocentric information. These differences between the active and passive conditions were eliminated in the present study, and a longitudinal design assessing performance at both 12 and 18 months was used. The hypothesis, however, remained the same – that active, self-produced movement would facilitate the ability of infants to coordinate perspectives and respond objectively.

## Experiment 1

### Method

*Subjects.* Subjects were twenty-three, 12½-month-old infants, twelve boys and eleven girls, ranging in age at first testing from 12.4 to 13 months with a mean of 12.6 months ($SD = 4.6$ days). Their names were drawn from birth announcements in papers from predominantly middle-class communities in northern California. All twenty-three of these infants returned 6 months later

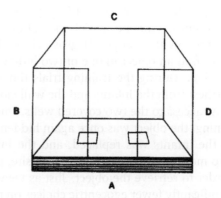

**Figure 1:** Experimental box: Wall A = front, Wall C = back

for retesting. Their ages at that time ranged from 18.4 to 19.3 months with a mean of 18.8 months (*SD* = 8.6 days).

*Materials.* The major piece of equipment used in the study was a 0.96 × 0.63-m box (38 × 25 in.), 0.63 m high, made of wood and Plexiglas (see Fig. 1). The wooden base of the box was 12.7 cm (5 in.) off the ground so that it could contain two 12.7 × 12.7-cm hiding wells, 30.5 cm (12 in.) apart, from center to center. The four corners of the box consisted of wooden tracks into which Plexiglas walls were inserted. In all conditions of the study one of the two long walls (called the front) was broken in the middle by a 30.5-cm (12 in.) opening through which the children could reach the hiding wells. The placement of the opening in the middle of the front wall ensured that the subjects would be viewing the wells with one to their left and the other to their right as they reached in to retrieve the object. The toys used in the hiding portion of the study included a Donald Duck top and a wind-up train. The only other materials were two white cloth diapers used to cover the hiding wells, and a round fence called a corral, 3.04 m (10 ft) in diameter, used to keep the children from wandering away from the apparatus.

*Procedure.* Infants were randomly assigned to one of the two groups with the result that 11 infants were tested in the active condition (5 boys and 6 girls) and 12 in the passive condition (7 boys and 5 girls). Their condition assignments remained the same at the 18 month testing session. At 12 months, 8 infants in each condition were walkers. Average age when walking began was 10.4 months for the active infants and 10.7 for the passive; these means were not significantly different.

The same experimental procedure was used at both ages. After an initial familiarization period inside the corral, the detour nature of the box was demonstrated to each subject. A toy was placed inside the box so that it was still visible from all angles and the child was placed just around the corner of the box. After the toy was retrieved, the same procedure was repeated, this time with the child closer to the back of the box. Finally, the child was placed in the middle of the back of the box, directly opposite the opening, and required to retrieve the toy three times by crawling or walking around the box to the opening. This movement was analogous to what would be required of subjects in the active condition and ensured that all subjects understood that the box was constructed to always allow access from one side. The direction in which the child was trained to go around the box was varied systematically across children. The hiding phase of the experiment was then begun.

At least five training trials and one test trial constituted the main phase of the experiment. Throughout all but the very end of this period the infant was seated in the middle of the long, back side of the box directly opposite the opening. His or her parent was seated behind the child, with the experimenter to the child's left or right. Access to the well for the training trials was provided by removing the Plexiglas wall.

The procedure for each of the training trials was the same. As the child was held back by the parent, the experimenter hid a toy in one of the two cloth-covered wells. The right well was used for half the infants in each condition, the left for the other half. The hiding place chosen was always on the side of the box around which the child had been trained to go during the familiarization phase. The object was hidden in the same well and the infant was encouraged to retrieve the toy and play with it until the child had successfully retrieved the toy five times. The test trial followed immediately.

The test trial was initiated by the replacement of the Plexiglas wall, thus denying the subjects direct access to the wells. The experimenter then moved around to the opening and hid the toy in the same well used for the training trials while the infant watched from the back of the box. Once the object was in place, one of two things happened. Infants in the active condition were set on their feet by their parent and encouraged to find the object. As the child moved around the box, the parent remained in her original place and the experimenter remained in the vicinity of the opening, far enough back to allow the child easy access. Infants in the passive condition were set on their feet by their parents, held under their arms, and carried around the box to the opening with their feet close to the floor. Parents were told that the child's path should be the same as though he or she were walking. As the child searched for the object from the new position, the parent remained directly behind the child and the experimenter moved to the parent's original position at the back of the box. Consequently, subjects in both conditions experienced one adult across from them and one adult behind them while they searched on the test trial.

Two types of data were collected on the test trial. The first was an evaluation of the infant's visual behavior as they moved around the box. Both the experimenter and another observer rated the degree to which the infants tracked the toy's location using the following scale: 0 = no tracking at all; 1 = occasional glances into the box; 2 = occasional glances *away* from the box; 3 = constant tracking throughout movement. The second measure was the accuracy of the child's search. The observer noted whether or not the infant succeeded in finding the toy (objective response) or instead chose the hiding place consistent with reliance on an egocentric frame of reference (egocentric response).

## Results and Discussion

Relevant data for each subject at each age included the number of training trials to criterion, the nature of the child's choice on the test trial, and the degree to which the child visually tracked the hidden object during movement to the other side of the box. Each point will be addressed in turn.

Training trials continued until each subject had successfully retrieved the toy five times. Overall, 92% of the subjects reached this criterion in five trials at 12 months and 95% at 18 months. The remaining infants took six or seven trials and were evenly distributed across conditions.

Responses on the test trial were categorized as egocentric (incorrect) or objective (correct). Presented in Table 1 are the numbers of children in the active and passive conditions falling into four response patterns, each pattern representative of a possible combination of responses at the two ages tested. For example, the EE category includes those subjects who responded egocentrically at both ages, and the EO category those who responded egocentrically at 12 months but objectively at 18 months.

Assuming that chance alone was operating, one would expect an equal number of subjects to fall into each category. However, a binomial test based on a probability of .25 that a subject would fall into a given category, indicated that the number of subjects in the active condition falling into the OO category was significantly greater than chance alone would predict ($p = .008$). In other words, a significant proportion of subjects in the active condition were able to find the object on the test trial at both ages. For the passive condition, significantly more subjects than would be expected by chance fell into the EO category ($p = .003$). Thus, in contrast to the subjects in the active condition, those in the passive condition tended to respond egocentrically at 12 months and then shift to objective responding at 18 months. A McNemar test of related

**Table 1:** Number of children in Experiment 1 exhibiting each of four possible response patterns on test trials across two ages

| Condition | Response pattern | | | | |
| --- | --- | --- | --- | --- | --- |
| | EE | EO | OE | OO | Total |
| Active | 1 | 2 | 1 | 7 | 11 |
| Passive | 1 | 8 | 1 | 2 | 12 |

Note: E = egocentric response; O = objective response; first letter represents response at 12 months; second letter represents response at 18 months.

samples also supported this finding of a developmental shift among subjects in the passive condition $\chi^2(1, N = 12) = 4.00, p < .05$. In addition, the difference between the active and passive conditions was demonstrated directly in a comparison of performance at 12 months: a Fisher's exact test indicated a significantly greater proportion of objective responders among subjects in the active than among subjects in the passive condition $(p < .05)$.

In sum, the results from the 12-month-olds of Experiment 1 support the hypothesis that active, self-produced movement facilitates objective responding in a simple spatial task requiring coordination of two perspectives. However, this facilitative effect no longer operates in this task at 18 months due to a ceiling effect; at this age the task was easily solved after either active or passive movement.

The question of what role visual tracking played in these results remains to be answered. The visual tracking scores were based on a 4-point rating scale (0–3) for which interrater reliability was 95%. The few discrepancies between observers were resolved through discussion. For purposes of analysis the values of the scale were collapsed into two categories: 0 and 1 = high tracking; 2 and 3 = low tracking. Presented in Table 2 are the numbers of children at each age exhibiting each of four possible combinations of visual tracking (low versus high) and search (egocentric versus objective). Statistical analyses (i.e., Fisher's exact tests and binomial tests) applied to the frequency data in Table 2 reveal a number of patterns significant at $p < .05$ or better. First, the data indicate that at 12 months, subjects in the active condition were more likely to track efficiently than those in the passive condition. Moreover, this tracking behavior seems to have been helpful to the infants. Across both the active and passive conditions and within the active condition alone, those infants who successfully found the object on the test trial (i.e., responded objectively) were significantly more likely to show high tracking than low tracking.[1] The reverse was also true at 12 months: those infants, both across conditions and within the passive condition, who responded egocentrically (i.e., did *not* find the object) were significantly more likely to show low levels

**Table 2:** Number of subjects at each age of Experiment 1 exhibiting each of four possible combinations of visual tracking behavior and search

| | | | Response | |
| --- | --- | --- | --- | --- |
| | Tracking | | Egocentric | Objective |
| 12 months | | | | |
| Active | Low | | 3 | 1 |
| | High | | 0 | 7 |
| Passive | Low | | 9 | 2 |
| | High | | 0 | 1 |
| 18 months | | | | |
| Active | Low | | 2 | 8 |
| | High | | 0 | 1 |
| Passive | Low | | 2 | 9 |
| | High | | 0 | 1 |

of tracking than high. Thus, the data at 12 months are consistent with the hypothesis that visual tracking is more likely to occur with active than with passive movement. Moreover, high levels of tracking are correlated with correct, objective search at this age.

Table 2 also reveals, however, that these relations among movement, search, and tracking do not continue at 18 months. Two things appear to have happened to change them. The first, a shift toward objective responding among the passive group, has already been discussed. The second is a shift toward low levels of tracking in the active condition where tracking was originally high. In support of this conclusion, binomial tests indicated that the proportion of active subject at 18 months showing *low* levels of tracking was significantly greater than would be expected by chance, both across response categories $(p < .005)$ and within the subgroups responding objectively $(p\text{'s} < .05)$. When one puts these two changes together, along with the continuation of objective responding among the active subjects and low tracking among the passive subjects, the following picture emerges: the children at 18 months were easily able to keep track of the location of the hidden object no matter what kind of movement was involved. Moreover, few if any infants bothered to track the location of the object as they moved.

The validity of this description of developmental change is also supported by the data as displayed in Table 3. Unlike Table 2, the data in Table 3 are grouped so as to show patterns of change across age in tracking and search for each individual subject. For example, the Hi/Lo tracking pattern includes those subjects who showed a high degree of visual tracking at 12 months but a low degree at 18 months, and the EE pattern includes subjects who responded egocentrically at both ages. Grouped in this way, the data are particularly clear in showing that visual tracking in the active condition declines with age: the Hi/Lo pattern is significantly more prevalent than would be expected by chance $(p < .05)$.

**Table 3:** Number of children in Experiment 1 falling into sixteen possible combinations of visual tracking and response patterns

| Condition | Tracking pattern | EE | EO | OE | OO | Total |
|---|---|---|---|---|---|---|
| Active | Lo/Lo | 1 | 2 | 0 | 1 | 4 |
|  | Lo/Hi | 0 | 0 | 0 | 0 | 0 |
|  | Hi/Lo | 0 | 0 | 1 | 5 | 6 |
|  | Hi/Hi | 0 | 0 | 0 | 1 | 1 |
| Passive | Lo/Lo | 1 | 8 | 1 | 1 | 11 |
|  | Lo/Hi | 0 | 0 | 0 | 0 | 0 |
|  | Hi/Lo | 0 | 0 | 0 | 1 | 1 |
|  | Hi/Hi | 0 | 0 | 0 | 0 | 0 |

*Note:* E = egocentric response; O = objective response. First entry in pattern label indicates behavior at 12 months; second entry indicates behavior at 18 months.

## Experiment 2

The results of Experiment 1 demonstrated that objective responding was more likely among infants in the active condition than the passive. However, in addition to the type of movement, these two conditions also differed in terms of the mother's position on the test trial. Mothers of infants in the active condition remained in their original position on Side C, whereas mothers of infants in the passive condition moved with their infants to Side A. The purpose of Experiment 2 was to determine whether the difference in search behavior between the active and passive groups of Experiment 1 could be explained on the basis of this difference rather than the type of movement involved.

## Method

Subjects included six 12-month-old infants (four males and two females) who had not been tested in Experiment 1. The apparatus and procedures used were identical to those of Experiment 1 with the exception that the infants were allowed to move themselves around the box on their own on the test trial while their mothers followed. Thus, all six infants were tested in the active condition with the mothers' position the same as experienced by infants in the passive condition of Experiment 1.[2]

## Results and Discussion

Five out of the six infants reached the training criterion of five successful searches in five trials. The 6th infant needed six trials. On the test trial, 5 out of the 6 infants searched accurately (objectively). A Fisher exact probability test was used to compare these data with those of the passive condition of Experiment 1 in which only 3 of 12 infants had searched accurately. The results indicated a significantly higher proportion of correct responses among the active subjects of Experiment 2 than among the passive subjects of Experiment 1 ($p = .04$). Thus, the type of movement and *not* the mother's position on the test trial appears to be the determining factor. These results do not support a suggestion made by Presson and Ihrig (1983) that egocentric search in paradigms of this sort is due to the child's reliance on the mother's maintenance of her position relative to the child as a cue that his or her own position in space has not changed and that the original search response is still appropriate.

## Experiment 3

The results of Experiment 1 also demonstrated that visual tracking is more likely to occur with active, self-produced movement at 12 months than with passive, other-directed movement. Moreover, both visual tracking and active movement are associated with objective search behavior at this age. It is very tempting to conclude from this pattern that it is the visual tracking at 12 months which facilitates objective responding, and that the advantage of active movement over passive at this age is due to active movement, for some as yet undetermined reason, tending to promote visual tracking while passive movement does not. Indeed, it was just this conclusion to which Campos, Svejda, Campos, and Bertenthal (1982) came based on their observations of locomotor and nonlocomotor infants: "it has been our impression that the infant who is passively carried is in a state of 'visual idle' – staring blankly straight ahead and not focusing on single objects in the environment" (p. 208).

However convincing such impressions might be, they unfortunately do not constitute proof that it is the tracking, and not the active movement per se, that most directly facilitates objective responding in our task. After all, it is entirely possible that the visual tracking is coincidental and that it is really the motor feedback from the self-produced movement which enables the 12-month-old infants in the active condition to maintain their orientation to the task materials. Indeed, the fact that at 18 months objective responding predominated despite little or no tracking behavior, could be interpreted as evidence supportive of this latter hypothesis.

It was the purpose of Experiment 3 to explore more precisely the relation among active movement, visual tracking, and objective responding. To this end, the transparent side walls of the box were replaced with opaque walls in order to disrupt the infants' attempts to keep their eyes on the target as they moved themselves around the box. If the infants, despite this disruption, were still able to find the object, then the results would suggest that active movement per se and not visual tracking is the crucial element. However, should the number of subjects searching correctly significantly decline in comparison to the active condition of Experiment 1, then it would seem likely that visual tracking and not active movement is the more direct facilitator of objective responding in this situation.

## Method

The subjects included 13 infants (7 boys and 6 girls), tested first at 12 months and later at 18 months of age. Their ages at the initial test ranged from 12.4 to 13.1 months with a mean of 12.7 months ($SD = 5.98$ days). At the second test the age range was 18.4 to 19.0 months with a mean of 18.69 months ($SD = 4.8$ days). None of the infants in Experiment 3 had been included in Experiment 1 or 2. Twelve of the infants were walkers; average age at onset of walking was 10.6 months.

The materials were the same as those used in Experiment 1 with the exception that the Plexiglas walls on the two short sides of the box were replaced with fiberboard. The procedure used at both testing sessions was identical to that used in Experiment 1 with the exception that the infants were only tested in the active, not the passive, condition. The mother remained in her original position on Side C, and the experimenter in the vicinity of the opening.

## Results

The criterion for training was five successful searches from the initial position. All but two of the infants reached this criterion in five trials; the remaining two took six trials. Once again the infants' choices on the test trial were categorized as objective (i.e., correct) or egocentric (i.e., incorrect), and the results for each subject for the two ages were combined into four patterns. Of the 13 subjects, 1 exhibited the EE pattern, 8 exhibited the EO pattern, 1 exhibited the OE pattern, and 3 exhibited the OO pattern. A binomial test applied to these data indicated that more subjects than would be expected by chance fell into the EO category $(p < .01)$, the pattern indicative of a shift from egocentric responding at 12 months to objective responding at 18 months. A McNemar's test of related samples also indicated that this shift was statisically significant, $\chi^2(1, N = 13), p < .05$.

Fisher's exact probability tests were used to compare the data from the opaque condition of Experiment 2 with the data from the active and passive transparent conditions of Experiment 1. These analyses revealed that the proportions of egocentric and objective responders in Experiment 2 did not differ significantly from the proportions among the passive subjects of Experiment 1 at either age. However, there was a significant difference between the two active groups at 12 months, the opaque condition of Experiment 2 producing a higher proportion of egocentric responders than the transparent condition of Experiment 1 $(p < .05)$. The shift to objective responding at 18 months by the infants in the opaque condition eliminated this difference.

The pattern which emerges from a comparison of the two experiments suggests quite strongly that active movement per se is not enough to guarantee objective responding at 12 months, at least not in our task. Twelve-month-old infants who were allowed to move on their own to the other side of the box, but whose efforts to track the location of the object were thwarted by opaque walls, were no better at finding the toy than the 12-month-old passive subjects of Experiment 1. It seems clear, then, that the visual tracking behavior exhibited at 12 months by the active subjects of Experiment 1 was a very important contributor to the high proportion of objective responders that resulted.

# General Discussion

The purpose of the present studies was to investigate the role active, self-produced movement might play in the type of rotation task typically used to assess spatial orientation during infancy. The results indicated that, at least at 12 months, spatial orientation was indeed faciliated by allowing the infants to move through the space on their own. The subjects in the active condition were significantly more likely than those in the passive condition to find the object on the test trial. These results for the 12-month-olds are clearly in line with the conclusions drawn by Benson and Uzgiris (1981) and Campos et al., (1982) based on their own investigations of the contribution that self-produced movement makes to infant spatial behavior. They also extend to infancy the pattern that has consistently emerged from studies of older children and adults (e.g., Acredolo & Feldman, 1979; Appleyard, 1970; Cohen, 1982). It appears that the facilitating effects of self-produced movement represent a continuity across development.

The present results, however, allow us to go beyond merely cataloging the existence of a relationship between active movement and spatial orientation during infancy. They also provide important insights into *why* the relationship exists. By recording the tracking behavior of the infants as they moved themselves or were moved around the box by their mothers, we were able to detect a highly significant three-way relationship at 12 months among objective responding, active movement, and visual tracking: those infants who tracked were more likely to find the object; those infants who moved themselves were more likely to find the object; and those infants who moved themselves were more likely to track. Moreover, the results of Experiment 3, in which the infants' view into the box was blocked, provided evidence that it was the tracking and not the movement itself that most directly facilitated objective responding at 12 months. Self-produced movement appears to aid the infant by increasing attention to relevant environmental information.

Of course, it is possible that our emphasis should not be on the possibility that active movement *promotes* tracking, but rather on the equally plausible hypothesis that being carried by an adult *hinders* tracking. This is a subtle but potentially important distinction. The implication for the present study is that the active/passive effect obtained may be very specific to passive movement involving being picked up by an adult. It may be that infants come to feel they have no control over where they go next in such situations, and that therefore no purpose is served by maintaining orientation to where they have just been. It is possible that visual tracking would be maintained under other conditions of passive movement, for example, when such movement still allows infants to predict their next location in space. Unfortunately, at this point all we can do is point out the distinction in the hope that others will provide data to clarify the issue.

The existence of these alternative explanations for our results does not diminish the importance of the discovery that tracking is related to superior performance on a spatial task at 12 months. In this sense our results are consistent with the results of several studies with infants. Both Goldfield and Dickerson (1981) and Bremner (1978) found that 9-month-old infants who visually tracked a target location as they were rotated around a table were more likely to search correctly (i.e., objectively). Visual tracking among the infants in the former study, however, was not very frequent when the two containers on the table were identical. Many of the infants at this age seemed to need a distinctive landmark to "hang on to" as they were moved. Bremner's data hint at another factor which may facilitate tracking in orientation tasks of this type. Successful search by his infants was correlated with both tracking and the elimination of training trials. It seems quite likely that the elimination of the training trials increased tracking. Why might that be? Acredolo (in press) suggests it may simply be that young infants find it easier to rely on well-practiced responses, such as result from training trials, than to make the effort to visually track.

The picture emerging from these two studies in combination with our own is that visual tracking is a crucial contributor to accurate spatial behavior from 9 to at least 13 months. Effective tracking, however, is not automatic. It tends to occur more often with active than with passive movement, with differentiated than with undifferentiated displays, and with less rather than with more experience searching in a particular direction relative to the body. Moreover, it seems unlikely that this list is exhaustive. It could well be, for example, that the infant's motivation to find an object would affect visual tracking. A highly valued object might induce a high degree of tracking even under conditions of passive movement, while a less valued object would not. It is also quite likely that the infant's anxiety level will affect tracking behavior. An infant who is frightened or ill at ease will not be as well able to organize effective attentional strategies. In fact, the results of two studies comparing the effect familiar versus unfamiliar environments have on performance in this type of task (Acredolo, 1979, 1982), provide indirect evidence to support such an hypothesis.

To this point we have focused exclusively on the results from the 12-month testing session, using the pattern we observed as evidence that visual tracking plays a role in infant spatial behavior. Of equal importance to the emerging storyline, however, is the fact that the relationships seen so clearly at 12 months disappeared completely at 18 months, being replaced by almost universal objective responding without the benefit of visual tracking. How can we account for such a dramatic shift? It seems quite likely that the development of mental representation skills (i.e., the symbolic function) plays a large role. In contrast to the 12-month-olds who had to keep their eyes on the target as they changed perspectives, at 18 months the infants were able to mentally represent the simple spatial relations involved in our task and easily predict the consequences of their movement. Such behavior is very reminiscent of some of Piaget's own descriptions of Stage 6 spatial behavior (Piaget, 1954). At 18 months, for example, his daughter Lucienne executed a complicated detour around a room in order to reach him without having to let go of the furniture she felt she needed to support her walking. Piaget's observation that, "The whole journey is made without looking at me" (p. 232), is clearly analogous to our own observations of infant spatial behavior at 18 months. At least under the simple conditions represented by our paradigm, "the whole journey" can be made at this age without even looking at the box. The infants have moved from reliance on direct perception to internal representations which allow the coordination of simple perspectives. It is our belief that this achievement is due at least in part to the mountains of information about spatial relations that visual tracking had provided over the previous months.

Of course, just because our 18-month-olds did not need to rely on tracking to solve our task does not mean that they would not need to do so in order to solve a task involving more complex spatial relations. What we suggest may remain constant across age and complexity is the ordering we observed so clearly within our simple task: purposeful attentional strategies (especially under conditions of active movement) followed by more automatic, internal, spatial problem solving. In fact, this was exactly the pattern found by Poag, Cohen, and Weatherford (1983) in their study of 5- and 7-year-old children required to remember the spatial layout of an entire room. It was only the 5-year-olds for whom self- versus other-directed movement and self- versus other-directed viewing made a difference. At this age, self-directed movement through the room resulted in superior recall regardless of whether the experimenter directed attention to salient features or not. Who controlled visual attention did, however, make a difference for 5-year-olds who were led through the environment by an adult. Among these subjects, self-directed viewing led to less accurate spatial memory than adult-directed viewing. In contrast, the 7-year-old subjects performed comparably across all conditions. This pattern of developmental change is entirely consistent with our own. At the younger age, active movement facilitated spatial knowledge; adult direction of attention was not needed because the children were *already* looking in the right places. In contrast, other-directed movement, like the passive condition of our own study, resulted in poor performance when the younger children's visual behavior was left entirely in their own hands. Only when an adult stepped in and specifically directed their attention as well as their movement, did these "passive" subjects retain adequate knowledge of the space. The older subjects, like our 18-month-olds, showed no such limitations. Thus, just as in every other domain of intellectual development, the nature of the task will in part determine the specific age differences one can expect.

# Notes

1. An interesting exception to this pattern is the fact that two of the three infants in the passive condition who searched correctly did so despite low levels of tracking. Unfortunately it is impossible with such small number to tell whether the behavior of these subjects was due to chance alone or to superior spatial skill. At this point there is no obvious reason to suspect the latter. In fact, one of these two subjects was among the few subjects who did not search correctly at 18 months. Superior ability seems particularly unlikely in this case.

2. Another logical possibility would have been to run the six subjects in a passive condition with the mother maintaining her original position. Such a group could then have been compared to the active group from Experiment 1 who also experienced a stationary mother. Unfortunately, allowing the mother to maintain her position in the passive condition would have made it necessary for someone else to move the infant to the other side of the box. It seemed likely that the sudden intrusion of a stranger in this way could create levels of anxiety high enough to prevent adequate attention to the task. Any egocentric responses that resulted could be due to this anxiety rather than to the passive movement per se. Because of this potential confound, we decided to run the six subjects in an altered version of the active rather than the passive condition.

# References

Acredolo, L. P. (1978). Development of spatial orientation in infancy. *Developmental Psychology*, **14**, 224–234.

Acredolo, L. P. (1979). Laboratory versus home: The effect of environment on the 9-month-old infant's choice of spatial reference system. *Developmental Psychology*, **15**, 666–667.

Acredolo, L. P. (1982). The familiarity factor in spatial research: What does it breed besides contempt? In R. Cohen (Ed.), *Children's perceptions of spatial relations,* (pp. 19–30). San Francisco: Jossey–Bass.

Acredolo, L. P. (in press). Coordinating perspectives on infant spatial orientation. In R. Cohen (Ed.), *The development of spatial cognition.* New York: Erlbaum.

Acredolo, L. P., & Evans, D. (1980). Developmental changes in the effects of landmarks on infant spatial behavior. *Developmental Psychology*, **16**, 312–318.

Appleyard, D. A. (1970). Styles and methods of structuring a city. *Environment and Behavior*, **2**, 100–116.

Benson, J. B., & Uzgiris, I. C. (1981). *The role of self-produced movement in spatial understanding.* Paper presented at the biennial meetings of the Society for Research in Child Development, Boston, MA.

Bremner, J. G. (1978). Egocentric versus allocentric spatial coding in 9-month-old infants: Factors influencing the choice of code. *Developmental Psychology*, **14**, 346–355.

Bremner, J. G. & Bryant, P. E. (1977). Place versus response as the basis of spatial errors made by young infants. *Journal of Experimental Child Psychology*, **23**, 162–171.

Campos, J., Bertenthal, B., & Benson, N. (1980). *Self-produced locomotion and the extraction of form invariance.* Paper presented at the meetings of International Conference on Infant Studies, New Haven, CT.

Campos, J., Svejda, M., Bertenthal, B., Benson, N., & Schmid, D. (1981). *Self-produced locomotion and wariness of heights: New evidence from training studies.* Paper presented at the meetings of the Society for Research in Child Development, Boston, MA.

Campos, J. J., Svejda, M. J., Campos, R. G., & Bertenthal, B. (1982). The emergence of self-produced locomotion: Its importance for psychological development in infancy.

In D. Bricker (Ed.), *Intervention with at-risk and handicapped infants*. Baltimore, MD: Univ. Park Press.

Cohen, R. (1982). The role of activity in the construction of spatial representations. In R. Cohen (Ed.), *Children's conceptions of spatial relations*, (pp. 41–55). San Francisco: Jossey–Bass.

Cornell, E. H., & Heth, C. D. (1979). Response versus place learning by human infants. *Journal of Experimental Psychology: Human Learning and Performance*. **5**, 188–196.

Feldman, A., & Acredolo, L. P. (1979). The effect of active versus passive exploration on memory for spatial location in children. *Child Development*, **50**, 698–704.

Goldfield, E. C., & Dickerson, D. J. (1981). Keeping track of locations during movement of 8- to 10-month-old infants. *Journal of Experimental Child Psychology*, **32**, 48–64.

Piaget, J. (1954). *The construction of reality in the child*. New York: Basic Books.

Poag, C. K., Cohen, R., & Weatherford, D. L. (1983). Spatial representations of young children: The role of self- versus adult-directed movement and viewing. *Journal of Experimental Child Psychology*, **35**, 172–179.

Presson, C. C., & Ihrig, L. H. (1983). Using mother as a spatial landmark: Evidence against egocentric coding in infancy. *Developmental Psychology*, **18**, 699–704.

Rieser, J. (1979). Spatial orientation of six-month-old infants. *Child Development*, **50**, 1078–1087.

Ruff, H. (1978). Infants' recognition of the invariant forms of objects. *Child Development*, **49**, 293–306.

# 42

# The Development of Relational Landmark Use in Six- to Twelve-Month-Old Infants in a Spatial Orientation Task

*Adina R. Lew, J. Gavin Bremner and Leonard P. Lefkovitch*

## Introduction

The ability to represent the location of an unseen target in relation to stable landmarks in the environment allows most adult mammals, including ourselves, to carry out a variety of spatial tasks. These include locating a goal from unique starting positions and novel route planning (Poucet, 1993). Such coding of spatial relations is normally referred to as allocentric spatial coding. If a strictly functional definition of allocentric spatial coding is used, then the number of landmarks necessary to code the location of a goal unambiguously depends on the situation. Generally, three distinct landmarks are necessary to locate a target on a two-dimensional plane (Pick, Montello, & Somerville, 1988), but if the position of the landmark is contiguous with the goal only one landmark is necessary. Such a landmark is commonly referred to either as a proximal cue (Rudy, Stadler-Morris, & Albert, 1987) or a beacon (e.g., Whishaw & Dunnett, 1985). Because the representational and computational implications of using two or more landmarks in a relational way are different from those involved in using a beacon, the term *allocentric coding* is here reserved for the situation in which two or more landmarks are needed to locate a goal, and the term *beaconing* is used to denote the case of orienting to a single landmark.

**Source:** *Child Development*, 71(5) (2000): 1179–1190.

The development of allocentric coding abilities in large-scale environments is the focus of the studies reported here. Unlike the paradigms used in the animal literature (Morris, 1981), no task has yet been developed for use with infants that can be solved *only* by using allocentric coding strategies. Instead, studies compare performance in an environment in which no distinctive landmarks are available so that a solution requires keeping track of one's own movements (referred to as egocentric spatial coding), with performance in which distinctive landmarks are present. Any improvements in performance with the indirect landmarks is attributed to their use. Acredolo and Evans (1980) made such a comparison by using a paradigm developed by Acredolo (1978). Infants learned to anticipate, after an auditory cue, the appearance of an adult playing peekaboo in one of two windows on either side of a square room and infants were then moved to the other side of the room (a rotation of 180° as well as a change of position in the room). After the auditory cue on test trials, their direction of looking was measured, this being taken as an index of where they expected the adult to appear. The two conditions of relevance to the present question were one in which the room contained no visual features apart from the windows and another in which the wall containing the nontarget window was marked by orange stripes with flashing lights surrounding the window itself. So as to be helped by the landmarks in the second condition, infants could code the position of the target window as being on the opposite side of the landmarked window. Eleven-month-old infants, but not 6- or 9-month-olds, performed significantly better in the indirect landmark condition, although a majority of 11-month-olds still looked to the incorrect, landmarked, window (but see Bushnell, McKenzie, Lawrence, & Connell, 1995, for failure by 12-month-old infants to use landmarks allocentrically in a search task). In a further beacon condition (in which the target window had the lights and stripes), 9-month-olds showed significant improvements in performance. Nine-month-olds were unable to benefit from a less salient beacon, however: a star shape forming a frame around the target window. In a separate study, Keating, McKenzie, and Day (1986) found that 8-month-old infants benefited from a beacon, comparable in salience with the "star" beacon of Acredolo and Evans (1980), relative to control conditions in both square and circular testing environments. Infants were rotated to different directions of facing from the center of the rooms, rather than the more complex rotation and translation movements of Acredolo and Evans (1980). Rieser (1979) found that even 6-month-olds benefited from a beacon in a task involving rotational movements only.

On the basis of this developmental timetable, Acredolo (1990) speculated that independent locomotion through crawling (which has an average onset age of 8.5 months) may be a critical factor in the development of allocentric spatial coding abilities, with ability to use beacons appearing early after crawling onset and relational use of landmarks a few months later. Bremner and Bryant (1985) have suggested that the earlier age of successful performance found in studies in which infants underwent simple rotation, as opposed to rotation together with translation, could be due to the achievement of the developmental milestone of sitting up unaided. This allows infants from about 6 months of age onward to explore actively the perceptual consequences of their own head rotations.

The suggestion in the Acredolo (1990) study is that independent locomotion leads to many problem-solving situations in which goals have to be located from novel positions. Acredolo also argued that infants pay a greater degree of attention to the perceptual changes occurring during transitions between spatial locations in active as compared with passive motion. Independent locomotion thus creates situations for infants to observe and learn how changes in landmark arrays are related to their own changes of position in the environment. The evidence for this view is equivocal, however, with some studies finding a link between locomotion onset and spatial or object search performance (Bai & Bertenthal, 1992; Bertenthal, Campos, & Barrett, 1984; Kermoian & Campos, 1988) and others not (McComas & Field, 1984; Roberts, Bell, & Pope, 1998). Bai and Bertenthal (1992) argue that degree of visual attention during task performance should be treated as independent from locomotor abilities because they found that both these factors contributed independently (and modestly) to successful object search performance. It is interesting to note that Nadel (1990; Nadel, Wilson, & Kurz, 1993) found that rat pups developed the ability to use beacons before the ability to use indirect landmarks relationally to locate a hidden escape platform in a tank of opaque liquid (Morris, 1981). Both these achievements occurred considerably later than independent locomotion (at 2–3 weeks of age as opposed to locomotion onset occurring a few days after birth), and were related to onset of exploratory behaviors and hippocampal maturation. In human infants, exploratory behaviors would be expressed in terms of visual scanning and attention, as opposed to rodent exploratory behaviors such as the visiting and sniffing of interesting locations.

Another potential problem with the role ascribed to locomotion onset by Acredolo (1990) is that some aspects of the procedures used in the original experimental paradigm might have led to an underestimation of the spatial coding abilities of younger, prelocomotor infants. In the early studies (Acredolo, 1978; Acredolo & Evans, 1980; Rieser, 1979), errors were not random (roughly equal to left and right directions) but consisted in a repetition of the previously rewarded and rehearsed response carried out during training trials. These effects are similar to the response perseveration effects seen in object search tasks and are particularly strong during the first year of life, during which Diamond (1990) argues that there is immaturity of the dorsolateral prefrontal cortex, responsible for inhibiting prepotent or previously reinforced responses. It is important to avoid confusion between response perseveration and egocentric spatial coding. Although Piaget (1936/1955) used the term and concept of egocentrism to explain *failure* to update the position of a target relative to self after movement of either self or target, in the wider spatial cognition literature, egocentric spatial coding now refers to *successful* updating of self movements in the absence of distinctive landmarks in the environment. Systematic errors in favor of initially successful responses are perhaps more parsimoniously accounted for by perseveration effects rather than an idiosyncratic spatial coding scheme particular to a stage of human infancy (e.g., egocentrism). The failure to inhibit a previously rewarded response not only leads to systematic errors when infants have not coded and remembered the target location but could also be masking knowledge of the target location. Two aspects of the original peekaboo paradigm might have acted to reinforce response perseveration tendencies. The first of these is that infants were trained only to anticipate the appearance of the adult from one position and orientation before being moved into the test location, which required a directionally opposite response to that made in training. Keating, McKenzie, and Day (1986) developed a training procedure whereby infants experienced peekaboo when the target location was both to the infant's left and right, before being tested in a new orientation relative to target (new in terms of angular extent rather than left or right direction). Although performance was high at 8.5 months when a beacon was present during this multilocational training procedure, it is not possible to tell whether this high level of performance was due to multilocational training or the fact that infants were only rotated in the center of the enclosure, as opposed to the rotation and translation movements in Acredolo (1978) and Acredolo and Evans (1980).

A second feature of the original paradigm that may have generated response perseveration in younger infants was the use of instrumental as opposed to associative training procedures. In the instrumental training regime of Acredolo and Evans (1980; also Acredolo, 1978), there is a 3–4 s interval between the auditory cue and the appearance of the adult on training trials. Infants have to reach a criterion of anticipatory looking within that interval before being moved on to a new training position or a test position (the average number of trials to reach a criterion of four consecutive anticipations is approximately 10). Tyler and McKenzie (1990) found that when they used associative rather than instrumental training procedures, even 6-month-olds were reasonably successful at turning to a target location following rotational movements from the center of a featureless cylindrical room. This associative training regime consisted of six training trials in which the experimenter appeared immediately after a cue, followed by test trials in which no peekaboo followed after the cue. The occurrence of peekaboo is entirely determined by the cue rather than any response on the infant's part. Despite this, infants still turn to look for the experimenter on test trials after the cue, a fact that can be used to assess their knowledge of the target location. Tyler and McKenzie (1990) also trained infants from more than one direction of facing prior to the test position, thus allowing infants to learn that the peekaboo event always occurred at the same place in the environment, whatever their viewing position.

Given the large effect of associative as opposed to instrumental training procedures in studies of egocentric spatial coding (Tyler & McKenzie, 1990), it seems necessary to apply these methodological changes to the question of infants' allocentric spatial coding abilities, particularly following complex movement involving both rotation and translation. If relational use of landmarks after complex movements can be demonstrated in infants who are not yet able to crawl by using procedures that minimize response perseveration, then factors other than independent locomotion are required to explain the development of allocentric spatial coding abilities.

The first study reported here uses a variant of the Acredolo (1978) paradigm to investigate allocentric coding abilities in 6- to 12-month-old infants, a younger age range than the 11- to 16-month-olds able to demonstrate allocentric coding in Acredolo and Evans (1980). A cylindrical curtained enclosure is used, divided at equal intervals by eight slits where an adult could potentially appear playing peekaboo. In one condition, four unpainted identical lanterns are positioned alongside alternate slits. In another, the lanterns on the two slits on either side of the target slit, where the adult appears playing peekaboo after an auditory cue on training trials, are replaced by distinctively painted lanterns. Infants are moved by their parents to different training and test positions on the perimeter of the enclosure. Success in turning to the target location from a novel starting position in the first condition can be achieved only by keeping track of one's own movements between training and test trials, whereas in the second condition the painted lanterns could be used as landmarks to locate the target. An important difference between this study and Acredolo (1978) is that an associative rather than an instrumental training regime is used. A further change from earlier studies is that training is from two different locations before the third, test location, with one of the training locations being to the left or right of the target and the other directly ahead of the target. The test position is then to whichever side was not used in training (e.g. the infant has to look left to locate the target on test trials if in one of the training positions the infant had to look right to the target). This method combines the advantage of the Acredolo (1978) paradigm of ensuring that the *direction* in which the infant has to look in test trials is *completely novel* with the benefit of multilocational training as advocated by McKenzie and her colleagues.

## Study 1

### Method

*Sample.* Parent and infant volunteers were recruited through advertisements in the local press and leaflets handed out by health visitors. Volunteers were initially told that the study involved babies' understanding of the space around them. A full debriefing occurred once the study was over. To be included in the final data set, infants had to be born within 37–43 weeks gestational age and had to change their direction of looking within 2 s of the end of the auditory signal on at least one of two test trials. There were three age groups of 6-, 8.5- and 12-month-olds. At each age, 32 infants took part, being assigned either to the Distinctive Landmarks condition or to the No Distinctive Landmarks condition. In the 6-month Distinctive Landmarks group there were 8 males and 8 females ($M$ = 24 weeks, 2 days; $SD$ = 5 days) and in the 6-month No Distinctive Landmarks condition there were 9 males and 7 females ($M$ = 24 weeks, 2 days; $SD$ = 4 days). In the 8.5-month Distinctive Landmark group there were 11 male and 5 female infants ($M$ = 36 weeks, 1 day; $SD$ = 1 week) and in the 8.5-month No Distinctive Landmarks group 10 male and 6 female infants ($M$ = 36 weeks, 1 day; $SD$ = 4 days). There were 10 male and 6 female infants in the 12-month Distinctive Landmarks condition ($M$ = 51 weeks, 3 days; $SD$ = 5 days) and 7 male and 9 female infants in the 12-month No Distinctive Landmarks condition ($M$ = 51 weeks, 5 days; $SD$ = 4 days). The ranges were 24 weeks ± 2 weeks, 36 weeks ± 2 weeks, and 52 weeks ± 2 weeks for the 6-, 8.5- and 12-month-olds, respectively. An additional six 6-month-olds were tested but did not change their direction of looking in either test trial. One 6-month-old became upset before completion of testing and one 6-month-old recording was lost due to experimenter error. Two additional 8.5-month-olds were excluded for not changing direction of look on either test trial, and the recordings of two 8.5-month-olds were lost because of experimenter error. A further three 12-month-olds were tested but were excluded from the final sample because of upset in one case and failure to change direction of looking on both test trials in the other two instances. All infants were White.

*Apparatus.* A cylindrical enclosure made of 100% cotton (fire retardant) curtain fabric was constructed of 2.30 m diameter and height 2.00 m. The perimeter walls of the enclosure were subdivided into eight equal sections with slits starting at a height of 0.25 m and finishing at 1.75 m. These were generally closed through having sprung-wire sown into the hems on either side but could be opened by the experimenter playing peekaboo. One of the slits could be fully opened to form an entrance flap. The ceiling of the enclosure was wooden and painted a uniform cream color with a circular light source at the center (a 28-W circular fluorescent tube). The floor was covered with a uniform gray carpet. Five centimeters to the right side of each slit, at a height of 1.25 m, eight 2-cm diameter camera holes were placed. A metal frame structure outside the enclosure supported the cameras in position. Those camera holes that were not covered by a camera lens were covered in "fake lenses" made of glass backed by black tape. In the No Distinctive Landmarks control condition, four identical beehive-shaped paper lanterns (length, 45.5 cm, maximal diameter, 27 cm) were hung on thin wire within the perimeter of the enclosure so that the top of each lantern was 25 cm below ceiling height.

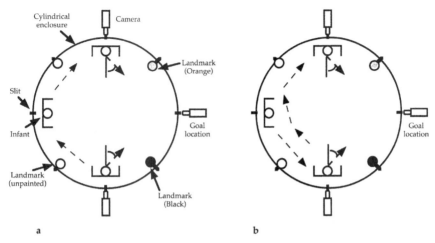

**Figure 1:** Experimental layout for the Distinctive Landmarks condition. (*a*) depicts a sequence of training trials at the six o'clock then nine o'clock positions followed by test trials at the twelve o'clock position. In (*b*) the order of the two training positions is reversed.

The lanterns were at an equal distance from each other, overlapping alternate slits in the curtained enclosure. In the Distinctive Landmarks condition two of the lanterns were replaced by identically shaped, painted lanterns, one Day-Glo orange and the other glossy black (see Figure 1). An infant car seat in an upright position was mounted onto a wheeled trolley for ease of movement between different positions within the enclosure (the height of infants' eye level was approximately 75 cm from the floor).

The video signals from the three color cameras were channeled through a quad unit for simultaneous recording. A video recorder with a built-in time code generator sensitive to one frame (25 frames/s) was used to record sessions. This contained a jog-shuttle facility for frame-by-frame and slow-motion viewing during analysis. A TV monitor was visible during recording so that the infants' direction of looking within the enclosure during testing could be monitored. Finally, a sound source emitting a signal of 250 Hz, 0.68-s duration, and 3-V peak-to-peak amplitude was placed on the outside of the ceiling of the enclosure at the center of the circular roof. This could be remotely controlled during testing by the experimenter.

*Design and procedure.* We used an independent samples design involving three age groups (6, 8.5 and 12 months) observed in two conditions, the No Distinctive Landmarks condition and the Distinctive Landmarks condition, yielding six experimental groups. Each infant had four training trials from two different positions in the enclosure (a block of two in each position), followed by two test trials from a novel position. During training, an adult appeared immediately after an auditory cue, playing peekaboo at the same target location each time. During test trials, the adult did not appear after the auditory signal. Figure 1 shows two possible sequences of training and test trials in the Distinctive Landmarks condition. In Figure 1a, the infant starts at the six o'clock position on the perimeter of the enclosure, having to look 45° to the right toward the goal. After two such trials, the infant is moved to the 9 o'clock position directly opposite the goal for a further two training trials. Finally, the infant is moved to the 12 o'clock position, in which a correct look to the goal would involve a look 45° to the left after the auditory cue. In Figure 1b, the "look ahead" training trials occur before the "look right" trials. A further two sequences of training and test positions were used in which the test position was to the right of the infant, i.e., the reverse of the sequences shown in Figure 1. The position directly opposite the goal was used only as a training position. The four possible sequences of training and test trials were counterbalanced within each age group and condition such that there were four infants in each of the six groups assigned to each sequence. The use of a position opposite the target location in training meant that two positions could be used during training (allowing the infant to learn that the experimenter appears at a particular *place*) and the test position could involve a completely novel direction of target location relative to the infant.

The parent and infant were introduced into the cylindrical enclosure by the experimenter. All three sat on the floor and the infant played with some toys while the experimenter explained to the parent the sequence of positions that should be followed during the experiment. This familiarization period lasted about 5 min. The experimenter then withdrew so that only the infant in an infant seat mounted on a trolley, with the parent standing behind, remained in the room. Parents were requested to give the infant two slow turns round the room in the trolley-mounted seat before coming to their first training position. This was carried out to disorient the infant relative to the enclosure entrance because infants had the opportunity of seeing the experimenter exiting from the entrance flap.

The experimenter controlled the onset time of the auditory cue. An intertrial interval of approximately 4–10 s was used (between the end of peekaboo and the cue for the next trial). This range allowed the experimenter to activate the auditory cue when the infant was looking away from the target location. If, however, during training trials an infant was still looking at the goal position after 10 s, the cue would be activated. A monitor outside the enclosure was used to check the infant's gaze. On training trials, the experimenter appeared immediately after the cue through the slit in the enclosure at the goal location, playing peekaboo for approximately 10 s. In practice, it was found subsequent to analysis that on a few occasions, some infants were already looking toward the target location just before the auditory cue during one of their test trials. There were five such trials (from three 12-month-olds and two 6-month-olds), all of which were excluded from the final data set.

Parents were asked not to initiate interactions with the infant, although they could give reassuring smiles if the infant looked up toward them. They were also asked to look down at the top of the infant's head, rather than up toward the target location, after the auditory cue.

*Measures.* The main dependent variable was the location of the infant's first look after the initiation of the auditory cue during test trials. A time window of 2 s after the end of the auditory cue was allowed for the infant to change direction of looking. If an infant failed to do so on one of the two test trials, this was scored as No Response. Failure to change direction of looking on both test trials resulted in exclusion from the sample. Locations were classified into five categories: Target; Undershoot; Opposite Direction; Ahead; and Other. Looks in the direction of the target could be reasonably accurate (approximately $45° ± 10°$) or they could undershoot the target. Undershoots ranged from eye movements only in the target direction in which the head remained forward to head and eye movements in the target direction (relative to the forward position) of about $20°–30°$. There were no overshoots. Looks of any magnitude that terminated in the half of the room opposite to the target direction (with the infant's ahead direction as a reference point) were classified as Opposite Direction. Finally, looks that ended straight ahead were classified as Ahead. The Other category included looks to the floor, ceiling, or up to the parent.

The latency (within the 2-s-plus duration of auditory cue time window) to make a first look was measured by subtracting the time of initiation of the auditory cue from the time of occurrence of the first frame at which movement to a new location could be detected. A measure of time spent looking at the target (within the above time window) allowed looks toward the target location to be taken into account even when the first look might not have been toward the target. The location of look before the auditory cue on test trials was measured in case this differed between experimental groups. Four categories were used: Opposite (i.e., opposite side to target); Ahead; Down at Hands; and Other (i.e., floor, ceiling or up to parent). Opposite and Ahead were the most frequent locations of prior look (44% Opposite, 40% Ahead). It should be remembered that the experimenter was waiting to activate the cue at the time when the infant was clearly not already looking to target within the intertrial interval, so it is to be expected that Opposite and Ahead positions should predominate. Prior look was analyzed as a dependent variable in preliminary analyses reported in Results sections below.

An interobserver agreement check was carried out by using 40% (102 test trials) of the data set from both Studies 1 and 2. The test trials were randomly selected within the constraints of having roughly equal numbers of each of the five response categories (No Response and Other were collapsed into one category, because there were only five trials classified as Other in the full data set) and of Trial 1 and Trial 2 data included in the analysis. The second scorer was naive to the aims of the study, and it was not possible to tell from the video records of the infant which experimental condition was being run. Cohen's κ for agreement on the full set of response categories for location of first look was .79. When the categories were collapsed into those to Target versus all the rest (Undershoot plus Ahead plus Opposite plus No Response), as is done for the statistical analyses reported, Cohen's κ was .73. The mean difference between observers for the latency of response measure was .00 s, $SD = 0.21$ s (five frames). Only those trials (out of the total of 102) in which both observers had scored a response were used for this analysis of latency differences.

## Results

Table 1 shows the number of first looks to each location category for each age and condition. The five trials in which an infant was already looking in the target direction (see procedure) and the three responses classified as other (see measures) have been added into the No Response category. The principal analysis carried out on these data was a three-way frequency analysis used to develop a logit model of the relation between Trial (test trial 1, test trial 2), Age (6, 8.5, and 12 months) and Landmark type (Distinctive Landmarks, No Distinctive Landmarks). The dependent variable of location of first look was used. Looks were either classified as correct if they were to Target or incorrect if they were an Undershoot, Ahead, Opposite Direction, or Other. No Responses (including already looking to target trials but excluding Other responses) were treated as missing data.

A hierarchical model-building approach was applied to data analyses in all the studies reported, performed by using Genstat 5 (release 3.2). For the main

**Table 1:** Frequency of types of first look in Study 1 for each age and condition (number of looks to target at any time within 2 s of the auditory cue are shown in parentheses)

| Group | Target | Undershoot | Ahead | Opposite | No response |
|---|---|---|---|---|---|
| First test trial | | | | | |
| 6 months | | | | | |
| DL | 2 (3) | 2 | 2 | 4 | 6 |
| NDL | 2 (2) | 1 | 4 | 5 | 4 |
| 8.5 months | | | | | |
| DL | 5 (7) | 4 | 0 | 3 | 4 |
| NDL | 1 (3) | 2 | 4 | 6 | 3 |
| 12 months | | | | | |
| DL | 11 (12) | 2 | 0 | 1 | 2 |
| NDL | 9 (10) | 2 | 3 | 1 | 1 |
| Second test trial | | | | | |
| 6 months | | | | | |
| DL | 0 (0) | 2 | 1 | 8 | 5 |
| NDL | 2 (2) | 0 | 5 | 6 | 3 |
| 8.5 months | | | | | |
| DL | 4 (5) | 3 | 3 | 4 | 2 |
| NDL | 0 (1) | 1 | 4 | 7 | 4 |
| 12 months | | | | | |
| DL | 8 (10) | 1 | 2 | 2 | 3 |
| NDL | 6 (6) | 3 | 2 | 1 | 4 |

*Note:* DL = Distinctive Landmarks condition; NDL = No Distinctive Landmarks condition.

analyses, a binomial distribution of data was assumed and a logit link function was used. For preliminary analyses on infants' direction of prior look as the dependent variable, a Poisson distribution with a logarithmic link function was used. This method of analysis was used because there were four possible categories for direction of Prior look, which led to a multinomial situation. Tests of significance were based on log-likelihood ratios and referred to the $\chi^2$ distribution (two tailed).

A preliminary analysis was conducted to verify that there were no systematic differences between groups on where infants were looking before the auditory cue. Prior look was the dependent variable, and Trial, Age, and Landmark were the factors in the analysis. No significant effects were found, which showed that there were no systematic differences between groups on where infants were looking before the buzzer. An initial model was constructed to analyze the dependent variable of looks to Target. This model included Trial, Sex, Landmark, and Position Sequence as factors. No significant effects due to Sex and Position sequence were found, so these factors were excluded from the main analyses.

Table 2 shows the results of the analysis of Looks to Target. The first factor included in the model was the main effect of Trial. Including Trial first was considered the most conservative approach because the main focus of interest were the factors of Age and Landmark and their interaction, so removing any effects due to Trial before considering these factors was preferred. There was a marginally significant main effect of Trial. Because there were no significant two- or three-way interaction effects involving Trial, the main effect can best be interpreted as one in which there were overall more correct responses to target in Test Trial 1 relative to Test Trial 2. Significantly more explanatory power was added to the model from the addition of the main effects of Age, Landmark, and their interaction. Post hoc tests showed that this interaction effect was mainly due to the 8.5-month age group, which was significantly better with the distinctive landmarks than without, although marginally so, given how few infants looked to target at this age (4% looks to Target out of all responses made in test trials 1 and 2 in the control condition and 35% correct looks in the distinctive landmarks condition; Test Trial 1, Fisher's exact test, $p < .07$; Test trial 2, Fisher's exact test, $p < .1$). The 6-month-olds were near

**Table 2:** Effects and significance tests for looks to target in Study 1

| Dependent variable | Effect name | df | $\chi^2$ | p |
|---|---|---|---|---|
| Looks to target | Trial | 1 | 3.0 | .09 |
| | Age | 2 | 33.9 | .0001 |
| | Landmark | 1 | 5.3 | .03 |
| | Trial × Age | 2 | .07 | ns |
| | Trial × Landmark | 1 | .2 | ns |
| | Age × Landmark | 2 | 6.7 | .04 |
| | Trial × Age × Landmark | 2 | 2.8 | ns |
| | Infant | 90 | 125.6 | .01 |
| | Residual | 52 | 16.6 | ns |

floor performance both with and without distinctive landmarks (16% correct in the control condition, 9.5% correct in the distinctive landmarks condition), and the 12-month-olds were performing at a high level in both conditions, although better with the distinctive landmarks (56% correct in control condition, 70% correct in the distinctive landmarks condition). There were no significant differences across landmark condition within the 6- or 12-month age groups. The Infant factor was significant, which suggests consistency of response across test trials within individual infants. As can be seen from Table 1, the data for looks to target when any look was included (within the 2-s time window after the end of the auditory cue) were very similar to the data for first look only, so this measure was not analyzed further.

It is possible that the older infants may be faster on average than younger infants so that a conservative time window of 2 s might not be appropriate for the latter. The latency to make a first look was analyzed by using a 3 × 2 × 2 ANOVA, with Age and Condition as between-subjects factors and Test Trial as a repeated measures factor. Although there were no significant differences between groups, with means ranging from 0.6s ($SD = 0.5$ s) to 1.3 s ($SD = 0.8$ s), there was a greater number of subject exclusions for the 6-month-olds (six infants) than the 8.5- or 12-month-olds (two infants at each age) because of failure to change direction of looking within 2 s on both test trials. A reexamination of the excluded 6-month-olds by using a 4-s response window showed that none of these infants changed his or her direction of looking within that time. Four of the infants were playing with their hands or looking up to mother and the remaining two continued to fixate the part of the room directly opposite to the actual target location in both test trials. These findings rule out the difference between the conservative time window used here and the looser one used in the earlier literature (4–5 s) as an explanation for the poor performance of 6-month-olds in the present study.

Although the analysis of looks to Target demonstrates a significant difference between landmarked and control conditions at 8.5 months of age, performance was still low when the landmarks were present (35% correct looks out of all responses made at 8.5 months in Test Trials 1 and 2). If a laxer criterion of correct responding is adopted whereby looks in the right direction (Target and Undershoot) are contrasted with directionally incorrect looks (Ahead and Opposite), then the difference between conditions at 8.5 months becomes 61.5% directionally correct looks in the distinctive landmarks condition versus 16% correct in the control condition. At 6 months of age there is little difference between conditions on this directionally correct measure (29% correct in the distinctive landmarks condition versus 20% correct in the control condition). At 12 months, there is a high level of performance in both experimental and control conditions as measured by looks in the correct direction (81% and 80% respectively). This qualitative analysis of directionally correct looks thus supports the pattern of results obtained by using the more conservative criterion of correct looks (looks to Target versus the rest).

*Analysis of errors.* If a directional error is made it is either a look ahead or a look in the direction opposite to target (this excludes looks classified as Other). These Ahead and Opposite looks could be repetitions of a look to the location experienced in the training trials immediately preceding the test trials, or they could be repetitions of the look to the location experienced in the first pair of training trials. The errors were fairly evenly divided between these two possibilities. Out of a total number of directional errors of 81 (collapsing across trials, ages, and conditions), 39.5% were repetitions of the responses made in the first training block and 55.5% were repetitions of the training block immediately preceding test trials (the three responses classified as Other account for the remaining errors). Taking only errors in which first looks were on the side opposite to target, out of a total of 48 such errors, 37.5% were repetitions of the first training block and 62.5% were repetitions of the training block before test trials. This pattern suggests that both of the previously successful responses could have a facilitating effect on test responses. The possible methodological implications of this finding will be considered below.

## Discussion

The findings from Study 1 suggest a two-step developmental progression. The first step, occurring between 6 and 8.5 months, involves the beginning of the ability to use landmarks to remain oriented after complex displacement (rotation and translation) within the environment. The second step, occurring between 8.5 and 12 months, involves being able to remain oriented after these complex displacements even without the aid of distinctive landmarks. Considering the latter achievement first, this indicates a considerably later development than that for rotational movements only, in which even 6-month-old infants seem proficient (Bremner & Hatton, 1996; Tyler & McKenzie, 1990. Both these authors obtained roughly 60% looks to target at 6 months). Caution is required in attributing all of this difference in performance to the type of displacement involved because of an important procedural difference between the present study and previous work. In the earlier studies, infants experienced the target to both their left and their right during training (although the actual degree of rotation away from the target in the test trial was novel). In the present study, because the "ahead of the infant" position for the goal was used in training, the *direction* of the goal relative to the infant in test trials was completely novel. Although care was taken in the earlier work that the training position immediately before test should not be in the same direction relative to target as the test trial, the pattern of errors found in Study 1 suggests that *any* prior experience of the target at a particular direction facilitates a movement in that direction during test trials. The accuracy of performance in the earlier studies (Bremner & Hatton, 1996; Tyler & McKenzie, 1990) was such that the findings are not fully explainable by this facilitation effect, but preliminary work (Woodcock, 1997) suggests that 6-month-olds are not so successful in locating a target after rotations when the test trial involves a completely novel *direction* of facing relative to the goal. More work is needed to disentangle the effects of training procedures from those due to the types of displacements involved in orientation tasks. The implications of the differences between Study 1 and studies using simpler displacements, and possibly more facilitating training regimes, for the question of the earliest age at which landmark use can be demonstrated in infants will be considered in the General Discussion.

The second major finding of Study 1, that of the beginnings of proficiency in use of indirect landmarks at 8.5 months, indicates an earlier age by several months for this capacity relative to previous work (Acredolo & Evans, 1980). Some doubt remains, however, as to how the landmarks were being used by the 8.5-month-olds. It is possible that the successful infants of Study 1 were solving the task in the distinctive landmarks condition by defining the target as being "to the right/left of" the orange or black lantern. This complex strategy involves coordinating a single landmark together with an egocentric code (e.g., to the left/right of landmark), rather than defining the target as being between the two colored lanterns. To address this possibility, two further experimental conditions with 8.5-month-olds were added in Study 2. These involved one group experiencing the orange landmark only, with the black landmark being substituted by an unpainted lantern (see Figure 1) and the other having the black landmark only, with the orange substituted by the nondistinctive landmark. If infants are able to use a combined beacon plus egocentric code strategy to locate the target (e.g., the target is to the right of the orange lantern), performance in Study 2 may be similar to the distinctive landmarks condition of Study 1. If infants are unable to use such a strategy, performance may be intermediate between the control condition of Study 1 (all landmarks the same), and the distinctive landmarks condition of Study 1. This is because a single landmark can indicate a region in the room where the target is (e.g., on one side or the other near to the landmark), thus being more helpful to infants in comparison with the control condition, although not being as helpful as both distinctive landmarks.

## Study 2

### Method

*Sample.* Volunteer recruitment and inclusion criteria were the same as for Study 1. There were sixteen 8.5-month-old infants in each of two conditions, the Orange landmark only condition ($M$ = 36 weeks, 1 day; $SD$ = 5 days;

10 males and 6 females), and the Black landmark only condition ($M$ = 36 weeks, $SD$ = 6 days; 12 males and 4 females). The range was within 34–38 weeks for both groups. All infants were White. A further three infants were tested, two of whom failed to change their direction of look within 2 s on both test trials and one of whom became upset during the procedure.

*Apparatus, design, and procedure.* Infants were tested by using the same enclosure and procedures as those used in Study 1, except that a single distinctive landmark was used. For one group ($N$ = 16), the black lantern shown in Figure 1 was replaced by an unpainted lantern (the Orange-Only group). In the other group ($N$ = 16), the orange lantern was replaced by an unpainted lantern (the Black-Only group).

## Results and Discussion

Preliminary logit analyses found no significant differences between experimental groups for Prior look. Initial models including the dependent variable of Looks to Target and Trial, Sex, Landmark, and Position Sequence as factors found no significant effects due to Sex and Position Sequence, so these factors were eliminated from further analyses. Table 3 shows the number of first looks to each location category, both for Orange-Only and Black-Only landmark conditions. As can be seen from Table 3, the proportion of looks to Target out of all responses in Test Trials 1 and 2 in the Orange-Only condition was 12% and in the Black-Only condition was 19%. This is greater than the control condition of Study 1 (4%) but less than the distinctive landmarks condition of Study 1 (35%). If directionally correct responses are considered (Target plus Undershoot), the proportion of such responses in the Orange-Only condition was 36% and in the Black-Only condition was 35% – again, intermediate between control and distinctive landmarks condition for 8.5 months in Study 1 (16% control; 61.5% distinctive landmarks).

To determine if frequency of looks to Target with a single landmark was intermediate between control and both landmarks conditions for the 8.5-month-olds of Study 1, the following logit model-building approach

**Table 3:** Frequency of types of first look in Study 2 for the single landmark conditions

| Group | Target | Undershoot | Ahead | Opposite | No response |
|---|---|---|---|---|---|
| First test trial | | | | | |
|     Black-only | 3 | 3 | 1 | 7 | 2 |
|     Orange-only | 3 | 3 | 1 | 4 | 5 |
| Second test trial | | | | | |
|     Black-only | 2 | 1 | 2 | 6 | 6[a] |
|     Orange-only | 0 | 3 | 5 | 5 | 3[b] |

[a] Includes 1 response classified as Other and one trial in which the infant was already looking to target.
[b] Includes 1 response classified as Other.

was applied to the Study 2 data and the relevant conditions of Study 1. The main effect of Trial was added to the model first, followed by a numerical factor labeled Landmark (Linear), in which the landmarks were treated as a quantitative variable with three levels, namely, the number of landmarks (0, 1, and 2). These three levels, in ascending order, were the No Distinctive Landmarks control condition from Study 1, both Single Landmark conditions (Orange-Only and Black-Only) from Study 2, and finally the Two Distinctive Landmarks condition from Study 1 (a linear regression was performed to fit a line to the four points provided by the four conditions). A Landmark (separate regressions) numerical factor in which two regressions were carried out, one for the black landmark and the other for the orange, was then included. This factor allowed the two regression lines to have different slopes. Finally, a further nominal Landmark factor that accounts for the remaining one degree of freedom was fitted. This factor should be significant only if the Black and Orange single landmark conditions differed from each other independently of the control and two-landmark conditions.

There was no significant main effect of Trial. The only significant Landmark effect was the Linearly Ordered Landmark factor, $\chi^2(1, N = 64) = 5.9, p < .008$. Neither of the two other Landmark factors added significant explanatory power to the model. There were no significant Trial by Landmark interaction effects or significant Infant and Residual effects. Thus, the hypothesis that performance on single landmark conditions (whatever the color of the single landmark) should be intermediate between control and two-landmarks conditions is confirmed. This result suggests that the 8.5-month-olds in Study 1 were probably using both the landmarks to locate the goal.

## General Discussion

The aim of the present series of studies was to establish the youngest age at which relational use of landmarks could be demonstrated in infants. This achievement was in evidence by 8.5 months of age, although only at 12 months were the majority of responses correct. The findings of Tyler and McKenzie (1990) of prelocomotor (6-month) competence in spatial performance have not been obtained in the present research, which leaves open the possibility that crawling onset has some influence on the development of allocentric spatial coding abilities. Further longitudinal studies charting the relation between locomotion onset and success on spatial cognition tasks would be required to investigate whether there is a link between the two behaviors. Other factors should also be considered, however. As with other mammalian species, it is possible that patterns of exploration, in particular visual exploration of the environment, is a critical variable in the development of allocentric spatial coding. Exploration of the environment can be considered as a behavioral index of the development of areas of the brain particularly related to spatial processing (e.g., the hippocampus and areas of parietal cortex; Rolls & Treves, 1998).

The question remains as to whether 8.5 months is in fact the youngest age at which relational use of landmarks occurs. Within the literature reporting a variant of the peekaboo paradigm, two factors emerge that may reveal a 6-month-old competence not found in the studies reported here. The first is the visual saliency of the landmarks (Acredolo & Evans, 1980, used the "hypersalient" landmark of flashing lights and stripes), and the second is the complexity of the movement involved during changes of position in the task. It is possible that rotations together with translations make the task too complicated for 6-month-olds, whatever landmarks are provided in the environment (Bremner & Bryant, 1985). With simpler movements, such as those involving rotation only, it may be possible to detect differential performance between landmark and control conditions (Rieser, 1979). Studies that both manipulate the saliency of the landmarks used and involve rotational movements only need to be carried out with 6-month-olds to examine these possibilities. However, it should be noted that the factors of landmark salience and complexity of movement have been found to influence only beacon use in earlier studies, with negative findings relating to indirect landmark use.

It is also important to take into account how a particular training regime may influence performance during test trials. Response perseveration within the context of object search tasks has been viewed in terms of the difficulties younger infants have in inhibiting a previously successful or learned response in favor of a novel response (Diamond, 1990). The other side of this process is that previously learned responses facilitate the repetition of those responses. In the context of the peekaboo paradigm, if the training regime involves viewing the target location from both left and right directions relative to the target (Tyler & McKenzie, 1990), this will have a facilitating effect on responses during test trials to the left or right (possibly bringing baseline performance up to .5 levels for directionally correct left or right responses). Such effects were found when the types of errors made in Study 1 were analyzed. Both responses made during the first or final block of training trials could affect the direction of looking during test trials. Studies are needed with infants in the 6-month age range involving rotational movements only to directly investigate the influence of training regime on test trial performance. A conservative criterion for good performance would require that 6-month-olds should be successful when a correct response during test trials involves looking in a completely new direction, as is the case in the training regimes used in the present studies.

A necessary approach to the question of early spatial competence is to develop paradigms that are less prone to the potentially confounding effects of response perseveration. Some steps in this direction have been made in investigations of memory for spatial location in small-scale space that use habituation-novelty paradigms (Wilcox, Rosser, & Nadel, 1994). These studies found that infants as young as 6.5 months could remember the location at which they had encountered an attractive object. The challenge is to develop such paradigms to investigate the question of allocentric spatial coding abilities in young infants.

Another direction for further research is to investigate whether infants of 8.5 months and older are still able to use indirect landmarks to locate a goal after inertial disorientation (for example after being turned slowly without vision of the environment). Recent work by Hermer and Spelke (1996) suggests that infants of 18-to 24-months tend to override unambiguous landmark information in favor of potentially ambiguous large-scale spatial information such as room shape when reorienting after inertial disorientation procedures. It has yet to be established whether this effect is obtained with younger infants, as well as whether it occurs when room shape on its own is completely uninformative as to target location (as is the case in the studies reported here; Hermer and Spelke used a rectangular room). If infants were still successful at using indirect landmarks in conditions such as those of Study 1 following inertial disorientation, this would argue against a strong version of the modular hypothesis put forward by Hermer and Spelke (1996) to explain their results. Under this view, inertial disorientation instantiates a "geometric module" for spatial reorientation that uses only large-scale features of the environment (for example, corners and length of walls). This is regardless of how informative such geometric features are compared with individual landmark information (e.g., brightly colored corner panels). An alternative view would be that it is only when certain relations hold between goal location and room shape (e.g., a toy being hidden in the corner of a rectangular room) that large-scale spatial layout overrides individual landmark use because of the saliency of the large-scale features overriding that of landmarks. Thus, the inertial disorientation procedure may not lead solely to the use of a "geometric" reorientation strategy as suggested by Hermer and Spelke (1996).

In conclusion, the present series of studies demonstrate that infants as young as 8.5 months are able to use the relation between a goal and indirect landmarks to locate that goal from a novel starting position. The question of even earlier competence in allocentric spatial coding is left open. Studies with 6-month-old infants using rotational displacements and highly salient landmarks are required, together with the development of paradigms that are less prone to perseveration effects compared with the peekaboo paradigm used here and in previous studies.

# References

Acredolo, L. P. (1978). Development of spatial orientation in infancy. *Developmental Psychology, 14,* 224–234.

Acredolo, L. P. (1990). Behavioral approaches to spatial orientation in infancy. In A. Diamond (Ed.), *Annals of the New York Academy of Sciences: Vol. 608. The developmental and neural bases of higher cognitive functions* (pp. 596–612). New York: The New York Academy of Sciences.

Acredolo, L. P., & Evans, D. (1980). Developmental changes in the effects of landmarks on infant spatial behavior. *Developmental Psychology, 16*, 312–318.

Bai, D. L., & Bertenthal, B. I. (1992). Locomotor status and the development of spatial search skills. *Child Development, 63*, 215–226.

Bertenthal, B. I., Campos, J. J., & Barrett, K. C. (1984). Self-produced locomotion: An organizer of emotional, cognitive, and social development in infancy. In R. N. Emde & R. J. Harmon (Eds.), *Continuities and discontinuities in development* (pp. 175–210). New York: Plenum.

Bremner, J. G., & Bryant, P. E. (1985). Active movement and development of spatial abilities in infancy. In H. M. Wellman (Ed.), *Children's searching: The development of search skill and spatial representation.* Hillsdale, NJ: Erlbaum.

Bremner, J. G., & Hatton, F. (1996, September). *The contribution of visual flow and vestibular information to spatial orientation by 6- and 9-month-old infants.* Paper presented at the Annual Conference of the Developmental Psychology Section of the British Psychological Society, Oxford, U.K.

Bushnell, E. W., McKenzie, B. E., Lawrence, D. A., & Connell, S. (1995). The spatial coding strategies of one-year-old infants in a locomotor search task. *Child Development, 66*, 937–958.

Diamond, A. (1990). Developmental time course in human infants and infant monkeys, and the neural bases of, inhibitory control in reaching. In A. Diamond (Ed.), *Annals of the New York Academy of Sciences: Vol. 608. The developmental and neural bases of higher cognitive functions* (pp. 637–676). New York: The New York Academy of Sciences.

Hermer, L., & Spelke, E. (1996). Modularity and development: The case of spatial reorientation. *Cognition, 61*, 195–232.

Keating, M. B., McKenzie, B. E., & Day, R. H. (1986). Spatial localization in infancy: Position constancy in a square and circular room with and without a landmark. *Child Development, 57*, 115–124.

Kermoian, R., & Campos, J. J. (1988). Locomotor experience: A facilitator of spatial cognitive development. *Child Development, 59*, 908–917.

McComas, J., & Field, J. (1984). Does early crawling experience affect infants' emerging spatial orientation abilities? *New Zealand Journal of Psychology, 13*, 63–68.

Morris, R. G. M. (1981). Spatial localization does not require the presence of local cues. *Learning and Motivation, 12*, 239–260.

Nadel, L. (1990). Varieties of spatial cognition: Psychobiological considerations. In A. Diamond (Ed.), *Annals of the New York Academy of Sciences: Vol. 608. The developmental and neural bases of higher cognitive functions* (pp. 613–636). New York: The New York Academy of Sciences.

Nadel, L., Wilson, L., & Kurz, E. M. (1993). Hippocampus: Effects of alterations in timing of development. In G. Turkewitz & D. A. Devenny (Eds.), *Developmental time and timing* (pp. 233–252). Hillsdale, NJ: Erlbaum.

Piaget, J. (1955). The child's construction of reality (M. Cook, Trans.). London: Routledge and Kegan Paul. (Original work published 1936).

Pick, H. L., Jr., Montello, D. R., & Somerville, S. C. (1988). Landmarks and the coordination and integration of spatial information. *British Journal of Developmental Psychology, 6*, 369–393.

Poucet, B. (1993). Spatial cognitive maps in animals: New hypotheses on their structure and neural mechanisms. *Psychological Review, 100*, 163–182.

Rieser, J. J. (1979). Spatial orientation of six-month-old infants. *Child Development, 50*, 1078–1087.

Roberts, J. E., Bell, M. A., & Pope, S. (1998, April). *Infant displacement and table displacement object search skills in infants 8 & 10 months of age.* Poster presented at the 11th International Conference on Infant Studies, Atlanta, GA.

Rolls, E. T., & Treves, A. (1998). *Neural networks and brain function.* Oxford, U.K.: Oxford University Press.

Rudy, J. W., Stadler-Morris, S., & Albert, P. (1987). Ontogeny of spatial navigation behaviors in the rat: Dissociation of "proximal" – and "distal" – cue based behaviors. *Behavioral Neuroscience, 101,* 62–73.

Tyler, D., & McKenzie, B. E. (1990). Spatial updating and training effects in the first year of human infancy. *Journal of Experimental Child Psychology, 50,* 445–461.

Whishaw, I. Q., & Dunnett, S. B. (1985). Dopamine depletion, stimulation or blockade in the rat disrupts spatial navigation and locomotion dependent upon beacon or distal cues. *Behavioural Brain Research, 18,* 11–29.

Wilcox, T., Rosser, R., & Nadel, L. (1994). Representation of object location in 6.5-month-old infants. *Cognitive Development, 9,* 193–209.

Woodcock, A. (1997). *Spatial orientation in 6-month-old infants.* Unpublished bachelor of science dissertation, University of Wales, Bangor, U.K.

# 43

# Spatial Updating and Training Effects in the First Year of Human Infancy

*D. Tyler and B.E. McKenzie*

Maintenance of one's bearings while moving through a stable environment requires monitoring spatial relationships that change with the movements that are executed. Adults and other animals have a variety of strategies that serve this function. These include the use of a continuously visible marker at the site of an invisible target, of a landmark or system of landmarks that bears an invariant spatial relationship with the invisible target, and of an updating system that depends on the revision of an initial self-target relationship in accordance with subsequent displacements. Most research on the development of these strategies in infancy has been concerned with the first two of these (Acredolo, 1978, 1987; Acredolo & Evans, 1980; Bremner, 1982; Rieser, 1979). The development of the third is the major focus of the experiments reported here.

In a visually impoverished setting with few external cues for spatial reference, orientation is largely dependent on information arising from movement of the body. Rieser (1979) tested 6-month-old infants in an unpatterned cylindrical chamber. They lay supine with four idential windows above them. When these windows were unmarked infants were unable reliably to relocate a particular window after they had been rotated through a 90° turn. Most infants responded as they had done prior to rotation, seemingly taking no account of their subsequent movement. Rieser concluded that, in these circumstances, 6-month-old infants showed no evidence of an ability to update their initial relation to the target in conjunction with their own

**Source:** *Journal of Experimental Child Psychology*, 50(3) (1990): 445–461.

movements. Keating, McKenzie, and Day (1986) drew a similar conclusion for 8-month-old infants. Although infants were successful in localizing a target in a round room with a landmark at the target site and in a square room both with and without the landmark, they did not succeed in a round featureless room. Keating et al. noted that their results did not support an interpretation of localization in terms of an updating strategy based on proprioceptive information. Evidence for the operation of such a strategy was provided by Rieser and Heiman (1982) for infants aged from 14 to 18 months. Unlike the preceding studies, this study involved a locomotor response and premobile infants were necessarily excluded.

While the major purpose of our investigation was to examine the development of the ability to localize in the absence of distinctive visual cues, a further aim was to establish a method suitable for testing infants over a wide age range. Traditionally most studies have used an instrumental training procedure with reinforcement contingent on the emission of a specific response (Acredolo, 1978; Rieser, 1979). In these studies it is assumed that infants learn that they are required to code a particular location in space. This assumption may not be justified since non-spatial strategies could be involved (Acredolo, 1985; Bremner, 1978; McKenzie, Day, & Ihsen, 1984). In an attempt to overcome this problem McKenzie et al. (1984) adapted the method so that infants were trained to anticipate the occurrence of an event first from a direction of facing on one side of the event and then from the opposite side. After reaching a criterion of learning infants were then faced in a new direction for test trials. The purpose of this adaptation was to avoid the likelihood that infants would repeat the one response that had been reinforced in training. This procedure was also used by Keating et al. (1986). However, the possibility was raised in the latter study that, when there are few visual referents, infants may learn a complex response rule rather than a spatial location. They are much less likely to do so when visual cues are available.

In the first study reported here a new procedure was compared with that of Keating et al. (1986). It involved a pairing of two events, one signalling the occurrence of the other independent of any response by the infant. The signal event always immediately preceded the experimenter's appearance. It occurred at three different locations but the experimenter appeared at only one, the target location. If infants had learned the association between the two events, we reasoned that they would relocate the site of the experimenter's appearance after viewing the signal event in a fourth novel location. Since the occurrence of the second event was not contingent on the infant's response as in the earlier procedure, the acquisition of non-spatial responding might be avoided.

The aims of the first experiment were twofold: first, to compare the effects of the two training procedures in a round featureless room and second, to examine the emergence of an updating strategy in infants of different ages. The second experiment was designed to ensure that any localization that occurred in the first could not be attributed to subtle cues emanating from the mother. The aim of the final study was to compare the effects on localization of the two training procedures in the presence and absence of distinctive visual information, that is, with and without a landmark at the site.

## Experiment 1

In order to satisfy the two purposes of this experiment there were four experimental groups in an unbalanced two-factor design. Groups of infants aged 4, 6, and 8 months each received association training. The fourth group, aged 8 months, received instrumental training.

## Method

*Subjects.* Each group was composed of six boys and six girls recruited from municipal infant welfare centers. The mean ages of the 4- and 6-month-old groups were 17.9 ($SD$ = 1.0) and 25.5 ($SD$ = 1.4) weeks, respectively. The 8-month-old infants were randomly allocated to either the instrumental or association training condition. The mean age of the former was 34.1 weeks ($SD$ =1.1) and of the latter, 34.3 weeks ($SD$ = 1.5). Four additional infants became distressed prior to completion of the procedure and another three failed to satisfy the instrumental training criteria (see below). Infants together with a parent were brought to the laboratory for testing.

*Apparatus.* The experimental environment was the same for all groups and consisted of a round enclosure centered within a round room. There were therefore no corners or walls that could serve as a frame of reference. This arrangement has been described earlier (Keating et al., 1986). The enclosure, 2 m in diameter and 1.3 m in height, was lined internally with the same white opaque material that formed the wall of the surrounding room. A hinged section of the enclosure permitted access and, when closed, was not distinguishable from the remainder of the wall. The ceiling of the room was also white. A shelf around the external wall of the enclosure supported a moveable video camera that was used to monitor and record infants' head–eye movements. Since its lens protruded slightly through the wall near the event site, seven false lenses were placed at 45° intervals around the enclosure at infant eye level so that the site was not distinctively marked. Eight identical red polystyrene balls 5 cm in diameter hung from the internal perimeter of the enclosure. These were level with, and 5 cm to the right of, the false or real camera lenses. Each ball was suspended by a fine teflon thread passing through a system of eyelets. These threads could be manipulated independently by the experimenter from her position outside the enclosure at the event site. When a particular thread was pulled and released, the ball attached to it moved up and down. The purpose of this movement was to attract infants' attention so that the direction of looking at the beginning of each trial was controlled.

The mother with her infant on her lap was seated on a swivel chair placed on a circular platform, 1.6 m in diameter and 40 cm in height, in the middle of the enclosure. Uniform illumination was provided by fluorescent light units located beneath the platform and in the gap between the enclosure and the surrounding wall. A television monitor was also positioned in this gap to allow on-line monitoring of infants' responses by the experimenter.

The target event was the appearance of the experimenter above the wall of the enclosure playing peek-a-boo. Only her head was visible at this time. The target event occurred at the same fixed location for any one infant but was located variously at one of three sites.

## Procedure

*Association training.* All infants in the three groups received a total of six training trials, two from each of the three directions of facing. An example of one sequence of trials is given in the right panel of Fig. 1. The mother with her infant on her lap was seated on a swivel chair in the center of the enclosure. The mother was instructed that she would be required to turn the chair so that she and her infant faced in the direction of any ball that moved. She was told to remain facing in that direction until a different ball was moved. No further instructions were given during the session.

Prior to the first trial the mother and her infant were seated facing toward the target site. The experimenter disappeared from view behind the enclosure wall at the target site and, from this position, jiggled a ball located either 45° or 90° to the right or left of the target site. The mother turned the chair so that she and her infant faced this moving ball. Once the experimenter had ascertained from the television monitor that the infant was looking at

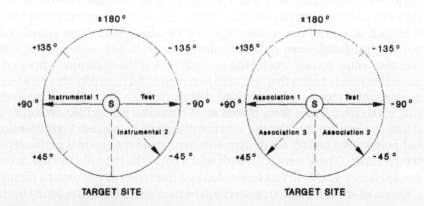

**Figure 1:** An example of the training and test sequences in Experiment 1. Association training is illustrated in the right panel and instrumental training in the left panel. S is the subject and the arrow heads indicate the facing direction at the beginning of the trial.

the moving ball, it was made stationary and the experimenter appeared immediately at the target site to initiate a game of peek-a-boo. She waved a musical toy, said "Peek-a-boo. Here I am." and then disappeared behind the wall of the enclosure. This procedure of pairing attention on the moving ball with the experimenter's appearance at the target site was then repeated. Next a ball 45° from the target site but on the opposite side of it was jiggled. The mother turned the chair past the target site to face toward this moving ball and two trials were completed from this direction of facing. Finally the experimenter jiggled the ball that was either 45° or 90° on the same side of the target site as that of the first two trials but at the alternate location. The mother rotated past the target site to face toward this ball. Again there were two trials from this facing direction.

Thus at the end of association training the experimenter's appearance at the one location had been paired twice with fixation on each of three different moving balls. These were located 45° to the left, 45° to the right, and 90° either to the left or right of the target site. The geographical site where the experimenter appeared, the site of the first moving ball, and the order of presentation of the 90° and 45° moving balls were counterbalanced over subjects. On each trial the experimenter appeared at the target site immediately after infants had fixated on the moving ball that they were facing. Anticipatory looking by the infant was not required on any of the six trials.

*Instrumental training.* The 8-month-old infants in this group received a three-phase training procedure identical to that of Keating et al. (1986). One phase of training was with the infant facing to the left of the target site, another when facing to the right of it and the third, a sequence of alternation between the two. The purpose of this procedure was to train infants to anticipate the appearance of the experimenter by looking toward the site before she appeared. Appropriate anticipations were immediately reinforced. The experimenter stood up so that she was visible above the enclosure wall. She waved a musical toy and said "Good boy/girl, you found me." If the infant did not look toward the site within 4 s the experimenter appeared saying "Here I am, are you looking for me?" An example of one sequence of training trials is given in the left panel of Figure 1.

In the first training phase, infants were faced either 45° or 90° to the left or right of the target site. Their attention was attracted by the movement of the ball immediately ahead of them. When the jiggling of the ball had stopped, the experimenter waited out of sight until either the infant turned to look at the site or 4 s had elapsed. Trials from the same facing direction continued until two successive anticipations were recorded within a maximum of 14 trials.

The second phase began immediately after reaching this criterion. If the first facing direction was 45° to one side of the target site, the second was 90° to the other and vice versa. The procedure and criterion were the same as in the first phase.

In the third training phase infants were rotated in a pseudo-random sequence between the two facing directions of phases one and two until there were four successive anticipations or until 12 trials were completed. In this sequence the constraint was imposed that there were no more than two consecutive trials from the one facing direction. Only infants reaching the criteria of learning of all three phases proceeded into the test phase.

*The test trial.* There was one test trial for each subject that was begun immediately after the six association training trials or after completion of the third phase of instrumental training. Infants were rotated to face 90° from the target site but on the opposite side from the 90° direction used in the earlier training trials. The ball that they were now facing was jiggled as before until infants had fixated on it. The experimenter neither appeared nor spoke during the ensuing test period. Two measures were scored from the video records. The first concerned where infants looked first after the ball ceased moving. It was reasoned that infants would look first toward the site where the experimenter had formerly appeared. This required a single head–eye turn of 90° from the ball that they faced to the target site. The direction of first look was scored independently by two judges from videotaped recordings played, if necessary, in slow motion. The one instance of disagreement was resolved by a third judge.

The second measure concerned the total duration of fixation on the target site throughout a 5-s interval that began after the first change in direction of looking. This was included as an index of localization since it was possible that infants would look more often or more persistently at the target site even though they did not look there first.

## Results

Preliminary analyses showed that sex of the subject was associated with neither of the dependent variables. In the following analyses the data were therefore collapsed across this factor.

*First looks.* The number of infants in each group whose first fixation was directly at the target site is given in Table 1. These data were analyzed by planned contrasts on proportions (Rodger, 1969). The first contrast concerned the effect of training. A greater proportion of 8-month-old infants looked first at the site after association than after instrumental training trials, $F(1, \infty) = 10.82, p < .001$. Whereas 10 infants in the association training group looked first to the site where the experimenter had appeared on earlier trials, only 2 from the instrumental training group did so. This was despite the fact that the former group had received only 6 training trials while the latter had a mean of approximately 15 trials. The mean numbers of training trials to reach criterion in phases 1, 2, and 3 for the instrumental training group were 5.33, 3.42, and 6.00, respectively. Two further contrasts were concerned with age trends in the three association training groups. There was a significant linear

**Table 1:** The frequency of types of first look and mean duration of looking at the target site in Experiments 1, 2, and 3

| | Type of first look | | | Mean duration of looking |
|---|---|---|---|---|
| Group | At site | Wrong direction | Undershoot | |
| Experiment 1 | | | | |
| Association | | | | |
| 4 months | 2 | 1 | 9 | 0.51 (1.05) |
| 6 months | 7* | 1 | 4 | 1.81 (1.81) |
| 8 months | 10* | 0 | 2 | 2.44 (1.19) |
| Instrumental | | | | |
| 8 months | 2 | 1 | 8 | .83 (1.37) |
| Experiment 2 | | | | |
| Association | | | | |
| 8 months | 10* | 1 | 1 | 2.59 (1.39) |
| Experiment 3 | | | | |
| Association | | | | |
| Landmark | 11* | 0 | 1 | 2.69 (1.32) |
| No landmark | 11* | 1 | 0 | 2.84 (1.26) |
| Instrumental | | | | |
| Landmark | 8* | 1 | 3 | 2.53 (1.23) |
| No landmark | 2* | 3 | 7 | 0.60 (1.42) |

Note: $n = 12$ in each group. Maximum duration of looking was 5 sec. Standard deviations are given in parentheses.
* $p < .05$.

trend over age, $F(1, \infty) = 10.82$, $p < .001$, but the quadratic trend was not significant, $F(1, \infty) < 1$.

Binomial tests were used to establish whether the numbers looking first at the site exceeded chance expectation. A chance level of .25 was selected; considering only the balls within 90° from the facing direction on the test trial four others served as possible sites. The obtained frequencies were greater than expected by chance in the 6- and 8-month-old association training groups.

The direction of first looks that were not at the target site is given in Table 1. These were classified as wrong direction, i.e., in the direction opposite to that of the site; undershoots, i.e., in the appropriate direction but stopping short of the site; and other. Only one "other" response was obtained in the 8-month instrumental training group. This response is not included in Table 1. Very few infants looked first in the wrong direction. Undershoots were the most frequent type of first look in the 4-month group and in the 8-month instrumental training group.

*Duration of visual fixation on the site.* The mean duration of looking at the target site throughout the test interval is given in Table 1 for each group. These data were analyzed by the same planned contrasts as before. Infants who received instrumental training looked at the site for a shorter period than infants of the same age who had received association training, $F(1, 44) = 2.85$, $p < .01$. For the association groups there was a significant linear trend over age, $F(1, 44) = 3.42$, $p < .001$. Newman-Keuls post hoc comparisons showed that 6- and 8-month-old infants looked significantly longer than 4-month-old infants. There was no significant quadratic trend, $F(1, 44) < 1$.

The pattern of responses was similar for both outcome measures. The number of infants looking first at the site and the duration of looking at it increased linearly between 4 and 8 months. At 8 months looking first to the site and persistence of looking at it were greater after association than after instrumental training.

## Discussion

At 8 months of age, localization of a target after reorientation in an environment with no distinctive landmarks or distinguishing room features varied according to pretest experience. As in the corresponding group in Keating et al. (1986), infants in this situation were generally unable to locate the site after instrumental training. They did not look first to the place where the experimenter had formerly appeared and throughout the test period they looked at it for only very brief periods. In contrast, after only six association pairings infants of the same age were able to locate the site. They looked first toward it and spent almost half the test period looking at it. Since there were no distinctive visual referents it seems likely that localization was achieved by means of visual–proprioceptive information deriving from body movement. Revision of the coding of the spatial relationship between self and target in terms of both direction and extent of reorientation was required. The results of Experiment 1 suggest that this was accomplished by almost all of the 8-month-old infants, by more than half of the 6-month-olds, but by few of the 4-month-olds. In terms of both dependent variables there was a linear increase in localization over the age range studied here. This is considerably earlier than was suggested by Rieser and Heiman (1982). However, since infants in our study were seated on their mother's lap, there is the possibility that their responding was influenced by maternal cues. The next experiment was concerned with this issue.

## Experiment 2

The results of Experiment 1 indicated that, after association training, infants aged 8 months were best able to locate a target after reorientation in a visually impoverished setting. The purpose of Experiment 2 was to examine performance in infants of this age when there was no possibility that subtle cues from the mother could have aided their responding. An additional sample was drawn from the same source as before and exposed to the same association training while seated in a standard infant seat rather than on their mother's lap.

## Method

*Subjects.* Six boys and six girls served as subjects. Their mean age was 34.4 weeks (*SD* = .9). A further nine infants (six boys and three girls) were seen but became distressed prior to completion of testing.

*Apparatus and procedure.* The same featureless environment was used. Infants were seated in a standard infant chair that was swivel mounted so that their eye height was level with the suspended balls. The mother stood behind the chair throughout the session. She rotated the chair to the appropriate direction of facing according to which ball was jiggled. Mothers were instructed not to touch or communicate with their infants except as necessary between trials.

## Results

*First looks.* As in the association training group of Experiment 1 a significant number of infants looked first to the target site. Ten infants looked first to the site, one infant looked first in the appropriate direction but not far enough, and the other looked in the opposite direction (see Table 1).

*Duration of looking at the target site.* The mean duration of looking at the target site throughout the test period was 2.59 s (see Table 1). There was no significant difference in the duration of looking at the site for these infants and those in the corresponding training group of Experiment 1, $t(22) < 1$.

## Discussion

In all respects other than subject attrition rate, infants seated on their own performed as well as those seated in contact with their mothers. This outcome indicates that they are not using subtle unspecified cues from their mothers as a means of relocating the target site after reorientation. In the final experiment we continued to seat infants with their mothers because the incidence of infant distress was reduced in this procedure.

## Experiment 3

The results of the first two experiments indicated successful localization of the target site by nearly all of the 8-month-old infants after association training. These results contrast with those of the instrumental training group in Experiment 1 and the corresponding group in Keating et al. (1986). However, in this latter study after identical instrumental training, infants were more successful in the same round room when a distinctive visual stimulus marked the target site. Together these results suggest that localization after instrumental training was dependent on visual information while that after association training was not. The aim of the final experiment was to assess the effects of type of training and availability of visual spatial referents. A further four groups of infants were tested. These were an instrumental training group with a landmark, an instrumental training group without a landmark, an association training group with a landmark, and an association training group without a landmark. The procedure was altered in two respects. First, instead of using an arbitrary estimate of chance expectation of looking first to the target site, a baseline measure of looking at the site prior to its association with the game of peek-a-boo was obtained. Second, the red balls were replaced by lights that were visible only when activated. This was to remove the possibility that infants might detect and use information associated with the balls to relocate the target on the test trial.

## Method

*Subjects.* The sample consisted of 48 infants ranging in age from 33.4 to 36.6 weeks. Six boys and six girls were randomly allocated to each of the four experimental conditions. Six additional infants (all males) were tested but failed to reach criterion in the final training phase in the instrumental–no landmark condition. The mean ages and standard deviations of the instrumental–landmark, instrumental–no landmark, association–landmark, and association–no landmark groups were 34.9 (1.0), 34.5 (0.9), 34.8 (0.8), and 34.8 (0.8) weeks, respectively.

*Apparatus.* All infants were tested in the same circular room as before except that the eight red balls were each replaced by red lights concealed behind a 15-cm strip of white mesh extending around the internal wall of the enclosure. The top of this mesh strip was 28 cm from the top of the enclosure. This mesh also concealed the lens of the television camera located at the target site and therefore made the provision of false lens unnecessary. The lights were placed at 45° intervals around the perimeter of the enclosure. Each light could be individually activated by the experimenter using a remote control facility. When activated, a light flashed on and off accompanied by a loud buzzing sound. The purpose of the light and sound was to control the direction of visual fixation at the beginning of each trial. Infants in the no landmark conditions were tested in the unmarked white circular room. Neither a landmark nor a frame of reference associated with the room was available. Infants in these conditions had therefore to rely on other than visual information to locate the target site on the test trial.

A distinctive visual stimulus was provided in the two landmark conditions. This was a red and white diagonally striped cardboard arrow 75 cm in height and 11 cm in width. This arrow was suspended on the white wall of the circular room 1.8 m from the floor and vertically above the target site, thus providing a visual cue that could be used as a spatial referent.

*Procedure.* Infants were seated on their mother's lap throughout the session. During a brief period of familiarization in the experimental enclosure, the mother was instructed that she would be required to turn the chair so that she and her infant faced any light that flashed. She was told to remain facing in this direction until the next light flashed. No further instructions were given during the session.

A pretest measure of where each infant looked in the absence of the experimenter's appearance at a particular site was then obtained. The light that was to be used later to initiate the test trial was flashed and the mother turned the chair to face it. This light was 90° to the left or right of the target site. Once the infant fixated on the light it was switched off. Where infants looked first after the light was extinguished was then recorded. The number looking first to the site within each of the four experimental groups was used as the estimate of chance responding for that condition. This replaced the arbitrary estimate used in Experiments 1 and 2.

The instrumental or association training trials were then completed as in Experiment 1, and followed by the test trial. As before, two indices of localization were scored from the video records by two independent judges one of whom was naive as to the experimental condition. A first look was judged correct if it was within approximately 5° either side of the target site and at the level where the experimenter's head had previously appeared. There were no disagreements as to the direction of first looks for each infant. The Pearson Product Moment correlation of the two judges' estimates of duration of total fixation on the target site was .96. The scores of the first judge were used in subsequent analyses.

## Results

Preliminary analyses again showed no association of the subject's sex with either of the dependent variables. In all the following analyses the results for the two sexes were combined.

*First looks.* The number of infants in each group looking first at the target site is given in Table 1. These data were analyzed using the method of planned contrasts on proportions (Rodger, 1969). The three contrasts concerned the effect of training, of landmark, and the interaction of the two factors. A greater proportion of infants looked first at the target site after association training, $F(1, \infty) = 10.82$, $p < .001$. The mean numbers of training trials to reach the learning criteria of phases 1, 2, and 3 in the instrumental training groups were 4.79, 3.33, and 5.33, respectively. Again the greater number of exposures to the appearance of the experimenter at the site did not lead to superior performance. Neither the availability of the landmark, $F(1, \infty) = 3.38, p > .05$, nor the interaction of the two factors, $F(1, \infty) = 3.38, p > .05$, was significantly related to looking first to the site.

**Table 2:** Number of infants looking first to the target site in the test trial and in the pretest (in parentheses)

| | Type of training | | |
| --- | --- | --- | --- |
| | Association | | Instrumental |
| Landmark | 11　(3) | | 8　(3) |
| | p = .000 | | p = .002 |
| No landmark | 11　(2) | | 2　(1) |
| | p = .000 | | p = .192 |

*Note: n = 12 in each group; p = binomial probability.*

Binomial tests were used to establish whether the numbers looking first at the target site exceeded chance expectation. The number of infants in each group who looked first to the target site prior to training was used as the chance estimate. These numbers and the corresponding binomial probabilities are given in Table 2. The number of association-trained infants looking first to the site exceeded chance expectation both when the landmark was present and when it was not. In contrast, the number of instrumentally trained infants differed from chance only if a landmark were present.

The responses of infants whose first fixation was not at the target site are given in Table 1. The predominance of undershoots is evident. It is also worthy of note that all three infants who made undershoots in the instrumental–landmark condition spent part of the test period looking at the event site while none of the seven in the instrumental–no landmark condition did so.

*Duration of looking at the target site.* The mean duration of looking at the target site for each group is given in Table 1.

Analysis of planned contrasts showed that there was a significant effect of type of training, $F(1, 44) = 9.93, p = .03$, of landmark, $F(1, 44) = 5.50$, $p = .024$, and a significant interaction between the two factors, $F(1, 44) = 7.54, p = .009$. The presence of a landmark resulted in longer looking times but only when infants were instrumentally trained.

In summary, the training effect was evident in both dependent variables: more infants looked first to the target site and looked at it longer after association training. Total looking time at the site, but not first looks at it, was greater in the presence of the landmark for instrumentally but not associatively trained infants.

## Discussion

These results show superior localization after association training both when a visual landmark is present and when it is not. More infants looked first to the location where the experimenter had appeared after association training whether or not there was a visual marker at that location. The presence of the marker was associated with longer looking only after instrumental training.

Without a landmark and without cues associated with room shape, infants in the association group were able to relocate the target site after their spatial relationship with it was changed. Moreover it is clear that they were not relying on information provided by the red balls since the two indices of localization were similar in the association training conditions of the three experiments. Substitution of red balls with lights that were not visible in the test trial was not associated with a deterioration in performance.

After instrumental training localization varied with the availability of a visual cue. The duration of looking at the target site increased when the landmark was present and the number of infants looking first to the site differed from the baseline frequency only when the landmark was available. Keating et al. (1986), using the same instrumental procedure, also concluded that visual information was necessary. On the pretest trial when the landmark was not associated with the site where the experimenter would later appear, infants looked longer at the site in the landmark as compared with the no landmark conditions. The respective means were 1.68 and 0.52 s. After the three phases of instrumental training this mean duration increased to 2.53 s in the landmark condition but remained virtually unchanged from baseline in the no landmark condition. These results together with the frequency of first looks indicate that it is not the landmark itself but the landmark as an indicator of the target that is influential in controlling infants looking behavior.

In summary, at 8 months of age associatively trained infants succeeded in localization both in the presence and absence of a distinctive visual cue, whereas instrumentally trained infants were only successful when the visual cue was present.

## General Discussion

Two major findings arise from these experiments. The first is the early emergence of a spatial updating strategy and the second is the difference in outcomes associated with the training procedures.

An updating strategy involving egocentric referencing was successfully used by 8-month-old infants. There were no distinctive visual cues in the round room without the landmark since, after rotation, all directions of facing resulted in an identical view. The results of the control study (Experiment 2) indicated that cues from the mother were not the critical factor in localization and the results of Experiment 3 indicated that cues associated with the balls were not necessary. We therefore conclude that infants used information arising from their rotatory movements to determine the site of the target. The results of Experiment 1 suggest that this ability begins to emerge at about 6 months. This is considerably earlier than was suggested by Rieser and Heiman (1982). The many differences in method between the two studies hinder explanation of the variation in findings. It is possible that the development of an updating strategy for looking precedes that for locomotion, or that exposure to a target from multiple perspectives promotes spatial encoding. Whatever the reason for the difference, our results clearly indicate that an updating strategy based on proprioceptive–vestibular information becomes operative early in the second half of the first year.

For egocentric referencing to be reliable over rotatory movement, it must be revised by input relating to the direction and extent of that movement. It has been shown that the vestibular system provides information relevant to the extent of angular displacements (Howard & Templeton, 1966; Potegal, 1982). The maturation of this system in human infants has not been well documented. From the results of our studies, it is not possible to determine the basis of developmental improvement in localization. It is of interest to note that even 4-month-old infants rarely turned in the wrong direction. Whether older infants better monitor the extent of the movement, better integrate this information with the visual–motor system, or better learn the inter-relation between the optic flow accompanying rotation and the associated proprioceptive–vestibular input, remains to be determined.

The second finding concerns the effect of type of training on localization. The updating strategy evident after only a few association trials is not exhibited after more extensive instrumental training. The training procedures differ in several respects. First, in association training the target event was seen from three different perspectives, and in instrumental training, from two. This difference is not thought to be critical since McKenzie, Day, Colussa, and Connell (1988), using a similar association procedure, found successful localization by 8-month-old infants who had seen the target event from only two different perspectives. Second, the procedures differed in the number of training trials. In association training the total number of trials was 6, whereas in instrumental training in the no landmark groups it ranged from 8 to 22. Other research has shown that the number of trials prior to testing has an effect on spatial responding (Bremner, 1978; Cornell & Heth, 1979; Landers, 1971). However, localization did not depend solely on the number of training trials in our studies. In Experiment 3 (see Table 1) persistence of looking at the site was similar in the landmark groups even though the instrumental group had received an average 13 trials and the association group only 6. It is possible that infants may lapse into a learned motor habit when training is prolonged in a visually impoverished setting. They do not do so when a visible cue is available and continuous updating is not necessary. There is yet another difference between the two procedures that may be critical in determining the different outcomes. In association training the target event immediately followed the signal event regardless of the behavior of the infant. In instrumental training the target event occurred after the infant had looked toward its site or, on the early trials, after a delay of 4 s. The purpose of the training was to shape responding so that anticipatory looking to the target site occurred. Infants did not proceed into the test trial until they had done so on 4 consecutive trials. Thus event occurrence became contingent on a motor response. When there are no visual referents to guide localization, this form of training apparently inhibits operation of the spatial updating strategy.

The most common error in first looks after instrumental training was an undershoot – that is, a look in the direction of the target but not far enough. This error was particulary apparent when the landmark was not available. It is possible that infants under these conditions were repeating the response that had been correct in training. For example, when turned to face –45° (see left panel, Figure 1) they had to turn to their right by 45°. On the test trial a 45° right turn would result in an undershoot. It seems that infants may have learned a specific response from the right and left starting positions. This was not the case when there was a landmark at the target site. In these circumstances infants detected the invariant landmark–target relation and undershoots were less frequent.

Whatever the reason for the different outcomes following the two types of training, the most important conclusion is that a localization strategy based on proprioceptive–vestibular input is within the repertoire of 8-month-old infants. These findings challenge current views (e.g., Acredolo, 1985; Lepecq & Lafaite, 1989) concerning the spatial localization processes that are available to infants at this age. Although it has been accepted that localization in an environment containing landmarks developmentally precedes that in which there are none (e.g., Acredolo, 1978; Bremner, 1982) our results suggest otherwise. From the second half of their first year both an environmentally specified system and a self-referent system are operative. Neither would seem to depend on a prolonged history of self-produced locomotion. The results reported here indicate that extensive training in which motor responses are consistently reinforced inhibits operation of the self-referent but not the environment-referent system. These results together with those of other studies in progress in our laboratory lead us to suggest that in 8-month-old infants, as in many other animals, there is a preferential association between spatial responding and visual cues.

## References

Acredolo, L. P. (1978). Development of spatial orientation in infancy. *Developmental Psychology, **14**,* 224–234.

Acredolo, L. P. (1985). Co-ordinating perspectives on infant spatial orientation. In R. Cohen (Ed.), *The development of spatial cognition* (pp. 115–140). Hillsdale, NJ: Erlbaum.

Acredolo, L. P. (1987). Early development of spatial orientation in humans. In P. Ellen & C. Thinus-Blanc (Eds.), *Cognitive processes and spatial orientation in animals and man* (Vol. 2, pp. 185–201). Dordrecht, Holland: Martinus Nijhoff Publishers.

Acredolo, L. P., & Evans, D. (1980). Developmental changes in the effects of landmarks on infant spatial behaviour. *Developmental Psychology, **16**,* 312–318.

Bremner, J. G. (1978). Egocentric versus allocentric spatial coding in 9 month old infants: Factors influencing the choice of code. *Developmental Psychology, **14**,* 346–355.

Bremner, J. G. (1982). Object localization in infancy. In M. Potegal (Ed.), *Spatial abilities: Developmental and physiological foundations* (pp. 79–106). New York: Academic Press.

Cornell, E. H., & Heth, C. D. (1979). Response versus place learning by human infants. *Journal of Experimental Psychology, 5,* 188–196.

Howard, I. P., & Templeton, W. B (1966). *Human spatial orientation.* London: Wiley.

Keating, M. B., McKenzie, B. E., & Day, R. H. (1986). Spatial localization in infancy: Position constancy in a square and circular room with and without a landmark. *Child Development, 57,* 115–124.

Landers, W. F. (1971). Effects of differential experience on infants' performance in a Piagetian stage 4 object-concept task. *Developmental Psychology, 5,* 48–54.

Lepecq, J. C., & Lafaite, M. (1989). The early development of position constancy in a no-landmark environment. *British Journal of Developmental Psychology, 7,* 289–306.

McKenzie, B. E., Day, R. H., Colussa, S., & Connell, S. (1988). Spatial localization by infants after rotational and translational shifts. *Australian Journal of Psychology, 40,* 165–178.

McKenzie, B. E., Day, R. H., & Ihsen. E. (1984). Localization of events in space: Young infants are not always egocentric. *British Journal of Developmental Psychology, 2,* 1–19.

Potegal, M. (1982). Vestibular and neostriatal contributions to spatial orientation. In M. Potegal (Ed.), *Spatial orientation: Development and physiological foundations* (pp. 361–387). New York: Academic Press.

Rieser, J. J. (1979). Spatial orientation in 6-month-old infants. *Child Development, 50,* 1078–1087.

Rieser, J. J., & Heiman, M. L. (1982). Spatial self-reference systems and shortest route behaviour in toddlers. *Child Development, 53,* 524–533.

Rodger, R. S. (1969). Linear hypotheses in 2 × a frequency tables. *British Journal of Mathematical and Statistical Psychology, 22,* 29–48.

# 44

# The Contribution of Visual and Vestibular Information to Spatial Orientation by 6- to 14-Month-Old Infants and Adults

*J. Gavin Bremner, Fran Hatton, Kirsty A. Foster and Uschi Mason*

## Introduction

When adults move around the world, they are adept at maintaining a sense of their position in space despite extensive bodily displacements and reorientations. It is easy to overlook this process, given its frequently effortless nature. But it is clearly a fundamental component of spatial processing and, in addition to reaching an understanding of its basis in adults, it is important to understand its developmental origins from infancy onwards.

Typically, research on infant spatial orientation investigates infants' ability to relocate a target following some form of bodily movement and/ or reorientation. One method (Cornell & Heth, 1979; Keating, McKenzie & Day, 1986; McKenzie, Day & Ihsen, 1984; Rieser, 1979) measures infants' anticipation of an event at a constant position; infants are trained to look towards a fixed locus and are then rotated to a new direction of facing, and direction of anticipatory looking is measured. This and similar methods reveal that between 4 and 8 months infants show an increasing ability to take account of bodily rotation (Keating *et al.*, 1986; McKenzie *et al.*, 1984; Meuwissen & McKenzie, 1987; Rieser, 1979).

One important gap in our knowledge concerns the relative contribution of visual and vestibular[1] information to infant spatial orientation. Although there

**Source:** *Developmental Science,* 14(5) (2011): 1033–1045.

is evidence regarding visual–vestibular interaction in early infancy (Rosander & von Hofsten, 2000), this concerns the effects on gaze adjustment during stimulation and not spatial orientation as such. On the one hand, evidence regarding the importance of landmarks in spatial orientation (Acredolo, 1978; Acredolo & Evans, 1980; Bremner, 1978a, 1978b; Meuwissen & McKenzie, 1987) suggests a visual component to performance. However, the fact that infants (Lew, Foster & Bremner, 2006) and toddlers (Hermer & Spelke, 1996) have difficulty using landmarks following inertial stimulation raises the possibility that the updating process is at least partially based on vestibular input.

In addition, evidence that young infants are capable of taking account of body rotation in featureless environments (Lepecq & Lafaite, 1989; Tyler & McKenzie, 1990) has led to the suggestion that early spatial orientation is based on vestibular input (Tyler & McKenzie, 1990). However, body rotation gives rise to visual flow information even in finely textured environments, and it has been demonstrated that visual flow simulating linear body movement affects postural stability. Lee and Lishman (1975) showed that if adult participants were put in a moving room in which the floor was stable but the walls moved, they reported the feeling that it was they who were moving rather than the walls. Lee and Aronson (1974) found that infants who had just learned to stand upright fell over when the walls moved, and Butterworth and Hicks (1977) obtained evidence for adjustment of sitting posture resulting from wall movement from 9- and 18-month-old infants. Further work indicates developmental changes in the amount of visual flow needed to trigger postural adjustment, with 7-month-olds requiring global flow whereas peripheral or central flow is sufficient at 9 months (Bertenthal & Bai, 1989), and also in the degree of attunement to optical flow between 5 and 13 months (Bertenthal, Rose & Bai, 1997). This raises the possibility that visual flow is also important in the maintenance of heading.

The literature on animal and human maintenance of heading is equivocal regarding the likely basis of infant spatial orientation. Some work on path integration and maintenance of heading suggests that vestibular information is of primary importance in both animals (Stackman & Herbert, 2002; Wallace, Hines, Pellis & Whishaw, 2002) and humans (Cohen, 2000; Klatsky, Loomis, Beall, Chance & Golledge, 1998; Simons & Wang, 1998). However, there also is growing evidence that adults can use visual information alone for spatial updating during rotational transformations (Riecke, von der Heyde & Bülthoff, 2004, 2005) and that they use optical flow preferentially in navigating visually rich environments (Bruggeman, Zosh & Warren, 2007). Furthermore, there is considerable evidence that, rather than using one sensory channel preferentially, adult humans (Ernst & Banks, 2002) and monkeys (Gu, Angelaki & DeAngelis, 2008) integrate information from different sensory channels in an optimal manner with the weighting given to different channels depending on their reliability (Ernst & Bülthoff, 2004; Morgan, DeAngelis & Angelaki,

2008). Such integration appears to be a general principle of adult intersensory perception, but applies in the specific case of integration between visual and vestibular channels (Fetsch, Turner, DeAngelis & Angelaki, 2009). Cases in which one sensory channel appears to dominate appear to be explained by the fact that when sensory cues are disparate in the extreme, one will be discounted in favour of the other (Banks & Backus, 1998; Blake, Bülthoff & Sheinberg, 1993).

However, integration of intersensory information appears to be relatively late in development. Gori, Del Viva, Sandini and Burr (2008) found that optimal integration of haptic and visual form information only occurred at around 8 years of age, and Nardini, Jones, Bedford and Braddick (2008) found that, in contrast to adults, children up to 8 years of age did not integrate vestibular and visual landmark information in navigation, tending to alternate between using one source of information or the other. This evidence suggests that although infants are unlikely to integrate information from visual and vestibular modalities in the way adults do, they may well be capable of using both sources of information. Thus there is a clear need to investigate directly the relative contribution of vestibular and visual information in infant spatial orientation. The aim of the present research is to begin to address this issue through a series of studies in which Lee and Lishman's methodology is adapted to make it applicable to spatial orientation testing. Using Tyler and McKenzie's basic technique, infants are trained to anticipate the appearance of a fixed event within a cylindrical enclosure. Following training, several forms of test trial are presented so as to isolate or put in opposition visual flow and vestibular information. Specifically, if the surround is rotated rather than the infant, only visual information for movement is provided. Or if the surround and infant are rotated simultaneously, only vestibular information is provided. Finally, if both infant and surround are rotated in the same direction, but the latter at twice the rate, vestibular information specifies one direction of rotation and visual flow information the opposite direction of rotation.

In the main studies we tested infants between the ages of 6 and 14 months, this being the age range that has been the focus of most prior research. However, it seemed important to provide an adult baseline. Previous research has investigated the effects of visual and vestibular information on adults' sense of body position, orientation (Ivanenko, Grasso, Israel & Berthoz, 1997; Wertheim, Mesland & Bles, 2001) heading (Blouin, Gauthier & Vercher, 1995), and subjective impressions of rotation (Wong & Frost, 1981), and also on their control of arm movement in pointing to a target (Guillaud, Gauthier, Vercher & Blouin, 2006). However, these studies either investigate perception and motor adaptation during the sensory stimulation itself rather than on spatial orientation following stimulation. And when they do investigate spatial orientation they tend to compare performance with and without vestibular (Riecke *et al.*, 2004) or visual information (Rieser, Ashmead, Talor & Youngquist, 1991) and so do not make all the comparisons we have in mind here. Thus we began our investigation with an adult version of the infant task.

# Experiment 1

The aim of this experiment was to evaluate the relative contribution of visual flow versus vestibular information in a task requiring adults to relocate a target following movement. Because the purpose was to provide an adult baseline for subsequent infant experiments, the task was designed so as to be easily adaptable for use with infants. Four conditions were run, a baseline condition and three others that manipulated visual flow information and vestibular information for bodily rotation separately or in combination.

## Method

### Participants

Forty-eight adults, 38 female and 10 male in the age range 20–30 years took part in the study. Twelve were assigned to each of the four conditions in such a way as to ensure that the mean age and gender balance were comparable across conditions.

### Apparatus

The experimental environment consisted of a circular enclosed room with a chair at its centre. The entire room was raised 26 cm from the ground, and was 244.2 cm in diameter and 191.5 cm in height, from floor to ceiling. The chair seat was 57 cm above the floor of the enclosure. The room was lined internally with off-white opaque fabric, forming the cylindrical wall of the room. This was divided by nine openable elasticized vertical slits extending from floor to ceiling at 30-degree intervals over a total angle of 240 degrees. Three movable video cameras were attached at a height approximately equivalent to participants' eye level to a support rail outside the material wall, to monitor and record participants' head and eye movements. To ensure that the sites at which the cameras were positioned were not distinctive, six false camera lenses were placed at the remaining sites. The fabric was stretched over a frame, eliminating sway during rotation but resulting in minor uniform undulations top to bottom that provided shading texture in the surround. Nine red LED lights were positioned at each of the nine sites directly above the camera positions, which were adjacent to the elasticized slits. The resulting texture and uniformly spaced features provided noticeable visual flow information when participant or surround was rotated. The lights could be activated singly from outside the circular room. Once activated the light flashed in order to attract participants' attention. A television monitor and three-channel mixer located outside the circular room and near the event site allowed the experimenter to monitor the participants' responses via the three cameras.

The chair was mounted on a central bearing that could be rotated by the experimenter. The enclosure was also connected to this central bearing, allowed it to be rotated as a whole. A belt system could be engaged that locked chair and surround together, either so that they rotated in the same direction at the same rate or so that the surround rotated at twice the speed of the chair. In these cases, the combined movements were achieved by the experimenter rotating the surround manually. All rotations occurred soundlessly.

## Design

Because the aim was to provide an adult baseline to which infant performance would be compared, we adopted the same basic procedure as used by Tyler and McKenzie with infants, in which initial training involved learning to anticipate appearance of a target at a fixed location from two directions of facing, followed by a single test trial. The test trial involved a transformation that provided either congruent or conflicting information in the visual and vestibular modalities. The form of the test trial differed for each of the four groups of participants. A *baseline condition* similar to the test trial used by Tyler and McKenzie (1990) contained both visual and vestibular information of movement to a new direction of facing (see Figure 1), a *visual change condition* provided only visual information of movement, a *vestibular change condition* provided only vestibular information of movement, and an *opposed visual and vestibular condition* provided visual and vestibular information specifying equal but opposite directions of rotation. These test trials were designed so as to make it possible to establish the relative contribution of vestibular and visual information to participants' response, and whether this varied depending on whether vestibular and visual information for movement were presented in isolation or in opposition.

## Procedure

The target event was the appearance of the experimenter's head at one of the elasticized slits between the panels of the enclosing wall, at the same location in the laboratory frame for every trial. Participants were provided with a pointer and were instructed not to point to the event site on the first trial, but to point as accurately as possible on subsequent trials, touching the wall, so that the experimenter could mark the position. They were told that they would be rotated to different positions and that, after the practice trials, the event would occur in the same place in the laboratory frame each time.

Participants received two practice trials and six training trials. The practice trials and the practice event site were different from those used in training

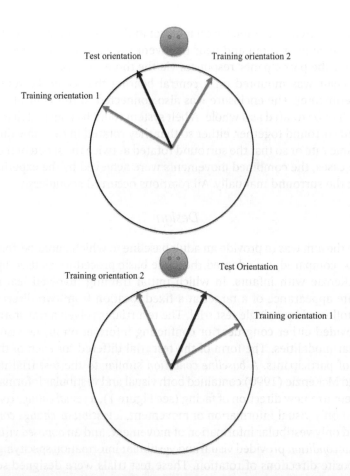

**Figure 1:** A diagram to illustrate the two versions of the training sequence that applied in all conditions and the associated test trial in the baseline condition. The face symbol indicates the fixed location at which the experimenter appeared during training trials.

and test. The chair was manually rotated to the first practice position, 30, 60, or 90 degrees to the right or left of the starting point. To cue the start of the trial the light in front of the participant flashed for 3 seconds, and 2 seconds later the experimenter appeared at the target site. A transformation phase followed in which the chair was rotated to the next practice position, past the event site and 120 degrees from the first training position. Again, to signal the start of the trial the light in front of the participant was activated for 3 seconds, and this time the participant was asked to point to the anticipated event location (target). Two seconds following the participant's point, the experimenter appeared at the event location.

The training sequence is illustrated in Figure 1. Before the first training trial, the participant was oriented to face the target site used during training and test. The chair was then manually rotated to the first training position,

60 degrees to the right or left of the target direction. The light in front of the participant flashed for 3 seconds to cue the start of the trial. The participant was asked to point to the anticipated event location (target), and 2 seconds later target feedback was provided by the experimenter appearing at the target site. A transformation followed in which the chair was then rotated clockwise or anticlockwise to the next training position, past the event site and 90 degrees from the first training position (thus 30 degrees to right or left of the event site). The light in front of the participant was then activated for 3 seconds to cue the start of the next trial, whereupon the participant pointed to their estimate of the target. Again, the experimenter appeared at the event site 2 seconds after the participant had pointed. This procedure was repeated until the participant had received a total of six training trials, three from each side of the target event site. (Training from two directions of facing is typically used in infant work to prevent establishment of perseveration of a single response.)

The single test trial followed immediately. The form of the transformation in this trial differed between conditions, as indicated in Figure 2. To allow measurement of anticipatory looking the experimenter did not appear at the target position. In the *baseline condition*, the chair was rotated past the target event site and 60 degrees from the last training position to a new test position (30 degrees to right or left of the event site), providing both visual and vestibular information for a change in orientation. In the *visual change condition*, the room was rotated 60 degrees clockwise or anticlockwise, while the chair remained stationary in the position of the last training trial. This provided visual flow information but no vestibular information for a change in orientation. If the last training trial had occurred with the participant oriented to the left of the target event site, the room was rotated anticlockwise (generating the visual flow direction that would result from a clockwise body rotation), and if to the right, the room was rotated clockwise. In the *vestibular change condition*, the chair was rotated 60 degrees past the target event site, and the room was simultaneously moved 60 degrees in the same direction (chair and surround were locked together in this condition, allowing no movement of the chair relative to the surround). This provided vestibular information but no visual information for a change in orientation. If the last training trial had occurred to the left of the target event site, the room and chair were rotated clockwise, and if to the left, they were rotated anticlockwise. In the *opposed visual and vestibular condition*, the chair and the room were also rotated simultaneously but through different extents. The chair was rotated 60 degrees past the target event site, and the room was rotated 120 degrees in the same direction. This provided visual flow information for a change of orientation in one direction and vestibular information for a change in the opposite direction. If the last training trial had occurred with the participant oriented to the left of the target event site, chair and surround were rotated clockwise, and if to the right, they were rotated anticlockwise. All chair and

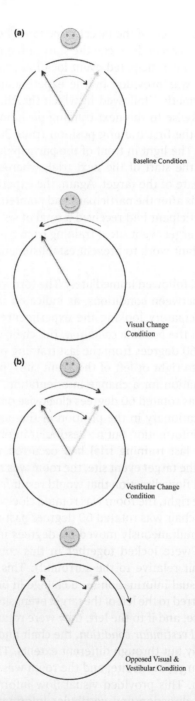

**Figure 2:** Test trial transformations for the four conditions in Experiments 1 and 2. The face symbol indicates the fixed location at which the experimenter had appeared during training. For simplicity, the transformations are illustrated for the case in which the final training trial took place with the participant oriented 30 degrees to the left of the appearance site.

surround rotations took place at a peak velocity of approximately 45 degrees/ sec, with smooth acceleration and deceleration phases during approximately the first and last 15% of the movement, apart from the test trial in the surround-twice-self condition in which the surround was rotated at a peak velocity of approximately 90 degrees/sec and the chair at half that rate.

Following each of these transformations, the cue light in front of the participant was activated for 2 seconds, whereupon the participant pointed to the anticipated location of the target. In each condition, the locations were identified that participants could be expected to point to depending on whether they were relying accurately on visual or vestibular information. In all but the *baseline condition*, reliance on vestibular or visual information predicted opposite directions of updating and different locations at which event prediction should occur. Note that reliance on vestibular information in the *visual change condition* and on visual information in the *vestibular change condition* would result in perception of no change in orientation and thus would result in an anticipatory look in the same direction as on the last training trial. To allow comparison with infant *location* responses, participants' point locations were coded as accurate according to vestibular or visual information if they fell within an area 15 cm either side of the slit in the curtains at a particular site and between 50 cm from the roof of the circular room and 80 cm above the floor, and area corresponding to that taken up by the appearance of the investigator during training. Any other responses were coded as angular departures from whichever target location (visual or vestibular) they were closest to.

## Results and Discussion

In the baseline condition visual flow and vestibular information specified the same rotation and hence would be expected to prompt identification of the same target location. All other conditions were designed so that reliance on visual information would lead to identification of the target at a specific position to one side of midline whereas reliance on vestibular information would lead to identification of the target at a specific position to the opposite side of midline. Table 1 displays the data coded for both directional and positional accuracy. The data are so clear that statistical analysis was unnecessary.

On the *direction* measure the overwhelming majority of participants looked in the direction specified by visual flow. The only exception was one individual in the *vestibular change condition* who pointed straight ahead. On the more exact *location* measure (15 cm either side of the surround slit) all but three of those who had pointed in the direction specified by visual information pointed at the target location specified by visual information. Those who did not were in the *opposed visual and vestibular condition*, and pointed to the location 30 degrees closer to midline than that specified by visual cues,

**Table 1:** Number of participants (/12) in Experiment 1 pointing to target (Baseline condition) and to visual versus vestibular positions (other conditions), coded according to direction and location (±15 degrees of target) criteria

| | | Rotation condition | | | | | |
| | | Visual | | Vestibular | | Opposed vis. & vest. | |
| Look coding | Baseline target | vis. | vest. | vis. | vest. | vis. | vest. |
|---|---|---|---|---|---|---|---|
| Direction | 12 | 12 | 0 | 11 | 0 | 12 | 0 |
| Location | 12 | 12 | 0 | 11 | 0 | 9 | 0 |

in keeping with a small effect of vestibular cues. Otherwise, the majority of participants responded in terms of visual flow information and appeared to show no awareness of the conflict between visual and vestibular cues. Apart from the baseline condition, the majority of participants were pointing at a location that was 60 degrees from the target location: their reliance on visual flow information made them very poor at identifying a position that had been indicated to be stable within the laboratory framework. This suggests that they discounted information from one sensory channel (in this case vestibular information) when it was markedly incongruent with information from another channel (Banks & Backus, 1998; Blake *et al.*, 1993).

## Experiment 2

Here we moved to investigating infants' performance in the same conditions used in Experiment 1. In this case, the dependent measure, in parallel with work by McKenzie and colleagues, was anticipatory looking on the test trial. But apart from the lack of verbal explanation given to adults, essentially the same procedure was followed as in Experiment 1. In order to investigate possible developmental change, we tested groups of infants of mean age 7, 9, and 12 months, covering the age range 6 to 14 months.

## Method

### Participants

A total of 216 infants took part in the experiment: 72 6- to 8-month-olds ($M$ = 213.3 days; range 184–240 days; 36 girls and 36 boys), 72 8- to 11-month-olds ($M$ = 279.4 days; range 244–332 days; 36 girls and 36 boys), and 72 12- to 14-month-olds ($M$ = 371.5 days; range 349–428 days; 35 female and 37 male). A further 36 infants failed to complete the session due to fussiness. Within each age group, 18 infants were assigned to each of the four experimental conditions in such a way as to ensure that the mean age and gender balance were comparable across conditions.

## Apparatus

The same equipment was used as in Experiment 1, with the addition of a VCR to record images of the infant captured by the three cameras. In order to maximize the accuracy of judgment of gaze direction, camera positions were varied depending on condition so that, following the test trial manipulation, one camera was straight ahead of the infant, and the other two were at the fixation points predicted by reliance on visual and vestibular information, respectively.

## Procedure

The procedure was largely the same as in Experiment 1, but was adapted to make it appropriate for infant testing. A short play session of about 5 minutes took place in the enclosure before testing commenced, so that the infant became accustomed to the surroundings and the investigator.

All infants received a total of eight training trials, four from each direction of facing. The parent was directed to sit on the chair in the centre of the room with her/his feet on the foot-rest. The infant sat on the parent's knee, facing forwards. The seat of the chair was 57 cm from the floor, so that when seated on the parent's lap the infant's eye level was approximately the same as the camera heights. Parents were asked to look forward, and not to communicate with their infant. Before the first trial, the parent and infant were seated facing the target site. The chair was then rotated to the first training position, 60 degrees to the left or right of the starting point (see Figure 1). At the start of the trial, the light facing the infant flashed until the infant was fixating it. Immediately following this the experimenter appeared at the target site, saying 'Boo. Here I am. Hello . . . (child's name).' A transformation phase followed in which the chair was rotated to the next training position, past the event site and 90 degrees from the first training position (hence 30 degrees to right or left of the event site). The next trial then commenced with the light cue in front of the infant, followed by the target event. The target event occurred at the same location in the laboratory frame for every trial. This procedure was repeated until the infant had received a total of eight training trials, four from each side of the target event site.

The single test trial followed immediately. The transformation phase of the test trial differed between conditions, as specified in Experiment 1, and to allow measurement of anticipatory looking the experimenter did not appear at the target position following the light cue. In all cases, following the test trial spatial transformation, the straight-ahead light cue flashed until the experimenter verified from the video data that the infant was fixating it. Measurements of anticipatory gaze direction followed once the light stopped flashing.

## Predictions

The results of Experiment 1 indicated that adults relied on visual information, whether this specified movement or stability, and even when vestibular information specified an opposite movement. This is consistent with strong effects of visual information on postural stability in adults and infants, and we might assume that infants should show similar reliance on visual information in the present task. However, predictive orientation to a target is a fundamentally different behaviour from maintenance of postural stability. Our finding with adults is consistent with the conclusion that when there is a large disparity between information from two sensory channels, adults discount information from one sense. However, work with children suggests that discounting does not occur, with instead a tendency to alternate between using one sensory channel and the other (Nardini *et al.*, 2008). If this is also true of infants, we would expect to find less consistency in responding in the three conditions in which vestibular and visual information is incongruent than in the *baseline condition* in which information about movement is congruent across the senses. Second, we might expect response consistency to be lower in the *opposed visual and vestibular condition*, in which vestibular and visual information specify opposite movements, and in the *visual change* and *vestibular change* conditions in which one sensory channel specifies a movement and the other specifies stability. Finally, although infants may be sensitive to both vestibular and visual information, one source of information may have more influence than the other, and this may vary depending on how visual and vestibular information is combined in the different test conditions.

## Measures and Coding

Recognizing that infants might look to more than one location on the test trial, Tyler and McKenzie (1990) measured both direction of first look and total duration of looking to target within a 5 second period following onset of the first look. In their work these measures yielded essentially the same outcomes. However, in the present work, particularly in conditions in which visual and vestibular information were uncorrelated, it was evident that many infants looked to more than one location during the test trial. Thus, we judged that a long look should be a more reliable indicator of sustained trained anticipation than a fleeting first look. Also, we found that longest looks tended to be quite sustained, averaging 2.27 s across ages and conditions, and their analysis yielded similar outcomes to analyses based on the total duration of looking measure used by Tyler and McKenzie. Two measures were derived from longest look data. First, looks were coded simply for *direction*. In the baseline condition this involved recording the number of infants who looked towards the target. In the other conditions, this involved recording the number of infants who looked in the direction specified by visual flow versus the number that looked in the direction specified by vestibular information. Because the two sources of information always specified opposite directions of looking, and because no infants looked straight ahead, all infants fell into one of these categories. Second, looks were coded according to a stricter *location* criterion. Because there were camera and light positions every 30 degrees, most infants looked quite directly at one of these positions. However, all looks were coded in terms of which of these positions was most closely fixated, and the number of infants looking to target was recorded. In the baseline condition, this involved recording the number of infants whose fixation was closer to the actual target than other locations. In the other conditions, this involved recording the number of infants who looked to the target as specified by visual flow and vestibular information, respectively. Because in this case our interest was in the relative proportions of accurate responding according to visual versus vestibular cues, infants who did not look to target according to this criterion were omitted from the *location* analyses. Our reason for adopting these two criteria was that it is possible for infants to use visual and/or vestibular information at two levels: (a) to simply identify *direction* of movement and (b) to identify *direction and extent* of movement.

In this experiment and the two that follow, 20% of video records were scored by a second scorer naïve to the aims and hypotheses. Inter-scorer reliability was high, with 91% agreement on exact measures and 95% agreement on directional measures.

## Results

Table 2 displays the data, subdivided by age and condition. For both directional and location codings, a binary logistic model was fitted to the data using the Generalized Linear Interactive Modelling (GLIM) Package (Francis, Green & Payne, 1993). In each case, the model was first constructed by adding each factor (Age and Condition) individually. Then, changes in deviance were assessed by addition of the interaction between factors to the model.

**Table 2:** Experiment 2: Number of infants (/18) making longest looks coded according to the direction and location (±15 degrees) criteria relative to target (baseline condition) and relative to visual versus vestibular positions (other conditions)

| | | Baseline | Visual | | Vestibular | | Opposed vis. & vest. | |
| | | | | | Look direction/Location | | | |
| Age | coding | target | visual | vestibular | visual | vestibular | visual | vestibular |
|---|---|---|---|---|---|---|---|---|
| 7m | Direction | 13 | 15 | 3 | 10 | 8 | 12 | 6 |
| | Location | 12 | 9 | 3 | 7 | 3 | 4 | 6 |
| 9m | Direction | 17 | 8 | 10 | 5 | 13 | 6 | 12 |
| | Location | 16 | 7 | 8 | 4 | 8 | 2 | 10 |
| 12m | Direction | 15 | 9 | 9 | 14 | 4 | 11 | 7 |
| | Location | 8 | 8 | 6 | 13 | 4 | 2 | 5 |

The first set of analyses included the data for the *baseline condition,* to provide a reference for performance in the other (experimental) conditions. In these analyses, we were interested in two things; first, how performance in the experimental conditions compared to that in *the baseline condition,* and second, whether performance in the *baseline condition* varied as a function of age. Thus we report condition and age effects for the whole data sets and just age effects for the *baseline condition.* However, given that the *baseline condition* confounds vestibular and visual information, further analyses to tease apart vestibular and visual effects were also carried out omitting the *baseline condition.*

## Analyses Including Baseline Condition

The *direction* measure yielded a significant condition effect, $\chi^2$ (3, N = 216) = 27.15, $p$ < .0001. More infants in the *baseline condition* responded in the direction specified by congruent visual and vestibular cues than responded to either cue singly in the *visual change condition,* $\chi^2$ (1, N = 108) = 20.0, $p$ < .0001, the *vestibular change, and opposed visual and vestibular conditions,* $\chi^2$ (1, N = 108) = 14.66, $p$ = .0001, and there were no other differences in performance between conditions, $\chi^2$ (1, N = 108) .15, $p$ = .69. The age × condition interaction was not significant, $\chi^2$ (6, N = 216) = 7.42, $p$ = .28. There was no significant difference in performance on the *baseline condition* between the three age groups, $\chi^2$ (2, N = 45) = .53, p = .77.

The *location* measure yielded a significant condition effect, $\chi^2$ (3, N = 145) = 51.67, $p$ < .0001, and the data suggest that this arose from more infants responding to congruent visual and vestibular cues in the *baseline condition* than to either cue singly in the experimental conditions. However, parameter estimates and standard errors were inflated, so this effect cannot be interpreted with confidence. The age × condition interaction was not significant, $\chi^2$ (6, N = 145) = 1.96, $p$ = .92. There was no significant difference in performance on the baseline condition between the three age groups, $\chi^2$ (2, N = 36) = 2.67, $p$ = .26.

In summary, performance on the *direction* measure was more strongly polarized in the baseline condition than the experimental conditions, and there were no age effects in performance on the baseline condition. The same appeared to be true of the *location* measure, though the condition effect was hard to evaluate.

## Analyses Omitting Baseline Condition

The *direction* measure yielded a significant age effect, $\chi^2$ (2, N = 216) = 14.07, $p$ = .0008. There was no difference in performance between 7- and 12-month-olds, $\chi^2$ (1, N = 108) = .16, $p$ = .69, but there was significantly more vestibular responding by 9-month-olds than by both 7-month-olds,

$\chi^2$ (1, $N = 108$) $= 10.72$, $p = .001$, and 12-month-olds, $\chi^2$ (1, $N = 108$) $= 7.26$, $p = .007$. The condition effect was not significant, $\chi^2$ (2, $N = 216$) $= .45$, $p = .79$, and the interaction between age and condition was not significant, $\chi^2$ (4, $N = 216$) $= 7.15$, $p = .13$.

The *location* measure yielded a significant age effect, $\chi^2$ (2, $N = 110$) $= 8.05$, $p = .018$. There was no difference in performance between 7- and 12-month-olds, $\chi^2$ (1, $N = 70$) $= .006$, $p = .94$, but there was more vestibular responding by 9-month-olds than by both 7-month-olds, $\chi^2$ (1, $N = 71$) $= 4.89$, $p = .027$, and 12-month-olds, $\chi^2$ (1, $N = 77$) $= 4.68$, $p = .03$. There was also a significant condition effect, $\chi^2$ (2, $N = 109$) $= 9.25$, $p = .01$. There was no difference in performance between the *visual change* and *vestibular change* conditions, $\chi^2$ (1, $N = 80$) $= .02$, $p = .89$, but there were significantly fewer accurate looks in the *opposed visual and vestibular condition* than both the *visual change*, $\chi^2$ (1, $N = 70$) $= 5.37$, $p = .02$, and *vestibular change* conditions, $\chi^2$ (1, $N = 68$) $= 5.7$, $p = .017$.

In summary, for both the *direction* and *location* measures, there was more vestibular responding at 9 months and more visual responding at other ages. Additionally, across all ages and relative to other conditions fewer infants in the *opposed visual and vestibular condition* satisfied the more precise *location* criterion, whether specified by visual or vestibular information.

## Discussion

On the *direction* measure in particular, infants are more accurate in the baseline condition than the other conditions in which vestibular and visual information are manipulated independently. Although the condition effect for the *location* measure was hard to interpret, it appears that the same trend was present there. At first sight, such a finding might seem predictable: when visual and vestibular information combine to specify the same location, performance could be expected to be better. However, the result is important in comparison with adult performance in Experiment 1, which was overwhelmingly guided by visual information. Thus, even though infants showed a clear tendency to rely more on one type of information, it was never such a strong tendency as to be uninfluenced by absent or conflicting information from another sensory channel.

The difference in results for adults and infants is in keeping with the conclusion that adults discount information from one sensory channel when it is particularly disparate from that in another (Banks & Backus, 1998; Blake *et al.*, 1993) whereas children are sensitive to both vestibular and visual information but do not integrate optimally (Nardini *et al.*, 2008) and do not discount disparate information. Additionally, the particularly low frequency of accurate looks in the *opposed visual and vestibular condition* suggests that responding in this task is not guided by one source of information or the other, but by a non-optimal integration of both.

The most striking finding is that, whereas the youngest and oldest age groups responded predominantly according to visual flow information, the 9-month-old group responded predominantly according to vestibular information. In the general discussion, we expand on a possible explanation for this different and unexpected finding at 9 months, by reference to arguments in the literature on locomotion and spatial cognition.

## Experiment 3

Evidence from 7-month-olds in Experiment 2 suggests some influence of vestibular information that leads to rather inconsistent responding across conditions. The question that follows from this is whether younger infants are capable of using vestibular information in a consistent way in spatial orientation. To investigate this we probably need a more sensitive test than included in the current set of conditions. In the *vestibular change condition*, vestibular information for body rotation is present, but visual information specifies non-movement. Although visual information predominates in this condition, that does not mean that infants could not use vestibular information if visual information did not conflict with it. Thus in Experiment 3 we repeated the *vestibular change condition* but turned off the lighting during the test transformation, yielding vestibular information for movement with no conflicting visual information.

## Method

### Participants

Eighteen 6- to 8-month-olds (*M* = 204.6 days; range 183–241 days; 10 girls and eight boys) took part in the experiment. A further four infants did not complete testing due to fussiness.

### Apparatus and Procedure

The same experimental environment was used as in Experiment 2. The procedure was the same as in the *vestibular change condition*, except that the enclosure lighting was extinguished for the duration of the test trial transformation.

## Results and Discussion

Table 3 displays the *direction* and *location* results. These data were analysed relative to chance and relative to comparable conditions in Experiment 2. On

**Table 3:** Number of infants (/18) making longest looks coded according to direction and location criteria relative to target in Experiment 3

| Measure | Direction | Location |
|---|---|---|
| Longest look | 13 | 5 |

the *direction* measure, a significant majority of infants look in the direction specified by vestibular information (*binomial p* = .048). The most marked increase in use of vestibular information relative to the *vestibular change condition* of Experiment 2 is on the *direction* measure, though this difference is not significant, $\chi^2$ (1, $N$ = 36) = 1.83, $p$ = .18. However, there is a significant difference on this measure between the present experiment in which only vestibular information for movement is provided and the *visual change condition* of Experiment 2 in which only visual information for movement is provided, $\chi^2$ (1, $N$ = 36) = 9.11, $p$ = .0025.

This experiment provides evidence that the youngest infants are capable of using vestibular information for movement provided visual information does not specify absence of movement. The effects of vestibular and visual information are not symmetrical, however, because infants in the *visual change condition* of Experiment 2 showed strong reliance on visual information even though vestibular information specified no movement. There are two possible reasons for this asymmetry. First, vestibular information may be less salient than visual information for this age group. Second, beyond considerations of salience, a stable visual field possibly provides more direct positive information for stability than a lack of vestibular input.

## Experiment 4

In the final experiment we turned to clarification of the predominantly vestibular responding by the 9-month-old group in Experiment 2. It seems unlikely that this occurred because the visual flow information arising from structure and texture in the surround was insufficient to be detected by this group. However, we can test the strength of the vestibular tendency by enhancing visual information for movement. If the vestibular tendency were particularly strong we would expect little or no effect of enhancing visual information, whereas if we are dealing with the outcome of relative salience of different forms of information, enhancement of visual information might produce a significant shift to visual responding.

The *opposed visual and vestibular condition* in Experiment 2 provided strongest evidence of vestibular responding by the 9-month-old group. Thus in Experiment 4 we presented this condition to a group of 8- to 10-month-olds, enhancing visual differentiation by attaching black discs to the surround.

**Table 4:** Number of infants (/18) making longest looks coded according to direction and location criteria relative to target in Experiment 4

| Measure | Direction | | Location | |
|---|---|---|---|---|
| | visual | vestibular | visual | vestibular |
| Longest look | 8 | 10 | 4 | 7 |

## Method

### Participants

Eighteen 8- to 10-month-old infants ($M$ = 272.9 days; range 247–314 days; seven girls and 11 boys) took part in the experiment. A further three did not complete testing due to fussiness.

### Apparatus and Procedure

The same experimental environment was used as in previous experiments, with the addition of 24 black fabric discs, measuring 25 cm in diameter. The discs were attached to the walls of the circular room at 30-degree intervals, the centres half-way between each camera lens. The discs were attached in two rows, with the centres of the top row 45 cm from the roof of the room and those of the bottom row 70 cm from the floor of the room. This arrangement ensured that none of the discs provided the infants with a beacon landmark to the target location. The experimental procedure was the same as in the *opposed visual and vestibular condition* of Experiment 2.

### Results and Discussion

Table 4 displays the *direction* and *location* results. Although the vestibular tendency is somewhat reduced relative to the equivalent condition in Experiment 2, vestibular responding still predominates. On neither measure is there evidence of a significant reduction in vestibular responding relative to Experiment 2 as a result of the enhanced visual flow information, *direction*, $\chi^2$ (1, $N$ = 36) = 0.12, $p$ = .73; *location*, $\chi^2$ (1, $N$ = 36) = 0.36, $p$ = .55. The absence of any clear evidence of response to what might be assumed to be highly salient information for visual flow adds support to the conclusion that this age group is responding in a very different way from 7-month-olds, 12-month-olds, and adults.

## General Discussion

In common with adults, 7- and 12-month-olds in Experiment 2 responded predominantly to visual flow information. However, unlike adults, they showed different performance relative to baseline in conditions in which visual and vestibular cues were incongruent, particularly on the location measure in the condition in which visual and vestibular cues were in direct opposition. This suggests partial sensitivity to information in both modalities rather than the total reliance on visual information seen in adults, and Experiment 3 shows that 6-month-olds used vestibular information when there was no conflicting visual information. The most striking finding is the predominance of vestibular responding by 9-month-olds, which persists even when visual information is enhanced (Experiment 4). The findings of Experiment 2 are of primary importance and also provide the greatest theoretical challenge. In particular, why do 9-month-olds rely primarily on vestibular information whereas 12-month-olds and 7-month-olds rely primarily on visual flow information?

First, we conclude that this effect is specific to spatial orientation, because no such developmental pattern is evident in the case of maintenance of posture, in which visual flow information appears primary across age (Bertenthal & Bai, 1989; Bertenthal *et al.*, 1997; Butterworth & Hicks, 1977; Lee & Lishman, 1975). To understand our effect, it may help to consider the forms of spatial orientation that infants are engaged in, both before and after the onset of locomotion. Interpretations of spatial orientation and maintenance of heading tend to be couched in terms of infants constructing new ways of organizing space that are appropriate for their new-found postural or motor capabilities (Bremner, 1993; Bremner & Bryant, 1985; Newcombe & Huttenlocher, 2000). And other approaches portray children and adults as engaged in processes of calibrating perceptual information in relation to action (Pick, Rieser, Wagner & Garing, 1999; Rieser, Pick, Ashmead & Garing, 1995). In both cases, action is central to development, and investigating spatial cognition in relation to developing action may provide the best means of explaining the present data.

Two milestones in development may be particularly important. Once infants can sit unaided (at around 6–7 months) they are able to inspect the world through controlled movements of eyes, head, and trunk. It has been argued elsewhere (Bremner, 1993; Bremner & Bryant, 1985; Newcombe & Huttenlocher, 2000) that this may be an important milestone in spatial development, and those movements now under the infant's control bring about the same sorts of visual flow as occur in the current task. It is noteworthy that the vestibular sense provides good information regarding rotational accelerations of this sort (Bresciani, Gauthier, Vercher & Blouin, 2005; Ivanenko *et al.*, 1997).

This analysis explains how infants might begin to take account of body rotation, but does not explain the temporary dominance of vestibular information around 9 months. A possible reason for this arises from another milestone in motor development. The onset of locomotion has been widely identified as a likely contributor to various aspects of spatial ability (Bertenthal & Campos, 1990; Bremner, 1993; Bremner & Bryant, 1985; Clearfield, 2004;

Horobin & Acredolo, 1986). Around 9 months, most UK infants begin to crawl, and their attentional resources are likely to be focused on this new activity. We believe that it is possible to develop a plausible explanation of our developmental effect that relates to the onset of locomotion, though we recognize that, because we did not have data on the locomotor status of our infants at the time of testing, this explanation must remain tentative.

While crawling, visual and vestibular inputs are congruent, so one might assume that there is no advantage in abandoning previous reliance on visual information. However, Bertenthal and Campos (1990) argue that experiences accompanying the onset of independent locomotion lead infants to expect specific correlations between visual and vestibular information during loco-motion. And, in time, they experience negative emotional reactions when the correlation is perturbed, such as when the infant approaches a visual drop-off (Campos, Anderson, Barbu-Roth, Hubbard, Hertenstein & Witherington, 2000). To become aware of correlations between visual and vestibular information it is likely necessary to attend to how both relate to kinaesthetic information about limb position and movement during locomotion. In consequence, vestibular information may acquire greater salience than earlier in development.

This, however, does not explain why this age group use vestibular information preferentially. But a possible reason for reliance on vestibular information for heading during early locomotion arises from consideration of factors that contribute to variability of visual information. Whereas vestibular information should be more or less constant for a given rate of locomotion, visual information depends also on the structure of the environment. As pointed out by Campos and colleagues, visual flow information is perturbed when infants approach a drop-off. Also, visual information is likely less salient in visually sparse environments, it having been shown that adults are less likely to use visual flow information under these circumstances (Bruggeman et al., 2007). Finally, the precise form of visual flow information will depend on the size and shape of the environment. These considerations suggest that, even if vestibular information for movement is subtle relative to visual information, constructing an active mapping between vestibular information and kinaesthetic information for movement may call on fewer resources because of the more or less constant relationship between the two. In contrast, the construction of a mapping to visual information is liable to be more complex through having to deal with variations in visual information resulting from differences in structure of the environments in which locomotion takes place, and its calibration to kinaesthetic information generated by movement may even depend on the presence of vestibular information that is unaffected by changes in environmental structure.

But why is there a shift to visual responding by 12 months? Once locomotion is achieved, there are at least two reasons why visual information can be expected to become dominant. First, because the vestibular system is an inertial sensor stimulated by acceleration forces, it provides no direct information about linear velocity, and even vestibular information about linear accelerations is ambiguous, being confusable with body tilts (Wertheim *et al.*, 2001). This provides good reasons why visual information would ultimately be relied upon more as a means of keeping track of translatory movements during crawling. Second, vision provides information regarding the spatial layout in which the infant is moving, whereas vestibular information does not. Thus, for the mobile infant, vision provides accurate information about displacements and the layout of the environment, effectively providing veridical information about the infant's orientation and movement in space.

We should not conclude that vestibular information about linear displacements is inferior to visual information in all respects. Although visual information provides better information about linear (constant) velocity, vestibular information provides better information for linear accelerations, and both forms of information may be important in the perception of linear movement (Schaffer & Durgin, 2005). The conclusion that both sources provide important information for movement is in keeping with the fact that, even at 12 months, there was evidence for at least some influence of vestibular information and with work indicating that adults tend to integrate intersensory information in an optimal manner (Ernst & Banks, 2002). One puzzle is why adults are so exclusively influenced by visual information in our task, particularly when the experimental manipulation involves just the form of rotational movements that the vestibular system seems well equipped to detect. The answer may be that in normal environments visual input provides veridical information about the relationship between the individual and environmental features, providing direct information about the spatial relationship between self and the targets of action. Thus it is likely to receive a higher weighting on the basis of its greater reliability (Ernst & Bülthoff, 2004; Morgan *et al.*, 2008) and when large disparities between visual and vestibular information are introduced, vestibular information is liable to be discounted.

## Note

1. Body movements are signalled by body pressure sensation as well as the vestibular system. It is not the aim to distinguish these sources and throughout the paper the term vestibular information is used to include both sources.

## References

Acredolo, L.P. (1978). Development of spatial orientation in infancy. *Developmental Psychology*, **14**, 224–234.
Acredolo, L.P., & Evans, D. (1980). Developmental changes in the effects of landmarks on infant spatial behavior. *Developmental Psychology*, **16**, 312–318.
Banks, M.S., & Backus, B.T. (1998). Extra-retinal and perspective cues cause the small range of induced effect. *Vision Research*, **38**, 187–194.

Bertenthal, B.I., & Bai, D.L. (1989). Infants' sensitivity to optical flow for controlling posture. *Developmental Psychology*, **25**, 936–945.

Bertenthal, B.I., & Campos, J.J. (1990). A systems approach to the organizing effects of self-produced locomotion during infancy. In C. Rovee-Collier & L.P. Lipsitt (Eds.), *Advances in infancy research* (Vol. 6, pp. 1–60). Norwood, NJ: Ablex.

Bertenthal, B.I., Rose, J.L., & Bai, D.L. (1997). Perception–action coupling in the development of visual control of posture. *Journal of Experimental Psychology: Human Perception and Performance*, **23**, 1631–1643.

Blake, A., Bülthoff, H.H., & Sheinberg, D. (1993). Shape and texture: ideal observer and human psychophysics. *Vision Research*, **33**, 1723–1737.

Blouin, J., Gauthier, G.M., & Vercher, J.-L. (1995). Failure to update the egocentric representation of the visual space through labyrinthine signal. *Brain and Cognition*, **29**, 1–22.

Bremner, J.G. (1978a). Egocentric versus allocentric spatial coding in nine-month-old infants: factors influencing the choice of code. *Developmental Psychology*, **14**, 346–355.

Bremner, J.G. (1978b). Spatial errors made by infants: inadequate spatial cues or evidence for egocentrism? *British Journal of Psychology*, **69**, 77–84.

Bremner, J.G. (1993). The emergence of new motor activities as a cause of cognitive development in infancy. In G.J.P. Savelsbergh (Ed.), *The development of coordination in infancy* (pp. 47–77). Amsterdam: Elsevier/North Holland.

Bremner, J.G., & Bryant, P.E. (1985). Active movement and development of spatial abilities in infancy. In H. Wellman (Ed.), *Children's searching: The development of search skill and spatial representation* (pp. 47–78). New York: Lawrence Erlbaum Associates.

Bresciani, J.-P., Gauthier, G.M., Vercher, J.-L., & Blouin, J. (2005). On the nature of the vestibular control of arm-reaching movements during whole-body rotations. *Experimental Brain Research*, **164**, 431–441.

Bruggeman, H., Zosh, W., & Warren, W. (2007). Optic flow drives human visuo-locomotor adaptation. *Current Biology*, **17**, 2035–2040.

Butterworth, G., & Hicks, L. (1977). Visual proprioception and postural stability in infancy: a developmental study. *Perception*, **6**, 255–262.

Campos, J.J., Anderson, D.I., Barbu-Roth, M.A., Hubbard, E.M., Hertenstein, M.J., & Witherington, D. (2000). Travel broadens the mind. *Infancy*, **1**, 149–221.

Clearfield, M.W. (2004). The role of crawling and walking experience in infant spatial memory. *Journal of Experimental Child Psychology*, **89**, 214–241.

Cohen, H.S. (2000). Vestibular disorders and impaired path integration along a linear trajectory. *Journal of Vestibular Research*, **10**, 7–15.

Cornell, E.H., & Heth, C.D. (1979). Response versus place learning in human infants. *Journal of Experimental Psychology: Human Learning and Memory*, **5**, 188–196.

Ernst, M.O., & Banks, M.S. (2002). Humans integrate visual and haptic information in a statistically optimal fashion. *Nature*, **415**, 429–433.

Ernst, M.O., & Bülthoff, H.H. (2004). Merging the senses into a robust percept. *Trends in Cognitive Sciences*, **8**, 162–169.

Fetsch, C.R., Turner, A.H., DeAngelis, G.C., & Angelaki, D.E. (2009). Dynamic reweighting of visual and vestibular cues during self-motion perception. *Journal of Neuroscience*, **29**, 15601–15612.

Francis, B.J., Green, M., & Payne, C. (Eds.) (1993). *The GLIM system release 4 manual*. Oxford: Oxford University Press.

Gori, M., Del Viva, M., Sandini, G., & Burr, D.C. (2008). Young children do not integrate visual and haptic form information. *Current Biology*, **18**, 694–698.

Gu, Y., Angelaki, D.E., & DeAngelis, G.C. (2008). Neural correlates of multisensory cue integration in macaque MSTd. *Nature Neuroscience*, **11**, 1201–1209.

Guillaud, E., Gauthier, G., Vercher, J.-L., & Blouin, J. (2006). Fusion of visuo-ocular and vestibular signals in arm motor control. *Journal of Neurophysiology*, **95**, 1134–1146.

Hermer, L., & Spelke, E. (1996). Modularity and development: the case of spatial reorientation. *Cognition*, **61**, 195–232.

Horobin, K., & Acredolo, L. (1986). The role of attentiveness, mobility history, and separation of hiding sites on stage IV search behavior. *Journal of Experimental Child Psychology*, **41**, 114–127.

Ivanenko, Y., Grasso, R., Israel, I., & Berthoz, A. (1997). Spatial orientation in humans: perception of angular whole-body displacements in two-dimensional trajectories. *Experimental Brain Research*, **117**, 419–427.

Keating, M.B., McKenzie, B.E., & Day, R.H. (1986). Spatial localization in infancy: position constancy in a square and circular room with and without a landmark. *Child Development*, **57**, 115–124.

Klatsky, R.L., Loomis, J.M., Beall, A.C., Chance, S.S., & Golledge, R.G. (1998). Spatial updating of self-position and orientation during real, imagined, and virtual locomotion. *Psychological Science*, **9**, 293–298.

Lepecq, J.-C., & Lafaite, M. (1989). The early development of position constancy in a no landmark environment. *British Journal of Developmental Psychology*, **7**, 289–306.

Lee, D.N., & Aronson, E. (1974). Visual proprioceptive control of standing in human infants. *Perception & Psychophysics*, **15**, 529–532.

Lee, D.N., & Lishman, J.R. (1975). Visual proprioceptive control of stance. *Journal of Human Movement Studies*, **1**, 87–95.

Lew, A.R., Foster, K.A., & Bremner, J.G. (2006). Disorientation inhibits landmark use in 12–18–month-old infants. *Infant Behavior and Development*, **29**, 334–341.

McKenzie, B.E., Day, R.H., & Ihsen, E. (1984). Localization of events in space: young infants are not always egocentric. *British Journal of Developmental Psychology*, **2**, 1–9.

Meuwissen, I., & McKenzie, B.E. (1987). Localization of an event by young infants: the effects of visual and body movement information. *British Journal of Developmental Psychology*, **5**, 1–8.

Morgan, M.L., DeAngelis, G.C., & Angelaki, D.E. (2008). Multisensory integration in macaque visual cortex depends on cue reliability. *Neuron*, **59**, 662–673.

Nardini, M., Jones, P., Bedford, R., & Braddick, O. (2008). Development of cue integration in human navigation. *Current Biology*, **18**, 689–693.

Newcombe, N.S., & Huttenlocher, J. (2000). *Making space: The development of spatial representation and reasoning*. Cambridge, MA: MIT Press.

Pick, H.L., Jr., Rieser, J.J., Wagner, D., & Garing, A.E. (1999). The recalibration of rotational locomotion. *Journal of Experimental Psychology: Human Perception and Performance*, **25**, 1179–1188.

Riecke, B.E., von der Heyde, M., & Bülthoff, H.H. (2004). Spatial updating in real and virtual environments – contribution and interaction of visual and vestibular cues. *Proceedings of the 1st Symposium on Applied Perception in Graphics and Visualization* (pp. 9–17). New York: ACM Press.

Riecke, B.E., von der Heyde, M., & Bülthoff, H.H. (2005). Visual cues can be sufficient for triggering automatic, reflexlike spatial updating. *ACM Transactions on Applied Perception*, **2**, 183–215.

Rieser, J.J. (1979). Spatial orientation of six-month-old infants. *Child Development*, **50**, 1078–1087.

Rieser, J.J., Ashmead, D.A., Talor, C., & Youngquist, G. (1990). Visual perception and the guidance of locomotion without vision to previously seen targets. *Perception*, **19**, 675–689.

Rieser, J.J., Pick, H.L., Jr., Ashmead, D.H., & Garing, A.E. (1995). Calibration of human locomotion and models of perceptual-motor organization. *Journal of Experimental Psychology: Human Perception and Performance*, **21**, 480–497.

Rosander, K., & von Hofsten, C. (2000). Visual–vestibular interaction in early infancy. *Experimental Brain Research*, **133**, 321–333.

Schaffer, E.S., & Durgin, F.H. (2005). Visual–vestibular dissociation: differential sensitivity to acceleration and velocity. *Journal of Vision*, **5**, 332a.

Simons, D.J., & Wang, R.F. (1998). Perceiving real-world viewpoint changes. *Psychological Science*, **9**, 315–320.

Stackman, R.W., & Herbert, A.M. (2002). Rats with lesions of the vestibular system require a visual landmark for spatial navigation. *Behavioral Brain Research*, **128**, 27–40.

Tyler, D., & McKenzie, B.E. (1990). Spatial updating and training effects in the first year of human infancy. *Journal of Experimental Child Psychology*, **50**, 445–461.

Wallace, D.G., Hines, D.J., Pellis, S.M., & Whishaw, I.Q. (2002). Vestibular information is required for dead reckoning in the rat. *Journal of Neuroscience*, **22**, 10009–10017.

Wertheim, A.H., Mesland, B.S., & Bles, W. (2001). Cognitive suppression of tilt sensations during linear horizontal self-motion in the dark. *Perception*, **30**, 733–741.

Wong, S.C.P., & Frost, B.J. (1981). The effect of visual–vestibular conflict and the latency of steady-state visually induced subjective rotation. *Perception & Psychophysics*, **30**, 228–236.

# 45

# Effect of Self-Produced Locomotion on Infant Postural Compensation to Optic Flow

*Carol I. Higgins, Joseph J. Campos and Rosanne Kermoian*

I n recent years the field of perceptual development has focused on the relation between perception and action, as well as on the identification of processes underlying perceptual development (Bertenthal, 1993). One perceptual motor phenomenon drawing increasing attention is that of visual proprioception, the process whereby visual stimulation elicits a sensation of self-motion and provides vital information for the control of posture (Dichgans & Brandt, 1978). Although proprioceptive sensory information is available from the muscular system through the inertia of the limbs and from the vestibular system through registering angular and linear accelerations of the head, the most powerful proprioceptive sensory information originates externally from the pattern of optical information flowing across the retina when observers move their heads (Gibson, 1966; Lishman & Lee, 1973). When muscular and vestibular information specify that the self is not moving, but optic flow information specifies self-motion, observers respond with postural adjustments (Butterworth & Hicks, 1977; Lee & Aronson, 1974; Lishman & Lee, 1973) and report sensations of self-motion (Lee & Lishman, 1975; Lishman & Lee, 1973). Observer postural adjustment is a sway of the torso and head in the direction of the optic flow, and often a compensatory sway in the opposite direction that returns the observer's center of gravity to a balanced position (Lishman & Lee, 1973). In adults, such postural adjustments occur in

**Source:** *Developmental Psychology*, 32(5) (1996): 836–841.

response to motion of the entire optic field, as well as to motion of portions of the optic field (Stoffregan, 1985). These findings suggest that optic flow is important not only for sensing self-motion but also for providing feedback critical to postural control.

The visual control of posture undergoes a critical development between the ages of 7 and 9 months: 9-month-olds, but not 7-month-olds are able to use partial optic flow fields for postural control (Bertenthal & Bai, 1989). Despite 7-month-olds' visual ability to perceive motion (Aslin & Shea, 1990; Bertenthal & Bradbury, 1992) and muscular ability to make postural adjustments (Bertenthal & Bai, 1989), they do not use the information available from partial optic flow fields in the service of postural control.

Gibson (1979) suggested that motoric experience can influence whether available stimulus information will be noticed and therefore used by observers. Experience related to self-locomotion may allow infants to convert potentially effective information from the optic flow field into information useful for postural control. Bertenthal and Campos (1990) elaborated on how motor experience might influence whether infant observers will notice and use information in the optic display: They suggested that infants' experience with voluntary self-produced locomotion acted as a "setting event" that allowed infants to make use of information available in the optic display of the visual cliff. In the same way, experience associated with self-produced locomotion may function as a "setting event" for the use of optic flow information for postural control. Self-produced locomotion, as compared with passive locomotion, provides the setting in which the visual cues for postural control are most useful: Passively moved observers, as exemplified by infants carried over adults' shoulders, need not attend to visual cues in the same way self-moving observers must attend to the optic display in order to navigate through the environment.

Self-moving observers' tendency to look in the direction of locomotion is particularly pronounced in newly self-mobile infants. Infants observed in laboratory locomotion evaluations who were moving themselves by either hands-and-knees creeping or using a walker device routinely directed their gaze at a specific target object and moved toward that object without deviation (Higgins, 1993). Such a consistent head and eye orientation while locomoting creates a highly reliable pattern of optic flow information, characterized by radial (i.e., starlike, as the spokes at the center of a bicycle wheel) flow in the central visual field and lamellar (i.e., almost parallel, as the spokes of a large bicycle wheel at its perimeter) flow in the peripheral visual field (Gibson, 1966). If the direction of looking shifts away from the direction of locomotion, then the area of the retina experiencing lamellar or radial optic flow also shifts. Because of the interaction between the direction of looking and the structure of optic flow experienced, nascent self-locomotor infants, as compared with passively moved infants, have different probabilistic levels of experience with the structure of optic flow generated by looking in the direction of locomotion.

We hypothesized that early self-locomotion and the perceptual experience associated with it may provide the "setting event" for the observed developmental transition in the use of optic flow for postural control. To test our hypothesis, we conducted two studies using the moving-room paradigm, in which stationary observers experience optic flow as a result of the motion of the walls and ceiling of the small room in which they stand or sit. Such optic flow results in reliable and measurable postural adjustments in the same direction as the motion of the room (Bertenthal & Bai, 1989; Lee & Lishman, 1975; Stoffregen, 1985). By manipulating the direction of the observer's gaze and which walls of the room move during a given experimental trial, we can present optic flow to the entire visual field or to a specific portion of the visual field (e.g.. central or peripheral).

In the first study, we pinpointed the age of the developmental transition in sensitivity to optic flow by using a cross-sectional design to compare the postural responsiveness of 7-, 8-, and 9-month-old infants. In the second study, we held age constant and manipulated locomotor experience in quasiexperimental fashion by contrasting postural responses to differing conditions of optic flow in three groups of infants: (a) infants who had no self-produced locomotor experience (prelocomotor infants), (b) infants who had experience with hands-and-knees creeping but did not use a walker (creeping infants), and (c) infants who had no creeping or crawling experience but were proficient at moving about in a walker (walker infants). This design allowed us to determine whether self-produced locomotor experience influenced postural responses independent of age and whether artificial self-produced locomotor experience was effective for infants who could not crawl or creep.

## Study 1

To specify the age of the developmental shift in visual control of posture, we used a cross-sectional design to compare the postural responsiveness of 7-, 8-, and 9-month-old infants to four conditions of optic flow. We predicted that age would affect response to optic flow created by the side-wall-motion condition, but it would not affect response to the other three conditions of optic flow – whole-room motion, front-wall motion, and no motion. From previous results (Bertenthal & Bai, 1989), we expected the side-wall-motion condition to elicit greater responses in 9-month-olds than in 7-month-olds. However, the behavior of 8-month-olds was unknown.

# Method

## Participants

Participants were twelve 9-month-olds (mean age = 39.9 weeks), twelve 8-month-olds (mean age = 34.5 weeks), and twelve 7-month-olds (mean age = 30.4 weeks). One additional 7-month-old was tested but did not complete the moving-room paradigm because of discomfort from extreme diaper rash. All participants were healthy full-term infants whose ethnicity was African American, Asian, Caucasian, Hispanic, or Filipino.

## Apparatus

The major pieces of equipment were a moving room, an infant seat supported by four pressure transducers, and a 386/33 MHz personal computer. The moving room was a 1.2 × 1.2 × 2.1 m (Height × Width × Length) room with a stationary floor and one wall removed. Wheels beneath the side walls allowed the room to move forward and backward in the direction of its long axis. The interior walls and ceiling of the room were covered with blue fabric having white polka-dots; the stationary floor of the room was covered with white padded fabric. The room was illuminated with two light tubes located at the top center of the two side walls. A box located in a recess of the front wall contained a mechanical toy dog that lit up and made noise to direct the infant toward the front wall during wall movement. At its farthest distance, the front wall was 39 in. (95.55 cm) from the infant, subtending a visual angle of 50° × 50°; at its nearest distance, the front wall was 24 in. (62.5 cm) from the infant, subtending a visual angle of 63° × 63°.

The construction of the moving room permitted the front wall to move either independently of or in conjunction with the two side walls. This allowed presentation of optic flow to different sections of the observer's visual field. Moving the front and side walls together presented global optic flow to the entire visual field. Moving only the front wall presented radial optic flow to the central visual field. Moving only the side walls and ceiling presented lamellar optic flow to the visual periphery. Both the side walls and the front wall were attached to a potentiometer that measured any motion of the room in either direction. Outputs were digitally sampled from the potentiometer at a rate of 50 Hz.

Any motions made by infants were measured by voltage offsets from four pressure-sensitive transducers located at the corners of a force plate under a plastic infant chair. Postural adjustments made by infants seated in the chair changed the distribution of the forces on the pressure transducers, altering the pattern of voltage offsets. The voltage-offset patterns reflecting infant motion were digitally sampled at a rate of 50 Hz and were time-locked with the samples of room motion.

## Procedure

Infants remained seated in the infant chair through 14 trials of wall movement. During the 14 trials, parents either stood outside the moving room watching their infant on a video monitor or sat in the moving room, behind and out of the infant's view. In the first and last trials the room did not move: These were control trials to assess the infant's baseline postural adjustment in the absence of room motion. In the other 12 trials the room moved 14 in. (35.5 cm) in a single direction over the course of 2.0 s. To manipulate the location of optic flow in the infant's visual field, there were three conditions of wall motion (global motion, front-wall motion, and side-wall motion), in which the walls moved toward the infant twice and away from the infant twice. Each infant received three blocks of four trials in each condition, with the order of conditions across blocks randomized across infants.

Before each trial, the toy dog in the front wall was activated to gain the infant's attention. To control for retinal location of optic flow stimulation, the trial began only after the infant looked toward the front wall, The infant's center of pressure and the location of the moving room were sampled for 2.0 s prior to the onset of wall motion, as well as for 2.0 s during wall motion and 2.0 s after the cessation of wall motion. Because a shift in direction of looking changes the retinal location of optic flow, a trial was repeated if the infant looked away from the front wall prior to the onset of wall motion or during the period of wall motion. Direction of infant gaze was monitored by both an experimenter looking through a hole in the back of the box containing the toy dog and an experimenter viewing the infant on a video monitor.

After being tested in the moving room, infants' locomotor status was determined by means of a parental interview concerning his or her infant's locomotor history, which was validated by a videotaped assessment of the infant's ability to creep forward on hands and knees 10 ft, without stopping to rest or untangle limbs, to obtain a desired object (based on Kermoian & Campos, 1988). For infants who used a walker at home, the assessment was repeated with the infants moving a walker.

## Analysis

We assessed infant postural response as a function of age and the different conditions of optic flow. Cross-correlations of the postural motion of the infant with the motion of the room on each trial were used to assess the amount of infant sway predictable by the room motion. Sampling every 20 ms, the 2.0-s trial generated 100 data points for infant sway as well as for room motion. These data points were analyzed with the DADiSP data analysis program (1990), which computed cross-correlations.

The cross-correlation values were normalized as Z scores (to fulfill the analysis of variance [ANOVA] assumption of normal distribution) and subjected to a 3 × 4 ANOVA comparing responses across three age groups using four conditions of wall motion as a within-subject variable.[1] Significant interactions were further investigated by looking at the simple effects of age at each of the four conditions of wall motion. Significant simple effects were followed by Tukcy tests for simple comparisons. We evaluated whether infants made significant responses to whole-room, side-wall, and front-wall motion by making Dunnett comparisons to the no-motion control condition at each age.

## Results and Discussion

Infant response to optic flow was found to interact with age and condition of wall motion. $F(6.99) = 3.3, p < .005$. Infant response to side-wall motion was found to be a function of age, $F(2, 33) = 4.8, p < .01$; however, response to the other three conditions of wall motion was not found to be affected by age (see Figure 1). Nine- and 8-month-olds showed significantly higher responses to the side-wall condition than did 7-month-olds ($p < .05$). Additionally, 9- and 8-month-olds showed significantly greater responses to the side-wall-motion condition (9-months: $M = .540$; 8-months: $M = .516$) than to the no-motion condition (9-months: $M = .126$; 8-months: $M = .121$; $p < .05$). In contrast, 7-month-olds showed no significant difference between response to side-wall motion ($M = .239$) and to the no-motion control condition ($M = .167$). These results suggest that between the ages of 7 and 8 months, there is a developmental shift in infants' ability to use a peripheral optic flow field for postural control.

In contrast to the findings for side-wall motion, age was not significantly related to infant response to whole-room motion, front-wall motion, or the

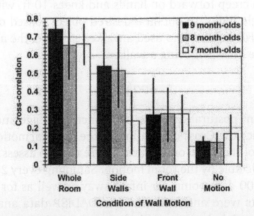

**Figure 1:** Mean postural sway (measured as cross-correlation) as a function of condition of wall motion for three age groups ($n = 12$). Error bars represent standard deviations. Group means and standard deviations are based on raw data, not normalized data.

no-motion control condition. Global optic flow did not elicit differential effects among 9-month-olds ($M = .741$), 8-month-olds ($M = .653$), and 7-month-olds ($M = .662$). Neither did central optic flow elicit differential effects among 9-month-olds ($M = .271$), 8-month-olds ($M = .278$), and 7-month-olds ($M = .277$). Nor did the control condition elicit differential effects among 9-month-olds ($M = .126$), 8-month-olds ($M = .121$), and 7-month-olds ($M = .167$). These results suggested developmental stability in response to whole-room motion, front-wall motion, and the no-motion control condition between 7 and 9 months of age.

All age groups' responses to global optic flow were significantly greater than their responses to the no-motion condition ($p < .05$). This level of response suggested that global optic flow fields were effective elicitors of postural response and that by 7 months of age, infants had the postural control necessary to respond to optic flow.

In the front-wall-motion condition, only 8-month-olds showed significantly higher responses to the front-wall than to the no-motion condition ($p < .05$). Despite their ability to make postural responses, 7- and 9-month-olds showed no significant response to the front wall. Considering that previous moving-room studies have not found significant responses to the front wall in infants (Bertenthal & Bai, 1989; Study 2 of this article) or adults (Stoffregen, 1985). The anomalous response pattern of the 8-month-olds was treated as a random event.

As all age groups received the same stimulus conditions, stimulus-based explanations, such as stimulus size or geometric structure, cannot adequately explain the variation in response to the side-wall condition. To further explore possible factors affecting response to optic flow, we examined the possibility that response to side-wall motion developed as a function of self-produced locomotor experience, which typically begins around 8 months of age. On closer examination of the 8-month-olds in Study 1, we found three major categories of locomotor experience: infants who were able to creep and had no experience moving a walker ($n = 5$), infants who had no creeping experience but were able to move themselves in a walker ($n = 2$), and infants who had no forward progression experience ($n = 3$). From these very small groups of participants, we conducted an exploratory comparison of the postural responses of the three groups of 8-month-olds. We observed that the mean response to side-wall motion was higher for the two groups of infants with self-locomotor experience (creeping, $M = .669$ and walker, $M = .546$) than for the group of infants without self-locomotor experience (prelocomotor, $M = .266$). Although exploratory in nature, the difference between infants with and without self-locomotor experience suggested that the differential responsiveness to the side-wall-motion condition might have been a function of self-produced locomotor experience rather than merely a function of age.

# Study 2

To investigate the role of self-produced locomotor experience in the development of the visual control of posture, we used an age-held-constant study to compare the fore–aft postural responses of three groups of 8-month-old infants who differed in self-produced locomotor experience. One group of infants had experience with hands-and-knees creeping, one group of infants had experience moving a walker, and one group of infants had no self-produced locomotor experience. From our hypothesis of the role of-self-produced locomotor experience in the developmental shift in the use of optic flow, we predicted that locomotor experience would affect responses to the side-wall-motion condition but not responses to the other conditions of optic flow. Specifically, we expected infants with experience creeping and infants with experience moving about in walkers to show greater response than prelocomotor infants to the side-wall-motion condition.

## Method

### Participants

Participants were thirty 8-month-old infants (mean age = 34.2 weeks; range = 33–36 weeks). There were three locomotor classifications: 10 participants were able to creep forward on their hands and knees 10 ft without stopping and had no experience moving a walker; 10 were able to move forward in a walker 10 ft without stopping and had no experience creeping on their hands and knees; and 10 had no experience with forward progression. All participants were healthy full-term infants whose ethnicity was African American, Asian, Caucasian, Hispanic, or Filipino.

We tested 63 infants to obtain the sample of 30. Of the 33 infants not included in the sample, 2 did not complete the procedure because of distress in the moving room, and 16 exhibited locomotor behavior that did not conform to the requirements of the three locomotor groups (e.g., infants who were proficient at moving themselves in a walker prior to becoming proficient at creeping or crawling). An additional 15 infants were classified into locomotor groups that were already filled with 10 participants. The data from these 15 infants were not included in the analysis for reasons explained later in the *Analysis* section.

### Apparatus

The apparatus was the same as in Study 1.

## Procedure

The procedure was the same as in Study 1.

## Analysis

We assessed 8-month-olds' postural response as a function of locomotor experience and the different conditions of optic flow. To hold the amount of locomotor experience constant across the two locomotor groups, walker infants were matched with creeping infants who had an equal number of weeks' experience moving themselves forward 10 ft without stopping. For example, a walker infant with 1 week of experience moving forward was matched with a creeping infant with 1 week of experience moving forward, and a walker infant with 4 weeks of experience moving forward was matched with a creeping infant with 4 weeks of experience moving forward. Thus the 10 walker infants were compared with 10 creeping infants who had roughly equivalent experience with self-produced locomotion. The use of this matching procedure resulted in obtaining data from 15 surplus infants, the data from whom were not analyzed because the infants could not be matched for locomotor experience.

The two locomotor-experienced groups were also compared with a group of 10 prelocomotor infants. We calculated cross-correlations as in Study 1 and analyzed the normalized data for three locomotor groups and four conditions of wall motion as in Study 1.

## Results and Discussion

Infant response to optic flow was found to interact with locomotor status and condition of wall motion, $F(6, 81) = 2.79, p < .016$. Self-produced locomotor experience affected infant response to side-wall motion, $F(2, 27) = 7.98, p < .002$, but did not affect response to the other three conditions of optic flow. In the side-wall-motion condition, prelocomotor infants ($M = .319$) were significantly less responsive than creeping ($M = .646, p < .01$) or walker ($M = .557, p < .01$) infants (see Figure 2).

Prelocomotor infants showed no significant difference in response to the side-wall-motion condition and to the no-motion condition. Conversely, creeping and walker infants showed significantly higher responses to the side-wall-motion condition than to the no-motion condition ($p < .05$). Means for the no-motion condition for prelocomotor, creeping, and walker infants were .117, .167, and .126, respectively. These results suggest that experience related to self-produced locomotion facilitates infants' use of peripheral optic flow for postural control.

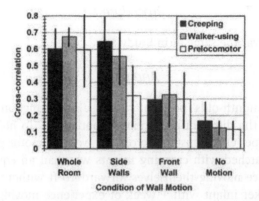

**Figure 2:** Mean postural sway (measured as cross-correlation) as a function of condition of wall motion for three locomotor groups (n = 10). Error bars represent standard deviations. Group means and standard deviations are based on raw data, not normalized data.

In contrast, locomotor experience had no significant effect on infants' response to whole-room motion or to front-wall motion. All locomotor groups showed significantly higher responses to the whole-room-motion condition than to the no-motion condition ($p < .05$); no locomotor group showed significantly higher responses to the front-wall-motion condition than to the no-motion condition. These results suggest that locomotor experience does not affect response to the motion of the front wall or the whole room.

Taken together, the results of this study implicate the effects of self-produced locomotor experience, rather than age, as an effective factor facilitating sensitivity to peripheral optic flow.

## General Discussion

Results of these studies implicate experience associated with early self-produced locomotion as a factor influencing the ability to use partial optic flow fields for postural control. Infants with self-produced locomotor experience typically shifted their posture in response to side-wall motion, whereas infants without self-produced locomotor experience did not shift their posture to side-wall motion.

These results suggest that the developmental shift in the use of optic flow for postural control may be more closely linked to experience than to maturational factors alone. With age held constant, only infants with self-produced locomotor experience responded to the side-wall-motion condition. Furthermore, infants with no creeping experience, those who received artificial self-produced locomotor experience with the use of a walker, showed responsiveness equivalent to those who had creeping experience. Factors proposed by maturational theories (Butterworth, 1992) do not explain why artificial self-produced locomotor experience should facilitate the use of optic flow to the same degree as endogenous self-produced locomotor experience.

To explain the observed developmental shift in the visual control of posture, we propose that early self-produced locomotion generates a unique structure of perceptual input, which in turn facilitates a change in the visual control of posture in one of two ways. First, the extensive experience nascently self-locomoting infants have with specific structures of optic flow located in specific regions of the visual field may sensitize infants to portions of the visual field that are sufficient for postural control. Second, constant looking in the direction of locomotion may correlate vestibular proprioceptive stimulation specifying forward linear motion of the observer with specific forms of optic flow (e.g., lamellar peripheral). In such a process, information from the active vestibular system would lend proprioceptive meaning to specific forms of optic flow, thereby making it possible for infants to respond to specific portions of the optic flow field. In either of these cases, the developmental transition in the use of optic flow reflects an ability to differentiate and use portions of the optic flow field.

The developing ability to use portions of the visual field could be interpreted as the resolution of a conflict of optical information arising when one portion of the visual field moves and the supplementary portion remains static (as in the side- or front-wall conditions). The presence of conflicting optical information might inhibit or suppress the postural response. Inversely, the absence of a conflict of cues in the whole-room-motion condition would explain the postural responses made by 7-month-olds in Study 1 and prelocomotor infants in Study 2. However the conflicting optical information interpretation alone does not adequately explain (a) the process by which the conflict is resolved, and (b) why 9-month-old infants in Study 1 and locomotor infants in Study 2 showed postural response to the side-wall condition but not to the front-wall condition.

Although failure to respond to the front wall of the moving room would seem to contradict the hypothesized role of experience as facilitating the use of portions of the optic flow field, we believe that it is a characteristic of the stimulus that impedes response to the front wall of the moving room. Prior research has shown that both infants' and adults' responses to the front wall in moving-room studies have generally been nonsignificant (Bertenthal & Bai, 1989; Stoffregan, 1985). The low level of response to the front wall of the moving room has been attributed to characteristics of the observer, such as a tendency to code motion in the central visual field as motion of an object rather than motion of the self (Brandt, Dichgans, & Koenig, 1973) or an inability of the central retina to process radial information (Stoffregan, 1985). Yet, adults have shown response to radially structured, centrally projected optic flow patterns when the paradigm uses computer-generated flow fields (Anderson & Braunstein, 1985; Warren & Kurtz, 1992). These adult findings suggest that a characteristic of the moving-room paradigm, rather than of the observer, is responsible for limiting responses to front-wall motion. Computer displays provide size, density, and velocity gradients in magnitudes not available from the front wall of the moving room. The depth information provided by these gradients may be critical for perceiving self-motion with the central visual field (Anderson, 1986; Anderson & Braunstein, 1985) and may account for the lack of response to front-wall motion in moving-room studies.

Although our results suggest that experiences associated with self-produced locomotion influence the developmental shift in the use of optic flow, we believe that additional factors, such as hard-wired visual-vestibular connections and the size of the optic flow stimulus, influence the use of optic flow prior to the developmental shift, explaining the whole-room responses of the 7-month-olds of Study 1 and the prelocomotor infants of Study 2. Before self-produced locomotor experience, infants make postural responses to motion of global optic flow fields. This response is not unusual given evidence suggesting inborn circuits connecting the movement detection system of the retinal-cortical pathways to the vestibular mechanisms in young infants (Ornitz, Kaplan, & Westlake, 1985; Tauber & Koffler, 1966). These connections could help infants to interpret visual proprioceptive information through their vestibular counterparts. However, the mere presence of these connections does not determine that they will function for proprioception in the absence of visual experience.

Visual experience can be a factor in the use of optic flow independent of whether observers move passively or actively. Any moving observer's global optic flow pattern changes as a function of changes in the direction of looking relative to the direction of locomotion. As such, moving observers experience a variety of optic flow patterns depending on the angle of difference between their direction of looking and the direction of their motion. Passively moved observers' freedom to look in any direction during locomotion allows them to experience any and all of the possible global optic flow patterns. The extent of passively moved observers' experience with the family of global optic flow patterns may facilitate their use of global optic flow fields and contribute to prelocomotor infants' response to the whole-room-motion condition.

Also affecting the pattern of responsiveness observed in the moving room is the size of the optic flow stimulus. In adult studies, the size of the area of retinal stimulation has been shown to influence response to optic flow (Paulus, Straube, & Brandt, 1984; Post, 1988). In our studies, the side- and front-wall motion conditions each stimulated approximately one third of the area stimulated by the whole-room-motion condition. The enormous size of the whole-room-motion stimulus may have contributed to prelocomotor infants' responses. However, specific relations between the size of optic flow stimulus and usefulness for postural control at different ages remain unspecified.

Although our studies do not distinguish which factor (neural connections, visual experience, size of the stimulus, absence of conflicting visual cues) or combination of factors best explains prelocomotor infants' response to the moving room, we can rule out the possibility that responses result from the "looming" phenomenon. *Looming,* the optical expansion of an object as it approaches the eye, could not have controlled postural responses, as the approaching wall never reached the visual angle necessary to qualify as "explosive" expansion in the visual field (Gibson, 1979).

As a final note, we must also acknowledge the suggestion that the onset of self-locomotion may be stimulated by a visual-vestibular correlation rather than being the "setting event" that allows a particular development in the visual control of posture. A true experiment would be necessary to distinguish such direction of causality.

## Note

1. None of the data on direction of room motion reported in this article reached significance at the .05 level. Directional effects did not reach significance in $3 \times 4 \times 2$ ANOVAs comparing three levels of age (in Study 1) or locomotor status (in Study 2), four levels of condition of optic flow, and two levels of direction of room motion. Therefore, data in each of the studies were collapsed across the two directions of room motion.

## References

Anderson, G. J. (1986). Perception of self-motion: Psychophysical and computational approaches. *Psychological Bulletin, 99*, 52–65.

Anderson, G. J., & Braunstein, M. L. (1985). Induced self-motion in central vision. *Journal of Experimental Psychology: Human Perception and Performance, 11*, 122–132.

Aslin, R. N., & Shea, S. L. (1990). Velocity thresholds in human infants: Implications for the perception of motion. *Developmental Psychology, 26*, 589–598.

Bertenthal, B. (1993, March). *Emerging themes in perceptual development.* Master lecture presented at the meeting of the Society for Research in Child Development, New Orleans, LA.

Bertenthal, B., & Bai, D. (1989). Infants' sensitivity to optic flow for controlling posture. *Developmental Psychology, 25*, 936–945.

Bertenthal, B., & Bradbury, A. (1992). Infants' detection of shearing motion in random-dot displays. *Developmental Psychology, 28*, 1056–1066.

Bertenthal, B., & Campos, J. (1990). A systems approach to the organizing effects of self-produced locomotion during infancy. In C. Rovee-Collier & L. Lipsett (Eds.), *Advances in infancy research* (Vol. 6, 1–60). Norwood. NJ: Ablex.

Brandt, T., Dichgans, J., & Koenig, E. (1973). Differential effects of central versus peripheral vision on egocentric and exocentric motion perception. *Experimental Brain Research, 16*, 476–991.

Butterworth, G. (1992). Origins of self-perception in infancy. *Psychological Inquiry, 3*, 103–111.

Butterworth, G., & Hicks, L. (1977). Visual proprioception and postural stability in infants: A developmental study. *Perception, 5*, 255–263.

DADiSP data analysis program. (1990). Cambridge, MA: DSP Development Corporation.

Dichgans, J., & Brandt, T. (1978). Visual–vestibular interaction: Effects on self-motion and postural control. In R. Held, H. Leibowitz, & H. Teuber (Eds.), *Handbook of sensory physiology* (Vol. 8, pp. 755–804). Heidelberg, Germany: Springer-Verlag.

204 **Spatial Orientation**

Gibson, J. (1966). *The senses considered as perceptual systems.* Boston: Houghton-Mifflin.
Gibson, J. (1979). *The ecological approach to visual perception.* Boston: Houghton-Mifflin.
Higgins, C. (1993). [Assessment of direction of looking during early locomotion]. Unpublished raw data.
Kermoian, R., & Campos, J. (1988). Locomotor experience: A facilitator of spatial cognitive development. *Child Development, 59,* 908–917.
Lee, D., & Aronson, E. (1974). Visual proprioceptive control of standing in human infants. *Perception and Psychophysics. 15,* 529–532.
Lee, D., & Lishman, J. (1975). Visual proprioceptive control of stance. *Journal of Human Movement Studies, 1,* 26–30.
Lishman, J., & Lee, D. (1973). The autonomy of visual kinaethesis. *Perception, 2,* 287–294.
Ornitz, E., Kaplan, A., & Westlake, J. (1985). Development of the vestibule-ocular reflex from infancy to adulthood. *Acta Otolaryngol, 100,* 180–193.
Paulus, W., Straube, A., & Brandt, T. (1984). Visual stabilization of posture: Physiological stimulus characteristics and clinical aspects. *Brain, 107,* 1143–1163.
Post, R. (1988). Circular vection is independent of stimulus eccentricity. *Perception, 17,* 737–744.
Stoffregan, T. (1985). Flow structure versus retinal location in the optical control of stance. *Journal of Experimental Psychology: Human Perception and Performance, 11,* 554–565.
Tauber, E., & Koffler, S. (1966). Optomotor response in human infants to apparent motion: Evidence for innateness. *Science, 152,* 382–384.
Warren, W., & Kurtz, J. (1992). The role of central and peripheral vision in perceiving the direction of self-motion. *Perception and Psychophysics, 51,* 443–454.

# 46

# Travel Broadens the Mind

*Joseph J. Campos, David I. Anderson,*
*Marianne A. Barbu-Roth, Edward M. Hubbard,*
*Matthew J. Hertenstein and David Witherington*

When infants begin to locomote voluntarily, they undergo an extraordinary psychological reorganization. The onset of prone progression, especially hands-and-knees crawling, is followed by a staggering array of changes in perception, spatial cognition, and social and emotional development. This article delineates the major changes and consequences of self-produced locomotor experience that we identified using a variety of research designs and methods. The article updates previous reviews that we published (e.g., Berthenthal & Campos, 1990; Bertenthal, Campos, & Barrett, 1984; Campos, Kermoian, Witherington, Chen, & Dong, 1997), and includes the findings from many investigations that have been hitherto unpublished, or that we recently completed. Furthermore, in response to the challenge posed by some researchers (e.g., McKenzie, 1987), we go into greater depth than we have to date in elucidating the links between locomotor experience and psychological transitions.

The research we describe is relevant to our broad understanding of how development takes place. Most approaches to developmental origins and transitions are either monistic or domain specific. A monistic view, typically exemplified by stage theories, leads a person to expect broad psychological changes to result from a single organismic process. Usually, monistic views propose that development occurs synchronously across domains (Emde, Gaensbauer, & Harmon, 1976). Domain-specific approaches, by contrast,

**Source:** *Infancy*, 1(2) (2000): 149–219.

consider development as the accrual of quite specific changes in discrete domains, with little relation of one domain to the other, and with no necessary synchrony or sequence among the domains (Smith & Thelen, 1993).

We propose a hybrid of the monistic and the domain-specific approaches. We argue that a single, universal, developmental acquisition – the onset of locomotion – produces a family of experiences, with each member of the family being implicated in some psychological changes but not in others. In addition, we note that in some cases several processes coalesce, sometimes in apparent synchrony with each other, sometimes one preceding another in an orchestrated fashion, to generate a specific psychological change. So, even though a number of psychological phenomena are related to a single pacer or organizer (in this case, locomotor experience), each outcome is dissociable from the other. The outcomes need not be correlated very highly despite commonality of origin.

Thus, as we conceive it, locomotion is a setting event, a control parameter, and a mobilizer that changes the intrapsychic states of the infant, the social and nonsocial world around the infant, and the interaction of the infant with that world. In our view, locomotion is not by itself a causal agent. The developmental changes chronicled in this article are not a function of locomotion per se; rather, the changes stem from the experiences that are engendered by independent mobility.

## Is Locomotor Experience Necessary or Sufficient for Producing Psychological Changes?

We believe that locomotor experience is a crucial agent of developmental change, but ironically, it might be neither necessary nor sufficient for bringing about these transitions. There are at least four reasons why locomotor experience might not be necessary for developmental change, and one reason for its insufficiency.

First of all, locomotor experience does not create new psychological skills ex nihilo. In virtually every domain we investigated, infants show some evidence of the perceptual, cognitive, or emotional characteristic in question before the onset of locomotion. Following Haith (1993), we call the existence of perceptual, cognitive, or emotional biases and precocities the principle of *partial accomplishment*. We refer to this principle many times in the course of this article. Although locomotor experience might not be responsible for the origins of a phenomenon, it can elevate some psychological skills to a much higher level. Such experiences thus are important for psychological advancement, but not necessarily for emergence.

Second, locomotor experience might not always be sufficient for producing a psychological skill because in a few cases infants can acquire the full-blown skill that ordinarily follows locomotor experience even prior to locomotion. For example, in our research we found that occasionally an infant will acquire wariness of heights prior to locomotor onset, although they usually do not. We call this state of affairs the principle of *precocious exposure*. This state of affairs is different from the principle of partial accomplishment. It is not a matter of locomotion improving an existing psychological skill; rather, it is a case of the causal processes usually produced by locomotor experience being recruited in nonlocomotor ways. Whether by serendipity or by design, the causal agents in locomotor experience can be brought about other than by locomotion, although they typically are not.

Third, we believe that human development shows the operation of alternative developmental pathways to the ones that usually bring about transition. This is the well-known, though little studied, principle of *equipotentiality*. This principle differs from the precocious exposure insofar as equipotentiality reflects the production of a particular psychological outcome by a different process than that linked to locomotion. In precocious exposure, it is the same process. (An example of equipotentiality is the development of wariness of heights in prelocomotor infants because of a particularly painful fall instead of the more typical process involving the decoupling of visual and vestibular proprioceptive information that we describe later.) Equipotentiality has been implicated in the apparent normal development of Piagetian sensorimotor skills ordinarily thought to depend on manual and locomotor exploration in infants whose mothers had taken thalidomide in the 1960s (e.g., Decarie, 1969; Kopp & Shaperman, 1973). These children were apparently able to acquire functionally identical end-states by using their feet, heads, mouths, or in some cases orthopedic appliances to replace the locomotor and other motoric experiences they lacked.

Finally, in a few cases, locomotor experience might not be required to induce or facilitate a psychological skill, but can be necessary for updating the skill and preventing it from eventual loss from disuse. This is the principle of *maintenance by experience*. There has been remarkably little research with humans on this principle; we elaborate on its developmental significance in the response article later in this issue. Suffice it to say here that phenomena such as calibration of perceptual skills or attainment of psychological goals require a constant availability of locomotor experience or its surrogate to update the relation of persons to their environment. The need for locomotor experience thus can be indispensable throughout life.

There are also likely to be many instances in which locomotor experience might not be sufficient to bring about psychological changes. In some cases, the insufficiency of locomotor experience stems from the hierarchical integration and organization of development (Fischer & Biddell, 1998). That is, the process of development often involves integrating a number of component subskills into a higher order one that links together the previous dissociated skills. (An example of hierarchical development is the development of means–ends relations, wherein a skill such as lifting a cloth, and a second skill such as reaching for a toy, are coordinated and sequenced into a single complex act of uncovering and capturing a hidden toy.) The principle of hierarchical organization implies that if any crucial subskill has not yet developed, and if locomotor experience requires that subskill to mobilize a psychological reorganization, then locomotor experience will not result in a particular psychological transition. The locomotor experience will need to await other developments to effect a change. In short, hierarchical integration imposes constraints on developmental transitions; hence, a person should not expect precocious locomotor experience to bring about precocious psychological changes of the sort ordinarily seen when locomotion develops at normative ages. As with psychological maintenance and equipotentiality, there have been very few studies on the effects of timing of a locomotor acquisition on psychological development (for an exception, see Biringen, Emde, Campos, & Appelbaum, 1995).

Are we minimizing the importance of locomotor experience as an agent of developmental change by arguing against the certainty of its causal role in infancy and later? We think not. Rather, we propose that the absence of necessity and sufficiency is probably the rule in most of human psychological and biological development. Indeed, that is a central tenet of systems approaches to development. Our argument for the importance of locomotor experience rests on evidence, which we are about to present, demonstrating that locomotor experience (a) is typically the agent of transition in many different psychological domains in most infants, and (b) has an extraordinarily widespread spectrum of consequences. The rest of this article is an attempt to substantiate these two propositions.

## Two Caveats about the Course of Development

Before beginning our description of the findings linking locomotor experience to psychological development, two other important caveats are in order. First, locomotor experience should be expected to show neither a monotonic nor a linear relation with any psychological outcome. Because of the hierarchical nature of developmental change, development will often take place by spurts, rather than by slow accretions. If so, correlation coefficients might be misleading in describing or testing the relation between the duration of locomotor experience and psychological change (see Bertenthal & Campos, 1984, for a more detailed discussion of this point). Linear relations will be inadequate descriptors of these functional relations under at least two conditions. One occurs when development follows a course that is more like a step preceded and followed by a plateau (i.e., an ogive); the second, when intermediate states of developmental flux and disorganization bridge two stable states, one prior to locomotion, and another after locomotor experience.

Failure to consider nonlinear developmental functions can account for many of the negative findings in the literature on locomotion and psychological change (e.g., Arterberry, Yonas, & Bensen, 1989; Rader, Bausano, & Richards, 1980; Scarr & Salapatek, 1970).

The second caveat draws us into the classic but still remarkably relevant issue of the role of genetics and experience in human development. The period of life surrounding the onset of locomotion appears to be one of the major life transitions in early development (Emde et al., 1976). As we have noted elsewhere (Bertenthal et al., 1984), there has been an implicit assumption that when broad-scale changes occur, maturation invariably must be posed as the underlying cause. Indeed, a number of the skills that we link to locomotor experience (e.g., search for hidden objects, secondary intersubjectivity, reactions to heights) have been said to be the result of maturation. However, the converging research designs used to document this point corroborate that this life transition is not necessarily mediated by maturational factors (i.e., by the unfolding of a genetic blueprint for psychological changes), but instead, is intimately linked to experience. The studies on the consequences of self-produced locomotion (SPL) do not minimize the importance of genetically mediated changes; however, they do point, at the very least, to ecological and transactional sources of *coaction* (Gottlieb, 1991) between genes and early experiences. In sum, a major objective of this article is to illustrate in a major psychological transition in infancy the role of experience – a role that has been relatively underemphasized recently. However, nothing that we say in this article should be construed as an argument against intraorganismic biological contributions to development. It is merely that our methods are more suited to discovering experiential contributions to development, rather than endogenous ones.

## Converging Research Operations Pointing to the Importance of Locomotor Experience

In earlier reviews of this work, we referred to some of the converging research operations by which one can infer the role of locomotor experience in psychological development. The objective of these converging operations is to determine whether locomotor experience plays a role as a concomitant or an antecedent of psychological changes. The simplest approach is to hold age constant and classify infants into those with and without locomotor experience. A second approach is the opposite of holding age constant – allowing age to vary along with locomotor experience. This approach, called the lag-sequential research design, results in classifying infants into a number of groups. For example, one group is early in crawling relative to locomotion norms for the population being studied; a second group is late in locomotion onset (also relative to population norms); and a third group acquires locomotion at the normative age. Infants are tested at the onset of locomotion and after selected amounts of locomotor experience, thereby permitting the assessment of the role of age, locomotor experience, and their interaction on the targeted psychological skill. The lag-sequential approach differs from the classic longitudinal design in oversampling early and late crawlers, so that the role of locomotor extremes might best be quantified without undue influence from the center of the normal distribution.

There are two other converging research operations that can help identify the role of locomotor experience. One of these involves the study of prelocomotor infants who have used wheeled carts or walkers that permit self-locomotion, often in a very skillful and goal-directed fashion. Higher levels of performance on psychological tests between these walker infants and matched prelocomotors who have had no such walker experience strengthens conclusions about locomotor experience as an antecedent of psychological change. The other converging operation is the study of locomotor delay and what takes place psychologically upon the delayed acquisition of locomotor experience. The study of locomotor delay assesses whether infants who are normatively slow to locomote show corresponding psychological delays, followed by an elevation in function after the delayed acquisition of locomotion.

In this article, we instantiate the study of locomotor delays with two types of populations. One is in urban China, where for ecological and cultural reasons, infants show a 3.3-month delay in the onset of locomotion, relative to Bayley Scale norms (Bayley, 1969). The delay results from the constrained living arrangements in contemporary urban apartments. Infants in China are typically placed on a bed, surrounded by thick pillows to prevent falling. Moreover, the bed is often soft, like a featherbed, and does not provide enough resistance to the child's efforts to push up, resulting in delayed development of the musculature in the shoulders and upper trunk – musculature needed to support locomotion. The use of bulky clothing to provide warmth to the infant also might impair movement and muscular development. In addition, parents in China do not engage in activities that involve reciprocal innervation of the musculature on the sides of the trunk, such as tipping the infant first to one side, then to the other. Such reciprocal activity is also a prerequisite for locomotion. Furthermore, the Chinese parents are very concerned about the child's cleanliness and discourage crawling to prevent dirty hands.

The second population of infants we studied has a neurological basis for the locomotor delay. One such neurological problem is menygomyelocele or spina bifida. A neural tube defect, menygomyelocele results in a locomotor delay – the higher the lesion in the spinal cord, the later the age of onset of locomotion. If the defect is quite low, for example, at the sacral level, the spina bifida condition is typically not associated with severe cerebral involvement, although spina bifida increases its likelihood. Sacral lesions can bring about locomotor delays ranging from 4 to 7 months (Shurtleff, 1986). To minimize higher central nervous system confounds, we focused on infants with low, sacral, lesions.

These converging operations reflect our conceptual focus on the importance of early experience. However, we reiterate that biological and maturational factors are likely to be important as coactants in the developmental process. Research must therefore be designed to do justice to the concept of coaction of genes and environment. Consequently, at the end of this article, we present some of our preliminary ideas on how to conduct research that might reveal the separate and interactive contributions of endogenous, genetic factors along with experience in the transitions we describe.

In the subsequent sections, we point out the consequences of locomotor experience for (a) the child's social and emotional development, (b) the perception of self-movement and its consequences, (c) distance perception, (d) the infant's manual search for hidden objects, such as in the A-not-B error with a delay, and (e) the infant's spatial coding strategies. In each section, we outline the specific experiences that locomotion generates and that, in turn, help to bring about the psychological changes seen in each specific domain. We suggest, where possible, new hypotheses about linkages between locomotor experience and psychological function. Next, we describe an experimental approach to the issue of whether locomotor experience is a cause or only an antecedent of the observed psychological changes. Finally, we note how other achievements that change the relation of the child to that child's social and physical world are also likely to lead to major psychological reorganizations.

## Self-Produced Locomotor Experience and Socioemotional Development

### Crawling as the "Psychological Birth of the Human Infant"

Many psychoanalytic theorists consider locomotion crucial for emotional development. Mahler, Pine, and Bergman (1975) went so far as to consider locomotion as the event that brings about the "psychological birth" of the human infant. By that they mean that locomotion breaks the symbiosis of infant with mother, creates autonomy and willfulness in the infant, and initiates a period of glee and a "love affair with the world." The onset of locomotion creates new challenges for the parents as well. One of these is the need to encourage exploration while discouraging the prohibitable. Another is to cope with the infant's new autonomy, which is welcome by some parents and regretted by others. We agree with Mahler et al. and differ from them in only one way: We propose that the origins of these changes in the infant, the parent, and the family system come from prone progression, and not, as they maintained, principally from upright locomotion.

*Locomotion and social signaling.* In addition to autonomy and willfulness, locomotor experience profoundly affects the infant's social cognition. When the child begins to crawl, there is a dramatic change in the type and source of social signaling that the child receives. Crawling increases the number of opportunities for the caregivers to communicate facially and vocally in the service of regulating the infant's explorations. Indeed, we speculated that crawling is the cradle of the social referencing phenomenon (Campos & Stenberg, 1981). It is principally after crawling that the child receives social signals that have a clear distal referent; prior to crawling there is little need for distal emotional communication. The importance of the origin of such distal communication for semantic comprehension and the "catching" of emotions cannot be underestimated (Moore, 1999).

*Locomotion and attachment.* The acquisition of SPL is a watershed in the formation of the attachment relationship. Bowlby (1969) spoke of locomotion marking the onset of the phase of discriminated attachment figures, as did Ainsworth and her colleagues (Ainsworth, Blehar, Waters, & Wall, 1978). Perhaps the most basic role of locomotion in attachment is in proximity seeking, which is the hallmark of the attachment relationship. Although proximity seeking might be attained through the indirect effects that social signaling can have on others, it is only through locomotion that the child can directly control distance from the attachment figure. Furthermore, the functions of the attachment relationship, to permit a secure base for exploration and a haven of safety in times of fear, require locomotion for their implementation.

*Locomotion and motivation.* If emotions reflect the fate of a person's goals (Lazarus, 1991), the onset of locomotion must markedly enrich the infant's emotional life. Crawling creates many new goals and enables the attainment and frustration of many others. Thus, crawling onset makes many familiar emotions much more prevalent, results in linking existing emotions to new objects (e.g., through the catching of emotions mentioned earlier), and creates the context for the emergence of new emotions (e.g., shame, pride, and other emotions that depend on distal social signaling).

*Reorganizing the family system.* Parents readily acknowledge that the onset of crawling brings about major social and emotional changes in the infant, the parents, and their interaction. Locomotion thus reorganizes the family system. The infant not only "gets into everything," but also makes happy the mother who strives for her baby's independence, saddens the mother who likes the prelocomotor infant's dependency, and imposes a demand on all parents to socialize the infant to explore what is safe and avoid what is dangerous. In this section, we review work on the reorganizations in the infant and the family following the onset of locomotion. We also describe a number of studies that show how locomotor experience is linked to the infant's growing sense of social understanding.

## An Interview Study Linking Locomotor Experience and Socioemotional Development

In this section, we review work on the reorganizations in the infant and the family system following the onset of locomotion. We begin by describing an interview study that shows how mothers attribute to the infant a growing sense of internal responsibility, change their behavior toward the infant as a result of the infant's new attributions, and thus bring about changes in the infant's behaviors toward them. This interview includes data related to the role of locomotion in the development of what Trevarthen (1993) called secondary intersubjectivity, and what others believe to be the origins of theory of mind (Moore & Dunham, 1995).

The interview study (Campos, Kermoian, & Zumbahlen, 1992) used a 2 × 2 design, crossing prelocomotor versus locomotor status of the infants with use of walker or not. The mothers were thus classified into one group if their infants were entirely prelocomotor, a second if their infants had at least 5 weeks of crawling experience, a third if the infants were crawling for 5 weeks and had at least 4 weeks of walker experience, and a fourth if the infants were prelocomotor and had at least 4 weeks' use of a walker. All infants were 8.5 months of age, and numbered 16 per group. Because there were few differences in the results of locomotor infants with and without walker experience, the data from these two groups were pooled. Its nature as an interview study constrains interpretation of the findings to parental perceptions and attributions. However, the study was designed to minimize the possibility of tapping into mothers' naive theory of locomotor consequences by including many questions on developmental changes in the infant besides those on locomotor experience.

*Results related to changes in the infant.*   With reference to three major areas – emotional expression, attachment, and attentiveness to distal events – the study revealed a number of differences as a function of whether the mothers were reporting on prelocomotor or locomotor infants. In the emotional realm, the number of locomotor infants reported to have recently shown a large increase in anger was significantly greater than prelocomotors. Locomotor infants changed in terms of the frequency of angry responses to events and the manner by which they expressed anger. Mothers of locomotor infants reported an increase in the intensity of their infants' anger. As one mother stated, her infant was "showing the beginning of temper tantrums." These data are presented in Figure 1.

In the attachment realm, locomotor infants were reported more often to show increased, new, or intense forms of affection to the primary caregiver, a greater sensitivity to maternal departures and whereabouts, and increased checking back in social situations. Increased checking back to the mother and

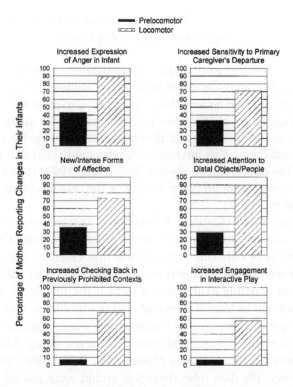

**Figure 1:** Reports by mothers of prelocomotor and locomotor infants of recent changes in their infants' emotional expression, attachment, and attentiveness to distal events. Adapted from "Socioemotional transformations in the family system following infant crawling onset" by J. J. Campos, R. Kermoian, & M. R. Zumbahlen. In N. Eisenberg & R. A. Fabes (Eds.), 1992, *Emotion and its regulation in early development* (pp. 25–40). San Francisco: Jossey-Bass. Copyright 1992 by Jossey-Bass. Adapted with permission.

increased wariness of maternal departures accompanied a significant elevation in locomotor infants' attending to distal events.

*Changes in the parent.*   Crawling produced changes in the mother as well, as indicated by parental reports summarized in Figure 2. Mothers of crawlers stated that they began to expect compliance from their infants; they felt that their infants were now responsible for their actions, and hence, they were expected to obey the mother. Mothers of locomotors also reported increasing their use of verbal prohibitions and mentioned how they used their voice predominantly as the means of conveying prohibition. Most strikingly, they reported a sharp increase in their expression of anger toward their infants, stating in many cases that it was the first time in their relationship that they had been angry toward the infant. In some instances, the expression of anger went so far as to lead to the use of physical punishment. Coincident with these increases in negative expressions, mothers of locomotor infants showed new

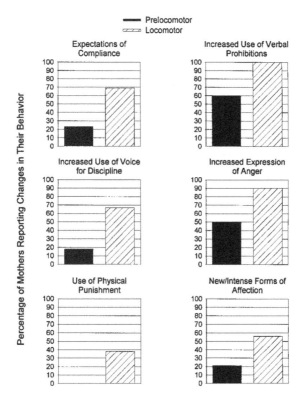

**Figure 2:** Reports by mothers of prelocomotor and locomotor infants of recent changes in their own (maternal) behaviors directed toward their infants. Adapted from "Socioemotional transformations in the family system following infant crawling onset" by J. J. Campos, R. Kermoian, & M. R. Zumbahlen. In N. Eisenberg & R. A. Fabes (Eds.), 1992, *Emotion and its regulation in early development* (pp. 25–40). San Francisco: Jossey-Bass. Copyright 1992 by Jossey-Bass. Adapted with permission.

and intense forms of affection toward their infants, manifested as increased frequency and intensity of hugging.

*Changes reported in family interaction.* This study portrayed the relationship between the parent and the locomotor infant as involving reciprocal changes in expression of anger and an apparent tug-of-war between infant willfulness and parental demands for compliance. Furthermore, the interview revealed some noteworthy changes in other interactive domains as well. One was the degree of interactive play reported as a function of locomotor status (see Figure 2). Interactive play referred to games involving reciprocity on the part of the child, such as peek-a-boo. Maternal reports indicated that more locomotor infants initiated interactive games and showed more intense forms of positive affect including "glee" in these games.

*The role of walker experience.* Interestingly, in this study, few differences were found between infants who were prelocomotor but had experience moving about in walkers, when compared to prelocomotor infants with no walker experience. However, there were two noteworthy findings in which the mothers of prelocomotors with walkers reported behaviors in their infants that were more like the reports of mothers of locomotor infants. Prelocomotors with walkers were reported to have shown increases in attention to distal objects and people, and increased checking back to the mother in previously prohibited contexts.

This lack of difference on most variables between prelocomotor infants with and without walker experience was not expected. We suspect that walker experience might not mimic crawling in ways significant for affecting social interaction. We propose several reasons for these negative findings. One is ecological. For instance, the tray surrounding the walker minimizes the number of objects the infant can inappropriately handle, reducing the need for the mother to use distal communication for emotional regulation. Furthermore, infants might use the walker more for its intrinsic "function pleasure" of locomoting, and much less for other purposes, such as playing with the stereo or electric outlets, that have more affective valence for the mother. Moreover, we believe that mothers can often use walkers as distractors or sources of entertainment for the baby; we suspect that they monitor the behavior of walker infants much less than they do that of a crawling infant. Nevertheless, the interview study proved to be one of the few instances in which walker experience did not yield findings similar to those for crawling infants.

## Locomotor Experience and Socioemotional Development: Direct Observation

To provide confirmatory evidence on socioemotional changes in the family following crawling onset, Zumbahlen (1997) conducted for her dissertation a short-term longitudinal study directly observing mother–infant interaction prior to and following the onset of hands-and-knees locomotion. She observed 41 infants at 6 and 8 months. All 6-month-old infants were prelocomotor, and of the 8-month-olds, 18 had not begun hands-and-knees crawling, and 23 had been hands-and-knees crawling for an average of 5 weeks.

Zumbahlen (1997; Zumbahlen & Crawley, 1997) confirmed four major findings from the interview study. For example, she observed that the number of prohibitions increased following hands-and-knees crawling onset, and that these prohibitions took place most often in distal contexts. She also reported a sharp increase in the locomotor infant's expression of anger and also in the incidence of checking back when the mother initiated emotional communication with the infant.

Zumbahlen (1997) did not confirm the reported increase in the use of physical punishment by the parents of locomotor infants. Rather, she discovered that parents, to regulate the child's behavior toward prohibitable objects, distracted their children and moved the infant away from such contexts. Nevertheless, her study confirmed the general findings of the interview. The interested reader is referred to Zumbahlen for more details of this important study.

## Locomotor Experience and the Origins of Referential Gestural Communication

There is a finding reported in this article that has a major bearing on the social and emotional development of the infant that is also very consistent across the transitions centering on locomotion. The finding has to do with changes with locomotor experience in the nature of the infant's attentiveness to distal events, illustrated in the interview study by the findings on checking back to the mother. These changes in attentiveness prove to be relevant to the ontogeny of referential gestural communication and "joint attention."

In the opening of Churcher and Scaife's (1982) review of literature on the phenomenon of joint attention, they used an illuminating analogy, citing a French proverb indicating that when the finger points at the moon, the idiot looks at the finger. The data and the rationale we discuss suggest that, on the whole, the prelocomotor infant is like the child in the French proverb, while the locomotor infant is more adult-like in following a referential gestural communication toward a distal target.

*Why a link between locomotor experience and responsiveness to referential gestures?* The interview and longitudinal study confirmed the observations of Mahler et al. (1975) about a sharp increase in checking back to the mother following the onset of prone progression. This pattern of checking back and forth is a component of the information-seeking aspect of social referencing (Campos & Stenberg, 1981), and as such, is relevant to understanding how values are imparted to the infant and how social regulation is effected by means of distal communications. It is through such emotional signaling that the mother can share meanings – affective and linguistic – with her infant. Thus, the pattern is important to investigate more formally (Corkum & Moore, 1998; Moore, 1999).

Consistent with the principle of partial accomplishments mentioned earlier, recent reviews (e.g., Moore, 1999) have noted that even prelocomotor infants have some capacity to respond to referential gestural communication. For instance, there appear to be three steps in the development of correct responsiveness to referential gestural communication (Moore, 1999). One step takes place well before locomotion onset – as early as 3 months – and is evident in successful responding of the infant to head and eye movements so long as the tester's head and the target of the communication are in the same visual field (D'Entremont, Hains, & Muir, 1997). There is a second level, beginning around 9 months, when the infant can respond to such communications when there is no target to the gestures of the experimenter. (Alternatively, in our view, the second level occurs when the gesturer is in one visual field, and the target of the gesture in another.) A final level, seen in the second year of life, involves correct localization of the target of referential communication even when the target is behind the infant.

We initiated a series of investigations on the second of these three levels and tested whether changes in referential gestural communication followed locomotor onset (Campos et al., 1997; Tao & Dong, 1997; Telzrow, 1990; Telzrow, Campos, Kermoian, & Bertenthal, 1999). These investigations involved an age-held-constant design, and the converging operations involving walker experience and locomotor delay in handicapped and Chinese infants. We initiated this line of research on the assumption, documented in the interview study, that crawling experience results in an increase in distal communication from a mother who is now typically at some distance from the infant and the referent of her utterance. More specifically, when the infant begins to locomote, the infant inevitably encounters prohibitable objects and contexts. As already noted previously, these encounters typically result in the parent using distal affective information to distract or inhibit the infant from the behavior. As the infant initially becomes exposed to this form of communication, the infant orients toward the parent. Orienting is the first phase in the development of the infant's attention to the mother's affective messages. Repeated often enough, such orienting to affective messages motivates the infant to determine the object of the mother's communication. Concern with the referent of the affective message is the second phase in the development of the gestural communication phenomenon. The second phase is further facilitated by the infant's new levels of attentiveness to distal displays, as well as new spatial understanding (e.g., to landmarks) made possible by distinct processes linked to locomotor experience. (The development of spatial attentiveness and understanding of landmarks are elaborated on in subsequent sections of this article. Suffice it here to note that the direction of the head and eyes, and that of the arm and pointing finger, constitute landmarks for localizing an object.) The outcome of these conjointly operating processes of distal attentiveness and understanding of spatial relations is the infant's growing understanding first of the general direction, and subsequently, the more specific target of the parent's head turn, gaze, or pointing gesture that invariably accompanies distal affective messages. Early locomotor experience seems to play a role in the first of these changes.

*Following the gaze and point gesture: Age-held-constant study.* The hypothesis that locomotor experience should facilitate the infant's following of the gaze or pointing gesture was investigated in a study of 8.5-month-old infants (Campos et al., 1997). There were three groups of 22 infants: infants crawling on their hands and knees for 6 weeks, prelocomotor infants, and prelocomotor infants with 40 or more hr of walker experience. The testing situation involved a 5-foot-square curtained area in which there were eight toys. Two were placed 45° to the infant's left, one 45° above the infant's eye level and one 45° below eye level. Two other toys were placed 45° to the infant's right, at homologous positions relative to the infant's eye level. Another two toys were placed 90° to the infant's left, one of which was again 45° above and one 45° below eye level. Finally, a seventh and eighth toy were placed in homologous positions 90° to the right. Looking at one of the eight toys, a female experimenter drew the infant's attention and simultaneously uttered a statement, such as "Look over there," while turning her head and eyes, and using an across-the-body pointing gesture. In her gesture, the finger of the pointing hand did not extend beyond the periphery of her body. The dependent variables were whether the infant looked to the same side as the experimenter, toward the experimenter's face, or toward the opposite side of the room from where the experimenter looked in the 3 sec following the experimenter's statement. A contrast between looking to the same side as the experimenter and to the opposite side is widely considered to be the minimal prerequisite for demonstrating referential gestural communication. Without such a comparison, following the point or gaze to the same side as the experimenter looked might be a spurious "pseudo-following" response (Moore, 1999).

The results of the study are presented in Figure 3 (taken from Campos et al., 1997). Both locomotor and prelocomotor infants with walker experience

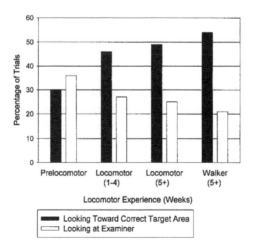

**Figure 3:** Following of a gaze and pointing gesture as a function of locomotor experience in 8.5-month-old infants. Adapted from "Activity, attention, and developmental transitions in infancy" by J. J. Campos, R. Kermoian, D. Witherington, H. Chen, & Q. Dong. In P. J. Lang & R. F. Simons (Eds.), 1997, *Attention and orienting: Sensory and motivational processes* (pp. 393–415). Mahwah, NJ: Lawrence Erlbaum Associates, Inc. Copyright 1997 by Lawrence Erlbaum Associates, Inc. Adapted with permission.

looked to the correct side on significantly more trials than did the totally prelocomotor infants. Each of the two groups with locomotor experience also looked significantly more often to the correct side than to the opposite side of the room; the prelocomotor infants did not look to the correct side more than to the incorrect. In sum, the prelocomotor infants behaved like the impaired child in the French proverb, whereas infants with locomotor experience looked at least in the general direction of the moon in the metaphor. This study thus confirmed two points: (a) There is a developmental shift in referential gestural communication between 8 and 10 months, as Moore proposed; and (b) locomotor experience is implicated in the shift.

Two qualifications of the findings of this study need to be mentioned. First, the infants did not look to the correct target (the specific toy that the experimenter was looking at), but rather at the region in which the target was embedded. Second, the findings, although statistically significant, were not robust. It is clear that the phenomenon of joint attention, although affected by locomotor experience, awaits further developments.

*Following the gaze and point: Infants with spina bifida.*    The findings of this study were confirmed in a study of infants with menygomyelocele (reported in Telzrow, 1990; Telzrow et al., 1999; Telzrow, Campos, Shepherd, Bertenthal, & Atwater, 1987). The study used the same paradigm as did the study just described (Campos et al., 1997). The infants in this study were recruited at approximately 5 months and were tested longitudinally every month for the period of the locomotor delay, and for 2 months after the delayed onset of locomotion. Locomotion occurred at 10.5, 11.5, 10.5, 8.5, 10.5, 13.5, and 10.5 months for infants 1 through 7 respectively. Locomotion was defined as intentional prone progression of 4 feet within 2 min. The group data are presented in Figure 4.

As is evident in the figure, prior to the delayed onset of locomotion, the spina bifida infants tended to look at the experimenter's face, and not toward the general region of the head turn, point, and gaze. However, upon the delayed acquisition of locomotion, the tendency to look at the experimenter's face dropped precipitously and the tendency to look in the general direction of the gaze and point increased significantly. (The numbers in this figure do not total to 100% because infants were also scored as doing nothing, or looking around at their bodies, etc.) In this study, 5 of the 7 infants showed the tendency to look in the general direction of the gaze or point; the 2 who did not show the shift toward rudimentary joint attention continued to look at the experimenter's face. The 2 infants who responded to the correct side even before locomotor onset might have been showing pseudo-following. Alternatively, they might be examples of the principle of precocious exposure we mentioned at the opening of this article (if their parents engaged in training the infants in referential gestural communication well before locomotion). Nevertheless, despite these two exceptions, a highly significant effect of delayed locomotor experience was found in this study.

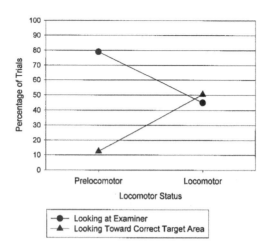

**Figure 4:** Following the gaze and point gesture in infants with spina bifida (data from Telzrow et al., 1999).

*Following the gaze: Locomotor delay in Chinese infants.* The same paradigm used in the study cited in Campos et al. (1997) was also used in a cross-sectional study conducted in Beijing on 90 Chinese infants ranging in age from 8 to 11 months (Tao & Dong, 1997). There were two major differences from the prior work. One was that in China, only the experimenter's gaze was used to refer to the target; the across-the-body point gesture was omitted in the study. The second was that in China only 8 trials were used, not 16. Despite the differences in procedure, the findings from China were similar to those obtained in the United States. Regardless of the age when the infants began to crawl (which in this study averaged 9.5 months), infants crawling on hands and knees for 5 weeks or more significantly outperformed precrawlers. The mean number of trials to follow the head turn and gaze to the correct side was 3.55 trials out of 8 for crawlers, compared to only 1.50 for prelocomotors – a significant difference. Infants crawling for 5 weeks or more also significantly outperformed infants crawling for 3 weeks or less (who searched in the correct direction on 1.54 trials). The Chinese infants rarely looked to the side opposite the experimenter's head turn and gaze. An analysis of covariance (ANCOVA) revealed a significant effect ($p < .03$) of crawling experience when age was statistically controlled.

A second investigation was conducted in China on following the gaze gesture of a female experimenter (Tao & Dong, 1997). The purpose of this study was to contrast the performance of two groups of locomoting infants of the same age. One group was constrained to the parent's bed (and thus had very limited experience with locomotion). The second group lived in apartments that permitted the infants to locomote on the floor; these infants were presumed to have more locomotor experience than the first group of infants. This study revealed a statistically significant difference ($p < .02$) between the two groups in following the gaze gesture, with floor crawlers searching to the correct side on 6.3 trials, and those confined to the bed searching only on 4.1 trials. As in the earlier study, Chinese infants rarely looked in the direction opposite to the direction of the experimenter's head turn and gaze.

Taken as a whole, these findings consistently implicate locomotor experience in the development of referential gestural communication. Similar findings were obtained regardless of whether the investigation dealt with infants who crawl at normative ages, infants with spinal lesions, or infants delayed in locomotion onset because of cultural and ecological factors. In every study, hands-and-knees crawling infants with approximately 5 weeks of locomotor experience responded appropriately to referential gestural communication, and did so whether the gesture involved head turn, gazing, and pointing, or the head turn and gaze alone. We thus conclude that locomotor experience greatly facilitates the development of the child's social cognition and lays the basis for the future development of skills crucial for social referencing, emotional development, and language acquisition. Furthermore, because the understanding of referential gestural communication is a necessary component of "secondary intersubjectivity" (i.e., a two-person communication about a third event), we propose that the development of secondary intersubjectivity can depend at least partly on experience; explanations solely emphasizing "maturation" (Trevarthen, 1993) are likely incomplete.

## Overview of Findings on Socioemotional Development

In this section, we described perhaps the broadest set of changes in infants following the onset of locomotion. Infants become more willful, more autonomous, more prone to anger and glee, more sensitive to maternal separations, more intense in their display of attachment behaviors, more likely to encounter the mother's wrath, more prone to begin social referencing, and more likely to initiate interactive games and processes. In addition, infants with locomotor experience perform better on a task assessing the tendency to follow referential gestural communications. Finally, because changes in the infant accompany changes in the family system, it is clear that the development of crawling is a crucial milestone for all family members. We now turn to a discussion and an explanation of a different emotional change in the child following locomotor onset.

## Self-Motion Perception, Self-Produced Locomotor Experience, and Why Infants Come to Fear Heights

In this section we consider the development of two perceptual abilities whose relation to self-produced locomotor experience appears to be particularly robust – wariness of heights and postural responsiveness to peripheral optic flow. Although most psychologists would agree that the latter ability falls clearly within the perceptual domain, many would argue that wariness of heights constitutes an emotional reaction rather than a perceptual phenomenon (Rader et al., 1980; Walk, Shepherd, & Miller, 1988). We do not make such a hard-and-fast distinction between perception and emotion; in fact, we argue that wariness of heights is brought about by a very specific, but hardly extraordinary discrepancy among visual, vestibular, and somatosensory information when a drop-off is encountered. The discrepancy also appears to be related to an individual's responsiveness to peripheral optic flow and, hence, wariness of heights is very much rooted in the perceptual domain. We elaborate on this argument subsequently.

As independent mobility emerges and develops, infants discover many new facts about themselves and their environment. These discoveries include what new information might be picked up from the environment; what information in the environment is relevant to the control of locomotion; and what objects, places, and events have consequences for a mobile organism. It should not be surprising, then, that the development of control over locomotion constrains perceptual development (the development of information pickup) just as perceptual development constrains the ability to control locomotion. Such interdependence between perception and action, referred to as *perception–action coupling*, and its implications for understanding human development, have recently captured the interest of psychologists (e.g., Bertenthal & Clifton, 1998; Bertenthal, Rose, & Bai, 1997; Reed, 1982; Schmuckler, 1993; von Hofsten, 1989).

## The Development of Height Avoidance in Kittens

Locomotion is an excellent phenomenon for studying the ontogeny of perception–action coupling, as demonstrated by the now-classic kitten studies initiated by Held and Hein (1963). In a yoked-control design, two groups of dark-reared kittens were exposed in dyads to the same pattern and amount of visual stimuli during locomotion. One kitten roamed freely (though in a circular trajectory) in self-directed locomotion, while the second kitten was passively yoked to and moved about by the first kitten. The results of the study indicated that only those kittens with active locomotor experience developed avoidance of heights (Held & Hein, 1963). Conversely, once the kittens previously deprived of locomotor experience were allowed to locomote freely, height avoidance became evident within 24 hr. In sum, specific experiences provided by active SPL allowed the kitten to respond in a new, more developmentally advanced manner to environmental stimuli such as a drop-off. These findings were confirmed and extended in a subsequent study by Hein, Held, and Gower (1970).

## Locomotor Experience and the Development of Wariness of Heights in the Human Infant

The findings by Held and Hein (1963) generalize to the human infant. In a variety of studies using the age-held-constant design, including walker manipulation, the study of motorically delayed infants, and lag-sequential longitudinal investigations, Campos, Bertenthal, and Kermoian (1992) documented that the role of experience is indeed crucial in mediating the development of wariness of heights. Using heart rate as an index of wariness of heights – an index that can be used with either prelocomotor or locomotor infants – Campos, Bertenthal, and Kermoian (1992) reported cardiac accelerations in infants lowered toward the deep side of a visual cliff, so long as the infants had experience crawling or controlling a walker. On the other hand, prelocomotor infants without any walker experience did not show any significant heart rate change. In a second study described in their article, Campos et al. tested infants who started to crawl at a relatively early age (6.5 months), at a normative age (7.5 months), and at a relatively late age (8.5 months). The dependent variable in this study was not heart rate, but rather the difference in the latency to cross to the mother when she called the infant to cross to her from across either the deep or the shallow side of the visual cliff. In all three groups, infants were tested after either 11 or 41 days of locomotor experience. The findings revealed that it was crawling experience and not age of locomotion onset that was associated with hesitation to crawl onto the deep side of a visual cliff. At no age or testing time was any hesitation observed in crawling onto the shallow side of the cliff when the mother called the infant to cross to her in that situation. These studies replicated and extended the findings from a previous longitudinal study (Campos, Hiatt, Ramsay, Henderson, & Svejda, 1978) that showed after only a few weeks of locomotor experience infants began to avoid crossing the deep side of the visual cliff to reach their mothers. Taken together, these studies support the notion that the onset of wariness of heights develops as a result of the specific experiences engendered by SPL, rather than visual experiences in general.

## The Concept of Optic Flow

Although the onset of wariness of heights was one of the earliest developmental changes to be linked to experience with SPL, the development of postural responsiveness to peripheral optic flow is one of the most recent. J. J. Gibson (1966, 1979) first introduced the concept of optic flow (i.e., the continuously changing ambient optic array produced by a continuously moving point of observation) in his discussion of the visual information available for the control of action. Gibson suggested that vision serves three major functions in locomotion to a destination. First, it allows an animal to steer an appropriate course such that obstacles are avoided and the most economical route is taken. Second, vision provides information specifying whether a surface can be traversed. Not surprisingly, there is evidence that prelocomotor and locomotor infants differ in the properties of surfaces to which they attend (Schmuckler, 1993). Finally, vision provides an essential source of information for the maintenance of postural stability. This latter function is perhaps the least obvious of the three because the vestibular and somatosensory systems have traditionally been imbued with the role of providing information for postural control. However, there is considerable evidence that postural compensations can be induced in adults and children, if they are exposed to simulated optic flow in a "moving room," despite the fact that vestibular and somatosensory information specify postural stability (Bertenthal & Bai, 1989; Lee & Aronson, 1974; Lee & Lishman, 1975; Stoffregen, 1985).

The moving room is a large enclosure, open at one end, that is suspended just above the floor. Usually, the walls are lined with some type of patterned (striped, polka-dotted) material, and lights positioned on the side walls illuminate from the room within. Lee and Aronson (1974) were the first to show that infants as young as 13 months, who were just learning to stand, would sway and fall in a directionally appropriate manner when the room was moved back and forward along the line of sight. In other words, the infants took the movement of the surrounding environment as an indication that they were moving and attempted to compensate for what was only an illusion of movement (see Figure 5). Butterworth and Hicks (1977) subsequently provided evidence that standing was not a prerequisite for responsiveness to optic flow, as infants who could not yet stand showed similar postural compensations when tested in the moving room in a seated position. Subsequent research has shown that the visual control of posture is specific to the geometric structure of the optic flow in concert with the region on the retina that is stimulated (Bertenthal & Bai, 1989; Dichgans & Brandt, 1974; Stoffregen, 1985, 1986), and possibly to the magnitude of the retinal area stimulated (Crowell & Banks, 1993).

When the eyes look in the direction of movement, the central regions of the retina are exposed to a melon-shaped family of curves that radiate out in an expanding starburst pattern from the point where the mover is heading (illustrated in Figure 6). This type of pattern has been referred to as *radial flow* (J. J. Gibson, 1979). In contrast, at the periphery (the edges of the visual field), the lines of flow are nearly parallel to the line of movement, having a lamellar structure (Cutting, 1986) similar to the lines of longitude at the equator of a

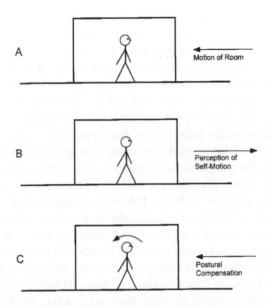

**Figure 5:** Demonstration of illusion of self-movement and postural compensation in a moving room. When the side walls of the room move from right to left (A), the observer perceives motion of the self in the direction opposite to side wall movement (B), and compensates for the perceived but illusory self-movement by adjusting the body in the same direction as side wall movement (C).

globe (also illustrated in Figure 6). When adults and children face the front wall of the moving room, they show much greater postural responsiveness to peripheral lamellar flow caused by movements of the side walls alone than by central radial flow caused by movements of the front wall alone (Stoffregen, 1985, 1986; Stoffregen, Schmuckler, & Gibson, 1987). However, there appears to be a developmental shift in responsiveness to spatially delimited portions of the optic flow between 5 and 9 months of age (Bertenthal & Bai, 1989).

## Locomotor Experience and the Development of Postural Responsiveness to Peripheral Optic Flow

Using an enclosure that permitted independent movement of the front and side walls, Bertenthal and Bai (1989) exposed 5-, 7-, and 9-month-old infants to global optic flow (whole-room motion), central flow (front-wall motion only), and peripheral flow (side-wall motion only). Although 5-month-olds showed no systematic postural compensation to any of the room movement conditions, both 7- and 9-month-olds compensated in a directionally appropriate manner to whole-room movement. Most important, 9-month-olds, but not 7-month-olds, responded with systematic postural compensations to side wall movements, suggesting a developmental trend between 7 and 9 months in

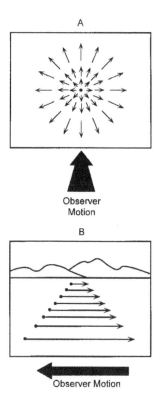

**Figure 6:** Patterns of optic flow. Radial optic flow presented to the central retina (A) and lamellar optic flow presented to the retinal periphery (B) when the head is aligned in the direction of forward motion.

the ability to use peripheral optic flow for postural control. Not surprisingly, Bertenthal and Bai suggested that SPL experience might play an important role in this perceptual shift; a suggestion that was subsequently tested in an experiment by Higgins, Campos, and Kermoian (1996).

Using the same type of moving-room apparatus as Bertenthal and Bai (1989) and a refined technique that permitted calculation of the correlation between infant sway and wall movements, Higgins et al. (1996) reported that 8.5-month-old infants without locomotor experience showed minimal postural compensation to peripheral optic flow. In contrast, 8.5-month-old infants with hands-and-knees crawling experience or walker experience showed significantly higher degrees of postural compensation to peripheral flow. The differences between the three groups of infants can be seen clearly in Figure 7. Because infants in all three groups showed postural compensation to testing conditions other than those involving peripheral optic flow, Higgins et al. ruled out the possibility that prelocomotor infants were incapable of postural compensation at all. The relative unresponsiveness of prelocomotor infants

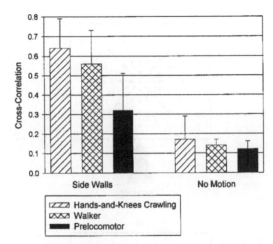

**Figure 7:** Responsiveness to side-wall motion and no motion in the moving room as a function of locomotor status. Adapted from "Effect of self-produced locomotion on infant postural compensation to optic flow" by C. I. Higgins, J. J. Campos, & R. Kermoian, 1996, *Developmental Psychology, 32,* 836–841. Copyright 1996 by the American Psychological Association. Adapted with permission.

in the moving room was specific to peripheral, lamellar flow conditions – namely, those conditions that typically and maximally inform the visual system of self-motion.

## The Link between Peripheral Optic Flow and Wariness of Heights

There is preliminary evidence that the developmental shift in infants' responsiveness to peripheral optic flow is related to the emergence of wariness of heights. Witherington, Campos, and Kermoian (1995) explicitly tested this relation in an experiment in which infants were tested in both the moving-room apparatus and the visual cliff. Twenty-two 8.5-month-olds with varying amounts of hands-and-knees crawling experience were exposed to side-wall movement in the moving room to assess the degree of coupling (i.e., correlation) between their body sway and the movement of the walls. In addition, the infants were tested to determine their latency to move off the centerboard of the visual cliff and across the deep or shallow side toward their mother. A latency score was devised by subtracting shallow-side trials from deep-side trials such that a high latency reflected behavioral avoidance of the deep side but not the shallow side of the cliff. The most important result was that postural response to peripheral optic flow correlated positively and significantly with behavioral avoidance on the deep side of the visual cliff ($r = .58$), implicating the development of responsiveness to peripheral optic flow as a mediator of the emergence of wariness of heights. This relation is not trivial and subsequently we address its implications in more detail.

So far, we have provided evidence that locomotor experience brings about changes in postural responsiveness to peripheral optic flow, which in turn leads to changes in reactions to heights. Little has been said about how or why locomotion engenders such changes. Specifically, by what process(es) does self-produced locomotor experience foster these important perceptual changes? As we have already implicated responsiveness to peripheral optic flow in the emergence of wariness of heights, we begin by suggesting the means by which locomotor experience facilitates the infant's ability to attend to and use specific portions of the optic array for the various functions involved in locomotion to a destination. We then return to the specific mechanism by which wariness of heights can emerge.

## How Does Locomotor Experience Facilitate Responsiveness to Peripheral Optic Flow?

Relative to maintaining stability in one place, the task of transporting the body from place to place is quite demanding on attention. Recall that J. J. Gibson (1979) suggested three major functions for vision during locomotion to a destination: steering, detection of surface traversability, and maintenance of postural stability over a dynamically changing base of support. These functions highlight the number of visual informational sources that must be processed concurrently as an infant moves through the environment. However, locomotion can be accomplished efficiently if the various sources of information are partitioned to those areas of the retina specialized to detect them. For example, the center of the retina is thought to be specialized to detect object properties and object motion (e.g., Leibowitz & Post, 1984), whereas, as is obvious from the preceding discussion, the retinal periphery is thought to be specialized to detect self-motion. Hence, a moving observer might maintain heading and steer an appropriate course using central radial flow and concurrently maintain postural stability by attending to lamellar flow presented to the retinal periphery. It is highly likely that the ability to differentiate the central radial optic flow and peripheral optic flow is learned during the acquisition of locomotor skill (Gibson & Schmuckler, 1989; Schmuckler, 1993). In other words, locomotion compels the infant to differentiate central and peripheral optic flow for the various functions involved in moving from place to place, if those functions are to be performed effectively and efficiently.

The foregoing argument does not imply that infants are insensitive to peripheral optic flow prior to the acquisition of locomotor skill; indeed, consistent with the principle of partial accomplishment mentioned earlier, Jouen (1988, 1990) elegantly showed that infants as young as 3 days of age show sensitivity to peripheral optic flow. Rather, we suggest, as have others (Bertenthal, 1990; J. J. Gibson, 1966; Jouen & Gapenne, 1995), that locomotor experience plays a role in the subsequent development of visual–postural coupling. Stated otherwise, locomotion brings about a marked shift in the utilization of spatially delimited portions of optic flow for controlling posture. Through a process of "optimization of attention" (E. J. Gibson, 1969), infants differentiate and fine-tune perceptual control of action during the actual practice of locomotion. Such fine-tuning or refinement of perception occurs to a degree hitherto unnecessary until the ability to locomote emerges. Furthermore, it is likely that the mapping between vision and posture that results from crawling experience will need to be remapped as the infant acquires new motor skills such as standing and walking (Adolph, Vereijken, & Denny, 1998; Bertenthal et al., 1997; Goodale, 1988; Milner & Goodale, 1995). In fact, remapping is likely to occur with the acquisition of every new motor skill in a continuously coevolving perception–action cycle.

## Does Responsiveness to Peripheral Optic Flow Play a Role in Wariness of Heights?

Returning now to the role of locomotor experience in the emergence of wariness of heights, we suggest that the ability to use peripheral optic flow for postural control is a prerequisite for showing a fearful reaction on the visual cliff. This hypothesis hinges on the different relations among visual, vestibular, and somatosensory information to which an infant is exposed during both active and passive locomotion. When infants move toward a destination, they will generally look in the direction of motion so as to steer appropriately and keep the target of locomotion in view (e.g., Higgins et al., 1996). As such, infants who actively locomote will receive the typical optic flow patterns described previously: radial flow projected to the center of the retina and lamellar flow projected to the periphery of the retina. In addition, there will be congruence among visual, vestibular, and somatosensory feedback specifying the angular acceleration of the body and head in the direction of locomotion. Thus, infants who actively locomote will increasingly experience a strong degree of correlation among patterns of visual, vestibular, and somatosensory information. In contrast, nothing demands that passively moved infants (in strollers, cars, or parents' arms) direct their attention toward the direction of motion. In many cases, passively moved infants face in a direction opposite to the direction of motion and quite often peripheral optic flow is at least partially blocked as the infant is moved. As a result, visual input received during passive transport can be very different from input received by the vestibular and somatosensory systems. In other words, correspondence among visual, vestibular, and somatosensory information will be relatively low in the prelocomotor infant, and in contrast to actively locomoting infants, it is unlikely that any consistent expectations will develop as to the typical pattern of relations among them.

When locomotor infants confront a drop-off, or depth at an edge, their expectation of correlated visual, vestibular, and somatosensory information will be violated. When approaching the edge, the vestibular and somatosensory systems will specify motion, but the visual system will specify relative stasis, because visual contours at the site of the drop-off are too distant to provide much in the way of proprioceptive information about self-motion. The key to understanding this violation is that the rate of angular displacement of optical texture on the retina, which specifies visually perceived acceleration, is related to distance (Bertenthal & Campos, 1990; Brandt, Bles, Arnold, & Kapteyn, 1979). Remember also, that it is the lamellar flow projected to the retinal periphery that efficaciously specifies self-motion. The fact that infants who show greater postural response to peripheral optic flow also display more avoidance on the deep side of the visual cliff (Witherington et al., 1995) provides compelling evidence that the violation of expectancy among patterns of visual, vestibular, and somatosensory feedback is, at least in part, responsible for locomotor infants' fearful reactions on the visual cliff. Uncorrelated feedback is not only responsible for postural instability but also for a range of physiological reactions including fear (Bertenthal & Campos, 1990; Guedry, 1974; Mayne, 1974).

In summary, we have provided evidence that the development of wariness of heights and postural responsiveness to peripheral optic flow are related to locomotor experience. Furthermore, we argued that these two phenomena are related to each other in that responsiveness to peripheral optic flow is considered a prerequisite to fearful reactions on the visual cliff. The former developmental change is thought to result from the increasing need to discriminate spatially delimited portions of the optic flow field if the important subtasks involved in locomoting to a destination are to be controlled effectively and efficiently. The latter change is thought to result from a violation in the expectation of correlated input from the visual, vestibular, and somatosensory systems when a drop-off is encountered. It is important to point out here that the expectation of correspondence among visual, vestibular, and somatosensory information is a direct consequence of locomotor experience. The arguments we presented here highlight the mutual interdependence between perception and action in the developmental process.

## The Role of Locomotor Experience in the Perception of Distance

In this section, we discuss the role of self-produced locomotor experience in the development of distance perception – the ability to gauge veridically how far an object is from the perceiver. The problem of distance perception is a classic issue that dates back at least to Berkeley (1709). At one time it was believed that information provided by vision about distance is too impoverished to allow for veridical perception of how near or how far an object is, let alone to direct spatially appropriate behavior. The motoric factors of accommodation (the thickening and thinning of the lens of the eye in response to image blur), convergence (the extent to which the two eyes are turned inward to fixate an object), reaching, and locomotion were deemed critical in providing information about distance that the visual system failed to provide by itself.

Following Berkeley (1709), Piaget (1954) described how the infant, after coordinating vision with reaching, constructed the perception of planes of depth, but only within the zone of reach and a little beyond (what Piaget called "near space"[1]). Beyond this range, according to Piaget, the world looks to the prelocomotor child as flat as the night sky does to an adult – a plane in which the relatively close moon, the more distant planets, and the even more distant stars appear equally far from the perceiver. Slowly, locomotor experience provides the information to disambiguate "far space," and the infant can thus estimate the sizes and distances of objects veridically. Such motoric enrichment of visual information involves scaling visual information in terms of motoric units. Such scaling is called *calibration*. Thus, the objective distance of a toy from a baby is calibrated in terms of such variables as the length of a reach required or the number of strides that must be taken to get to it (Kaufman, 1974).

The impoverished vision hypothesis also predicts that size constancy, which is related to accurate distance perception (Holway & Boring, 1941; Rock, 1977), will require calibration. Until such calibration takes place by motoric enrichment of visual information, according to this hypothesis, an object receding from a prelocomotor infant must create an ambiguous percept. For example, without calibrating distance, the infant cannot tell whether the departing mother is shrinking or maintaining the same size while moving farther away. Although infants will possess size constancy in near space once reaching and vision are coordinated, they will lack it in space well beyond reach. Similar considerations apply to shape constancy. Specifically, the perception of any object will show a developmental trend ranging from absence of any constancy prior to reaching, to presence of shape constancy in near space, then to elaboration of shape constancy at ever greater distances subsequent to the infant's expanding locomotor experiences, and ultimately ending with the intervention of more cognitive triangulations permitting distance to be calculated precisely.

The classic view represented by Berkeley (1709) and Piaget (1954) is now discredited. For example, J. J. Gibson (1979) and others have claimed that the visual system, far from being impoverished, has all the information required for veridical perception. Although Gibson's view is not universally accepted (e.g., Palmer, 1999; Rock, 1997), he and his followers have uncovered numerous previously unexamined sources of information available for distance perception. Furthermore, an impressive array of empirical studies documented that even the newborn has the ability – within limits – to perceive correctly the size and shape of objects despite variations in distance and slant (e.g., Slater, Mattock, & Brown, 1990; Slater & Morison, 1985). Because the newborn has little reaching, poor convergence and accommodation, and no locomotor ability, the neonate's visual system must be capable of sufficiently accurate distance information to mediate the level of correct size and shape perception assessed in these investigations.

Do these findings suggest that locomotor experience is not relevant to the development of distance perception? We have already alluded to a tendency for the infant to possess a skill in some measurable way prior to locomotion but to show a dramatic tuning of that skill upon the acquisition of locomotion. We saw this tendency to be the case for visual proprioception – evident, though weakly, in the newborn, yet showing step-function increases following a few weeks of locomotor experience. This tuning and subsequent step-function improvement in a psychological skill might be even greater in infants' perception of distance for, as Banks (1988) noted, the first year of life is a period of dramatic ocular growth and neural migration, which requires continuous recalibration if the infant is to perceive the world veridically.

We argue that the perception of size and shape constancy, and more generally, the perception of distance, show similar developmental improvements following the acquisition of locomotion, despite the reports of rudimentary neonatal skills in these domains. Our prediction is based on the premise that the prelocomotor infant's visual system can detect the information for veridical distance perception only within a limited range. Beyond that range, the distance-specifying visual information either is unattended to, or might be beyond the powers of resolution of the prelocomotor infant's visual system. Locomotion thus can calibrate distance information after all, but only for distances relatively far from the infant, and not in the fashion Piaget expected. Rather than adding information to an impoverished visual system, locomotion can help to calibrate distance by drawing attention to previously undetected depth-specifying information.

## Locomotor Experience and the Redeployment of Attention

Prior to the onset of locomotion, the child might not notice the information in the distal optic array. Motoric factors, especially locomotion, might thus have a role in what J. J. Gibson (1966) called the "education of attention" to information that resides in visual input, but is not initially used by the visual system. Locomotion can be a parameter in the development of veridical distance perception in large-scale spaces provided that locomotion helps direct attention to distal displays. Several studies have discovered precisely such a change in the deployment of attention. One suggestive result can be found in the Campos, Kermoian, and Zumbahlen (1992) interview study mentioned earlier. More mothers of locomotor infants reported that their infants attended to distant objects and events than did mothers of prelocomotor infants. Several other lines of research, which we now describe, directly addressed the issue of changes in attention to distant events and reported differences between prelocomotor and locomotor infants.

*Locomotion and deployment of attention to a destination.* As discussed in the previous section, Higgins (1994; Higgins et al., 1996) found that infants with locomotor experience directed their gaze almost exclusively in the direction of motion as they crawled toward a distal goal. Hence, locomotion lures attention to far space, especially to the location toward which the infant is moving. If distracted, infants will discontinue forward motion and assume a "side-sit" posture to examine the distraction. In contrast, the passively moved prelocomotor infant is not engaging in goal-directed locomotion and so has no need to maintain a specific focus of attention. Higgins's observations thus provide preliminary evidence that locomotor infants and passively moved prelocomotor infants have different foci of attention during movement through the environment.

*Locomotion and attention to far space.* In addition to this differential focus on specific portions of far space as a function of goal-directed locomotion, locomotor infants demonstrate general changes in attentiveness to far space compared to prelocomotor infants (Freedman, 1992; Gustafson, 1984). In two experiments, Gustafson (1984) studied the social and exploratory behaviors of 20 prelocomotor infants. In the first experiment, infants between 6.5 and 10 months were tested for 10 min in a walker and 10 min out of a walker. Gustafson found that during the time that they were in the walker, infants spent significantly more time looking at far space, that is, at distant toys, people, and other features of the room. In the second experiment, Gustafson compared the behavior of the prelocomotor infants while in the walker with that of locomotor infants. She found no significant differences in the extent to which the walker infants and hands-and-knees crawlers looked to far space. Again, these findings indicate that there is a difference in the allocation of attention to space that is brought about by SPL.

Other research, conducted in our lab by Freedman (1992), further demonstrates that deployment of attention varies as a function of locomotor experience. Using an age-held-constant design, thirty 8.5-month-old infants were assigned to one of three groups of 10 each: prelocomotor, prelocomotor with walker experience, and hands-and-knees crawling. Infants in the hands-and-knees crawler group had at least 5 weeks of locomotor experience. Infants in the walker group had similar amounts of experience through use of a walker. The infants' task was to manipulate a canister in front of them that activated a display either in front of them and within reach, or two displays to the infants' side and beyond reach. One of the out-of-reach canisters was 5° to the right of midline, and the second was 60° from midline. Freedman obtained a number of noteworthy findings. For example, she found that prelocomotor infants were just as likely to look away to far space as locomotors, but they differed in what they focused on in far space. More specifically, she found that infants in the two groups with locomotor experience looked in the direction of objects in far space, whereas infants without locomotor experience when looking beyond reach tended to look at nothing in particular – at vacant parts of the room (see Figure 8). In addition, both hands-and-knees crawler and walker infants were more likely than prelocomotor infants to look toward far space while manipulating objects in near space. The results of the walker infants were not significantly different from those of the hands-and-knees crawlers, indicating that the walker group was as likely as the hands-and-knees crawlers to deploy attention differentially to far space. Overall, these results indicate that locomotor infants are more discriminating in their attentional deployment than prelocomotor infants.

*Further links between development and deployment of attention to distances.* Taken in conjunction with the findings by Higgins (1994) and Gustafson (1984), Freedman's (1992) results strongly suggest that infants direct their attention differently to near and far space as a function of locomotor experience. These results are also consistent with some observations of infants' allocation of attention early in life. For example, McKenzie and Day (1972) examined 6- to 20-week-old infants' looking time to objects at 30, 50, 70, and 90 cm. The infants were tested with a series of objects that were either constant in size (and therefore varied in retinal size as a function of distance) or increased in size systematically so that they projected the same retinal size. For both conditions, there was a linear decrease in looking times as a function of distance from the infant. Furthermore, there was no difference in looking time between the younger (6–12 weeks) and older (13–20 weeks) infants. These results have been confirmed with 22-week-old infants by Field (1975)

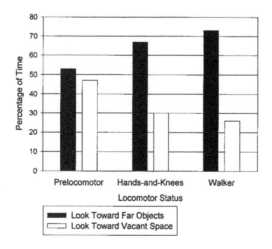

**Figure 8:** Time spent looking at objects in far space versus at vacant areas in far space as a function of locomotor status

and with 9- and 16-week-old infants by McKenzie and Day (1976). However, the latter authors also showed that as the distance of the object from the infant increased, there were no decrements in looking time to a moving object. The latter finding raises the interesting possibility that motion in general (motion of the environment and motion of the infant) facilitates the deployment of attention to far space.

In fact, Walk et al. (1988) confirmed a relation between environmental motion, attention, and perceptual development. Walk et al. found that the number of days required to show wariness of heights in dark-reared kittens is profoundly affected by the allocation of attention, as well as by locomotor experience. Using a modification of the original Held and Hein (1963) experiment discussed earlier, Walk et al. tested kittens in six different groups, of which only two are critical to our concerns. Both groups of kittens were reared in total darkness, except for 3 hr a day during which they were exposed to the experimental manipulation while restrained in a specially built box. For one group (the go-cart group), the box was placed on a motorized skateboard that moved forward if the kitten raised its head to close a switch. For the other (the car-watching group), the kittens were not given any sort of self-motion, but instead were presented with an interesting display consisting of toy cars moving around a figure-8 track.

There were two critical findings in this study. First, the car-watching and go-cart groups avoided the deep side of the visual cliff with significantly fewer days of testing than kittens that were raised in total darkness or that received no self- or environmental motion. These findings demonstrate that, even in the absence of locomotor experience, attention to the environment can be critical for this developmental transition. Second, Walk et al. (1988) demonstrated that in the absence of either a moving environment that captures attention or locomotor experience avoidance of heights does not develop normally. These results indicate that although locomotor experience might be sufficient for the development of wariness of heights on the visual cliff, it is not necessary. Walk et al.'s data can also document the principle of equipotentiality described in the introduction: It seems that adaptive reactions to heights can result from the mediation of attention, in addition to the locomotion-generated proprioceptive decoupling process described in the previous section.

If, as suggested by these studies, locomotion encourages a reallocation of attention to near and far space, then we would predict three changes in perceptual abilities following the onset of locomotion. First is improved size and shape constancy at relatively large distances from the infant, second is a change in the use of monocular static information specifying depth relations, and third is an increase in veridical distance perception, as consequences of changes in the use of depth information. We now detail our rationale for expecting such changes.

## The Redeployment of Attention in the Perception of Size and Shape Constancy

In support of our claim that an ability demonstrated early in infancy will undergo subsequent developmental changes as a function of specific experiences, there is evidence that size constancy improves until 10 or 11 years of age (Beryl, 1926; Day, 1987; Shallo & Rock, 1988; Wohlwill, 1963). In addition, highlighting the relation between size constancy and distance perception, Wohlwill (1963) noted that distance constancy develops throughout childhood. Other research (Granrud, 1986) showed improvements in an extant perceptual constancy ability even within infancy. Granrud (1986) reported that with the onset of stereoscopic perception at approximately 4 months, there is a step-function increase in infants' size constancy. Specifically, Granrud found that 4-month-olds sensitive to retinal disparity showed better evidence of size constancy than infants of the same age who were not yet sensitive to disparity. Extending the logic of Granrud's study, we maintain that following the onset of locomotion there might well be further calibration of size constancy at greater distances than used by Granrud, especially because Granrud habituated infants over distances of only 30 to 155 cm and tested them at distances of 55 to 105 cm. These distances are still within the range of near space as defined by Johansson (1973). In other words, with the onset of disparity sensitivity, size constancy improves; why, then, should constancies not improve further with the acquisition of locomotor as well as other experiences?

Finally, McKenzie, Tootell, and Day (1980) reported a failure of size constancy in 6- and 8-month-old infants at relatively great distances from the infant (3 m), but not at relatively close ones (1 m). Interestingly, in a second experiment, McKenzie et al. showed that 4-month-old infants, given a dynamic display that is more likely to attract attention, demonstrated constancy at a larger distance. We take this pair of investigations as suggesting the importance of the role of self- or environmental motion in educating or optimizing attention. Specifically, only when the infant's attention is attracted toward the display is information for constancy used veridically.

Taken as a whole, the previously mentioned studies highlight Haith's (1990, 1993) notion of *partial accomplishments*. As Haith (1993) noted,

> The problem is that we find a shred of evidence that a piece of a process is functional and then infer that the whole process is intact, at least implicitly. But, we only have evidence for a partial accomplishment, and we need conceptual schemes that will accommodate such partial accomplishments.... In addition, we often fail to recognize that a baby might "have" a skill at one moment and not the next. (p. 358)

We feel that this reconceptualization of development is critical to understanding the role of locomotor experience in the transitions we are discussing here.

## Locomotor Experience and the Development of Sensitivity to Monocular Static Information

On a priori grounds alone, we would not predict that there should be any relation between locomotor experience and the use of monocular static information, because the normative age for the development of sensitivity to this source of information precedes the normative age for the onset of prone progression. Between the ages of 5 and 7 months, infants begin to reach toward the "apparently nearer" of two objects specified by monocular static information such as linear perspective, texture gradients, and familiar size (Granrud, Haake, & Yonas, 1985; Granrud & Yonas, 1984; Yonas & Granrud, 1985; Yonas, Granrud, Arterberry, & Hanson, 1986). However, with increasing experience, children and adults are acutely aware of the illusion of depth and no longer make this error (Haber, 1980; Koenderink, 1999). Curiously, there is evidence that a reduction in the tendency to reach for the apparently nearer of two objects on the basis of monocular static information is related to locomotor experience. This decline can result from the increasing effectiveness of motion parallax following the onset of SPL.

Using an age-held-constant design, Arterberry, Yonas, and Bensen (1989, Experiment 2) reported that prelocomotor infants, belly crawlers, and hands-and-knees crawlers reached for an object that was apparently nearer on the basis of information contained in linear perspective and texture gradients, on 74.5%, 66.9%, and 63.1% of the trials, respectively. Although suggesting that greater locomotor experience results in less reaching for the apparently nearer of two objects, this trend was not significant. However, a study conducted independently by Thomas and Crow (1988), using similar methodology, did obtain significant results. These authors reported that infants with locomotor experience were significantly less likely to reach toward an apparently nearer object on the basis of the monocular static information associated with familiar size. Taken together, these findings not only implicate locomotor experience in infants' increasing resistance to the illusion of depth but also suggest that such resistance is evident across different sources of monocular static information. It is possible, as Arterberry et al. (1989) noted, that

> With increasing motor experience, infants become more sensitive to the conflicting information for the orientation of the surface. Whereas static-monocular information specifies depth, accommodation and motion parallax provide information that the upper and lower objects are at the same distance. (p. 981)

*Explaining the decline in effectiveness of pictorial depth information for reaching.* We predict that infants will attend more to motion parallax information following the onset of locomotion and consequently will be fooled less by monocular static information presented in pictorial displays. This argument is premised on the increasing ease with which motion parallax information can disambiguate surface relations following refinements in visual–vestibular coupling (improvement in this coupling following locomotor experience was discussed in the previous section). There is considerable evidence in the adult literature to support the important role of vestibular information in the utilization of motion parallax (Cornilleau-Pérès & Gielen, 1996; Hayashibe, 1991; Rogers & Graham, 1979; Rogers & Rogers, 1992). Generally, this evidence suggests that surface relations specified by motion parallax alone are ambiguous unless augmented by nonvisual sources of information specifying self-motion.

Therefore, with locomotor experience, information from the vestibular system might be increasingly utilized by the visual system to disambiguate motion parallax information specifying surface layout. Although seated infants might make use of vestibular information stemming from small head motions to disambiguate motion parallax, we believe that the self-motion that takes place over larger distances in locomotion serves as a much better disambiguator of motion parallax. Consequently, locomotor infants can become more aware than prelocomotors of the discrepancy between the depth relations specified by monocular static information and those specified by motion parallax. Growing sensitivity to discrepant depth relations would then lead to a reduction in infants' reaching behavior toward pictorial displays containing illusory depth relations. We feel that this hypothesis should be tested in future research.

## Self-Produced Locomotor Experience, Attention, Depth, Distance, and Constancy

Thus, it seems plausible that the role of locomotor experience in the calibration of distance perception is not the ability to detect invariants per se. Rather, it is the ability to integrate the information from those invariants into a coherent perception of space. It must be noted here that our entire discussion is premised on the distinction between depth and distance information.

Traditional accounts of visual development indicate that infants are sensitive to a number of sources of depth information very early in life (e.g., Timney, 1988; Yonas, Arterberry, & Granrud, 1987; Yonas, Granrud, & Pettersen, 1985). However, there is no evidence that infants perceive distance relations in a wholly veridical manner. The problem is that most of the traditional accounts have examined sources of information that specify only relative depth relations. An example of relative depth perception is the perception that a person's hand is farther than a person's outstretched arm, but closer than an object a person is reaching for. Relative depth information, as its name implies, specifies relations between surfaces and objects in ordinal terms. However, to perceive distance veridically, a person also needs to perceive absolute distance information. That is, a person must know exactly how far to stretch an arm to reach an object. For absolute distance perception, the various sources of relative depth information must be calibrated by one or another type of metric information. One type of metric information can be provided by motoric factors, including locomotor experience. We thus expect major changes in absolute distance perception as a function of locomotor experience, even in infants whose relative depth perception is already quite good. If our reasoning is correct, Berkeley and Piaget might not have been entirely wrong in their suppositions about distance perception – at least not for the perception of relatively large distances.

In summary, we have provided evidence in this section to show that locomotor experience can be responsible for changes in allocation of attention. This change in attention will modify the use of various sources of depth information, which are related to accurate distance perception. Accurate distance perception also leads to marked improvements in size and shape constancy. Our argument implies that distance perception and each of its component factors do not operate effectively over large ranges until the infant has had sufficient locomotor experience to disambiguate those features of the environment that remain invariant following large changes in perspective. Interestingly, our analysis again implicates attention to the environment as a critical mechanism by which developmental changes occur. Some evidence suggests that movement in the environment can elicit precocious perceptual abilities or facilitate their development. Perhaps such a finding should not surprise us. The invariant features of objects, places, and events can be detected both by noticing characteristic patterns of change in global optic flow (i.e., when the observer is moving through the environment) and local optic flow (i.e., when objects and other people are moving through the environment). No doubt, infants' predisposition to attend to movement facilitates the detection of environmental invariants. Finally, we should note the important role of visual–vestibular coupling in the veridical perception of distance. Like attention, such coupling between visual and vestibular information can be a general mechanism underlying the development of a range of perceptual changes.

## Locomotor Experience and Spatial Search

Infants between the ages of 8 and 12 months are able to retrieve an object hidden within reach at one location but often have difficulty finding an object when it is hidden under one of two adjacent locations, even when those hiding locations are perceptually distinct (Bremner, 1978; Piaget, 1954). Most curious, however, is that following repeated object retrievals at one location (conventionally denoted as A), infants often make an erroneous reach back to hiding location A when they observe the object moved to a second hiding location (denoted as B). The error, commonly referred to as the A-not-B error, becomes more pronounced as the delay between hiding and search at location B increases. Observed by Piaget (1954) and made an important basis for his stress on the role of action in sensorimotor development, the error was the focus of intense scientific scrutiny during the 1970s and 1980s (Wellman, Cross, & Bartsch, 1987) and has recently received attention anew (Munakata, 1998; Smith, Thelen, Titzer, & McLin, 1999). Piaget (1954) explained the A-not-B error on the assumption that infants younger than 8 months coded object positions relative to the self (egocentrically) and were unable to relate objects to each other (allocentrically or geocentrically). Contemporary explanations suggest that this notion is too simplistic and implicate a number of other relevant factors (e.g., Munakata, 1998; Smith et al., 1999). It is also important to note that the explanation involving an egocentric to allocentric shift in localization cannot account for an infant's failure on the two-position hiding task described initially, suggesting, perhaps, that different mechanisms underlie performance on this task and the more difficult A-not-B task. Most important for the present purposes, however, is the robust link that has been established between locomotor experience and performance on the A-not-B task (e.g., Smith et al., 1999), as well as variants of the task that tap spatial search skills.

## The Initial Evidence for a Link between Self-Produced Locomotor Experience and Spatial Search

A link between locomotor experience and spatial search was suggested long ago by Piaget (1954), and more recently postulated by Campos et al. (1978), Acredolo (1978, 1985) and Bremner (e.g., Bremner, 1985; Bremner & Bryant, 1977). However, Horobin and Acredolo (1986) were the first to directly test whether locomotor experience had any bearing on the ability to find hidden objects. Horobin and Acredolo tested 34- to 41-week-old infants with varying amounts of locomotor experience, using three variations of the A-not-B task; one in which the two hiding locations were spaced close together, one in which the hiding locations were far apart, and one in which six hiding locations were used. The results showed clearly that infants who had more experience moving independently were more likely to search correctly on the B trials across all three conditions. Furthermore, the most attentive infants in the study were those who had been sitting and moving independently for the longest period. Not surprisingly, the authors speculated that locomotor experience mediated performance on this type of task by facilitating general attentiveness as well as the deployment of attentional strategies such as "keeping an eye" on the correct hiding location.

The findings reported by Horobin and Acredolo (1986) were replicated and extended in a rigorous series of studies by Kermoian and Campos (1988). Experiments 1 and 2 in the Kermoian and Campos series compared the performance of 8.5-month-old prelocomotor infants, prelocomotor infants with walker experience, and locomotor infants with hands-and-knees crawling experience on a series of spatial search tasks designed by Kagan, Kearsley, and Zelazo (1978). The tasks varied in difficulty from retrieving an object partially hidden under one cloth, to the classic A-not-B task with a 7-sec delay between hiding and search, to a variation of the A-not-B task involving the substitution of an object for the one originally hidden. Infants were given a score based on the number of tasks that were passed. The results indicated that the infants with hands-and-knees and walker-assisted locomotor experience performed significantly better than the prelocomotor infants. Furthermore, when the hands-and-knees and walker-assisted groups were divided further based on the amount of locomotor experience (1–4 weeks, 5–8 weeks, and 9+ weeks), there was clear evidence for improved spatial search scores the longer the infant had been locomoting independently. Again, there were no differences between the hands-and-knees crawling and walker groups.

Analysis of performance on selected individual tasks further highlighted the important role of locomotor experience on spatial search. Forty-two percent of prelocomotor infants failed to find an object slid under a single cloth compared to only 12% of infants who had been hands-and-knees crawling for 9 or more weeks. Eighty-seven percent of the prelocomotor infants failed the A-not-B task with a 3-sec delay compared to only 24% of the infants who had been hands-and-knees crawling for 9 or more weeks. Data from Experiment 3 must be considered to understand completely the implications of the Kermoian and Campos (1988) studies. Thirty 8.5-month-old infants with 1 to 9 weeks of belly-crawling experience (a more effortful, much less efficient form of prone locomotion) performed similarly to the prelocomotor infants from Experiments 1 and 2 on the spatial search tasks. Further, unlike hands-and-knees crawling and walker experience, weeks of belly-crawling experience had no effect on search performance. There is a connection here between Horobin and Acredolo's (1986) suggestion that the deployment of attention mediates spatial search and the data from Experiment 3. The more effortful belly crawling can consume nearly all attentional resources, leaving limited attention to notice features of the environment and their characteristic patterns of change (e.g., occlusion and reappearance) that might facilitate spatial search in other contexts.

## Evidence from Delayed Crawlers in China

The previous findings have received additional support from a converging line of research in China that was designed to disentangle the role of the age at which locomotion was acquired from the duration of locomotor experience. This project capitalized on the ecologically and culturally mediated delay described earlier in the acquisition of prone progression in urban Chinese infants.

Two studies were conducted. One was cross-sectional and involved testing 34 infants on only one occasion in a modification of the Kermoian and Campos (1988) procedure (the modification primarily involving the addition of delays of up to 13 sec between hiding and finding the toy in the A-not-B delay test). In this study, the infants' ages ranged from 9 to 12 months, and averaged 10.6 months. All 34 infants were able to crawl on hands and knees for 2.5 m. The infants' data were expressed as a function of the weeks of locomotor experience the mothers reported when the infants were tested. Age was controlled statistically by an ANCOVA.

The second study, which was cross-sectional, revealed two noteworthy findings. First, age had no significant effect on A-not-B delay performance, whereas locomotor experience did. A follow-up analysis, which partialed out the effects of age on A-not-B delay, revealed a robust effect of the duration of locomotor experience ($p < .008$). Second, when the data were graphed and analyzed in terms of the duration of locomotor experience reported by the mothers, there was a clear monotonic trend between infants' performance and the duration of locomotor experience (see Figure 9). This study thus suggested

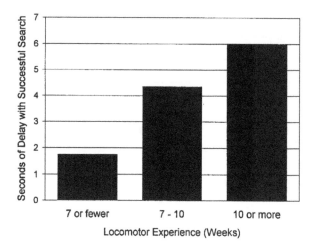

**Figure 9:** Performance of Chinese infants tested once cross-sectionally on the A-not-B delay task as a function of locomotor experience (data from Tao & Dong, 1997)

that the trend reported by Kermoian and Campos (1988) for infants at 8.5 months of age is evident even when infants begin to crawl at somewhat later ages. Indeed, within the limits of age tested (which in China extended to ages when some Western infants have begun to walk, not just crawl), age had no evident influence on the obtained results.

This cross-sectional work was followed up in China with a longitudinal study. Infants were recruited for the study when they were 7 months of age, and followed up by home visits until the investigators determined that the infant had begun to crawl on hands and knees for 2.5 m without stopping, slipping, or untangling the legs. This locomotor milestone was achieved at different ages, allowing the Chinese investigators to perform a lag-sequential analysis of their data. That is, regardless of the age when the infants began to crawl, they were tested on the A-not-B delay test used in the cross-sectional study after they had approximately 4 weeks, 7 weeks, and 10 or more weeks of locomotor experience. The results of the longitudinal study, averaged across all participants, are presented in Figure 10. As can be seen, there is again a clear monotonic trend indicating improvement in A-not-B delay performance as a function of locomotor experience.

The lag-sequential analysis of this longitudinal study allowed a test of the effects of age of crawling onset separately from the duration of locomotor experience. This dissociation was accomplished by dividing the infants into those who began to crawl at an age that is normatively early for China (approximately 8.5 months), normatively late for China (approximately 11 months), and an in-between age. These data are presented in Figure 11. As can be seen, each of the early, normative, and late-crawling-onset groups

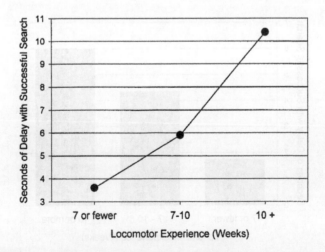

**Figure 10:** Performance of Chinese infants tested longitudinally on the A-not-B delay task as a function of locomotor experience (data from Tao & Dong, 1997)

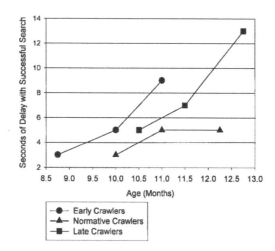

**Figure 11:** Performance of Chinese infants tested longitudinally on the A-not-B task as a function of both age of onset of crawling, and locomotor experience. Each curve represents data from three infants (data from Tao & Dong, 1997).

shows the same monotonic increase in performance as a function of locomotor experience. The only suggestion of an age effect is the steeper gradient in improvement in performance for the normatively late-crawling-onset group. Although the sample size in the lag-sequential analysis is small ($n = 3$ per group), these data suggest that the duration of locomotor experience facilitates tolerance of increasing durations of delay between hiding and finding an object on an A-not-B task. Furthermore, a potential criticism of the longitudinal data (viz., that the improvement with locomotor experience involves the effects of repeated testing) cannot apply to the highly similar findings from the cross-sectional study, in which infants were tested only once, and in which the sample size was much larger.

*Evidence from infants with motor disabilities.* The study of motoric delays in China resulting from ecological and cultural factors raises important questions about the consequences of locomotor delays in children with neurological, orthopedic, or other medical conditions that delay the onset of locomotion. For many years, researchers have questioned whether locomotor experience is necessary for the development of aspects of sensorimotor intelligence. As mentioned in the introduction, the work of Decarie (1969) and Kopp and Shaperman (1973) suggested that locomotor experience is not necessary for the development of sensorimotor skills. However, our research, taken as a whole, suggests strongly that crawling experience can be an important organizer of psychological development, especially in the realm of manual search for hidden objects. We confirmed that implication in the aforementioned study of 7 infants with spina bifida by Telzrow (Telzrow, 1990; Telzrow et al., 1987; Telzrow et al., 1999).

In addition to studying referential gestural communication, Telzrow's study examined spatial search on a two-position hiding task (patterned after a study by Bremner & Bryant, 1977), in which an object was hidden under one of two perceptually distinct covers (Telzrow et al., 1987; Telzrow et al., 1999). In this paradigm, infants saw the object hidden only in one location; the second location served only as a distractor. As mentioned earlier, infants were tested once a month, at the same session as the one assessing referential gestural communication. Testing began at the age of entry into the study until 2 months after the onset of SPL.

The results showed unequivocally a dramatic improvement in spatial search performance following the onset of locomotion. Prior to locomotion, infants passed only 14.3% of the trials; following locomotion, infants passed 64.3% of the trials. This trend was evident in 6 of the 7 infants tested. As in the work of Horobin and Acredolo (1986), Telzrow et al. (1999) noted that after the onset of locomotion, the infants with spina bifida tended to be much less distractible, more task oriented, and more likely to align their heads, eyes, and bodies toward the hiding location during the delay between hiding and search than before the onset of locomotion.

The study by Telzrow et al. (1999) was conducted simultaneously in Denver, using an age-held-constant study of 8-month-olds, with the same two-position hiding procedure. Infants were divided equally into three groups: crawling ($n = 16$), prelocomotor with walker experience ($n = 12$), and prelocomotor ($n = 24$; Campos, Benson, & Rudy, 1986). The two groups with locomotor experience performed almost identically (around 72% correct search on the hiding trials), and very differently from the prelocomotor infants without locomotor experience (who successfully retrieved the object hidden under one of the two cloths only 17% of the time).

In sum, regardless of whether infants are tested with a two-position hiding task or an A-not-B task with a few seconds of delay, crawling infants and prelocomotor infants with walker experience far outperform infants with no locomotor experience. Furthermore, these findings are obtained cross-sectionally, longitudinally, across at least two cultures, and appear to be independent of the age of onset of crawling, within the age limits investigated to date.

## By What Processes Are Spatial Search and Locomotor Experience Linked?

Despite the intense scrutiny given to the A-not-B error, and to a lesser extent, performance on two-position hiding tasks, the processes by which spatial search ability improves are still poorly understood. Without doubt the phenomenon is extremely complicated, especially when a person considers that it is necessary to explain the spatial component of spatial search (i.e., how is the correct location selected?) in addition to the temporal component (i.e., why do increasing delays between hiding and search degrade performance?). Nevertheless, several processes have been proposed to account for the development of spatial search performance and here we outline our view of how locomotor experience mobilizes these processes. The processes underlying improvements in spatial search include: (a) shifts from egocentric to allocentric coding, (b) learning of new attentional strategies, including improved discrimination of task-relevant features, (c) refinements in means–ends behavior and an associated tolerance of longer delays in goal attainment, and (d) improved understanding of others' intentions. We discuss the relation between each of these processes and locomotor experience.

*Shift from egocentric to allocentric coding.* Piaget (1954) was one of the first to suggest that improvements in spatial search represent the infant's emerging ability to shift from egocentric to allocentric coding strategies. The idea stems from an observation of the prelocomotor infant's world, a world that is very proximal and generally acted on from a stationary position. Under such conditions, an egocentric reference system is sufficient to learn how to move body parts relative to one another and to reach for objects. However, remaining oriented once mobile is a different problem, because an egocentric reference system, unless updated, will not be as useful as an allocentric reference system in which the positions of environmental features are coded relative to each other. Although a simple shift from egocentric to allocentric referencing can partly explain improvements in spatial search, it should be kept in mind that it cannot explain the improvements in search performance on two-position hiding tasks following locomotor experience (e.g., Campos et al., 1986; Telzrow, 1990). The two-position hiding task involves no trials in which a toy first hidden at A is subsequently hidden at B; as said before, the second position is a mere distractor. Our findings with the two-position task suggest that the transition engendered by locomotion is likely to result from multiple processes.

*The role of attention.* Acredolo and colleagues (e.g., Acredolo, 1985; Acredolo, Adams, & Goodwyn, 1984; Horobin & Acredolo, 1986) were the first to note a relation between locomotor experience and visual attention during "hide-and-seek" tasks like those used in the A-not-B paradigm. Quite simply, infants who kept an eye on the correct hiding location tended to search correctly for the hidden object. For a mobile infant, keeping an eye on objects and the places where they have disappeared is an effective way to find them again. However, there is more to attention than simply keeping an eye on certain targets. As Acredolo (1985) suggested, visual tracking of spatial locations can simply be a transitional strategy as infants learn what information from the self and the environment must be attended to in order to refine egocentric and allocentric coding strategies.

Earlier, it was noted that through a process akin to the education of attention, infants learn to use spatially delimited portions of the optic array for controlling the important subtasks involved in locomoting to a destination. The same type of selective attention is likely involved in the spatial discriminations necessary to localize distal targets and successfully steer a course to a target and return. Not surprisingly, the increasing ability to make fine-grained spatial discriminations has been suggested as one means by which locomotor experience might contribute to improved performance on the A-not-B task (Smith et al., 1999). The premise here is that the classic A-not-B task presents a perceptually confusing context in which reaching and search errors are very likely to occur. This argument is bolstered by the observation that search on B trials improves when the A and B hiding locations are perceptually distinct and easily discriminated (Wellman et al., 1987).

Related to this idea is the notion that better discrimination might also facilitate performance on the two-position hiding task, even when the hiding locations in these tasks are perceptually distinct. This argument is tenable if a person assumes that the learning of new motor skills initially directs an infant's attention to the features of the environment that specify the affordances for the new skill (e.g., Gibson & Schmuckler, 1989; Schmuckler, 1993). These features include the physical properties of the environment to which movements must conform, what Gentile (1987) referred to as the regulatory features of the environment. In a spatial search task, the position of the target relative to the infant, and the size, shape, weight, and texture of the hiding cover would be regulatory features. Once infants have become attuned to the important regulatory features of the environment, they might begin to notice the background or nonregulatory (Gentile, 1987) features of the environment, such as the color of an object. In other words, the infant would show a progression in the detection of information as skill proficiency improves from those features directly related to the control of action to those that are indirectly related but can nevertheless facilitate performance on tasks like spatial search.

With reference then to spatial search performance, locomotor experience likely has a broad impact on the development of attentional skills that generalizes to contexts other than those involving locomotion. Locomotor experience facilitates the development of new attentional strategies and leads to the detection and extraction (discrimination) of information most relevant to the task at hand. This argument is supported further by the common observation that locomotor infants are generally more attentive and less distractible during hide-and-seek tasks than prelocomotor infants. The argument also explains why belly crawling (which is an inefficient means of prone locomotion that consumes considerable energetic and attentional resources) should facilitate neither the development of attentional skills nor the subsequent development of spatial search skills.

*Refinements in means–ends behavior and tolerance of delays in goal attainment.*  Although the previous explanations can adequately explain the spatial component of the A-not-B error, they do not account for the observation that the likelihood of the error increases as the delay between hiding and search lengthens and that older infants and those with more locomotor experience are capable of tolerating longer delays. What role does locomotor experience play here? Quite possibly, locomotor experience demands and sets up the contingencies associated with the development of more sophisticated means–ends behavior and the ability to tolerate delays in goal attainment.

When an infant locomotes toward an environmental goal, the goal must be kept in mind over the period of time necessary to reach the objective, particularly if the target is somehow occluded during any portion of the movement toward it. Furthermore, the act of locomotion requires sophisticated means–ends behavior. Contrary to a discrete behavior such as reaching for a single object, locomotion demands a concatenation of movements over time – specific movements are nested within higher order movement sequences in the service of goal attainment. That deficits in means–ends behaviors have been implicated in the A-not-B error (e.g., Diamond, 1991; although see Munakata, McClelland, Johnson, & Siegler, 1997) is of special interest in the proposal here. However, the primary suggestion we make is that the establishment of action intermediaries in means–ends behavior has a counterpart in the time domain that is then associated with the ability to tolerate longer delays in goal attainment. In other words, locomoting to achieve a goal takes time. The infant must keep the goal in mind and must sequence (concatenate) a number of movements over time if the goal is to be achieved. It may be in this sense that locomotor experience leads to improvements in means–ends behaviors and to the ability to tolerate longer delays in goal attainment.

*The development of interintentionality.* The final process linked to locomotion and underlying improvements in spatial search performance is the development of interintentionality. The phenomenon of interintentionality is similar to the social referencing phenomenon and the understanding of referential gestural communication in that it involves the processing of communicative signals from others. However, interintentionality refers specifically to an understanding that others have intentions and the nature of such intentions. Based on observations of infants performing the A-not-B task in our lab, locomotor infants appear not only more attentive and less distractible than prelocomotor infants but they appear also to actively search for communicative signals from the experimenter. It is as if they work harder to understand the "game," as it were, and try to glean such an understanding from the experimenter. Perhaps this observation should not be surprising given the evidence provided previously for increased checking back and increased understanding of referential gestural communication following locomotor experience. Although based only on serendipitous observation, we feel strongly that the role of interintentionality in spatial search performance should be examined further, especially in two-position hiding tasks, where our serendipitous observations have been made.

To recapitulate, a number of converging research operations have shown a robust link between experience with self-produced locomotion and performance on spatial search tasks. The onset of locomotion leads to a number of new encounters with the environment and an accompanying need to extract new information and solve new problems. We have argued that the experiences associated with these encounters lead to general changes in attentiveness, to the specific deployment of attentional strategies as well as the education of attention to important features in the environment, to refinement of means–ends behaviors, and to the development of interintentionality. Consequently, these processes are implicated in the development of more sophisticated spatial search strategies and the appropriate deployment of such strategies across changing tasks and contexts. The specific role of these processes in the development of spatial search skills, as well as the interactions among them, awaits further research.

## Experience with Self-Produced Locomotion, Spatial Coding Strategies, and the Development of Position Constancy

In this section, we discuss spatial coding strategies and position constancy. The former refers to the means by which infants search for objects in space following self-movement, and the latter refers to the accurate outcome of a search strategy after self-movement. Here, we explain why there should be a robust link between SPL and spatial coding strategies. We also place the data on the use of such strategies in early infancy into a developmental context. Finally, we highlight a number of variables that might mediate the effects of locomotor experience on the development of spatial coding strategies and position constancy.

### Self-Referent and Environmental Referent Coding Strategies

In the previous section, we discussed Piaget's (1954, 1970) ideas about how the infant in early life undergoes a developmental sequence in which objects are first localized through the use of egocentric or self-referent (SR) spatial search strategies. An SR strategy involves the infant locating objects either by determining where it is in relation to the infant's body, or by repeating the actions that were previously successful. For example, an infant who finds an object on the right will continue to look to the right in subsequent attempts, even if the infant moves so that a rightward search is no longer appropriate. During the second step of Piaget's developmental sequence, which is thought to occur during the third quarter of the first year of life, the infant begins to replace SR strategies and use evironmental referent (ER) strategies to locate objects. Unlike SR strategies, search based on ER involves relating at least two environmental events or objects to each other, independent of the position of the self. ER strategies are much more likely to result in position constancy, because an object's position in space relative to other objects is generally invariant despite shifts in body movement. However, it was also noted previously that an egocentric strategy is not always inaccurate, provided the egocentric reference system is updated following self-movement. In other words, spatial orientation can be maintained if (a) the position of the self relative to the target location is noted prior to displacement, and (b) the direction and extent of movement of the self is continuously monitored. With such monitoring of self-movement, the new position of the target location relative to the self can be computed. Note, however, that in this section we do not discuss the role of locomotor experience on updating SR strategies, because evidence has yet to be provided for a link between these two variables, at least not at the ages we are concerned with here.

Piaget (1954) implied, and Acredolo (1985) and Bertenthal et al. (1984) explicitly proposed, that motoric activity, especially locomotion in space, facilitates the construction of ER strategies. In this section, we review some hitherto-undiscussed research on the role of locomotor experience on SR and ER use and draw two conclusions. One is that there is a developmental shift toward increasing probability of ER strategy use, and the second is that locomotor experience, contrary to some reviews (McKenzie, 1987), does play a role in that shift.

Several researchers have studied infants' use of these different strategies using two different types of displacements: rotations up to 180° and rotations up to 180° combined with translation (see Figure 12 for clarification of these two different kinds of displacements). Typically, the infant is taught to localize a target object from an initial vantage point, then displaced and tested to determine whether that infant can relocalize the target from the new vantage point. The task can be accomplished using a looking or a reaching movement with or without the aid of specific landmarks. The general consensus is that before 6 months of age, infants are unable to show position constancy after any of the types of displacement shown in Figure 12 (for reviews, see Acredolo, 1985; Bremner, 1993b). Between 6 and 8 months, infants are more successful at such constancy, but only if they are minimally rotated – no more than 90° (J. G. Bremner, personal communication, March 18, 1999; McKenzie, 1987; Rieser, 1979). After 8 months, infants are shown to be progressively more capable of relocalizing a target after larger rotations, with or without translation, as long as the landmark is available to the infant (Acredolo, 1985; Acredolo & Evans, 1980; Cornell & Heth, 1979; Lepecq & Lafaite, 1989).

Given the prior findings, locomotor experience does not seem necessary for the development of some degree of ER use and hence position constancy. Rather, this early use of ER search can be linked to the development of sitting and reaching (Bremner, 1993a). Our reading of the literature suggests that

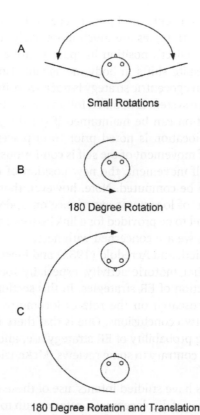

A

Small Rotations

B

180 Degree Rotation

C

180 Degree Rotation and Translation

**Figure 12:** Illustrations of rotation (defined as the infant pivoting left or right, but staying in the same place) versus rotation and translation (defined as the infant pivoting left or right and also moving from one place to another). A small rotation is one that is less than 180°.

position constancy and ER use is likely to be evident precociously (relative to Piaget's expectations) under the following four circumstances:

1. The environmental referent is close to, or even adjacent to, the searched-for object, rather than at some distance from it (Acredolo & Evans, 1980; Bremner, 1978).
2. The landmarks are salient (Acredolo & Evans, 1980).
3. Infants are tested in familiar environments, such as the home (Acredolo, 1979, 1982).
4. No training trials are presented during initial localization of the target (Bremner, 1978).

## Limitations in Prelocomotor Use of ER Strategies

Given that several studies have shown the ability to use ER strategies quite early in life, why have several authors hypothesized a strong link between locomotor experience and the development of spatial skills? (For reviews, see Acredolo, 1978, 1985; Bremner, 1993a; Bremner & Bryant, 1977; Lepecq, 1990, but for a sharp objection, see McKenzie, 1987). One reason is that the extent of ER use by infants who can sit and turn their heads and torsos will be constrained because of the limited nature of the experiences made possible by sitting, turning, and reaching. A second reason is that SPL contributes to ER use in situations where the landmarks are well beyond reach or in the extreme periphery of the infant's vision. (We have already seen the possible importance of growth of the infant's peripheral visual field in the research described previously on referential gestural communication. In that work, an infant capable of success when signaler and target are in the same visual field cannot succeed when signaler and target are in different visual fields.) Demands on the locomotor infant are very different from demands on the prelocomotor, seated infant. In addition, the deployment of ER strategies is especially likely when the infant is displaced in a forward direction by some minimal distance. Such forward displacements are common after prone progression, and rare prior to it.

There can be yet another reason for expecting a link between locomotor experience and spatial coding strategy use. To relocalize targets, and hence show position constancy, mobile infants must pay close attention not only to the environmental layout but also to their own movement with respect to the environmental layout. We discussed already the refined coupling between various sources of perceptual information following locomotor experience. Such coupling should facilitate the ability to track a person's own movement, and therefore, contribute to the ability to update egocentric responding after larger and larger displacements. Furthermore, attention will be directed increasingly toward far space as the infants' targets of locomotion become more distal. Hence, we predict that the ability to use distal landmarks to relocalize target positions should improve markedly following locomotor experience.

Spatial coding strategies provide thus another example of a skill (in this case ER or landmark search strategies) present early in life but not yet fully developed. As a function of specific experiences and adaptation to new contexts, the skill undergoes further development and is deployed in settings where it was not previously evident. We believe that locomotor experience creates new contexts that call for deployment of an existing skill in a more complex way. What empirical evidence, then, supports the role of self-produced locomotor experience in the development of spatial coding strategies?

## A Study of Locomotor Experience and Position Constancy

One of the first studies to examine the link between locomotor experience and the use of external referent strategies was carried out in our laboratory by Enderby (1984). Using a paradigm developed by Acredolo (1978; Acredolo & Evans, 1980), Enderby tested, in an age-held-constant design, three groups of 36-week-old infants. One group had no locomotor experience, one had at least 3 weeks of crawling experience, and one had no crawling experience but at least 40 hr of walker use. There were 20 infants per group. Each infant was trained to anticipate the appearance of a person at one of two windows (about 75° to the left or right) within a curtained enclosure. Salient landmarks, including flashing lights around the window, brightly colored stripes, and a blue star on the wall, were used to highlight the target window in an otherwise homogenous 2.7-m × 2.7-m enclosure. Note that in this study, the landmark was distal from the infant, which met one criterion for the type of testing context that would require locomotor experience for successful ER use. A cartoon of the paradigm is presented in Figure 13.

There were two parts to the study by Enderby (1984) – training trials and test trials. On training trials, a buzzer sounded, followed 5 sec later by the appearance of an experimenter at the target window. Training was repeated until the infant correctly anticipated the appearance of the experimenter on four out of five trials. Immediately after the training criterion was met, infants were both translated by about 1.3 m and rotated 180° to face the other side of the enclosure, and test trials began. When the buzzer sounded on each of the five test trials, the experimenter no longer appeared at the window. The direction of the infant's looking was examined as the dependent variable.

Results from this experiment revealed that, over all five test trials, 40% of infants with crawling experience correctly anticipated the appearance of the experimenter at the labeled window compared to only 15% of the same-aged prelocomotor infants. Infants with walker experience fell in between (35%).

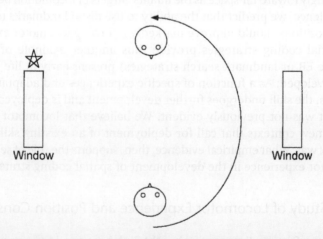

**Figure 13:** Visual depiction of the Acredolo paradigm, in which the infant is rotated 180° and translated by 1.3m. The starred window represents the landmarked location where the infant initially learned on training trials to expect the emergence of an experimenter.

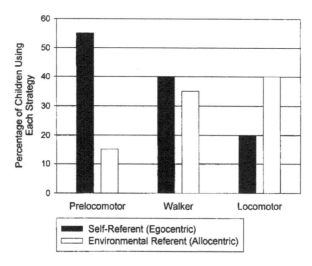

**Figure 14:** Egocentric and allocentric responses of 8.5-month-old infants as a function of locomotor status (data from Enderby, 1984)

These results, presented in Figure 14, showed that locomotor infants had significantly better position constancy than prelocomotors. A similar pattern of findings was obtained for the first test trial data (Enderby, 1984).

## Subsequent Research on Locomotor Experience and Spatial Coding

The results of Enderby's (1984) study were replicated in a study conducted at the University of Virginia by Bertenthal et al. (1984). Using very similar procedures to those of Enderby, the authors reported results for locomotor and prelocomotor infants that showed a trend similar to Enderby's. However, there were two noteworthy differences between the studies. First, Bertenthal et al. reported that walker experience resulted in looking at the correct window on the test trials a greater percentage of time than crawling experience. In that sense, the Bertenthal et al. study obtained stronger findings than did Enderby's. Second, Bertenthal et al. reported that locomotor infants used an allocentric (ER) strategy on many more trials than did Enderby (74% of trials compared to 40%); on the other hand, the prelocomotor infants used an allocentric code on 56% of trials, compared to 15% for Enderby. Despite these differences, the two studies converge in linking locomotor experience to position constancy on a displacement-plus-rotation task. Adding further strength to the link between locomotor experience and position constancy, Bertenthal et al. described a longitudinal study of an infant with an orthopedic handicap. That infant performed poorly on the Acredolo paradigm until a heavy cast impeding locomotion was removed and the infant became capable of locomotion at a somewhat later than average age.

The results of a study by McComas and Field (1984), also using a paradigm based on Acredolo's (1978) study, are often cited as evidence against the role of locomotor experience in the development of spatial referencing strategies. Their findings superficially appear to fail to replicate the studies by Enderby (1984) and Bertenthal et al. (1984). However, there are several reasons to be cautious about the findings of the McComas and Field study. First, the study seriously confounded locomotor experience and age, in that the older group had more locomotor experience. Second, all infants in that study had some locomotor experience (either 2 or 8 weeks); no prelocomotor group was included to provide a benchmark for comparison with the work of Enderby and Bertenthal et al. Third, the landmark used to specify the target window (a star around the window) was much less salient than the landmarks used in the Enderby and Bertenthal et al. studies. The relevance of the McComas and Field study to the evaluation of the role of locomotor experience on deployment of ER strategies is thus uncertain.

Also uncertain is the relevance of a study by Glicksman (1987) on the ability of 35-week-old locomotor and prelocomotor infants to relocalize a target object in a spatial rotation task that involved no landmarks. Glicksman's groups included prelocomotor infants, prelocomotors with walker experience, crawlers, and crawlers with additional walker experience. Infants were seated in the middle of a homogenous 2-m × 2-m square enclosure, centered between two identical brass bells, one on the left and the other on the right. One of the bells was movable, and thus, could be manipulated freely by the infant, whereas the other bell was invisibly secured to the floor. First, infants were required to retrieve the movable bell two times in succession during a training period. Then, after watching the bell being replaced in its original position, the infants were rotated 180°. Results from three consecutive training and test trial sequences revealed no differences between the groups in terms of the proportion of infants in each group who reached for the movable bell following rotation. Half of the infants in each group reached for the movable bell, and half reached for the stationary bell.

Given the demanding nature of Glicksman's (1987) task, we are not surprised by her results. Because there are no landmarks, success on this task requires that infants use a sophisticated SR strategy involving the updating of body position – a strategy beyond the capability of infants with limited locomotor ability. Furthermore, body position must be updated following a large rotation, that is, 180°. With a rotation of this magnitude, coupled with the absence of landmarks, it is unlikely that infants would succeed on this task prior to 12 months of age (Acredolo, 1978; Lepecq & Lafaite, 1989).

We thus conclude that the weight of the evidence favors a role for locomotor experience in facilitating correct performance in tasks such as the Acredolo rotation plus displacement task. But do these findings imply that locomotor experience is effecting a developmental shift in spatial coding strategies? Or is there another explanation possible for the findings using the Acredolo paradigm?

The most crucial concern raised about the research on the effects of locomotor experience on spatial coding is the possibility that the Acredolo paradigm involves infants learning a motor habit. As several investigators note (e.g., Bai & Bertenthal, 1992; Bremner & Bryant, 1985; McKenzie, Day, & Ibsen, 1984), a motor habit or response set can conceivably mask an ER or landmark-based coding strategy that the infant in fact possesses. If so, locomotor experience can have more to do with overcoming motor habits than facilitating the deployment of more complex spatial cognitive skills. To overcome this problem, a paradigm should be used that assesses position constancy without using training trials or generating motor habits.

## Overcoming the Motor Habit Confound in Spatial Coding Studies

Bai and Bertenthal (1992) conducted precisely such a study and found an effect for locomotor experience on the type of spatial coding strategies used by their infants. Their study adapted a paradigm from Bremner (1978) that minimizes the likelihood of teaching infants an incorrect egocentric response. Infants were tested in a square homogeneous room (2.5-m × 2.5-m) that was free of landmarks. Each infant was seated in the center of the room in a chair attached to a table. The chair allowed the infant to be rotated and locked in two positions 180° apart. Although the paradigm used a set of warm-up trials, in which infants were trained to search for a toy hidden in a single cup, there was no training in the part of the study that assessed position constancy.

In the position constancy test, two different colored cups (different also from those used in training trials) were placed side by side on the table in front of the baby. The infant watched the toy being hidden in one of the two cups and was immediately rotated 180° around the table (corresponding to a translation of approximately 1 m) before being allowed to search (see Figure 15 for a cartoon of the task). Three groups of 33-week-old infants were tested. One group of 20 infants was prelocomotor, a second group of 10 infants had 2.7 weeks of belly-crawling experience, and the third group of 18 infants had 7.2 weeks of creeping experience.

Results revealed that search performance varied as a function of locomotor status, especially on the first trial, with 72% of the creeping infants, compared to 25% of prelocomotors and 30% of belly crawlers showing position constancy (see Figure 16). These findings provide evidence that locomotor experience affects the deployment of spatial coding strategies, even when motor habits play no confounding role. Taken in conjunction with the work

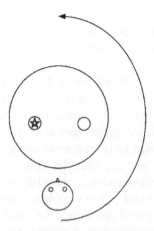

**Figure 15:** Cartoon of the testing apparatus used in the Bai and Bertenthal (1992) study

of Enderby (1984) and Bertenthal et al. (1984), the role of hands-and-knees locomotor experience is evident in spatial displacement tasks that also involve a rotation.

As in the Kermoian and Campos (1988) study, belly crawling did not seem to affect performance in this study. However, the confound in the belly-crawling group between duration of locomotor experience and quality of locomotion precludes any strong inferences about the role of belly crawling on position constancy.

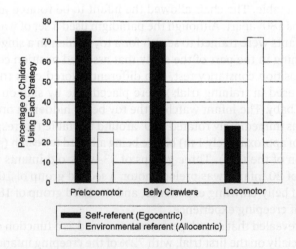

**Figure 16:** Performance of infants differing in locomotor status on a rotation translation task that involved no training trials. Adapted from "Locomotor status and the development of spatial-search skills" by Bai, D. L., & Bertenthal, B. I., 1992, *Child Development, 63,* 215–226. Copyright 1992 by the Society for Research in Child Development. Reprinted with permission from John Wiley and Sons Ltd.

There was another aspect to the Bai and Bertenthal (1992) study that deserves brief mention. They reported no differences between the locomotor and prelocomotor infants when the table, rather than the infant, was rotated. We are not surprised by this result: Rarely would prelocomotor or locomotor infants of this age experience environmental movements involving a static observer and a rotating hiding surface. At some point in development, correct search following table rotation should be evident; however, locomotor experience should not be linked to table rotations in front of a static observer. The effects of locomotor experience should be much more strongly related to position constancy following subject movement.

## Making More Robust the Link between Locomotor Experience and ER Deployment

In sum, the results of the studies cited in this section suggest a positive link between locomotor experience and the use of external landmarks that underlie the development of allocentric or ER spatial coding strategies. However, we believe that the link between locomotor experience and spatial referent strategies following displacements should be even more robust than has been the case in studies conducted to date.

Why is the link not as robust as we might expect? There are at least three factors that can mediate the effects of SPL on the development of new spatial referent strategies. First, it is likely that the amount of experience needed to bring about a shift in spatial coding strategies has been underestimated. Infants should not be expected to effectively switch from 0% to 100% position constancy. After locomotion emerges, the infant learns through experience that referencing objects and people to themselves as static observers will reliably work under some conditions, but not others (e.g., when moving from place to place). A transitory period is likely to follow, during which infants learn to differentiate those situations that can successfully employ a static self-referent system from those requiring the use of external landmarks to update orientation within the environment. It should not be surprising if, during this period, infants switch back and forth between the two strategies of SR and ER before they begin to consistently show position constancy. Only a longitudinal study will definitively show whether the predominant use of one spatial reference strategy is followed by a period of use of a more complex strategy, with a period of extensive instability in coding strategy use in between. In the meantime, cross-sectional studies should ensure that comparisons are made between infants who are clearly prelocomotor versus those who have considerable locomotor experience.

The second factor that might mediate the effects of locomotor experience on emergence of different spatial referent systems is the type of displacements used by researchers versus the displacements that are typically encountered by actively locomoting infants. The specificity of displacements experienced in locomotion is critical to understanding the limitations of previous studies. Displacements generated by a creeping infant are predominantly linear in nature (involving forward translation). However, the testing situations used in studies of position constancy and locomotion have used large *rotations* (of 180°) accompanied by translations. Translations with rotations are not likely to be experienced very often by creeping infants, although walking infants doubtless often experience them. Consequently, we believe that a more robust link between locomotor experience and spatial reference strategies following displacement can be established if infants are tested in tasks that involve linear displacements, as opposed to rotations or combinations of rotation and translation.

This is not to suggest that rotations are never experienced prior to upright locomotion; certainly, sitting infants regularly experience rotations when they pivot the trunk relative to the base of support and the head relative to the trunk. However, these are small rotations, not on the order of 180°, as used in studies cited previously; nor is translation involved, again as in the studies cited earlier. In fact, some evidence shows clearly that prelocomotor infants are capable of relocalizing targets after only partial rotations.

The third factor relevant to this discussion is the type of landmarks that can be used to maintain spatial orientation. It is important to note the success in relocalizing a target has been most reliably linked to locomotor experience in experiments where landmarks were very salient. Furthermore, it must be noted that in all experiments in which prelocomotors were found to use ER strategies, the landmarks used were spatially coincident with the target and relatively close to the infant. The landmark surrounded the target, and could not be visually separated from it. It is more likely that, relative to prelocomotors, locomotor infants will notice and be more able to use landmarks separated from targets and distal from the infant. The latter part of this hypothesis is based on Freedman's (1992) study, showing that locomotor infants directed more attention to far space than prelocomotor infants. Hence, differences between locomotor and prelocomotor infants' use of ER strategies can be much more apparent in paradigms that make use of distal landmarks, particularly those placed outside of the reaching envelope that typically constrains the perceptual-motor workspace of prelocomotor infants. Another possibility is that locomotor experience will lead to greater sensitivity to landmarks in the peripheral visual field than those in the central visual field.

In summary, we believe that the capacity to show position constancy and landmark- or environmentally based referencing following a displacement is present in narrowly specified contexts quite early in life. As suggested by others (e.g., Bremner, 1993a), the development of motor abilities such as sitting can facilitate the development of spatial coding strategies to some degree. However, we expect that the onset of self-produced locomotion will markedly influence the subsequent development of spatial coding. Specifically, locomotor experience leads to the refinement of strategies and to the development of knowledge about the appropriateness of a given strategy for a specific task and situation.

## Can Locomotor Experience Be Manipulated in a True Experiment?

Despite the extraordinary number of converging research operations we used in this research project, all of the studies linking locomotor experience and psychological development are quasi-experimental. In no study was random assignment of participants to conditions used (not even in the walker groups, which tested infants whose mothers had decided to provide such devices to their infants). Given the limitations of quasi-experimental research designs for making any strong inferences about causality, we are currently investigating whether locomotor experience can be manipulated in a true experiment to assess the effects of such experience on responsiveness to peripheral optic flow, wariness of heights, and spatial search strategies. Evidence has been provided already that training can accelerate the development of creeping and that such training has an impact on intellectual development (Lagerspetz, Nygård, & Strandvik, 1971). However, rather than manipulate the onset of crawling, we have taken our lead from an ingenious experiment by Woods (1975) that tested whether self-produced locomotion had reinforcing properties for prelocomotor infants between the ages of 88 and 109 days. Using a motorized infant carriage, controllable by sucking on the nipple of a bottle that housed a pressure transducer, Woods clearly showed that infants produced higher rates of sucking and longer burst lengths when motion of the carriage was contingent on sucking than when it was not. These findings suggest strongly that prelocomotor infants can learn to control their motion in a powered mobility device (PMD), a notion at the heart of our current endeavors to manipulate locomotor experience in a true experiment.

Some of our preliminary results (Anderson, Campos, Barbu-Roth, & Uchiyama, 1999) showed that prelocomotor infants are quite adept at controlling their forward motion by pulling on a brightly colored joystick mounted at the front of a PMD (refer to Figure 17 for a photograph of the PMD). Briefly, we have used two variations of a transfer design to determine whether infants actually learn the contingency between pulling on the joystick and moving in the PMD. In both designs, infants are initially placed in the PMD (in either a prone position or a seated position) for a 5-min period and observed to determine the frequency and duration with which they pull on a single joystick. (The PMD can be set to follow a linear path toward the mother or a circular trajectory around the mother when the joystick is pulled.) Following a 3-min rest, the infants are again placed in the PMD for a 5-min period under one of two conditions. In the first condition, the single joystick

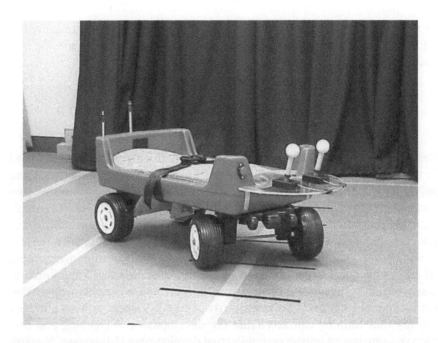

**Figure 17:** Photograph of the powered mobility device used in the Anderson, Campos, Barbu-Roth, and Uchiyama (1999) study

is either active or inactivated, and in the second, an additional, inactive, joystick is added.

The data for a sample of 8 infants during the second 5-min period of the design in which an additional inactive joystick is added (note that the position of the active joystick, right or left side, is counterbalanced across infants) are presented in Figure 18. In this particular design, the infants are in a prone position, and as noted earlier, move in a circular trajectory around the mother. The data show clearly that the infants spend a much greater proportion of time pulling on the active as opposed to the inactive joystick. This finding suggests that infants were not simply motivated to pull a joystick but were motivated to pull a joystick that would lead to forward motion in the PMD.

Based on the Anderson et al. (1999) results, we are very encouraged that the consequences of locomotor experience can be tested in a true experiment. One might wonder why we chose to manipulate locomotor experience in a PMD at this time rather than to train infants to crawl, as was done by Lagerspetz et al. (1971). A crawling manipulation certainly has ecological validity, however, given the drastic changes in the family ecology following the onset of crawling, many parents are disinclined to want a precocious crawler. Furthermore, the PMD has several advantages over a crawling manipulation. First, it is less cumbersome and time consuming on the infant and the experimenter – our data are quite clear in showing that most infants learn to control their motion

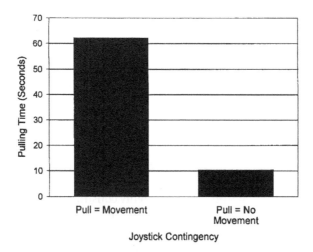

**Figure 18:** Time spent pulling the active and inactive joystick during the second 5-min period of the transfer design used by Anderson et al. (1999)

in the PMD relatively quickly. Related to this point, learning to locomote in the PMD is much less effortful and attention demanding than learning to crawl, freeing the infant to attend to the environment and its characteristic patterns of change during the course of locomotion.

Perhaps the greatest advantage of the PMD paradigm, though, is the ability to run a yoked-control design, similar to the classic Held and Hein (1963) experiment in which one infant receives active locomotor experience and another receives the same locomotion passively. We intend to perform such a study with monozygotic twins to control for maturational changes that can be involved in developmental changes relevant to our interests. Using such a design the researcher can tease apart the role of locomotion per se from the role of self (in the genesis of behavior) on changes in the developmental phenomena that have been chronicled in this article. We predict that the developmental changes described in this article are critically dependent on self-produced locomotion rather than locomotion in general. A twin design is also one of the few means available to the researcher on human infants to tease apart the role of genetics and environment on psychological development. A twin study crossing the factors of heredity with type of movement is clearly called for to study the role of gene–environment interaction. Such a study involves comparing monozygotic and dizygotic twins, some of whom are given active and some given passive movement experience. Such an investigation is one of the most sensitive means we can think of to assess the separate and conjoint influences of genes and experience on the psychological outcomes we described.

# Conclusions

The foregoing review clarifies that the onset of crawling heralds major changes in the psychology of the child. We present a summary of the findings from the work we conducted in our laboratory in Table 1, along with the converging research operations used to determine how consistent the link is between locomotor experience and psychological consequences. However, does this empirical work, with the conceptualizations that it has engendered, have broader implications than documenting that crawling experience is important during a rather narrow age range? Do the phenomena delineated in this article have long-lasting consequences for the infant? Are there major conceptual lessons to be learned that transcend this highly constrained phenomenon? Are there analogous events earlier or later in life that, like crawling onset, have major unanticipated or uninvestigated sequelae? We believe that the answer to these questions is an emphatic "yes," and we delineate some of these broad implications in the final section of the article.

When asked what makes a phenomenon important, most developmentalists would emphasize whether events early in life are successful in forecasting later characteristics. Indeed, the study of child development is largely the study of predictors of later personality, intelligence, social characteristics, and brain function. Viewed in this way, the research on the correlates and consequences of crawling can seem modest in scope and significance. And indeed, we are not claiming that individual differences in the age of onset of a motoric skill predict future intelligence or emotionality. No one has ever documented such a predictive link. So, have we just finished an article with only a narrow focus?

We believe not and argue that locomotor experience might well have enduring consequences, but of a vastly different nature than those focused on typically by developmentalists. The long-term significance of locomotor experience is that once attained, it is typically maintained. Except under extraordinary circumstances, once a child begins to locomote, crawling, walking, running, and other forms of moving about produce a constant developmental framework. This framework helps to maintain skills that locomotor experience helped to generate in the first place, and often require recurrent updating and pervasive maintenance. Viewed in this way, locomotor experiences can have far more enduring significance than most, if not all, of the phenomena that developmentalists typically study. In short, developmentalists often talk of "scaffolding" as a needed or helpful short-term support for development; locomotor experience is more than a scaffold. It is like the supporting frame of a building, always necessary for the building's integrity. If this analogy is correct, research needs to be conducted on what occurs when locomotor experience becomes unavailable to the human. What occurs in the psychological states of the person who, by reason of lesion or

**Table 1:** Summary of our findings linking locomotor experience to psychological functions

| Consequences of locomotor experience | How demonstrated | | | | | | How locomotor experience brings about psychological change |
|---|---|---|---|---|---|---|---|
| | A | B | C | D | E | F | |
| Changes in family social dynamics | + | – | | | | + | Increase in infant autonomy → need for infant autonomy vs. caregiver regulation |
| Referential gestural communication | + | + | | + | + | + | Increased opportunities to relate objects and events to parental communication |
| Wariness of heights | + | + | + | + | + | + | Reaction to discrepancy between visual and vestibular information specifying self-motion |
| Postural compensation to peripheral optic flow | + | + | | | | | Differentiation of regions of optic flow for efficient control of locomotion |
| Attention to far space | + | + | | | | | Distal events become attainable and so increasingly functional |
| Spatial search performance | + | + | + | + | + | + | Use of strategies like "keeping an eye" on target |
| | | | | | | | Discrimination of relevant environmental features |
| | | | | | | | Locomotion requires new coding strategies |
| | | | | | | | Longer locomotor excursions lead to tolerance of longer delays in goal attainment |
| | | | | | | | Improved understanding of others' intentions |
| Spatial coding strategies | + | + | | + | | | Environmental-referent strategies are problematic for prelocomotor infants |

*Note:* A = locomotor vs. prelocomotor; B = walker vs. prelocomotor; C = lag-sequential; D = Locomotor Delay (neurological/orthopedic); E = locomotor delay (ecological); F = longitudinal; + = positive findings; – = predicted relation not confirmed.

illness, loses locomotor ability and experience? It is noteworthy that we know of no research on this topic.

There is a second broad implication to the work we described. It forces a different view of the processes by which development takes place. Notice that in almost every phenomenon we discussed, crawling brings about developmental change by recruiting processes that are available in ways other than by locomoting. For example, attention to distal events, use of parallax information, social interactions involving referential communication, and differential attentiveness to new affordances of events in the world can and doubtless do occur even when the child is unable to crawl. The significance of locomotion is in making the operation of such processes almost inevitable. However, the process analyses we described also make efforts to understand alternative developmental pathways equally inevitable.

The processes of developmental change can also be quite independent of each other. The factors that account for the flowering of the child's affectivity following locomotor onset are dramatically different from those that enter into the shifts in successful search following a delay, those related to spatial cognition, or those linked to improvements in distance estimation. Even within the domain of affective development, the processes that bring about fear of heights differ from those that produce anger and frustration, or for that matter, fears of animals and insects "caught" from the mother.

If we are correct in construing how locomotion brings about psychological changes, we will also need to begin viewing development in probabilistic rather than fixed ways. We are proposing that development involves the orchestration of processes to bring about new levels of psychological function. The best illustration of the orchestration principle in the studies we described involves the explanation of the wariness of heights phenomenon. Fear of heights is not just the outcome of depth perception. If depth perception alone generated avoidance of heights, 5-month-old infants would show wariness of heights and they do not (Schwartz, Campos, & Baisel, 1973). The avoidance of drop-offs results from the development, first of increased responsiveness to peripheral optic flow, second from the mismatches with vestibular input that such new responsiveness makes possible, and third, the vertigo or sense of postural instability that the mismatch engenders. Development of phenomena like wariness of heights cannot be explained in monistic terms (e.g., as due to "depth perception," or the maturation of the frontal lobes, or falling experiences). Development involves organizing (orchestrating) many component processes into more and more complex levels. We have illustrated the process of orchestration and showed how each domain involves the interplay of different segments of experience. We have also shown how a relatively neglected developmental event – locomotor experience – plays the role of an organizer or orchestrator. In so doing, we hope we have shown how fruitful it is to conceptualize a variety of enduring psychological changes in ways that are both domain specific and yet under a single agent of control.

So, locomotor experience has effects that can be enduring, even though they are not necessarily predictive of the future; locomotor experience also can explain developmental transitions, even though it cannot determine them; and locomotor experience dramatically changes the relation of the person to that person's environment. This last point is particularly broad and heuristic. It highlights the importance of studying any life event that changes the relation between the person and the environment. The more profoundly the developmental acquisition changes such relations, the more significant is that life event, and the richer that age period is for a developmental analysis of how the life event results in psychological changes.

There are many life events likely to have major consequences for person–environment reorganizations in infancy. Some are motoric; others are not. The motoric attainments with developmental implications include the experiences made possible by reaching and those by upright locomotion. Neither has been studied systematically or even extensively, although Witherington (1998) and Biringen et al. (1995) began to study the correlates and consequences of reaching and walking, respectively. A nonmotoric attainment – learning to speak – is yet another life event with profound psychological consequences (Bloom, 1993). Although language acquisition is a major area of investigation, few of the myriad studies in the area have focused on the consequences of language acquisition for other psychological characteristics. Surely, the changes following language onset must be as pervasive and profound as those discovered to date for crawling. A major implication of the work described in this article is the analogy that it provides for conceptualizing and investigating other periods of rapid developmental transition in infancy and early childhood.

Our language often systematizes in the form of idiomatic expressions major aspects of our lives. Lakoff and Johnson (1980) referred to these as "metaphors we live by." Perhaps it is no accident that we have idioms such as "making great strides," "step-function improvement," and "moving ahead" to refer to accomplishments. Locomotion connotes progress and advance, in the person's relation to the environment and in the person's mind. In this article, we tried to make a case for invigorating the investigation of the role of motoric attainments for psychological development. Such investigations of functional consequences of motor-skill acquisition have been seriously neglected. We maintain that the neglect has been brought about by inappropriate beliefs, of which three stand out. One is the confusion of partial accomplishments with full-blown skills; a second is the restricted way of construing how events can have long-term significance; the third is an overemphasis on single-factor explanations of development. We hope that this article provided evidence against each of these beliefs, and that the developmentalist's typical concern with origins and long-term outcomes can be supplemented again by the currently unfashionable study of developmental transitions in infancy. The rejuvenation of concern with transitions and the processes by which they come about can be the most valuable legacy of the study of locomotor experience in infancy.

## Note

1. Johansson (1973) defined near space in adults to be less than 2 m. This definition is relevant later when we discuss the results of McKenzie, Tootell, and Day (1980). It seems that near space, in this case, is defined by the limits of sensitivity to the two sources of absolute information mentioned before, accommodation and convergence, which are effective in adults to about 2 m (6–8 ft).

## References

Acredolo, L. P. (1978). Development of spatial orientation in infancy. *Developmental Psychology, 14,* 224–234.

Acredolo, L. P. (1979). Laboratory versus home: The effect of environment on the 9-month-old infant's choice of spatial-reference system. *Developmental Psychology, 15,* 666–667.

Acredolo, L. P. (1982). The familiarity factor in spatial research. *New Directions for Child Development, 15,* 19–30.

Acredolo, L. P. (1985). Coordinating perspectives on infant spatial orientation. In R. Cohen (Ed.), *The development of spatial cognition* (pp. 115–140). Hillsdale, NJ: Lawrence Erlbaum Associates, Inc.

Acredolo, L. P., Adams, A., & Goodwyn, S. W. (1984). The role of self-produced movement and visual tracking in infant spatial orientation. *Journal of Experimental Child Psychology, 38,* 312–327.

Acredolo, L. P., & Evans, D. (1980). Developmental changes in the effects of landmarks on infant spatial behavior. *Developmental Psychology, 16,* 312–318.

Adolph, K. E., Vereijken, B., & Denny, M. A. (1998). Learning to crawl. *Child Development, 69,* 1299–1312.

Ainsworth, M. S., Blehar, M.C., Waters, E.,& Wall, S. (1978). *Patterns of attachment: A psychological study of the strange situation.* Hillsdale, NJ: Lawrence Erlbaum Associates, Inc.

Anderson, D. I., Campos, J. J., Barbu-Roth, M. A., & Uchiyama, I. (1999, June). *Motor behavior and psychological function.* Paper presented at the North American Society for the Psychology of Sport and Physical Activity, Clearwater Beach, FL.

Arterberry, M., Yonas, A., & Bensen, A. S. (1989). Self-produced locomotion and the development of responsiveness to linear perspective and texture gradients. *Developmental Psychology, 25,* 976–982.

Bai, D. L., & Bertenthal, B. I. (1992). Locomotor status and the development of spatial search skills. *Child Development, 63,* 215–226.

Banks, M. S. (1988). Visual recalibration and the development of contrast and optical flow perception. In A. Yonas (Ed.), *Perceptual development in infancy* (pp. 145–196). Hillsdale, NJ: Lawrence Erlbaum Associates, Inc.

Bayley, N. (1969). *Manual for the Bayley scales of infant development.* New York: Psychological Corporation.

Berkeley, G. (1709). *An essay towards a new theory of vision* (2nd ed.). Dublin, Ireland: Aaron Rhames for Jeremy Pepyat.

Bertenthal, B. I. (1990). Application of biomechanical principles to the study of perception and action. In H. Bloch & B. I. Bertenthal (Eds.), *Sensory-motor organizations and development in infancy and early childhood* (pp. 243–260). Dordrecht, Netherlands: Kluwer Academic.

Bertenthal, B. I., & Bai, D. L. (1989). Infants' sensitivity to optical flow for controlling posture. *Developmental Psychology, 25*, 936–945.

Bertenthal, B. I., & Campos, J. J. (1984). Are examination of fear and its determinants on the visual cliff. *Psychophysiology, 21*, 413–417.

Bertenthal, B. I., & Campos, J. J. (1990). A systems approach to the organizing effects of self-produced locomotion during infancy. In C. Rovee-Collier & L. P. Lipsitt (Eds.), *Advances in infancy research* (Vol. 6, pp. 1–60). Norwood, NJ: Ablex.

Bertenthal, B. I., Campos, J. J., & Barrett, K. C. (1984). Self-produced locomotion: An organizer of emotional, cognitive, and social development in infancy. In R. Emde & R. Harmon (Eds.), *Continuities and discontinuities in development* (pp. 175–210). New York: Plenum.

Bertenthal, B. I., & Clifton, R. (1998). Perception and action. In D. Kuhn & R. Siegler (Eds.), *Cognition, perception and language* (Vol. 2, 5th ed., pp. 51–102). New York: Wiley.

Bertenthal, B. I., Rose, J. L., & Bai, D. L. (1997). Perception-action coupling in the development of visual control of posture. *Journal of Experimental Psychology: Human Perception & Performance, 23*, 1631–1643.

Beryl, F. (1926). Uber die Grossenauffasung bei Kindern [On the size perception of young children]. *Zeitschrift fur Psychologie, 100*, 344–371.

Biringen, Z., Emde, R. N., Campos, J. J., & Appelbaum, M. I. (1995). Affective reorganization in the infant, the mother, and the dyad: The role of upright locomotion and its timing. *Child Development, 66*, 499–514.

Bloom, L. (1993). *The transition from infancy to language: Acquiring the power of expression.* New York: Cambridge University Press.

Bowlby, J. (1969). *Attachment and loss: Attachment.* New York: Basic Books.

Brandt, T., Bles, W., Arnold, F., & Kapteyn, T. S. (1979). Height vertigo and human posture. *Advances in Oto-rhino-otolaryngology, 25*, 88–92.

Bremner, J. G. (1978). Egocentric versus allocentric spatial coding in 9-month-old infants: Factors influencing the choice of code. *Developmental Psychology, 14*, 346–355.

Bremner, J. G. (1985). Object tracking and search in infancy: A review of data and a theoretical evaluation. *Developmental Review, 5*, 371–396.

Bremner, J. G. (1993a). Motor abilities as causal agents in infant cognitive development. In G. J. P. Savelsbergh (Ed.), *The development of coordination in infancy* (pp. 47–77). Amsterdam, Netherlands: Elsevier Science.

Bremner, J. G. (1993b). Spatial representation in infancy and early childhood. In C. Pratt & A. F. Garton (Eds.), *Systems of representation in children: Development and use* (pp. 67–89). Chichester, England: Wiley.

Bremner, J. G., & Bryant, P. E. (1977). Place versus response as the basis of spatial errors made by young infants. *Journal of Experimental Child Psychology, 23*, 162–171.

Bremner, J. G., & Bryant, P. E. (1985). Active movement and development of spatial abilities in infancy. In H. M. Wellman (Ed.), *Children's searching: The development of search skill and spatial representation* (pp. 53–72). Hillsdale, NJ: Lawrence Erlbaum Associates, Inc.

Butterworth, G., & Hicks, L. (1977). Visual proprioception and postural stability in infancy: A developmental study. *Perception, 6*, 255–262.

Campos, J. J., Benson, J., & Rudy, L. (1986, April). *The role of self-produced locomotion in spatial behavior.* Paper presented at the International Conference of Infant Studies, Beverly Hills, CA.

Campos, J. J., Bertenthal, B. I., & Kermoian, R. (1992). Early experience and emotional development: The emergence of wariness of heights. *Psychological Science, 3*, 61–64.

Campos, J. J., Hiatt, S., Ramsay, D., Henderson, C., & Svejda, M. (1978). The emergence of fear on the visual cliff. In M. Kewis & L. Rosenblum (Eds.), *The development of affect* (pp. 149–182). New York: Plenum.

Campos, J. J., Kermoian, R., Witherington, D., Chen, H., & Dong, Q. (1997). Activity, attention, and developmental transitions in infancy. In P. J. Lang & R. F. Simons (Eds.), *Attention and orienting: Sensory and motivational processes* (pp. 393–415). Mahwah, NJ: Lawrence Erlbaum Associates, Inc.

Campos, J. J., Kermoian, R., & Zumbahlen, M. R. (1992). Socioemotional transformations in the family system following infant crawling onset. In N. Eisenberg & R. A. Fabes (Eds.), *Emotion and its regulation in early development* (pp. 25–40). San Francisco: Jossey-Bass.

Campos, J. J., & Stenberg, C. (1981). Perception, appraisal, and emotion: The onset of social referencing. In M. Lamb & L. Sherrod (Eds.), *Infant social cognition: Empirical and theoretical considerations* (pp. 274–313). Hillsdale, NJ: Lawrence Erlbaum Associates, Inc.

Churcher, J., & Scaife, M. (1982). How infants see the point. In G. E. Butterworth & P. Light (Eds.), Social cognition: Studies of the development of understanding (pp. 110–136). Sussex, England: Harvester.

Corkum, V., & Moore, C. (1998). The origins of joint visual attention in infants. *Developmental Psychology, 34*, 28–38.

Cornell, E. H., & Heth, C. D. (1979). Response versus place learning by human infants. *Journal of Experimental Psychology: Human Learning & Memory, 5*, 188–196.

Cornilleau-Pérès, V., & Gielen, C. C. A. M. (1996). Interactions between self-motion and depth perception in the processing of optic flow. *Trends in Neurosciences, 19,* 196–202.

Crowell, J. A., & Banks, M. S. (1993). Perceiving heading with different retinal regions and types of optic flow. *Perception & Psychophysics, 53*, 325–337.

Cutting, J. E. (1986). The shape and psychophysics of cinematic space. *Behavior Research Methods, Instruments & Computers, 18*, 551–558.

Day, R. H. (1987). Visual size constancy in infancy. In B. E. McKenzie & R. H. Day (Eds.), *Perceptual development in early infancy: Problems and issues* (pp. 67–91). Hillsdale, NJ: Lawrence Erlbaum Associates, Inc.

Decarie, T. (1969). A study of the mental and emotional development of the thalidomide child. In B. Foss (Ed.), *Determinants of infant behavior* (Vol. 4, pp. 167–187). London: Methuen.

D'Entremont, B., Hains, S. M. J., & Muir, D. W. (1997). A demonstration of gaze following in 3- to 6-month-olds. *Infant Behavior and Development, 20*, 569–572.

Diamond, A. (1991). Neuropsychological insights into the meaning of object concept development. In S. Carey & R. Gelman (Eds.), *The epigenesis of mind: Essays on biology and cognition* (pp. 67–110). Hillsdale, NJ: Lawrence Erlbaum Associates, Inc.

Dichgans, J., & Brandt, T. (1974). The psychophysics of visually induced perception of self-motion and tilt. In F. O. Schmidt & F. G. Worden (Eds.), *The neurosciences* (Vol. III, pp. 123–129). Cambridge, MA: MIT Press.

Emde, R. N., Gaensbauer, T. J., & Harmon, R. J. (1976). Emotional expression in infancy: A biobehavioral study. *Psychological Issues, 10*(1, Whole No. 34).

Enderby, S. F. (1984). *The effects of self-produced locomotion on the development of spatial orientation in infancy.* Unpublished honors thesis, University of Denver, Denver, CO.

Field, J. (1975, May). *The adjustment of reaching behavior to object distance in early infancy.* Paper presented at the Second Experimental Psychology Conference, Sydney, Australia.

Fischer, K., & Biddell, T. (1998). Dynamic development of psychological structures in action and thought. In R. Lerner (Ed.), *Theoretical models of human development* (Vol. 1, pp. 467–562). New York: Wiley.

Freedman, D. L. (1992). *Locomotor experience and the deployment of attention to near and distant space.* Unpublished honors thesis, University of California, Berkeley.

Gentile, A. M. (1987). Skill acquisition: Actions, movements, and neuromotor processes. In J. H. Carr & R. B. Shepherd (Eds.), *Movement science: Foundations for physical therapy in rehabilitation* (pp. 93–154). Rockville, MD: Aspen.

Gibson, E. J. (1969). *Principles of perceptual learning development.* Englewood Cliffs, NJ: Prentice Hall.

Gibson, E. J., & Schmuckler, M. A. (1989). Going somewhere: An ecological and experimental approach to development of mobility. *Ecological Psychology, 1,* 3–25.

Gibson, J. J. (1966). *The senses considered as perceptual systems.* Boston: Houghton Mifflin.

Gibson, J. J. (1979). *The ecological approach to visual perception.* Boston: Houghton Mifflin.

Glicksman, M. (1987). The relation between locomotor experience and spatial knowledge in infancy. In P. Ellen & C. Thinus-Blanc (Eds.), *Cognitive processes in spatial orientation in animal and man: Vol. 1. Experimental animal psychology and ethology* (pp. 264–273). Dordrecht, Netherlands: Martinus Nijhoff.

Goodale, M. A. (1988). Hemispheric differences in motor control. *Behavioural Brain Research, 30,* 203–214.

Gottleib, G. (1991). Experiential canalization of behavioral development: Theory. *Developmental Psychology, 27,* 4–13.

Granrud, C. E. (1986). Binocular vision and spatial perception in 4- and 5-month-old infants. *Journal of Experimental Psychology: Human Perception & Performance, 12,* 36–49.

Granrud, C. E., Haake, R. J., & Yonas, A. (1985). Infants' sensitivity to familiar size: The effect of memory on spatial perception. *Perception and Psychophysics, 37,* 459–466.

Granrud, C. E., & Yonas, A. (1984). Infants' perception of pictorially specified interposition. *Journal of Experimental Child Psychology, 37,* 500–511.

Guedry, F. E. (1974). Psychophysics of vestibular sensation. In H. H. Kornhuber (Ed.), *Handbook of sensory physiology: Vestibular system, part 2: Psychophysics, applied aspects, and general interpretations* (pp. 3–154). Berlin: Springer-Verlag.

Gustafson, G. E. (1984). Effects of the ability to locomote on infants' social and exploratory behaviors: An experimental study. *Developmental Psychology, 20,* 397–405.

Haber, R. N. (1980). How we perceive depth from flat pictures. *American Scientist, 68,* 370–380.

Haith, M. M. (1990). Progress in the understanding of sensory and perceptual processes in early infancy. *Merrill-Palmer Quarterly, 36,* 1–26.

Haith, M. M. (1993). Preparing for the 21st century: Some goals and challenges for studies of infant sensory and perceptual development. *Developmental Review, 13,* 354–371.

Hayashibe, K. (1991). Reversals of depth caused by motion parallax. *Perception, 2,* 17–28.

Hein, A., Held, R., & Gower, E. C. (1970). Development and segmentation of visually controlled movement by selective exposure during rearing. *Journal of Comparative and Physiological Psychology, 73,* 181–187.

Held, R., & Hein, A. (1963). Movement-produced stimulation in the development of visually guided behavior. *Journal of Comparative and Physiological Psychology, 56,* 872–876.

Higgins, C. I. (1994). *The origins of visual proprioception.* Unpublished doctoral dissertation, University of California, Berkeley.

Higgins, C. I., Campos, J. J., & Kermoian, R. (1996). Effect of self-produced locomotion on infant postural compensation to optic flow. *Developmental Psychology, 32,* 836–841.

Holway, A. H., & Boring, E. G. (1941). Determinants of apparent visual size with distance variant. *American Journal of Psychology, 54,* 21–37.

Horobin, K., & Acredolo, L. (1986). The role of attentiveness, mobility history, and separation of hiding sites on Stage IV search behavior. *Journal of Experimental Child Psychology, 41,* 114–127.

Johansson, G. (1973). Monocular movement parallax and near-space perception. *Perception, 2*, 135–146.

Jouen, F. (1988). Visual-proprioceptive control of posture in newborn infants. In B. Amblard, A. Berthoz, & F. Clarac (Eds.), *Posture and gait: Development, adaptation and modulation* (pp. 59–65). Amsterdam: Elsevier Science.

Jouen, F. (1990). Early visual-vestibular interactions and postural development. In H. Bloch & B. I. Berthenthal (Eds.), *Sensory-motor organizations and development in infancy and early childhood* (pp. 199–215). Dordrecht, Netherlands: Martinus Nijhoff.

Jouen, F., & Gapenne, O. (1995). Interactions between the vestibular and visual systems in the neonate. In P. Rochat (Ed.), *The self in infancy: Theory and research* (pp. 277–301). Amsterdam, Netherlands: Elsevier Science.

Kagan, J., Kearsley, R. B., & Zelazo, P. R. (1978). *Infancy: Its place in human development.* Cambridge, MA: Harvard University Press.

Kaufman, L. (1974). *Sight and mind: An introduction to visual perception.* New York: Oxford.

Kermoian, R., & Campos, J. J. (1988). Locomotor experience: A facilitator of spatial-cognitive development. *Child Development, 59*, 908–917.

Koenderink, J. J. (1999). *Pictorial relief.* Paper presented at the Oxyopia symposium, University of California, Berkeley.

Kopp, C. B., & Shaperman, J. (1973). Cognitive development in the absence of object manipulation during infancy. *Developmental Psychology, 9*, 430.

Lagerspetz, K., Nygård, M., & Strandvik, C. (1971). The effects of training in crawling on the motor and mental development of infants. *Scandanavian Journal of Psychology, 12*, 192–197.

Lakoff, G., & Johnson, M. (1980). *Metaphors we live by.* Chicago: University of Chicago Press.

Lazarus, R. S. (1991). *Emotion and adaptation.* New York: Oxford University Press.

Lee, D. N., & Aronson, E. (1974). Visual proprioceptive control of standing in human infants. *Perception and Psychophysics, 15*, 529–532.

Lee, D. N., & Lishman, J. R. (1975). Visual proprioceptive control of stance. *Journal of Human Movement Studies, 1*, 87–95.

Leibowitz, H. W., & Post, R. B. (1984). The two modes of processing concept and some implications. In J. Beck (Ed.), *Organization and representation in perception* (pp. 343–363). Hillsdale, NJ: Lawrence Erlbaum Associates, Inc.

Lepecq, J.-C. (1990). Self-produced movement, position constancy, and the perceptual-learning approach. In H. Bloch & B. I. Berthenthal (Eds.), *Sensory-motor organizations and development in infancy and early childhood* (pp. 445–453). Dordecht, Netherlands: Kluwer Academic.

Lepecq, J.-C., & Lafaite, M. (1989). The early development of position constancy in a no-landmark environment. *British Journal of Developmental Psychology, 7*, 289–306.

Mahler, M. S., Pine, F., & Bergman, A. (1975). *The psychological birth of the human infant: Symbiosis and individuation.* New York: Basic Books.

Mayne, R. (1974). A systems concept of the vestibular organs. In H. H. Kornhuber (Ed.), *Handbook of sensory physiology: Vestibular system, part 2: Psychophysics applied aspects, and general interpretations* (pp. 493–580). Berlin: Springer-Verlag.

McComas, J., & Field, J. (1984). Does crawling experience affect infants' emerging spatial orientation abilities? *New Zealand Journal of Psychology, 13*, 63–68.

McKenzie, B. E. (1987). The development of spatial orientation in human infancy: What changes? In B. E. McKenzie & R. H. Day (Eds.), *Perceptual development in early infancy: Problems and issues* (pp. 125–142). Hillsdale: NJ: Lawrence Erlbaum Associates, Inc.

McKenzie, B. E., & Day, R. H. (1972). Object distance as a determinant of visual fixation in early infancy. *Science, 178*, 1108–1110.

McKenzie, B. E., & Day, R. H. (1976). Infants' attention to stationary and moving objects at different distances. *Australian Journal of Psychology, 28*, 45–51.

McKenzie, B. E., Day, R. H., & Ihsen, E. (1984). Localization of events in space: Young infants are not always egocentric. *British Journal of Experimental Psychology, 2*, 1–19.

McKenzie, B. E., Tootell, H. E., & Day, R. H. (1980). Development of visual size constancy during the 1st year of human infancy. *Developmental Psychology, 16*, 163–174.

Milner, A. D., & Goodale, M. A. (1995). *The visual brain in action*. Oxford, England: Oxford University Press.

Moore, C. (1999). Gaze following and the control of attention. In E. P. Rochat (Ed.), *Early social cognition: Understanding others in the first months of life* (pp. 241–256). Mahwah, NJ: Lawrence Erlbaum Associates, Inc.

Moore, C., & Dunham, P. (1995). *Joint attention: Its origins and role in development*. Hillsdale, NJ: Lawrence Erlbaum Associates, Inc.

Munakata, Y. (1998). Infant perseveration and implications for object permanence theories: A PDP model of the A-not-B task. *Developmental Science, 1*, 161–211.

Munakata, Y., McClelland, J. L., Johnson, M. H., & Siegler, R. S. (1997). Rethinking infant knowledge: Toward an adaptive process account of successes and failures in object permanence tasks. *Psychological Review, 104*, 686–713.

Palmer, S. E. (1999). *Vision science: Photons to phenomenology*. Cambridge, MA: MIT Press.

Piaget, J. (1954). *The construction of reality in the child*. New York: Basic Books.

Piaget, J. (1970). Piaget's theory. In W. Kessen (Ed.), *History, theory, and methods* (pp. 103–126). New York: Wiley.

Rader, N., Bausano, M., & Richards, J. E. (1980). On the nature of the visual-cliff-avoidance response in human infants. *Child Development, 51*, 61–68.

Reed, E. S. (1982). An outline of a theory of action systems. *Journal of Motor Behavior, 14*, 98–134.

Rieser, J. (1979). Spatial orientation of 6-month old infants. *Child Development, 50*, 1078–1087.

Rock, I. (1977). In defense of unconscious inference. In W. Epstein (Ed.), *Stability and constancy in visual perception* (pp. 321–373). New York: Wiley.

Rock, I. (Ed.). (1997). *Indirect perception*. Cambridge, MA: MIT Press.

Rogers, B., & Graham, M. (1979). Motion parallax as an independent cue for depth perception. *Perception, 8*, 125–134.

Rogers, S., & Rogers, B. J. (1992). Visual and nonvisual information disambiguate surfaces specified by motion parallax. *Perception and Psychophysics, 52*, 446–452.

Scarr, S., & Salapatek, P. (1970). Patterns of fear development during infancy. *Merrill-Palmer Quarterly, 16*, 53–90.

Schmuckler, M. A. (1993). Perception-action coupling in infancy. In G. J. P. Savelsbergh (Ed.), *The development of coordination in infancy* (pp. 137–173). Amsterdam: Elsevier Science.

Schwartz, A. N., Campos, J. J., & Baisel, E. J. (1973). The visual cliff: Cardiac and behavioral responses on the deep and shallow sides at 5 and 9 months of age. *Journal of Experimental Child Psychology, 15*, 86–99.

Shallo, J., & Rock, I. (1988). Size constancy in children: A new interpretation. *Perception, 17*, 803–813.

Shurtleff, D. (Ed.). (1986). *Myelodysplasias and extrophies: Significance, prevention, and treatment*. Orlando, FL: Grune & Stratton.

Slater, A., Mattock, A., & Brown, E. (1990). Size constancy at birth: Newborn infants' responses to retinal and real size. *Journal of Experimental Child Psychology, 49*, 314–322.

Slater, A., & Morison, V. (1985). Shape constancy and slant perception at birth. *Perception, 14*, 337–344.

Smith, L. B., & Thelen, E. (1993). *A dynamic systems approach to development: Applications.* Cambridge, MA: MIT Press.

Smith, L. B., Thelen, E., Titzer, R., & McLin, D. (1999). Knowing in the context of acting: The task dynamics of the A-not-B error. *Psychological Review, 106,* 235–260.

Stoffregen, T. A. (1985). Flow structure versus retinal location in the optical control of stance. *Journal of Experimental Psychology: Human Perception & Performance, 11,* 554–565.

Stoffregen, T. A. (1986). The role of optical velocity in the control of stance. *Perception and Psychophysics, 39,* 355–360.

Stoffregen, T. A., Schmuckler, M. A., & Gibson, E. J. (1987). Use of central and peripheral optic flow in stance and locomotion in young walkers. *Perception, 16,* 113–119.

Tao, S., & Dong, Q. (1997). *Referential gestural communication and locomotor experience in urban Chinese infants.* Unpublished manuscript, Beijing Normal University, Beijing, China.

Telzrow, R. (1990, April). *Delays and spurts in spatial-cognitive development of the locomotor handicapped infant.* Paper presented at the Annual Meeting of the International Conference on Infant Studies, Montreal, Canada.

Telzrow, R., Campos, J. J., Shepherd, A., Bertenthal, B. I., & Atwater, S. (1987). Spatial understanding in infants with motor handicaps. In K. Jaffe (Ed.), *Childhood powered mobility: Developmental, technical and clinical perspectives* (pp. 62–69). Washington, DC: Rehabilitation Engineering Society of North America.

Telzrow, R. W., Campos, J. J., Kermoian, R., & Bertenthal, B. I. (1999). *Locomotor acquisition as an antecedent of psychological development: Studies of infants with myelodysplasia.* Unpublished manuscript, University of California, Berkeley, CA.

Thomas, D. G., & Crow, C. D. (1988, April). *The effects of self-produced locomotion on depth perception in infants.* Paper presented at the International Conference on Infancy Studies, Washington, DC.

Timney, B. (1988). The development of depth perception. In P. G. Shinkman (Ed.), *Advances in neural and behavioral development* (Vol. 3, pp. 153–208). Norwood, NJ: Ablex.

Trevarthen, C. (1993). The self born in intersubjectivity: The psychology of an infant communicating. In U. Neisser (Ed.), *The perceived self: Ecological and interpersonal sources of self-knowledge* (pp. 121–173). New York: Cambridge University Press.

von Hofsten, C. (1989). Mastering reaching and grasping: The development of manual skills in infancy. In S. A. Wallace (Ed.), *Perspectives on the coordination of movement* (pp. 223–258). Amsterdam: North-Holland.

Walk, R. D., Shepherd, J. D., & Miller, D. R. (1988). Attention and the depth perception of kittens. *Bulletin of the Psychonomic Society, 26,* 248–251.

Wellman, H. M., Cross, D., & Bartsch, K. (1987). Infant search and object permanence: A meta-analysis of the A-not-B error. *Monographs of the Society for Research in Child Development, 51,* 1–51.

Witherington, D. (1998). *Visually guided reaching and the development of anger in infancy.* Unpublished doctoral dissertation, University of California, Berkeley.

Witherington, D., Campos, J. J., & Kermoian, R. (1995, March). *What makes a baby afraid of heights?* Paper presented at the Society for Research in Child Development, Indianapolis, IN.

Wohlwill, J. F. (1963). Overconstancy in distance perception as a function of the texture of the stimulus field and other variables. *Perceptual and Motor Skills, 17,* 831–846.

Woods, T. E. P. (1975). *Locomotor reinforcement of non-nutritive sucking in human infants.* Unpublished master's thesis, San Francisco State University, San Francisco.

Yonas, A., Arterberry, M. E., & Granrud, C. E. (1987). Four-month-old infants' sensitivity to binocular and kinetic information for three-dimensional-object shape. *Child Development, 58,* 910–917.

Yonas, A., & Granrud, C. A. (1985). Reaching as a measure of infants' spatial perception. In G. Gottlieb & N. A. Krasnegor (Eds.), *Measurement of audition and vision in the first year of postnatal life: A methodological overview* (pp. 301–322). Norwood, NJ: Ablex.

Yonas, A., Granrud, C. E., Arterberry, M. E., & Hanson, B. L. (1986). Infants' distance perception from linear perspective and texture gradients. *Infant Behavior and Development, 9,* 247–256.

Yonas, A., Granrud, C. E., & Pettersen, L. (1985). Infants' sensitivity to relative size information for distance. *Developmental Psychology, 21,* 161–167.

Zumbahlen, M. (1997). *The role of infant locomotor onset in shaping mother–infant communication.* Unpublished doctoral dissertation, University of Illinois at Urbana-Champaign, Urbana.

Zumbahlen, M., & Crawley, A. (1997, April). *Infants' early referential behavior in prohibition contexts: The emergence of social referencing.* Paper presented at the invited symposium on social referencing at the Meetings of the International Conference on Infant Studies, Providence, RI.

# 10. Multisensory Perception

# The Development of Intersensory Temporal Perception: An Epigenetic Systems/Limitations View

*David J. Lewkowicz*

Most of our perceptual experiences consist of concurrent and multiple sensations in different sensory modalities. Despite this fact, we do not perceive a collection of singular sensations. Instead, we perceive a world of multimodally unified objects and events. For example, when we watch a bouncing a ball, we do not perceive the ball's separate visible and audible attributes; rather, we perceive a moving object that has a certain rhythmic quality to it. Likewise, when we interact with another person our perceptual experience is that of a talking person rather than that of a separate voice and face that happen to occur together in space and time.

Undoubtedly, the ability to perceive the integral nature of multimodally specified objects and events has evolved because it is highly adaptive. An organism that can perceive objects and events in an intermodally integrated fashion is at an adaptive advantage because such integration reduces the overall amount of information that has to be processed to more manageable proportions and makes processing more efficient and rapid. Indeed, it is interesting to note that evolution has capitalized on this advantage by incorporating intersensory interactions into the neural architecture of most species. This fact was noted by Stein & Meredith (1990), who observed that they knew of no organism with a nervous system in which the sensory modalities maintain absolute exclusivity from one another. In other words, intersensory interaction

**Source:** *Psychological Bulletin*, 126(2) (2000): 281–308.

is a basic neural design feature that is found at most phyletic levels. One impressive example of the advantage that intersensory interaction confers on an organism is the male gypsy moth, which is able to find a female at distances of 1–2 miles. He is able to do so because he constantly integrates information about his position in space vis-à-vis the olfactory gradient created by the female, the wind speed gathered by his tactile and proprioceptive senses, and his position in space determined from visual cues (Stein & Meredith, 1993). Obviously, the male moth would have a much harder time finding the female on the basis of smell alone. At the human level, a good example that illustrates the advantage of intersensory interaction can be found in speech perception. Under normal conditions, our perception of a talking person is dependent on the synchrony between the audible and visible aspects of the speech produced by that person. This is evident by a decrease in identification accuracy when the synchrony between the audible and visible aspects of the person's speech is disrupted (Dodd, 1977). Similarly, identification of a speech signal on the basis of its audible features is considerably less accurate than when the visible features of that signal are added (Summerfield, 1979).

Marks (1978) has argued that underlying the ability to integrate information across different modalities is the fundamental process that enables us to perceive similarity. In other words, whenever we integrate information across different modalities we perceive similar qualities regardless of which sensory modality registered the information. For example, when a person can be seen and heard uttering a word, the visible and audible duration of the word is the same. Likewise, when we touch and look at an object, we perceive the same shape, spatial extent, and texture in each modality. In general, any attribute that can specify similar information across modalities is considered to be amodal in nature. Intensity, spatial location, rate, and rhythmic structure are other common types of amodal attributes. The similarity specified by amodal attributes has been variously referred to as *intermodal invariance* (J. J. Gibson, 1966), *common sensibles* (Marks, 1978), or *intersensory equivalence* (Lewkowicz, 1994a).

Although the perception of intersensory equivalence is the best known and most important way in which integration of information across modalities can occur, other forms of intersensory integration such as facilitation, inhibition, or association are possible as well. This suggests that intersensory integration is not a unitary process and that distinct mechanisms might be involved depending on the specific type of intersensory interaction (Lewkowicz & Turkewitz, 1980; Ryan, 1940; Turkewitz, 1994; Turkewitz & Mellon, 1989; Walker-Andrews, 1994). For example, facilitation occurs when stimulation in one modality produces greater responsiveness to (usually concurrent) stimulation in another modality and does not involve the detection of similarity. Thus, adults' judgments of visual intensity can be markedly enhanced by the concurrent presentation of an auditory stimulus (Stein, London, Wilkinson, & Price, 1996), adults' comprehension of audible linguistic information is usually facilitated by the simultaneous availability of visual information (Summerfield, 1979), infants' responses to bimodal compared with unimodal cues are invariably more robust (Lewkowicz, 1988a, 1988b, 1992b, 1996a, 1998), and cats' spatial localization responses are greatly facilitated by the concurrent presentation of auditory and visual cues (Stein, Meredith, & Wallace, 1994). Inhibition occurs when stimulation in one modality produces decreased responsiveness to input in a different modality, such as when intense stimulation in one modality inhibits responsiveness to stimulation in another modality (Welch & Warren, 1986). Finally, modality-specific attributes in different modalities can be associated together to signify a single object (e.g., the sight, smell, and sizzle of a steak on a grill).

Although intersensory integration based on equivalence detection, or facilitation, inhibition, or association processes is a common way of thinking about intersensory integration, a different way of thinking about it has recently been suggested by Calvert, Brammer, and Iversen (1998). According to Calvert et al., there are two distinct behavioral and neural intersensory integration processes and mechanisms. One is concerned with the localization of multimodally specified objects or events, whereas another is concerned with their identification. The principal advantage of this way of thinking about intersensory interactions is that it helps to distinguish between distinct neural mechanisms underlying such interactions. Calvert et al.'s distinction is not, however, incompatible with the traditional ways of conceptualizing intersensory integration because the perception of equivalence, intersensory facilitation/inhibition, and intersensory association all are involved in both object localization and identification.

## Intersensory Perception in Adults and Infants: Empirical Findings

An extensive literature has documented the very impressive abilities of human adults to integrate information across modalities, both through the perception of equivalence and through facilitation/inhibition and association (Freides, 1974; Jones, 1981; Marks, 1978; Massaro, 1998; Ryan, 1940; Welch & Warren, 1980, 1986). Two of the best known examples of intersensory integration in adults are the ventriloquism and the McGurk effects, both of which illustrate how powerful the perceptual system's proclivity for intersensory and perceptual unity is. The ventriloquism effect occurs when participants are presented with a sound that is spatially displaced from a concurrently presented visual stimulus. Despite the fact that the sound does not emanate from the same place as the visual stimulus, participants report hearing the sound as actually being closer to the visual stimulus than it really is (Jack & Thurlow, 1973; Radeau & Bertelson, 1977, 1978). An everyday example of this tendency to fuse spatially discrepant auditory and visual inputs is the common experience of hearing the voice of the ventriloquist as coming from the puppet's mouth rather than from his own voice box. The McGurk effect (McGurk & MacDonald, 1976) also illustrates the proclivity of the perceptual system to achieve a unified experience. When adults are presented with different audible and visible syllables simultaneously, there are a number of different ways in which they can perceive them depending on the specific syllables presented. For example, the auditory perception of a syllable either can be completely dominated by the concurrent presentation of a different visible syllable (i.e., participants report hearing "va" when a visible "va" and an audible "ba" are presented) or can be partly influenced by a different visible syllable and thus result in a blend (i.e., participants report hearing a "da" when a visible "ga" and an audible "ba" are presented). These types of "biasing" effects where input in one sensory modality tends to dominate responsiveness to input in a different modality are ubiquitous in that they also have been demonstrated for vision and touch in the perception of shape (E. A. Miller, 1972), size (Rock, 1965), depth (Singer & Day, 1969), orientation (Over, 1966), and texture (Lederman, Thorne, & Jones, 1986). Perhaps the most dramatic example of intersensory integration is synesthesia – a phenomenon reported by a small minority of individuals who, following stimulation in a given modality, experience sensations in other modalities even though no physical stimulation in those other modalities is presented (Marks, 1978). The most common form of synesthesia is known as *colored hearing,* where speech sounds and music produce not only auditory perceptions but colored visual images as well.

In contrast to the voluminous literature demonstrating intersensory perceptual abilities in adults, the experimental literature demonstrating intersensory perceptual abilities in infants is relatively recent and small. This is despite the fact that a number of writers have over the years called attention to the central role that intersensory integration plays in the development of perception and behavior (Birch & Lefford, 1963, 1967; Piaget, 1952; H. Werner, 1973). There are at least two reasons for this state of affairs. One is that sufficiently rigorous and reliable experimental techniques for studying various aspects of infant behavior were only developed during the 1960s. The other is that it was not until E. J. Gibson (1969) published her book *Principles of Perceptual Learning and Development* that researchers interested in development became interested in the problem of intersensory perception in human infancy. Gibson argued in her book that the perception of invariant intersensory relations was crucial to understanding the development of perception and learning. Following Gibson, other theorists have argued that the ability to perceive the unified nature of multimodal information provides the foundation for the development of perception, cognition, and action. For example, Edelman (1992) and Thelen and Smith (1994) have proposed that intersensory interactions provide the basis for the development of novel elemental behavioral capacities that, in turn, are critical to the development of higher level perceptual and cognitive functions.

Over the past two decades, research has shown that intersensory integration does occur in early development (Lewkowicz & Lickliter, 1994a; Rose & Ruff, 1987). One of the problems in organizing the results of this research, however, is that different investigators have used different methods and that these different methods may tap different kinds of processes and skills. In addition, different studies have presented infants with different levels of stimulus complexity, adding further to interpretive difficulty. Therefore, an attempt to organize this evidence must first and foremost examine the principal methods that have been used in this area of research.

## Methodological Considerations

One of the principal experimental procedures used in studies of intersensory perception in infants has been the intersensory paired-preference procedure (Spelke, 1976). It involves presenting for a set amount of time (typically between 30 s and 2 min) two side-by-side visual events that differ along some dimension together with a sound centered between them. For example, two objects might be seen bouncing out of phase with respect to one another, and the sound might be synchronized with the bounce that one of the visual objects makes each time it reaches bottom. By recording the amount of time that an infant looks at each of the two objects, it is possible to tell whether the infant perceived the relation between the sound and the visual information. The assumption is that if the infant did, then he or she should have looked longer at the object that is synchronized with the sound. Usually, investigators using this procedure refer to positive results as reflecting either intersensory matching, cross-modal matching, intersensory perception of equivalence, or intersensory integration. Successful performance in this type of task means that the infant had to have detected and discriminated the difference between the two visual objects and recognized the intersensory relation between one of them and the concurrent sound.

The habituation/test procedure, and its variant, the familiarization/test procedure, are also used frequently. Both rely on first allowing an infant to become familiar with a certain stimulus and then presenting a novel stimulus to determine, by looking for response recovery, whether the infant can discriminate between them. The habituation/test procedure involves first presenting a stimulus repeatedly during discrete trials, either for a predetermined number of trials or until responsiveness declines to some criterion, whereas the familiarization procedure involves presenting the stimulus for some predetermined amount of time. There are at least three different ways in which the two procedures can be implemented: (a) the multimodal component variation method, (b) the switch method, and (c) the cross-modal transfer method.

The multimodal component variation method (Lewkowicz, 1988a, 1988b, 1996a, 1996b; Walker-Andrews & Lennon, 1991) involves first habituating infants to an auditory–visual (A-V) compound stimulus and then presenting a series of test trials. Two of these trials are unimodal change trials during which some attribute of either the auditory or visual component is changed while the other component remains unchanged. The third type of test trial is a bimodal change trial during which some attribute of both components is changed simultaneously, thus permitting an assessment of the differential contribution of unimodal versus bimodal information to responsiveness. This method makes it possible to determine whether infants are sensitive and responsive to (a) a specific stimulus attribute in a given sensory modality in the context of information in a different modality and (b) to the intersensory relationship (because the change in a unimodal test trial also produces a change in the intersensory relationship). The simultaneous change in stimulus attribute and intersensory relationship makes it essential to conduct additional control studies to see whether the effects of the unimodal component change are due to the change in that modality and/or to the change in the intersensory relationship.

The switch method was first introduced by Younger and Cohen (1983) to study visual perception. It has been adapted for intersensory perception studies and involves habituating infants to two different compound A-V stimuli (e.g., $A_1 + V_1$ and $A_2 + V_2$) with the explicit goal of teaching infants that the two components making up each compound are related in some way. Then, during the test trials, the components of the two compounds are switched and infants are now presented with two compounds composed of $A_1 + V_2$ and $A_2 + V_1$ (Gogate & Bahrick, 1998). If infants encoded the specific relationship between the audible and visible components during habituation, then they should exhibit a novelty response to the switched components.

Finally, the cross-modal transfer method (Allen, Walker, Symonds, & Marcell, 1977) involves habituating infants to information in one sensory modality (e.g., a given rhythm) and then testing for recognition of that information by comparing responsiveness to the same and different information in a different modality. Successful cross-modal transfer is indicated by significant response recovery to the different information and no recovery to the same information.

Positive findings from any studies utilizing the habituation/test procedure allow only the conclusion that an infant detected and discriminated a change. They do not allow the conclusion that infants can use the information to recognize an intersensory relationship. Only the paired-preference procedure permits this conclusion because it explicitly requires infants to first recognize the intersensory relation and then make a choice based on it. According to Walker-Andrews (1997), the distinction between detection and discrimination, on the one hand, and recognition, on the other, is important because it forces one to specify more precisely the processes that are involved in a response in an experiment using a particular method. Similar to Walker-Andrews' distinction between detection and discrimination, detection here means that an infant is sensitive and responsive to some kind of stimulation, whereas discrimination means that an infant is able to tell the difference between two or more objects or events. Recognition, on the other hand, involves more. It means that infants are not only able to detect and discriminate between different features of the stimulation but also able to recognize the relationship between one of the visual stimuli and a concurrently presented auditory stimulus on the basis of some common feature and to perform an explicit response (e.g., choose to look longer at one of the stimuli and thus show a preference for it). Consistent with the distinction between detection and discrimination, on the one hand, and recognition, on the other, Bahrick and Pickens (1994) have argued that the habituation/test method is less demanding than the paired-preference method because the latter requires greater attentional mobility and more sophisticated cognitive skills.

## Infant Findings

Overall, infant research has shown that some intersensory capacities are present at birth, some emerge within the first months after birth, and that the specific age at which certain ones emerge depends on the characteristics of the information to be integrated. Table 1 provides a summary of the results of the studies examining infant intersensory functioning discussed in this article (other reviews may be found in Lewkowicz & Lickliter, 1994a).

One historically early example documenting the operation of intersensory integration shortly after birth comes from a study by Lewkowicz and Turkewitz (1980), who showed that infants as young as 3 weeks of age can perceive the equivalence of auditory and visual inputs on the basis of intensity. Other studies have shown that newborns can associate objects and sounds on the basis of the combined cues of colocation and synchrony (Morrongiello, Fenwick, & Chance, 1998), that 4-month-olds can perceive the equivalence of the audible and visible information specifying a syllable (Kuhl & Meltzoff, 1982), that 5-month-olds exhibit the McGurk effect (Rosenblum, Schmuckler, & Johnson, 1997), and that 7- but not 5-month-old infants can recognize A-V relations in multimodally specified emotional expressions (Walker-Andrews, 1986). Studies also have shown that, when presented with simple objects and sounds, infants between 3 and 4 months of age can detect intersensory synchrony and temporal microstructure (Bahrick, 1983, 1988, 1992; Lewkowicz, 1992a). It appears, however, that they can do so as long as the visual stimulation is spatially dynamic. If the visual stimulation is spatially static, it is not until 6 months of age that they can recognize a synchrony/duration-based A-V relation (Lewkowicz, 1986). Initial studies of visual–tactile transfer showed that both 6- and 12-month-old infants could transfer shape information (Gottfried, Rose, & Bridger, 1977; Rose, Gottfried, & Bridger, 1981a, 1981b) but that the younger infants needed more time to encode the information in

**Table 1:** Summary of results from selected studies of intersensory perception in human infants

| Study | Ages tested | Modalities | Results |
|---|---|---|---|
| Lewkowicz & Turkewitz (1981) | Newborn | A-V | Modification of visual preferences for brightness following auditory stimulation |
| Gardner, Lewkowicz, Rose, & Karmel (1986) | Newborn | A-V | Modification of visual preferences for temporal frequencies following auditory stimulation with different temporal frequencies |
| Morrongiello, Fenwick, & Chance (1998) | Newborn | A-V | Association of objects and sounds based on combined colocation and synchrony cues |
| Slater, Quinn, Brown, & Hayes (1999) | Newborn | A-V | Association of objects and speech tokens |
| Lewkowicz & Turkewitz (1980) | 3 weeks | A-V | Matching of A and V stimulation on the basis of intensity |
| Streri (1987) | 2–3 months | T-V | Transfer of shape from vision to touch |
| Lewkowicz (1992b) | 2, 4, 6, 8 months | A-V | Discrimination of rate/synchrony differences in the A, V, and A-V components of a simple compound A-V stimulus composed of a moving/sounding disk |
| Lewkowicz (1996b) | 2, 4, 6, 8 months | A-V | Detection of synchrony relations; identification of synchrony/asynchrony threshold at ~350 ms. |
| Bahrick (1988) | 3 months | A-V | Matching based on temporal synchrony and temporal microstructure specifying object composition |
| Bahrick (1992) | 3.5 months | A-V | Matching based on temporal synchrony and temporal microstructure specifying object composition; no matching based on modality-specific cues (pitch & color) |
| Spelke (1979) | 4 months | A-V | Matching based on rate and synchrony |
| Spelke, Born, & Chu (1983) | 4 months | A-V | Matching of discontinuous object motion and sounds (on the basis of synchrony) |
| Mendelson & Ferland (1982) | 4 months | A-V | Matching based on simple rhythm |
| Lewkowicz (1996a) | 4, 6, 8 months | A-V | When presented with continuous bimodal utterances, discrimination of only V and A-V attributes at younger ages but of A, V, and A-V at the oldest age |
| Lewkowicz (1998) | 4, 6, 8 months | A-V | When presented with isolated bimodal syllables, discrimination of only A and A-V attributes at 4 & 6 months but of A, V, and A-V at 8 months |
| Lewkowicz (1992a) | 4 & 8 months | A-V | Failure to make rate-based matches (moving V stimuli and punctate sounds); successful synchrony-based matching |
| Lewkowicz (1985a) | 4 months | A-V | Failure to make rate-based matches (flashing checkerboards/pulsing tones) |
| Kuhl & Meltzoff (1982) | 4.5 months | A-V | Matching of A and V attributes of syllables |
| Rosenblum, Schmuckler, & Johnson (1997) | 5 months | A-V | McGurk effect |

| Study | Ages tested | Modalities | Results |
|---|---|---|---|
| Bahrick (1983) | 4–5 months | A-V | Matching on the basis of synchrony and substance |
| Streri & Pecheux (1986) | 5 months | T-V | Transfer of shape from touch to vision but not from vision to touch |
| Walker-Andrews & Lennon (1991) | 5 months | A-V | Discrimination of vocal expressions of emotion when presented together with the face |
| Lewkowicz (1986) | 3, 6, 8 months | A-V | 6- & 8-month-olds, but not 3-month-olds, performed duration-based matching |
| Lewkowicz (1988a) | 6 months | A-V | Rate/synchrony-based discrimination of only the A and A-V components of an A-V compound stimulus made up of a flashing checkerboard and pulsing tone |
| Lewkowicz (1994b) | 4, 6, 8 months | A-V | Despite prior familiarization, failure to make rate/synchrony-based matches of moving visual stimuli and punctate sounds |
| Bahrick (1994) | 3, 5, 7 months | A-V | Only 7-month-olds matched color/shape of objects & pitch |
| Rose, Gottfried, & Bridger (1981b) | 6 months | T-V | Tactual to visual transfer of shape but not oral to visual |
| Rose, Gottfried, & Bridger (1981a) | 12 months | T-V | Visual to tactual transfer of shape |
| Allen, Walker, Symonds, & Marcell (1977) | 7 months | A-V | Cross-modal transfer of rhythm |
| Humphrey & Tees (1980) | | | Failure to make rate-based matches of spatially static visual stimuli & sounds |
| Pickens & Bahrick (1995) | 7 months | A-V | Discrimination of A-V rhythm |
| Pickens & Bahrick (1997) | 7 months | | Discrimination of A-V rate against variations in A-V rhythm, but not rhythm against varying tempo |
| Phillips, Wagner, Fells, & Lynch (1990) | 7 months | A-V | Metaphorical matching of facial emotional expression and sound quality |
| Walker-Andrews (1986) | 5 & 7 months | A-V | 7- but not 5-month-olds matched the A & V attributes of emotion |
| Lewkowicz (1988b) | 10 months | A-V | Rate/synchrony-based discrimination of the A, V, and A-V components of an A-V compound stimulus (flashing checkerboard and pulsing tone) |
| Wagner, Winner, Cicchetti, & Gardner (1981) | 11 months | A-V | Metaphorical matching of abstract visual stimuli and sounds |
| Gottfried, Rose, & Bridger (1977) | 12 months | T-V | Successful cross-modal transfer from touch to vision |

*Note:* A-V = auditory–visual; T-V = tactual–visual.

one modality before performing the cross-modal transfer. More recent studies have found cross-modal transfer between these two modalities at younger ages, but they also have found a transfer asymmetry that was attributed to the differential development of the visual and tactile modalities: 2-month-old infants could only transfer information about shape from vision to touch (Streri, 1987), whereas 5-month-old infants could only transfer shape information from touch to vision (Streri & Pecheux, 1986).

Evidence of such impressive infant intersensory performance has led Radeau (1994) and Slater and Kirby (1998) to propose that intersensory integrative abilities are innate. Likewise, Marks, Hammeal, and Bornstein (1987) have made the claim that metaphorical cross-modal matching (e.g., pitch–brightness, loudness–brightness) is based on innate intersensory connections. As discussed later, this view is not new. For example, one key feature of E. J. Gibson's (1969) invariance detection view is that detection of amodal invariants is present at birth. To those inclined to dichotomous developmental thinking (i.e., that a particular behavioral capacity is either learned or innate), such a view could be interpreted to mean that the detection of amodal invariants is innate.

Although a nativistic view is an attractive one, it may be unwarranted on both empirical and theoretical grounds. First, some failures to obtain intersensory integration have been reported (Humphrey & Tees, 1980; Lewkowicz, 1985a, 1992a, 1994b, 1994c; Spelke, 1994), and these should not be ignored for they may indicate that intersensory integration of some types of information is not possible or may be possible only later in development. Second, Marks et al.'s (1987) claim that metaphorical matches reflect innate intersensory connections implies that even newborn infants should be able to make metaphorical matches, but only two reports of successful cross-modal, metaphorical matching have so far been published (Phillips, Wagner, Fells, & Lynch, 1990; Wagner, Winner, Cicchetti, & Gardner, 1981), and the youngest age at which such matches have been reported is 7 months. Finally, if intersensory integration is truly innate, then this means that integration of any sort should be possible at birth. This is not the case. For example, Bahrick (1994) has found that integration based on the association of certain modality-specific properties of objects such as their pitch and shape/color does not emerge until 7 months of age. E. J. Gibson's (1969) increasing specificity principle (see a more detailed discussion of this in the section entitled Theoretical Views on the Development of Intersensory Perception below) holds that infants are responsive to amodal invariants, and thus it could be argued that the ability to associate modality-specific attributes does not depend on the perception of amodal invariants but rather requires a learning phase. In other words, one could argue that this example does not really refute the nativist view. The fact is, however, that, as already shown, perception of some amodal invariants (e.g., those specifying affect or some temporal attributes) also does not emerge until later in infancy. The Gibsonian increasing specificity principle could be invoked to explain such findings by arguing that perceptual differentiation during the months following birth allows infants to perceive increasingly finer and more complex amodal invariants, but this only dilutes the nativist position by admitting that a little bit of innate and a little bit of acquired are both necessary. Perhaps the emergence of some intersensory skills later in development depends not so much on the differentiation of these kinds of amodal invariants per se as on the prior perceptual differentiation of the relevant information in each modality.

The nativistic view, or the innate-acquired dichotomy, is antithetical to achieving an ultimate understanding of the developmental process (Johnston,

1987; Oyama, 1985). A newborn infant is essentially an altricial organism whose central nervous system (CNS) and sensory/perceptual apparatus are immature and inexperienced. The development, differentiation, and sharpening of the infant's sensory/perceptual and cognitive capacities are slow and gradual processes that last a relatively long time. This means that substantial changes in the way infants respond to intersensory relations could reasonably be expected and probably have not as yet been uncovered because the focus of most of the work to date has been on demonstrating the existence of intersensory abilities rather than on exploring their limits. A nativistic approach discourages searching both for the limits of intersensory perceptual abilities in early development and for the processes underlying their development.

The general aim of this article is to present a different view of intersensory perception in early development. Instead of making nativistic assumptions, this article asks what developmental processes might be involved in the emergence of intersensory perceptual abilities. The principal focus of interest here is the perception of equivalence because, as noted earlier, the perception of similarity is a fundamental problem for psychology regardless of whether one deals with sensory, perceptual, cognitive, or linguistic questions. Furthermore, this article focuses on how and under what conditions infants perceive equivalent intersensory temporal relations. There are two reasons for choosing the perception of temporal intersensory equivalence. One is the universality of the time dimension. As Marks (1978) has noted, "if there is any attribute that truly deserves to be called a common sensible, any attribute of objects or events that really can manifest itself through *all* of the senses, it is time" (p. 32; italics in original). Indeed, the temporal dimension of stimulation is a fundamental basis for intersensory integration that cuts across sensory, perceptual, cognitive, social, and linguistic experiences. The second reason is that many of the empirical investigations of infants' intersensory perceptual abilities have either directly or indirectly explored the role of temporal information in intersensory integration. As a result, a substantial body of research findings has become available on this question, and a relatively detailed and formal analysis of temporally based intersensory perception in early development is now possible. It is hoped that such an analysis might permit the generation of some general principles for the development of intersensory integration and the specification of underlying processes with a degree of precision that has not been attempted to date.

## Perception of Temporal Information in Development

The temporal flow of events is an inescapable part of our life. By virtue of their temporal character, events can usually be characterized in terms of duration, rate, and overall rhythmic quality. In addition, because most temporally organized objects and events are represented by multimodal sensory qualities, the sensory representations of these objects and events in each modality normally occur at the same time and, thus, are temporally contiguous. A good example illustrating the intersensory temporal properties of a multimodal event is a person playing the violin. As the violinist draws the bow across the strings, an observer can see and hear that the visible actions of the arm are temporally contiguous with the heard actions of the arm and that each discrete up-and-down movement of the arm has a specific duration. In addition, as the violinist repeatedly moves the bow up and down, the observer can see and hear that the action occurs at a certain rate over time and that it has a specific rhythmic quality to it.

The fact that a human observer usually has little difficulty perceiving the equivalent nature of the visible and audible aspects of such an event is testimony to our general ability to integrate the multimodal properties of temporal events into unified perceptual experiences. With specific regard to the integration of multimodal temporal inputs, studies have shown that adults are sensitive to the temporal synchrony of heteromodal inputs (Dixon & Spitz, 1980; Massaro, 1998; Massaro, Cohen, & Smeele, 1996; McGrath & Summerfield, 1985), respond to temporal variations in one modality differently in the presence of temporal stimulation in another modality than in its absence (Myers, Cotton, & Hilp, 1981), and can make intersensory matches based on the specific temporal pattern of stimulation (Gebhard & Mowbray, 1959; Handel & Buffardi, 1969). In contrast, infants find it more difficult, if not impossible in some cases, to perceive the integral nature of certain forms of multimodal temporal structure (Lewkowicz, 1994a). This raises two questions. First, what abilities might infants lack and adults possess that make it possible to perceive the integral nature of multimodal, temporal structure? Second, how do such abilities come about in development?

To be sure, such questions have been asked before, but they were asked of children, not of infants, and were specifically concerned not with intersensory integration but with the general question of the perception and understanding of time. Piaget (1969, 1970) carried out the classic investigations of these types of questions in children, and it was he who first pointed out the theoretical importance of such questions for understanding the development of general perceptual and cognitive skills. Based on his work on the perception of duration, Piaget proposed that children initially cannot perceive time directly because they cannot coordinate the distance that an object travels and the speed of its motion in estimating time. He based this conclusion on the results from his trains problem where children were shown two moving trains and were asked to estimate the relative duration of travel when the trains' start and stop points, speed, and distance were varied. He found that young children had difficulty coordinating the various indicators of duration and concluded that children must construct the concept of time from information extracted about speed and distance. In other words, he assumed that inferential processes must operate on temporally discrete sense data and that, as a result, the perception of time and its duration is not directly available to the perceptual system but must be inferred from other knowledge. This theoretical position led Piaget to believe that children do not attain a mature concept of time until middle childhood, when they begin to understand the relationship between time, speed, and distance.

In contrast to Piaget and his theory, E. J. Gibson (1969) posited that duration is directly available to perception right from birth. Even more importantly, and in direct contrast to Piaget, Gibson proposed that various temporal dimensions are amodal in nature and, as a result, that they are available to all sensory modalities right from birth. In fact, the results from subsequent studies investigating children's perception of time are generally consistent with this view in showing that children do not need to understand the relationship between time, speed, and distance to have at least a rudimentary understanding of time. They show that as long as children understand the relative start and stop times of moving objects, they are able to judge relative durations (Acredolo, 1989; Levin, 1982). What is not clear from these results, however, is how early in development the ability to process multimodally represented, temporal information emerges. According to Gibson's theory, infants could be expected to perceive and integrate the multimodal attributes of temporal experience such as temporal synchrony, duration, rate, and rhythm. Gibson takes it as a given that infants perceive intermodal invariants and thus, by extension, that they perceive the temporal relation between inputs in different modalities.

At the time that Piaget and Gibson put forth their theoretical positions, there was little, if any, empirical information on infants' perception and responsiveness to multisensory temporal information. Since that time, however, a great deal of empirical evidence has been gathered on this question, allowing it to be revisited. I review this empirical evidence and show that infants are capable of responding to intersensory temporal relations but that responsiveness to some types of temporal relations emerges earlier than responsiveness to others. Also, I show that, although Gibson's theory predicts that infants should be able to pick up temporal intersensory relations right from birth and that they should become more adept at picking up increasingly more complex intersensory relations as they develop, the theory does not go far enough. It does not specify when responsiveness to specific intersensory temporal relations emerges, what processes underlie the emergence of responsiveness to increasingly more complex intersensory temporal relations, and what processes are responsible for the observed developmental transitions. The principal aim of the remainder of this article is to address these issues. This is done by (a) reviewing the empirical evidence on infants' responsiveness to intersensory temporal relations, (b) discussing extant theoretical approaches to the development of intersensory perception and to the development of behavior in general, and (c) proposing a model and a set of developmental principles designed to account for the developmental emergence of responsiveness to intersensory temporal relations.

## A Taxonomy of Intersensory Temporal Relations and Their Perception in Early Development

As events flow over time, they provide an observer with a steady stream of temporally organized and intermodally integrated information (Ashton, 1976; Lashley, 1951; Lewkowicz, 1989; C. L. Miller & Byrne, 1984). For example, when infants interact with their caretakers they must constantly deal with a wealth of multimodal, temporally organized information. That is, each time a caregiver talks and interacts with an infant, the multimodal information specifying the caretaker can be specified in terms of the temporal synchrony between audible and visible attributes, their duration, rate, and rhythmic quality. Figure 1 illustrates this fact in schematic form. As can be seen, when the caregiver produces a word, the voice starts and stops at the same time that the lips start and stop moving. In addition, each individual visible and audible instantiation of a given word has a specific and equal duration. On a more global level (i.e., at the level of the entire utterance), two types of intermodally integrated, temporal information are available. First, as the caregiver speaks, he or she utters the words at a certain temporal rate, and that rate is the same regardless of whether it is heard or seen. Second, the caregiver's utterance is usually imbued with an overall rhythmic quality that also is the same whether it is heard or seen. One key aspect of the temporal information characterizing the utterance illustrated in Figure 1 is that it is embedded. For example, the temporal synchrony between the audible and visible attributes of the utterance depicted in Figure 1 is embedded within intersensory duration, rate, and rhythm equivalence. Put differently, in order

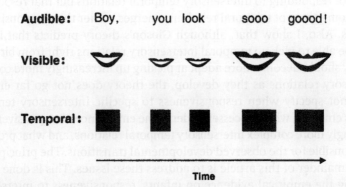

**Figure 1:** A typical temporally organized event illustrating the various types of intersensory temporal relations

for the infant to perceive the equivalence of the audible and visible components of the utterance in terms of either their duration, rate, or rhythmic structure, the infant must be able to perceive their synchronous onsets and offsets. Likewise, in order for the infant to perceive A-V equivalence based on the overall rhythmic quality of the utterance, the infant must be able to perceive the equivalence of the audible and visible components and of the intervals separating them in terms of their duration.

Are infants sensitive and responsive to the various types of temporal information shown in Figure 1? This is a two-part question. One part is whether infants are sensitive and responsive to temporal information regardless of whether it is uni- or multimodal. The other is whether infants are sensitive and responsive to intersensory temporal relations. In general, evidence indicates that infants are sensitive and responsive to different types of temporal variations. For example, infants exhibit sensitivity to a change in the temporal distribution of stimulation (Brooks & Berg, 1979; Clifton, 1974; Davies & Berg, 1983; Donohue & Berg, 1991) and can perform anticipatory responses based on temporal information. The latter ability is evident in the fact that they can preform their hands in anticipation of the future position of an object as it moves through space (Lockman, Ashmead, & Bushnell, 1984; von Hofsten, 1980, 1985) and can learn to anticipate the spatial position of an object as evidenced by anticipatory eye movements (Canfield & Haith, 1991). Finally, infants can organize their behavioral actions in a temporally meaningful way (Stern, Beebe, Jaffe, & Bennet, 1977) and to such an extent that their interactions with a caregiver are usually characterized by relatively precise temporal interlocking (Lester, Hoffman, & Brazelton, 1985). Indeed, it appears that these types of temporally based perceptual and motor capacities in infancy may provide an important developmental foundation for the emergence of cognitive abilities later in life. Thus, Haith and his colleagues (Dougherty & Haith, 1997) have shown that there is a relationship between infant visual reaction time/visual anticipation at 3.5 months of age and childhood full-scale IQ on the Wechsler Preschool and Primary Scale of Intelligence – Revised at 46 months of age.

Given that infants can perceive and respond to temporally organized information, it might be expected that they also could perceive the types of intersensory equivalence relations illustrated in Figure 1. In general, findings regarding infants' responsiveness to these types of relations indicate that infants are, in fact, sensitive and responsive to some of these intersensory temporal relations. In addition, the findings indicate that the ability to respond to different aspects of multimodal temporal structure emerges at different times in development. Specifically, it seems that intersensory responsiveness to temporal synchrony emerges first, followed by the emergence of responsiveness to duration, rate, and rhythm in that order.

## Perception of A-V Temporal Synchrony and the Intersensory Temporal Contiguity Window

Intersensory temporal synchrony is a fundamental temporal dimension that is likely to serve as an important foundation for intersensory integration in early development (Edelman, 1992; Thelen & Smith, 1994) because it can provide a simple and relatively easy basis for the perception of intersensory unity. Perhaps it is for this reason that responsiveness to temporal synchrony is one of the most intensively studied aspects of intersensory perception in infants. In general, empirical findings have shown that infants are sensitive and responsive to intersensory temporal synchrony (Bahrick, 1988; Lewkowicz, 1986, 1992a, 1992b, 1996b; Spelke, 1988; Spelke, Born, & Chu, 1983) and that responsiveness to it emerges very early in life. Moreover, Bahrick (1998) has recently reported that A-V temporal synchrony has developmental priority over other intersensory relations. She showed that infants as young as 4 weeks of age respond to the disruption of the synchronous relationship between an object's motion and the sound that it makes but that it is not until 7 weeks of age that infants exhibit sensitivity to the disruption of the association between a specific sound and a specific object.

Most recently, Slater, Quinn, Brown, and Hayes (1999) have reported that newborn infants can associate objects and linguistic tokens on the basis of synchrony. Each of two groups of infants was familiarized with two different object/sound pairings; in one group, the sound was presented contingent on the infant's looking at the visual object (and thus synchronously with it), and in the other group, the sound was presented noncontingently (by repeatedly presenting the sound every second for 25 s regardless of looking during each familiarization trial). Then, using the switch method, Slater et al. gave infants two test trials during which sound presentation was contingent on looking. The familiar object/sound pairing was presented in the familiar test trial, but it was switched in the novel test trial. The contingent familiarization group exhibited response recovery to the object/sound switch, but the noncontingent familiarization group did not. This finding was interpreted as evidence that infants detected the synchrony-based intersensory relation. There are two problems, however, that make it unclear whether these findings constitute evidence of synchrony-based matching. One is that a critical control group that would make the conclusion that infants had learned the association on the basis of synchrony more certain was not run. The critical data that allowed Slater et al. to conclude that synchrony mediated the making of the intersensory association came from the contingent familiarization group, which was familiarized to the synchronous presentation of the object and sound and then tested to the synchronous but switched object/sound pair. What is missing is a condition where the object and sound are presented synchronously during familiarization and then the same object and sound are presented asynchronously during testing. In addition, there is a confound in the study that raises the opposite possibility that the reason that the infants in the noncontingent group failed to make the intersensory association was because they experienced an overall greater amount of stimulation (they heard the sound every second regardless of looking) that exceeded their optimal level of preferred stimulation. Studies by myself and associates (Gardner, Lewkowicz, Rose, & Karmel, 1986; Lewkowicz & Turkewitz, 1981) have shown that neonates regulate the amount of visual stimulation that they look at depending on the amount of auditory stimulation. Indeed, consistent with this fact is the report by Slater et al. that many more participants in the noncontingent group dropped out of the experiment. Given these problems, it is still not certain whether newborn infants can respond to temporal intersensory synchrony.

If intersensory temporal synchrony is such an important and basic type of intersensory relation, one important question is what exactly constitutes temporal synchrony for infants. Put differently, one could ask whether the audible and visible attributes of an object or event have to occur at precisely the same time for infants to perceive them as synchronous, or whether they can have some "temporal slippage" between them and still be perceived as synchronous. Fraisse (1982a) showed that adult observers can tolerate some temporal slippage. On the basis of this observation, he postulated the "psychological present" concept to capture the idea that the heteromodal components specifying a multimodal event do not have to physically occur at the same time to be psychologically perceived as simultaneous. Indeed, the same is true for infants except that they can tolerate greater amounts of temporal intersensory slippage than adults can.

The psychological present for adults depends on the order in which the audible and visible attributes of a multimodal event occur. Studies show that when adults watch an object bouncing on a surface and listen to an impact sound associated with that object, they perceive the sound and bounce as occurring in synchrony as long as the sound does not precede the visible bounce by more than 80 ms. If the sound is delayed with respect to the visible bounce, adults perceive the two as synchronous as long as the delay does not exceed 140 ms (McGrath & Summerfield, 1985; Summerfield, 1979). Thus, an intersensory temporal contiguity window (ITCW) appears to govern responsiveness to the temporal relation between the auditory and visual components of an A-V compound stimulus; as long as the audible and visible components of an A-V event fall within this temporal window, they are perceived as synchronous. To determine how wide the ITCW might be in infants, I (Lewkowicz, 1996b) conducted a series of studies in which I investigated infants' responses to different intersensory temporal asynchronies. There were a priori reasons to suspect that the window might be substantially wider in infants. First, conditioning studies have shown that, compared with adults, infants require longer conditioned stimulus-unconditioned stimulus intervals for successful classical conditioning (Caldwell & Werboff, 1962; Ingram, 1978). Second, the nervous system undergoes dramatic structural and functional changes during postnatal life (Garey & Yan, 1993; Scheibel, 1993; Yakovlev & Lecours, 1967), with changes in conduction velocity being one important and prominent feature (Karmel, Gardner, Zappulla, Magnano, & Brown, 1988).

To assess possible developmental changes in responsiveness to A-V temporal synchrony relations, I studied infants between 2 and 8 months of age. Using an infant-controlled habituation/test procedure, infants were first habituated to a synchronous A-V event consisting of a visual object (a green disk) moving up and down on a TV monitor and a percussive sound that occurred each time the object reversed direction at the bottom of the screen. During the test trials, the visible bounce and the sound were temporally offset by different amounts. Results indicated that there were no age differences in responsiveness and showed that infants required a minimum asynchrony interval of 350 ms to exhibit discrimination when the sound preceded the visible bounce and a minimum interval of 450 ms when the sound followed the visible bounce. Figure 2 shows the results from an experiment in which asynchronies of 150, 250, and 350 ms were presented and indicates that infants discriminated an asynchrony of 350 ms but not lower ones.

To determine how infants' responsiveness might compare to that of adults, I conducted a separate study with the identical stimuli and a modified procedure in which I exposed adult participants first to the synchronous event and then to a series of asynchronous test events. I then asked them to indicate which of the test events was asynchronous. In contrast to infants, adults required an asynchrony of only 65 ms when the sound preceded the visible bounce and an asynchrony of 112 ms when the sound followed the visible bounce to discriminate the test events from the synchronous one. These values are in general agreement with previous findings from studies with adult participants (Dixon & Spitz, 1980; Summerfield, 1979).

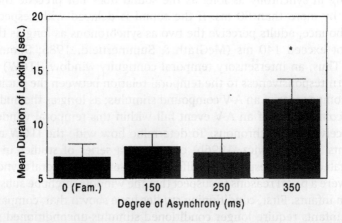

**Figure 2:** Mean duration of looking at different auditory–visual asynchronies. Asterisk indicates significant response recovery. Fam. = Familiar test trial.

One of the interesting aspects of the findings from both infants and adults is that they required a longer temporal separation between the audible and visible bounce when the audible bounce followed the visible bounce. I (Lewkowicz, 1996b) interpreted this effect to reflect both the longer neural transduction speed of the visual as opposed to the auditory signals at the receptor level and the ensuing longer response latency to visual signals at the cortical level (Regan, 1989). I argued that if the differential neural processing of the auditory and visual signals is taken into account, then the psychological size of the ITCW ends up being the same regardless of signal order, and the resulting infant ITCW is equal to approximately 350 ms.

## Perception of Duration-based Intersensory Equivalence

Very limited information regarding developmental changes in infants' responsiveness to duration, and particularly their responsiveness to intersensory duration-based equivalence, is available. Indirect evidence suggests that infants can respond to unimodally specified differences in duration in both auditory and visual modalities and that this value is below 100 ms (Karmel, Lester, McCarvill, Brown, & Hofmann, 1977; Lewkowicz, 1985b; Morrongiello & Trehub, 1987; L. A. Werner, Marean, Halpin, & Spetner, 1992). For example, infants have been shown to attend differentially to visual stimulation differing in its temporal rate of presentation, implying that they can use interstimulus duration differences to discriminate between different rates. In fact, Regal (1981) has reported that the critical flicker frequency in 4-week-old infants is as high as 40.7 Hz, implying that infants as young as 1 month of age are sensitive to interpulse durations as small as 25 ms. Similarly, in the auditory modality, infants can discriminate auditory duration changes of as little as 20 ms (Morrongiello & Trehub, 1987).

Only one study has investigated whether infants can perceive the intersensory equivalence of duration (Lewkowicz, 1986). In this study, I gave 3-, 6-, and 8-month-old infants two kinds of paired-preference trials. During the first 6 silent trials, infants viewed pairs of checkerboards flashing at the same rate but for different durations. During the next 12 sound trials, infants viewed the same pairs of checkerboards but this time accompanied by a sound whose duration, onset, and offset corresponded to one of the checkerboards. The checkerboards were flashed at one of three durations (400, 800, and 1,600 ms), and all possible pairs of the three durations were presented. Clear evidence of intersensory matching was found in the 6- and 8-month-old infants for the 400–1,600 ms and the 800–1,600 ms pairs. For each pair, infants looked longer at the visual stimulus whose duration was the same as the duration of the auditory stimulus, and they also looked at it longer in the presence of the matching sound than in the absence of sound. Interestingly enough, the results also indicated that the onset and offset synchrony between the matching visual and auditory stimuli contributed to intersensory matching. This was indicated by the results from a second experiment where infants were tested with the identical stimuli except that the onset and offset of the sound occurred 300 ms after the onset and offset of the corresponding visual stimulus. In this case, infants no longer performed intersensory matching. This latter finding suggests that what appeared to be duration-based matching in the first experiment was actually synchrony-based matching. When the results from studies of infant rate-based intersensory matching are discussed later in this article, it is shown that the results from the asynchrony experiment actually mean that infants required both synchrony and duration cues to detect the duration-based intersensory equivalence.

The only other research on the intersensory perception of duration comes from animal studies. For example, adult rodents have been found to perceive the duration of a signal in the visual or auditory modality and to then transfer that information to the other modality (Meek & Church, 1982; Roberts, 1982; Tees & Symons, 1987). On the basis of this finding, some have made the assumption that the cross-modal transfer of duration reflects the operation of an underlying clock mechanism common to all modalities and that this ability is dependent on genetically determined neural circuits. The evidence cited in support of this nativist position comes from studies showing that dark-reared rats display no deficits in their cross-modal transfer of duration (Tees & Symons, 1987). Despite the fact that dark rearing has no effect on cross-modal transfer of duration in rats, however, the question of the developmental origins of intersensory responsiveness to duration is still very much an open one. First, if cross-modal transfer of duration reflects the operation of an underlying clock that is common to all modalities, then it is possible that dark-reared rats might acquire the ability to distinguish between different durations in the auditory or somesthetic modalities and that this might then generalize to other modalities including the visual. Second, tests to determine whether developmental experience is necessary for the differentiation of intersensory duration have not been done in other species, including humans. Third, my (Lewkowicz, 1986) finding that a response to the intersensory equivalence of duration does not emerge before 6 months of age in human infants suggests that intersensory responsiveness to duration in humans may depend on experience.

## Perception of Rate-based Intersensory Equivalence

Discrimination of temporal rate differences appears to be relatively easy for infants, regardless of whether these differences are represented by unimodal or bimodal attributes. For example, studies have shown that infants (even right after birth) can discriminate between different visually (Gardner et al., 1986; Karmel et al., 1977; Lewkowicz, 1985b) and bimodally specified rates

(Lewkowicz, 1988a, 1988b; Pickens & Bahrick, 1997). Other studies have shown that infants can respond to unimodal rate differences in the context of unchanging rate information in a second sensory modality (Lewkowicz, 1988a, 1988b, 1992b) and to the invariant properties of bimodally specified temporal rate against variations in bimodally specified rhythm (Pickens & Bahrick, 1997).

If infants can discriminate unimodally and bimodally specified temporal rates and if temporal rate can provide an important basis for relating sensory inputs across modalities, the obvious question is whether infants can perceive rate-based intersensory equivalence. Unfortunately, the answer to this question is equivocal because of a number of contradictory findings in the literature. The only positive findings on infants' intersensory perception of rate-based equivalence come from a study by Spelke (1979). She presented 4-month-old infants with two side-by-side puppets bouncing against a surface at different rates and a percussive sound that was synchronized with the bounce of one of these puppets. Spelke reported that infants looked longer at the puppet whose rate of bouncing was the same as the rate at which the sound occurred and concluded that they detected the A-V temporal relation. In contrast to Spelke's findings, however, both Humphrey and Tees (1980) and I (Lewkowicz, 1985a) failed to obtain evidence of rate-based intersensory matching. There was one possible reason for the different outcomes. Whereas Spelke (1979) presented moving visual stimuli, Humphrey and Tees (1980) and I (Lewkowicz, 1985a) presented spatially static visual stimuli. Visual motion happens to be a highly salient stimulus attribute for infants (Kaufmann, Stucki, & Kaufmann-Hayoz, 1985) and allows infants to extract certain types of information that they cannot extract when only spatially static information is presented (Kellman, 1984; Kellman, Spelke, & Short, 1986). This makes it possible that the lack of motion made intersensory matching difficult in the Lewkowicz (1985a) and Humphrey and Tees (1980) studies.

To determine whether motion might be the critical variable that makes rate-based intersensory matching possible, I (Lewkowicz, 1992a) conducted a set of experiments that investigated infants' rate-based intersensory matching with moving visual stimuli. Four-and 8-month-old infants were given a series of twelve 30-s paired-preference trials during which pairs of stimuli bouncing up and down on each side of a computer monitor were shown. During each trial, the two visual stimuli bounced at different rates. All possible pairs of three rates (.22, .42, and .98 Hz) were presented across trials. As the stimuli bounced, a tone was sounded each time one of the two visual stimuli reached bottom and reversed trajectory. Thus, the rate at which the auditory stimulus was sounded corresponded to the rate at which one of the visual stimuli bounced. Results indicated that despite the fact that the visual stimuli were spatially dynamic, no evidence of intersensory matching was obtained. In response to these findings, Spelke (1994) revisited the question of whether infants were capable of making rate-based intersensory matches and concluded that her original conclusions regarding infants' intersensory matching based on rate were perhaps unwarranted.

What might be the reason for the difficulty that infants appear to have in making rate-based intersensory matches? One possibility is that it may be too difficult for them to process the differential rate of visual motion at the same time that they have to process the synchrony/rate relation between the sound and the corresponding visual stimulus. I (Lewkowicz, 1992a) addressed this possibility in another experiment by reducing the complexity of the task. This time both visual stimuli were made to bounce at the same rate but were made to bounce out of phase with respect to one another during a given test trial. This was done by having one of them appear on the screen at the start of a trial followed a short time later by the appearance of the other stimulus. In this way, the visual stimuli making up a given pair no longer differed in terms of motion velocity and thus rate. Across trials, the two visual stimuli were moved at one of three rates (either .32, .49, or .73 Hz). In one block of 6 trials, the sound occurred in conjunction with the bounce of the visual stimulus that appeared first on the screen (i.e., the leading visual stimulus), whereas, in the other block, the sound occurred in conjunction with the bounce of the visual stimulus that appeared second (i.e., the lagging visual stimulus). Results supported the hypothesis that the complexity of the task might have prevented infants from making intersensory matches because both the 4- and the 8-month-old infants exhibited intersensory matching. Specifically, they looked longer at the sounding/leading stimulus when the leading visual stimulus was associated with the sound, both in the slow-motion and in the medium-motion condition. In addition, infants did not look longer at the leading stimulus when the sound did not correspond to it, indicating that they were responding to the intersensory relation rather than to the fact that this stimulus appeared first on the screen. Taken together, the findings from this (Lewkowicz, 1992a) study showed that infants as young as 4 months of age can recognize the temporal relation of spatially dynamic sights and corresponding sounds but that this ability is limited to synchrony-based, rather than synchrony/rate-based, relations.

Although making synchrony/rate-based intersensory matches may be difficult for infants, it may be possible that this difficulty might be overcome with some prior experience with such complex temporal relationships. This is suggested by the findings from a study by Bahrick (1988). She showed that when infants are first given a familiarization procedure and then given an intersensory equivalence perception task, they exhibit matching even though they do not exhibit matching without prior familiarization. To determine whether prior short-term experience might make it possible for infants to detect the kinds of rate-based relations presented in my earlier study (Lewkowicz, 1992a), I conducted another series of experiments (Lewkowicz, 1994b) in which infants first were familiarized with a rate-based intersensory relation and then were tested with the same procedures as in the earlier

(Lewkowicz, 1992a) study. Despite the initial familiarization, the results from this set of experiments indicated that infants still did not recognize the rate-based A-V relationship.

There was yet a third possible reason for the failure to exhibit rate-based intersensory matching. The kinds of stimuli used by Humphrey and Tees (1980) and myself (Lewkowicz, 1992a) were rather "impoverished." In the case of my (Lewkowicz, 1992a) study, the visual stimuli were identical, flat, green disks that differed only in their speed of motion. The sound was the same regardless of which stimulus it was associated with and differed only in terms of its temporal relation to a given visual stimulus. Thus, one possibility is that infants need a set of distinctive features to distinguish the visual and auditory information to detect rate-based intersensory relations. Although, as shown earlier, this is not the case for the perception of duration- and synchrony-based intersensory relations, it may be the case for the perception of more complex temporal relations. To investigate this possibility, I (Lewkowicz & Lickliter, 1998) recently conducted a series of studies in which, prior to testing for intersensory matching, I gave separate groups of 4-, 6-, and 8-month-old infants an opportunity to become familiar with each of the multimodal events that they would see and hear in the subsequent paired-preference trials. To accentuate the differences between the two visual stimuli, I rendered them on a computer monitor as three-dimensional objects that differed in color and size. The sounds also differed from each other in that the sound that corresponded to one of the objects was a low-pitched, resonant, complex sound, whereas the other sound was a higher pitched, tinny, complex sound. Results showed that despite the use of the familiarization procedure and the presentation of highly distinctive events, infants did not make intersensory matches. Consistent with the prior findings (Lewkowicz, 1992a), however, when rate differences were removed and only synchrony specified the intersensory relation, infants did make intersensory matches and did so even without a prior familiarization phase.

When all the findings on intersensory rate matching are considered together, they suggest that the perception of rate-based intersensory equivalence is difficult for infants as old as 8 months of age. It should be noted, however, that all the studies reviewed so far employed the intersensory paired-preference task, which, according to Bahrick and Pickens (1994), is a difficult one for infants and might belie their true competence. Indeed, in studies using the multimodal component variation method, I (Lewkowicz, 1988a, 1988b) did find some evidence that infants perceive rate-based intersensory relations. Infants were habituated to a flashing checkerboard and a sound pulsing at the same rate and were then tested with a change in the rate of one or the other of the two components. This resulted in a change in the rate-based relation between the audible and visible components and thus could serve as a test of whether the infants could discriminate the change in that relation. Results showed that 10-month-old, but not 6-month-old, infants responded to the change in the intersensory rate relation, suggesting that 10-month-old infants can perceive a rate-based A-V relation.

One factor that might possibly complicate this interpretation is that when the rate of one of the components was changed in these studies, the synchrony relation between the auditory and visual components also changed. Therefore, it might be argued that rather than responding to a rate change, infants responded either to a change in the synchrony relation and/or to a change in the synchrony/rate relation. It is unlikely, however, that responsiveness was based on the synchrony change alone because if that were the case, then the 6-month-old infants should have been able to detect the changes. That they did not suggests at a minimum that the perception of intersensory relations on the basis of temporal rate depends on the joint attributes of rate and synchrony and that such perception may not emerge until late in infancy. This conclusion is supported by my (Lewkowicz, 1985a) failure to find intersensory matching by 4-month-old infants in a study in which a sound corresponded both in terms of synchrony and rate to one of two flashing checkerboards. If synchrony were sufficient as a relational cue and even if infants were unable to make the matches based solely on rate, they should have been able to perform them. The fact that they did not suggests that synchrony alone is not sufficient when rate covaries with it. Furthermore, these findings are consistent with the findings from my (Lewkowicz, 1988a, 1988b) studies in showing that infants younger than 10 months of age do not perceive intersensory temporal relations based on joint synchrony/rate relations.

## Perception of Rhythm-based Intersensory Equivalence

Questions about the processes underlying the perception of rhythmic structure, as well as about structure in general, are fundamental to the study of perception because structure is an abstract property that transcends any particular stimulus and gives meaning to events (Pomerantz & Lockhead, 1991). Rhythmic structure is also fundamental on the production side because most of our motor behaviors are rhythmically organized. Despite structure's obvious importance, it is curious that the developmental foundations underlying the perception of temporal structure are virtually unexplored and that most theorists (Bregman, 1990; Fraisse, 1982a; Handel, 1989; Martin, 1972) simply posit an innate basis for it with very scant empirical support for this position.

As in the case of rate, there is some evidence indicating that infants can discriminate differences in rhythm. For example, Demany, McKenzie, and Vurpillot (1977) and Washburn and Cohen (1984) reported that infants as young as 2 months of age can discriminate between different auditory rhythmic sequences, and Mendelson (1986) reported that infants as young as 4 months of age can discriminate between different visual rhythmic sequences.

Interpretation of the results from these studies is problematic, however, because the type of temporal structure presented was very simple and, thus, did not exemplify the kind of hierarchically organized temporal structure characteristic of typical rhythmic patterns (see the subsection *Rhythm* under *Differential Informational Complexity* below).

There are, however, three studies that are exceptions to this shortcoming. One is a study conducted by Morrongiello (1984) in which infants' response to relatively complex auditory rhythmic patterns that did meet the requirements of true rhythmic structure was investigated. Infants' discrimination between different rhythmical patterns that differed either in absolute terms (i.e., the interelement intervals changed) or in relative terms (i.e., the interelement intervals were presented in novel combinations) was tested. Both 6- and 12-month-old infants detected the difference when it was an absolute one, but only 12-month-olds detected the difference when it was a relative one. Pickens and Bahrick (1995) found successful discrimination of relatively complex A-V rhythmic sequences in 7-month-old infants. Finally, Bahrick and Lickliter (in press), using the same rhythms used by Pickens and Bahrick (1995), showed that 5-month-old infants could discriminate between them as well. Together, these studies suggest that discrimination of rhythmic patterns emerges by the 5th month of life and that the specific time when responsiveness emerges may depend on pattern complexity and on whether the stimulation is specified unimodally or bimodally.

It is not clear whether and at what age infants can extract the invariant properties of a specific rhythm. On the one hand, Trehub and Thorpe (1989) have found that 7- and 9-month-old infants can successfully categorize auditory sequences on the basis of rhythm. In contrast, Pickens and Bahrick (1997) have found equivocal evidence of 7-month-old infants' ability to categorize bimodal, A-V rhythmic sequences. They habituated infants to a single rhythm presented at three different rates and then tested for discrimination by presenting either a novel rhythm at a novel rate or a familiar rhythm at a novel rate. Results from the two test conditions indicated no successful discrimination and were interpreted to mean that infants of this age cannot abstract the property of rhythm.

Like rate, rhythm can serve as an important basis for the perception of intersensory equivalence. The key question from the present perspective is when the ability to recognize rhythm-based intersensory equivalence emerges. On the basis of the distinctions made earlier between detection, discrimination, and recognition, the most demanding and most developmentally advanced skill is the recognition of rhythm-based intersensory equivalence. Only two studies have investigated infants' perception of rhythm-based intersensory equivalence. Both studies, however, used a cross-modal transfer technique, thus making it impossible to determine whether infants can recognize rhythm-based intersensory equivalence and making it possible to determine only whether they can detect a particular rhythmic pattern and discriminate it from another. Moreover, neither study investigated developmental changes, and each confounded rhythmic structure with another feature. In the first of these two studies, Allen, Walker, Symonds, and Marcell (1977) reported transfer of rhythm between audition and vision in 7-month-old infants. Infants were habituated to either a regularly or an irregularly occurring sequence and then were tested to determine whether they could detect an intra- or intersensory change in the sequence. The sequences consisted of three flashing lights or sounds. In one of the sequences, the elements were separated by two .9-s intervals. In the other sequence, the first and second elements were separated by a .3-s interval, and the second and third elements were separated by a 9-s interval. As a result, the two sequences differed in terms of the first interelement interval and in terms of their overall length. This makes it possible that infants discriminated the two sequences either on the basis of the "local" features of the stimulus sequences (i.e., the first interelement interval) or on the basis of their different lengths, rather than on the basis of their overall rhythmic structure. In the second of these studies, Mendelson and Ferland (1982) familiarized 4-month-old infants with a syllable that was presented repeatedly according to either a regular or an irregular temporal pattern. Then they were tested for transfer of the specific familiarization pattern by viewing a film of a puppet moving its mouth according to one or the other temporal pattern. Although Mendelson and Ferland found transfer, this was only the case in one direction. In addition, the regular sequence used in this study was an isochronous, concatenated sequence of stimuli and thus did not meet the relative timing requirement of a true rhythmic sequence (see the subsection *Rhythm* under *Differential Informational Complexity* below for further discussion of rhythmic structure).

## Summary of Findings on Perception of Intersensory Temporal Relations

The findings on infants' responsiveness to temporally related auditory and visual information show that infants as young as 1 month of age are sensitive to A-V temporal synchrony relations and that they can tolerate considerably larger intersensory temporal asynchronies than adults can. The early ability to detect intersensory temporal synchrony enables infants as young as 4 weeks of age to discriminate between synchrony and asynchrony; by 4 months of age, infants can make intersensory matches in a paired-preference task. In contrast to this early ability to detect temporal synchrony relations, young infants (between 3 and 4 months of age) show no evidence of making duration- or rate-based intersensory matches. This is the case even when these types of temporal relations covary with temporal synchrony. It is only at 6 months of age that infants begin to exhibit duration/synchrony-based intersensory matching. Rate/synchrony-based intersensory matching appears to be difficult even for infants as old as 8 months of age, and it is only at 10 months of age that infants exhibit detection of intersensory rate/synchrony relations. Finally, the available evidence concerning infants' response to rhythm-based intersensory relations does not make it possible to draw any definitive conclusions at this time. Overall, the empirical evidence to date suggests that intersensory perception of synchrony-based relations emerges the earliest and that temporal synchrony is involved in infants' perception of duration-based and rate-based equivalence in matching tasks. The evidence also suggests that the ability to detect and discriminate the different forms of intersensory temporal relations emerges earlier in development than the ability to use the temporal information to recognize intersensory equivalence.

What processes may underlie these kinds of abilities, and what theoretical constructs could be helpful in uncovering these processes? To answer this question, first I describe some theoretical approaches that have been put forth to account for the development of intersensory integration, thus putting this question into a general theoretical framework. I then argue that one contemporary theory of development known as epigenetic systems theory may provide helpful conceptual tools for uncovering the mechanisms and processes underlying the development of intersensory perception. Because epigenetic systems theory requires that a search for putative determinants underlying the development of a particular function be conducted at many different levels of organization (ranging from the unicellular to the organismic one) and because development is considered to start at conception, I next consider the contribution of prenatal experience and neural development to the development of intersensory development. I then return to a consideration of the development of intersensory perception of temporal relations by proposing a tentative model and end with a consideration of its generalizability.

## Theoretical Views on the Development of Intersensory Perception

Historically, two diametrically opposed theoretical positions have been put forward on the question of the developmental origins of intersensory perception. One, known as the differentiation view and primarily championed by H. Werner (1973), Bower (1974), and E. J. Gibson (1969), maintains that the different sensory systems are unified at birth and that, as development progresses, they become gradually differentiated from one another. A radical version of this view is that infants are synesthetes (Maurer, 1993; H. Werner, 1973) and that the senses are thus completely merged at birth. The opposing view, championed by Piaget (1952) and Birch and Lefford (1963, 1967), maintains that the sensory systems are uncoupled at birth and that over time, through self-initiated action (Piaget, 1952), they gradually become increasingly more coupled as they participate together in coordinated action.

Currently, the most influential theoretical view on the development of intersensory perception is embodied in E. J. Gibson's (1969) general theory of perceptual development. This theory is an extension and direct outgrowth of J. J. Gibson's (1966, 1979) direct perception theory, which, in a radical departure from traditional views that considered perception to be a collection of separate sensations, held that behavior is governed by a set of perceptual systems operating in an ecologically meaningful and structured world. The perceptual systems, using sensations from multiple sensory modalities to discover the amodal properties of objects and events, allow the organism to discover structure and thus the affordances of objects and events. According to J. J. Gibson (1979):

> The affordance of an object is what the infant begins by noticing. . . . An affordance is an invariant combination of variables, and one might guess that it is easier to perceive such an invariant unit than it is to perceive all of the variables separately, (p. 134)

E. J. Gibson (1969, 1982, 1984) further proposed that infants are sensitive and responsive to amodal structure right from birth and that as development progresses, through the process of perceptual differentiation, they become increasingly more capable of picking up increasingly more complex amodal invariants. According to this increasing specificity principle, initially in development, infants are sensitive to global amodal invariant relations and, as development progresses, they become more sensitive to finer, embedded aspects of amodal structure. The mechanism that makes the discovery of increasingly finer perceptual structure possible is a mutual interdependence between an actively perceiving infant and its structured environment. In other words, the infant is seen as an active seeker of perceptual structure, and the structure is seen as actively influencing the way infants seek it out. This idea of mutuality is central to a whole class of developmental theories.

## Developmental Systems Theory, Epigenesis, and the Role of Limitations

According to a group of theories, all of which can be classified under the rubric of systems theories of development (Gottlieb, 1991; Johnston, 1987; Lehrman, 1970; Lerner & Kaufman, 1985; Sameroff, 1975; Schneirla, 1957), the emergence of new structures and functions at multiple, hierarchically organized levels is the essence of development. In other words, development occurs at the cellular up through the organismic levels of organization, and one must understand all these processes and their interactions if one is to reach an ultimate understanding of development. This is the essence of Gottlieb's (1991) probabilistic epigenesis view of development according to which the developmental emergence of new structures and functions is the result of horizontal (e.g., gene–gene, cell–cell, organism–organism) and vertical (e.g., gene–neuron, behavioral activity–nervous system) reciprocal coactions among existing constituents. For example, sensory experience can shape the ultimate structural and functional properties of the developing nervous system (Greenough & Juraska, 1979; Merzenich, Allard, & Jenkins, 1990), and, reciprocally, the more developed and elaborate a nervous system is, the greater the behavioral capacity of the organism (Maier & Schneirla, 1964). The results of these bidirectional/reciprocal coactions are increased complexity and the elaboration of new emergent properties. A critical feature of Gottlieb's (1991) view is that development is a process driven by the engine of coaction between two or more components and thus that one must study the relationship of the components through time to achieve an understanding of how a specific structure or function develops. As noted earlier, the direct perception view (E. J. Gibson, 1988; J. J. Gibson, 1979) also considers the mutuality between the organism and its ecology to be crucial. Although this mutuality concept is similar to Gottlieb's concept of coaction, Gottlieb's probabilistic epigenesis approach is broader in scope in that it calls for analyses to be conducted not only at the perceptual level but at all levels of structural and functional organization.

According to epigenetic systems theory, one of the most important concepts in the study of development is the concept of experience. As organisms develop, they are constantly exposed to self-generated and externally generated multisensory inputs. This constant exposure to stimulative inputs creates an experiential milieu that may or may not lay the foundation for the subsequent development of new structures and functions. Thus, one of the central questions for a developmental analysis is what role antecedent conditions play in the emergence of subsequent outcomes. By asking what role an earlier experience (e.g., in utero exposure to the maternal voice) may have on subsequent outcome (e.g., a preference for a maternal voice over a stranger's voice at birth), one is asking about the relationship between the two developmental events. In other words, an analysis of the effects of experience on developmental outcome focuses on the processes underlying the interaction of at least two components through developmental time.

Turkewitz and Kenny (1982, 1985) proposed that an important aspect of developmental experience, particularly for perceptual development, is the timing of sensory function onset. This idea is based on the observation that the different sensory systems become functional at different times and develop at different rates in both avian and mammalian species (Gottlieb, 1971). Turkewitz and Kenny suggested that this differential developmental timing creates a context in which earlier developing sensory modalities develop without competition from later developing modalities. For example, in the bobwhite quail (an avian species), the auditory modality develops earlier than the visual modality, and introduction of earlier than usual visual stimulation leads to changes in the developmental trajectory of the auditory modality (Lickliter & Lewkowicz, 1995). The most significant feature of Turkewitz and Kenny's limitations view, however, is that the immaturity of the various components of a developing system and the resulting absence of or diminished function in some sensory modalities compared to others are actually advantageous. The absence or diminished function of a given sensory modality makes it possible for another, earlier developing modality to develop without competition. As described later in this article, the general concept of limitations is a powerful idea that can be used to construct a theoretical model that can account for the development of intersensory temporal processing.

## Putative Prenatal Sources of Intersensory Temporal Integration

Epigenetic systems theory considers development as a continuous process that begins at conception, and many, if not all, behavioral functions observed at birth have their antecedents in prenatal development. Because responsiveness to temporal synchrony relations emerges very early in development and may be fundamental to the development of responsiveness to the other, more complex types of intersensory temporal relations, one could ask whether such responsiveness may serve as a basis for intersensory integration in prenatal life.

The somesthetic and vestibular modalities are the first to become functional in prenatal life and are followed in order of functional emergence by the chemosensory (oral and nasal), auditory, and visual modalities (Gottlieb, 1971). This limits the opportunities for concurrent multimodal stimulation until quite late in gestation when all but the visual modality are functional. Empirical studies show that the human fetus can respond to vibrotactile, acoustic (Kisilevsky, 1995; Lecanuet, Granier-Deferre, & Busnel, 1995), and chemical stimulation (Schaal, Orgeur, & Rognon, 1995) by the third trimester and that the fetus also can produce its own tactile and kinesthetic stimulation as a result of spontaneous cyclic motor activity (Bekoff, 1995; Robertson & Bacher, 1995). Thus, the prenatal environment of the third-trimester human fetus is rich in external, internal, and self-generated stimulation, and the fetus is responsive to this multimodal array. This makes it possible, for example, for a fetus to experience the consequences of its own motion (kinesthesis) in synchrony with the tactile consequences of that motion (i.e., sucking a thumb or feeling one of its limbs moving across some body surface). It should be noted, however, that when concurrent multimodal stimulation becomes possible, its effects are likely to change continually during gestation because the sensory systems mature and develop and the intrauterine environment changes as the fetus grows and the amount of amniotic fluid decreases.

In addition, the types of intersensory interactions are limited to a great extent by the nature of the fetal nervous system. Both synaptogenesis and neural differentiation occur well into the first year of life (Bourgeois, 1993; Scheibel, 1993), and the fetal and neonatal CNS is immature, undifferentiated, and unmyelinated (Garey & Yan, 1993; Yakovlev & Lecours, 1967). Indeed, on the basis of this immature state of the fetal and neonatal CNS, some have argued that neonatal behaviors are largely governed by subcortical systems and that gradually, over several months, these systems are supplanted by cortical control systems (Bronson, 1974; Morton & Johnson, 1991; Woodruff, 1978). Consistent with this view, results from behavioral studies show that neonates exhibit nonspecific patterns of responsiveness that generalize across sensory modalities (Kaplan, Fox, Scheuneman, & Jenkins, 1991; Lewkowicz, 1985a; Lewkowicz & Turkewitz, 1980, 1981) and that neonatal responsiveness appears to be controlled by the infant's general state of arousal and the overall amount of stimulation (Gardner & Karmel, 1995; Karmel, Gardner, & Magnano, 1991; Lewkowicz, 1991; Turkewitz, Gardner, & Lewkowicz, 1984). As a result, prenatal stimulation most likely provides the fetus with only the basic features of the stimulus array such as intensity and/or its temporal features. In fact, it is probably these two stimulus features that provide the principal basis for prenatal intersensory integration, although no empirical information is available on the possible role of temporal synchrony in prenatal intersensory integration.

The only direct evidence showing that prenatal intersensory interactions do occur comes from studies in birds. For example, Gottlieb, Tomlinson, and Radell (1989) found that mallard embryos did not learn the maternal call (something they normally do while in the egg) if concurrent and premature visual stimulation was presented at the same time as the call but that they did if the two types of stimulation were presented in an alternating fashion. Likewise, Radell and Gottlieb (1992) found that mallard embryos failed to learn the maternal call in the presence of relatively intense concurrent vestibular stimulation but that they did learn the call when the amount of vestibular stimulation was reduced to species-specific levels and that this was the case even though the vestibular stimulation was presented concurrently. Lickliter and Hellewell (1992) also found detrimental effects of concurrent premature visual stimulation on learning the maternal call in bobwhite quail embryos. No studies have directly assessed the effects of concurrent, heteromodal stimulation presented at species-typical levels during prenatal development on responsiveness to the temporal relation between heteromodal inputs during postnatal development.

In sum, given that the human fetus is sensitive and responsive to stimulation in different sensory modalities, it is not difficult to imagine how the co-occurrence of stimulation in different modalities might contribute to the early appearance of postnatal responsiveness to temporally contiguous heteromodal inputs. The problem, of course, is that in avian and vertebrate species, the visual modality is not functional prior to birth, so the embryo or the fetus does not have the opportunity to experience the temporal synchrony between visual stimulation and stimulation in the other sensory modalities. Moreover, on the basis of the fact that human infants can detect the temporal synchrony of auditory and visual stimulation very early in development, it is hard to imagine how prenatal experience could contribute to this ability. One possibility is that the prenatal experience with temporally contiguous inputs in the somesthetic, vestibular, and auditory modalities provides the developmental precursor for subsequent responsiveness to A-V temporal synchrony relations after birth.

## Neural Mechanisms of Intersensory Integration

There is no doubt that the neural mechanisms required for the perception of intersensory relations are widespread throughout the animal kingdom. It is the rule rather than the exception that the various sensory pathways send their information from different subcortical areas to common and convergent areas of the cortex and that intersensory integration is the ultimate result of sensory processing (Stein & Meredith, 1993). In the invertebrate nervous system, modality-specific afferents converge on central interneurons and efferent neurons, both of which are largely intersensory in their response properties. In the vertebrate nervous system, modality-specific afferents converge on an even greater array of subcortical and cortical multimodal regions. For example, at the brain stem level of the mammalian brain, multimodal neurons are widespread throughout the reticular activating system and provide the organism with the capacity for generalized arousal by means of any sensory route. In the midbrain, the deep laminae of the superior colliculus contain cells that respond solely to concurrent visual, auditory, and tactile input and provide the organism with the ability to orient toward meaningful multimodal events (Stein & Meredith, 1993). In the thalamus, regions in the posterior and lateral thalamus respond to multimodal signals. At the cortical level in the primate brain, the superior temporal, intraparietal, frontal, and prefrontal cortices all contain multimodal neurons and thus are known as "association" areas.

The mechanisms underlying the perception of multimodal information have been and continue to be a matter of considerable debate and controversy (Damasio, 1989; Edelman, 1992; Ettlinger & Wilson, 1990; Freides, 1974; Marks, 1978; Thelen & Smith, 1994; Welch & Warren, 1986). Historically, the general assumption has been that intersensory integration in the association areas mediates the higher level cognitive, perceptual, and attentive behaviors and thus provides the observer with the "final," unified view of the world. More recently, however, this view has been challenged. Instead of viewing intersensory integration as a unidirectional flow of information from lower, sensory-specific neural sites to higher level association areas where intermodally integrated information is stored, some have proposed that there are no neural sites that act as the repository of uniquely intersensory information in the brain. For example, Damasio (1989) has proposed that the integration of the various aspects of perceptual experience, be they unimodal or multimodal, is dependent on the "time-locked co-activation of geographically separate sites of neural activity within sensory and motor cortices, rather than on a neural transfer and integration of different representations towards rostral integration sites" (p. 39). Likewise, Edelman (1992) has proposed a theoretical model in which the brain is organized into neuronal groups that represent assemblages of neurons distributed throughout the brain that function as a single unit. The neuronal groups receive modality-specific inputs and communicate with one another constantly by means of massive, reentrant interconnections. Different neuronal groups are formed as a developing organism interacts with the external world, and those whose functions have positive consequences are selected, strengthened, and retained for future use. The continuous reentrant intersensory interactions that occur during early development are postulated to lead, in turn, to the emergence of a set of global mappings whose main function is to integrate the elemental functions into whole, integrated patterns of behavior. Thus, according to Edelman's theory, intersensory integration is the result of massive parallel interactions between modality-specific regions. In a similar vein, Ettlinger and Wilson (1990) have proposed the notion of "leakage," according to which sensory-specific representations become available to other modalities through sensory convergence (i.e., association) areas of the brain using circuits similar to Edelman's reentrant networks. Ettlinger and Wilson explicitly rejected the notion that intersensory integration is mediated by representations in polysensory neural convergence areas. Whether this "new" view of the neural mechanisms underlying intersensory integration is correct is still very much an open question and awaits empirical confirmation.

How likely is it that similar neural mechanisms mediate intersensory perception in early development? The available evidence, although mostly indirect, suggests that this is not likely. The developing brain, which is a highly plastic organ, is the result of both constructive and destructive processes. Although until recently it was thought that brain development resulted only from the growth of new neurons, it has now become clear that destructive processes play an important part as well. Initially during development, there is an overproduction of neurons that turn out to be transient and that eventually the (Frost, 1990). As a result, the mature organization of the brain is achieved through selective destruction of these transient neurons and their connections, in part guided by sensory input and intrinsic biological processes. For example, Frost (1990) has shown that in the newborn hamster, retinal ganglion cells send out projections to several nonvisual brain nuclei such as the inferior colliculus (the main relay station for auditory signals) and the ventrobasal body of the thalamus (the main way station for somesthetic signals). Both of these transient connections disappear by the end of the first postnatal week. Similar types of transient connections have been shown to exist between the auditory and visual cortex in kittens (Innocenti & Clarke, 1984). In the primate brain, transient connections apparently exist for several years after birth (Kennedy & Dehay, 1993). Based on the existence of such transient, intersensory connections, Stein, Meredith, and Wallace (1994) suggested that from an anatomical perspective, the fetal and newborn brains of some animals are more multisensory than when they become mature. Maurer (1993) went so far as to suggest that human neonates are synesthetes and that because of this fact, they actually confuse sensations in different sensory modalities. She ascribed this state of neonatal synesthesia in part to the presence of transient intersensory connections in the neonatal brain. Tees (1994), however, maintained that there is no evidence to suggest that these transient projections exist in human infants or that they are involved in the intersensory functions so far observed in infants. Until more direct evidence is obtained in the human fetus and infant, it will be impossible to tell whether transient connections do exist in humans during early development and whether they in some way lay the groundwork for the eventual development of stable, mature forms of intersensory organization.

Regardless of whether transient connections play a role in intersensory development, there is little doubt that experience plays an important role in the development of intersensory connections at the anatomical level. For example, Knudsen and Knudsen (1985) showed that the correction of auditory localization errors resulting from the insertion of an earplug into one ear of young barn owls was critically dependent on the visual spatial cues that were available at the same time. Furthermore, Knudsen (1985) demonstrated that the spatial tuning of the auditory and visual maps in the bimodal tectal units of the barn owl became misaligned following removal of the earplug, but as the animal's behavioral localization errors diminished, the neural maps became aligned again. Similar results have been reported by King and Carlile (1993), who found that ferrets deprived of visual experience during early development showed abnormal topography and precision in the spatial tuning of individual acoustically tuned neurons in the superior colliculus resulting in the misalignment of the auditory and visual spatial maps.

Recently, Wallace and Stein (1997) have reported on single cell responses in the deep layer neurons of the superior colliculus in kittens between postnatal Days 3 and 135. They found that there are major developmental changes in the way these cells respond to multimodal inputs. The primary functions of 75% of these cells in the adult cat are to integrate visual, auditory, and somatosensory inputs and to provide the neural substrate for spatially directed action. A unique feature of these neurons is that their response to multimodal inputs is far greater than their response to unimodal inputs. No multimodal neurons were found during the first 10 days of postnatal life, and it was not until 12 days after birth that the first type of multisensory neurons appeared. These nascent multimodal neurons responded only to concurrent somatosensory and auditory stimulation. Not until 20 days after birth were multisensory neurons that responded to visual stimulation found. Even when multisensory neurons first began to appear, their response properties were largely immature; they exhibited weak responses to sensory stimuli and had long response latencies, large receptive fields, and poorly developed response selectivities. Moreover, when these multisensory neurons first began to appear, they did not produce the kind of response enhancement normally found in the adult consisting of much more vigorous responses to multimodal, spatially coincident inputs than to unimodal ones and of response depression to spatially disparate stimulation. It was not until 28 days after birth that some of the multisensory neurons began to integrate combinations of multimodal cues and exhibited response enhancement when these cues were spatially coincident and response depression when the cues were spatially disparate. Even at this age, however, the number of multisensory neurons responding in an adultlike fashion was still low and increased gradually during the following 2 months.

Wallace and Stein's (1997) findings indicate that the neural substrate for intersensory spatial integration is immature and not fully developed in early infancy. Of course, it is not clear how these findings might apply to the human infant because there are vast differences between the kitten and the human infant in terms of both the very different ecological pressures that each species has to contend with and the structural and functional status of the sensory systems at birth in each species. Nonetheless, because evolution tends to be conservative, it is likely that some of the features of intersensory neural organization observed in the kitten have some parallels in human development, and it is probably safe to assume that the development of these neural structures follows a rather protracted course in human development.

## Responsiveness to Intersensory Temporal Relations: A Developmental Model

Although there is no longer any question that infants can perceive intersensory relations in general and temporal relations in particular, most of the research to date on infants' intersensory perceptual capabilities has been concerned with demonstrating the existence of such abilities. In the words of Smith (1991), until now investigators have been asking the "what" question, but as is evident from the earlier review of the evidence, a sufficiently large body of empirical findings has accumulated by now that it is possible to begin to ask the "how" question. In other words, it is now possible to begin to specify the processes underlying the developmental changes in infants' responsiveness to intersensory temporal relations.

With this goal in mind, I propose a preliminary model. The model offers a taxonomy of intersensory temporal equivalence relations and proposes that different psychological processes underlie responsiveness to them. The model is based on three related premises: (a) The development of responsiveness to different kinds of intersensory temporal equivalence occurs in a sequential, hierarchical manner; (b) the development of later emerging temporal processing skills is dependent on the development of earlier emerging ones; and (c) as development progresses, infants become capable of processing increasingly more complex forms of intersensory temporal equivalence. The assumption that intersensory perception of temporal equivalence is built up over developmental time in a hierarchically dependent fashion makes this a constructivist type of model and is based on the notion that an understanding of the earliest determinants of multisensory temporal experience can best be achieved by breaking that experience up into its subcomponents.

The theoretical perspective behind the model has a good deal in common with the Gibsonian view of the development of intersensory perception in that it too considers differentiation and increasing responsiveness to greater complexity to be important. It differs from the Gibsonian view, however, in three important respects. First, whereas the Gibsonian view holds that perception is amodal right from birth, the current view does not make such an assumption. Second, the current view considers development as a system of epigenetic interactions where structural and functional limitations are seen as advantageous. Third, the current view considers the development of intersensory perception to result both from the coaction of developmental differentiation and developmental integration and from the interaction of factors that are intrinsic and extrinsic to the organism.

The model makes no a priori assumptions regarding the time of developmental emergence of responsiveness to a specific intersensory relation. Rather, it attempts to specify the conditions that lead to the emergence of a particular intersensory perceptual capacity once it is identified. Whether an infant can or cannot perceive a given intersensory relation is presumed to be due to any number of factors, including the relative immaturity of neural structures, a relative lack of developmental experience, the absence of essential unimodal processing skills, and so on. In its search for the conditions necessary for the emergence of successful intersensory integration, the current view relies on a convergent-operations approach that examines the question of intersensory perception at multiple levels of organization and across different species (Lewkowicz & Lickliter, 1994b; Lickliter & Lewkowicz, 1995).

The currently available evidence indicates that infants become sensitive to synchrony-based A-V relations by the 1st month of life, to duration/synchrony-based A-V relations sometime between the 3rd and the 6th month of life, and to rate/synchrony A-V relations by the 10th month of life. Furthermore, intersensory temporal synchrony appears to play a key role in infants' intersensory response because when it is absent, infants do not respond to duration- and rate-based intersensory relations. On the basis of this core set of facts, I propose that the developmental emergence of the ability to detect the four types of intersensory temporal relations occurs in the sequential, hierarchic fashion depicted in Figure 3. The series of increasingly larger and overlapping

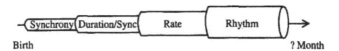

Birth                                                                    ? Month

**Figure 3:** Schematic representation of the developmental emergence of responsiveness to the four types of intersensory temporal relations

pipes is meant to capture the key developmental principle that the emergence of responsiveness to a given temporal relation is dependent on the emergence of responsiveness to a prior and different intersensory temporal relation. This means that once infants become capable of responding to a given intersensory temporal relation, they can rely on it to "discover" the next and more complex one. Thus, for example, the model explicitly assumes that the discovery of duration as a temporal basis for intersensory equivalence depends on the fact that heteromodal inputs are usually temporally contiguous in their onsets and offsets and that this onset/offset synchrony makes it possible for infants to discover the duration-based relation. Only sometime later in development is duration differentiated as an independent intersensory temporal attribute, and that is when response to duration-based intersensory equivalence can be made without relying on synchrony. Finally, as can be seen in Figure 3, the model assumes that responsiveness to complex temporal structure, such as that inherent in a rhythmic sequence, is not expected to emerge until the infant first perceptually differentiates the other three intersensory temporal relations. This last prediction is based on a number of a priori processing constraints rather than on empirical evidence because such evidence is not available at this time.

## The Possible Role of the ITCW in Intersensory Temporal Integration

One basic assumption of the model is that the ITCW provides an initial basis for the integration of the audible and visible features of multimodally specified events. Specifically, if the audible and visible components of an event fall inside the ITCW they are perceived as belonging together. If, however, one of them falls outside the window, they are perceived as belonging to different events. Based on this assumption, the ITCW helps explain responsiveness to rate-based intersensory equivalence. For example, let us assume that an infant sees and hears a bouncing ball. If the ball bounces at a rate that has a longer cycle time than the infant's ITCW (i.e., if the rate at which the ball bounces is lower than 3 Hz), the infant does not have to detect the specific temporal rate of each of the components. That is, given a 350-ms wide ITCW, the infant should be able to detect the intersensory equivalence of the audible and visible components of the bouncing ball on the basis of synchrony alone. This idea is illustrated in the top part of Figure 4, which shows in schematic

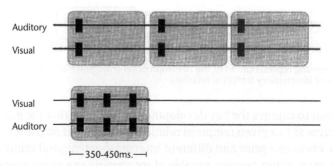

**Figure 4:** The effect of the intersensory temporal contiguity window (ITCW) on the integration of the auditory and visual components of an auditory–visual event. The gray rectangle represents the ITCW.

form the temporal distribution of this kind of A-V event. If the ball bounces at a rate of approximately 2 Hz, the infant should perceive the audible and visible attributes of the ball as belonging together. If, however, the ball bounces at a higher rate (see the bottom part of Figure 4), the infant may no longer be able to integrate the audible and visible attributes of the ball as a unified event on the basis of synchrony alone because each occurrence of the audible and visible components of the event falls within the same ITCW and is too close to the occurrence of the next set of audible and visible components. It is as if each discrete bounce specified by its audible and visible attributes is perceptually "smeared" from the infant's standpoint.

Because the faster bounce of the ball depicted in the bottom part of Figure 4 can no longer be processed in terms of temporal synchrony alone, other temporal attributes of the event have to be processed. Among these are the specific rate at which the audible and visible components occur and whether their rate is the same or different. The evidence already reviewed shows that infants respond to unimodal rate differences, making it more likely that their failure to respond to intersensory rate equivalence may be due to other reasons. One such reason could be that infants cannot determine the specific rate of a given event in each modality. As a result of this inability, they may not be able to determine whether the temporal rates of the audible and visible components are the same or different. Alternatively, it could be that infants, although able to detect the temporal rate of the audible and visible components, may be unable to detect their equivalence.

The model also accounts well for the results from the duration/ synchrony matching studies and for the earlier emergence of duration/synchrony-based intersensory matching. It predicts that the easiest duration/synchrony-based intersensory matches should be those involving durations that are longer than the ITCW. In the studies of intersensory matching of duration/synchrony (Lewkowicz, 1986), I found that 6- and 8-month-old infants made intersensory matches on the basis of duration/synchrony. This was the case when infants

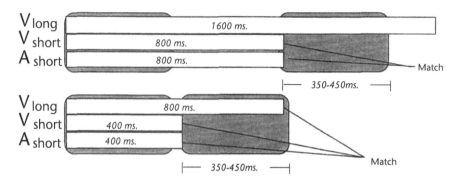

**Figure 5:** The effect of the intersensory temporal contiguity window (ITCW) on intersensory matching of duration. The gray rectangle represents the ITCW.

were presented with the 400–1,600-ms and the 800–1,600-ms pair of stimuli. In contrast, I found no intersensory matching when infants were presented with the 400–800-ms pair. Figure 5 shows how the model might account for the differential effects. In the case of successful matching, the top part of Figure 5 shows that the matching may be performed on the basis of the offset of the stimuli in the two modalities. If it is assumed that the ITCW that is critical for intersensory matching begins with the offset of the short auditory and the short visual stimulus and continues for between 350 and 450 ms, these two stimuli are perceived as belonging together because they fall within the same ITCW. In contrast, the long visual stimulus is not perceived as belonging together with the short auditory stimulus because it continues outside the ITCW. Similarly, the bottom part of Figure 5 shows why matching was not possible in the case of the 400–800-ms pair. The offsets of the short and the long visual stimuli occurred within the same ITCW in which the offset of the auditory stimulus occurred, and, as a result, the infant had no basis for distinguishing between the two visual stimuli in relation to the auditory stimulus. The important point to note here is that the onsets and offsets of the stimuli in each modality provide the critical information regarding intersensory correspondence. If that is the case, then it is likely that the onset of the three stimuli in Figure 5 also causes the start of an ITCW that runs for 350–450 ms. This ITCW does not, however, help to distinguish between the three stimuli as all three begin at the same time and do not have an offset at the end of the window.

In sum, the foundational nature of intersensory temporal synchrony and the ability of the ITCW to account for intersensory integration on the basis of temporal synchrony provide an initial basis for the sequential emergence of responsiveness to what appear to be qualitatively different multimodal temporal features of the world. The ITCW may reflect some basic underlying periodicity of the nervous system that is postulated to be the product of the continuous coaction of the nervous system and experience during the organism's prenatal and postnatal development. The periodicity appears to give rise to a variety of heretofore seemingly disparate phenomena and provides a unifying principle for understanding the developmental changes observed in infants' intersensory responsiveness to temporally distributed multimodal events.

## Differential Informational Complexity

Some might argue that the elementaristic approach of breaking down the organizational structure of the temporal flow of multimodal information into its subcomponents (e.g., temporal synchrony, duration, rate, and rhythm) is not useful in explaining the psychological effects of temporal experiences (Friedman, 1990). The current theoretical position runs counter to this view and holds that an elementaristic approach is useful, and perhaps essential, to understanding the development of intersensory temporal perception and its underlying processes. Furthermore, the current position assumes that the subcomponents of multimodal temporal experience represent different levels of informational complexity and that this is the principal reason why responsiveness to each emerges at different times in development and in the order depicted in Figure 3.

*Intersensory temporal synchrony.* The basic assumptions of the model are that responsiveness to intersensory temporal synchrony emerges first in development and that its developmental primacy lays the foundation for the development of responsiveness to the other three types of intersensory temporal relations. Furthermore, the model assumes that the perception of the concurrent occurrence of two events is relatively simple both because it does not require complex processing skills and because it can be performed relatively quickly.

*Duration.* In contrast to the perception of intersensory temporal synchrony, the perception of duration-based intersensory equivalence requires that an infant detect the temporal extent of each heteromodal component making up a compound stimulus. It is assumed that an infant, when faced with a temporally extended multimodal event, takes longer to perceive the temporal extent of each of the components and their relation than to perceive the temporal synchrony of the heteromodal components. Developmentally, the perception of intersensory duration equivalence is hypothesized as initially depending on the concurrent occurrence of the heteromodal components of an A-V event. Eventually, however, as perceptual experience with temporally organized events increases and accumulates, the perception of duration-based intersensory equivalence becomes independent of temporal synchrony, and the heteromodal components of an A-V compound stimulus no longer have to occur at the same time to be perceived as equivalent.

*Temporal rate.* When a multimodal event occurs repeatedly over time, it can do so in either a regular or an irregular fashion. Martin (1972) refers to the first kind of temporal structure as concatenated (i.e., successive) and to the second as rhythmic. Although the property of temporal structure has traditionally been associated with rhythmically organized stimulus sequences, there is no reason why the concept of temporal structure cannot include concatenated sequences as well. On the one hand, a concatenated sequence represents the simplest case of a temporal pattern. On the other hand, a concatenated temporal sequence is qualitatively different from a rhythmic sequence because the former is made up of equal interelement intervals whereas the latter is not. As a result, a concatenated sequence is mainly characterized by local (adjacent) dependencies that do not lead to the formation of a holistic, hierarchically organized temporal structure. The absence of a hierarchically organized temporal structure places lower processing demands on the infant.

Figure 6 shows a typical multimodal concatenated sequence of stimulation. As can be seen, this kind of sequence can be quantified in terms of the number of elements occurring over a given period of time and is usually expressed in terms of a specific temporal rate. Psychologically, a given physical temporal rate is usually experienced as a certain speed of stimulation. In a formal sense, the nature of a multimodal concatenated sequence is determined by at least three different properties. First, as noted above, the interelement durations of a concatenated sequence are isochronous (Fraisse, 1982b), meaning that the elements of the sequences are separated by a single, specific duration. The faster the sequence, the shorter the interelement durations. Second, the elements of a concatenated sequence are, by definition, ordered in time. This becomes particularly important when the elements making up a concatenated sequence are different (e.g., three different people producing three different sounds in sequence). Third, under normal conditions, the heteromodal components of multimodal concatenated sequences are temporally synchronous (e.g., the lips move in synchrony with the sound whenever each person speaks). A complete understanding of infants' perceptual response to concatenated temporal sequences requires an examination of how each of

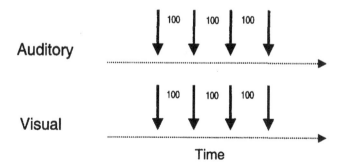

**Figure 6:** Schematic representation of an auditory–visual concatenated sequence. The numbers indicate the interelement intervals in milliseconds.

these three properties contributes to the perception of multimodally specified temporal rate. Results from such an examination would provide much-needed clarification of the inconsistent findings reviewed earlier on infants' response to multimodal rate.

The fact that isochrony, temporal order, and temporal synchrony each contribute to an event's specific rate and intersensory integrity makes the perception of rate-based intersensory relations more complicated than the perception of synchrony- or duration-based relations. In addition, these three properties and the need to process them to perceive intersensory equivalence most likely require even more extended exposure to the information than that required for the perception of synchrony- and duration-based intersensory relations. That is, when faced with a multimodal concatenated sequence, an infant must determine whether the heteromodal components are temporally contiguous. If they are, the infant must perceptually extract the specific temporal rate of each heteromodal component, determine the temporal order of the elements comprising the sequence in each modality (if they are different), determine if the temporal ordering is the same in each modality, and determine if the rate of each component is the same or different. Whether the infant does this in a parallel or serial fashion is not clear at this point, but the assumption that more extended exposure is needed implies that the discovery of the temporal properties of a concatenated sequence may occur serially. As in the case of duration, temporal synchrony plays a pivotal role in the case of rate in early development because it provides infants with the first entree into the processing of the intersensory temporal relation. As development progresses, however, the influence of temporal synchrony is presumed to wane and the child becomes capable of detecting intersensory temporal rate relations without the aid of temporal synchrony.

*Rhythm.* Figure 7 shows a typical rhythmic sequence. According to Martin (1972), the unique property of this, as well as all, rhythmic sequences is that it is characterized by *relative timing.* The property of relative timing first means that the interelement intervals of a rhythmic sequence are all related to each other and that this makes it possible to predict the length of the others. Second, the property of relative timing imposes on rhythmic sequences the perceptual quality of grouping, which means that a change in one interelement interval can lead to a perceptual reorganization of the entire sequence (Handel, 1989). Finally, the property of relative timing confers on rhythmic sequences the perceptual quality of relative temporal order such that the temporal locus of a specific element of a rhythmic sequence is determined relative to the locus of all the other elements in the sequence regardless of whether they are adjacent to it or not. As a result of all of these properties, the perception of rhythm-based intersensory equivalence is more complicated than the perception of intersensory equivalence based on the other three types of intersensory temporal relations.

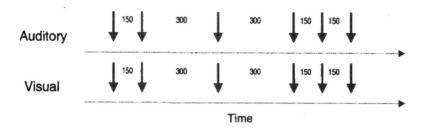

**Figure 7:** Schematic representation of an auditory–visual rhythmic sequence. The numbers indicate the interelement intervals in milliseconds.

To perceive the intersensory equivalence of an audibly and visibly specified rhythmic structure, the current model requires that the infant first detect the intersensory onset and offset synchronies of the individual elements comprising the multimodal rhythmic sequence. Indeed, Bahrick and Lickliter (in press) recently have found that 5-month-old infants did not discriminate between two different bimodal rhythms when the A and V components making up these rhythms were out of synchrony, but that they did discriminate between these rhythms when the components were in synchrony. Synchrony itself, however, is obviously not sufficient for the perception of the other, embedded properties of a rhythmic sequence such as the durations of each of the individual elements, the durations of the interelement intervals, the temporal order of the elements, and the overall rhythmic structure resulting from the relative timing of the elements comprising the sequence. Because the rhythmic structure presents the infant with the most complex temporal information and the most complex intersensory relations, it is likely that its perception would demand more processing time than the perception of the other three types of intersensory relations.

## Advantage of Model

The kind of process-oriented approach espoused by the current model offers some clear advantages over the direct, amodal perception approach. It specifies what steps might be involved in the perception of a given intersensory temporal relation and can generate empirically testable hypotheses. Its advantage is that in cases of a failure to perform intersensory integration, it does not merely assume that the infant has not yet perceptually differentiated that specific amodal invariant. Rather, by specifying what processes might be involved in the perception of that particular intersensory relation, it provides the investigator with specific processes that might be deficient.

## Developmental Changes in the ITCW, Its Effects on Perception, and Possible Qualifications

As was shown earlier, the ITCW narrows with development from an initial width of approximately 350 ms in infancy to the ultimate width of approximately 80 ms in adulthood. It might be argued that part of the reason that infants have difficulty making rate-based intersensory matches is because the ITCW is too wide and that the eventual emergence of such a matching ability is due to the narrowing of the ITCW. This argument assumes that all rate-based matches are, in reality, synchrony-based matches. This might be the case given an ITCW of 80 ms because the maximum temporal rate that an observer would be able to match purely on the basis of synchrony would be 12.5 Hz. The problem with this explanation is that even though this rate is well within the temporal rate range that adults are able to match across modalities (Myers et al., 1981), the ITCW is not likely to narrow this rapidly during infancy. Furthermore, it was argued earlier that responsiveness to temporal extent eventually becomes independent of temporal synchrony relations. The same must be true for rate-based relations.

The problem of detecting intersensory relations purely on the basis of temporal synchrony is particularly serious for the perception of rhythm-based intersensory equivalence. The periodicity of each individual element, and thus its local ITCW, is too short for integration to occur purely on the basis of temporal synchrony. Therefore, other processes must operate to permit the perception of rhythmic structure and the integration of that structure across modalities. This suggests that the role that temporal synchrony plays during development changes from a major and foundational one in the beginning to a supportive and secondary one later. Thus, I propose that when the ability to detect intermodal relations first emerges, it is performed solely on the basis of temporal synchrony and that all the higher level, embedded temporal relations are ignored. With development, perceptual differentiation, and experience, however, temporal synchrony enables infants to begin to notice temporal extent and permits the emergence of duration-based intersensory integration. With further development, differentiation, and experience, infants begin to acquire the capacity to detect rate-based intersensory relations, and at this point, the influence of intersensory temporal synchrony on perception begins to wane. It wanes even further when the ability to perceive intersensory rhythmic relations emerges. Although, as in the case of duration and rate, the ITCW may govern the integration of the heteromodal attributes of each individual element of the sequence, it is the more complex, higher level, organizational features that take over and begin to dominate responsiveness. In sum, the current model proposes that the ITCW lays the developmental foundation for the perception of intersensory temporal relations but that once infants perceptually master such basic relations, temporal synchrony takes on a secondary though still important role.

The developmental scenario just outlined is admittedly neat and orderly in that it considers only what happens when infants are faced with one of the intersensory temporal relations at a given age. What happens, however, when infants are faced with higher level aspects of embedded temporal structure and have not as yet developed the ability to respond to them? One possible answer to this question is suggested by the foregoing model – they simply ignore these complex, embedded features and respond only to the information in terms of its lower level temporal properties. This is similar in principle to other constructivist information-processing views of development (Cohen, Amsel, Redford, & Casasola, 1998), which allow for the possibility that infants resort to developmentally earlier types of processing when faced with events that demand processing beyond their current capability. An alternative possible answer is that the higher level, embedded features may confuse or distract the infant from responding to the lower level features altogether. This is suggested by findings from studies in my laboratory of infants' response to the audible and visible attributes of talking faces (Lewkowicz, 1996a, 1998). In one study, infants were habituated to a videotaped display of a person uttering a continuous prepared text and were then given three types of test trials: an auditory test trial during which they heard another person saying something new but saw the familiar person, a visual test trial during which they saw a new person mouthing a new text but heard the familiar person uttering the familiar text, and a bimodal test trial during which they saw and heard a new person uttering a new text. Despite the fact that the temporal synchrony between the auditory and visual components was disrupted in the auditory and visual test trials, infants even as old as 8 months did not respond to this disruption. Likewise, in more recent studies (Lewkowicz, in press) involving the presentation of isolated syllables, infants as old as 6 months did not respond to one of the unimodal changes and thus to the disruption of synchrony. It seems, however, that responsiveness to temporal synchrony relations interacts with and is affected by other concurrent features of stimulation. This is suggested by the finding that when the stimulation was made more "relevant" by having the person speak in an infant-directed manner or by having the person sing, infants did respond to the changes in the unimodal test trials during which the synchrony relation was disrupted (Lewkowicz, 1996a, 1998). Moreover, in an experiment where responsiveness to face/voice asynchrony was tested directly (Lewkowicz, in press), the age at which infants first responded to it was affected by concurrent featural information specifying the face and voice (i.e., whether the face and voice presented during the test trial were familiar or novel). These findings show clearly that the model put forth in this article eventually must be broadened to incorporate the effects of other nontemporal, modality-specific factors.

## Relationship between the Model and the Epigenetic Systems/Limitations View

Rather than viewing the developing infant as an immature organism, the current model sees the infant as developmentally adapted (Oppenheim, 1981) despite inherent limitations that play a continuing role throughout development. For example, the fact that a young infant's sensory/perceptual capacities are rather primitive is seen not as a disadvantage but as an advantage that initially makes integration of auditory and visual information in terms of their synchronous occurrence in time (and space) possible. As noted earlier, the processing of intersensory temporal synchrony does not require any sophisticated perceptual mechanisms. Nonetheless, it enables infants to discover the basic properties of the world. In other words, this limited ability makes it possible to begin to organize and integrate the temporal multimodal world in a relatively simple and straightforward way without having to determine whether inputs in different modalities are related in more complex ways. The principles of developmental adaptations, timing, and limitations make it possible to understand why responsiveness to the various types of intersensory temporal relations emerges in the order proposed.

Needless to say, in the long run, synchrony-based integration is not sufficient for the perception and construction of a world of unified objects and events because the environment is rich in temporal structure and in much more complex information (J. J. Gibson, 1966, 1979). Given the bidirectional/reciprocal nature of the epigenetic process of development and the importance of contextual factors in shaping behavioral outcome, the structured environment is assumed to "push" the organism and its nervous system into elaborating more complex response and processing mechanisms. These mechanisms then permit the infant to deal with greater perceptual and cognitive complexity.

Although the structured environment pushes infants to develop more sophisticated temporal response skills, the complexity of information and the developmental processing limitations at a given time in development constrain the degree of temporal complexity that infants may be able to perceive. In fact, it is these two opposing forces – (a) the push by the structured environment and (b) the inherent developmental limitations at a given point in development – that together determine the sequential, hierarchic emergence of responsiveness to the different intersensory temporal relations. For example, the interaction of these two processes means that the developmental emergence of skills needed for the perception of duration-based intersensory equivalence depends on the prior development of skills that permit the discovery and perception of intersensory temporal synchrony. The discovery of temporal extent and its relational property is not, however, sufficient for the perception of intersensory relations based on temporal rate. Thus, when the environment pushes infants to detect intersensory temporal rate and when the requisite synchrony- and duration-based intersensory perceptual skills have developed, infants must then acquire new skills that make it possible to process periodic phenomena. Finally, when faced with rhythmically organized events, infants, in addition to being able to perceive temporal synchrony, duration, and rate, must also develop the ability to perceive the intersensory equivalence of rhythmically organized events. What the current model does not consider is how spatial relations contribute to the perception of intersensory unity. As the ventriloquism effect shows, spatial factors play a very important role in integration as well. It is likely that the combination of spatial and temporal intersensory relations is a very powerful but complex one in the development of intersensory development (Lewkowicz, 1999).

## Generalizability of Model to Other Modality Pairs

Can the principles outlined above be applied to other modality pairs? For example, how might they apply to the relationship between vision and touch or to that between audition and touch during early development? It is certainly highly likely that intersensory temporal synchrony provides an important, if not the initial, basis for the integration of inputs in these modality pairs. It is also likely that temporal synchrony continues to serve a facilitative role when infants begin to differentiate the finer aspects of perceptual structure (e.g., texture) and to integrate its properties in vision and touch. In other words, it is probably important for infants to have initially temporally contiguous experiences of the same features of stimulation in both modalities before they become capable of recognizing intersensory equivalence even when inputs into the two modalities do not occur at the same time. As far as the other intersensory temporal relations such as duration, rate, and rhythm are concerned, it is not known at the present time whether and how these types of temporal relations are involved in the integration of information between vision and touch or between audition and touch.

There is virtually no information on responsiveness to temporal relations in either the vision-touch or the audition–touch pair of modalities. For the vision–touch pair, only infants' perception of shape and texture equivalence (Rose, 1994; Rose & Ruff, 1987) has been studied. For the audition–touch pair, researchers have examined infants' response to voice and touch stimulation in interaction contexts (Muir & Hains, 1993), but no researcher has examined infants' response to temporal relations in these two modalities. Needless to say, research on the role of temporal relations in these two modality pairs would provide both important insights and a test of the generality of the proposed model.

Future research designed to address these issues should take into account the fact that each sensory modality is to some extent specialized for the processing of different features of stimulation. For example, vision is relatively better at processing spatial than temporal information, whereas the opposite is true for audition (Kubovy, 1988; Welch & Warren, 1986). Moreover, different sensory modalities are specialized for processing different aspects of a given feature. For example, vision is better than touch in processing the spatial density of texture, but touch is better than vision in processing the roughness of a surface (Lederman et al., 1986). Consequently, when studying responsiveness to a given sensory dimension, the appropriateness of the modality must be taken into account while conducting studies of intersensory integration (Welch & Warren, 1986). Also, it should be remembered that even though the temporal structure of the perceptual array is a fundamental part of our experience, the different modalities respond somewhat differently to such structure, and, thus, it is important to find out how the different modalities use such structure to integrate the information despite sensory specialization. At the same time, of course, there is no doubt that we are capable of overcoming the various specializations of the different sensory modalities and can integrate information across modalities. This suggests that the most reasonable conceptual approach in investigating intersensory integration is one that views intersensory interactions as being the product of specialization and intersensory integration processes working together.

## Relationship of Model to Other Contemporary Theoretical Views

The proposed model is consistent with other theoretical views that assign a foundational role for intersensory temporal synchrony in the development of not only intersensory perceptual organization but also general perception and action systems. For example, temporal synchrony has privileged status in Edelman's (1992) theory of neuronal group selection and is considered to lay the foundation for the development of the neural circuitry underlying all behavior. Likewise, Thelen and Smith (1994) considered temporal synchrony to have privileged status. Their dynamic systems theory of development builds on the principles of Edelman's theory and applies them to the development of perception, cognition, and action in human infants. With specific reference to the multisensory character of the world, Thelen and Smith pointed out that "The experience of any set of objects or events is nearly always multimodal" and that "If the responses to perceptual information of many types are to hang together, then information reaching the different collections of neuronal groups must be correlated." On the basis of this observation, Thelen and Smith then stated the fundamental tenet of their theory: "We believe, with Edelman, that this correlation is the primary link between the mind and the world" (p. 149). To illustrate how intersensory associations provide the foundations for the process of perceptual categorization of a given object and event, they presented the example of a person eating an apple. As the person eats the apple, he or she concurrently experiences sensations in the haptic and olfactory or taste modalities, and this, in turn, leads to similar neural representations in the neuronal groups responsive to the sensations in each modality. The intersensory associations are strengthened and selected because of their perfect temporal association, because of the processes of neural reentry, and because of the vast neural inter-connectivity leading to coherent patterns of firing across different sensory modalities. As a result, the person eating the apple acquires a long-lasting, dynamic association in memory of eating an apple. Thelen and Smith pointed out that the neural connections between the different senses already exist at birth and thus proposed the idea that intersensory integration may be the primitive state and that intersensory linkages do not have to be built. Furthermore, they proposed on the basis of Edelman's principle of selection that the infant's "developmental task may not be to construct, but to select from all the possible multimodal associations those that represent persistent real-life correlations of perception and action in the world" (p. 191).

If the idea that sensory integration is the primitive is accepted at face value and if sensory integration drives development and the infant selects from all possible multimodal associations those that represent persistent real-life correlations of perception and action, this does not require that the infant come into the world capable of detecting all classes of intersensory equivalence. As was argued earlier, some types of intersensory relations are more complex and embedded than others, and, as a result, not all intersensory relations are equally obvious to direct perceptual experience, particularly in an immature organism. Indeed, the current model proposes that some intersensory relations must be experienced, perceptually differentiated, and learned before they can be used for meaningful interaction with the world. Furthermore, sensitivity to the time-locked correlation of multimodal information may be sufficient for the perceptual categorization of some aspects of the multimodal world (e.g., intensity), but it is not sufficient for the categorization of other aspects. For example, infants do not associate certain modality-specific attributes of objects and events (e.g., color, shape, pitch) until quite late in infancy (Bahrick, 1994) even though these types of attributes are experienced in a time-locked fashion from the beginning. Furthermore, the time-locked correlation of multimodal information is not sufficient for perceptual categorization in some cases because of sensory salience hierarchies. Thus, when the concurrent attributes in different sensory modalities do not elicit attention equally well, infants may either (a) not attend to their time-locked relationship and instead respond to the information in one modality only or (b) respond to the information in one modality more than to the information in the other modality (Lewkowicz, 1988a, 1988b, 1992b). In other words, information in one modality can sometimes block the detection of the intersensory relation even though the heteromodal inputs are time-locked.

Thelen and Smith's (1994) notion that intersensory integration drives perceptual and cognitive development is also problematic in that it both fails to capture the full gamut of intersensory perceptual functioning during early development and endows the infant with a degree of perceptual power that may not be there. Thelen and Smith give the impression that intersensory integrative skills are in place from the very beginning of life. Although the overall assumption of the current model agrees with Thelen and Smith's view that infants possess some intersensory integration abilities, it differs in its central assumption that different types of intersensory integration abilities emerge at different times in development. Consistent with dynamical systems theory, however, the current model assumes that the emergence of skills for the perception of different types of temporal intersensory relations is based on experience and that the infant's discovery of the various intersensory temporal relations is to a large extent dependent on the specific context within which the infant has to process the information. In terms of the current model, the idea of context is embodied in the notion of the environmental push discussed earlier. Indeed, Thelen and Smith provide an excellent example of the importance of such an experience-based, context-dependent process. Infants who are crawlers appear to possess knowledge about depth in that they avoid it on the visual cliff. At the same time, they do not avoid steep slopes when allowed to traverse them; they plunge headfirst down steep slopes as if they do not understand the consequences of heights and of falling down the slope. Over time, crawlers learn the properties of slopes and no longer attempt to crawl down steep ones. What is interesting about this developmental *décalage* is that the knowledge and understanding of slopes acquired during crawling does not generalize to walking: When these same infants begin to walk, they have to learn the properties of slopes all over again. Thelen and Smith suggest that this is evidence against domain-general knowledge structures and is instead evidence that infants' actions and knowledge are selected dynamically from the context in which they find themselves. In fact, in dynamical systems theory, the role of context is central because it is the immediate here and now that is seen as setting the stage for all behavior and that incorporates the organism's past developmental history. If that is the case, then the fact that 3-month-old infants do not exhibit evidence of duration/synchrony-based intersensory matches but 6-month-old ones do suggests that something inherent in the infants and not the experimental task makes them respond differently. Whereas the experimental context is the same for both age groups, their developmental history is different.

## Conclusions

Theoretical views on the development of intersensory perceptual functions have ranged from those of Piaget (1952) and Birch and Lefford (1963, 1967) that the senses become gradually integrated in development to those of H. Werner (1973), Bower (1974), E. J. Gibson (1969), and Thelen and Smith (1994) that the senses are integrated and unified from birth. On the basis of the evidence reviewed in this article and the general body of research on the development of intersensory functions (Lewkowicz & Lickliter, 1994a), the current consensus is that intersensory perceptual abilities are present early in human development. Furthermore, the general notion that the infant's world and perceptual experience are largely, if not totally, multimodal in nature is undeniable. What has been lacking until recently in the vast majority of studies of perceptual development has been an acknowledgement of the pervasive role played by the multimodal character of perceptual experience in everyday perception. The danger of this is that scientists may have misrepresented the infant's true perceptual capacities.

Although most major theories of perceptual and cognitive development acknowledge the importance of intersensory perceptual functions, they do not provide specific details about the possible processes that may underlie the development of intersensory perceptual skills in early development. For example, E. J. Gibson's theory proposes that perceptual differentiation makes it possible for infants to pick up increasingly more complex amodal invariants and thus provides a theoretical framework for the study of the development of intersensory perception. It does not, however, specify precisely what processes enable infants to perceive increasingly more complex intersensory relations. The model proposed in this article attempts to partly address this shortcoming. It does so by first positing that the emergence of responsiveness to four fundamental intersensory temporal relations proceeds in a sequential, hierarchical fashion. It then offers a process-oriented approach to explain the sequential, hierarchical development of the perception of intersensory temporal equivalence relations. This approach capitalizes on the general principles of epigenetic systems theory, developmental limitations, and the differential complexity of the four types of intersensory temporal relations. Being situated in an epigenetic systems theoretical framework with its reliance on the concept of coaction and developmental limitations, the model is able to generate empirically testable hypotheses. These hypotheses can address such issues as the contribution of early experience to the subsequent emergence of intersensory temporal perceptual capacities, the role of sensory limitations on responsiveness, and the role of information complexity and processing constraints. The model's comparative, convergent operations approach also calls for studies to be carried out in different species at different points in development to provide insights into both similarities and differences in processes underlying the development of intersensory perceptual skills.

# References

Acredolo, C. (1989). Assessing children's understanding of time, speed and distance interrelations. In I. Levin & D. Zakay (Eds.), *Time and human cognition: A life-span perspective* (pp. 219–257). Amsterdam: North-Holland.

Allen, T. W., Walker, K., Symonds, L., & Marcell, M. (1977). Intrasensory and intersensory perception of temporal sequences during infancy. *Developmental Psychology, 13*, 225–229.

Ashton, R. (1976). Aspects of timing in child development. *Child Development, 47*, 622–626.

Bahrick, L. E. (1983). Infants' perception of substance and temporal synchrony in multimodal events. *Infant Behavior and Development, 6*, 429–451.

Bahrick, L. E. (1988). Intermodal learning in infancy: Learning on the basis of two kinds of invariant relations in audible and visible events. *Child Development, 59*, 197–209.

Bahrick, L. E. (1992). Infants' perceptual differentiation of amodal and modality-specific audio-visual relations. *Journal of Experimental Child Psychology, 53*, 180–199.

Bahrick, L. E. (1994). The development of infants' sensitivity to arbitrary intermodal relations. *Ecological Psychology, 6*, 111–123.

Bahrick, L. E. (1998, April). *Increasing specificity in the development of intermodal perception.* Paper presented at the International Conference on Infant Studies, Atlanta, GA.

Bahrick, L. E., & Lickliter, R. (in press). Intersensory redundancy guides attentional selectivity and perceptual learning in infancy. *Developmental Psychology.*

Bahrick, L. E., & Pickens, J. (1994). Amodal relations: The basis for intermodal perception and learning in infancy. In D. J. Lewkowicz & R. Lickliter (Eds.), *Development of intersensory perception: Comparative perspectives* (pp. 205–233). Hillsdale, NJ: Erlbaum.

Bekoff, A. (1995). Development of motor behavior in chick embryos. In J.-P. Lecanuet, W. P. Fifer, N. A. Krasnegor, & W. P. Smotherman (Eds.), *Fetal development: A psychobiological perspective* (pp. 191–204). Hillsdale, NJ: Erlbaum.

Birch, H. G., & Lefford, A. (1963). Intersensory development in children. *Monographs of the Society for Research in Child Development, 25*, (5, Whole No. 89).

Birch, H. G., & Lefford, A. (1967). Visual differentiation, intersensory integration, and voluntary motor control. *Monographs of the Society for Research in Child Development, 32*(2).

Bourgeois, J. P. (1993). Synaptogenesis in the prefrontal cortex of the macaque. In B. de Boysson-Bardies, S. de Schonen, P. Jusczyk, & J. Morton (Eds.), *Developmental neurocognition: Speech and face processing in the first year of life* (pp. 31–39). Dordrecht, The Netherlands: Kluwer Academic.

Bower, T. G. R. (1974). *Development in infancy.* San Francisco: Freeman.

Bregman, A. S. (1990). *Auditory scene analysis: The perceptual organization of sound.* Cambridge, MA: MIT Press.

Bronson, G. W. (1974). The postnatal growth of visual capacity. *Child Development, 45*, 873–890.

Brooks, P. R., & Berg, W. K. (1979). Do 16-week-old infants anticipate stimulus offset? *Developmental Psychobiology, 12*, 329–334.

Caldwell, D. F., & Werboff, J. (1962, June 29). Classical conditioning in newborn rats. *Science, 136*, 1118–1119.

Calvert, G. A., Brammer, M. J., & Iversen, S. D. (1998). Crossmodal identification. *Trends in Cognitive Sciences, 2*, 247–253.

Canfield, R. L., & Haith, M. M. (1991). Young infants' visual expectations for symmetric and asymmetric stimulus sequences. *Developmental Psychology, 27*, 198–208.

Clifton, R. K. (1974). Heart rate conditioning in the newborn infant. *Journal of Experimental Child Psychology, 18*, 9–21.

Cohen, L. B., Amsel, G., Redford, M. A., & Casasola, M. (1998). The development of infant causal perception. In A. Slater (Ed.), *Perceptual development: Visual, auditory, and speech perception in infancy* (pp. 167–209). Hove, England: Psychology Press.

Damasio, A. R. (1989). Time-locked multiregional retroactivation: A systems-level proposal for the neural substrates of recall and recognition. *Cognition, 33*, 25–62.

Davies, M. C., & Berg, W. K. (1983, April). *Developmental changes in mechanisms infants use to mark time.* Paper presented at the meeting of the Society for Research in Child Development, Detroit, MI.

Demany, L., McKenzie, B., & Vurpillot, E. (1977, April 21). Rhythm perception in early infancy. *Nature, 266,* 718–719.

Dixon, N. F., & Spitz, L. T. (1980). The detection of auditory visual desynchrony. *Perception, 9,* 719–721.

Dodd, B. (1977). The role of vision in the perception of speech. *Perception, 6,* 31–40.

Donohue, R. L., & Berg, W. K. (1991). Infant heart-rate responses to temporally predictable and unpredictable events. *Developmental Psychology, 27,* 59–66.

Dougherty, T. M., & Haith, M. M. (1997). Infant expectations and reaction time as predictors of childhood speed of processing and IQ. *Developmental Psychology, 33,* 146–155.

Edelman, G. M. (1992). *Bright air, brilliant fire.* New York: Basic Books.

Ettlinger, G., & Wilson, W. A. (1990). Cross-modal performance: behavioural processes, phylogenetic considerations and neural mechanisms. *Behavioural Brain Research, 40,* 169–192.

Fraisse, P. (1982a). The adaptation of the child to time. In W. J. Friedman (Ed.), *The developmental psychology of time* (pp. 113–140). New York: Academic Press.

Fraisse, P. (1982b). Rhythm and tempo. In D. Deutsch (Ed.), *The psychology of music* (pp. 149–180). New York: Academic Press.

Freides, D. (1974). Human information processing and sensory modality: Cross-modal functions, information complexity, memory, and deficit. *Psychological Bulletin, 81,* 284–310.

Friedman, W. J. (1990). *About time: Inventing the fourth dimension.* Cambridge, MA: MIT Press.

Frost, D. O. (1990). Sensory processing by novel, experimentally induced cross-modal circuits. *Annals of the New York Academy of Sciences, 608,* 92–112.

Gardner, J. M., & Karmel, B. Z. (1995). Development of arousal-modulated visual preferences in early infancy. *Developmental Psychology, 31,* 473–482.

Gardner, J. M., Lewkowicz, D. J., Rose, S. A., & Karmel, B. Z. (1986). Effects of visual and auditory stimulation on subsequent visual preferences in neonates. *International Journal of Behavioral Development, 9,* 251–263.

Garey, L. J., & Yan, X. X. (1993). Maturation of synapses and GABA-immunoreactive neurons in the perinatal human visual cortex. In B. de Boysson-Bardies, S. de Schonen, P. Jusczyk, & J. Morton (Eds.), *Developmental neurocognition: Speech and face processing in the first year of life* (pp. 41–49). Dordrecht, The Netherlands: Kluwer Academic.

Gebhard, J. W., & Mowbray, G. H. (1959). On discriminating the rate of visual flicker and auditory flutter. *American Journal of Psychology, 72,* 521–528.

Gibson, E. J. (1969). *Principles of perceptual learning and development.* New York: Appleton.

Gibson, E. J. (1982). The concept of affordances in development: The renascence of functionalism. In W. A. Collins (Ed.), *The concept of development: The Minnesota Symposia on Child Psychology* (pp. 55–81). Hillsdale, NJ: Erlbaum.

Gibson, E. J. (1984). Perceptual development from the ecological approach. In M. E. Lamb, A. L. Brown, & B. Rogoff (Eds.), *Advances in developmental psychology* (pp. 243–286). Hillsdale, NJ: Erlbaum.

Gibson, E. J. (1988). Exploratory behavior in the development of perceiving, acting, and the acquiring of knowledge. *Annual Review of Psychology, 39,* 1–41.

Gibson, J. J. (1966). *The senses considered as perceptual systems.* Boston: Houghton Mifflin.

Gibson, J. J. (1979). *An ecological approach to perception.* Boston: Houghton Mifflin.

Gogate, L. J., & Bahrick, L. E. (1998). Intersensory redundancy facilitates learning of arbitrary relations between vowel sounds and objects in seven-month-old infants. *Journal of Experimental Child Psychology, 69,* 133–149.

Gottfried, A. W., Rose, S. A., & Bridger, W. H. (1977). Cross-modal transfer in human infants. *Child Development, 48,* 118–123.

Gottlieb, G. (1971). Ontogenesis of sensory function in birds and mammals. In E. Tobach, L. R. Aronson, & E. Shaw (Eds.), *The biopsychology of development* (pp. 67–128). New York: Academic Press.

Gottlieb, G. (1991). Experiential canalization of behavioral development: Theory. *Developmental Psychology, 27,* 35–39.

Gottlieb, G., Tomlinson, W. T., & Radell, P. L. (1989). Developmental intersensory interference: Premature visual experience suppresses auditory learning in ducklings. *Infant Behavior and Development, 12,* 1–12.

Greenough, W. T., & Juraska, J. M. (1979). Experience-induced changes in brain fine structure: Their behavioral implications. In M. E. Han, C. Jensen, & B. C. Dudek (Eds.), *Development and evolution of brain size* (pp. 296–320). New York: Academic Press.

Handel, S. (1989). *Listening: An introduction to the perception of auditory events.* Cambridge, MA: MIT Press.

Handel, S., & Buffardi, L. (1969). Using several modalities to perceive one temporal pattern. *Quarterly Journal of Experimental Psychology, 21,* 256–266.

Humphrey, K., & Tees, R. C. (1980). Auditory–visual coordination in infancy: Some limitations of the preference methodology. *Bulletin of the Psychonomic Society, 16,* 213–216.

Ingram, E. M. (1978). The interstimulus interval in classical conditioning of young infants. *Developmental Psychobiology, 11,* 419–426.

Innocenti, G. M., & Clarke, S. (1984). Bilateral transitory projection to visual areas from auditory cortex in kittens. *Developmental Brain Research, 14,* 143–148.

Jack, C. E., & Thurlow, W. R. (1973). Effects of degree of visual association and angle of displacement on the "ventriloquism" effect. *Perceptual and Motor Skills, 37,* 967–979.

Johnston, T. D. (1987). The persistence of dichotomies in the study of behavioral development. *Developmental Review, 7,* 149–182.

Jones, B. (1981). The developmental significance of cross-modal matching. In R. D. Walk & J. H. L. Pick (Eds.), *Intersensory perception and sensory integration* (pp. 109–136). New York: Plenum.

Kaplan, P., Fox, K., Scheuneman, D., & Jenkins, L. (1991). Cross-modal facilitation of infant visual fixation: Temporal and intensity effects. *Infant Behavior and Development, 14,* 83–109.

Karmel, B. Z., Gardner, J. M., & Magnano, C. L. (1991). Attention and arousal in early infancy. In M. J. S. Weiss & P. R. Zelazo (Eds.), *Newborn attention: Biological constraints and the influence of experience* (pp. 339–376). Norwood, NJ: Ablex.

Karmel, B. Z., Gardner, J. M., Zappulla, R. A., Magnano, C. L., & Brown, E. G. (1988). Brain-stem auditory evoked responses as indicators of early brain insult. *Electroencephalography and Clinical Neurophysiology, 71,* 429–442.

Karmel, B. Z., Lester, M. L., McCarvill, S. L., Brown, P., & Hofmann, M. J. (1977). Correlation of infants' brain behavior response to temporal changes in visual stimulation. *Psychophysiology, 14,* 134–142.

Kaufmann, F., Stucki, M., & Kaufmann-Hayoz, R. (1985). Development of infants' sensitivity for slow and rapid motions. *Infant Behavior and Development, 8,* 89–98.

Kellman, P. J. (1984). Perception of three-dimensional form by human infants. *Perception & Psychophysics, 36,* 353–358.

Kellman, P. J., Spelke, E. S., & Short, K. R. (1986). Infant perception of object unity from translatory motion in depth and vertical translation. *Child Development, 57,* 72–86.

Kennedy, H., & Dehay, C. (1993). The relevance of primate corticogenesis for understanding the emergence of cognitive abilities in man. In B. de Boysson-Bardies, S. de Schonen, P. Jusczyk, & J. Morton (Eds.), *Developmental neurocognition: Speech and face processing in the first year of life* (pp. 17–30). Dordrecht, The Netherlands: Kluwer Academic.

King, A. J., & Carlile, S. (1993). Changes induced in the representation of auditory space in the superior colliculus by rearing ferrets with binocular eyelid suture. *Experimental Brain Research, 94,* 444–455.

Kisilevsky, B. S. (1995). The influence of stimulus and subject variables on human fetal responses to sound and vibration. In J.-P. Lecanuet, W. P. Fifer, N. A. Krasnegor, & W. P. Smotherman (Eds.), *Fetal development: A psychobiological perspective* (pp. 263–278). Hillsdale, NJ: Erlbaum.

Knudsen, E. I. (1985). Experience alters the spatial tuning of auditory units in the optic tectum during a sensitive period in the barn owl. *Journal of Neuroscience, 5,* 3094–3109.

Knudsen, E. I., & Knudsen, P. F. (1985, November 1). Vision guides the adjustment of auditory localization in young barn owls. *Science, 230,* 545–548.

Kubovy, M. (1988). Should we resist the seductiveness of the space: time:: vision: audition analogy? *Journal of Experimental Psychology: Human Perception and Performance, 14,* 318–320.

Kuhl, P. K., & Meltzoff, A. N. (1982, December 10). The bimodal perception of speech in infancy. *Science, 218,* 1138–1140.

Lashley, K. S. (1951). The problem of serial order in behavior. In L. A. Jeffress (Ed.), *Cerebral mechanisms in behavior: The Hixon Symposium* (pp. 112–136). New York: Wiley.

Lecanuet, J.-P., Granier-Deferre, C, & Busnel, M.-C. (1995). Human fetal auditory perception. In J.-P. Lecanuet, W. P. Fifer, N. A. Krasnegor, & W. P. Smotherman (Eds.), *Fetal development: A psychobiological perspective* (pp. 239–262). Hillsdale, NJ: Erlbaum.

Lederman, S. J., Thorne, G., & Jones, B. (1986). Perception of texture by vision and touch: Multidimensionality and intersensory integration. *Journal of Experimental Psychology: Human Perception and Performance, 12,* 169–180.

Lehrman, D. S. (1970). Semantic and conceptual issues in the nature-nurture problem. In L. R. Aronson, D. S. Lehrman, E. Tobach, & J. S. Rosenblatt (Eds.), *Development and evolution of behavior* (pp. 17–52). San Francisco: Freeman.

Lerner, R. M., & Kaufman, M. B. (1985). The concept of development in contextualism. *Developmental Review, 5,* 309–333.

Lester, B. M., Hoffman, J., & Brazelton, T. B. (1985). The rhythmic structure of mother–infant interaction in term and preterm infants. *Child Development, 56,* 15–27.

Levin, I. (1982). The nature and development of time concepts in children: The effects of interfering cues. In W. J. Friedman (Ed.), *The developmental psychology of time* (pp. 47–85). New York: Academic Press.

Lewkowicz, D. J. (1985a). Bisensory response to temporal frequency in 4-month-old infants. *Developmental Psychology, 21,* 306–317.

Lewkowicz, D. J. (1985b). Developmental changes in infants' visual response to temporal frequency. *Developmental Psychology, 21,* 858–865.

Lewkowicz, D. J. (1986). Developmental changes in infants' bisensory response to synchronous durations. *Infant Behavior and Development, 9,* 335–353.

Lewkowicz, D. J. (1988a). Sensory dominance in infants: I. Six-month-old infants' response to auditory–visual compounds. *Developmental Psychology, 24,* 155–171.

Lewkowicz, D. J. (1988b). Sensory dominance in infants: II. Ten-month-old infants' response to auditory–visual compounds. *Developmental Psychology, 24,* 172–182.

Lewkowicz, D. J. (1989). The role of temporal factors in infant behavior and development. In I. Levin & D. Zakay (Eds.), *Time and human cognition: A life-span perspective* (pp. 9–62). Amsterdam: North-Holland.

334 Multisensory Perception

Lewkowicz, D. J. (1991). Development of intersensory functions in human infancy: Auditory/visual interactions. In M. J. S. Weiss & P. R. Zelazo (Eds.), *Newborn attention: Biological constraints and the influence of experience* (pp. 308–338). Norwood, NJ: Ablex.

Lewkowicz, D. J. (1992a). Infants' response to temporally based intersensory equivalence: The effect of synchronous sounds on visual preferences for moving stimuli. *Infant Behavior and Development, 15*, 297–324.

Lewkowicz, D. J. (1992b). Infants' responsiveness to the auditory and visual attributes of a sounding/moving stimulus. *Perception & Psychophysics, 52*, 519–528.

Lewkowicz, D. J. (1994a). Development of intersensory perception in human infants. In D. J. Lewkowicz & R. Lickliter (Eds.), *The development of intersensory perception: Comparative perspectives* (pp. 165–203). Hillsdale, NJ: Erlbaum.

Lewkowicz, D. J. (1994b). Limitations on infants' response to rate-based auditory–visual relations. *Developmental Psychology, 30*, 880–892.

Lewkowicz, D. J. (1994c). Reflections on infants' response to temporally based intersensory equivalence: Response to Spelke (1994). *Infant Behavior and Development, 17*, 289–292.

Lewkowicz, D. J. (1996a). Infants' response to the audible and visible properties of the human face. I: Role of lexical–syntactic content, temporal synchrony, gender, and manner of speech. *Developmental Psychology, 32*, 347–366.

Lewkowicz, D. J. (1996b). Perception of auditory–visual temporal synchrony in human infants. *Journal of Experimental Psychology: Human Perception and Performance, 22*, 1094–1106.

Lewkowicz, D. J. (1998). Infants' response to the audible and visible properties of the human face: U. Discrimination of differences between singing and adult-directed speech. *Developmental Psychobiology, 32*, 261–274.

Lewkowicz, D. J. (1999). The development of temporal and spatial inter-modal perception. In G. Aschersleben, T. Bachman, & J. Müsseler (Eds.), *Cognitive contributions to the perception of spatial and temporal events* (pp. 395–420). Amsterdam: Elsevier.

Lewkowicz, D. J. (in press). Infants' response to the audible and visible properties of the human face: Perception of syllable differences. *Child Development.*

Lewkowicz, D. J., & Lickliter, R. (1994a). *The development of intersensory perception: Comparative perspectives.* Hillsdale, NJ: Erlbaum.

Lewkowicz, D. J., & Lickliter, R. (1994b). Insights into mechanisms of intersensory development: The value of a comparative, convergent-operations approach. In D. J. Lewkowicz & R. Lickliter (Eds.), *The development of intersensory perception: Comparative perspectives* (pp. 403–413). Hillsdale, NJ: Erlbaum.

Lewkowicz, D. J., & Lickliter, R. (1998, April). *The detection of inter-modal rate and synchrony relations in 6- and 8-month-old infants.* Paper presented at the International Conference on Infant Studies, Atlanta, GA.

Lewkowicz, D. J., & Turkewitz, G. (1980). Cross-modal equivalence in early infancy: Auditory–visual intensity matching. *Developmental Psychology, 16*, 597–607.

Lewkowicz, D. J., & Turkewitz, G. (1981). Intersensory interaction in newborns: Modification of visual preferences following exposure to sound. *Child Development, 52*, 827–832.

Lickliter, R., & Hellewell, T. B. (1992). Contextual determinants of auditory learning in bobwhite quail embryos and hatchlings. *Developmental Psychobiology, 25*, 17–31.

Lickliter, R., & Lewkowicz, D. J. (1995). Intersensory experience and early perceptual development: Attenuated prenatal sensory stimulation affects postnatal auditory and visual responsiveness in bobwhite quail chicks (*Colinus virginianus*). *Developmental Psychology, 31*, 609–618.

Lockman, J. J., Ashmead, D. H., & Bushnell, E. W. (1984). The development of anticipatory hand orientation during infancy. *Journal of Experimental Child Psychology, 37*, 176–186.

Maier, N. R. F., & Schneirla, T. C. (1964). *Principles of animal psychology.* New York: Dover.

Marks, L. E. (1978). *The unity of the senses.* New York: Academic Press.

Marks, L. E., Hammeal, R. J., & Bornstein, M. H. (1987). Perceiving similarity and comprehending metaphor. *Monographs of the Society for Research in Child Development, 52*(1).

Martin, J. G. (1972). Rhythmic (hierarchical) versus serial structure in speech and other behavior. *Psychological Review, 79,* 487–509.

Massaro, D. W. (1998). *Perceiving talking faces: From speech perception to a behavioral principle.* Cambridge, MA: MIT Press.

Massaro, D. W., Cohen, M. M., & Smeele, P. M. T. (1996). Perception of asynchronous and conflicting visual and auditory speech. *Journal of the Acoustical Society of America, 100,* 1777–1786.

Maurer, D. (1993). Neonatal synesthesia: Implication for the processing of speech and faces. In B. de Boysson-Bardies, S. de Schonen, P. Jusczyk, & J. Morton (Eds.), *Developmental neurocognition: Speech and face processing in the first year of life* (pp. 109–124). Dordrecht, The Netherlands: Kluwer Academic.

McGrath, M., & Summerfield, Q. (1985). Intermodal timing relations and audio-visual speech recognition by normal-hearing adults. *Journal of the Acoustical Society of America, 77,* 678–685.

McGurk, H., & MacDonald, J. (1976, December 23). Hearing lips and seeing voices. *Nature, 264,* 229–239.

Meek, W. H., & Church, R. M. (1982). Abstraction of temporal attributes. *Journal of Experimental Psychology: Animal Behavior Processes, 8,* 226–243.

Mendelson, M. J. (1986). Perception of the temporal pattern of motion in infancy. *Infant Behavior and Development, 9,* 231–243.

Mendelson, M. J., & Ferland, M. B. (1982). Auditory–visual transfer in four-month-old infants. *Child Development, 53,* 1022–1027.

Merzenich, M. M., Allard, T. T., & Jenkins, W. M. (1990). Neural ontogeny of higher brain function: Implications of some recent neuro-physiological findings. In O. Franzn & P. Westman (Eds.), *Information processing in the somatosensory system* (pp. 293–311). London: Macmillan.

Miller, C. L., & Byrne, J. M. (1984). The role of temporal cues in the development of language and communication. In L. Feagans, C. Garvey, & R. Golinkoff (Eds.), *The origins and growth of communication* (pp. 77–101). Norwood, NJ: Ablex.

Miller, E. A. (1972). Interaction of vision and touch in conflict and nonconflict form perception tasks. *Journal of Experimental Psychology, 96,* 114–123.

Morrongiello, B. A. (1984). Auditory temporal pattern perception in 6- and 12-month-old infants. *Developmental Psychology, 20,* 441–448.

Morrongiello, B. A., Fenwick, K. D., & Chance, G. (1998). Crossmodal learning in newborn infants: Inferences about properties of auditory–visual events. *Infant Behavior and Development, 21,* 543–554.

Morrongiello, B. A., & Trehub, S. E. (1987). Age-related changes in auditory temporal perception. *Journal of Experimental Child Psychology, 44,* 413–426.

Morton, J., & Johnson, M. (1991). CONSPEC and CONLERN: A two-process theory of infant face recognition. *Psychological Review, 98,* 164–181.

Muir, D. W., & Hains, S. M. J. (1993). Infant sensitivity to perturbations in adult facial, vocal, tactile, and contingent stimulation during face-to-face interactions. In B. de Boysson-Bardies, S. de Schonen, P. Jusczyk, & J. Morton (Eds.), *Developmental neurocognition: Speech and face processing in the first year of life* (pp. 171–185). Dordrecht, The Netherlands: Kluwer Academic.

**Multisensory Perception**

Myers, A. K., Cotton, B., & Hilp, H. A. (1981). Matching the rate of concurrent tone bursts and light flashes as a function of flash surround luminance. *Perception & Psychophysics, 30*, 33–38.

Oppenheim, R. W. (1981). Ontogenetic adaptations and retrogressive processes in the development of the nervous system and behavior: A neuro-embryological perspective. In K. J. Connolly & H. F. R. Prechtl (Eds.), *Maturation and development: Biological and psychological perspectives* (pp. 73–109). Philadelphia: Lippincott.

Over, R. (1966). An experimentally induced conflict between vision and proprioception. *British Journal of Psychology, 57*, 335–341.

Oyama, S. (1985). *The ontogeny of information*. Cambridge, England: Cambridge University Press.

Phillips, R. D., Wagner, S. H., Fells, C. A., & Lynch, M. (1990). Do infants recognize emotion in facial expressions? Categorical and "metaphorical" evidence. *Infant Behavior and Development, 13*, 71–84.

Piaget, J. (1952). *The origins of intelligence in children*. New York: International Universities Press.

Piaget, J. (1969). *The child's conception of time*. London: Routledge & Kegan.

Piaget, J. (1970). *The child's conception of movement and speed*. London: Routledge & Kegan.

Pickens, J., & Bahrick, L. E. (1995). Infants' discrimination of bimodal events on the basis of rhythm and tempo. *British Journal of Developmental Psychology, 13*, 223–236.

Pickens, J., & Bahrick, L. E. (1997). Do infants perceive invariant tempo and rhythm in auditory–visual events? *Infant Behavior and Development, 20*, 349–357.

Pomerantz, J. R., & Lockhead, G. R. (1991). Perception of structure: An overview. In G. R. Lockhead & J. R. Pomerantz (Eds.), *The perception of structure: Essays in honor of Wendell R. Garner* (pp. 1–20). Washington, DC: American Psychological Association.

Radeau, M. (1994). Auditory–visual spatial interaction and modularity. *Cahiers de Psychologie 13*, 3–51.

Radeau, M., & Bertelson, P. (1977). Adaptation to auditory–visual discordance and ventriloquism in semirealistic situations. *Perception & Psychophysics, 22*, 137–146.

Radeau, M., & Bertelson, P. (1978). Cognitive factors and adaptation to auditory–visual discordance. *Perception & Psychophysics, 23*, 341–343.

Radell, P. L., & Gottlieb, G. (1992). Developmental intersensory interference: Augmented prenatal sensory experience interferes with auditory learning in duck embryos. *Developmental Psychology, 28*, 795–803.

Regal, D. M. (1981). Development of critical flicker frequency in human infants. *Vision Research, 21*, 549–555.

Regan, D. (1989). *Human brain electrophysiology: Evoked potentials and evoked magnetic fields in science and medicine*. New York: Elsevier.

Roberts, S. (1982). Cross-modal use of an internal clock. *Journal of Experimental Psychology: Animal Behavior Processes, 8*, 2–22.

Robertson, S. S., & Bacher, L. F. (1995). Oscillation and chaos in fetal motor activity. In J.-P. Lecanuet, W. P. Fifer, N. A. Krasnegor, & W. P. Smotherman (Eds.), *Fetal development: A psychobiological perspective* (pp. 169–189). Hillsdale, NJ: Erlbaum.

Rock, I. (1965). Adaptation to a minified image. *Psychonomic Science, 2*, 105–106.

Rose, S. A. (1994). From hand to eye: Findings and issues in infant cross-modal transfer. In D. J. Lewkowicz & R. Lickliter (Eds.), *The development of intersensory perception: Comparative perspectives* (pp. 265–284). Hillsdale, NJ: Erlbaum.

Rose, S. A., Gottfried, A. W., & Bridger, W. H. (1981a). Cross-modal transfer and information processing by the sense of touch in infancy. *Developmental Psychology, 17*, 90–98.

Rose, S. A., Gottfried, A. W., & Bridger, W. H. (1981b). Cross-modal transfer in 6-month-old infants. *Developmental Psychology, 17*, 661–669.

Rose, S. A., & Ruff, H. A. (1987). Cross-modal abilities in human infants. In J. Osofsky (Ed.), *Handbook of infant development* (2nd ed., pp. 318–362). New York: Wiley.

Rosenblum, L. D., Schmuckler, M. A., & Johnson, J. A. (1997). The McGurk effect in infants. *Perception & Psychophysics, 59*, 347–357.

Ryan, T. A. (1940). Interrelations of the sensory systems in perception. *Psychological Bulletin, 37*, 659–698.

Sameroff, A. J. (1975). Transactional models in early social relations. *Human Development, 18*, 65–79.

Schaal, B., Orgeur, P., & Rognon, C. (1995). Odor sensing in the human fetus: Anatomical, functional, and chemoecological bases. In J.-P. Lecanuet, W. P. Fifer, N. A. Krasnegor, & W. P. Smotherman (Eds.), *Fetal development: A psychobiological perspective* (pp. 205–237). Hillsdale, NJ: Erlbaum.

Scheibel, A. B. (1993). Dendritic structure and language development. In B. de Boysson-Bardies, S. de Schonen, P. Jusczyk, & J. Morton (Eds.), *Developmental neurocognition: Speech and face processing in the first year of life* (pp. 51–62). Dordrecht, The Netherlands: Kluwer Academic.

Schneirla, T. C. (1957). The concept of development in comparative psychology. In D. B. Harris (Ed.), *The concept of development* (pp. 78–108). Minneapolis: University of Minnesota Press.

Singer, G., & Day, R. H. (1969). Visual capture of haptically judged depth. *Perception & Psychophysics, 5*, 315–316.

Slater, A., & Kirby, R. (1998). Innate and learned perceptual abilities in the newborn infant. *Experimental Brain Research, 123*, 90–94.

Slater, A., Quinn, P. C, Brown, E., & Hayes, R. (1999). Intermodal perception at birth: Intersensory redundancy guides newborn infants' learning of arbitrary auditory–visual pairings. *Developmental Science, 3*, 333–338.

Smith, L. B. (1991). Perceptual structure and developmental process. In G. R. Lockhead & J. R. Pomerantz (Eds.), *The perception of structure: Essays in honor of Wendell R. Garner* (pp. 297–315). Washington, DC: American Psychological Association.

Spelke, E. S. (1976). Infants' intermodal perception of events. *Cognitive Psychology, 8*, 553–560.

Spelke, E. S. (1979). Perceiving bimodally specified events in infancy. *Developmental Psychology, 15*, 626–636.

Spelke, E. S. (1988). Where perceiving ends and thinking begins: The apprehension of objects in infancy. In A. Yonas (Ed.), *Perceptual development in infancy: The Minnesota Symposia on Child Psychology* (Vol. 20, pp. 197–234). Hillsdale, NJ: Erlbaum.

Spelke, E. S. (1994). Preferential looking and intermodal perception in infancy: Comment on Lewkowicz (1992b). *Infant Behavior and Development, 17*, 284–286.

Spelke, E. S., Born, W. S., & Chu, F. (1983). Perception of moving, sounding objects by 4-month-old infants. *Perception, 12*, 719–732.

Stein, B. E., London, N., Wilkinson, L. K., & Price, D. D. (1996). Enhancement of perceived visual intensity by auditory stimuli: A psychophysical analysis. *Journal of Cognitive Neuroscience, 8*, 497–506.

Stein, B. E., & Meredith, M. A. (1990). Multisensory integration: Neural and behavioral solutions for dealing with stimuli from different sensory modalities. *Annals of the New York Academy of Sciences, 608*, 51–70.

Stein, B. E., & Meredith, M. A. (1993). *The merging of the senses.* Cambridge, MA: MIT Press.

Stein, B. E., Meredith, M. A., & Wallace, M. T. (1994). Development and neural basis of multisensory integration. In D. J. Lewkowicz & R. Lickliter (Eds.), *The development of intersensory perception: Comparative perspectives* (pp. 81–105). Hillsdale, NJ: Erlbaum.

Stern, D. N., Beebe, B., Jaffe, J., & Bennet, S. L. (1977). The infant's stimulus world during social interactions: A study of caregiver behaviors with particular reference to repetition and timing. In H. R. Shaffer (Ed.), *Studies in mother–infant interaction* (pp. 177–202). London: Academic Press.

Streri, A. (1987). Tactile discrimination of shape and intermodal transfer in 2- to 3-month-old infants. *British Journal of Developmental Psychology, 5,* 213–220.

Streri, A., & Pecheux, M.-G. (1986). Vision-to-touch and touch-to-vision transfer of form in 5-month-old infants. *British Journal of Developmental Psychology, 4,* 161–167.

Summerfield, A. Q. (1979). Use of visual information in phonetic perception. *Phonetica, 36,* 314–331.

Tees, R. C. (1994). Early stimulation history, the cortex, and intersensory functioning in infrahumans: Space and time. In D. J. Lewkowicz & R. Lickliter (Eds.), *Development of intersensory perception: Comparative perspectives* (pp. 107–131). Hillsdale, NJ: Erlbaum.

Tees, R. C., & Symons, L. A. (1987). Intersensory coordination and the effect of early sensory deprivation. *Developmental Psychobiology, 23,* 497–507.

Thelen, E., & Smith, L. B. (1994). *A dynamic systems approach to the development of cognition and action.* Cambridge, MA: MIT Press.

Trehub, S. E., & Thorpe, L. A. (1989). Infants' perception of rhythm: Categorization of auditory sequences by temporal structure. *Canadian Journal of Psychology, 43,* 217–229.

Turkewitz, G. (1994). Sources of order for intersensory functioning. In D. J. Lewkowicz & R. Lickliter (Eds.), *The development of intersensory perception: Comparative perspectives* (pp. 3–17). Hillsdale, NJ: Erlbaum.

Turkewitz, G., Gardner, J., & Lewkowicz, D. J. (1984). Sensory/perceptual functioning during early infancy: The implications of a quantitative basis for responding. In G. Greenberg & E. Tobach (Eds.), *Behavioral evolution and integrative levels* (pp. 167–195). Hillsdale, NJ: Erlbaum.

Turkewitz, G., & Kenny, P. A. (1982). Limitations on input as a basis for neural organization and perceptual development: A preliminary theoretical statement. *Developmental Psychobiology, 15,* 357–368.

Turkewitz, G., & Kenny, P. A. (1985). The role of developmental limitations of sensory input on sensory/perceptual organization. *Journal of Developmental and Behavioral Pediatrics, 6,* 302–306.

Turkewitz, G., & Mellon, R. C. (1989). Dynamic organization of intersensory function. *Canadian Journal of Psychology, 43,* 286–301.

von Hofsten, C. (1980). Predictive reaching for moving objects by human infants. *Journal of Experimental Child Psychology, 30,* 369–382.

von Hofsten, C. (1985). Perception and action. In M. Frese & J. Sabini (Eds.), *Goal-directed behavior: The concept of action in psychology* (pp. 80–96). Hillsdale, NJ: Erlbaum.

Wagner, S., Winner, E., Cicchetti, D., & Gardner, H. (1981). "Metaphorical" mapping in human infants. *Child Development, 52,* 728–731.

Walker-Andrews, A. S. (1986). Intermodal perception of expressive behaviors: Relation of eye and voice? *Developmental Psychology, 22,* 373–377.

Walker-Andrews, A. S. (1994). Taxonomy for intermodal relations. In D. J. Lewkowicz & R. Lickliter (Eds.), *The development of intersensory perception: Comparative perspectives* (pp. 39–56). Hillsdale, NJ: Erlbaum.

Walker-Andrews, A. S. (1997). Infants' perception of expressive behaviors: Differentiation of multimodal information. *Psychological Bulletin, 121,* 437–456.

Walker-Andrews, A. S., & Lennon, E. (1991). Infants' discrimination of vocal expressions: Contributions of auditory and visual information. *Infant Behavior and Development, 14,* 131–142.

Wallace, M. T., & Stein, B. E. (1997). Development of multisensory neurons and multisensory integration in cat superior colliculus. *Journal of Neuroscience, 17*, 2429–2444.

Washburn, K. J., & Cohen, L. B. (1984, April). *Infant perception of rhythmic form.* Paper presented at the International Conference on Infant Studies, New York.

Welch, R. B., & Warren, D. H. (1980). Immediate perceptual response to intersensory discrepancy. *Psychological Bulletin, 88*, 638–667.

Welch, R. B., & Warren, D. H. (1986). Intersensory interactions. In K. R. Boff, L. Kaufman, & J. P. Thomas (Eds.), *Handbook of perception and human performance: Sensory processes and perception* (Vol. 1, pp. 1–36). New York: Wiley.

Werner, H. (1973). *Comparative psychology of mental development.* New York: International Universities Press.

Werner, L. A., Marean, G., Halpin, C. F., & Spetner, N. B. (1992). Infant auditory temporal acuity: Gap detection. *Child Development, 63*, 260–272.

Woodruff, D. (1978). Brain electrical activity and behavioral relationships over the life span. In P. Baltes (Ed.), *Life-span development and behavior* (Vol. 1, pp. 111–179). New York: Academic Press.

Yakovlev, P., & Lecours, A. (1967). The myelogenetic cycles of regional maturation of the brain. In A. Minkowski (Ed.), *Regional development of the brain in early life* (pp. 3–70). Philadelphia: Davis.

Younger, B. A., & Cohen, L. B. (1983). Infant perception of correlations among attributes. *Child Development, 54*, 858–867.

# 48

# Intersensory Redundancy Guides the Development of Selective Attention, Perception, and Cognition in Infancy

*Lorraine E. Bahrick, Robert Lickliter and Ross Flom*

The world provides a richly structured, continuous flux of multimodal stimulation to your senses. Objects and events can be simultaneously seen, heard, smelled, and felt as you interact with your environment. Scientists have long been intrigued and challenged by issues arising from the specificity of stimulation from the different senses and the overlap among them. How are objects and events experienced as unitary when they stimulate receptors that give rise to different forms of information? How are different modes of sensory stimulation bound together? How do infants determine which sights, sounds, tastes, and smells belong together and constitute unitary events, and which are unrelated? Adults can use prior knowledge about objects and events to guide selective attention to meaningful, unitary patterns of stimulation. Experienced perceivers know that faces go with voices, that the sound of footsteps foretell the approach of a person, and that the breaking glass made the sharp crashing sound. How does the infant, who begins life with no prior knowledge to guide attention, make sense of this flow and focus on stimulation that is meaningful, coherent, and relevant? What guides and constrains perceptual development and provides the foundation for the knowledge of the adult perceiver?

One answer to these questions arises from the fact that the senses pick up overlapping, redundant information for objects and events in the environment.

**Source:** *Current Directions in Psychological Science,* 13(3) (2004): 99–102.

In a radical move from traditional perceptual theory, J.J. Gibson (1966) proposed that different forms of sensory stimulation are not a problem for the perception of unitary events but instead provide an important basis for it. He argued that the senses should be considered as a perceptual system whose components work together to pick up stimulation that is common across the senses.

In this view, the fact that the senses provide overlapping information for objects and events is therefore no extravagance of nature. Moreover, from our perspective, it is a cornerstone of perceptual development. One type of overlap involves amodal information, that is, information that is not specific to a single sense modality, but is completely redundant across more than one sense. The dimensions of time, space, and intensity are typically conveyed by multiple senses. For example, the rate and rhythm of hands clapping are conveyed visually and acoustically. The sights and sounds of a ball bouncing are synchronous, originate in the same location, and share a common rate, rhythm, and intensity pattern. Picking up this redundant, amodal information is fundamental to perceptual development. It allows naive perceivers to selectively attend to related aspects of stimulation that constitute unitary events and ignore concurrent stimulation from unrelated events nearby (Bahrick & Lickliter, 2002; E.J. Gibson & Pick, 2000).

For example, the face and voice of a person speaking share temporal synchrony, rhythm, tempo, and changing intensity. By selectively attending to these amodal properties, perceivers can attend to the unitary event, the person speaking, and ignore unrelated faces and objects nearby. This selectivity allows perception to get started on the right track in early development, providing a foundation for learning about meaningful, unitary objects and events.

Converging evidence from comparative and developmental psychology has shown that both animal and human infants are adept perceivers of amodal information (Lewkowicz & Lickliter, 1994; Lickliter & Bahrick, 2000). Infants detect temporal aspects of stimulation such as synchrony, rhythm, and tempo, as well as the spatial correspondence of objects and their sound sources. They also detect synchrony, affect, prosody, and changes in intensity of stimulation from faces and voices. Infants also participate in multimodal, temporally coordinated interactions with adults.

Despite the fact that perceptual, cognitive, social, and emotional development emerge within and rely upon this sensory overlap, most research in developmental psychology has focused on development of capabilities involving only a single sense modality (unimodal research). Such research demonstrates that infants are excellent perceivers of visual stimulation such as color, pattern, and faces and of acoustic stimulation such as the sounds of speech. Because of the historical focus on the specificity of the senses, there is currently a lack of integration between research on unimodal perception and emerging research on multimodal perception, and recent discoveries of important neural and behavioral interdependencies among the senses are not generally appreciated (Lickliter & Bahrick, 2000).

Consequently, no theories have yet addressed how and under what conditions people perceive amodal information versus modality-specific information (information that can be conveyed by only a particular sense) when events typically provide both types of information. For example, a bouncing soccer ball provides amodal synchrony, rhythm, and tempo across sights and sounds of impacts, as well as color and pattern that can be perceived only visually, and pitch and timbre that can be perceived only acoustically. How is detection of amodal information coordinated with detection of modality-specific information across development in a world that provides a constant flux of multimodal and unimodal stimulation from objects and events? How do people perceive faces in the context of speech, or voices in the context of moving faces? To date, research has not directly addressed the coordination of attention to different aspects of events in unimodal and multimodal stimulation.

## The Intersensory Redundancy Hypothesis

We have proposed an intersensory redundancy hypothesis (IRH), which addresses the nature of this coordination across development and bridges the gap between theories of unimodal and multimodal functioning. The IRH explains how the detection of amodal information can guide selective attention and learning during early infancy and how this process is coordinated with perception of information specific to a single sense (Bahrick & Lickliter, 2000, 2002). Intersensory redundancy refers to the spatially coordinated and temporally synchronous presentation of the same information across two or more senses and is therefore possible only for amodal properties (e.g., tempo, rhythm, duration, intensity). Thus, the sights and sounds of hands clapping provide intersensory redundancy because they are temporally synchronous, originate in the same place, and convey the same rhythm, tempo, and intensity patterns in vision and audition.

According to the IRH, during early infancy intersensory redundancy promotes detection of amodal information in multimodal events, and this causes amodal stimulus properties to become "foreground" and other properties to become "background." Intersensory redundancy affects selective attention, promoting earlier processing of redundantly specified properties than of other stimulus properties in early development. Thus, the infant's initial sensitivity to amodal information provides an economical way of guiding perceptual processing to focus on meaningful, unitary events.

Of course, not all exploration of objects and events makes multi-modal stimulation available. Sometimes only unimodal stimulation is provided (e.g., when listening to the radio or touching a hidden toy), and in this case, no intersensory redundancy is available. This unimodal stimulation makes modality-specific properties stand out. Attention to properties that are specific to vision is facilitated when an object is seen but not heard, and attention to properties that are specific to audition is facilitated when an event is heard but not seen. This facilitation occurs partly because there is no competition from intersensory redundancy, which makes amodal properties salient. Unimodal stimulation can also provide amodal information (e.g., the rhythm of music or a rapidly flashing light), but when amodal information is not redundantly specified, it is not particularly salient. Thus, amodal properties are less salient in unimodal stimulation than when they are experienced redundantly across two senses.

## Predictions of the IRH

Given that all events provide both amodal and modality-specific information, when and under what conditions do people perceive each type of information? According to the IRH, the nature of exploration (unimodal vs. multimodal) interacts with the type of property explored (amodal vs. modality-specific) to determine the attentional salience and processing priority given to various properties of sensory stimulation. As can be seen in Figure 1, multimodal (bimodal or trimodal) exploration of amodal properties and unimodal exploration of modality-specific properties should receive processing priority. The IRH makes two specific predictions regarding which stimulus properties

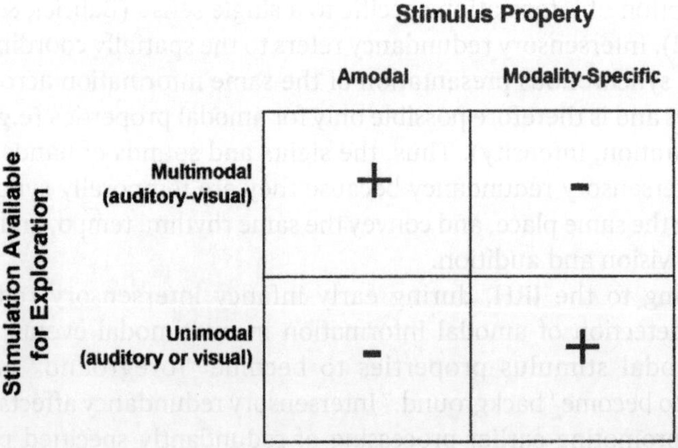

**Figure 1:** Predictions of the intersensory redundancy hypothesis. The combination of stimulus properties (amodal vs. modality-specific) and the nature of exploration (multimodal vs. unimodal) determines whether attention and perceptual processing are facilitated (plus signs) or attenuated (minus signs). Reprinted from "Intersensory Redundancy Guides Early Perceptual and Cognitive Development," by L.E. Bahrick and R. Lickliter, in R. Kail (Ed.), *Advances in Child Development and Behavior*, Vol. 30, p. 166, New York: Academic Press. Copyright 2002 by Academic Press. Reprinted with permission from Elsevier via Copyright Clearance Center's RightsLink service.

(amodal vs. modality-specific) are detected in multimodal versus unimodal stimulation. The first prediction is that processing and learning of amodal properties is facilitated in multimodal stimulation (in which intersensory redundancy is available) compared with unimodal stimulation (in which no redundancy is available; cf. the two left-hand quadrants in Fig. 1). In contrast, the second prediction is that processing and learning of modality-specific properties is facilitated when information is experienced unimodally, as compared with when stimulation is multimodal and redundant (cf. the two right-hand quadrants in Fig. 1). The IRH also makes a developmental prediction; as perceivers become more experienced, perceptual processing becomes increasingly flexible, such that both amodal and modality-specific properties are detected in unimodal and multimodal contexts. Thus, according to the IRH, the facilitation of attention we have described is most pronounced in early development (or when a task is difficult). These initial conditions can have far-reaching consequences for how perception is organized and develops.

## Research Supporting the IRH

Research indicates that human infants attend to different properties of an event depending on whether redundant bimodal stimulation or only unimodal stimulation is available (Lewkowicz, 2000; Lickliter & Bahrick, 2000). In this research, infants are typically tested in what is called a habituation procedure. They are repeatedly presented with an event until they are habituated to it, that is, until their amount of looking at the event decreases to some criterion (e.g., 50% of their initial looking level). Once this criterion has been met, the event is changed in some way on test trials. If infants notice the change, their level of looking at the novel event should increase significantly above the habituated level.

Using this procedure, we found greater sensitivity to amodal properties when intersensory redundancy was available than when it was not, supporting the first prediction of the IRH. Three-month-old infants discriminated a change in the tempo of a toy hammer tapping during redundant bimodal (audiovisual) but not during unimodal (auditory or visual) stimulation (Bahrick, Flom, & Lickliter, 2002). Similarly, 5-month-old infants discriminated a change in a complex rhythm in bimodal but not unimodal presentations (Bahrick & Lickliter, 2000). We also obtained results consistent with the developmental prediction of the IRH: Perception became more flexible with additional experience, and older infants discriminated the amodal properties of rhythm and tempo in both bimodal and unimodal stimulation (Bahrick & Lickliter, 2003).

Findings from studies of nonhuman animals converge with results obtained with human infants (Lickliter & Bahrick, 2000). Research with animals has shown enhanced neurophysiological and behavioral responsiveness to coordinated bimodal stimulation as compared with unimodal stimulation. Animal studies also indicate that the attenuation or uncoupling of multimodal experience can modify perceptual organization during early development. For example, results from studies of birds and mammals indicate that temporally or spatially separating auditory and visual stimulation alters infants' sensitivity to both unimodal and multimodal information. Further, animal-based research has demonstrated a dramatic facilitation of perceptual learning and memory following exposure to redundant, bimodally specified information, even during the prenatal period. Quail embryos learned an individual maternal call four times faster and remembered the call four times longer when intersensory redundancy was provided by synchronizing a light with the rate and rhythm of the maternal call than when the call was desynchronized with the light or presented alone (Lickliter, Bahrick, & Honeycutt, 2002).

Research has also illustrated the organizing influence of inter-sensory redundancy on early social and linguistic processing. Walker-Andrews (1997) reviewed evidence that infants initially need input from more than one sensory modality to recognize emotional expressions, but at a later age can use the voice alone and eventually facial expressions alone. Evidence for the importance of intersensory redundancy (e.g., synchrony between speech sounds and motions of objects) for the initial detection of the relation between speech sounds and the objects to which they refer has also been demonstrated (Gogate & Bahrick, 1998). The early emergence of infant sensitivity to prosody (Cooper & Aslin, 1989), a composite of amodal properties such as rhythm, tempo, and intensity changes in audiovisual speech, also highlights the salience of intersensory redundancy in guiding attention.

The complementary prediction of the IRH, that processing of modality-specific properties is facilitated in unimodal compared with multimodal stimulation, has also been supported by studies of human infants (Bahrick & Lickliter, 2002). We tested 5-month-olds' detection of orientation (a property available visually but not acoustically) under conditions of bimodal (audiovisual) and unimodal (visual) stimulation. After being habituated to films of a hammer tapping in one of two orientations (upward vs. downward), infants detected a change in orientation following unimodal visual habituation, but not following bimodal audiovisual habituation (Bahrick, Lickliter, & Flom, 2003). Optimal differentiation of visible qualities of an event occurs when there is no concurrent auditory stimulation, which creates intersensory redundancy and competes for attention.

This principle is especially apparent in the domain of person perception. In early development, differentiation of the appearance of a person's face (i.e., on the basis of facial features and their arrangement) should be optimal when the individual is silent, and differentiation of the person's particular voice (i.e., on the basis of pitch and timbre) should be optimal when his or her face is not visible. Research in progress in our lab indicates that this is indeed the case.

Young infants differentiate among moving faces under conditions of visual but not audiovisual stimulation and differentiate among voices under conditions of audio but not audiovisual stimulation. After a few months of additional perceptual experience, infants appear to discriminate among the faces and the voices when they experience either unimodal or multimodal stimulation. Enhanced unimodal discrimination of modality-specific properties thus characterizes early attention, and with experience perception becomes more flexible, such that modality-specific properties can be detected in unimodal and multimodal stimulation.

## Implications for Theory and Research

Converging evidence across species, developmental periods, tasks, and amodal properties suggests that the organizing influence of intersensory redundancy in guiding early attention, perception, and cognition likely constitutes a general developmental principle. Whether there remains a processing advantage for amodal properties in multimodal stimulation and for modality-specific properties in unimodal stimulation through childhood and adulthood is a topic worthy of investigation. Adults may retain the processing advantages of infancy when stimulation is novel or particularly difficult. These processing advantages likely have significant implications for perceiving, learning, and remembering and, if so, may have potential for educational applications across the life span.

The research highlighted here raises several important challenges for theories of learning and development. First, research on unimodal and multimodal functioning needs to be better integrated to develop unified theories relevant to the world outside the laboratory. Given that studies of multimodal functioning and studies of unimodal functioning often obtain different results, and that the environment is intrinsically multimodal, findings from unimodal research must translate to their natural, multimodal contexts to be more relevant (Lickliter & Bahrick, 2001). The IRH bridges this gap by promoting investigations of both unimodal and multimodal functioning in single research designs, making comparisons across these domains feasible. Second, theories of attention need to be better integrated with those of perception, learning, and memory. Selective attention provides the foundation for what is perceived and learned, and an understanding of what guides this process and how it changes developmentally seems essential for theories of learning and memory. The IRH provides testable predictions of how the allocation of attention affects the development of perception, learning, and memory. A third challenge is to develop more integrative theories; traditional divisions between areas, species, and levels of inquiry have allowed bodies of research to develop in isolation from other relevant knowledge. For example, behavioral research will benefit from incorporating recent discoveries from physiology and the neurosciences regarding interactions among the senses and the multimodal nature of the brain. The convergence of findings across species and levels of analysis will foster more biologically plausible theories and the discovery of more fundamental principles of development.

## Recommended Reading

Calvert, G., Spence, C., & Stein, B.E. (2004). Handbook of multisensory integration. Cambridge, MA: MIT Press.
Gibson, E.K., & Pick, A.D. (2000). (See References)
Lewkowicz, D.J., & Lickliter, R. (1994). (See References)
Stein, B.E., & Meredith, M.A. (1993). *The merging of the senses*. Cambridge, MA: MIT Press.

## References

Bahrick, L.E., Flom, R., & Lickliter, R. (2002). Intersensory redundancy facilitates discrimination of tempo in 3-month-old infants. *Developmental Psychobiology, 41*, 352–363.
Bahrick, L.E., & Lickliter, R. (2000). Intersensory redundancy guides attentional selectivity and perceptual learning in infancy. *Developmental Psychology, 36*, 190–201.
Bahrick, L.E., & Lickliter, R. (2002). Intersensory redundancy guides early perceptual and cognitive development. In R. Kail (Ed.), *Advances in child development and behavior* (Vol. 30, pp. 153–187). New York: Academic Press.
Bahrick, L.E., & Lickliter, R. (2003). *The development of infants' detection of amodal properties of events in unimodal and bimodal stimulation: A further test of the intersensory redundancy hypothesis*. Manuscript submitted for publication.
Bahrick, L.E., Lickliter, R., & Flom, R. (2003). *Up versus down: The role of intersensory redundancy in infants' sensitivity to object orientation and motion*. Manuscript submitted for publication.
Cooper, R.P., & Aslin, R.N. (1989). The language environment of the young infant: Implications for early perceptual development. *Canadian Journal of Psychology, 43*, 247–265.
Gibson, E.J., & Pick, A.D. (2000). *An ecological approach to perceptual learning and development*. New York: Oxford University Press.
Gibson, J.J. (1966). *The senses considered as perceptual systems*. Boston: Houghton Mifflin.
Gogate, L.J., & Bahrick, L.E. (1998). Intersensory redundancy facilitates learning of arbitrary relations between vowel sounds and objects in 7-month-old infants. *Journal of Experimental Child Psychology, 69*, 133–149.
Lewkowicz, D.J. (2000). The development of intersensory temporal perception: An epigenetic systems/limitations view. *Psychological Bulletin, 126*, 281–308.
Lewkowicz, D.J., & Lickliter, R. (1994). *Development of intersensory perception: Comparative perspectives*. Hillsdale, NJ: Erlbaum.
Lickliter, R., & Bahrick, L.E. (2000). The development of infant intersensory perception: Advantages of a comparative, convergent-operations approach. *Psychological Bulletin, 126*, 260–280.
Lickliter, R., & Bahrick, L.E. (2001). The salience of multimodal sensory stimulation in early development: Implications for the issue of ecological validity. *Infancy, 2*, 447–463.
Lickliter, R., Bahrick, L.E., & Honeycutt, H. (2002). Intersensory redundancy facilitates perceptual learning in bobwhite quail embryos. *Developmental Psychology, 38*, 15–23.
Walker-Andrews, A.S. (1997). Infants' perception of expressive behaviors: Differentiation of multimodal information. *Psychological Bulletin, 121*, 437–456.

# 49

# The Effects of Auditory Information on 4-Month-Old Infants' Perception of Trajectory Continuity

*J. Gavin Bremner, Alan M. Slater, Scott P. Johnson,*
*Uschi C. Mason and Jo Spring*

Infants' response to moving object occlusion events in which an object passes behind an occluder has a long history as an indicator of infants' awareness of object persistence or permanence (Bower, Broughton, & Moore, 1971; Goldberg, 1976; Moore, Borton, & Darby, 1978). This early work relied on detecting anticipation of object reemergence following occlusion. But alternative interpretations of anticipation were identified (Goldberg, 1976; Moore et al., 1978) that led to the conclusion that, on its own, anticipation of reemergence did not safely indicate that the infant had interpolated the missing segment of the object's trajectory. Instead, it was possible that infants were anticipating a repeated cycle of discrete events each side of the occluder rather than the emergence of a single persisting object (Goldberg, 1976).

More recently, precise eye-tracker measures of visual tracking (Gredebäck & von Hofsten, 2004; Johnson, Amso, & Slemmer, 2003; Rosander & von Hofsten, 2004) and habituation novelty data (Bremner et al., 2005; Bremner et al., 2007; Johnson, Bremner, et al., 2003) have produced converging evidence. This work has led to the conclusion that infants' ability to perceive an object's trajectory as continuous improves over the early months after birth (Figure 1 illustrates the habituation novelty displays used). Specifically, 2-month-olds appear unable to perceive trajectory continuity (Johnson, Bremner, et al.,

**Source:** *Child Development*, 83(3) (2012): 954–964.

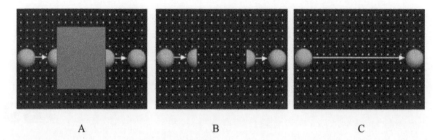

A                                    B                                    C

*Note:* (a) Habituation event. A ball moves behind an occluding screen and reemerges, then returns on a repetitive cyclic trajectory. (b) Discontinuous trajectory test event. The ball moves to the place occupied previously by the occluder and goes out of sight in the same manner. (c) Continuous trajectory test event. The ball moves back and forth as before but remains visible during the entire trajectory. The rationale is that if infants perceived trajectory continuity during habituation they should show a novelty preference for the discontinuous test trial.

**Figure 1:** Schematic depiction of events shown to infants in Johnson, Bremner, et al. (2003) to gage perception of trajectory continuity

2003), whereas 4-month-olds appear to perceive trajectory continuity when the spatial or temporal gap in perception is small (Bremner et al., 2005; Johnson, Bremner, et al., 2003), and 6-month-olds' ability appears to be well developed (Johnson, Amso, et al., 2003; Johnson, Bremner, et al., 2003). This has led some investigators to conclude that there are perceptual origins for object identity and permanence (Bremner et al., 2005; Bremner et al., 2007; Johnson, Bremner, et al., 2003). As infants become increasingly able to detect and retain information specifying perceptual completion, such as collinearity and temporal contiguity, their ability to recognize relations among disparate parts of a visual scene begins to improve. And these perceptual advances form the basis for development of awareness of object identity and permanence.

These studies presented information for the object's trajectory solely in the visual modality. However, there is evidence indicating modification of very young infants' response to visual stimuli following auditory stimulation, indicating intersensory matching and interaction of stimulus intensity (Lewkowicz & Turkewitz, 1980, 1981). Also there is strong evidence that redundant presentation of information across modalities recruits infant attention and enhances learning (the intersensory redundancy hypothesis [IRH]; Bahrick, Flom, & Lickliter, 2002; Bahrick & Lickliter, 2000; Bahrick, Lickliter, & Flom, 2004).

With respect to object movement, it has been demonstrated that 6-month-old infants are sensitive to congruence between timing of a sound and timing of a change in object movement direction, and that this sensitivity is dependent on spatial contiguity between auditory and visual stimuli (Lawson, 1980). Additionally, there is some work investigating detection of dynamic auditory–visual correspondences for movements in the near–far plane (Pickens, 1994; Walker-Andrews & Lennon, 1985). These studies indicate an ability to form correspondences between sound intensity and object distance at 4–5 months. And recently it has been demonstrated that infants from 2 to 8 months of age detect auditory–visual congruence and incongruence in events involving laterally moving visual objects and stereophonically simulated moving sounds (Bremner et al., 2011). During habituation trials, infants detected congruence of visual and auditory information for movement and showed recovery of attention when the two sources of information became incongruent, specifically when the auditory stimulus appeared to move left to right as the visual stimulus moved from right to left, and vice versa.

Evidence of infants' sensitivity to intersensory information about an object's trajectory raises the issue of whether providing auditory as well as visual information about an object's trajectory would enhance young infants' perception of trajectory continuity across an occlusion. According to the IRH, optimum conditions for deriving benefit from provision of multisensory information would be those in which both visual and auditory information provide congruent information about an object's trajectory. Under such conditions, visual and auditory information would specify the object's trajectory redundantly and so could be expected to enhance perception of trajectory continuity as the object passed behind an occluder. However, in the present case there is an additional reason why supplementing the visual event with auditory information might enhance perception of trajectory continuity. Specifically, although there is a discontinuity in visual perception of the object as it passes behind an occluder, auditory information arising from a sounding object need not show this discontinuity. And although sound intensity generally reduces when an object passes behind an occluder, sound is not usually eliminated and may not reduce sufficiently to be detected by infants.

In order to benefit from presentation of intersensory information regarding an object's trajectory, it is of course necessary that infants are capable of localizing sound with sufficient accuracy to detect change in location from sound alone. Some investigators have detected a more or less linear increase in localization ability with age (Morrongiello, 1988; Morrongiello, Fenwick, & Chance, 1990), whereas other work suggests that auditory localization is hard to elicit at around 2 months (Clifton, Morrongiello, Kulig, & Dowd, 1981; Field, Muir, Pilon, Sinclair, & Dodwell, 1980; Muir, Clifton, & Clarkson, 1989). However, although 4-month-olds' auditory localization ability falls well short of adult levels, it is well established, with a minimum discriminable auditory angle of around 18° (Morrongiello et al., 1990). And the fact that for static stimuli auditory–visual spatial colocation occurs in newborns (Morrongiello, Fenwick, & Chance, 1998) and older infants (Morrongiello, Fenwick, & Nutley, 1998), and that it occurs from 2 months upwards in the case of moving stimuli (Bremner et al., 2011), indicates that auditory localization is sufficient to detect information specifying object location and change in location.

In the series of experiments reported here we investigate different levels at which auditory information may benefit perception of trajectory continuity. In Experiment 1 we investigate the effect of supplementing visual information with continuous dynamic auditory information specifying the object's trajectory. In Experiment 2 we investigate whether effects of auditory information are limited to the case in which the sound provides dynamic information for movement, or whether such effects also occur when static auditory information specifies continuity over time but does not provide information for movement. In Experiment 3 we investigate two cases in which auditory information may be expected to detract from perception of continuity, one in which the sound ceases and resumes suddenly when the visual object disappears and reappears, and one in which the sound specifies motion in the opposite direction from that specified by vision.

## Experiment 1

In this and the following experiments, we adopted the habituation novelty technique that had proved successful in previous work on trajectory continuity. Infants are habituated to an event in which an object moves back and forth, disappearing and reappearing behind a centrally placed occluder. Following habituation, they are presented with sequential test trials with the occluder absent and the object moving either continuously or discontinuously, in the latter case disappearing and reappearing as it did during habituation (see Figure 1). The rationale is that if infants perceived the habituation event as an object moving on a continuous trajectory, they should show a novelty preference for the discontinuous test display, whereas if they perceived a discontinuous trajectory during habituation they should show a novelty preference for the continuous test display. Johnson, Bremner, et al. (2003) demonstrated that 4-month-olds' perception of trajectory continuity depended on the occluder width used, and Bremner et al. (2005) demonstrated that this age group appeared to perceive trajectory continuity provided either the time or distance out of sight was short. As the starting point for our investigation, we replicated conditions from earlier work, adding a continuous sound that stereophonically specified the object's trajectory. We selected two conditions from Johnson, Bremner, et al. (2003). One used a wide occluder that apparently led the 4-month-olds to perceive trajectory discontinuity, and the other used a narrow occluder that had resulted in an intermediate null response, suggesting that 4-month-olds neither perceived continuity nor discontinuity in the trajectory presented during habituation. A second reason for our choice of these conditions was that we knew that these effects without sound were robust: The result with the wide occluder was replicated by Johnson, Bremner, et al. (2003) and the null result with the narrow occluder was replicated in a subsequent study (Bremner et al., 2005). Thus, we were confident that we had reliable performance baselines without the need for further replication.

# Method

*Participants.* Twenty-four 4-month-old infants ($M = 120.5$ days, range $= 112$–$136$ days; 9 girls and 15 boys) took part in the experiment. A further 9 did not complete testing due to fussiness and 2 infants failed to habituate and so their data were not included. Twelve infants were assigned to each of the two experimental conditions in such a way as to ensure that the mean age and the gender balance were comparable across conditions. Throughout the series, infants took part in only one experiment. In all experiments, participants were recruited by personal contact with parents in the maternity unit when the baby was born, followed up by telephone contact near test age to those parents who volunteered to take part. Infants with reported health problems including visual and hearing deficits and those born 2 weeks or more before due date were omitted from the sample. The majority were from Caucasian, middle-class families.

*Apparatus and stimuli.* A Macintosh computer and a Samsung 100-cm color monitor were used to present stimuli and collect looking-time data. An observer viewed the infant on a second monitor, and infants were recorded onto videotape for later independent coding of looking times by a second observer. Both observers were unaware of the hypothesis under investigation. Using HABIT software (Cohen, Atkinson, & Chaput, 2000) the computer presented displays, recorded looking-time judgments, calculated the habituation criterion for each infant, and changed displays after criteria were met. The observer's judgments were input with a key press on the computer keyboard.

The habituation display consisted of a stationary centrally placed blue occluder with vertical extent 21.5 cm (12.3°) and horizontal extent either 17.7 cm (10.1°) or 14.8 cm (8.5°) and a 6.7 cm (3.8°) green ball undergoing continuous lateral translation back and forth at a rate of 16.8 cm/s (9.6°/s), the center of its trajectory concealed by the occluder (see Figure 2). In the case of the wide occluder the ball was visible on either side of the occluder in its entirety for 1,067 ms and was completely occluded for 667 ms. In the case of the narrow occluder, the ball was visible in its entirety for 1,200 ms and was completely occluded for 533 ms. In both conditions the transition from full visibility to full occlusion or the reverse took 400 ms. The animation was run as a continuous loop for the duration of the trial. During habituation trials, a repetitive musical sound was presented through two speakers located immediately to the left and right of the display monitor at the height of the object's trajectory, so that it appeared to a small sample of adults to move congruently with the object. This effect was achieved through varying the balance at constant rate from one extreme in which the sound came from only one speaker, through equal volume at each speaker (and hence equal intensity at both ears of the listener) to the other extreme when sound only came from the other speaker. Given the placement of the speakers directly at the extremes of visual object motion, and assuming the use of interaural intensity difference

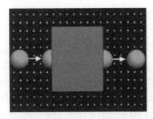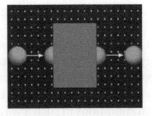

*Note:* Test displays were as illustrated in Figure 1, with the "gap" in the discontinuous display matched to the width of the habituation occluder.

**Figure 2:** The wide and narrow occluder habituation displays used in Experiments 1 and 2

to locate the sound, this provides objective colocation of visual and auditory information at the extremes and mid point. Furthermore, the smooth alteration in balance may be assumed to create a smooth change in apparent location between midpoint and extremes. In test displays, which occurred in silence, the box was removed and the ball translated back and forth in the same way as in the habituation display. In the continuous trajectory test display, the ball was always visible. In the discontinuous trajectory display, the ball went out of and back into view by progressive deletion and accretion at a vertical linear boundary, just as in the wide or narrow occluder habituation display (i.e., with a wide or a narrow gap in the trajectory), but without a visible (i.e., color- or luminance-defined) occluding edge (Figure 1b illustrates this for the wide occluder condition). Objects were presented against a black background with a 12 × 20 grid of white dots measuring 48.8 × 33.0 cm (27.4 × 18.7°) serving as texture elements.

*Design.* Infants were assigned randomly to one of the two conditions. They were first habituated to either the wide occluder or the narrow occluder ball-and-box stimulus, with synchronized auditory information for the object's location provided continually throughout each trial. The two test displays were then presented in alternation, three times each, for a total of six presentations. Test trials were presented in silence. Half the infants in each condition viewed the continuous trajectory first, and half viewed the discontinuous trajectory first. Because the test displays were identical to those used in Johnson, Bremner, et al. (2003), control conditions involving test displays alone were not conducted, since null results were obtained in these conditions previously.

*Procedure.* Each infant was seated 100 cm from the display and tested individually in a darkened room. During habituation trials the ball-and-box display was presented until looking time declined across four consecutive trials, from the second trial on, adding up to less than half the total looking time during the first four trials. After this criterion was achieved, the sequence of six test trials was commenced. Timing of each trial began when the infant fixated the screen after display onset. The observer pressed a key as long as the infant fixated the screen, and released when the infant looked away. A trial was terminated when the observer released the key for 2 s or 60 s had elapsed. Between trials, a beeping target was shown to attract attention back to the screen. The second observer coded looking times from videotape for purposes of assessing reliability of looking time judgments. Interobserver correlations were high across the five experiments in this report (*M* Pearson *r* = .99).

## Results and Discussion

Figure 3 presents average looking times to the two test displays for the wide and narrow occluder conditions, respectively. Infants in both conditions looked longer at the discontinuous test display. Looking time data in many cells were positively skewed, violating assumptions of homogeneity of variance required by analysis of variance (ANOVA), so scores were log-transformed prior to analysis in all the experiments in this report (data in the figures are based on raw scores). A 2 (display: wide vs. narrow occluder) × 2 (test trial order) × 2 (test trial type: continuous vs. discontinuous) × 3 (test trial block) mixed ANOVA yielded a significant effect of test trial type, $F(1, 20) = 15.01$, $p = .001$, $\eta_p^2 = .43$. This effect was general across conditions, because the interaction between test trial type and display was not significant, $F(1, 20) = 0.02$, $p = .89$, $\eta_p^2 = .001$. There were no other significant main effects or interactions.

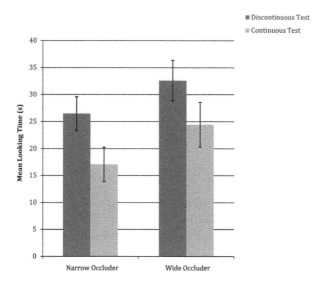

*Note:* Error bars in this and subsequent data figures display standard errors.

**Figure 3:** Mean looking times to the two test displays for wide and narrow occluder conditions in Experiment 1

The significant novelty preference across conditions for the discontinuous test display indicates that with the addition of auditory information for the object's trajectory, infants appeared to perceive trajectory continuity. This is in contrast to the results obtained by Johnson, Bremner, et al. (2003) in the absence of auditory information, in which case infants in the wide occluder condition showed a significant preference for the continuous test display, indicative of perception of trajectory discontinuity, and infants in the narrow occluder condition showed no preference for either display. To confirm the effect of auditory information we made direct comparisons between the present data and the data from conditions with equivalent occluder widths in Johnson, Bremner, et al. (2003). Separate ANOVAs for each occluder width yielded significant Test Trial Type × Experiment (sound vs. no sound) interactions for both the wide occluder condition, $F(1, 20) = 13.03, p = .002, \eta_p^2 = .39$, and the narrow occluder condition, $F(1, 20) = 5.25, p = .03, \eta_p^2 = .21$. Thus, we have a clear demonstration that provision of auditory information supported perception of trajectory continuity.

## Experiment 2

It is tempting to conclude that the effectiveness of auditory information in supporting perception of trajectory continuity was due to the fact that it provided dynamic auditory information for the changing location of the object as it moved along its path. In addition to providing redundant information for the object's changing location, auditory information provides dynamic location information even when the object is out of sight. However, it is possible that it was simply the continuity of the sound that provided information for continuity of the object's trajectory. If this were the case, provision of a stationary sound for the duration of each trial might also be effective in specifying trajectory continuity. Thus, in Experiment 2 we repeated the two conditions of Experiment 1 but replaced the stereophonically generated "moving" sound with a sound that appeared to come from the center of the display.

## Method

*Participants*. Twenty-four 4-month-old infants ($M = 125.3$ days, range = 109–134 days; 12 girls and 12 boys) took part in the experiment. A further 7 did not complete testing due to fussiness. Twelve infants were assigned to each of the two conditions in such a way as to ensure that the mean age and the gender balance were comparable across conditions.

*Apparatus, stimuli, design, and procedure.* These were identical to Experiment 1 in all respects other than the fact that the sound during habituation trials was presented with equal intensity at both speakers, and thus appeared to come from the middle of the display.

## Results and Discussion

Figure 4 presents average looking times to the two test displays for the wide and narrow occluder conditions, respectively. In the case of the narrow occluder infants looked longer at the discontinuous test display, and in the case of the wide occluder they looked approximately equally at the two test displays. A 2 (display: wide vs. narrow occluder) × 2 (test trial order) × 2 (test trial type: continuous vs. discontinuous) × 3 (test trial block) mixed ANOVA yielded no significant effect of test trial type, $F(1, 20) = 1.04, p = .32, \eta_p^2 = .05$. But there was a significant interaction between test trial type and test trial block, $F(2, 19) = 4.26, p = .03, \eta_p^2 = .31$. This interaction is illustrated in Figure 5. On the first test trial block, the effect of test trial type was not significant, $F(1, 20) = 2.19, p = .15, \eta_p^2 = .1$. However, on Blocks 2 and 3 there was a significant preference for the discontinuous test trial, $F(1, 20) = 5.56, p = .03, \eta_p^2 = .22$. There was also a significant main effect of test trial block, $F(2, 29) = 6.87, p = .006, \eta_p^2 = .42$, due to a reduction in looking at the test trials across blocks. Neither the interaction between test trial type and display, $F(1, 20) = 0.46, p = .5, \eta_p^2 = .02$, nor the interaction between test trial type, test trial block, and condition, $F(2, 19) = 0.59, p = .56, \eta_p^2 = .06$, was significant, so the significant effects can be taken to be general across conditions.

These results indicate that provision of a continuous stationary sound during habituation trials also enhanced perception of trajectory continuity. However, this was only evident after the first test trial block, suggesting a more subtle effect that took some time to become evident. A possible reason

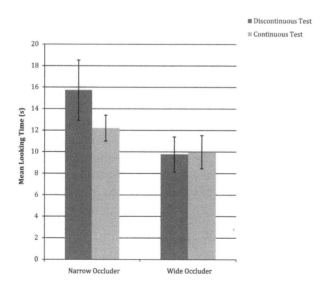

**Figure 4:** Mean looking times to the two test displays for wide and narrow occluder conditions in Experiment 2

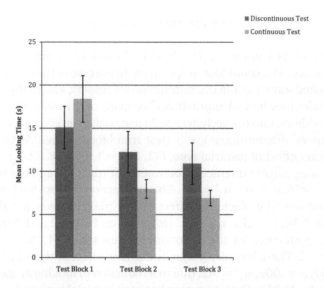

**Figure 5:** Mean looking times to the two test displays by test trial block in Experiment 2

for the delay in the effect relates to the novelty of both test trials relative to the habituation display: In both the occluder is absent and there is no sound. It is possible that one or both of these sources of novelty initially swamped a relatively subtle effect of a mono sound during habituation. However, note that no such effect was evident in Experiment 1, which adds to the conclusion that the effect of a static sound is less marked than that of a dynamic sound. To evaluate the effect of mono sound against a baseline of no sound, similar to Experiment 1, we made direct comparisons between the present data and the data from conditions with equivalent occluder widths in Johnson, Amso, et al. (2003) and Johnson, Bremner, et al. (2003). Separate ANOVAs for each occluder width yielded a significant Test Trial Type × Experiment (sound vs. no sound) interaction for the wide occluder condition, $F(1, 20) = 7.07, p = .015, \eta_p^2 = .26$, but not for the narrow occluder condition, $F(1, 20) = 0.75$, $p = .39, \eta_p^2 = .04$. It seems likely that this inconsistent pattern arises from the combination of a relatively subtle effect of mono sound and the fact that a relatively strong preference for the discontinuous test trial was needed in the sound condition to make for a significant departure from the near chance result in the narrow occluder baseline condition.

## Experiment 3

In our final experiment we posed the question of whether there were conditions under which provision of auditory information would impact negatively on perception of trajectory continuity. Given the conclusion from Experiment 2 that simply the continuity of a sound-enhanced perception of trajectory continuity, we might suppose that providing a discontinuous sound might have the opposite effect. Thus, in one condition we again presented a dynamic sound during habituation, but it terminated abruptly at the moment when the object disappeared and then commenced again when the object began to reappear from behind the occluder. Another condition that seemed likely to disrupt trajectory perception involves provision of auditory information for the object's location that conflicts with information provided by vision. Thus in a second condition we provided a dynamic auditory stimulus that was displaced relative to the visual object, and appeared to travel in the opposite direction to it.

We may consider both these conditions in relation to the IRH. In the first case, while the object is in view information about its path is specified redundantly across the two senses. However, there is a lower level of redundancy with respect to common onset and offset of both stimuli. As in Experiments 1 and 2, there is common onset and offset of visual and auditory stimuli at the beginning and end of each habituation trial. Additionally, in this condition there is common offset and onset when the object disappears and reappears from behind the occluder. At first sight, this suggests enhanced redundant presentation that should recruit attention. However, common offset and onset at the occluder boundaries presents redundant informa-tion for discontinuity. So this manipulation should increase the tendency to process the trajectory as discontinuous. In the second condition, there is common onset and offset of auditory and visual information at the beginning and end of each trial, however, there is no redundant information about the object's trajectory. In fact, across each trial the dynamic information is actually conflicting (dislocated) between modalities. Thus, again it can be predicted that such a condition should disrupt perception of trajectory continuity. In this experiment we chose to use only the narrow occluder display. Compared with the wide occluder display that led to perception of discontinuity when no auditory information was presented (Johnson, Bremner, et al., 2003), this occluder width led to a null result and thus constituted the condition most likely to reveal a detrimental effect of auditory information relative to unimodal presentation.

## Method

*Participants.* Twenty-four 4-month-old infants ($M = 124$ days, range = 107–139 days; 14 girls and 10 boys) took part in the experiment. A further 2 did not complete testing due to fussiness, and 1 infant failed to habituate and so the data were not included. Twelve infants were assigned to each of the two conditions in such a way as to ensure that the mean age and the gender balance were comparable across conditions.

*Apparatus, stimuli, design, and procedure.* These were identical to previous experiments other than in the form of the auditory information presented during habituation trials and in the fact that only the narrow occluder display was used. In the discontinuous sound condition, a dynamic sound of the sort used in Experiment 1 was presented, but it went off abruptly at the point when the object became fully hidden by the occluder and resumed abruptly when the object began to reemerge. In the dislocated sound condition, the same sound was used as in Experiment 1, but it cycled back and forward such that when the object was at the right hand end of its cycle the sound was at the left hand end, and vice versa.

## Results and Discussion

Figure 6 illustrates the results of Experiment 3. A 2 (condition: discontinuous vs. dislocated) × 2 (test trial order) × 2 (test trial type: continuous vs. discontinuous) × 3 (test trial block) mixed ANOVA revealed an overall trend toward perception of discontinuity, as shown by greater looking at the continuous display, $F(1, 20) = 2.85$, $p = .11$, $\eta_p^2 = .13$, qualified by a Test Trial × Test Trial Order interaction, $F(1, 20) = 11.58$, $p = .003$, $\eta_p^2 = .37$. Exploration of this interaction indicated that there was significant perception of discontinuity when the first test trial was continuous, $F(1, 20) = 12.24$, $p = .006$, $\eta_p^2 = .55$, but not for the opposite order, $F(1, 20) = 1.56$, $p = .24$, $\eta_p^2 = .13$ (see Figure 7). There was neither a significant interaction

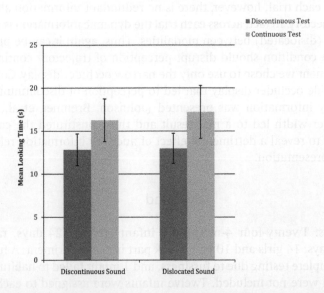

**Figure 6:** Mean looking times to the two test displays in the discontinuous and dislocated conditions of Experiment 3

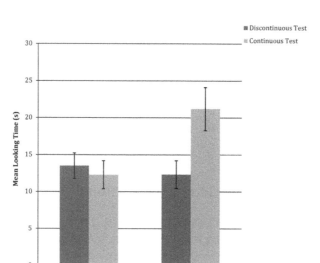

**Figure 7:** Mean looking times to the two test displays for the two test trial orders in Experiment 3

between test trial type and condition, $F(1, 20) = 0.31$, $p = .59$, $\eta_p^2 = .15$, nor a significant interaction between test trial type, condition, and test trial order, $F(1, 20) = 0.004$, $p = .95$, $\eta_p^2 = .0$. Thus, we may conclude that the significant interaction between condition and test trial order is general across the two conditions. This effect cannot be explained by a general decline in looking across test trials because there was no significant effect of test trial block, $F(2, 19) = 0.27$, $p = .76$, $\eta_p^2 = .03$.

These results confirm our prediction that presentation of both discontinuous and dislocated auditory information would have a detrimental effect on infants' perception of continuity of the visual event. However, the effect was limited to the case in which infants experienced the continuous test display first in the alternating sequence. Given that this cannot be interpreted as a simple order effect, the most plausible interpretation is that infants processed the habituation displays as discontinuous but only showed a novelty preference for the continuous test trial when it occurred first in the test trial sequence. When the discontinuous test trial was presented first, its novelty resulting from absence of occluder and sound may have attracted attention to these perceptual changes rather than continuity versus discontinuity. Of course, this effect did not occur in other experiments in this series. Although it is unclear just why it would have occurred in this experiment, we believe this constraint on the effect attests to the relatively weak negative effect of these forms of auditory information. This is in keeping with the conclusion that it is simpler to propel young infants along their developmental trajectory toward veridical perception than it is to do the opposite (Bremner et al., 2005). Specifically, once the ability to perceive trajectory continuity has begun to emerge, it may take relatively little to support its further emergence. In contrast, development of perceptual constraints may attune infants selectively to veridical information and reduce the effectiveness of nonveridical information such as incongruent or abruptly discontinuous auditory information. There is likely a parallel here with earlier work on auditory–visual learning in which it was demonstrated that young infants failed to learn incongruent auditory–visual temporal relationships (Bahrick, 1988).

## General Discussion

This series of experiments demonstrates clearly that the addition of auditory information can affect young infants' perception of trajectory continuity. The positive effects provide further evidence in keeping with the general argument that inter-sensory information, and specifically intersensory redundancy, has a vital role in directing and constraining development (Bahrick & Lickliter, 2002; Bahrick et al., 2004). The strongest positive effect was obtained in Experiment 1 in which dynamic auditory information about the object's trajectory apparently led to perception of trajectory continuity. The strength of this effect is in keeping with the predictions of the IRH, because in Experiment 1 information about the object's changing location was presented redundantly across auditory and visual modalities. However, a rather weaker effect also emerged in Experiment 2 when the sound was continuous but provided no information for the object's changing location. This finding is again consistent with the IRH, because redundancy existed in terms of common stimulus onset, offset, and duration. Infants were generally looking away when trials ended, meaning that common offset and common duration were unlikely to be detected. However, common onset may constitute sufficient redundancy to recruit attention to the visual event and enhance trajectory perception. An alternative possibility, also in keeping with the IRH, is that continuity of the sound across the period during which the object was out of sight supported perception of trajectory continuity. The result in the discontinuous sound condition of Experiment 3 supports this interpretation. A discontinuous dynamic sound, like a dislocated dynamic sound, had a negative effect on perception of trajectory continuity. Although in both these conditions there was common onset of auditory and visual events, in Experiment 3 this information is probably insufficient to support perception of trajectory continuity because conflicting information was also present. In the discontinuous sound condition auditory information specified discontinuity of trajectory, and the dislocated sound condition markedly eliminated the spatiotemporal relationship between visual and auditory information.

Rather than pointing to a shortcoming of the IRH, these results suggest an extension of the hypothesis for the particular case of perception of trajectory continuity. It seems likely that there is a hierarchy of auditory information that is more or less likely to influence perception of trajectory continuity. The most precise information for trajectory continuity is information about the continuous change in the object's location. Presenting this spatiotemporal information redundantly across the parts of the cycle in which the object is visible may act to fill in the gap in visual perception when the object passes behind the occluder (Experiment 1). However, dislocated or discontinuous presentation of this information (Experiment 3) provides conflicting or discontinuous spatiotemporal information and disrupts perception of continuity. At a lower level, providing a continuous stationary sound provides temporal information for continuity that enhances perception of trajectory continuity (Experiment 2). Finally, in all the current experiments, common onset information may have recruited attention to the habituation display. But if so, its effects were outweighed by the negative effects of discontinuity or dislocation of auditory information.

An important finding emerging from work on intersensory perception concerns the developmental sequence in which different intersensory properties are detected. Temporal synchrony is detected early and is followed by detection of information about stimulus duration, temporal rate and rhythm (Bahrick, 2001). And it is argued that temporal synchrony forms the basis for development of the later detected properties (Bahrick, 1987, 2001; Lewkowicz, 2000). In the present work, common onset is a case of temporal synchrony, and there is an interesting question of whether benefit from amodal auditory–visual information for trajectory would be lost if there was not common onset between auditory and visual information. However, the importance of synchrony between dynamic auditory and visual information for movement leads us to conclude that this cue may be primary in dynamic events of the sort we have investigated. This dynamic auditory–visual spatial colocation is a case of dynamic spatiotemporal synchrony, in which the auditory left–right cycle is in phase relative to the visual cycle. Future work should investigate the developmental relationship between this form of synchrony and detection of other properties of object trajectories such as rate and extent of movement. If there is a parallel with other work on intersensory perception, dynamic spatial colocation should form the basis for later development of sensitivity to other intersensory properties of object trajectories.

At a general level, these results both extend our understanding of young infants' perceptual abilities and attest to the importance of taking a multimodal approach. Existing work suggests that 4-month-olds have a rather fragile ability to perceive object trajectories but that this ability is readily facilitated and enhanced by reducing the processing demands of the task (Bremner et al., 2005; Johnson, Bremner, et al., 2003). The present results are a clear demonstration that supplementing visual information with auditory information can enhance 4-month-old infants' perception of object trajectories. Furthermore, many objects in the infant's everyday environment emit sounds as they move. We may speculate that infants first begin to interpolate the path of an object that is temporarily lost to sight under circumstances in which auditory information continues to provide information about its trajectory, and in general, when there is amodal auditory–visual information for the object's trajectory when the object is in view. In parallel with findings regarding infants' perception other spatio-temporal properties such as rhythm and tempo (Bahrick & Lickliter, 2004) we may predict that older infants will be less dependent on multimodal information for object trajectories, showing more robust unimodal perception of object trajectories. However, when auditory–visual information for movement is present, we may expect infants to develop increasing sensitivity to incongruence between the senses. Bremner et al. (2011) demonstrated that 2-month-olds were capable of learning an incongruent dynamic auditory–visual relationship whereas older infants only did so with additional training. We may speculate that this developmental effect is the result of accumulated experience of congruent auditory–visual information in everyday events. This, along with improvements in infants' capacity for auditory localization, may make them sensitive to increasingly subtle incongruence between auditory and visual information for object movement.

## References

Bahrick, L. E. (1987). Infants' intermodal perception of two levels of temporal structure in natural events. *Infant Behavior and Development, 10,* 387–416.

Bahrick, L. E. (1988). Intermodal learning in infancy: Learning on the basis of two kinds of invariant relations in audible and visible events. *Child Development, 59,* 197–209.

Bahrick, L. E. (2001). Increasing specificity in perceptual development: Infants' detection of nested levels of multimodal stimulation. *Journal of Experimental Child Psychology, 79,* 253–270.

Bahrick, L. E., Flom, R., & Lickliter, R. (2002). Intersensory redundancy facilitates discrimination of tempo in 30-month-old infants. *Developmental Psychobiology, 41,* 352–363.

Bahrick, L. E., & Lickliter, R. (2000). Intersensory redundancy guides attentional selectivity and perceptual learning in infancy. *Developmental Psychology, 36,* 190–201.

Bahrick, L. E., & Lickliter, R. (2002). Intersensory redundancy guides early perceptual and cognitive development. *Advances in Child Development and Behavior, 30,* 153–186.

Bahrick, L. E., & Lickliter, R. (2004). Infants' perception of rhythm and tempo in unimodal and multimodal stimulation: A developmental test of the intersensory redundancy hypothesis. Cognitive, Affective, & Behavioral Neuroscience, 4, 137–147.

Bahrick, L. E., Lickliter, R., & Flom, R. (2004). Intersensory redundancy guides infants' selective attention, perception, and cognition in infancy. *Current Directions in Psychological Science, 13,* 99–102.

Bower, T. G. R., Broughton, J., & Moore, M. K. (1971). Development of the object concept as manifested in changes in the tracking behavior of infants between 7 and 20 weeks of age. *Journal of Experimental Child Psychology, 11,* 182–193.

Bremner, J. G., Johnson, S. P., Slater, A. M., Mason, U., Cheshire, A., & Spring, J. (2007). Conditions for young infants' failure to perceive trajectory continuity. *Developmental Science, 10*, 613–624.

Bremner, J. G., Johnson, S. P., Slater, A. M., Mason, U., Foster, K., Cheshire, A., et al. (2005). Conditions for young infants' perception of object trajectories. *Child Development, 76*, 1029–1043.

Bremner, J. G., Slater, A. M., Johnson, S. P., Mason, U., Spring, J., & Bremner, M. (2011). Two- to eight-month-old infants' perception of dynamic auditory-visual spatial co-location. *Child Development, 82*, 1210–1223.

Clifton, R. K., Morrongiello, B. A., Kulig, J. W., & Dowd, J. M. (1981). Developmental changes in auditory localization in infancy. In R. Aslin, J. Alberts, & M. Petersen (Eds.), *Development of perception: Psychobiological perspectives* (Vol. 1, pp. 141–160). New York: Academic Press.

Cohen, L. B., Atkinson, D. J., & Chaput, H. H. (2000). *Habit 2000: A new program for testing infant perception and cognition. (Version 1.0)* [Computer software]. Austin: The University of Texas.

Field, J., Muir, D., Pilon, R., Sinclair, M., & Dodwell, P. (1980). Infants' orientation to lateral sounds from birth to three months. *Child Development, 51*, 295–298.

Goldberg, S. (1976). Visual tracking and existence constancy in 5-month-old infants. *Journal of Experimental Child Psychology, 22*, 478–491.

Gredebäck, G., & von Hofsten, C. (2004). Infants' evolving representations of object motion during occlusion: A longitudinal study of 6- to 12-month-old infants. *Infancy, 6*, 165–184.

Johnson, S. P., Amso, D., & Slemmer, J. A. (2003). Development of object concepts in infancy: Evidence for early learning in an eye-tracking paradigm. *Proceedings of the National Academy of Sciences of the United States of America, 100*, 10568–10573.

Johnson, S. P., Bremner, J. G., Slater, A. M., Mason, U. C., Foster, K., & Cheshire, A. (2003). Infants' perception of object trajectories. *Child Development, 74*, 94–108.

Lawson, K. R. (1980). Spatial and temporal congruity and auditory-visual integration in infants. *Developmental Psychology, 16*, 185–192.

Lewkowicz, D. J. (2000). The development of intersensory temporal perception: An epigenetic systems/limitations view. *Psychological Bulletin, 126*, 281–308.

Lewkowicz, D. J., & Turkewitz, G. (1980). Cross-modal equivalence in early infancy: Auditory-visual intensity matching. *Developmental Psychology, 16*, 597–607.

Lewkowicz, D. J., & Turkewitz, G. (1981). Intersensory interaction in newborns: Modification of visual preferences following exposure to sound. *Child Development, 52*, 827–832.

Moore, M. K., Borton, R., & Darby, B. L. (1978). Visual tracking in young infants: Evidence for object identity or object permanence? *Journal of Experimental Child Psychology, 25*, 183–198.

Morrongiello, B. A. (1988). Infants' localization of sounds in the horizontal plane: Estimates of minimum audible angle. *Developmental Psychology, 24*, 8–13.

Morrongiello, B. A., Fenwick, K. D., & Chance, G. (1990). Sound localization acuity in very young infants: An observer-based testing procedure. *Developmental Psychology, 26*, 75–84.

Morrongiello, B. A., Fenwick, K. D., & Chance, G. (1998). Crossmodal learning in newborn infants: Inferences about properties of auditory-visual events. *Infant Behavior & Development, 21*, 543–554.

Morrongiello, B. A., Fenwick, K. D., & Nutley, T. (1998). Developmental changes in associations between auditory-visual events. *Infant Behavior & Development, 21*, 613–626.

Muir, D. W., Clifton, R. K., & Clarkson, M. G. (1989). The development of a human auditory localization response: A U-shaped function. *Canadian Journal of Psychology, 43*, 199–216.

Pickens, J. (1994). Perception of auditory-visual distance relations by 5-month-old infants. *Developmental Psychology, 30*, 537–544.

Rosander, K., & von Hofsten, C. (2004). Infants' emerging ability to represent occluded object motion. *Cognition, 91*, 1–22.

Walker-Andrews, A. S., & Lennon, E. M. (1985). Auditory-visual perception of changing distance by human infants. *Child Development, 56*, 544–548.

# 50

# Crossmodal Learning in Newborn Infants: Inferences about Properties of Auditory-Visual Events

*Barbara A. Morrongiello, Kimberley D. Fenwick and*
*Graham Chance*

## Introdution

Most objects and events we encounter in the world provide for multimodal stimulation. Adults routinely integrate these diverse sensations into a unified percept. Not surprisingly, owing to the significance of these abilities for one's perceptual experiences, there has been considerable interest in establishing if cross-modal perception is present in less mature perceivers. Two opposing theoretical positions about the ontogenetic course of crossmodal learning and perception during infancy have received much attention in the literature. Piaget (1952), among others (e.g., McGurk, Turnure & Creighton, 1977), argues that the senses provide distinct and separate information at birth, with increasing integration of these sources of information emerging from accumulated sensori-motor experiences with events and objects. By contrast, Gibson (1969) argues that crossmodal learning and perception should be present at birth. Neonates presumably can detect higher-order amodal properties (i.e., invariant relations), such as temporal synchrony and colocation, which serve to unite auditory with visual events. Perceptual learning with accumulated experiences might result in increasing differentiation of distinctive features or refinements in detection of invariant

**Source:** *Infant Behavior & Development,* 21(4) (1998): 543–553.

relations. However, the basic ability to experience unified percepts when presented bimodal events should be evident at birth (see Gibson, 1992). Although these theories make different predictions as to whether newborns and young infants should show crossmodal learning and perception, there have been surprisingly few studies conducted with infants at very young ages. Toward this aim, in the present study we examined whether neonates would show crossmodal learning of arbitrary auditory-visual relations.

Although evidence reveals a number of links between auditory and visual functioning in human neonates (e.g., Clifton, Morrongiello, Kulig & Dowd, 1981; Mendelson & Haith, 1976; Morrongiello, Fenwick & Chance, 1994), there is no unequivocable evidence of auditory-visual crossmodal perception at birth (see Morrongiello, 1994 for review and discussion). Aronson and Rosenblum (1971) argued that 1-month-old infants experienced a unity of the senses and common mapping of auditory-visual space. However, their experiment was methodologically weak and the findings were not substantiated when more adequate procedures were employed (McGurk & Lewis, 1974). The earliest age at which auditory-visual crossmodal perception has been demonstrated under rigorous testing conditions is 3 weeks of age (Lewkowicz & Turkewitz, 1980). In fact, the only findings of which we are aware to support the claim that newborns are capable of crossmodal perception examined transfer of information about shape across visual-tactual modalities (e.g., Kaye & Bower, 1994; Meltzoff & Moore, 1977), although it bears noting that a number of important issues have been raised about Meltzoff and Moore's (1977) original demonstration of the effects (e.g., Anisfield, Master, Jacobsen & Kagan, 1979; Hayes & Watson, 1981). Suffice it to say, whether neonates demonstrate integration of auditory-visual information and show crossmodal learning remains to be determined.

Although there are no unequivocable demonstrations of auditory-visual integration at birth, a number of studies reveal abilities present at birth that are relevant to auditory-visual crossmodal perception. Research on visual functioning indicates that neonates extract information about object shape, remember objects over time, process relational information thereby perceiving similarities and differences between stimuli, and they recognize the constancy of an object's identity across transformations in orientation and movement (Slater & Morison, 1985; Slater, Morison & Rose, 1982, 1984; Slater, Morison, Town & Rose, 1985). Similarly, neonates readily localize and discriminate sounds, and remember sounds over time (Morrongiello & Gotowiec, 1990; Morrongiello et al., 1994; Swain, Zelazo & Clifton, 1993; Weiss, Zelazo & Swain, 1988). Thus, neonates enter the world with a number of abilities that could support auditory-visual crossmodal learning and their drawing inferences about properties of sight-sound events they encounter.

The focus in the present study was twofold: To determine if neonates can learn arbitrary sight-sound pairings, and to examine what some inferences might be that they make when repeatedly encountering such events. The ability to draw inferences about events and objects greatly increases the efficiency of and potential for learning: Detecting similarities between novel and familiar events or objects allows one to formulate expectations about features or characteristics of the novel exemplar, and eliminates the need to learn anew about underlying properties. Not surprisingly, therefore, research reveals infants reason about events and object properties at very young ages (Baillargeon, 1987a, b; Baillargeon & DeVos, 1991; Baillargeon, Spelke & Wasserman, 1985). Drawing on Baillargeon's research on infants' reasoning, in the present study we used a violation-of-expectancy procedure. Neonates were familiarized with sight-sound pairings and, following habituation, were presented two test trials to assess learning and the development of expectations about these bimodal events. Increased looking time (i.e., dishabituation) on test trials was taken as evidence that newborns had learned the sight-sound associations and made certain inferences about constraints on the identity and location of these bimodal events.

Three test conditions were included. In the *dis-location* condition, the sound was colocated with the toy during the habituation phase; across trials, the bimodal event was sometimes presented to the right of infant's midline and sometimes to the left of midline. During dishabituation, the toy and sound were presented on opposite sides of midline. The aim of this condition was to address the question of whether newborns expect that a toy and sound that have always been colocated will continue to co-occur together in space if they are presented from a new location. This condition also provided a test of infants' learning arbitrary sight-sound pairings. We hypothesized that if infants had learned to associate the sight with the sound during habituation, and they expected these sights and sounds to persist in being collocated, then they would respond with renewed looking during the dishabituation test when these stimuli were no longer colocated in space.

In the *change in toy* condition, two toys were presented during the habituation and test phases. The sound was colocated only with one of the toys during habituation and was shifted to be presented with the other toy during dishabituation. The purpose of this condition was to address the question of whether newborns recognize that a particular sound is unique to a particular object. This condition also provided a test of newborns' abilities to learn arbitrary sight-sound pairings based on colocation. We hypothesized that if they had learned to associate the original toy with the sound, and they expected that these would remain colocated together, then they would respond by renewed looking when the novel sight-sound pairing was presented during the dishabituation test.

Finally, in the *change in location* condition, only one toy was presented, and this was colocated with a sound. During the dishabituation test, the toy and sound continued to be presented in a colocated fashion but in another location than that used during habituation. The purpose of this condition was to address the question of whether newborns recognize that an object and its corresponding sound can change location in space and that the critical feature is that they remain colocated, not their spatial locus per se.

# Method

## Subjects

The final sample included 36 healthy full-term (38–42 weeks gestational age) newborn infants with birthweights higher than 2500 g and Apgar scores of 7 or higher at 1 and 5 minutes after birth. Infants were randomly assigned to one of three conditions, resulting in 12 neonates (6 males and 6 females) in each group. Data from an additional 5 infants were discarded due to inappropriate state (i.e., fussy or sleepy, $N = 1$) or failure to reach habituation criterion ($N = 4$); fussiness was operationalized as any sign of discomfort (e.g., crying, excessive movement) and sleepiness was defined as eyes closed, body limp, and slow rhythmical breathing. Exclusion based on these factors was distributed evenly across sex. Infants were recruited from the maternity ward at St. Joseph's Health Centre in London, Ontario and were tested within 2 days after birth before leaving the hospital. Males were tested either before circumcision or at least 24 hr after circumcision.

## Stimuli & Apparatus

Testing took place within a laboratory suite adjacent to the maternity ward; the suite was designed for biomedical research and was very well insulated to eliminate extraneous audio and electrical noise. During testing, infants were held upright on a hospital bed facing a custom-built apparatus similar to a puppet stage with a curtain rod extended horizontally across the top of the stage and a black curtain hanging from the rod. The puppet stage was positioned lengthwise on the bed. The distance from the surface of the bed to the top of the puppet stage was approximately 70 cm and the width of the stage was approximately 75 cm. The whole apparatus was painted flat black.

The auditory stimulus was a rattle sound produced by rhythmically shaking a small plastic jar 1/3 filled with popcorn kernels at a rate of twice per s. Spectrographic analysis indicated that the sound produced was a broadband signal containing frequencies ranging from 50 to 7000 Hz, with a peak around 2800 Hz. An audio cassette recording (AIWA F800C) was made of the rattle sound and used during testing. The sound was amplified (Realistic, SA-150) and played on an audio tape deck (AIWA F800C) at approximately 68 dB SPL over an ambient noise level of approximately 44 dB SPL, as measured by a Bruel and Kjaer sound-level meter having a 1-inch condensor microphone positioned at the approximate location of the infant's head during testing.

The visual stimuli consisted of 6 different brightly colored lightweight commercially available cloth toys (i.e., Sesame Street figures) having an average height of 14 cm, average width of 10 cm, and average depth (i.e., distance from front to back) of 4 cm. Velcro was used to attach the toys to the end of metal rods for presentation to subjects during test trials, each toy was attached to a separate rod and two rods were used during each trial. A miniature loudspeaker was attached to each metal rod directly behind each toy; the auditory stimulus was delivered over these loudspeakers.

Test sessions were video-and audio-recorded, although all scoring took place online during testing. A small hole at the midpoint of the curtain allowed a videocamera lens (Sony, AVC-1400) to poke through the curtain for recording (Panasonic, AG2200) a close-up view of the infant's face during testing. This view was available to one of the two experimenters on a 16-in black and white monitor (Commodore, 1802) and provided a basis for scoring during testing. A microphone positioned on the floor allowed for recording the start and stop of each trial on the video record.

Testing was controlled by a customized computer program run on a microcomputer (Tron 386). A custom-built three-switch apparatus interfaced with the computer and allowed the experimenter to initiate a trial and to record the infant's looking time to the right and left sides of the puppet stage; each switch was controlled by means of a foot press.

## Procedure & Design

Infants were tested when in a state of alert inactivity using an infant-control habituation procedure, followed by the presentation of test trials aimed at assessing their learning of sight-sound pairs and expectations with respect to some properties of these bimodal events. The general test procedure was adapted from that developed by Slater and Morison and colleagues to study a variety of aspects of newborn visual functioning (e.g., Slater & Morison, 1985; Slater et al., 1982).

Drawing on the work of Baillargeon and her colleagues with 3- and 5-month-old infants, each session began with a habituation phase consisting of at least six trials. Each trial during habituation was initiated when the infant looked at the stimulus display and was terminated when the infant had looked away from the event for 2 consecutive seconds after having looked at it for at least 6 cumulative seconds (cf. Baillargeon & DeVos, 1991; Baillargeon & Graber, 1987); we opted to use a termination criteria that forced a certain amount of looking as well as non-looking, as opposed to one that was predicated only on non-looking (e.g., looked away for 2 consecutive seconds, cf. Slater, Morison, Town & Rose, 1985), in order to allow us to minimize the number of habituation trials allowable while still ensuring a sufficient amount of study time by each infant. Looking times on the first two trials were averaged to establish a baseline level of looking. Subsequently, habituation trials were presented and continued until (a) the infant satisfied a criterion of habituation of a 50% decrease in looking time on 2 successive trials following baseline, or (b) completed 9 habituation trials (cf. Baillargeon & DeVos, 1991), after which time a session was terminated and the infant's data were discarded. It should be noted that although Baillargeon includes in her final sample infants who do not reach habituation criterion (e.g., Baillargeon & De Vos, 1991), we thought it best to aim for a more uniform sample and therefore to limit our final sample only to those infants who habituated; this decision was motivated too by findings suggesting cognitive differences among infants who demonstrate slow versus faster rates of visual processing (e.g., Columbo, Mitchell, Coldren & Freeseman, 1991). If the infant reached the habituation criterion within the allotted number of trials, a dishabituation phase was presented. Two trials were presented during the dishabituation phase, each lasting 30 s, and looking time was recorded in the same manner as during the habituation phase.

A between-subjects design was used, with different infants tested under each of the three conditions: *dis-location* condition, *change in toy* condition, and *change in location* condition. In all conditions, two rods were presented, one on either side of the infant's midline, and moved in synchrony with the sound. Thus, infants had to use colocation as a basis for crossmodal learning, since temporal synchrony was not a clue that differentiated between sides.

In the *dis-location* condition, two rods were presented during the habituation phase, one each on either side of the infant's midline. Both rods had a loudspeaker positioned near the end and one had a toy attached in front of the loudspeaker. During the habituation phase, the sound was colocated with the toy. Across trials, the same toy and sound were presented in a colocated fashion but the side of midline on which the toy-sound event was presented was varied. Prior to beginning the test session, the side on which the toy-sound event would be presented on each trial was randomly determined with the following constraints on randomization: (1) the toy-sound event be presented an equal number of times from each side, and (2) the toy-sound event be presented on the same side of midline on no more than two consecutive trials. During dishabituation, the toy was presented on one side of midline while the sound was presented on the opposite side of midline. The side of midline on which the toy was presented was randomly chosen for the first dishabituation trial, with a reversal of sides for the second dishabituation trial.

In the *change in toy* condition, two toys were presented, one on each rod on either side of midline, during the habituation and test phases; prior to the onset of the habituation phase, each toy was presented without movement or sound and at midline, each for 20 s, to familiarize the infants with each toy. During habituation, the sound was colocated only with one of the toys across trials. Side of sound presentation was randomized following the same procedure used in the *dis-location* condition. During the dishabituation phase, the sound was presented with the other toy on one side of the baby's midline and the toy that had been presented with the sound during habituation was presented from the opposite side of midline and without a sound; across the two test trials the novel pairing occurred once to the right of the infant's midline and once to the left of midline, with the order randomly determined for each baby.

In the *change in location* condition, two rods with loudspeakers were presented but only one toy was presented, colocated with a sound. The toy and sound were presented on the same side of midline across trials, and always in a colocated fashion. However, the exact location of the sight-sound event was varied randomly across habituation trials. The side of midline on which the stimuli were presented during habituation was determined randomly across infants with the constraint that half the infants receive the bimodal event on the right side of midline and half on their left side of midline. During the dishabituation test, the toy and sound were presented in a colocated fashion but on the side of midline opposite to where they had been presented during habituation; across test trials the exact location of the sight-sound event was varied although it remained on the novel side of midline in both cases.

Two experimenters were required for each test session: One experimenter held the infant, and the other operated the equipment and scored looking responses. Both wore headphones over which the sound was played, thereby allowing experimenters to know when the sound was playing but preventing them from determining on which side of the infant the sound was playing. Infants were swaddled in a receiving blanket from the shoulders downward with the neck and head completely uncovered to allow complete freedom of head movement. One experimenter was behind the baby, and positioned the newborn in an upright seated position facing the apparatus. The experimenter supported the infant's back with one hand and positioned the other hand under the baby's chin, holding the hand open in a flat position to provide a platform on which the baby rested his/her chin while maintaining full capability for side-to-side head movements. The experimenter briefly turned the baby away from the apparatus between trials and spoke her name or sang in order to maintain a quiet and alert state.

On each trial, the experimenter operating the equipment sat on the side of the curtain opposite the infant so she was not visible to the infant. At the start of a trial, this experimenter switched on the rattle sound by pressing the on/off switch on the amplifier and immediately slid the two rods underneath the curtain holding them in such a way that toys attached to the rods appeared upright in front of the infant. During all trials, the experimenter operating the equipment coded looking behavior by watching the video-monitor and using the footpedal apparatus to record the infant's looking behavior. The experimenter sat with her back to the computer screen so she had no knowledge of accumulated looking time during a trial. An audible beep, generated by the computer, sounded to indicate the beginning and end of a trial for the experimenters. At the end of a trial, the experimenter operating the equipment withdrew the rods behind the curtain and switched off the rattle sound. This experimenter then set up for the next trial and began the trial by depressing the appropriate pedal on the foot-pedal apparatus when the two experimenters agreed that the baby was positioned properly and looking straight ahead at the puppet display. If the baby was not looking toward the display area, the experimenter operating the equipment would call to the baby to get her visual attention forward facing before starting the trial. The test session typically lasted about 12 minutes.

During the session, state was coded independently by the two experimenters. The experimenter operating the equipment coded state either as positive (i.e., eyes open with baby quiet and alert) or negative (i.e., eyes closed or fussy or sleeping). Subsequently, the experimenter holding the baby indicated her rating of state. Disagreements (<1% of all trials) were resolved by discussion at the time. To minimize discarding the data of subjects due to poor state, no trial was initiated until the infant was judged to be in a positive state by both experimenters. The experimenter holding the baby was a nurse by training, had extensive experience with newborns, and was highly successful in coaxing infants to a positive state. In addition, much attention was paid to the timing of a test session in order to ensure the baby's comfort during the session (e.g., had been fed recently, diaper was clean).

Inter-rater reliability on coding infants' looking was established based on 22% of the sample by having a second coder score looking from the videorecords. Kappa statistic revealed 92% reliability, allowing for a difference of 200 msec on a trial. The data of the primary coder were analyzed.

# Results

## Familiarization Trials/Habituation Phase

To evaluate if infants across groups responded similarly to the familiarization events, an Analysis of Variance (ANOVA) was performed on the number of trials to habituation, with sex (2) and condition (3) as factors. Results revealed no significant differences across groups or due to the infant's sex ($ps > .05$). On average, following baseline, newborns habituated in 5.5 trials ($SD = .51$ trials). Consistent with this, an ANOVA on the total looking time revealed no significant differences due to sex or group assignment: Infants looked to the events an average of 72.20 s ($SD = 6.96$ s) before reaching habituation criterion. Similarly, a MANOVA on the total duration of looking during trial 1 as compared to the last trial of familiarization did not reveal any differences due to the neonate's sex or group assignment ($ps > .05$). The only significant finding was that looking times decreased across trials, as one would expect during habituation [$F (1, 30) = 211.34, p < .001$]. Infants looked about

17.56 s during the first trial and this declined to 7.08 s (*SD* = .77) by the last habituation trial. In summary, during familiarization, across conditions, neonates showed similar rates of habituation and total looking times to the events presented.

## Test Trials and Dishabituation

To analyze the results of the test phase, we initially compared looking on test trials 1 and 2. Separate MANOVAs were performed for each condition, with sex (2) and trial (2) as factors. Results for each condition revealed no differences in the mean looking time across test trials (*ps* > .05). Consequently, we averaged the data across test trials and then assessed for dishabituation and differences in looking behavior across conditions. In Figure 1 is shown the average looking times of infants in each condition during familiarization and testing.

With respect to looking at specific stimulus events during test trials, there did not seem to be any consistent preference that emerged across conditions regarding orienting to sound versus a sight per se: infants in the Dis-location condition looked at the silent familiar toy 67% of the time and at the loudspeaker from which the sound was presented on the other side of midline the remaining 33% of the time; for the change in toy condition, infants looked to the novel sight-sound pairing for 56% of the time, and to the toy that was presented without sound but had been previously paired with the sound for 44% of the time; for the change in location condition, infants looked to the sight-sound pairing 86% of the time, with the remaining time spent looking to the rod alone on the other side of midline.

To determine if looking during test trials varied across condition, we conducted an ANOVA with sex (2) and condition (3) as factors. Results revealed significant differences across conditions in infants' looking on test trials [$F(2, 30) = 224.74, p < .001$]. A Newman-Keuls test confirmed that there was significantly more looking on test trials in the dis-location (*M* = 17.31 s) and change in toy (*M* = 16.50 s) conditions, than for the change in location (*M* = 6.80 s) condition (*ps* < .05), as shown in Figure 1.

To further assess for differences in looking across conditions, a MANOVA was applied to infants' dishabituation scores (i.e., average looking time during test minus looking on the last habituation trial), with sex (2), condition (3) and trials (2) as factors. A significant effect of condition confirmed that dishabituation did not occur in all conditions [$F(2, 30) = 186.54, p < .001$]. One-sample *t* tests comparing dishabituation scores with a score of 0 (i.e., no dishabituation) revealed that infants dishabituated in the dis-location condition (*M* = 9.32 s) and the change in toy condition (*M* = 10.44 s; *ps* < .05). However, infants did not dishabituate in the change in location condition (*M* = .34; *p* > .05). Thus, infants apparently treated as novel a change in sight-sound pairing,

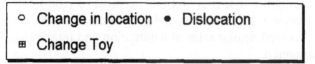

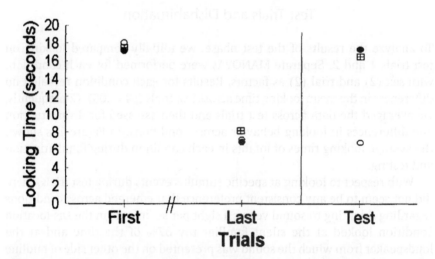

**Figure 1:** Looking times (seconds) during familiarization and test for infants in each condition

and a separation in location of sight and sound. However, they accepted as familiar changes in the absolute location of the sight-sound pair.

## Discussion

The present findings provide support for the notion that newborns are capable of learning sight-sound associations, and they do so with fairly limited exposure to bimodal events. The results suggest also that neonates develop certain expectations about properties of bimodal events based on repeated exposure to these events.

In the dis-location condition, neonates were habituated to a toy and sound that always occurred together, although they saw the toy and sound on one side of midline for half of the habituation trials, and on the opposite side of midline during the remaining trials. During testing, neonates saw the toy on one side and heard the sound on the opposite side. Neonates reacted with increased looking time to the separation of the sight and sound during the test phase, even though they had previously been exposed both to the sight and sound on each side of midline. Thus, neonates seem to develop the expectation that paired stimuli will remain spatially colocated.

In the change in toy condition, neonates were shown two toys and a sound paired with one of the toys. As in the dis-location condition, the absolute location of the toy-sound pair changed location over habituation trials but the pairing remained constant. Neonates habituated to this condition, indicating that they remembered the toy-sound pairing and were not surprised when the pair changed in absolute location. However, when the toy paired with the sound was switched, neonates dishabituated and responded with increased looking. This result suggests that infants had learned to associate a particular sight with a specific sound, and they expected this pairing to remain constant.

Finally, in the change in location condition, neonates habituated to a sight-sound pairing that occurred on the same side of midline but in different spatial locations. The infants apparently formed an association between the sight and sound and did not treat minor changes in absolute location as novel. During test trials, the sight-sound pairing was presented on the side of midline opposite to that during habituation, and infants did not show increased looking. These findings suggest that newborns accepted changes in absolute location of a sight-sound pairing as expected events, even if these involved the introduction of fairly dramatic changes in location (i.e., across midline).

Taken together, these findings suggest that infants very soon after birth are capable of crossmodal learning and of drawing inferences about properties of sight-sound events they encounter. Gibson (1969) has suggested that crossmodal perception should be evident at birth, with infants entering the world able to detect amodal invariant relations that serve to unite audible with visible events, such as temporal synchrony and colocation. By contrast, Piaget (1952) argues that crossmodal perception emerges much later during infancy, following an increasing integration of the senses with accumulated sensori-motor experiences. The present findings are consistent with Gibson's theoretical views. Although spontaneous integration of auditory-visual information was not evaluated, the results obtained indicate that newborns detect and utilize the amodal property of colocation in learning sight-sound associations. If they did not do so, they would have had no basis for associating the sound with a particular toy in the change in toy condition, since both toys moved in synchrony with the sound.

Previous research by Aronson and Rosenbloom (1971) suggested that by 1 month of age infants expect familiar sights and sounds (e.g., mother's voice and face) to be colocated. However, these findings were not replicated when more rigorous methodological constraints were imposed (e.g., Condry, Haltom & Neisser, 1977; McGurk & Lewis, 1974). Lyons-Ruth (1977) provided evidence that infants by 4-month-olds could learn sight-sound relations based on colocation. Lawson (1980) directly evaluated the necessity of colocation and how this interacts with temporal synchrony to influence 6-month-olds' learning about sight-sound associations. She presented infants with a number of conditions, including ones in which sights and sounds were colocated but asynchronous and ones in which they were synchronous but not colocated.

She found that synchrony alone did not result in learning in the absence of colocation, and colocation resulted in learning under only some synchronous conditions. Thus, both synchrony and colocation influence crossmodal learning in infants, and neither property is necessarily sufficient to ensure crossmodal learning. The two amodal properties obviously interact to influence infants' learning of sight-sound associations (see Morrongiello, 1994 for extensive discussion). In the present study, infants had both synchrony and colocation information available, and these cues were not made to conflict. Hence we cannot speak to the issue of whether one amodal property plays a more primary role than another in guiding crossmodal learning at birth. Suffice it to say, however, when temporal synchrony is present and provides ambiguous information as to which toy is associated with the sound (e.g., change in toy condition), neonates can utilize colocation information to disambiguate the situation, and they associate the sound with the toy with which it is colocated. Thus, the present findings extends downward the age at which infants had previously been show to utilize colocation in formulating sight-sound associations.

In previous research, Baillargeon and Spelke and their colleagues have demonstrated fairly sophisticated reasoning about physical properties of objects in infants as young as 3 and 4 months of age (see review in Spelke, 1991). Drawing on these findings, Spelke (1991) has argued for the notion of innate core principles that serve to guide infants' reasoning about properties of objects and events they encounter in the world. The present study yields findings consistent with the notion that infants, at birth, have a sufficiently developed inferential-reasoning system to represent and reason about objects and events they encounter. Specifically, newborns expect auditory and visual properties to be consistent characteristics of a given object and to remain so despite change in that object's spatial location. Future research, building on the success of the present methodology, may reveal other properties, apart from location and identity, about which neonates formulate expectations when they encounter bimodal events.

# References

Anisfield, M., Master, J., Jacobsen, S., & Kagan, J. (1979). Interpreting "imitative" responses in early infancy. *Science, 205*, 214–219.

Aronson, E., & Rosenblum, S. (1971). Space perception in early infancy: Perception within a common auditory-visual space. *Science, 172*, 1161–1163.

Baillargeon, R. (1987a). Object permanence in 3.5- and 4.5-month-old infants. *Developmental Psychology, 23*, 655–664.

Baillargeon, R. (1987b). Young infants' reasoning about the physical and spatial properties of a hidden object. *Cognitive Development, 2*, 179–200.

Baillargeon, R., & De Vos, J. (1991). Object permanence in young infants: Further evidence. *Child Development, 62*, 1227–1246.

Baillargeon, R., & Graber, M. (1987). Where is the rabbit: 5.5-month-old infants' representation of the height of a hidden object. *Cognitive Development, 2*, 375–392.

Baillargeon, R., Spelke, E., & Wasserman, S. (1985). Object permanence in 5-month-old infants. *Cognition, 20*, 191–208.

Clifton, R., Morrongiello, B. A., Kulig, J., & Dowd, J. (1981). Newborns' orientation to sounds: Possible implications for cortical development. *Child Development, 52*, 833–841.

Columbo, J., Mitchell, D. W., Coldren, J., & Freeseman, L. (1991). Individual differences in infant visual attention: Are short lookers fasters processors or feature processors? *Child Development, 62*, 1247–1257.

Condry, S., Haltom, M., & Neisser, U. (1977). Infant sensitivity to audio-visual discrepancy: A failure to replicate. *Bulletin of the Psychonomic Society, 9*, 431–432.

Gibson, E. (1969). *Principles of perceptual learning and development.* NY: Appleton-Century-Crofts.

Gibson, E. (1992). How to think about perceptual learning: Twenty-five years later. In H. Pick, P. vanden Broek, & D. Knill (Eds.), *Cognition: Conceptual and methodological issues* (pp. 215–239). Washington: American Psychological Association.

Hayes, L., & Watson, J. (1981). Neonatal imitation: Fact or artifact? *Developmental Psychology, 17*, 653–660.

Kaye, K., & Bower, T. G. R. (1994). Learning and intermodal transfer of information in newborns. *Psychological Science, 5*, 286–288.

Lawson, K. (1980). Spatial and temporal incongruity and auditory-visual integration in infants. *Developmental Psychology, 16*, 185–192.

Lewkowicz, D., & Turkewitz, G. (1980). Cross-modal equivalence in early infancy: Auditory-visual intensity matching. *Developmental Psychology, 16*, 597–607.

Lyons-Ruth, K. (1977). Bimodal perception in infancy: Response to auditory-visual incongruity. *Child Development, 48*, 820–827.

McGurk, H., & Lewis, M. (1974). Space perception in early infancy: Perception within a common auditory-visual space? *Science, 186*, 649–650.

McGurk, H., Turnure, C., & Creighton, S. (1977). Auditory-visual coordination in neonates. *Child Development, 48*, 138–143.

Meltzoff, A., & Moore, M. K. (1977) Imitation of facial and manual gestures by human neonates. *Science, 198*, 75–78.

Mendelson, M., & Haith, M. (1976). The relation between audition and vision in the human newborn. *Monograph of the Society for Research in Child Development, 41* (Serial No. 167).

Morrongiello, B.A. (1994). Effects of colocation on auditory-visual interactions and cross-modal perception in infants. In D. Lewkowicz, & R. Lickliter (Eds.), *The development of intersensory perception* (pp. 235–263). NY: Academic Press.

Morrongiello, B., Fenwick, K., & Chance, G. (1994). Sound localization in newborn infants. *Developmental Psychobiology, 27*, 519–538.

Morrongiello, B. A., & Gotowiec, A. (1990). Recent advances in the behavioral study of infant audition: Sound localization. *Journal of Speech and Language Pathology and Audiology, 14*, 187–208.

Piaget, J. (1952). *The origins of intelligence in children.* NY: International Universities Press.

Slater, A., & Morison, V. (1985). Shape constancy and slant perception at birth. *Perception, 14*, 337–344.

Slater, A., Morison, V., Town, C., & Rose, D. (1985). Movement perception and identity constancy in the new-born baby. *British Journal of Developmental Psychology, 3*, 211–220.

Slater, A., Morison, V., & Rose, D. (1982). Visual memory at birth. *British Journal of Developmental Psychology, 73*, 519–525.

Slater, A., Morison, V., & Rose, D. (1984). Newborn infants' perception of similarities and differences between two- and three-dimensional stimuli. *British Journal of Developmental Psychology, 2,* 287–294.

Spelke, E. (1991). Physical knowledge in infancy. In S. Carey, & R. Gelman (Eds.), *The epigenesis of mind* (pp. 133–169). NJ: Erlbaum.

Swain, I., Zelazo, P., & Clifton, R. (1993). Newborn infants' memory for speech sounds retained over 24 hours. *Developmental Psychology, 29,* 312–323.

Weiss, M., Zelazo, P., & Swain, I. (1988). Newborn response to auditory stimulus discrepancy. *Child Development, 59,* 1530–1541.

# 51

# Intermodal Perception at Birth: Intersensory Redundancy Guides Newborn Infants' Learning of Arbitrary Auditory–Visual Pairings

*Alan Slater, Paul C. Quinn, Elizabeth Brown and Rachel Hayes*

M ost of the objects and events that we experience are intermodal in that they provide information to more than one sensory modality. Such intermodal information can be broadly categorized into one of two types of relation, amodal and arbitrary. Amodal perception is where two (or more) senses provide information that is equivalent in one or more respects, and many types of amodal perception have been demonstrated in early infancy. Newborn infants reliably turn their heads and eyes in the direction of a sound source, indicating that spatial location is given by both visual and auditory information (Wertheimer, 1961; Butterworth, 1983; Muir & Clifton, 1985). By 4 months infants are sensitive to temporal synchrony specified intermodally in that they detect the common rhythm and duration of tones and flashing lights (Lewkowicz, 1986). Four-month-olds also detect and match appropriately the sounds made either by a single unitary element or by a cluster of smaller elements (Bahrick, 1987, 1988). Thus, there is evidence that infants, from birth, perceive a wide range of invariant amodal relations.

However, many of the intermodal relationships that we perceive appear to be quite arbitrary. For example, there is no information specifying *a priori* that a particular animal makes a certain sound, that a particular voice is associated with a particular face, or that an object makes a certain sound on making

**Source:** *Developmental Science*, 2(3) (1999): 333–338.

contact with a certain surface. Research suggests that arbitrary intermodal relations are learned in infancy: Spelke and Owsley (1979) found that 3.5-month-olds had learned to associate the sound of their mother's voice with the sight of her face, and Hernandez-Reif, Cigales and Lundy (1994) reported that 6-month-olds learned the face–voice pairings of same-sex female strangers; Reardon and Bushnell (1988) reported that 7-month-olds were able to learn the association between the colour of a container and the taste of the food it contained.

Many intermodal events give both amodal and arbitrary information. For instance, when a person speaks the synchrony of voice and mouth provides amodal information, whereas the pairing of the face and the sound of the voice is arbitrary. Infants' learning about intermodal relations, both amodal and arbitrary, has been investigated in detail in studies by Bahrick (e.g. 1987, 1988, in press; Bahrick & Pickens, 1994; Gogate & Bahrick, 1998). Gogate and Bahrick (1998) habituated 7-month-old infants to video films of vowel–object pairs in three conditions. In the moving-synchronous (amodal) condition intersensory redundancy was present and the movement of the object was temporally coordinated with the vowel sound, but in the other two conditions (still and moving-asynchronous) the infants saw stationary objects or objects and sounds that were out of synchrony. The results indicated that it was only in the first condition that the infants learned the arbitrary speech–object relations. Gogate and Bahrick (1998) relate their findings to early language acquisition and suggest that such temporal synchrony is 'an important precursor to the development of lexical comprehension in infancy' (p. 133).

The major conclusion resulting from this and other studies is that learning about intermodal relations appears to be most effective when amodal, redundant relations (in the above study temporal synchrony) are present. These findings lead to the view that, in a given domain, 'intermodal knowledge about arbitrary relations is differentiated only after amodal relations are detected' and that 'detection of amodal invariants precedes and guides learning about arbitrary object–sound relations by directing infants' attention to appropriate object–sound pairings and then promoting sustained attention and further differentiation' (Bahrick & Pickens, 1994, pp. 225–226).

Slater, Brown and Badenoch (1997) investigated the ability of newborn infants to learn arbitrary intermodal relations. In their experiment the infants were familiarized to two simple line stimuli (differing in colour and orientation) presented alternately, each accompanied by the presentation of its 'own' sound. In these familiarization trials amodal information was present in the form of temporal synchrony: the auditory stimulus was only presented when the infant looked at the visual stimulus. On subsequent test trials the infants were given alternate presentation of a familiar and a novel sight-sound combination, and attention recovered to the novel combination but not to the familiar one. This finding is a clear demonstration that newborn infants can learn arbitrary auditory–visual combinations. The findings and conclusions by Bahrick, described above, suggest that such learning should be facilitated and guided by the presence of amodal invariants, but we do not know if this principle applies to newborn infants, or if newborns are able to learn arbitrary auditory–visual relations in the absence of amodal information. The experiment described here was designed to test newborn infants' learning of arbitrary auditory–visual relationships in the absence versus presence of amodal information.

## Method

### Participants

The participants were 24 newborn babies, 11 females and 13 males, mean age 44 hours; range 5–93 hours). Sixteen were tested in the auditory-noncontingent condition, and eight in the auditory-contingent condition: this imbalance in numbers is because the auditory-contingent condition is the same as the condition reported by Slater *et al.* (1997), and it was therefore intended as a confirmation that the results of the 1997 study are replicable. A further 25 babies were seen but could not be tested because of fussing, crying or sleeping. Participants were selected from the maternity ward of the Royal Devon and Exeter Hospital, Heavitree, Exeter, Devon. They were all full-term healthy babies, and throughout testing were in the behavioural state of alert inactivity (Ashton, 1973).

### Stimuli and Apparatus

There were two visual and two auditory stimuli: these were the stimuli used by Slater *et al.* (1997). The visual stimuli were a green diagonal line (inclined 45° from vertical) and a red vertical line, each being 13 cm long and 2 cm wide, subtending a visual angle of 25° at the viewing distance of 30 cm. The red and green colours were approximately equated for brightness by adult observers. There is no 'natural' or unlearned preference for either of these stimuli, and it is known that newborn infants can discriminate between them (Slater, Mattock, Brown, Burnham & Young, 1991; Slater *et al.*, 1997). The stimuli were mounted on white cards and presented against a matte white screen. They were illuminated by two strip lights placed behind and to either side of the infant, and the luminances of the figures and the light background were, respectively, 70 and 137 cd m$^{-2}$. During both familiarization and test trials each visual stimulus was presented separately (see below) and was in the centre of the stimulus screen.

The two auditory stimuli were chosen to be dissimilar in a number of acoustic aspects, in order to facilitate easy discrimination between them, and were the word 'teat' spoken in a female voice and the word 'mum' spoken in a male voice. Each word was spoken at a rate of once per second, and each was recorded on a continuous tape loop in order that the presentation of each word could continue throughout the duration of a trial. Only one sound was presented on each trial (see below) from a speaker located above the centre of the stimulus screen.

## Procedure

Each infant was brought to the experimental room in the maternity ward of the hospital and seated upright on one experimenter's knee with his/her eyes 30 cm (±2 cm) from the centre of the stimulus screen. Half of the infants in each of the two conditions were familiarized to the auditory–visual stimuli of 'green-teat' (GT) and 'red-mum' (RM) alternately presented, with GT as the first pairing presented, and half were familiarized to the alternating order RM and GT, with RM as the first pairing presented. Other details of the procedure differed for those infants in the auditory-noncontingent and for those in the auditory-contingent conditions, and these are described next.

### Auditory-noncontingent Condition

In the first familiarization trial in the auditory-noncontingent condition the auditory stimulus (either 'teat' or 'mum') was presented as soon as the observer judged that the infant was in an alert attentive state, irrespective of whether the infant was judged to be looking at the visual stimulus (either the green diagonal or red vertical line) or not. The trial continued until 25 s of looking to the visual stimulus had accumulated. The next trial began with presentation of the second auditory stimulus ('mum' or 'teat') and its accompanying visual stimulus, and ended when 25 s of looking at the visual stimulus had accumulated. Alternating trials continued until each auditory–visual combination had been presented three times. Thus, the infants looked at each of the visual stimuli for a total of 75 s, but the auditory stimulus was available for the whole of the trial durations, which always totalled more than 75 s for each of the combinations.

### Auditory-Contingent Condition

On the first familiarization trial in the auditory-contingent condition the first visual stimulus was shown, and as soon as the observer judged that the infant was looking at it the paired sound (either 'teat' or 'mum') was presented. Presentation of the sound was contingent upon the infant looking at the visual stimulus, so that when the observer judged that the infant was no longer looking at the visual stimulus the sound stopped: this was accomplished by having the continuous tape loop connected to the speaker; the latter was activated only when the main observer pressed the recording button to indicate that the baby was looking. This contingency ensured that the arbitrary auditory–visual pairing provided the amodal invariant of synchronized onset and offset of both stimuli. Alternating familiarization trials continued, as described above, until each stimulus pairing had been presented three times. Each trial ended when the baby had looked at and heard the auditory–visual combination for 25 s. Thus, each of the familiarized auditory–visual stimulus combinations were looked at and listened to for a total of 75 s. Order of stimulus presentation was counterbalanced across subjects.

## Test Trials

When the familiarization trials ended each infant was given two test trials, one presenting a familiar auditory–visual combination and the other a novel combination: there were two novel combinations, 'red-teat' (RT) and 'green–mum' (GM). The test trials were identical for the auditory-noncontingent and auditory-contingent conditions. Equal numbers of infants had one of the two familiar combinations and one of the two novel combinations, giving four test conditions: these four, with the familiar combination given first, are GT and GM, GT and RT, RM and GM, RM and RT. For each of the test trials the visual stimulus and its paired sound were both presented, and the trial began when the infant first looked at the visual stimulus. From this point on the trial continued until 30 s had elapsed, and the paired sound was played only when the infant looked at the visual stimulus, therefore providing amodal synchronous (or contingent) information. Order of stimulus presentation was counterbalanced such that half the subjects were presented with the familiar stimulus combination first, and half with the novel combination.

## Inter-observer Reliability

Either one or two experienced observers recorded the infants' fixations from peepholes behind and to left or right of the stimulus screen. An additional experimenter ensured that the appropriate auditory–visual combination was presented on familiarization and test trials. The observers who recorded fixations were never visible to the infants and had no expectations as to the outcome of the experiment, and were blind to the placements of novel and familiar stimulus combinations on the test trials. For 38 of the test trials two independent observers recorded the infants' fixations on the stimuli, and the inter-observer agreement was high (Pearson $r = 0.926$).

# Results

## Main Analyses

Each infant looked at the two alternately presented visual stimuli on the six familiarization trials for a total of 150 s. The average time taken to accumulate this looking time (measured from the first look on each of the six trials until the 25 s of looking at each was reached) in the auditory-noncontingent condition was 194 s (SD = 52.2, range 151–369 s), and in the auditory-contingent condition was 173 s (SD = 15.84, range 150–194 s). There were no significant differences in the average time taken to accumulate the total of 75 s looking time to stimulus GT and to stimulus RM in either experimental condition.

The dependent variables of most interest are the times spent looking at the familiar and novel combinations on the post-familiarization test trials, and these are shown in Figure 1. In the auditory-noncontingent condition the familiar combination (either GT or RM) was looked at for 64.6% of the 30 s test trial, and the novel combination (either GM or RT) was looked at for 65.2% of the test trial. Ten of the infants looked more at the familiar combination, five looked more at the novel combination, and one looked the same time at each. Clearly, there is no difference in percentage looking times between the two test combinations: $t$ (15) = 0.10, ns. In the auditory-contingent condition the familiar combination was looked at for 62.5% of the test trial, and the novel combination was looked at for 82.3% of the time. Seven of the eight infants looked more at the novel combination. This difference in looking times between the two test combinations replicates the findings of Slater et al. (1997) and is significant: $t$ (7) = 2.31, $p$ = 0.023, one-tailed. In the auditory-noncontingent condition the mean percentage difference in looking

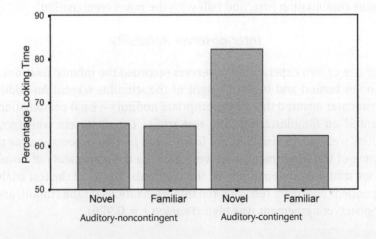

**Figure 1:** Percentage looking at familiar and novel auditory–visual combinations on the test trials, in the auditory-noncontingent and auditory-contingent conditions

times between the familiar and novel test trials was 0.6%, and in the auditory-contingent condition the difference was 19.8%. The difference between the two conditions is significant: $t$ (23) = 2.08, $p< 0.025$.

Additional analyses were carried out to test for order effects: whether the stimulus combination on the first test trial was familiar or novel; whether there was greater looking on the first test trial independently of whether it was novel or familiar. None of these differences approached statistical significance.

## Additional Analysis: Participant Drop-Out

The auditory-contingent condition was identical to, and intended as a replication of, the experimental conditions reported by Slater *et al.* (1997). In both studies the newborn infants spent more time looking at the novel auditory–visual combinations on the test trials (27 of the 32 infants gave a novelty preference). Given the replicability of the finding it is meaningful to combine the results from the two studies. In the combined auditory-contingent condition it was necessary to test 44 infants in order to have 32 who completed the experimental procedure (i.e. a participant loss of 12/44 infants). In the auditory-noncontingent condition it was necessary to test 37 infants in order to achieve 16 'completers', a participant loss of 21/37 infants. This differential participant loss between the two conditions is significant: $\chi^2 = 9.8, p< 0.01$.

## Discussion and Conclusions

The strong preferences for the novel visual–auditory pairings that were found on the post-familiarization test trials in the auditory-contingent condition, both in the present study and by Slater *et al.* (1997), are clear evidence that newborn babies are able to learn and remember arbitrary auditory–visual relations. It is important to note that the novelty responses could not have resulted if the infants had only processed the separate properties of the stimuli presented on the familiarization trials since the novel pairings consisted of stimuli (colour/orientation and sound) that had been presented earlier. However, in the auditory-noncontingent condition of the present experiment, the almost identical looking times to novel and familiar auditory–visual combinations on the test trials are a clear indication that the newborn infants *did not* learn the arbitrary association. This difference between conditions was present despite the fact that the auditory stimulus was available for longer in the auditory-noncontingent than the auditory-contingent condition. The observers who recorded infant looking in the two conditions, while they were unaware of the hypotheses being tested, spontaneously commented that it was more difficult to 'get the babies through' in the auditory-noncontingent condition, an observation that is confirmed by the significant difference in infant 'drop-out' rates between the two conditions.

These findings add to our understanding of newborn infants' perceptual abilities, and point to constraints on early (and possibly later) learning. They confirm that newborns are able to learn, in a short time in an experimental situation, arbitrary auditory–visual combinations. However, this learning is both facilitated and constrained by the presence or absence of amodal information. In the absence of amodal information (the auditory-noncontingent condition) newborns failed to learn the auditory–visual combinations that were presented, despite the fact that each visual stimulus was never presented on the familiarization trials unless its accompanying sound was also available. When amodal information was present – in this experiment by presenting the sound only when the infant looked at the visual stimulus (the auditory-contingent condition) – the infants readily learned the association.

The newborn infant has an enormous amount to learn and it is reasonable that such learning should be constrained by the contingencies that are found within the environment. It would be a complex and chaotic world if infants associated all arbitrary associations of sights and sounds, and other intermodal combinations, and clearly they do not: the presence of this 'learning constraint' prevents infants from learning irrelevant associations that simply happen to be co-jointly available but are otherwise unrelated. The fact that such arbitrary auditory–visual associations are most easily learned in the presence of amodal information gives strong confirmation to Bahrick's views, described earlier, and suggests that the presence or absence of amodal information – in the form of temporal contingency between looking and hearing in the present experiment – acts both as a powerful facilitator and a constraint on learning.

## References

Ashton, R. (1973). The state variable in neonatal research: a review. *Merrill-Palmer Quarterly*, **19**, 3–20.

Bahrick, L.E. (1987). Infants' intermodal perception of two levels of temporal structure in natural events. *Infant Behavior and Development*, **10**, 387–416.

Bahrick, L.E. (1988). Intermodal learning in infancy: learning on the basis of two kinds of invariant relations in audible and visible events. *Child Development*, **59**, 197–209.

Bahrick, L.E. (in press). Increasing specificity in the development of intermodal perception. In K. Lee, A. Slater & D. Muir (Eds), *Essential readings in psychology: Infancy*. Oxford: Blackwell.

Bahrick, L.E., & Pickens, J.N. (1994). Amodal relations: the basis for intermodal perception and learning in infancy. In D.J. Lewkowicz & R. Lickliter (Eds), *The development of intersensory perception: Comparative perspectives* (pp. 205–233). Hillsdale, NJ: Erlbaum.

Butterworth, G. (1983). Structure of the mind in human infancy. In L.P. Lipsitt & C.K. Rovee-Collier (Eds), *Advances in Infancy Research*, **2**, 1–29.

Gogate, L.J., & Bahrick, L.E. (1998). Intersensory redundancy facilitates learning of arbitrary relations between vowel sounds and objects in seven-month-old infants. *Journal of Experimental Child Psychology*, **69**, 133–149.

Hernandez-Reif, M., Cigales, M., & Lundy, B. (1994, June). Memory for arbitrary adult face–voice pairs at six months of age. Paper presented at the International Conference on Infant Studies, Paris.

Lewkowicz, D.J. (1986). Developmental changes in infants' bisensory response to synchronous durations. *Infant Behavior and Development*, **9**, 335–353.

Muir, D.W., & Clifton, R. (1985). Infants' orientation to the location of sound sources. In G. Gottlieb & N. Krasnegor (Eds), *The measurement of audition and vision during the first year of life: A methodological overview* (pp. 171–194). Norwood, NJ: Ablex.

Reardon, P., & Bushnell, E.W. (1988). Infants' sensitivity to arbitrary pairings of color and taste. *Infant Behavior and Development*, 11, 245–250.

Slater, A., Mattock, A., Brown, E., Burnham, D., & Young, A.W. (1991). Visual processing of stimulus compounds in newborn infants. *Perception*, **20**, 29–33.

Slater, A., Brown, E., & Badenoch, M. (1997). Intermodal perception at birth: newborn infants' memory for arbitrary auditory–visual pairings. *Early Development and Parenting*, **6**, 99–104.

Spelke, E.S., & Owsley, C.J. (1979). Intermodal exploration and knowledge in infancy. *Infant Behavior and Development*, **2**, 13–27.

Wertheimer, M. (1961). Psychomotor coordination of auditory and visual space at birth. *Science*, **134**, 1692.

# 52

# Preverbal Infants' Sensitivity to Synaesthetic Cross-Modality Correspondences

*Peter Walker, J. Gavin Bremner, Uschi Mason, Jo Spring,
Karen Mattock, Alan Slater and Scott P. Johnson*

S ynaesthesia occurs when stimulation of one sensory channel induces perceptions normally associated with a different sensory channel. Although there is much that is idiosyncratic about the experiences of individual synaesthetes, their experiences are constrained by a set of underlying cross-modality correspondences. These correspondences reflect the alignment of different dimensions of sensory experience (e.g., between visual brightness and auditory pitch) and can also be observed in nonsynaesthetes (where their influence is called *weak synaesthesia*; see Martino & Marks, 2001). Claims that neonatal perception is synaesthetic for all infants (James, 1890/1950; Maurer, Pathman, & Mondloch, 2006; Mondloch & Maurer, 2004) suggest that these cross-modality correspondences are an innate aspect of perception.

Cross-modality correspondences qualify most clearly as synaesthetic either when at least one of the dimensions involved is *metathetic* (i.e., concerned with a qualitative aspect of sensory experience) or when two *prothetic* dimensions (i.e., concerned with the amount of sensory experience) are aligned in opposition to their *more-than* interpretation (e.g., when less size is aligned with more brightness and more speed; see Walker & Smith, 1985).[1] When two prothetic dimensions are aligned according to their shared *more-than* interpretation (e.g., when more visual brightness is aligned with more auditory

**Source:** *Psychological Science*, 21(1) (2010): 21–25.

loudness), the cross-modality associations that arise need not be synaesthetic. Instead, they might reflect the fact that the two modalities are conveying equivalent (redundant) information about the same aspect of an object or event (as when vision and audition provide equivalent information about the strength of a stimulus). Lewkowicz and Turkewitz (1980) emphasized the latter interpretation in their seminal study demonstrating that 3- to 4.5-week-old infants respond to the equivalence of different levels of visual brightness and auditory loudness.

As a metathetic dimension, auditory pitch is involved in cross-modality correspondences with visuospatial height (Melara & O'Brien, 1987; Miller, Werner, & Wapner, 1958; Roffler & Butler, 1967), visual sharpness (Marks, 1987; O'Boyle & Tarte, 1980), visual brightness (Collier & Hubbard, 2001; Marks, 1978; Walker & Smith, 1984, 1985; Ward, Huckstep, & Tsakanikos, 2006), lightness in weight (Walker & Smith, 1984), and smallness in size (Parise & Spence, 2008; Perrott, Musicant, & Schwethelm, 1980; Walker & Smith, 1984). Some of these studies confirmed the impact of cross-modality correspondences on perception (e.g., Miller et al., 1958; Parise & Spence, 2008; Roffler & Butler, 1967). Strong evidence for this also comes from visual-hearing synaesthesia, where higher pitched sounds induce visual images that are brighter, smaller, higher in space, sharper, and more likely to be moving than those induced by lower pitched sounds (Karwoski & Odbert, 1938; Marks, 1987; Ward et al., 2006).

If neonatal perception is synaesthetic, then infants should reveal their sensitivity to these cross-modality correspondences. Wagner, Winner, Cicchetti, and Gardner (1981) claimed to have shown that 9- to 13-month-olds appreciate the correspondence between visual height (specifically, an up and down pointing arrow) and auditory pitch (an ascending and descending tone). As noted by Wagner et al., however, arrows are conventional symbols, whose significance needs to be learned, and the infants may not have interpreted them as representing ascending and descending change. Instead, Wagner et al. proposed that the infants looked at the top of an up arrow, and at the bottom of a down arrow, because these are the locations at which the highest density of visual information is found. Wagner et al. implied, therefore, that the difference in the elevation of infants' fixation is the critical factor in correspondence with the ascending and descending pitch of a sound. Wagner et al. offered no supporting evidence for the presence and significance of such a correspondence in adults and did not monitor the elevation of the infants' fixation, and so we contend that the youngest children in whom synaesthetic cross-modality correspondences have been confirmed with any certainty were 2- to 3-year-olds (Maurer, Pathman, & Mondloch, 2006; Mondloch & Maurer, 2004).

This age range does not preclude mediation through post-natal learning. Such learning could be based on a child's exposure to language, because synaesthetic cross-modality correspondences find expression in the visible, spoken, and conceptual aspects of language (Marks, 1978). For example, across a range of languages, smaller, brighter, sharper, and faster objects tend to have names with higher pitched vowel sounds (Marks, 1978; Maurer et al., 2006). To test the perceptual innateness of synaesthetic cross-modality correspondences, while avoiding any learning based on language comprehension, we used a preferential looking procedure to assess 3- to 4-month-old preverbal infants' sensitivity to two synaesthetic correspondences involving auditory pitch.

In the first of two experiments, we examined the correspondence between auditory pitch and visuospatial height. In the second experiment, we examined the correspondence between auditory pitch and visual sharpness. The existence of these two perceptual correspondences has been confirmed with several observations. For example, when adults point to the perceived visual location of a sound whose source is hidden from view, the elevation of this location is determined by the pitch of the sound, and not by the actual location of the source of the sound (Roffler & Butler, 1967). And when an incidental sound rises and falls in pitch, it induces corresponding visual illusory movement (i.e., upward vs. downward autokinetic movement, respectively) in a stationary spot of light (Miller et al., 1958). In addition to being observed in visual-hearing synaesthesia, the correspondence between auditory pitch and visual sharpness emerges when adults judge the sharpness of auditory tones varying in pitch using a scale defined by the polar adjectives *sharp* and *blunt* (Walker & Smith, 1985). And when, in a preliminary phase of the present study, people rated pointed and curved variants of several geometric shapes (including those in Fig. 1b) on a scale with endpoints defined as *would make a high/low-pitched sound if it came to life or was struck by another object*, pointedness was again associated with higher pitch.

## Method

### Participants

Eight male and 8 female infants completed the first (pitch-height) experiment (mean age = 128 days, range: 114 to 145 days). A further 2 infants were unable to complete this experiment because of excessive restlessness. Eight male and 8 female infants completed the second (pitch-sharpness) experiment (mean age = 129 days, range: 91 to 150 days). A further 3 infants were unable to complete the experiment because of excessive restlessness.

### Materials and Procedure

A Barco screen was integrated into one side of a 3-m² cubicle created with thick, black curtains. QuickTime animations appeared within a 48 × 48 cm

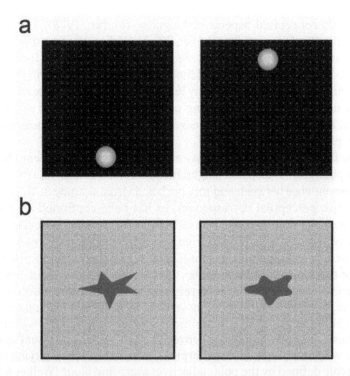

**Figure 1:** Examples of animations presented as stimuli in the (a) pitch-height and (b) pitch-sharpness experiments. In (a), the moving ball is shown at the extremes of its vertical trajectory. In (b), the extreme forms of pointedness of the static morphing shape are shown. All images are reproduced to scale.

screen area (25.6° × 25.6°), each lasting a maximum of 60 s. Each infant sat on her or his mother's knee, viewing the animations at eye level and from a distance of 1 m. The mothers fixed their own gaze on the top of their child's head. Each infant's eye fixations were monitored and recorded on video, and an animation was removed immediately after he or she looked elsewhere for a single period of 2 s or more. The total length of time an infant looked directly at an animation was later determined by two independent judges, who were unaware of the nature of the animation being observed by the infant.

In the pitch-height experiment, the infants watched a 7-cm (4°) diameter orange ball (average luminance = 39 cd/m$^2$) move up and down a 32-cm vertical trajectory in front of a 20 × 20 grid of small, white dots on an otherwise dark field (see Fig. 1a). The deletion and accretion of the dots served to strengthen the impression that the ball was a solid object moving in its own depth plane. The ball moved at a constant speed of 12.8 cm/s and paused for 50 ms at each endpoint. Each animation was accompanied by the sound of a sliding whistle, whose fundamental frequency changed at a constant rate, between 300 and 1700 Hz, over a period of time coinciding with an individual phase of the animation (2.5 s). The loudness of the sound increased and then decreased between 54 and 80 dB (against an uncontrolled ambient noise level of 42 dB) within each phase of the animation, peaking when the fundamental frequency of the sound was midrange. The natural sound of a sliding whistle has a loudness profile of this type, and this profile was retained during sound editing for two reasons: first, to preserve the naturalness of the sound (which we considered especially important for infants) and, second, in the absence of individual equal-loudness contours for our participants, to ensure that changes in perceived loudness were not confounded with changes in pitch. In the *congruent* condition, the pitch of the sound rose and fell as the ball rose and fell. In the *incongruent* condition, the pitch of the sound fell and rose as the ball rose and fell. Every infant viewed three congruent animations interleaved with three incongruent animations, with 8 infants viewing a congruent animation first and 8 viewing an incongruent animation first.

In the pitch-sharpness experiment, the infants watched computerized animations of a static, uniformly gray (13 cd/m$^2$) geometric shape morphing constantly between two extreme forms of pointedness (see Fig. 1b). The shape appeared against a beige, hopsack background (average luminance = 28 cd/m$^2$) and in its pointed and curved extreme forms had a surface area of 100.3 and 99.7 cm$^2$, respectively. With this small difference in surface area, the overall size of the shape did not appear to change as it morphed (as judged by a set of independent adult judges in a preliminary study). The morphing was accompanied by the same sound used in the pitch-height experiment. Each phase of the animation (morphing from one extreme to the other) again lasted 2.5 s, with a brief 50-ms pause at each extreme. In the *congruent* condition, the pitch of the sound rose and fell as the shape became more and less pointed. In the *incongruent* condition, the pitch of the sound fell and then rose as the shape became more and less pointed. Other aspects of the method were identical to the pitch-height experiment.

## Results

In both experiments, a high level of agreement was confirmed between the two judges in their estimates of each infant's individual viewing times across the six trials (mean Pearson $r = .99$, $p < .01$, in both cases).

### Auditory Pitch and Visuospatial Height

Twelve of the 16 infants looked longer at a congruent animation than at an incongruent animation ($p = .038$ on a binomial test, $p_{rep} = .90$). The average time infants looked at congruent and incongruent animations was 28.5 s ($SD = 10.5$) and 21.7 s ($SD = 11.9$), respectively. Because the looking times were positively skewed, they were log-transformed before analysis of variance confirmed the significance of the effect of congruity, $F(1, 15) = 9.22$, $p = .008$, $p_{rep} = .94$, $\eta_p^2 = .38$.

## Auditory Pitch and Visual Sharpness

Twelve of the 16 infants looked longer at a congruent animation than at an incongruent animation ($p = .038$ on a binomial test, $p_{rep} = .90$). The average time infants looked at congruent and incongruent animations was 20.1 s ($SD = 7.9$) and 15.9 s ($SD = 6.3$), respectively. Analysis of variance of the log-transformed looking times confirmed the significance of the effect of congruity, $F(1, 15) = 7.57$, $p = .015$, $p_{rep} = .96$, $\eta_p^2 = .34$. The percentage reduction in looking time caused by introducing incongruity was comparable across both experiments (i.e., 24% and 21% for the pitch-height and pitch-sharpness experiments, respectively).

## Discussion

Our results confirm young infants' sensitivity to the correspondences linking auditory pitch with visuospatial height and visual sharpness. They provide the strongest indication to date that synaesthetic cross-modality correspondences are an unlearned aspect of perception and are consistent with claims that neonatal perception is synaesthetic.

Some might wish to argue that our infants were old enough to have learned the correspondences. This raises two questions. First, where might the correspondences originate, if not in language? Second, could there be sufficient exposure to these origins to allow the correspondences to be learned within the first 3 or 4 months of life? It is possible that relevant co-occurrences exist in the real world, and exposure to these ensures perceptual learning of the underlying dimensional correspondences. For example, when they hear people or animals vocalize (Bee, Perrill, & Owen, 2000; Davies & Halliday, 1978; Harrington, 1987) and objects strike each other (Grassi, 2005; Perrott et al., 1980), infants will encounter co-occurrences reflecting the correspondence between size and pitch, and these encounters might be sufficient to establish perceptual expectations linking size and pitch. It is difficult, however, to identify natural co-occurrences capable of supporting other correspondences, including the two correspondences examined here. With regard to sharpness and pitch, a potentially relevant co-occurrence might be mediated by the hardness of natural materials. Sharp and pointed objects tend to be formed from hard materials, for which reason the objects are also likely to make relatively high-pitched sounds when struck (Freed, 1990; Klatzky, Pai, & Krotkov, 2000; van den Doel & Pai, 1998). Future research must explore the incidence of natural co-occurrences to determine if the typical environment to which young infants are exposed could support perceptual learning of the synaesthetic cross-modality correspondences observed in adulthood. Confirmation would not, of course, mean that sensitivity to the correspondences is acquired during infancy. Indeed, we doubt very much that infants' encounters with objects within the first 3 to 4 months could support such learning, in part because any relevant co-occurrences will not be in evidence with complete consistency (e.g., objects that look sharp will sometimes make a low-pitched sound, and vice versa). Furthermore, as implied by the claim that neonatal perception is synaesthetic, acquisition of the correspondences could be phylogenetic rather than ontogenetic, with appropriate neural circuitry in place at birth (Maurer & Mondloch, 2006).

## Note

1. The distinction between prothetic and metathetic dimensions (continua) of sensory experience is, in essence, a distinction between quantity and quality (Stevens, 1957). Prothetic dimensions are concerned with how much of a type of sensation is being experienced (e.g., how loud) and have been linked to variations in the level of excitation within a sensory channel. Metathetic dimensions deal with qualitative differences in sensory experience and have been linked to variations in the location of maximum excitation in a sensory channel.

## References

Bee, M.A., Perrill, S.A., & Owen, P.C. (2000). Male green frogs lower the pitch of acoustic signals in defense of territories: A possible dishonest signal of size? *Behavioral Ecology*, *11*, 169–177.

Collier, W.G., & Hubbard, T.L. (2001). Judgements of happiness, brightness, speed and tempo change of auditory stimuli varying in pitch and tempo. *Psychomusicology*, *17*, 36–55.

Davies, N.B., & Halliday, T.R. (1978). Deep croaks and fighting assessment in toads *Bufo bufo*. *Nature*, *274*, 683–685.

Freed, D.J. (1990). Auditory correlates of perceived mallet hardness for a set of recorded percussive sound events. *Journal of the Acoustical Society of America*, *87*, 311–322.

Grassi, M. (2005). Do we hear size or sound? Balls dropped on plates. *Perception & Psychophysics*, *67*, 274–284.

Harrington, F.H. (1987). Aggressive howling in wolves. *Animal Behavior*, *35*, 7–12.

James, W. (1950). *Principles of psychology*. New York: Dover. (Original work published 1890)

Karwoski, T.F., & Odbert, H.S. (1938). Color-music. *Psychological Monographs*, *50*(2, Whole No. 222).

Klatzky, R.L., Pai, D.K., & Krotkov, E.P. (2000). Perception of material from contact sounds. *Presence*, *9*, 399–410.

Lewkowicz, D.J., & Turkewitz, G. (1980). Cross-modal equivalences in early infancy: Auditory-visual intensity matching. *Developmental Psychology*, *16*, 597–607.

Marks, L.E. (1978). *The unity of the senses: Interrelations among the modalities.* New York: Academic Press.

Marks, L.E. (1987). On cross-modal similarity: Auditory-visual interactions in speeded discrimination. *Journal of Experimental Psychology: Human Perception and Performance, 13,* 384–394.

Martino, G., & Marks, L.E. (2001). Synesthesia: Strong and weak. *Current Directions in Psychological Science, 10,* 61–65.

Maurer, D., & Mondloch, C.J. (2006). The infant as synesthete? In Y. Munakata & M.H. Johnson (Eds.), *Attention and performance XXI: Processes of change in brain and cognitive development* (pp. 449–471). Oxford, England: Oxford University Press.

Maurer, D., Pathman, T., & Mondloch, C.J. (2006). The shape of boubas: Sound-shape correspondences in toddlers and adults. *Developmental Science, 9,* 316–322.

Melara, R.D., & O'Brien, T.P. (1987). Interaction between synesthetically corresponding dimensions. *Journal of Experimental Psychology: General, 116,* 323–336.

Miller, A., Werner, H., & Wapner, S. (1958). Studies in physiognomic perception: V. Effect of ascending and descending gliding tones on autokinetic motion. *The Journal of Psychology, 46,* 101–105.

Mondloch, C.J., & Maurer, D. (2004). Do small white balls squeak? Pitch-object correspondences in young children. *Cognitive, Affective, & Behavioral Neuroscience, 4,* 133–136.

O'Boyle, M.W., & Tarte, R.D. (1980). Implications for phonetic symbolism: The relationship between pure tones and geometric figures. *Journal of Psycholinguistic Research, 9,* 535–544.

Parise, C., & Spence, C. (2008). Synesthetic congruency modulates the temporal ventriloquism effect. *Neuroscience Letters, 442,* 257–261.

Perrott, D.R., Musicant, A., & Schwethelm, B. (1980). The expanding-image effect: The concept of tonal volume revisited. *Journal of Auditory Research, 20,* 43–55.

Roffler, S.K., & Butler, R.A. (1967). Localization of tonal stimuli in the vertical plane. *Journal of the Acoustical Society of America, 43,* 1260–1266.

Stevens, S.S. (1957). On the psychophysical law. *Psychological Review, 64,* 153–181.

van den Doel, K., & Pai, D.K. (1998). The sounds of physical shapes. *Presence, 7,* 382–395.

Wagner, S., Winner, E., Cicchetti, D., & Gardner, H. (1981). "Metaphorical" mapping in human infants. *Child Development, 52,* 728–731.

Walker, P., & Smith, S. (1984). Stroop interference based on the synaesthetic qualities of auditory pitch. *Perception, 13,* 75–81.

Walker, P., & Smith, S. (1985). Stroop interference based on the multimodal correlates of haptic size and auditory pitch. *Perception, 14,* 729–736.

Ward, J., Huckstep, B., & Tsakanikos, E. (2006). Sound-colour synaesthesia: To what extent does it use cross-modal mechanisms common to us all? *Cortex, 42,* 264–280.

# 53

# Sound Symbolism in Infancy: Evidence for Sound–Shape Cross-Modal Correspondences in 4-Month-Olds

*Ozge Ozturk, Madelaine Krehm and Athena Vouloumanos*

## Introduction

The mapping between labels and referents has been considered arbitrary in mainstream linguistics (De Saussure, 1916/1983). However, research findings suggest some systematicity between specific labels and referents; adults and toddlers spontaneously and consistently map particular shapes to particular words even when there appears to be no obvious physical basis for the mapping (e.g., Köhler, 1947; Maurer, Pathman, & Mondloch, 2006). However, because adults and toddlers already have significant experience with language mappings in their environment, it is unclear whether these biases are the result of an acquired sensitivity or an initial proclivity. Here we investigated the origins of these sound–shape mapping biases by examining whether 4-month-old infants share the same sound–shape mapping biases as adults and toddlers.

A fundamental tenet of modern linguistics is that there is no systematic relationship between linguistic labels and the meaning they convey (De Saussure, 1916/1983). Some have even proposed that this arbitrary connection between linguistic labels and their referents is a fundamental feature of human language (e.g., Monaghan, Fitneva, & Christiansen, 2011; Ramachandran & Hubbard, 2001) and the basis for its referential power (e.g., Gasser, 2004).

**Source:** *Journal of Experimental Child Psychology*, 114(2) (2013): 173–186.

Moreover, if the sound structure of words was related in a systematic way to their referents, we would expect similarities across languages, with similar inventories of sounds corresponding to similar types of meaning. This is clearly not the case because even a simple concept such as *tree* is realized with phonologically distinct words in different languages – *ağaç* in Turkish, *zuhaitza* in Basque, *árbol* in Spanish, and *dendro* in Greek. Indeed, most linguistic labels have different sound structures in different languages; these labels are conventions agreed on by the speakers of the languages with no apparent systematic relationship to their referents (Hockett, 1977).

However, not all label–referent mappings appear to be arbitrary. Cross-linguistic observations suggest that there are words in natural language whose sounds are systematically related to their meanings. Ideophones – words that are used by speakers to evoke vivid associations with particular sensory perceptions (e.g., smell, color, shape, sound, action, or movement across languages) – are widely attested in the languages of the world (Voeltz & Kilian-Hatz, 2001). West African, East Asian, and Southeast Asian languages, and to a lesser extent Amerindian languages, are known for their large inventories of ideophonic vocabulary, but many other languages also make use of ideophones (e.g., Turkish *citir citir* 'crispy'; Basque *mara mara* 'falling softly, said of rain'; Ewe *gbadzaa* 'flat, spreading out over a wide area'; English *bling bling* 'glitter, sparkle'). However, the sounds of these words evoke or imitate the meaning, creating systematic nonarbitrary connections.

People also systematically map particular speech sounds to properties of objects cross-linguistically. For instance, across languages, there are phonetic classes of speech sounds that are systematically found in vocabulary related to size (e.g., /i/ vs. /a/ for size as in Ewe *kitsikitsi* 'small' vs. *gbaggbagba* 'big', Greek *micros* 'small' vs. macros 'large') or distance (e.g., words for *here* are more likely to include an /i/ sound and words for *there* are more likely to include an /a/ sound; see Tanz, 1971). Experimental findings also support this idea of sound–size relations. Syllables containing low back vowels (e.g., *mal*) are consistently matched to large objects, whereas syllables containing high front vowels (e.g., *mil*) are consistently matched to small objects (Sapir, 1929). Recently, cross-modal mapping of sound and size has also been demonstrated in infants, with 4-month-olds matching [o] or [a] to large objects and [i] or [e] to small objects (Peña, Mehler, & Nespor, 2011). Thus, systematic mapping of sound to size is widespread and observed even during infancy.

Cross-modal correspondences between sound and size have been noted for centuries (Descartes, 1641/1986; Gibson, 1966; Ohala, 1997; Walker et al., 2010) and appear to be grounded in physical reality. High front vowels such as [i] and [e] tend to have higher fundamental frequencies ($F_0$) than low back vowels such as [o] and [a] (Whalen & Levitt, 1995). At the same time, objects that are physically thinner or smaller tend to produce a higher pitch than wider larger objects. For instance, the pitch of a cello is lower compared with the pitch made by its smaller cousin, the violin. Similarly, the vocal folds of a larger animal are longer, and longer vocal folds tend to generate sounds that are lower in pitch (Shayan, Ozturk, & Sicoli, 2011; Zbikowski, 1998). Peña and colleagues (2011) proposed that infants may map vowels to object size based on their experience in seeing mouths open to different extents when humans produce different vowels. The systematic mapping between vowels and object size appears to be grounded on observable physical relationships between the pitch of vowels and the size of objects and, therefore, may simply reflect associations based on participants' prior multisensory experiences.

Another type of cross-modal mapping that has been observed in adults, and recently in infants as young as 3 or 4 months, is a correspondence between auditory pitch and visuospatial height or visual sharpness (Marks, 1987; Walker et al., 2010). Infants (and adults) map higher pitched tones with sharper objects and objects that appear higher in space. Walker and colleagues (2010) proposed that the mapping between sharpness and pitch might be mediated by the hardness of natural materials. Sharp and pointed objects tend to be formed from hard materials, and they tend to produce high-pitched sounds when struck. These natural correspondences are also grounded on observable physical relationships and may reflect prior multisensory experience.

However, there are other cross-modal mappings between linguistic labels and their referents that may rely less on prior multisensory experience in a phenomenon known as sound symbolism. Adult Spanish speakers consistently matched curvy shapes with the novel word 'baluba' and angular shapes with another novel word 'takete' (Köhler, 1947). These mapping biases were later documented in American college undergraduates and Tamil speakers in India, with the vast majority of both groups (as many as 98%) selecting a curvy shape as 'bouba' and an angular shape as 'kiki', and this effect became known as the "bouba/kiki effect" (Köhler, 1947). These mapping biases also affect processing; adults are more accurate and faster at classifying a novel object if the category name matches the shape of the object (Kovic, Plunkett, & Westermann, 2010). Electrophysiological responses also differentiate between sound symbolic and non-sound symbolic categories, producing an early neural activation similar to that elicited by highly learned categories, possible evidence of auditory–visual integration (Kovic et al., 2010). Curvy and angular shapes may be related to the shape of a speaker's lips when producing the vowels (open and rounded or wide and narrowed; see Ramachandran & Hubbard, 2001). However, this would require attending to and mapping two sets of visual properties of two different entities (the object shape and the speaker's mouth) that are not spatially colocalized or even always temporally copresent – a much less straightforward mapping than noticing natural physical relationships between sounds and objects. Thus, sound–shape correspondences are less easily explained by observable physical relationships but are systematic nevertheless.

Nonarbitrary mappings between sound and shape extends into childhood. When asked to label Köhler-type curvy and angular drawings with the word 'takete' or 'uloomo', both English-speaking children (11–14 years old) from England and Swahili-speaking children (8–14 years old) from central Africa matched the curvy shape with the word 'uloomo' and the angular shape with the word 'takete' (Davis, 1961). This systematic sound–shape mapping has even been demonstrated in 2½-year-olds. Children systematically matched 'bouba' to curvier shapes and 'kiki' to more angular shapes (Maurer et al., 2006).

Both adults and children make systematic cross-modal mappings between linguistic labels and their referents. However, the origins of these sound–shape mappings are unknown. Because adults and toddlers have had significant experience with the statistics of label mappings that exist in their environment, it is unclear whether these systematic pairings are the result of language exposure or the product of an initial proclivity. Young infants who have yet to develop a lexicon have not been exposed to the statistical regularities in their language long enough to be biased by vocabulary-wide systematicity in labels for specific sound–shape patterns; for example, corpus analyses showed that velars are found more in words for angular – rather than rounded – objects. (Monaghan, Mattock, & Walker, 2012). Therefore, if infants share the same sound–shape mappings as adults and toddlers, these biases may precede and perhaps aid in word or category learning, narrowing the massive number of possible sound–shape correspondences that learners face (Imai, Kita, Nagumo, & Okada, 2008; Monaghan et al., 2012; Nygaard, Cook, & Namy, 2009; Parault, 2006; Parault & Schwanenflugel, 2006).

To investigate the origins of these biases, we examined whether prelinguistic infants exhibit the same sound–shape mapping biases as adults and toddlers. Furthermore, we systematically explored whether infant mappings are based on a combination of vowels and consonants, vowels alone, or consonants alone, and we compared these results with those for adults. In Experiment 1, we presented infants with a large red shape that was either curvy or angular, accompanied by a nonsense word, either 'bubu' or 'kiki'. We predicted that if 4-month-olds who have less language exposure and few, if any, word–object mappings in their receptive vocabulary (Fenson et al., 1994; see also Bergelson & Swingley, 2012) have the same biases as adults and toddlers, they would look differently at trials considered as congruent by adults (pairing the angular shape with 'kiki' or the curvy shape with 'bubu') and at incongruent trials (pairing the curvy shape with 'kiki' or the angular shape with 'bubu'). If, on the other hand, the biases demonstrated by adults and toddlers are developed through significant language experience, 4-month-olds should look equally at incongruent and congruent trials. In Experiments 2 and 3, we examined whether mappings are based on vowels or consonants. Finally, in Experiment 4, we tested adults on these materials and examined their use of vowels or consonants in making systematic mappings.

# Experiment 1

Experiment 1 examined whether prelinguistic infants make the same mappings between nonsense words and shapes as adults (Köhler, 1947; Ramachandran & Hubbard, 2001) and toddlers (Maurer et al., 2006). We presented 4-month-old infants with two sounds: 'kiki' and 'bubu'. These two sounds were paired with a curvy shape or an angular shape. We examined whether infants looked differently at pairings that adults and toddlers in prior studies had rated as incongruent (the curvy shape with 'kiki' and the angular shape with 'bubu') than at pairings that had been rated as congruent (the angular shape with 'kiki' and the curvy shape with 'bubu').

## Method

### Participants

The participants were 12 full-term 4-month-olds (mean age = 4 months 4 days, range = 3 months 22 days to 4 months 20 days, 5 girls and 7 boys). Infants were recruited at birth from local birthing hospitals. A research assistant subsequently contacted the families to participate in the study. Parents were compensated for transportation, and infants were given a small gift for participating. Infants' parents filled out a demographic information form and reported a range of educational backgrounds; of the 24 parents, 1 had not completed any high school, 1 had completed some high school, 2 had completed some college, 8 had completed college, 6 had completed graduate degrees, and 6 declined to answer). Of the 12 infants, 6 were reported as being White, 4 were of mixed ethnicity, 1 was Hispanic, and 1 parent declined to answer. An additional 13 infants were tested but excluded from the analysis because of fussiness (6), inattentiveness (2), equipment failure (3),[1] or experimenter error (2). All procedures were approved by the New York University institutional review board.

### Materials

*Auditory stimuli.* A female English–Turkish bilingual speaker recorded several productions of 'kiki' and 'bubu' in a sound attenuated room with a Shure SM58 microphone. We decided to use 'bubu' instead of 'buba', which had been used in previous studies (Maurer et al., 2006), to match the reduplicative structure of 'kiki'. Three 'kiki' and three 'bubu' tokens were selected and matched on duration ('kiki': $M = 415$ ms, range = 400–425; 'bubu': $M = 408$ ms, range = 400–417) and modified using Praat (Boersma & Weenink, 2010) to match on amplitude (all tokens were 70 dB) and pitch ('kiki': $M = 230$ Hz, range = 227–233; 'bubu': $M = 230$ Hz, range = 228–232). For each word, the three selected tokens were combined in a semirandomized order, with an interstimulus interval jittered around 1250ms (ranging from 1000 to 1500 ms), creating a 40-s 'kiki' string and a 40-s 'bubu' string, each of which contained 24 tokens.

*Visual stimuli.* We created two visual stimuli: one of a curvy shape and one of an angular shape (see Fig. 1). Both shapes were red and presented on a black background. The curvy and angular shapes filled 22.6% and 22.3% of the screen, respectively.

## Procedure

Infants were tested in a sound attenuated room. They sat on a parent's lap 1 m away from a 30-inch Apple monitor. Sounds were played from an M-Audio BX5a speaker located behind the monitor. A Sony DCR-HC96 camera mounted below the monitor recorded the infants and allowed the experimenter to watch the silent video feed in a nearby room. Parents wore Extreme Isolation Ex-25

**Figure 1:** Curvy and angular shapes

noise-canceling headphones that played music mixed with spoken words to mask experimental sounds.

Each infant was tested in an infant-controlled cross-modal matching paradigm with sequential presentation of congruent and incongruent trials. The infant controlled both the onset and the offset of the trials. When the infant oriented to the screen, the experimenter started the trial. The trial ended when the infant looked away from the screen for a minimum of 2 s or after a maximum trial length of 40 s. The experiment began with a red flashing light on a black background. The first trial was a pretest trial to familiarize the infant with the procedure. During the pretest trial, the infant saw a shape that had a combination of curvy and angular edges and also heard music. After the pretest trial, the experiment began. The experiment consisted of four identical blocks. Each block consisted of four trials with each of the four possible word/shape pairings: 'kiki' with a curvy shape, 'kiki' with an angular shape, 'bubu' with a curvy shape, and 'bubu' with an angular shape. The trials were in semirandom order such that each pair of stimuli within a block consisted of one congruent trial and one incongruent trial. Whether the first trial was congruent or incongruent was counterbalanced across infants. The red flashing light was presented between trials to draw the infant's attention back to the screen. An animated video clip was played between the blocks to retain the infant's attention. The experiment was presented using Habit X software (Cohen, Atkinson, & Chaput, 2004) on an iMac Apple computer, with the experimenter recording online looking time with a key press. Infant looking times were coded off-line by a coder naive to the experimental conditions, and the offline data were used in the analyses. Online and offline coding had a correlation of $r = .78$ across all three infant experiments, and 25% of trials for each infant were reliability coded by a second offline coder. Data from the two offline coders were highly correlated at $r = .87$.

## Results and Discussion

The 4-month-olds differentiated between incongruent word–object pairings (i.e., 'bubu' with an angular shape or 'kiki' with a curvy shape) and congruent word–object pairings (i.e., 'bubu' with a curvy shape or 'kiki' with an angular shape). Infants looked longer at incongruent pairings ($M = 16.8$ s, $SE = 2.3$) than at congruent pairings ($M = 13.0$ s, $SE = 2.0$), $t(11) = 2.77$, $p < .02$, $r = .64$, paired-samples t test (see Fig. 2, and see Table 1 for mean infant looking times by stimulus characteristics in Experiment 1). Of the 12 infants, 10 looked longer at incongruent trials, $p < .05$, using a binomial test. There were no effects of individual sounds or shapes as measured by a two-factor analysis of variance (AN-OVA) with shape (curvy or angular) and sound ('bubu' or 'kiki') (all $ps = ns$). There was no interaction between congruency and block in a repeated-measures ANOVA, $F(3, 21) = 0.47$, $p = .71$, indicating

**Table 1:** Mean infant looking times (in seconds) by stimulus characteristics in Experiments 1, 2, and 3

|  |  | Congruent | Incongruent |
|---|---|---|---|
| Combination of vowels and consonants | Curvy | 13.3 (1.9) | 17.6 (2.9) |
|  | Angular | 12.8 (2.4) | 13.6 (1.9) |
| Vowels | Curvy | 12.8 (1.8) | 12.1 (2.1) |
|  | Angular | 11.1 (2.1) | 11.9 (1.9) |
| Consonants | Curvy | 9.7 (1.5) | 6.9 (1.1) |
|  | Angular | 7.2 (0.9) | 8.5 (1.1) |

*Note:* Standard errors are in parentheses.

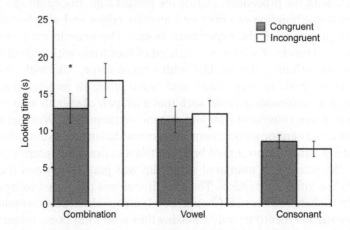

**Figure 2:** Mean infant looking times and standard errors for congruent and incongruent trials across the three experiments testing a combination of consonants and vowels (bubu or kiki), vowels only (kiki or kuku), and consonants only (bubu or kuku). Infants differentiated between incongruent and congruent trials only with a combination of consonants and vowels.

that the looking time difference between congruent and incongruent trials was not due to learning during the experiment. See Table 2 for a summary of the looking times by block and congruency. There was a significant effect of block, $F(3, 21) = 5.74, p < .01$, partial $\eta^2 = .45$, because infants' looking times decreased as the experiment progressed.

These results indicate that infants may have some of the same sound–shape associations as adults and toddlers even before they have learned reliable

**Table 2:** Mean infant looking times (in seconds) in Experiment 1 for each of the four blocks

|  | Congruent | Incongruent |
|---|---|---|
| Block 1 | 18.6 (3.5) | 21.4 (3.5) |
| Block 2 | 13.6 (2.5) | 18.0 (3.2) |
| Block 3 | 10.9 (2.6) | 13.9 (2.9) |
| Block 4 | 5.7 (1.5) | 8.9 (2.5) |

*Note:* Standard errors are in parentheses.

word–object mappings. This pattern of results differs from that of a prior study showing that 4-month-olds look longer at congruent trials (matching [o] or [a] to large objects and [i] or [e] to small objects) than at incongruent trials (Peña et al., 2011). However, this difference may stem from significant methodological differences between the two studies in the number of stimuli presented and in the mode of presentation. The previous study presented six different sounds with four different shapes presented in four different colors, whereas the current study presented two sounds with two shapes. Infants presented with more variables and more complex stimuli tend to look longer at relatively familiar or congruent pairings, whereas infants presented with simpler stimuli tend to look longer at relatively novel or incongruent pairings (Hunter & Ames, 1988). In addition, in the previous study, the two objects were presented simultaneously with one sound, which encourages matching behavior (e.g., Patterson & Werker, 2003). In contrast, in the current study, sound–object pairs were presented sequentially, which can lead infants to look longer at inconsistent audiovisual pairings (e.g., Stager & Werker, 1997). However, both studies provide converging evidence that 4-month-olds differentiate between congruent and incongruent sound–object mappings.

## Experiment 2

Infants in Experiment 1 showed the same sound–shape mappings as adults and toddlers. However, the words tested in Experiment 1 varied on both vowels (u/i) and consonants (b/k); therefore, it is unclear which segments of the words infants use to make the mappings – consonants, vowels, or a combination of vowels and consonants.

In Experiment 2, we examined whether infant mappings are based on vowels. Vowels are generally longer in duration and have more intensity than consonants (Lagefoged & Johnson, 2010). Moreover, infants can map different vowels onto small and large objects reliably (Peña et al., 2011). Thus, infants may be more likely to use information from the vowels than from the consonants to map sounds to shapes. In Experiment 2, we presented infants with the same two shapes but now did so with two words that differed only in their vowels: 'kiki' and 'kuku'.

### Method

#### Participants

The participants were 12 full-term 4-month-olds (mean age = 4 months 8 days, range = 3 months 22 days to 4 months 23 days, 7 girls and 5 boys). Infants were recruited in the same way as in Experiment 1. Of the infants' parents, 1 had completed some high school, 2 had completed some college,

11 had completed college, 8 had completed graduate degrees, and 2 declined to answer. Of the 12 infants, 8 were White, 2 were of mixed ethnicity, 1 was Hispanic, and 1 infant's parent declined to answer. An additional 10 infants were tested but excluded from the analysis because of fussiness (6), inattentiveness (1), or experimenter error (3).

## Stimuli

*Auditory stimuli.* The stimuli for Experiment 2 were recorded during the same session as the stimuli for Experiment 1. The tokens for each word were matched on duration ('kuku': $M$ = 435 ms, range = 433–439; 'kiki': $M$ = 434 ms, range = 431–437), amplitude (all tokens were 70 dB), and pitch ('kuku': $M$ = 232 Hz, range = 231–233; 'kiki': $M$ = 232 Hz, range = 231–232). We selected /k/ as the carrier vowel rather than /b/ to limit the variation in rounding information in the vowel and to reduce any coarticulation of rounding from the bilabial consonant /b/ on the vowel. We created 40-s strings in the same way as in Experiment 1.

*Visual stimuli.* We used the same stimuli as in Experiment 1.

## Procedure

The procedure was identical to that in Experiment 1.

## Results and Discussion

Infants looked equally at incongruent pairings ($M$ = 12.3 s, $SE$ = 1.8) and congruent pairings ($M$ = 11.6 s, $SE$ = 1.8), $t(11)$ = 0.64, $p$ = .54, $r$ = .19 (see Fig. 2, and see Table 1 for mean infant looking times by stimulus characteristics in Experiment 2). Of the 12 infants, 6 looked longer at the congruent trials, $p$ = 1.00, using a binomial test. There was no effect of individual sounds or shape as measured by a two-factor ANOVA with shape (curvy or angular) and sound ('kuku' or 'kiki') (all $ps$ = ns). Even though infants in prior studies systematically matched vowels to the size of objects (Peña et al., 2011), we found no evidence that infants matched vowels alone to the shape of objects.

# Experiment 3

Vowel information was not sufficient for infants to match words and shapes. In Experiment 3, we examined whether infants use the consonant information to map words and shapes. Adults prefer using consonants to vowels when making sound–shape pairings (Nielsen & Rendall, 2011). Infants' use of consonants to make label–shape mappings would be consistent with the role that consonants have been proposed to play in lexical processing, as compared with the role of vowels in indexical, prosodic, and grammatical processing (Bonatti, Peña, Nespor, & Mehler, 2005; Nespor, Peña, & Mehler, 2003). We presented infants with the same two shapes but now did so with two words that differed only in their consonants: 'bubu' and 'kuku'.

## Method

### Participants

The participants were 12 full-term 4-month-olds (mean age = 4 months 9 days, range = 3 months 27 days to 4 months 19 days, 7 girls and 5 boys). Of the infants' parents, 1 had completed some high school, 4 had completed some college, 9 had completed college, 7 had completed graduate degrees, and 3 declined to answer. Of the 12 infants, 5 were Hispanic, 4 were White, 2 were of mixed ethnicity, and 1 infant's parents declined to answer. An additional 4 infants were tested but excluded from the analysis because of fussiness (1), parental interference (1), or experimenter error (2).

### Stimuli

*Auditory stimuli.* The stimuli for Experiment 3 were recorded at the same session as the stimuli for Experiments 1 and 2. The tokens for each word were matched on duration ('kuku': $M = 398$ ms, range = 387–409; 'bubu': $M = 398$ ms, range = 390–407), amplitude (all tokens were 70 dB), and pitch ('kuku': $M = 231$ Hz, range = 228–238; 'bubu': $M = 230$ Hz, range = 228–232). We selected /u/ rather than /i/ as the carrier vowel because velars such as /k/ have especially low resistance to coarticulation from /i/ (Fowler & Brancazio, 2000). We created 40 s strings in the same way as in Experiment 1.

*Visual stimuli.* We used the same stimuli as in Experiment 1.

### Procedure

The procedure was identical to that in Experiment 1.

### Results and Discussion

Infants looked equally at incongruent pairings ($M = 7.5$ s, $SE = 1.0$) and congruent pairings ($M = 8.5$ s, $SE = 0.9$), $t(11) = 0.87, p = .40, r = .25$ (see Fig. 2, and see Table 1 for mean infant looking times by stimulus characteristics in Experiment 3). Of the 12 infants, 7 looked longer at congruent trials ($p = .77$) using a binomial test. There were no effects of individual sounds or shape as measured by a two-factor ANOVA with shape (curvy or angular) and sound ('bubu' or 'kuku') (all $ps = ns$). Despite the importance of consonants in lexical processing (Bonatti et al., 2005; Nespor et al., 2003), we found no evidence that infants matched consonants alone to the shape of objects.

## Comparison of Infants' Performance across the Three Infant Experiments

To compare the three infant experiments, we derived each infant's relative looking time to incongruent trials by calculating a difference score between incongruent and congruent looking times (Incongruent Looking Time – Congruent Looking Time). A one-way ANOVA comparing difference scores across the three experiments revealed a reliable effect of experiment, $F(2, 33) =$ 4.66, $p = .02$, $\eta^2 = .22$). Post hoc least-squares differences tests confirmed that infants looked relatively longer to incongruent trials in Experiment 1, which combined both vowels and consonants, than in Experiment 2, which compared vowels ($p = .02$, $r = .45$), and in Experiment 3, which compared consonants ($p = .01$, $r = .48$). Infants differentiated between congruent and incongruent trials only when the labels differed on both consonants and vowels (see Fig. 2).

# Experiment 4

Previous work examining the features of speech sounds used by adults to make sound–object mappings found that participants were more likely to respond based on consonant quality than on vowel quality when the two made opposite predictions (Nielsen & Rendall, 2011). The current experiments with infants used different words ('bubu', 'kiki', and 'kuku') from those used in previous studies. In Experiment 4, we tested adults on these new materials to confirm that adults generalize sound–shape mappings to these words. Furthermore, we examined adults' use of vowels or consonants in making systematic mappings.

## Method

### Participants

The participants were 10 undergraduate students (9 women and 1 man) either enrolled at New York University or participating in a summer internship program at the university. All of the participants were native English speakers and between 18 and 22 years old. An additional 3 participants' data were not included in the analysis because they were not native English speakers (2) or did not follow task instructions (1).

## Stimuli

*Auditory stimuli.* These were the same as those used in the previous experiments with the addition of 'bibi'. The tokens were adjusted using Praat (Boersma & Weenink, 2010) to be similar in duration ($M$ = 425 ms, range = 423–438), pitch ($M$ = 227 Hz, range = 225–230), and intensity (all 70 dB).

*Visual stimuli.* These were the same shapes as those used in the previous experiments except that we included more colors to encourage independent judgments for each trial: red, light pink, bright pink, maroon, brown, rust, orange, mustard, marigold, yellow, bright green, seafoam green, emerald green, olive green, teal, turquoise, French blue, royal blue, light gray, dark gray, gray–green, blue–purple, and purple.

## Procedure

*One-label task.* Participants sat at a desktop computer wearing Extreme Isolation Ex-25 noise-canceling headphones. They were presented with two shapes: a curvy shape and an angular shape of the same color, one on each side of the computer screen. The shapes remained consistent across all of the trials but varied in color between trials. The two objects presented in any given trial were of the same color. Below these shapes was a teardrop (half curvy and half angular). Participants were instructed to click on the teardrop to hear a word and then to record whether the word was a better match for the shape on the left or the right. Two trials for each of the nonwords used in the infant experiments ('bubu', 'kiki', or 'kuku'), with the addition of 'bibi', were presented for a total of eight experimental trials.[2]

*Two-label task.* Participants sat at a desktop computer wearing Extreme Isolation Ex-25 noise-canceling headphones. They were presented with the same two shapes as in the one-label task but with an additional teardrop above the objects. The second teardrop played a different word when clicked. Participants were instructed to click on the two teardrops to hear two words and then to pair each of the words with one of the two objects. This procedure allowed the isolation of specific features for word–object pairings. For example, a trial with 'kiki' and 'kuku' measured whether participants could use vowel information alone to make consistent pairings without conflicting or supporting consonant information. There was a total of six test trials – one trial for each permutation of /b/ and /k/ combined with /i/ and /u/ (kiki/kuku, bibi/bubu, kuku/bubu/, kiki/bibi, bibi/kuku, and bubu/kiki).

# Results and Discussion

## *One-label task*

Trials were scored according to whether participants used a vowel (e.g., pairing /i/ with the angular shape), a consonant (e.g., pairing /k/ with the angular shape), or a combination of the two (e.g., pairing /kiki/ with the angular shape). Participants had the highest score using the combinations ($M = 95\%$), followed by consonants ($M = 88\%$). Scores on trials comparing vowels ($M = 63\%$) were significantly lower than either consonant trials, $t(9) = 4.58$, $p < .01$, $r = .84$, or combination trials, $t(9) = 9.80$, $p < .01$, $r = .96$.

## *Two-label Task*

Trials were scored according to whether participants assigned the words to the congruent shapes (/i/ or /k/ with the spiky shape and /u/ or /b/ with the curvy shape). Accuracy was equivalent between trials when only vowel information distinguished the words (kiki/kuku or bibi/bubu, $M = 90\%$), when only consonant information distinguished the words (kiki/bibi or kuku/bubu, $M = 90\%$), and when the consonant–vowel combination distinguished the words (bubu/kiki, $M = 100\%$). However, when words contained conflicting vowel and consonant information (kuku/bibi), 8 of the 10 participants matched the words according to consonant information ($p < .05$) using a binomial test.

Adults' use of consonants and vowels differed from results of some previous studies in which adults used only consonant information to match shapes and sounds (Nielsen & Rendall, 2011). This may be because previous studies used different materials with multiple consonants and vowels – 'takete' and 'maluma' rather than 'bubu'/'buba' and 'kiki'. However, the difference in findings is more likely due to the different tasks. The task used by Nielsen and Rendall (2011) is more similar to the one-label task, in which participants need to choose whether to use vowels or consonants to match the shapes. The one-label task results are consistent with Nielsen and Rendall's findings in showing that participants will use consonants instead of vowels. However, Nielsen and Rendall did not contrast labels differing only on vowels; thus, their results cannot speak to whether participants can use vowel information at all. Our results suggest that participants prefer to match using consonant information but can use vowels when no consonant information is available (see also Monaghan et al., 2012).

# General Discussion

We predicted that if 4-month-old infants have the same sound–shape mapping biases as adults and toddlers, they would differentiate between congruent trials (pairing the angular shape with 'kiki' or the curvy shape with 'bubu') and incongruent trials (pairing the curvy shape with 'kiki' or the angular shape with 'bubu'). Infants looked longer at incongruent pairings than at congruent pairings. This mapping appears to be based on a combination of vowels and consonants given that neither vowels alone nor consonants alone elicited systematic mapping. Our results indicate that adult sound–shape mapping biases have their origins during infancy and might not result uniquely from language exposure creating statistical regularities in the lexicon.

Adults in our study, like infants, used a combination of consonant and vowel information to match the labels they heard with the shapes they saw. Their better performance with a combination of consonants and vowels rather than either vowels or consonants alone may be because the combination of vowels and consonants contained more sound symbolic phonemes, thereby inducing a stronger sound symbolism effect (Thompson & Estes, 2011). However, this was not the only strategy that was available to them. Adults, unlike infants, were also able to use consonant information alone and vowel information alone to match the labels to the shapes, albeit less frequently than the consonant–vowel combination. When vowels and consonants were put in conflict, adults used consonants more often than vowels. Adults' primary use of consonants is consistent with the role that consonants have been proposed to play in lexical processing, as compared with the role of vowels in indexical, prosodic, and grammatical processing (Bonatti et al., 2005; Nespor et al., 2003). Specifically, consonants and vowels are processed differently; adults extract statistical regularities from consonants but not from vowels (Bonatti et al., 2005; Toro, Shukla, Nespor, & Endress, 2008; but see Newport & Aslin, 2004), whereas rule extraction is privileged over vowels but not over consonants for adults and infants (Bonatti et al., 2005; Hochmann, Benavides-Varela, Nespor, & Mehler, 2011; Pons & Toro, 2010; Toro et al., 2008).

Where do these biases for systematically mapping sounds to shapes come from? One possibility is that sound symbolism is related to cross-modal synesthetic tendencies (e.g., Ramachandran & Hubbard, 2001; Spector & Maurer, 2009). An adult with synesthesia experiences additional involuntary sensations in one sensory modality when another sensory modality is stimulated (Cytowic & Eagleman, 2009; Cytowic & Wood, 1982). Synesthetic associations are stronger in younger infants than in older infants (Wagner & Dobkins, 2011), indicating that these associations may play a larger role in the perceptions of prelinguistic infants than of toddlers or adults. However, because synesthesia occurs in only 4 to 5% of the adult population (Simner & Ward, 2006), whereas 90% to 98% of adults show systematic sound–shape mapping biases (Köhler, 1947), our results are unlikely to be explained by adult synesthesia. At the same time, the human proclivity for systematically mapping sounds to shapes is also consistent with data from nonhuman primates showing biased cross-modal correspondences in chimpanzees (Ludwig, Adachi, & Matsuzawa, 2011). Thus, sound symbolism may be an intrinsic feature of primate sensory systems.

Another potential explanation for the origins of cross-modal biases comes from theories claiming links between perception and production mechanisms (Calvert & Campbell, 2003; Keysers et al., 2003; Kohler et al., 2002; Liberman & Mattingly, 1985; Wilson, Saygin, Sereno, & Iacoboni, 2004) and is supported by studies with individuals with autism spectrum disorder and patients with brain lesions. These individuals do not show as systematic a bias for sound–shape mappings as typical individuals do. Where typically developing individuals agree with the standard result 90% to 98% of the time, individuals with autism or lesions to the angular gyrus agree only 56% of the time (Ramachandran, Azoulai, Stone, Srinivasan, & Bijoy, 2005). Children with autism spectrum disorder also do not show the sound–shape mapping biases that neurologically typical adults and children show (Oberman & Ramachandran, 2008). Individuals with autism spectrum disorder or brain lesions are proposed to have a dysfunction in the mirror neuron system linking perception and production that prevents the systematic bias for sound–shape mappings that typical adults show (Altschuler et al., 2000; Nishitani, Avikainen, & Hari, 2004; Oberman et al., 2005; Theoret et al., 2005).

The current results provide evidence that prelinguistic infants show adult-like nonarbitrary mapping biases between speech labels and objects. Infants in our experiments showed these biases only when the two labels differed in both consonants and vowels. Our results differ from those of prior studies in which vowels alone were sufficient to convey object size to 4-month-olds (Peña et al., 2011). The use of vowels alone in prior studies may be grounded in observable physical relationships between the pitch of vowels and the size of objects built through participants' prior multisensory experiences. The relationship between vowel quality and object shape, in contrast, might not be as easily observable, consistent with findings that consonants, and not vowels, are preferred in adult sound–shape mappings (Experiment 4 in the current study; see also Nielsen & Rendall, 2011). It must be noted that our experiments used only two consonants (/b/ and /k/) and two vowels (/i/ and /u/). Although these data are consistent with previous infant studies linking vowel and object size (Peña et al., 2011) and pitch and object shape (Walker et al., 2010), further research with different consonants and vowels is needed to understand what may drive infants' sound–shape mapping biases.

Our perceptual system must combine or segregate concurrent sensory inputs from different modalities to quickly and accurately detect objects or events and to choose appropriate responses (Evans & Treisman, 2010). In a world full of multisensory experiences, developing infants must be able to integrate multisensory inputs (e.g., Bahrick, Lickliter, & Flom, 2004; Lewkowicz, 2000). The early biases for cross-modal correspondences during infancy provide a basis for processing the multisensory nature of our daily experiences.

## Notes

1. The relatively higher attrition rate for Experiment 1 was due to data loss from equipment failure. Specifically, there was no sound played during the experiment. This was corrected in subsequent experiments.
2. Participants were also presented with trials where they heard the non-English vowels (/i/ and /y/) combined with both /b/ and /k/, but these trials were not analyzed.

## References

Altschuler, E. L., Vankov, A., Hubbard, E. M., Roberts, E., Ramachandran, V. S., & Pineda, J. A. (2000). *Mu wave blocking by observer of movement and its possible use as a tool to study theory of other minds.* In Poster session presented at the 30th annual meeting of the Society for Neuroscience, New Orleans, LA.

Bahrick, L. E., Lickliter, R., & Flom, R. (2004). Intersensory redundancy guides the development of selective attention, perception, and cognition in infancy. *Current Directions in Psychological Science, 13*, 99–102.

Bergelson, E., & Swingley, D. (2012). At 6–9 months, human infants know the meanings of many common nouns. *Proceedings of the National Academy of Sciences of the United States of America, 109*, 3253–3258.

Boersma, P., & Weenink, D. (2010). *Praat: Doing phonetics by computer* (Version 5.3.08) [computer program]. Retrieved 26 July 2010 from http://www.praat.org.

Bonatti, L., Peña, M., Nespor, M., & Mehler, J. (2005). Linguistic constraints on statistical computations: The role of consonants and vowels in continuous speech processing. *Psychological Science, 16*, 451–459.

Calvert, G. A., & Campbell, R. (2003). Reading speech from still and moving faces: The neural substrates of visible speech. *Journal of Cognitive Neuroscience, 15*, 57–70.

Cohen, L. B., Atkinson, D. J., & Chaput, H. H. (2004). *Habit X: A new program for obtaining and organizing data in infant perception and cognition studies (Version 1.0).* Austin: University of Texas.

Cytowic, R. E., & Eagleman, D. M. (2009). *Wednesday is indigo blue: Discovering the brain of synesthesia.* Cambridge, MA: MIT Press.

Cytowic, R. E., & Wood, F. B. (1982). Synesthesia: I. A review of major theories and their brain basis. *Brain and Cognition, 1*, 23–35.

Davis, R. (1961). The fitness of names to drawings: A cross-cultural study in Tanganyika. *British Journal of Psychology, 52*, 259–268.

De Saussure, F. (1983). *Course in general linguistics.* In C. Bally & A. Sechehaye (Eds), R. Harris, Trans. La Salle, IL: Open Court. (Original work published 1916).

Descartes, R. (1986). *Meditations on first philosophy.* New York: Cambridge University Press (Original work published 1641).

Evans, K. K., & Treisman, A. (2010). Natural cross-modal mappings between visual and auditory features. *Journal of Vision, 10*, 1–12.

Fenson, L., Dale, P. S., Reznick, J. S., Bates, E., Thal, D. J., & Pethick, S. J. (1994). Variability in early communicative development. *Monographs of the Society for Research in Child Development, 59*(5), 1–173 (discussion, pp. 174–185).

Fowler, C. A., & Brancazio, L. (2000). Coarticulation resistance of American English consonants and its effects on transconsonantal vowel-to-vowel coarticulation. *Language and Speech, 43*, 1–41.

Gasser, M. (2004). The origins of arbitrariness in language. In *Proceedings of the annual conference of the Cognitive Science Society* (Vol. 26). Mahwah, NJ: Lawrence Erlbaum.

Gibson, J. J. (1966). *The senses considered as perceptual systems*. Boston: Houghton Mifflin.

Hochmann, J. R., Benavides-Varela, S., Nespor, M., & Mehler, J. (2011). Consonants and vowels: Different roles in early language acquisition. *Developmental Science, 14*, 1445–1458.

Hockett, C. F. (1977). *The view from language: Selected essays* 1948–1974. Athens: University of Georgia Press.

Hunter, M. A., & Ames, E. W. (1988). A multifactor model of infant preferences for novel and familiar stimuli. *Advances in Infancy Research, 5*, 69–95.

Imai, M., Kita, S., Nagumo, M., & Okada, H. (2008). Sound symbolism facilitates early verb learning. *Cognition, 109*, 54–65.

Keysers, C., Kohler, E., Umilta, M. A., Nanetti, L., Fogassi, L., & Gallese, V. (2003). Audiovisual mirror neurons and action recognition. *Experimental Brain Research, 153*, 628–636.

Kohler, E., Keysers, C., Umilta, M. A., Fogassi, L., Gallese, V., & Rizzolatti, G. (2002). Hearing sounds, understanding actions: Action representation in mirror neurons. *Science, 297*, 846–848.

Köhler, W. (1947). *Gestalt psychology* (2nd ed.). New York: Liveright.

Kovic, V., Plunkett, K., & Westermann, G. (2010). The shape of words in the brain. *Cognition, 114*, 19–28.

Lagefoged, P., & Johnson, K. (2010). *A course in phonetics* (6th ed.). Boston: Wadsworth.

Lewkowicz, D. J. (2000). The development of intersensory temporal perception: An epigenetic systems/limitations view. *Psychological Bulletin, 126*, 281–308.

Liberman, A. M., & Mattingly, I. G. (1985). The motor theory of speech perception revised. *Cognition, 21*, 1–36.

Ludwig, V. U., Adachi, I., & Matsuzawa, T. (2011). Visuoauditory mappings between high luminance and high pitch are shared by chimpanzees (*Pan troglodytes*) and humans. *Proceedings of the National Academy of Sciences of the United States of America, 108*, 20661–20665.

Marks, L. E. (1987). On cross-modal similarity: Auditory–visual interactions in speeded discrimination. *Journal of Experimental Psychology: Human Perception and Performance, 13*(3), 384–394.

Maurer, D., Pathman, T., & Mondloch, C. J. (2006). The shape of boubas: Sound–shape correspondences in toddlers and adults. *Developmental Science, 9*, 316–322.

Monaghan, P., Christiansen, M. H., & Fitneva, S. A. (2011). The arbitrariness of the sign: Learning advantages from the structure of the vocabulary. *Journal of Experimental Psychology: General, 140*, 325–347.

Monaghan, P., Mattock, K., & Walker, P. (2012). The role of sound symbolism in language learning. *Journal of Experimental Psychology: Learning, Memory, & Cognition*. http://dx.doi.org/10.1037/a0027747. [Epub ahead of print].

Nespor, M., Peña, M., & Mehler, J. (2003). On the different roles of vowels and consonants in speech processing and language acquisition. *Lingue & Linguaggio, 2*, 203–231.

Newport, E. L., & Aslin, R. N. (2004). Learning at a distance. I. Statistical learning of non-adjacent dependencies. *Cognitive Psychology, 48*, 127–162.

Nielsen, A., & Rendall, D. (2011). The sound of round: Evaluating the sound–symbolic role of consonants in the classic takete–maluma phenomenon. *Canadian Journal of Experimental Psychology, 65*, 115–124.

Nishitani, N., Avikainen, S., & Hari, R. (2004). Abnormal imitation-related cortical activation sequences in Asperger's syndrome. *Annals of Neurology, 55*, 558–562.

Nygaard, L. C., Cook, A. E., & Namy, L. L. (2009). Sound to meaning correspondences facilitate word learning. *Cognition, 112*, 181–186.

Oberman, L. M., Hubbard, E. M., McCleery, J. P., Altschuler, E. L., Ramachandran, V. S., & Pineda, J. A. (2005). EEG evidence for mirror neuron dysfunction in autism spectrum disorders. *Cognitive Brain Research, 24*, 190–198.

Oberman, L. M., & Ramachandran, V. S. (2008). Reflections on the mirror neuron system: Their evolutionary functions beyond motor representation. In J. A. Pineda (Ed.), *Role of mirroring in social cognition*. Totowa, NJ: Humana.

Ohala, J. J. (1997). Sound symbolism. In *Proceedings of the 4th Seoul International Conference on Linguistics* (pp. 98–103). SICOL: Seoul, Korea.

Parault, S. J. (2006). Sound symbolic word learning in context. *Contemporary Educational Psychology, 31*, 228–252.

Parault, S. J., & Schwanenflugel, P. J. (2006). Sound symbolism: A possible piece in the puzzle of word learning. *Journal of Psycholinguistic Research, 35*, 329–351.

Patterson, M. L., & Werker, J. F. (2003). Two-month-old infants match phonetic information in lips and voice. *Developmental Science, 6*, 191–196.

Peña, M., Mehler, J., & Nespor, M. (2011). The role of audiovisual processing in early conceptual development. *Psychological Science, 22*, 1419–1421.

Pons, F., & Toro, J. M. (2010). Structural generalizations over consonants and vowels in 11-month-old infants. *Cognition, 116*, 361–367.

Ramachandran, V. S., Azoulai, S., Stone, L., Srinivasan, A. V., & Bijoy, N. (2005, April). *Grasping metaphors and thinking with pictures: How brain damage might affect thought and language*. In Poster presented at the 12th annual meeting of the Cognitive Neuroscience Society, New York.

Ramachandran, V. S., & Hubbard, E. M. (2001). Synaesthesia: A window into perception, thought, and language. *Journal of Consciousness Studies, 8*, 3–34.

Sapir, E. (1929). The status of linguistics as a science. *Language, 5*, 209.

Shayan, S., Ozturk, O., & Sicoli, M. A. (2011). The thickness of pitch: Crossmodal metaphors in Farsi, Turkish, and Zapotec. *Senses & Society, 6*, 96–105.

Simner, J., & Ward, J. (2006). The taste of words on the tip of the tongue. *Nature, 444*, 438.

Spector, F., & Maurer, D. (2009). Synesthesia: A new approach to understanding the development of perception. *Developmental Psychology, 45*, 175–189.

Stager, C. L., & Werker, J. F. (1997). Infants listen for more phonetic detail in speech perception than in word-learning tasks. *Nature, 388*, 381–382.

Tanz, C. (1971). Sound symbolism in words relating to proximity and distance. *Language & Speech, 14*, 266–276.

Theoret, H., Halligan, E., Kobayashi, M., Fregni, F., Tager-Flusberg, H., & Pascual-Leone, A. (2005). Impaired motor facilitation during action observation in individuals with autism spectrum disorder. *Current Biology, 15*, 84–85.

Thompson, P. D., & Estes, Z. (2011). Sound symbolic naming of novel objects is a graded function. *Quarterly Journal of Experimental Psychology, 64*, 2392–2404.

Toro, J. M., Shukla, M., Nespor, M., & Endress, A. (2008). The quest for generalizations over consonants: Asymmetries between consonants and vowels are not the by-product of acoustic differences. *Perception and Psychophysics, 70*, 1515–1525.

Voeltz, F. K. E., & Kilian-Hatz, C. (Eds.). (2001). *Ideophones*. Amsterdam: John Benjamins (Typological Studies in Language, Vol. 44).

Wagner, K., & Dobkins, K. R. (2011). Synaesthetic associations decrease during infancy. *Psychological Science, 22*, 1067–1072.

Walker, P., Bremner, J. G., Mason, U., Spring, J., Mattock, K., Slater, A., et al. (2010). Preverbal infants' sensitivity to synaesthetic cross-modality correspondences. *Psychological Science, 21*, 21–25.

Whalen, D. H., & Levitt, A. G. (1995). The universality of intrinsic $F_0$ in vowels. *Journal of Phonetics, 23*, 349–366.

Wilson, S. M., Saygin, A. P., Sereno, M. I., & Iacoboni, M. (2004). Listening to speech activates motor areas involved in speech production. *Nature Neuroscience, 7*, 701–702.

Zbikowski, L. M. (1998). Metaphor and music theory: Reflections from cognitive science. *Music Theory Online, 4*(1).